D1088678

TECHNICAL COLLEGE OF THE LOWCOUNTRY
LEARNING RESOURCES CENTER
POST OFFICE BOX 1288
BEAUFORT, SOUTH CAROLINA 29901-1288

PARALEGAL LITIGATION AND PRACTICE LIBRARY FROM WILEY LAW PUBLICATIONS

PARALEGAL DISCOVERY
PROCEDURES AND FORMS
SECOND EDITION

SUBSCRIPTION NOTICE

This Wiley product is updated on a periodic basis with supplements to reflect important changes in the subject matter. If you purchased this product directly from John Wiley & Sons, Inc., we have already recorded your subscription for this update service.

If, however, you purchased this product from a bookstore and wish to receive (1) the current update at no additional charge, and (2) future updates and revised or related volumes billed separately with a 30-day examination review, please send your name, company name (if applicable), address, and the title of the product to:

Supplement Department
John Wiley & Sons, Inc.
One Wiley Drive
Somerset, NJ 08875
1-800-225-5945

For customers outside the United States, please contact the Wiley office nearest you:

Professional and Reference
   Division
John Wiley & Sons Canada, Ltd.
22 Worcester Road
Rexdale, ONT M9W 1L1
CANADA
(416) 236-3580
Phone: 1-800-263-1590
Fax: 1-800-675-6599

John Wiley & Sons, Ltd.
Baffins Lane
Chichester
West Sussex, PO19 1UD
UNITED KINGDOM
Phone: (44) (243) 779777

Jacaranda Wiley Ltd.
PRT Division
P.O. Box 174
North Ryde, NSW 2113
AUSTRALIA
PHONE: (02) 805-1100
Fax: (02) 805-1597

John Wiley & Sons (SEA)
   Pte. Ltd.
37 Jalan Pemimpin
Block B # 05-04
Union Industrial Building
SINGAPORE 2057
Phone: (65) 258-1157

PARALEGAL DISCOVERY
PROCEDURES AND FORMS
SECOND EDITION

PAT MEDINA

San Francisco, California

Wiley Law Publications
JOHN WILEY & SONS, INC.
New York • Chichester • Brisbane • Toronto • Singapore

TECHNICAL COLLEGE OF THE LOWCOUNTRY
LEARNING RESOURCES CENTER
POST OFFICE BOX 1288
BEAUFORT, SOUTH CAROLINA 29901-1288

This text is printed on acid-free paper.

Copyright © 1994 by John Wiley & Sons, Inc.

All rights reserved. Published simultaneously in Canada.

Reproduction or translation of any part of this work beyond
that permitted by Section 107 or 108 of the 1976 United
States Copyright Act without the permission of the copyright
owner is unlawful. Requests for permission or further
information should be addressed to the Permissions Department,
John Wiley & Sons, Inc., 605 Third Avenue, New York, NY
10158-0012.

This publication is designed to provide accurate and
authoritative information in regard to the subject
matter covered. It is sold with the understanding that
the publisher is not engaged in rendering legal, accounting,
or other professional services. If legal advice or other
expert assistance is required, the services of a competent
professional person should be sought.

Library of Congress Cataloging-in-Publication Data

ISBN 0-471-31076-X

Printed in the United States of America

10 9 8 7 6 5 4 3 2 1

This book is gratefully dedicated to my husband, Nick, my daughters, Debbie and Suzie, and all my friends whose encouragement helped me hang in there and complete this project.

PREFACE

Paralegal Discovery—Procedures and Forms was first written in 1989 and supplemented in 1991. Since that time I have noticed a trend towards more liberal pretrial discovery, and a trend towards appointing special discovery commissioners in many superior courts whose sole function is to research and review discovery motions. Discretionary powers of discovery commissioners vary from court to court, but most commissioners can issue discovery orders granting and/or denying various discovery motions and awarding sanctions.

This emphasis on pretrial disclosure of discoverable evidence presents new challenges for the litigation paralegal who, as the evidence custodian, investigator, and factual research specialist, is responsible for preservation of evidence and protection of client confidentiality. Litigation paralegals are on the frontline in the paper chase of discovery wars, and must sharpen their skills and knowledge regarding case law decisions, local court rules, and procedural requirements in pretrial discovery in order to keep pace in today's litigious society.

In this second edition you will find new sections on today's hot discovery issues as well as more sample forms, letters, and checklists addressing the everyday discovery problems faced by my students and working paralegals laboring in the trenches of discovery wars and trial preparation. There are in-depth views and new sections on:

- Demand letters as settlement tools
- Legal calendaring—problems with proper computation of time
- Computerized conflict of interest systems
- Interviewing techniques for clients and witnesses
- Discovery plan samples for contract and personal injury actions
- Privilege protection checklists for corporate clients
- Limits of corporate confidentiality
- Discovery of witness statements
- Electronic work product
- FAX communications—are they privileged?
- Computerized screening of documents for privilege
- Factual investigation
- Public records searches and specialized data bases
- Locating information on privately held companies and financial institutions
- Sample deposition notices for state and federal courts
- Subpoena preparation for nonparty depositions and documents
- Out-of-state depositions

- Client deposition preparation
- Avoiding drafting objectionable interrogatories
- Specific ways to avoid the overbroad objection and eliminate the "any and all" language in drafting interrogatories
- Enlarged section of "problem interrogatories" and "problem requests for admissions" with student samples, accompanied by analysis of problem and corrected interrogatory
- Sample interrogatories for a government entity—both plaintiff and defendant
- New sample meet and confer letters for resolving interrogatory disputes
- Sample requests for admissions correlated to interrogatory responses as part of overall discovery plan
- Sample discovery motions complete with points and authorities (interrogatories and requests for admissions)
- Criteria for identifying privileged documents
- Comprehensive list of the universe of documents available in construction and real estate cases
- New section on electronic media discovery, the litigation weapon of the 90's
- Coordinating document production with interrogatories
- Sample motion to compel production of documents, complete with points and authorities
- New section on protecting your client from subpoena abuse

There is also a new chapter on expert witnesses, **Chapter 7,** which discusses their integral roles in trial preparation as well as the litigation paralegal's role in working with the expert witness.

San Francisco, California   PAT MEDINA
January 1994

ACKNOWLEDGMENTS

I want to thank Linda Sutliff, a paralegal student whose original suggestion and encouragement started this entire project. Thanks to all of my paralegal students for their thoughtful questions and comments which helped me to focus on common discovery problems and concerns. I have had the pleasure and good fortune of working with hundreds of paralegal students in my 12 years as an instructor for the San Francisco State University Paralegal Program. They have challenged me with the sophistication of their questions and concerns. Discovery is a "gray" area of the law, evolving and emerging as specific case decisions shape case law and become Black Letter Law.

Special thanks to Carol Willis, my typist, without whom my words would have remained on tape and not appeared on the pages you are about to read.

P.M.

ABOUT THE AUTHOR

Pat Medina received her B.A. from San Francisco State University; she then received a secondary teaching credential from California State University at Hayward and began a 10 year career as a high school English teacher. In 1979 she began her legal career upon graduating from St. Mary's College in Moraga, an A.B.A. approved program. Specializing in litigation, she has worked in personal injury, medical malpractice, product liability, commercial torts, wrongful termination, real estate litigation, bad faith insurance and contract law. She is currently employed as a Senior Litigation Legal Assistant at the Law Offices of Cartwright, Slobodin, et al, in San Francisco, California.

Pat has worked for both defense and plaintiff firms, which has broadened her understanding of discovery devices and given her the advantage of being able to "think like the opponent" in plotting discovery strategy.

In 1981, Pat Medina joined the faculty of San Francisco State University's Paralegal Program as a litigation instructor, and in 1990 became the director of field studies/internships for paralegal students in the San Francisco State Paralegal Certificate Program. In this capacity, she arranges internship placements in both the private and public sectors of the law community. Pat has always believed in the professionalism of legal assistants and has been a staunch supporter and officer in various professional legal assistant associations. Over the course of the past 10 years, Pat has served as president of the East Bay Association of Legal Assistants and Director, Secretary, and Chairperson of the Education Committee and the Paralegal Educator's Committee for the San Francisco Association of Legal Assistants.

Pat is a member of the American Association for Paralegal Education (AAfPE), a national organization composed of educational institutions offering paralegal study programs, and spoke at the 1992 annual convention in Denver, Colorado. She organizes and conducts various educational seminars for the San Francisco Association of Legal Assistants and frequently is a guest speaker at various legal events.

Pat is a member of the Advisory Board for St. Mary's College Paralegal Program in Moraga, California, and a member of the Paralegal Advisory Board for the California State University at Hayward Paralegal Program, and has conducted resume workshops and career counseling sessions for their paralegal students. She has written numerous articles for publication in paralegal journals such as *California Paralegal,* and contributed to various articles in *Legal Assistant Today.*

SUMMARY CONTENTS

DETAILED CONTENTS

CHAPTER 1

COMMENCING LITIGATION

§ 1.1   Introduction

Civil litigation is based on two main theories of liability—tort and contract. A complaint may incorporate both tort and contract elements in its theories of liability. A wrongful termination complaint could include allegations of breach of contract (oral or written), breach of implied covenant of good faith and fair dealing, and damages for physical injuries (stress, ulcers, cardio-vascular, and so forth), emotional distress, damage to business reputation, and lost wages.

Complaints may be filed in the judicial arena of small claims, municipal, or superior court, or in the nonjudicial arena of an administrative agency, contractual arbitration board, or the American Arbitration Association. Irrespective of where the complaint has been filed, the necessity for filing required preliminary documents and for discovery remains the same.

§ 1.2   Prelawsuit Notices and Claims

Certain actions require the filing of notices and/or claims within a given statutory time period or a client may forfeit their rights to a specific remedy. Claims must be filed against:

Government entities

Public agencies

Public employees acting within the scope of public employment at the time of the alleged wrong

Decedent's estate—a creditor's claim must be filed in probate proceedings

Notices of intent to commence actions against health care professionals and

Notices of intent to commence actions for professional negligence.

§ 1.3   Government Claims

The purpose of the formal claim requirement is to give governmental entities an opportunity to investigate a claim and attempt to settle meritorious claims prior to incurring the costs of litigation. In reality, 99 percent of all claims presented to governmental entities are denied. Litigation begins because compliance with the formal claim requirement is an essential element of any cause of action for money or damages against a governmental entity. Compliance must become a part of a complaint and be affirmatively pled and proved at trial. Suits against public entities are subject to dismissal for failure to file a timely claim.

Filing claims against government entities and/or public agencies must be done in a timely fashion with service of the notice of claim on a person authorized to accept on behalf of the entity—usually an employee or designated agency representative. If uncertain of the proper name, address, list of officers, or persons who can accept service of a claim for a particular entity, contact the Secretary of State and and ask them to research their Roster of Public Agencies. Each Secretary of State's office has a duty pursuant to Government Code §§ 53050 and 53051(c) to maintain a current Roster of Public Agencies listing the name, address, current list of officers, and designated representatives for agencies within the state.

If you need to research a city or county agency, contact the county clerk for information. Their office has an obligation to maintain an up-to-date Roster of Public Agencies for all agencies within their county. These rosters are updated yearly and contain all of the information necessary to file proper claims.

Many public entities provide preprinted claim forms. For those agencies who do not provide a form, prepare a form on pleading paper stating:

1. The name and address of the claimant
2. The date and place of the accident or the event out of which the claim arose
3. A general description of the damage, loss, or indebtedness
4. Names of any public employees allegedly responsible
5. The amount of the claim as then known and
6. Address where notices and other communications may be sent.

Forms 1–1 through **1–4** illustrate samples of government claims.

FORM 1-1
SAMPLE CLAIM FOR DAMAGE, INJURY, OR DEATH

CLAIM FOR DAMAGE, INJURY, OR DEATH	INSTRUCTIONS: Please read carefully the instructions on the reverse side and supply information requested on both sides of this form. Use additional sheet(s) if necessary. See reverse side for additional instructions.	FORM APPROVED OMB NO. 1105-0008

1. Submit To Appropriate Federal Agency:	2. Name, Address of claimant and claimant's personal representative, if any. *(See Instructions on reverse.)* *(Number, street, city, State and Zip Code)*

3. TYPE OF EMPLOYMENT ☐ MILITARY ☐ CIVILIAN	4. DATE OF BIRTH	5. MARITAL STATUS	6. DATE AND DAY OF ACCIDENT	7. TIME (A.M. OR P.M.)

8. Basis of Claim *(State in detail the known facts and circumstances attending the damage, injury, or death, identifying persons and property involved, the place of occurence and the cause thereof) (Use additional pages if necessary.)*

PROPERTY DAMAGE

9. NAME AND ADDRESS OF OWNER, IF OTHER THAN CLAIMANT *(Number, street, city, State, and Zip Code)*

BRIEFLY DESCRIBE THE PROPERTY, NATURE AND EXTENT OF DAMAGE AND THE LOCATION WHERE PROPERTY MAY BE INSPECTED. *(See instructions on reverse side.)*

PERSONAL INJURY/WRONGFUL DEATH

10. STATE NATURE AND EXTENT OF EACH INJURY OR CAUSE OF DEATH, WHICH FORMS THE BASIS OF THE CLAIM. IF OTHER THAN CLAIMANT, STATE NAME OF INJURED PERSON OR DECEDENT.

11. WITNESSES

NAME	ADDRESS (Number, street, city, State, and Zip Code)

12. (See instructions on reverse) AMOUNT OF CLAIM (in dollars)

12a. PROPERTY DAMAGE	12b. PERSONAL INJURY	12c. WRONGFUL DEATH	12d. TOTAL (Failure to specify may cause forfeiture of your rights.)

I CERTIFY THAT THE AMOUNT OF CLAIM COVERS ONLY DAMAGES AND INJURIES CAUSED BY THE ACCIDENT ABOVE AND AGREE TO ACCEPT SAID AMOUNT IN FULL SATISFACTION AND FINAL SETTLEMENT OF THIS CLAIM

13a. SIGNATURE OF CLAIMANT (See instructions on reverse side.)	13b. Phone number of signatory	14. DATE OF CLAIM

CIVIL PENALTY FOR PRESENTING FRAUDULENT CLAIM	CRIMINAL PENALTY FOR PRESENTING FRAUDULENT CLAIM OR MAKING FALSE STATEMENTS
The claimant shall forfeit and pay to the United States the sum of $2,000, plus double the amount of damages sustained by the United States. (See 31 U.S.C. 3729.)	Fine of not more than $10,000 or imprisonment for not more than 5 years or both. (See 18 U.S.C. 287, 1001.)

95-107
Previous editions not usable.

NSN 7540-00-634-4046

STANDARD FORM 95 (Rev. 7-85)
PRESCRIBED BY DEPT. OF JUSTICE
28 CFR 14.2

FORM 1–2
SAMPLE CLAIMS AGAINST A CITY—NUMBER 1

CLAIM AGAINST THE CITY AND COUNTY OF [name]

Charter Section [number] and the Government Code Sections 910 to 911.2 require that all claims must be presented to the CONTROLLER or to the CLERK OF THE BOARD OF SUPERVISORS within six months from date of accident or incident.

CLAIMANT'S NAME

CLAIMANT'S ADDRESS   TELEPHONE

AMOUNT OF CLAIM $ _____

ADDRESS TO WHICH NOTICES ARE TO BE SENT

DATE OF INCIDENT

EXACT LOCATION & DESCRIPTION SUFFICIENT TO IDENTIFY

HOW DID IT OCCUR?

DESCRIBE DAMAGE OR INJURY

NAME OF PUBLIC EMPLOYEE(S) CAUSING INJURY OR DAMAGE, IF KNOWN

GIVE LICENSE NUMBER, IF VEHICLE INVOLVED

ITEMIZATION OF CLAIM (List items totaling amount set forth above)

_____ $ _____
_____ $ _____
_____ $ _____
_____ $ _____
_____ $ _____

                                        TOTAL $ _____

Signed by or on behalf of Claimant _____

FORM 1–3
SAMPLE CLAIM AGAINST A CITY—NUMBER 2

[name and address of law firm]

[attorneys for claimant]

CLAIM AGAINST THE CITY OF [name]

NAMES AND ADDRESS OF CLAIMANT:

ADDRESS TO WHICH NOTICES ARE TO BE SENT:
[attorney name]
[law firm]
[address]

DATE, PLACE, AND CIRCUMSTANCES OF OCCURRENCE:
   On [date], [claimant], while on board a MUNI-operated cable car near the end of the [street] line, was thrown from said cable car. The accident and subsequent harm was caused by the carelessness and negligence of the operator of the City vehicle.

AMOUNT OF CLAIM:
[dollar amount]

GENERAL DESCRIPTION OF INJURIES AND BASIS OF COMPUTATION OF DAMAGES:
   Fracture and other injuries to the arm requiring medical treatment, hospital, and other medical expenses, as well as loss of time from gainful employment.

DATED: [date]

                                        [law firm]
                                        By: [attorney name]

FORM 1–4
SAMPLE CLAIM FOR PERSONAL INJURIES

[name and address of law firm]

[attorneys for claimant]

[claimant name]

CLAIM OF:
[name]   )   CLAIM FOR PERSONAL INJURIES
)   (Government Code § [code number])
                        Claimant,   )
)
        vs.   )
STATE OF [name],   )

[state] HIGHWAY and TRANSPOR-)
TATION DISTRICT.   )
)
_____)

TO THE STATE OF [state name] AND THE [city]
HIGHWAY & TRANSPORTATION DISTRICT:

You are hereby notified that [claimant], whose address is [street, city & state], claims damages from the State of [name] and the [city] Highway & Transportation District.

This claim is based on personal injuries sustained by claimant on or about [date], approximately 105 feet north of light pole no. 11 at [location] Bridge under the following circumstances:

At approximately [time] claimant was northbound on the [name] Bridge. At that time, a southbound vehicle crossed into claimant's lane and struck his vehicle head on. Claimant's vehicle was then rear-ended by the vehicle directly behind his own.

The accident and subsequent harm was caused by the State of [name] and [city] Highway & Transportation District's negligent creation, maintenance, and failure to warn of a dangerous condition on the [name] Bridge. The State of [name] and [city] Highway & Transportation District had actual or constructive notice of the dangerous condition a sufficient time prior to claimant's injury to have taken measures to protect against the dangerous condition. Said dangerous condition was created and allowed to exist due to the State of [name] and [city] Highway & Transportation District's careless and negligent failure to provide appropriate barriers, guard rails, lights, devices, and warnings.

The names of the public employees causing claimant's injuries under the described circumstances are at this time unknown.

The injuries sustained by claimant, as far as known, as of the date of presentation of this claim, consist of extensive injuries to the body, including fractured ribs and fractured wrist, and general damages. Additionally, claimant is a practicing doctor who by reason of his injuries has lost wages as well as suffered a decrease in his future earning capacity. Based on the amount of claimant's injuries, jurisdiction over this claim rests with the Superior Court.

All notices or other communications with regard to this claim should be sent to the Law Offices of (name of law firm) at the above address.

Dated: [date]

                                                  [law firm]
                                                  By: [attorney name]

§ 1.4   Federal Government Claims

Federal statutes require that a Notice of Claim be formally submitted to an administrative agency before an action may be filed to give the agency an opportunity to resolve the matter without litigation. Agencies such as the Equal Employment Opportunity Commission (EEOC) and the Social Security Administration are examples of administrative agencies with precise claim requirements. If you represent a client with a claim against either of these agencies, you may obtain the proper form for presenting your claim by contacting the agency headquarters directly. Be mindful of the particular statutes governing your claim. For example, 42 U.S.C. § 200E-5 is the governing statute for requirements and time constraints for claims presented to the EEOC.

The more common federal tort claim is brought by a person injured by an act or omission of a federal employee acting in the course and scope of employment with a federal agency. Procedures for filing tort claims against the United States are governed by 20 U.S.C. §§ 1346, 2671–80. A federal tort claim must be filed within two years of the circumstances giving rise to the claim. The government then has six months to act on the claim. If the claim is not officially denied within that six-month period, it is deemed automatically denied by operation of law 28 U.S.C. § 2675(a). The claimant then has one year after the date of the denial, or denial date by operation of law, to file a lawsuit.

§ 1.5   Procedures for Filing Federal Tort Claims

When filing a federal tort claim, you can opt to use either a preprinted form or create your own and present it formatted on pleading paper. Either form is correct and acceptable if the minimal required information is set forth. (Certain agencies have preprinted forms and will furnish them upon request.) Federal tort claims require precise information which can be more easily set forth in a long form on pleading paper. All claims against public entities and governmental agencies must contain the following information:

1. Name and address of claimant.
2. Address where person presenting claim desires notices to be sent (usually the name of your law firm).
3. Date, place, and circumstances of occurrence which gave rise to the claim.
4. Name of any public vehicle involved in this claim (include here not only obvious public vehicles such as state highway patrol cars, but any private vehicles owned by governmental agencies, public entities or any vehicles driven by government employees in the course and scope of that employment).
5. A general description of the injury, obligation, damage, loss or indebtedness incurred, as far as is presently known (at the time of presentation of the claim).
6. Name or names of public employees responsible for injury, loss, indebtedness, and so forth, and if names are unknown at the time of the presentation of the claim, that should be so stated.

7. Specific description of the location of public property involved in the occurrence.

8. The amount claimed including estimates of future loss with the basis of computation. If the amount of loss exceeds $10,000 a statement to that effect may be made and the dollar amount may be excluded from the claim.

Once this form is completed, serve it on the district counsel, or other responsible party for that governmental agency against whom the claim is being made. Consult the federal yellow pages or other government directories to obtain a name and title before sending the claim. Send claims by certified mail, return receipt requested, to guarantee proof of service. The automatic six-month denial pursuant to 28 U.S.C. § 2675(a) should be calendared as six months from the date received by the governmental agency as shown on the return receipt or on the receipt portion of your enclosure letter. **Form 1–5** is an example of a claim enclosure letter.

FORM 1–5
SAMPLE ENCLOSURE LETTER

CERTIFIED MAIL [number]

[date]

[city] Park District
Attn: Director
[address]

RE: [claimant] v. [city] Park District

Dear Sir:

Enclosed please find the original and one copy of a Claim Against the [city] Park District on Behalf of [claimant].

Please acknowledge receipt of this claim by completing and returning the additional copy of this letter to our office. The enclosed envelope is for your convenience.

If you have any questions, do not hesitate to call.

Very truly yours,

_____

[legal assistant name]

Enclosure-Claim

Receipt of the above-referenced claim is hereby acknowledged.

Dated: [date]

[name]

[title]

§ 1.6   Requirements for Perfecting a Federal Tort Claim

Requirements for perfecting a federal tort claim are set forth at Title 28, Code of Federal Regulations (C.F.R.), part 14, § 14.4, and Title 38, Code of Federal Regulations, part 14, §§ 14.606 and 14.607. This supporting data must be furnished before a public entity/federal agency will consider your claim "properly submitted." In addition to that information, you may submit a brief statement supporting the legal basis of the claim and justifying the amount demanded. This may include a settlement figure which is understood to be used for settlement negotiations only and not to be referred to in any subsequent litigation of the claim. Requirements for perfecting a federal tort claim are similar to a detailed settlement demand letter and include the following:

1. A written report by the attending physician, or other health care provider, setting forth the nature and extent of treatment, any degree of temporary or permanent disability, the prognosis, period of hospitalization, and any diminished earning capacity.

2. Itemized bills for medical, dental, and hospital expenses incurred, or itemized receipts of payment for such expenses, invoices, and other damage documentation.

3. If the prognosis reveals the necessity for future treatment, a statement of expected expenses for such treatment, or other future expense documentation.

4. If a claim is made for loss of time from employment, a written statement from the employer showing actual time lost from employment, whether they are a full- or part-time employee, and wages or salary actually lost.

5. If a claim is made for loss of income and the claimant is self-employed, documentary evidence showing the amount of earnings actually lost.

6. Claimant may be requested to furnish a copy of a medical opinion supporting the contention of malpractice, or future basis of liability claim.

7. Any other evidence or information which may have a bearing on either the responsibility of the United States for the personal injury, or the damages claimed.

In addition to the foregoing, the claimant may be required to submit to a physical or mental examination by a physician employed by the agency or another federal agency. A copy of the report of the examining physician shall be made available upon the claimant's written request, provided that the claimant furnished the report referred to in subparagraph (1) above and has made or agrees to make available to the agency any other physician's reports previously or thereafter made of the physical or mental condition which is the subject matter of the claim.

Failure to submit the required information or evidence may result in a determination that the claim has not been properly perfected, and the claim will be denied for failure to comply with C.F.R. § 14.4 et seq. An action may not be filed without seeking relief from those provisions and resubmitting the claim with the required supporting documentation.

§ 1.7   Rejecting a Federal Tort Case

Circumstances may arise requiring you to file a federal tort claim, or a claim against a state governmental agency or public entity, on behalf of a client whose case you may decide not to handle. Filing the claim to protect the statute for a prospective client may be done as a good-will gesture and is frequently necessary to buy time while you investigate the client's claim to decide whether or not your office will represent them. Rejecting a case is discussed in § **1.40** of this text, and those general principles apply in this instance. However, in the case of government claims, certain specific statutory deadlines must be *precisely set forth* in a rejection letter to avoid any misunderstanding or give rise to a potential malpractice action brought by the client who may think that by filing the government claim you have become "their attorney" and will be handling their case.

Form 1–6 is an example of a sample letter to send to a client when rejecting an action based on a federal tort claim. This letter should be sent certified mail, return receipt requested, with enclosures as indicated.

FORM 1–6
SAMPLE REJECTION LETTER

[date]

CERTIFIED MAIL
RETURN RECEIPT REQUESTED

PERSONAL AND CONFIDENTIAL

[claimant name]
[address]

RE: [claimant v. U.S.A.
      Reference [number]]

Dear [claimant]:

As you know, this office filed a claim on your behalf against [agency name] on [date]. Thereafter you provided us with medical records which we have reviewed along with your narrative letter enclosing further documentation.

To date, this office has received the enclosed letter from [name], [agency] District Counsel. After reviewing this matter, we have decided that we are unable to represent you in a medical malpractice action against the United States of America and the [agency]. As you know, a claim must be filed within two years of the date of accrual of injury. The government then has six months to deny your claim or the claim will be automatically denied by operation of law. 28 U.S.C. § 2675(a). If your claim is not formally denied by letter, but rather is deemed denied by operation of law, the date of that denial will be

[date], six months from the date of filing of your claim on [date]. You must then file your lawsuit by [date], one year after that denial. If you do not file within one year after the date of denial or the deemed denial date, your claim will be forever barred by the statute of limitations.

I strongly urge you to seek other counsel regarding this matter. I would be happy to discuss it further with you or your new counsel. With this letter, I am enclosing all materials you have provided to this office, and all correspondence we have received relating to this claim including copies of our certified letters to the [agency] presenting your claim, along with copies of certified mail return receipts indicating receipt of the claim.

Thank you for contacting our office. I am sorry we could not be of further assistance and hope that this matter is resolved satisfactorily for you.

Very truly yours,

[attorney name]

§ 1.8 Late Claims

The need to file late claims and to petition for relief from the provisions set forth in the Government Code for the timely filing of claims against public entities is a fact of life in many law firms. A client may be aware of the one-year statute of limitations from the date of his accident for filing of an action against particular defendants, but may be unaware of the fact that a potential defendant may be a public entity. The time limit for filing a claim against a public entity is less than one year, and, therefore, a client may not contact your office in time for the timely filing of a claim. The average unsophisticated client is also usually unaware that a public entity can be named as a defendant in a civil action for maintaining dangerous and defective conditions of public property, roadways, bridges, public overcrossings, freeway exits, public parks, and so forth, as part of a personal injury or wrongful death action.

To preserve your client's right to file against a public entity, an application for leave to present a late claim must be presented to the public entity involved as soon as you accept the client's case. An Application for Leave to Present a Late Claim must contain all of the information required by the governing code sections for government claims. The public entity then has the right, pursuant to statute, to accept or deny the Application for Leave to Present a Late Claim. Should the public entity reject the application, the effect is that no claim has been made, and while the plaintiff is not completely barred from filing an action naming that public entity, an estoppel defense may be raised by the public entity citing failure to comply with the technical requirements for filing a claim in a timely fashion.

If your application for permission to file a late claim is denied, consult your state's statutes regarding time requirements for filing a Petition to Seek Relief. In California, for example, a Petition for Relief from the provisions of Government

Code § 945.4 may be brought, pursuant to Government Code § 946.6, within six months after the denial of an application for permission to present a late claim.

California courts have held that the remedial provisions of Government Code § 946.6 should be liberally construed to grant relief upon a good cause showing of mistake, inadvertence, surprise or excusable neglect, or physical disability of petitioner. The statute provides for "judicial discretion" in granting relief from the bar to sue public entities. In order to prevail, the plaintiff (petitioner) must demonstrate that the original mistake (failure to file claim in a timely fashion) was due to *excusable neglect,* that an application seeking permission to file a late claim was made promptly upon recognition of the mistake, and that the public entity has not been prejudiced in any way by this late filing of a claim. If the claim concerns a dangerous or defective condition of public property, it is important that the condition which caused the original injury still be in the same condition as on the day of the injury, so that investigation by the public entity will not be hampered in any way by the delay.

Generally speaking, applications for permission to file late claims are granted if they are made within a reasonable time frame, and if it can be demonstrated that they were made as soon as counsel of record became aware of a cause of action against that particular public entity. Petitions for relief are usually granted unless extraordinary circumstances exist which would prejudice the investigation of the occurrence by the responding public entity.

Forms for application for permission to file a late claim, notice of motion for order relieving petitioner from the provisions of Government Code § 945.4, petition, memorandum of points and authorities and supporting declarations of attorney and petitioner as would be appropriate for California statutes are included in the following section. Consult form books of pleading and practice for your state to modify the sample. **Forms 1–7** through **1–11** are samples of pleadings required for permission to file late claims.

FORM 1–7
SAMPLE NOTICE OF MOTION

SUPERIOR COURT OF THE STATE OF [name]
COUNTY OF [county name]

[petitioner],	No. [case number]
Petitioner,	NOTICE OF MOTION FOR ORDER RELIEVING PETITIONERS FROM
-vs-	PROVISIONS OF GOVERNMENT CODE § 945.4
COUNTY OF [county name], CITY OF [city name] DEPARTMENT OF PUBLIC WORKS,	_____,
	[date] [time]
Respondents.	[department]

TO RESPONDENTS HEREIN:

YOU WILL PLEASE TAKE NOTICE that on [date] at [time] in Department [number] of the above-entitled court, petitioner will move the court for an order relieving petitioner from the provisions of Government Code Section [section number] on the grounds that the failure to present the claim was due to petitioner's mistake, inadvertence, surprise, excusable neglect, physical disability, and respondents have suffered no prejudice thereby.

Said motion will be based upon this notice, the petition for order relieving petitioner, the declarations of [name] and [petitioner], and the memorandum of points and authorities submitted herewith and upon such further oral and documentary evidence as may be presented at the hearing.

Dated: [date]

[attorney]

FORM 1–8
SAMPLE PETITION

SUPERIOR COURT OF THE STATE OF [state name]
COUNTY OF [county name]

[petitioner],	No. [case number]
Petitioner,	PETITION FOR RELIEVING PETITIONERS FROM THE
-vs-	PROVISIONS OF GOVERNMENT CODE § 945.4
COUNTY OF [county name] CITY OF [city name] DEPARTMENT OF PUBLIC WORKS,	[date] [time]
Respondents.	[department number]

TO THE HONORABLE SUPERIOR COURT AFORESAID:

Comes now petitioner, [name], by and through petitioner's attorneys, and petition this court for relief pursuant to Government Code Section [number] from having to present a claim for damage against the County of [name], City of [city name], and the [city] Department of Public Works and in support of said petition represent to the court as follows:

1.   Petitioner is a resident of the County of [county name], state of [state name]; the parties against whom the claim is asserted are the County of [county

name], the City of [city name], and the [city] Department of Public Works, local public entities of the State of [state name] within the meaning of [code section] of the Government Code.

2. Petitioner's claim is based on causes of action for negligence, premises liability, and dangerous and defective conditions of public property arising out of personal injuries sustained in a fall on [date] in [location]. Pursuant to the provisions of Government Code Section [number], on [date], petitioner presented to the City of [city name], City Council, petitioner's application for leave to file a late claim. This application was denied by the City of [city name] on [date], and a notice thereof was sent on [date].

3. Petitioner presented to the County of [county name], Board of Supervisors on [date], an application for leave to file a late claim setting forth the same facts, circumstances, and date provided to the City of [city name]. This application was denied by the County of [county name] on [date] and notice thereof was sent on [date].

4. Petitioner presented to the [city] Department of Public Works on [date], an application for leave to file a late claim. This application was denied by the [city] Department of Public Works on [date] and notice thereof was sent on [date].

5. Petitioner's failure to present petitioner's claim within the time limit specified by Government Code Section [number], such failure was due to petitioner's mistake, inadvertence, surprise, and excusable neglect in that petitioner was hospitalized at General Hospital [city, state] for open reduction of multiple leg fractures and placement of fifteen surgical screws and a surgical plate in petitioner's leg, through approximately [date], after which time petitioner was restricted to home until [date]. After petitioner was able to leave the house, petitioner still required substantial bodily assistance; petitioner was not able to consult with counsel regarding this matter until [date], after which consultation a claim was properly submitted.

6. The information required by Government Code Section [number] is contained in petitioner's proposed claims attached as Exhibits A, B, and C and incorporated by reference.

7. Petitioner has fulfilled both requirements of Government Code Section [number], namely, petitioner's reason for failure to file a timely claim is justified on the grounds of mistake, inadvertence, surprise, and excusable neglect, as is set forth in subpart [number], and petitioner filed an application for leave to file a late claim within a reasonable time. Said application and said claim were presented less than five months after the occurrence at issue. Further, the City of [city name], the County of [county name], and the [city] Department of Public Works will not be prejudiced if this court relieves petitioner from the provisions of Government Code Section [number] because the dangerous condition which caused petitioner's

TECHNICAL COLLEGE OF THE LOWCOUNTRY
LEARNING RESOURCES CENTER
POST OFFICE BOX 1288
BEAUFORT, SOUTH CAROLINA 29901-1288

injury is still in existence, uncured, and in the same condition as on the date of petitioner's injury, so that investigation may be pursued forthwith.

WHEREFORE, petitioner respectfully requests that this court exercise its discretion and relieve petitioner from the provisions of Section [number] and grant petitioner leave to file a suit for damages against the City of [city name], the County of [county name], and the [city] Department of Public Works.

Dated: [date]

[attorney name]

FORM 1–9
SAMPLE POINTS AND AUTHORITIES

SUPERIOR COURT OF THE STATE OF [state name]
COUNTY OF [county name]

[name],	No. [case number]
Petitioner,	MEMORANDUM OF POINTS AND AUTHORITIES IN SUPPORT OF
-vs-	PETITION FOR ORDER RELIEVING PETITIONER FROM PROVISIONS OF GOVERNMENT
COUNTY OF [county name], CITY OF [city name] DEPARTMENT OF PUBLIC WORKS,	CODE SECTION [number]
	[date]
	[time]
Respondents.	[department]

_____/

I. INTRODUCTION

Petitioner [name] seeks relief pursuant to Government Code Section 946.6 from the requirements set forth in Government Code Section 945.4 that petitioner file an administrative claim with the County of [county name], the City of [city name], and the [city] Department of Public Works prior to initiating suit against those entities.

On [date] petitioner was a pedestrian lawfully walking in the vicinity of Main and Elm Streets in the City of [city name] when petitioner fell into an uncovered, unmarked drainage hole. As a result of this fall, petitioner suffered severe personal injuries including multiple leg fractures. This required hospitalization for nine days and subsequent restriction to petitioner's home until late July.

After that time, petitioner still required substantial bodily assistance to ambulate and to this day still requires the aid of a cane. Petitioner anticipates further surgery being necessary in the future.

As set forth in petitioner's claim served on all the above-named parties on [date], petitioner contends that as a result of the creation and maintenance of the dangerous condition of the above-mentioned public property by all of the respondents petitioner was caused to suffer these severe personal injuries.

Petitioner seeks relief from the claim filing requirements on the grounds of mistake, inadvertence, surprise, or excusable neglect and physical disability in that petitioner was hospitalized and severely restricted in mobility throughout the 100-day period and was unable to consult with counsel within that time. A claim was submitted promptly after consultation with counsel and less than five months after the occurrence of the injury. Because the dangerous condition which caused petitioner's injury is still uncured, respondents can claim no prejudice.

II. THE REMEDIAL PROVISIONS OF GOVERNMENT CODE SECTION [number] SHOULD BE LIBERALLY CONSTRUED TO GRANT RELIEF UPON A SHOWING OF MISTAKE, INADVERTENCE, SURPRISE OR EXCUSABLE NEGLECT AS WELL AS PHYSICAL DISABILITY.

Government Code Section [number] provides for judicial discretion to grant relief from the bar to suit against public entities when an injured person fails to file a claim within one hundred days of the occurrence, stating in pertinent part:

> (a) Where an application for leave to present a claim is denied or deemed to be denied . . . a petition may be made to the court for an order relieving the petitioner from the provisions of section 945.4 . . .
>
> (b) The court shall relieve the petitioner from the provisions of section 945.4 if the court finds that the application to the Board under section 911.4 was made within a reasonable time not to exceed that specified in subdivision (d) of section 911.4 and was denied or deemed denied pursuant to section 911.6, and that:
>
> (1) the failure to present the claim was through a mistake, inadvertence, surprise, or excusable neglect unless the public entity established that it would be prejudiced if the court relieves the petitioner from the provisions of section 945.4 . . . and
>
> (3) the person who sustained the alleged injury, damage or loss was physically . . . incapacitated during all of the time . . . .

In the landmark case of Viles v. State 66 Cal. 2d 24, 56 Cal. Rptr. 666 (1967), the Supreme Court considered the intent of the legislature in including mistake, inadvertence, surprise, or excusable neglect (hereinafter referred to as "mistake") as a ground for relief. In Viles, the plaintiff's wife was killed in a highway collision on September 13, 1963. The collision allegedly resulted from a dangerous and defective condition of the state highway. After the accident, plaintiff was contacted by insurance adjusters who told him he had one year to bring suit for wrongful death. Relying on their information, plaintiff did not consult an attorney until June 1, 1964, when he first learned of the one-hundred-day claim structure.

The Supreme Court, in reversing the trial court's refusal to grant relief from the claims provisions, noted that in adding mistake as a ground, the legislature was undoubtedly influenced by the Law Revisions Commission's warning that the inflexible time limits of the claims statute provided a trap for the unwary and ignorant claimant and that the Commission intended to alleviate the harshness of strict compliance with the claims presentation statute by those who were excusably neglectful. The Court observed:

> Based on information received from insurance adjusters experienced in claims work that he had a year in which to bring an action, plaintiff erroneously concluded that an action against the State could be brought in the same manner and in the same time limits as one against a private person, and we cannot say that this was an unreasonable conception nor one that the average prudent man in the conduct of important business affairs would not have formed. . . .
>
> We are of the opinion that the mistake made by plaintiff was of the type foreseen by the legislature and that his neglect to present his claim within one hundred days because of his honest belief that he had a year to act was excusable. Viles, *supra,* at pp. 29–31.

Finally, the Viles court concluded:

> Under the well-recognized policy of the law to liberally construe remedial statutes designed to protect persons within their purview and the modern trend of judicial decisions in favor of granting relief unless absolutely forbidden by statute, we are of the opinion that the trial court's denial of the petition defeats the legislative objective and was an abuse of discretion. (Id., 32–33.)

See also Tammen v. County of San Diego, 66 Cal. 2d 468, 58 Cal. Rptr. 249, (1967), 480 and State v. Superior Court, 86 Cal. App. 3d 475, 481, 150 Cal. Rptr., 308 (1978).

An honest mistake is excusable if it is reasonably foreseeable that the claimant would so act. Viles at 29. It is completely reasonable that a person as severely injured as Mrs. Brown would not be able to file a claim within the 100-day period. She was hospitalized and housebound throughout this period and unable to consult with counsel regarding any causes of action she might have or to ascertain who might have been responsible for creating the dangerous condition causing her injuries. Petitioner then pursued her claim with reasonable diligence once her physical condition permitted.

In State v. Superior Court, 86 Cal. App. 3d 475, 150 Cal. Rptr. 308 (1978), the claimant was injured in July of 1976 and hospitalized until December of 1976. He did not file his late claim until August of 1977—13 months after the incident on the grounds of physical incapacitation. The trial court relieved him from the late claim requirement and the appellate court affirmed stating that hospitalization time during which the claimant is incapacitated, must be deducted. The claim must be reasonably filed after this period is ended. Id. at 483. Mrs. Brown's situation is analogous to this situation. She, too, was unable to file her claim while disabled and promptly filed her claim once her disability was alleviated. If the period of her disability is deducted, petitioner clearly filed her claim within the 100-day limit.

Public policy in this state also compels a holding that petitioner be relieved from the requirements of the late claim statute. Section 946.6 is a remedial statute designed to provide relief from technical pleading rules. The policy underlying this statute is that cases should be heard on their merits and not decided on technical rules. All doubts must be resolved in favor of the statute's application. Moore v. State, 157 Cal. App. 3d 715, 721, 203 Cal. Rptr. 847 (1984). Petitioner was seriously injured and unable to technically comply with the strict requirements of the statute. The gravity of her injuries and the dangerous condition of the public property on which she was injured, mandates an opportunity for her cause to be adjudicated on its merits. Clear frustration of the public policy underlying Section 946.6 will be the result if petitioner is not allowed to file her suit.

III. PETITIONER'S APPLICATION TO FILE A LATE CLAIM WAS MADE WITHIN A REASONABLE TIME AFTER THE INCIDENT AND RESPONDENTS HAVE NOT BEEN PREJUDICED BY THE DELAY.

Once petitioner was able to consult with counsel, petitioner's claim was promptly filed. The public entities were put on notice of her claim less than five months after the occurrence of the injury and only 46 days after the 100-day claim period expired. Courts allowing relief from the claim statute have stressed that the public entity must now be prejudiced by the delay in presentation of the claim. *See generally* Moore v. State at 721 and Segal v. Southern California Rapid Transit District, 12 Cal. App. 3d 509, 512, 190 Cal. Rptr. 720 (1970). Respondents here have in no way been prejudiced by petitioner's slight delay in presenting petitioner's claim. The dangerous condition created by the uncovered, unmarked drainage hole continue unabated as of this date. There can be no claim, then, that respondents are unable to investigate the facts surrounding petitioner's claim.

IV. CONCLUSION

Petitioner has presented ample evidence to show that petitioner's failure to file a claim prior to [date], was due to petitioner's physical disability and excusable neglect. The evidence herein presented suggests that as soon as petitioner's physical condition allowed, petitioner acted diligently in consulting with counsel and filing a claim with each public entity. Further, respondents have not been prejudiced by this delay as the dangerous condition causing petitioner's injuries continues unabated.

In the event that this petition is not granted on the grounds heretofore presented, petitioner prays for leave of court to prove that the County of [county name], the City of [city name], and the [city] Department of Public Works should be estopped from raising the defense of failure to comply with Government Code Section [number], *et seq.* Petitioner is informed and believes and thereon alleges that the evidence will show that these public entities do not consider such claims in good faith and routinely deny them without substantial investigation or determination of their validity.

In view of the foregoing authorities, it is respectfully requested that this court pursuant to Government Code Section [number] relieve [petitioner] from the requirements of Government Code Section [number] and grant petitioner leave to file an action against the County of [county name], the City of [city name], and the [city] Department of Public Works.

Dated: [date]

[attorney name]

FORM 1–10
SAMPLE DECLARATION OF PETITIONER

SUPERIOR COURT OF THE STATE OF [state name]
COUNTY OF [county name]

[name]	No. [case number]
Petitioner,	DECLARATION OF [Petitioner] IN SUPPORT OF
-vs-	PETITION FOR RELIEF
COUNTY OF [county name] CITY OF [city name] DEPARTMENT OF PUBLIC WORKS,	[date] [time]
Respondents.	

_____/

I, [petitioner name], declare under penalty of perjury that the following is true and correct:

I was hospitalized at General Hospital in [city, state] from [date] to [date], for open reduction of multiple leg fractures and placement of fifteen surgical screws and a surgical plate in my leg.

I was restricted to my home until [date]. After this time, I was able to leave my house only with substantial bodily assistance.

I first consulted my attorney regarding this matter on [date], when I met with [attorney name].

I still require the use of a cane in ambulation and have been informed that my injuries will require future surgical correction next spring.

Executed [date], at [city], [state].

[Petitioner]

FORM 1–11
SAMPLE DECLARATION OF PETITIONER'S ATTORNEY

SUPERIOR COURT OF THE STATE OF [state name]
COUNTY OF [county name]

[name]	No. [case number]
Petitioner,	DECLARATION OF [petitioner's attorney] IN SUPPORT OF PETITION FOR RELIEF
-vs-	
COUNTY OF [county name], CITY OF [city name] DEPARTMENT OF PUBLIC WORKS, Respondents.	[date] [time]

_____/

I, [petitioner's attorney], declare under penalty of perjury that the following is true and correct:

I am a member of the law firm of [name of law firm], attorneys of record for petitioner herein, and I am duly licensed to practice law in the State of [state name].

On [date], I was first contacted by [petitioner] regarding any possible causes of action petitioner might have as a result of petitioner's injuries.

On [date], an application for leave to present a late claim was presented to the City of [city name], the County of [county name], and the [city] Department of Public Works. Copies of these documents are attached hereto and labeled as Exhibits A, B, and C.

On [date], the City of [city name] sent notice that the application for leave to present a late claim was denied by the City Council on [date]. A copy of said document is attached as Exhibit D.

On [date], the County of [county name] sent notice that the application for leave to present a late claim was denied by the Board of Supervisors on [date]. A copy of said document is attached as Exhibit E.

On [date], the [city] Department of Public Works sent notice that the application for leave to present a late claim was denied by the [county name] County Board of Supervisors on [date]. A copy of said document is attached as Exhibit F.

Petitioner's application for leave to present a late claim (Exhibits A, B, and C) contains all the information required by Government Code Section [number].

This petition is made within six months following rejection of the application for leave to file a late claim in conformity with Government Code Section [number]. Furthermore, the above-named public entities will not be prejudiced by the granting of the relief sought, since they received actual notice of the petitioner's claim less than five months after the incident and less than two months after the 100-day claim statute had run.

Since the dangerous condition of the public property giving rise to the claim has not been abated, the information necessary remains available to the County.

It is respectfully requested that the subject petition for relief under the provisions of the Government Code be granted.

Executed [date[, at [city], [state].

[petitioner's attorney]

§ 1.9   Petitions for Appointment of a Guardian Ad Litem

Before a cause of action can be initiated for a minor, or for a person judged to be incompetent, a petition must be filed for the appointment of a guardian ad litem. A minor or an incompetent has no standing on their own to bring a cause of action; they must do so through a court-appointed guardian ad litem who is then responsible for protecting their interests and pursuing the action. Although it differs from state to state (check you local code), minors over a certain age must give their consent to the appointment. Petitions for the appointment of a guardian ad litem:

1. Can be made ex parte to be presented to court for approval without the necessity of a hearing
2. Must contain declarations by the guardian ad litem(s) (parents can both be appointed), and a brief description of the cause of action
3. Must be prepared with an ex parte order that is presented to the court along with the executed petition.

Forms 1–12 and **1–13** illustrate a sample ex parte petition and an order for an appointment of a guardian ad litem.

FORM 1–12
SAMPLE EX PARTE PETITION FOR APPOINTMENT
OF A GUARDIAN AD LITEM

[name and address of law firm]
Attorneys for [plaintiffs A and B]
as guardians ad litem for
[minor A] and [minor B]

IN THE SUPERIOR COURT OF THE STATE OF [state name]
IN AND FOR THE COUNTY OF [county name]

[plaintiff A] and [plaintiff B]	)	
as guardians ad litem for	)	No. [case number]
[minor A] and	)	
[minor B],	)	
	)	EX PARTE PETITION
	)	FOR APPOINTMENT OF
Plaintiffs,	)	GUARDIAN AD LITEM
	)	OF MINOR TO PROSECUTE ACTION
vs.	)	BY PARENT CCP § 1373
	)	
[defendant A], [defendant B],	)	
[defendant C],	)	
DOES 1 through 10, inclusive,	)	
	)	
Defendants.	)	
_____	)	

Petitioners [plaintiffs A and B] respectfully represent:

1. Petitioners are the mother and father of [minor A], and [minor B], minors.

2. That minor [A], was born [date], and is [number] years of age. That minor [B] was born on [date], and is [number] years of age.

3. The minors have a cause of action against the above-named defendants on which a suit should be brought in this court. The cause of action arises out of physical injuries suffered by plaintiff [minor A], as a result of an accident which occurred when he was struck and dragged by a motor vehicle operated by defendant [A]. This accident occurred in the street near [address] in [city, state] on [date]. Plaintiff [minor A] sustained physical and mental injuries and was forced to expend certain costs for medical treatment.

4. The minor [B] has a cause of action against the above-named defendants on which a suit should be brought in this court. The cause of action arises out of the emotional distress that [minor B] suffered due to the shock resulting from the direct emotional impact upon her from the sensory and contemporaneous observation of the accident to her younger brother.

5. [Plaintiffs A and B] are willing to serve as the guardians ad litem for the minors and are fully competent to understand and protect the rights of the minors and have no interest adverse to that of the minors.

6. WHEREFORE, petitioners pray that [plaintiff A and B] be appointed guardians ad litem for [minor A] and [minor B] to prosecute the above-described causes of action on behalf of these minors, and for such other and further relief as the court may deem proper.

DATED: [date]   [plaintiff A]

DATED: [date]   [plaintiff B]

DATED: [date]   [plaintiff's attorney]

VERIFICATION

[Plaintiff A] and [plaintiff B] state they are the petitioners in the above-named proceeding. We have read the foregoing petition and know the contents thereof. The same is true of our own knowledge, except as to those matters which are therein represented on information and belief, and as to those matters, we believe them to be true.

We declare under penalty of perjury under the laws of the State of [state name] that the foregoing is true and correct.

DATED: [date]   [plaintiff A]

DATED: [date]   [plaintiff B]

CONSENT OF NOMINEES

We, [plaintiff A] and [plaintiff B], the nominees of petitioners in the above petition, consent to serve as guardians ad litem for [minor A] and [minor B], and to prosecute the above-entitled cause of action on their behalf.

DATED: [date]   [plaintiff A]

DATED: [date]   [plaintiff B]

FORM 1–13
SAMPLE ORDER FOR APPOINTMENT
OF A GUARDIAN AD LITEM

[name and address of law firm]
[attorneys for plaintiffs]
[plaintiff A] and [plaintiff B]

as guardians ad litem for
[minor A] and
[minor B]

IN THE SUPERIOR COURT OF THE STATE OF [state name]
IN AND FOR THE COUNTY OF [county name]

[plaintiff A] and [plaintiff B])	
as guardians ad litem for)	No. [case number]
[minor A] and)	
[minor B],)	ORDER FOR APPOINTMENT
)	OF GUARDIAN AD LITEM
Plaintiffs,)	OF MINOR (CCP § 1373)
vs.)	
[defendant A], [defendant B],)	
[defendant C],)	
DOES 1 through 10, inclusive,)	
)	
Defendants.)	
_____)	

The verified petition of [plaintiff A] and [plaintiff B] to be appointed guardians ad litem of [minor A] and [minor B], minors, was considered by the court on this date. Petitioners appeared by counsel, [name of attorney]. On proof made to the satisfaction of the court, the court finds the appointment is expedient.

IT IS ORDERED that the petition of [plaintiff A] and [plaintiff B] be granted, and [plaintiff A] and [plaintiff B] are appointed guardians ad litem for [minor A] and [minor B], to prosecute the above-entitled action for them.

Dated: [date]

[name of judge]
Judge of the Superior Court

§ 1.10   Procedures for Bringing Suit Against Minors

Bringing a tort action against a minor is possible only by naming the parents or guardians of that minor as defendants. Liability for the actions of a minor, whether or not that minor is living at home, is imputed to the parents, guardians, or other persons responsible for that minor. The most common tort actions filed against minors and their parents are negligent entrustment of a motor vehicle and negligent supervision and training of a minor child resulting in destruction of public or private property. In negligent entrustment of motor vehicle actions, parents are often the registered owners and the minor child is the driver of the vehicle involved in an accident. In that case, a cause of action against the parents exists as registered owners of the vehicle, and a second cause of action exists against the parents for the negligent entrustment of that vehicle to the minor child. Where a minor is the responsible party for the destruction or vandalism of public or private property, parental liability stems from negligent supervision of the minor child. Case law varies from state to state, both enlarging and restricting the liability of parents for the actions of their children. Once an action has been brought by the filing of a complaint naming the parents, guardians, or other responsible adults along with naming the minor, a petition for guardian ad litem must be filed by the parents before answering the complaint. The purpose of the appointment of a guardian ad litem is to afford a minor the opportunity not only to bring an action against others, but also to defend against any actions brought against them.

§ 1.11 Emancipated Minors

Minors who become emancipated through operation of law are treated as individuals with the same rights and obligations as an adult. They may bring an action on their own behalf without benefit of a guardian ad litem, and likewise, they may be named as a defendant in an action without being sued through a guardian ad litem. Emancipated minors may enter into contracts on their own signature and be held liable to fulfill contractual obligations. Likewise, they may bring an action for breach of contract. The age of emancipation varies from state to state. By seeking emancipation, a minor declares before the courts that the minor wishes to be considered in all respects legally an adult responsible for their own actions. By declaring their emancipation, minors forego the protection offered by case law and statute to minors involved in litigation.

§ 1.12 Appointment of a Guardian Ad Litem for an Incompetent Person

The most common situation requiring the appointment of a guardian ad litem arises when parents of a minor child wish to bring a tort action on behalf of that child. A less common situation arises when it is necessary to bring an action on behalf of an incompetent person. The person may have become incompetent due to age or infirmity, or have been rendered incompetent as a result of a serious accident. An application for appointment of a guardian ad litem for an incompetent follows the same procedures as outlined in § 1.9 with the exception that an order must first be obtained by the superior court of the county in which the action is to be brought appointing petitioner the conservator of the incompetent person. A Petition for Conservatorship is a preprinted form available in the probate departments of all superior courts. The appointment of a conservator is done by the probate commissioner. Once the petitioner has been appointed the conservator of the incompetent person, follow statutory procedures as outlined in your state Code of Civil Procedure for appointment of a guardian ad litem. The precise wording of the statute and specific procedure required may vary from state to state; however, the substance will remain the same as exemplified in **Forms 1–14** and **1–15.** Consult form books of pleading and practice for your state, and make necessary modifications to conform to statutes and local court rules.

FORM 1–14
SAMPLE PETITION FOR APPOINTMENT OF
GUARDIAN AD LITEM FOR INCOMPETENT

IN THE SUPERIOR COURT OF THE STATE OF [state name]
IN AND FOR THE COUNTY OF [county name]

[Plaintiff A]   No. [case number]
by and through his guardian
ad litem, [guardian],

           Plaintiff,

                                                      PETITION FOR APPOINTMENT
-vs.-   FOR GUARDIAN AD LITEM
                                                      OF INCOMPETENT PERSON
                                                      TO PROSECUTE ACTION

[defendant A]; [defendant B];
[defendant C]; [defendant D];
and DOES 1
through 20, inclusive,

           Defendants.
_____/

Petitioner [plaintiff B] respectfully represents:

1. Petitioner is the duly appointed and acting conservator of the body and the estate of [plaintiff A], an incompetent person in [county name] County, and plaintiff in the above-entitled action.

2. [Plaintiff A] is a 19-year-old [sex], [date of birth] who was declared incompetent on [date], by an order of the Superior Court of [county name] County [case number] in which petitioner was appointed the conservator of the body and the estate of [plaintiff A] (see Exhibit "A" attached hereto and made a part of this Petition).

3. The incompetent, [plaintiff A], has a cause of action and a claim for damages against the above-named defendants on which a suit should be brought in this court. The causes of action arise out of an automobile accident in which [Plaintiff A] was a passenger in an automobile which went off the road and crashed into a utility pole in [county name] County, State of [state name], causing severe physical and mental injuries, which have placed him in a coma.

4. [Guardian] is the [mother/father] of [plaintiff A] and is willing to serve as the guardian ad litem for the incompetent, [plaintiff A], and is fully competent to understand and protect [plaintiff A]'s rights and has no interest adverse to that of the incompetent.

WHEREFORE, petitioner prays that [plaintiff B] be appointed guardian ad litem for [plaintiff A] to prosecute the above-described cause of action on behalf of [plaintiff B], and for such other and further relief as the court may deem proper.

Dated: [date]   [plaintiff B]

Dated: [date]   [plaintiff A]

VERIFICATION

[Guardian] states that [guardian] is the petitioner in the above-named proceeding. I have read the foregoing petition and know the contents thereof. The same is true of my own knowledge, except as to those matters which are therein represented on information and belief, and as to those matters, I believe them to be true.

I declare under penalty of perjury under the laws of the State of [state name] that the foregoing is true and correct.

Dated: [date]

[plaintiff B]

CONSENT OF NOMINEE

I, [guardian], the nominee of petitioner in the above petition, consent to serve as guardian ad litem for [plaintiff A] and to prosecute the above-entitled causes of action on [plaintiff A]'s behalf.

Dated: [date]

[plaintiff B]

FORM 1–15
SAMPLE ORDER FOR APPOINTMENT OF
GUARDIAN AD LITEM OF AN INCOMPETENT

IN THE SUPERIOR COURT OF THE STATE OF [state name]
IN AND FOR THE COUNTY OF [county name]

[Plaintiff A]   No. [case number]
by and through his guardian

ad litem, [plaintiff B],

        Plaintiff,

-vs-

[defendant A]; [defendant B];
[defendant C]; [defendant D];
and DOES 1 through 20,
inclusive,

        Defendants.
_____/

                ORDER FOR APPOINTMENT
                OF GUARDIAN AD LITEM
                OF INCOMPETENT CCP § 1373

The verified petition of [plaintiff B] to be appointed guardian ad litem of [plaintiff A], an incompetent, was considered by the court on this date. On proof made to the satisfaction of the court, the court finds the appointment is expedient.

IT IS ORDERED that the petition of [plaintiff B] be granted, and [plaintiff B] is appointed guardian ad litem for [plaintiff A], to prosecute the above-entitled action for [plaintiff A].

Dated: [date]

                [name of judge]
                Judge of the Superior Court

§ 1.13   Deceased Plaintiffs and Defendants

In the special circumstance of a deceased plaintiff or deceased defendant, the executor or special administrator may bring or defend an action on their behalf. This is only possible after an order appointing an executor or special administrator has been signed by the probate judge, with letters of special administration issued. An order appointing a special administrator for the sole purpose of bringing or defending an action can be granted even if the decedent's will has not been filed or admitted to probate. This appointment of a special administrator is considered limited to one function, representing and protecting the interests of a decedent. Once that has been done, a complaint can be filed on behalf of the decedent by the person named executor or special administrator. That person then "stands in the shoes" of the decedent just as the guardian ad litem "stands in the shoes" of the minor or incompetent. Not only can that person initiate or defend an action, but that person also may propound and respond to discovery on behalf of the named litigant and exercise all privileges on behalf of the minor, incompetent, or decedent. This becomes especially important in the discovery arena and protects against the disclosure of sensitive information. For example, in California the Evidence Code provides that an executor as personal representative of a decedent can claim a privilege against disclosure of confidential medical and psychiatric records. The privilege remains intact and outlives the patient, as long as the executor is claiming the privilege to protect the interests of the estate.

§ 1.14   Claims Against a Decedent's Estate

In general, a lawsuit cannot be maintained against a decedent's estate. A lawsuit pending against a decedent at the time of his death cannot be continued, unless plaintiff files a timely creditor's claim in the probate proceedings of the decedent's estate. There are exceptions to this rule, and local rules must be consulted. Official forms are available for claims at the Probate Commissioner's office, and they must be used.

Timely filing of creditor's claims, like government claims, is an essential element of a cause of action against a decedent's estate and must be affirmatively pleaded as part of the complaint, and proved at trial. Contents of a creditor's claim are:

Claimant's name and address

Amount of money/damages

Description of the circumstances of the damage or debt, and

A verified statement that no monies have been paid to claimant and no offsets are known to exist.

§ 1.15   Civil Actions Against a Decedent's Estate

Actions may be filed against a decedent's estate by filing a creditor's claim. However, in some situations a cause of action may exist which can be satisfied through assets held by the decedent independent of those considered "part of his estate." An example of this would be when the decedent was the driver of a vehicle involved in an automobile accident causing serious injuries to others and the decedent's own death. If the decedent driver was protected by liability insurance at the time of the accident, permission may be sought to file an action against the decedent which will not prejudice the assets of the estate and seek recovery only against decedent's insurer (the policy limits of the liability insurance). An *ex parte* petition may be presented to the court seeking permission to file such a complaint. (The proposed complaint must be attached to the petition.) Consult your local court rules, confer with the probate commissioner, and check probate rules for your state before filing such a petition. **Forms 1–16** through **1–18** are samples of these documents.

FORM 1–16
SAMPLE EX PARTE PETITION AND COMPLAINT

SUPERIOR COURT OF THE STATE OF [state name]
COUNTY OF [county name]

[plaintiff A] and [plaintiff B],   No. [case number]

Plaintiffs,	EX PARTE PETITION TO FILE
	AGAINST DECEDENT WITH
-vs-	INSURANCE PROTECTION AND
	ORDER (PROBATE CODE [section number])

ESTATE OF [defendant A], Deceased;
DOE ONE, DOE TWO, DOE THREE,
DOE FOUR, inclusive,

        Defendants.

_____/

Petitioners [plaintiff A] and [plaintiff B] allege:

1. Petitioners received severe personal injuries on or about [date] when the vehicle in which they were traveling was struck head-on due to the negligence of the decedent, [defendant A]. Petitioners believe they have a good cause of action against decedent for damages incurred as a result of said negligence.

2. Petitioners are informed and believe and thereon allege that at the time of the subject accident the decedent, [defendant A], was protected by liability insurance with respect to the subject accident.

3. Petitioners are informed and believe and thereon allege that at the time of her death, decedent, [defendant A], was a resident of the City of [city name], County of [county name], State of [state name].

4. The interests of the Estate of [defendant A] will not be prejudiced if petitioners are granted leave to file an action for personal injuries resulting from the negligence of the decedent, [defendent A].

5. Petitioners agree to seek no recovery against the decedent's estate or against any heir or beneficiary of the decedent, and agree and hereby stipulate to recover or seek judgment only as against decedent's insurer and, specifically, to seek no relief from the decedent's estate or decedent representative or heirs or beneficiaries other than to the extent coverage is provided by the insurer or insurers in question.

I declare under penalty of perjury that the foregoing is true and correct.

Executed this [date] day of March, [year], at [city, state].

                [plaintiff A]

                [plaintiff B]

POINTS AND AUTHORITIES

Probate Code [code number] provides:

Dated: [date]

By: [attorney for plaintiffs]

FORM 1–17
SAMPLE COMPLAINT FOR DAMAGES

SUPERIOR COURT OF THE STATE OF [state name]
COUNTY OF [county name]

[plaintiff A] and [plaintiff B]	No. [case number]
Plaintiffs,	(Proposed) COMPLAINT FOR DAMAGES (Personal Injury)
-vs-	
ESTATE OF [defendant A], Deceased; DOES 1 through 20, inclusive	
Defendants.	
_____/	

CAUSE OF ACTION FOR NEGLIGENCE BROUGHT BY
PLAINTIFFS AGAINST ALL DEFENDANTS

1. Defendants DOES 1 through 20, inclusive, are sued herein under fictitious names; plaintiffs do not at this time know the true names or capacities of said defendants, but pray that the same may be inserted herein when ascertained.

2. At all times herein mentioned, each defendant was the agent, servant, employee, partner, and joint venturer of each of the other defendants and at all of said times as acting within the course and scope of such agency, service, employment, partnership, and joint venture.

3. At all times herein mentioned, decedent [defendant A] and DOE ONE owned, entrusted, controlled, serviced, repaired, and maintained the 1988 Honda Prelude automobile herein mentioned; at all of said times said automobile was being driven and operated by decedent [defendant A] by and with the permission and consent of, and as agent, servant, and employee of said defendant owners.

4. On or about [date], plaintiff [B] was operating a 1980 Chevrolet southbound on [route number] at or near the [location] on the [name] Bridge, in the City and County of [name], State of [state name]. Plaintiff [A] was a passenger in said vehicle.

5. At said time and place, defendant [A] was operating said Honda automobile in a generally northerly direction on [route number], at or near [location] on the [name] Bridge, City and County of [name].

6. At said time and place, decedent [defendant A] so carelessly and negligently owned, entrusted, controlled, serviced, repaired, maintained, drove, and operated said Honda automobile as to cause the same to cross into the northbound lane and to collide with the vehicle in which plaintiffs were riding, thereby causing plaintiffs to be thrown in and about said vehicle and to sustain the injuries and damages hereinafter mentioned.

7. Defendant [A] died in the aforementioned collision and by order of the within Court duly made and entered, plaintiffs were given leave to file this complaint against [defendant A]'s estate.

8. By reason of the premises, plaintiffs were caused to sustain severe personal injuries and to undergo a course of pain and suffering and have sustained general damages.

9. By reason of the premises, plaintiffs have been compelled to incur obligations as and for medical services, medicines, x-rays, hospitalization, and medical supplies and will in the future be compelled to incur additional obligations therefor; plaintiffs do not at this time know the reasonable value thereof, but pray that the same may be inserted herein when ascertained.

10. By reason of the premises, plaintiffs have been deprived of their respective earnings and earning capacities and will in the future be deprived thereof; plaintiffs do not at the time know the reasonable value thereof, but pray that the same may be inserted herein when ascertained.

11. By reason of the premises plaintiffs claim prejudgment interest; plaintiffs do not at this time know the reasonable value thereof, but pray that the same may be inserted herein when ascertained.

WHEREFORE, plaintiffs pray for judgment against decedent [defendant A]'s estate for general damages, for the items of special damage and loss of earnings above mentioned when ascertained, for interest according to law, for costs of suit herein, and for such further relief as the Court deems just and proper.

Dated: [date]

[attorney for plaintiffs]

FORM 1–18
SAMPLE ORDER GRANTING LEAVE TO FILE
ACTION AGAINST DECEDENT

SUPERIOR COURT OF THE STATE OF [state name]
COUNTY OF [county name]

[plaintiff A] and [plaintiff B],	No. [case number]
Plaintiffs,	ORDER GRANTING LEAVE TO FILE ACTION AGAINST DECEDENT WITH INSURANCE PROTECTION
-vs-	
ESTATE OF [defendant A], Deceased; DOE ONE, DOE TWO, DOE THREE, DOE FOUR, Inclusive,	
Defendants.	

Upon reading the verified Petition of [plaintiff A] and [plaintiff B], and finding that the interests of the Estate will not be prejudiced, IT IS HEREBY ORDERED that petitioners are granted leave to file an action against the ESTATE OF [defendant A].

Dated: [date]

[name of judge]
Judge of the Superior Court

§ 1.16   Considerations Before Filing a Lawsuit

Prior to filing a lawsuit there are several factors which should be considered and evaluated. The objective of filing is to obtain a favorable result for the client at the least cost in both attorney/paralegal time and money. The main factors to be considered include:

1. Cost effectiveness
2. Attorney evaluation of credibility of client
3. Likelihood of recovery should the case go to trial, and
4. Amount of damages versus potential recovery.

Questions to consider in evaluating these factors are:

1. Can a client afford, emotionally and financially, to see this case through the discovery necessary to bring it to trial?

2. Can damages be documented by supporting papers, files, reports, and testimony of witnesses?

3. Is there any possibility that this case can be settled through effective informal discovery such as use of public records, client documents, and a carefully prepared demand letter?

4. Is the client emotionally stable enough to withstand the vigorous demands of protracted litigation on the client's mental and emotional state?

5. What are the client's main motivations for seeking recovery for this wrong? Is it a matter of principle? Revenge? Justifiable reliance? How will this motivation influence the client's rationality?

6. Is this a case that will "sell" well to a jury? Are the fact patterns and story line of this case plausible to the average juror in the sense that they can identify with the situation?

7. Last of all, money. Is it realistic to expend $21,000 when the chances of recovery might be limited to $19,000?

§ 1.17   Evaluation of Damages

Evaluating damages is an important aspect of deciding whether or not to undertake representation of a particular client. In order to successfully prove your client's case, liability must be established; however, in cases of clear and/or undisputed liability where substantial damages may not exist or cannot be proven; the client may win "on paper only" and end up losing since the cost of the litigation would exceed the potential recovery. In cases of this nature, it is advisable to recommend that the client consider representing himself by filing a pro per action. The amount of recovery available in Small Claims Court has recently been raised in many states. If liability is clear and damages are nominal, filing in pro per in Small Claims Court is a means of obtaining a moral victory and damages. The amount of potential damages should always exceed the costs of litigation for the client to be a "winner".

There are many elements of damages as well as many different types of damages. **Damage** is defined as:

> A loss, injury or deterioration caused by the negligence, design or accident of one person to another. An injury produces a right in them who have suffered any damage to demand reparation of such damage from the authors of the injury. By damage it is understood to be every loss or diminution of what is a man's own, occasioned by the fault of another.[1]

Damages which may be recovered in litigation are further defined as "a pecuniary compensation or indemnity, which may be recovered in the courts by any person who has suffered loss, detriment, or injury whether to his person, property, or rights through the unlawful act or omission or negligence of another person."[2]

---

[1] Black's Law Dictionary 406 (4th ed. 1951).

[2] *Id.* 467–69.

Categories of damages set forth in *Black's Law Dictionary*[3] which may be recovered in the courts include:

Actual damages—real, substantial and just damages for actual and real loss or injury as opposed to nominal, exemplary, special or punitive damages.

Compensatory damages—those damages that will compensate the injured party for the injury sustained and nothing more. Damages that will simply make good or replace the loss caused by the wrong or injury, or which will make them "whole" again.

Consequential damages—such damage, loss or injury as does not flow directly and immediately from the act of the party, but only from some of the consequences or results of such act or omission, that damage which may be remote and does not follow immediately in point of time upon the doing of the act which is complained of.

Continuing damages—those damages which accrue from the same injury or from repetition of similar acts (a continuing course of conduct), between specified periods of time.

Direct damages—same as actual damages. These damages immediately follow the act or omission.

Exemplary damages—also known as excessive damages, or punitive damages; these are damages on an increased scale which are awarded to the plaintiff over and above what will compensate him for his property loss, injury to person, business reputation, or rights. These damages are usually awarded in cases of oppression, malice, fraud, or wanton or wicked conduct on the part of the defendant and are intended to compensate the plaintiff for mental anguish, injury to his feelings, humiliation, embarrassment, shame, slanderous conduct, or aggravations of the original wrongdoing. The purpose of these damages is also to punish the defendant for evil behavior and make an example of the defendent.

General damages—these damages are such as the law itself implies or presumes to have accrued from the wrong complained of for the reason that they are its immediate, direct, and proximate result or such as necessarily result from the injury or did in fact result from the wrong, directly, and proximately, without reference to the special character, condition or circumstance of the plaintiff. General damages are similar to actual and direct damages.

Intervening damages—these are damages to an appellee which result from the delay caused by an appeal from a judgment in a lower court which was in appellee's favor.

Irreparable damages—damages pertaining to injunctions for which no certain pecuniary standard exists for measurement. These damages are frequently awarded in actions concerning public nuisances, condemnation actions, land use questions, and so forth. The term *irreparable damages* is defined as wrongs of a repeated and continuing character or which occasion damages which can be estimated only by conjecture, and not by any accurate standard.

---

[3] *Id.* 466–69.

Land damages—this term is often applied to the amount of compensation to be paid for land (real property) taken under the power of eminent domain, or for the injury to or depreciation of that land which adjoins that which has been taken.

Liquidated damages and penalties—this term applies when the amount of the damages has been ascertained by the judgment in the action, when a specific sum of money has been expressly stipulated by the parties to a bond or other contract as the amount of damages to be recovered by either party for a breach of the agreement by the other. The purpose of this penalty is to secure performance (specific performance of a particular contractual obligation), while the purpose of stipulating damages as liquidated damages in a contract is to fix the amount to be paid in lieu of performance.

Nominal damages—nominal damages are a "trifling sum" awarded to a plaintiff in an action, when there is no substantial loss or injury to be compensated, but still the law recognized a technical invasion of the defendant's rights or a breach of the defendant's duty, or where there has been a real injury and the plaintiff's evidence entirely fails to show its actual amount. In evaluating a case when it is determined that nominal damages are all that plaintiff can hope to recover, plaintiff should be advised to seek relief in small claims courts or municipal courts by filing an action in proper.

Permanent damages—those damages which are awarded on the theory that the cause of injury is fixed and that the property will always remain subject to it, for example, crop damage, land erosion, and damages caused by toxic waste disposal. Permanent damages also arise in personal injury and product liability actions, where a person who has been injured has not made a 100 percent recovery and is left with a permanent disability.

Prospective damages—also defined as remote and/or speculative damages. They are damages which are similar to future damages and which are expected to flow from the act or state of facts which made the basis of a plaintiff's action. These damages are not accrued at the time of the trial, but given the nature of things, a reasonable man would conclude that these damages would necessarily or probably result from the acts or state of facts which has been complained of in the action.

Special damages—those damages which are the actual, but not the necessary, result of the injury complained of, and which, in fact, follow it as a natural and proximate consequence in the particular case, that is, by reason of the special circumstances or conditions. These damages include all of those expenses and hardships which plaintiff has incurred as a result of the original act or omission, and that, "but for" the act or omission would not necessarily have been incurred.

§ 1.18   Calculating Damages

Damages suffered by the majority of clients can be grouped into actual or special damages, general damages, compensatory damages, future damages, and, in some cases, punitive damages. Clients should be instructed to save all documents which can be used in proving items of damage, such as:

All cancelled checks

All receipts for items purchased which in any way relate to the incident and/or dispute

Copies of contracts for goods or services which relate in any way to the nature of the dispute (breach of contract, remodeling contracts, service contracts for housekeepers, and so forth)

Job diaries, logs, pain and suffering diaries

Phone bills, date books, appointment books, Visa card statements, and so forth

Contracts for services which were arranged prior to the incident and subject to a cancellation fee (for example, nonrefundable deposit on vacations, ski rentals, health club memberships, and so forth)

All wage verification information, pay stubs, W-2 forms, and so forth. Documents vary for self-employed individuals and independent contractors. Your client is your best source of information as to how to prove any and all wage losses suffered.

Items of special damages in personal injury cases include, but are not limited to, costs of examination, surgery, care, treatment or evaluation by any health care provider, prescriptions and medications, prosthetic devices including artificial limbs and cosmetic replacement items, orthopedic appliances such as crutches and braces, equipment purchase or rental including wheelchairs, hospital beds, special auto equipment, or any other item recommended by a health care practitioner. Nonprescription, injury-related items purchased at the suggestion of a health care professional such as a heating pad, hearing aid, ointments, vitamins, lumbar supports, and so forth are also included. Medical mileage, cost of replacement services for those jobs and chores that the client would normally perform such as housekeeping, gardening, and home maintenance can be considered in special damages.

Special damages in business litigation include cost of replacement items, cost of repair, salaries for extra employees, warehouse space, loss of commissions, lost contracts due to inability to complete work on schedule, lost promotions, lost opportunities for job advancement, lost opportunities to submit bids and/or contract proposals, and so forth.

Consequential damages are often the most difficult to calculate. These damages would not have occurred "but for" the original incident. For example, Mary and Bob Smith hire Jim Jones to remodel their bathroom. A contract is drawn up calling for the installation of a new stall shower and a double sink. Unfortunately the remodeling does not go as scheduled, is delayed and is not done properly. Several months after the remodeling is completed, Mary notices water damage on the walls and ceiling of the bedroom directly below the remodeled bathroom. After investigation, it is found that the shower was not properly installed or sealed and has caused the leaking. This water damage has resulted in consequential damages and was caused by the remodeling work done by Jones. Not only does the bathroom have to be completely redone, but the water damages to the walls and ceiling to the bedroom immediately below the bathroom must also be remedied.

Compensatory damages may occur without actual money being spent. For example, an independent contractor may commit to a contract for a set price and allow the time necessary to complete that contract only to be delayed by injuries and/or lack of ability to obtain the supplies and materials necessary to do the job. The contractor may then be sued for breach of contract and not be permitted to do the job. An element of damage will be detrimental reliance. That is, in relying upon that contract, the independent contractor may have not bid on other jobs. The amount of those contracts represent lost income even though no money has exchanged hands. "But for" the reliance upon the original contract, the contractor would not have lost these business opportunities and the contractor needs to be compensated.

General damages are those items of damage which in personal injury cases are considered pain and suffering, emotional trauma, mental anguish, and a general loss of enjoyment and quality of life. General damages are those items for which no monetary amount can be easily ascertained. It is a common mistake to restrict a claim for general damages for pain and suffering and mental anguish to personal injury and product liability actions. In reality they are part and parcel of every tort action. Every litigant, even a sophisticated business person, experiences the stress and strain, changes in lifestyle, and pressure on family life and personal relationships, which are brought on by litigation.

Future damages (speculative damages) lack specific documentation. In assisting a client in calculating future damages, consider the following regarding wages:

1. Employment contracts with specified increases per steps in salary schedule such as union contracts for electricians, carpenters, plumbers, and so forth.

2. Bid proposals for jobs that plaintiff would have been able to accept "but for" the injuries.

3. Contracts for specific future work projects. For example, plaintiff has completed phase one of a contract and included is the option of performing work for phases two, three, and so forth on the same project.

4. Promotions which may have entailed relocating and attaining a higher salary and the next rung up in the corporate ladder. This may now be impossible due to the injuries that plaintiff has received in this accident.

5. Commissions, merit pay increases, opportunity for overtime work, pay incentives, and any other policy or system in existence at plaintiff's place of employment which would have given him the opportunity to earn more money and which plaintiff now is unable to participate in due to restrictions on the hours plaintiff is able to work, and/or not having worked during the time period necessary to qualify for a particular salary incentive plan.

6. Cumulation of credits, points, and so forth into a company's retirement or annuity program which may have been adversely affected by plaintiff's absence from work.

7. The entire fringe benefit package calculated in monetary terms should be factored into both present and future wage loss.

Calculation of future damages is often an area which requires expert testimony, especially at trial. Expert actuaries can forecast with reasonable certainty a person's lifetime wage loss based on age and life expectancy tables factoring in inflation and cost of living. It is important that legal assistants work closely with experts in obtaining the necessary documentation from the client to enable the expert to forecast with the highest degree or accuracy.

§ 1.19   Alternate Dispute Resolution

Alternate dispute resolutions such as arbitration or mediation should be discussed with the client. Many actions involving a noncomplex fact situation and a minimal amount of damages are best suited to small claims court or nonjudicial arbitration. Arbitration is provided for by statute in the federal court and all state court systems. Additionally, arbitration is available through the American Arbitration Association for specialty cases such as construction claims. Finally, all attempts should be made at settlement through informal means such as:

Letter from attorney to opposing party (this can be done only if the opposing party is not represented by counsel).

Written notice of breach of warranty to manufacturer, vendor, and so forth. (*See* **Form 1–19.**)

Written notice of rescission of contract to all parties involved in a contract dispute. Most state statutes set forth the specific grounds that a consumer must state in order to rescind a contract. (*See* **Form 1–20.**)

Settlement demand letter to insurance adjustor (frequently done as a matter of procedure in personal injury claims).

FORM 1–19
SAMPLE NOTICE OF BREACH OF WARRANTY

NOTICE OF BREACH OF WARRANTY

DATED: [date]

TO: [seller/manufacturer]

   YOU ARE HEREBY NOTIFIED that the goods you delivered to me on or about [date] under the contract of sale dated [date] are defective in the following regards, among others: [detail of defects]. Such defects breach the [express/implied] warranties contained in the aforesaid contract as follows: [type of warranty breach such as merchantibility, fitness for a particular purpose, and so forth]

DATED: [date]

[name of buyer]

FORM 1–20
SAMPLE NOTICE OF RESCISSION

NOTICE OF RESCISSION

TO: [parties as to whom contract rescinded]

YOU ARE HEREBY NOTIFIED that [name] rescinds that certain [written/oral] contract entered into on or about [date] between [names], pertaining to [subject matter].

This rescission is upon the following grounds, among others: [one or more of grounds enumerated in local state statutes, city ordinances, or written terms of rescission as stated in contract].

The undersigned herewith offers to restore to you everything of value that has been received by the undersigned from you under the aforesaid contract, to-wit: [money, specific description of property, and so forth] upon condition that you restore to the undersigned everything of value that you have received from the undersigned under the said contract, to-wit: [money, specific description of property, and so forth].

DATED: [date]

[name of rescinding party]

§ 1.20   Demand Letters

A settlement package, or demand letter (see **Form 1–21**), is a common and inexpensive negotiating tool which is most commonly used in personal injury disputes, but should not be limited to only those types of actions. Demand letters are a necessary first step for a litigant wishing to prove their case in small claims court. It is not only useful in attempting to settle a dispute, but it also provides the best opportunity to lay out the facts of your case in a carefully organized manner and present those facts in their most favorable light. There is no way you lose when submitting a demand letter or settlement package. Litigating a claim is a risk for both sides of a dispute. Settlement is a means of risk control because it allows both sides an opportunity to reduce the risk of all the intangibles and unknowns that occur as a case proceeds through discovery and trial preparation towards resolution.

Usually demand letters are sent prior to filing an action and are directed to insurance adjusters; however, demand letters may also be sent after an action has been filed. Undertaking settlement after litigation has begun affords both parties an opportunity to minimize the total amount of loss in the case and the insurance company's legal fees and costs. Frequently such demands are for policy limits, and are based by plaintiffs upon the argument that should a carrier fail to accept a settlement demand within policy limits, any judgment ultimately rendered for a verdict higher than the policy limit becomes the responsibility of the carrier. The plaintiff usually offers to discount their claim to fit within policy limits in an attempt to save both sides those fees and costs which would be expended in proceeding to trial. A useful argument for plaintiffs is to promote the idea that monies saved on litigation costs can be used to maximize the settlement offer so that the injured party receives the full benefit of an early settlement.

§ 1.21   —Demand Letter Checklist

Prior to sending a demand letter to an insurance carrier, adverse party, or opposing counsel, be certain you have included the following:

_____ Documentation for all damages claimed which may include the following:

     _____ Photographs depicting damage to a vehicle, person, property, and so forth

     _____ Invoices

     _____ Billing statements

     _____ Contracts

     _____ Leases

     _____ Letters, fax and/or other written documentation concerning the incident such as accident reports, reports of injury, OSHA reports, medical records, and so forth

     _____ Canceled checks

     _____ Evidence of any payments made for goods, services, or any other expenses related to the incident

     _____ Witness statements

     _____ Claim forms

     _____ Verification of wage loss, loss of business, and any related expenses

_____ Remember to send your demand letter, or settlement package, certified mail return receipt requested. This is particularly important if you are sending to an insurance claims adjuster or private party, rather than a law firm. Also be sure to itemize all enclosures and include a separate list of attachments with your demand letter. Your file copy should be an exact duplicate of what was sent.

_____ Calendar 10 to 15 days for a response. If there has been no response to your demand letter within that time frame, send a follow-up letter enclosing the complaint you intend to file within 10 days of the date of your letter unless you hear otherwise. (*See* **Form 1–23.**)

§ 1.22   —Elements of a Demand Letter

It is important that demand letters contain all of the information necessary to be used as an efficient negotiating tool. (*See* **Form 1–22.**) These elements are:

Statement of Your Case.   A brief, narrative, factual summary of the incident which is the cause of the dispute.

Liability.   Incorporate in narrative form those statutes, jury instructions, or case law supporting your client's position. Police reports, accident reports, witness statements, and so forth can be included in this section.

Damages.   Include names of medical care providers, if applicable, date of expense, and amount of expense. Also include an itemization of all expenses related to the dispute—all expenses that would not have been incurred "but for the dispute."

Wage Loss.   Nontraditional wage loss claims may require different documentation (self-employed individuals, small business owners, and so forth) Consider sending Schedule C of the 1040 Income Tax Form.

Replacement Cost.   This may include costs for replacing merchandise, repairing damage, or hiring someone to perform simple household tasks such as cooking, cleaning, child care, and so forth.

Residual Damages.   Future prognosis is most applicable in personal injury, product liability, medical malpractice, and other cases where a person's physical and/or mental well being has been compromised and it is uncertain what will be needed in the future to stabilize their physical condition. A business can also sustain a residual loss such as loss of customers, damage to reputation within the business community, and so forth. Future damages could also include a need for new marketing, advertising, and new product lines among other needs.

FORM 1–21
SAMPLE DEMAND LETTER

[Date]

[name of insurance adjuster]
[insurance company address]

   RE: [client A]
   Your Insured: [insured B]
   Date of Loss: [date]
   Claim No: [claim number]

Dear [insurance adjuster]:

The condition of my client, [A], has now stabilized to the extent that we are able to make a settlement demand. Enclosed for your review are copies of [client A]'s medical records and bills from [name] General Hospital and Dr. G. We have also enclosed wage loss verifications from [client A]'s employers.

As you know, [client A] suffered physical juries to the lower back and neck in the accident which occurred on [date], when he was a passenger in a vehicle driven by N.W.

FACTUAL SUMMARY

This accident occurred when [client A], who was sitting with [client A]'s seatbelt on in the front passenger seat, was injured when a vehicle driven by [insured B] pulled out unexpectedly, hitting the right front fender of N.W.'s vehicle. [Client A] was able to get out of the car without difficulty and noted no symptoms until the following morning at which time [client A] noted considerable stiffness of the lower back area with associated soreness and pain prompting him to seek treatment at [name] General Hospital's Emergency Department. Examination at that time revealed mild paracervical and upper trapezium tenderness in the neck area and a mild lumbar strain and tenderness, particularly in the lower back. Dr. D., the emergency room physician, prescribed heat, aspirin, and rest as well as further examination by [client A]'s regular doctor if the pain persisted.

On [date], [client A] consulted Dr. G. complaining of considerable stiffness in the lower back area. [Client A] also had been unable to return to work, because [client A]'s job required carrying heavy objects. [Client A] also noted difficulty in sitting for long periods of time. Dr. G's examination revealed considerable spasms of the lower lumbar muscles and limitation in forward bending, backward bending, and sideward bending with discomfort and tenderness on percussion over the lumbar spine area. Dr. G.'s diagnosis was acute back strain and Dr. G. applied tape for relief of the local pain and discomfort. [Client A] was advised to continue using the heating pad and aspirin and to remove the tape in about 5 days.

Treatment was continued with Dr. G through [date], at which time [client A] was able to bend forward, backward, and sidewards without limitation and had no residual muscle spasms in the lumbar region. At that time, Dr. G. released [client A] to return to work.

[Client A] was advised to continue with caution to [client A]'s back, and return on an as needed basis for treatment. At this time, [client A] appears to have recovered from the injuries suffered to the lower back.

DAMAGES
[name] General Hospital		$ 95.00
Dr. G.		$ 123.00
	TOTAL	$ 218.00

WAGE LOSS

At the time of the accident, [client A] was employed through [name] Corporation as a concessionaire at the [location] selling beer and soft drinks. Because of the physical demands of this position, [client A] was unable to work for a total of 15 days. A wage and salary verification form signed by Joan N. for [name] Corporation establishes the wage loss [client A] suffered as a result of injuries received in this accident at $1,628.00.

[Client A] also worked at a temporary position through [business name] as a demonstrator. At the time of the accident, [client A]'s wages were $7.40 per hour. As a result of the accident, [client A] was unable to work from [date] through [date] and lost a total of 43 hours, or $307.10 in wages. This amount is verified by the wage verification signed by the assistant service supervisor of [business name].

In addition to the medical expenses previously itemized, [client A]'s damages consist of a total wage loss in the amount of $1,935.10.

LIABILITY

It is clear that the cause of this accident was the inattentiveness of the driver of the [insured B]'s vehicle who was a 16-year-old minor driving on a license that [insured B] had for three weeks. At the time of the accident [insured B] told [client A] [insured B] was driving [insured B]'s mother's car and simply "didn't see you guys." At the time of the accident, N.W.'s vehicle, in which [client A] was a passenger, was proceeding at approximately 30 miles per hour on [street], going west. As the vehicle travelled up the hill to make a turn at [intersection name], [insured B]'s vehicle driven by the 16-year-old minor failed to stop at [street name] and proceeded to come out of [street name] Street and attempt a left turn. [Insured B]'s vehicle instead turned diagonally, almost hitting N.W.'s vehicle head on. The left front of [insured B]'s vehicle hit the right front of N.W.'s vehicle causing extensive damage to the right front of the car, the frame, the left fender, and the left door. It does not appear that a police report was made concerning this accident, however, [client A] gave a statement recounting the accident to [insurance company].

My client has authorized me to demand $5,000.00 in full settlement of this case. I look forward to your prompt reply to this settlement demand.

Very truly yours,

[name of attorney]

FORM 1–22
SAMPLE DEMAND LETTER (PROMISSORY NOTE)

[date]

VIA CERTIFIED MAIL
RETURN RECEIPT REQUESTED

Ms. Pamela S.
132 Elm Street
Anytown, USA

RE: Promissory Note Dated [date]

Dear Ms. S.:

Please be advised that the above-referenced Promissory Note became due and payable on [date], and is presently due and owing. We have been requested by [client], hereinafter known as the lender and the holder of the note, to make this demand on you for payment in full of all amounts currently owing on and under the Note. The conditions of payment as set forth in the Note required monthly payments to be made in the amount of $85.00. These payments are due and owing as of the first of each month and are considered delinquent by the tenth of that month. Your signature on line 27 of the enclosed Promissory Note indicates your acceptance of the terms set forth therein.

We have been informed by our client that no payments have been tendered in the past nine months. Our client has also informed us that [client] has attempted to informally resolve this matter with you on numerous occasions through telephone contact and letter. Furthermore, our client has agreed to accept partial payment in lieu of full monthly payments.

Should you continue to ignore your obligations, our client, the lender, will institute and prosecute litigation designed to enforce your obligations under the enclosed Promissory Note. You are hereby specifically notified that your failure to pay your obligations herein will result in increased liability by way of attorney's fees and costs of court incurred by the lender and prosecution of litigation designed to enforce your obligations.

Nothing herein shall be deemed a waiver of any other default, whether matured or unmatured, and whether enumerated above or not, existing or hereafter arising under the Note or any other agreement, instrument or document executed in connection with or as security for the Note, or a waiver or abandonment of any rights or remedies available to the lender (whether against you or any other person or any property), each of which rights or remedies is hereby specifically reserved (including without limitation the right to seek judgment and/or to proceed against personal property).

If payment is not received from you of all sums now due and payable on the Note on or before [time] [date], lender will exercise lender's right to accelerate the entire amount due and owing along with the accrued, earned, and unpaid interest as of the date of acceleration pursuant to the terms and conditions of the Note.

If you have any questions or need further information regarding the exact amount now due and payable on and under this Note, please contact this office immediately so that we may discuss prompt resolution of this claim.

Sincerely,

[name of attorney]

FORM 1–23
SAMPLE FOLLOW-UP LETTER

[date]

[name of insurance adjuster]
[insurance company]
[address]

> RE: [Client A]
> Your Insured: [Insured B]
> Date of Loss: [date]
> Claim No: [claim number]

Dear [insurance adjuster]:

Please be advised that we have yet to receive a reply to our demand letter and settlement package forwarded to you at the above address on [date]. If you have any questions or need further information in order to properly review this claim, please contact our office.

My client authorized me to demand $5,000 in full settlement of the claim, and our settlement demand letter included documentation of all damages sustained by [client A] in the accident which occurred on [date] and was caused by your insured driver, [insured B]. If you do not admit liability in this matter, and are not desirous of attempting to resolve this case prior to expending litigation costs, please contact this office immediately so that we may proceed accordingly.

I have included for your review a copy of the complaint that I intend to file within ten (10) days of the date of this letter. On that date, [client A]'s previous offer of $5,000 will expire, be withdrawn, and will not be offered again. That figure constitutes a substantial savings to defendant from the amount of damages which will ultimately be recovered at trial.

If you are interested in attempting to resolve this matter prior to expending litigation costs, please immediately contact this office.

Sincerely,

[name of attorney]

§ 1.23 Legal Calendaring

Accurate and dependable calendaring is vital to the proper operation of any law firm or legal department. Although most law firms have secretaries and/or calendar clerks responsible for the overall calendar, every paralegal should keep their own calendar on each case to which they have been assigned. Many law firms often practice the policy and procedure of dual or triple calendaring at the suggestion of their malpractice carrier. Calendaring mistakes can cost a firm money, clients, and reputation. A missed statute of limitations can be prima facia evidence of legal malpractice. Although many other calendar dates are not as crucial, it is still vitally important to calendar properly and promptly.

In addition to calendaring court dates, statute of limitations dates, date responses due to particular pleadings, dates to file a particular motion or responsive documents, and so forth, it is also important to calendar other dates as reminder dates. Reminder dates have traditionally been known in many law firms as part of a *tickler system.* The origin of this term is unknown, but one may presume it is to tickle your memory. A tickler system works in conjunction with the calendar, and is used to remember dates such as:

> File review and status letter to client
>
> Check to see if client has completed medical treatment
>
> Check status of investigator's report
>
> Check status of witness statements
>
> Check on the status of any records or documents that have been requested under the Federal Freedom of Information Act or any other public records, and send follow-up letters when necessary
>
> Remind client to give promised documents to the office
>
> Remind of dates 10 or 15 days in advance of the last day for filing particular motions to compel discovery, move for protective orders, and/or move for summary judgment.

A tickler file becomes individualized to a particular case and/or client depending upon case strategy, discovery plan, litigation budget, and most importantly, individual working styles of attorney/paralegal litigation teams. It is a good practice to calendar in your tickler system the date any information gathering letter is generated by your office to any other entity. This type of calendaring is invaluable when you are preparing case status memos and/or letters to clients.

§ 1.24   Time Computation

Computation of the time for performing an act provided or required by law such as serving, filing, and responding to documents on time is both frustrating and confusing to many. Simply put, the time within which any act provided by law is to be done is computed by *excluding the first day and including the last day, unless the last day is a holiday, in which case the period is extended to the next day which is not a holiday.* For example, a complaint arrives in your office by hand service or fax service on May 1. You know that as defendant you have thirty days from the date of service within which to respond. Day one for counting purposes is May 2. If the thirtieth day, May 31, is a Monday through Friday and not a holiday, then that is the date your response is due. If on the other hand, May 31 was a Saturday, Sunday or other holiday, the time period would be extended to the *next day* which is not a holiday, Monday June 1 or June 2.

The term *holiday* as used in most Civil Codes of Procedures means all day on Saturdays, all day on Sundays, and all holidays as specified your local Government Code.

Beware of case law which may include language such as "not less than" or "not later than" when speaking about the number of days to perform an act before a designated time. An example of the use of this statutory language in California is found at Code of Civil Procedure § 473(c). This statute pertains to summary judgments and states that, "the motion shall be heard *no later than* thirty days before the date of trial, unless the court for good cause orders otherwise." Code of Civil Procedure § 473(c)(a) further states, "any opposition to the motion shall be served and filed *not less than* fourteen days preceding the noticed or continued date of hearing, unless the court for good cause orders otherwise." Based on a reading of this specific code section, the time for performing the act (filing summary judgment motion and/or filing opposition to the motion) is not extended to the next day if the thirtieth or fourteenth day falls on a Saturday, Sunday or holiday. In this specific case, the filing date would be the twenty-ninth day rather than the thirtieth day if the thirtieth day were a holiday.

Other problems occur when the word "prior" is used in an ordinance or statute and the last day is a holiday. If the word prior is used, the act must be performed prior to the last day which is usually the Friday before a weekend.

Based on the unclarities of many statutes using language such as "not less than" or "not later than" or "prior to", it is safest to file papers in conformity with the "Friday-before" concept rather than the "Monday-after" concept.

Generally speaking, there is a difference of five days between hand service and service by mail. In today's electronic age, FAX service has become the preferred method of service for many last minute attorneys, law firms, and legal departments. Service by FAX is generally considered to be the same as hand service. However, to be certain when filing, serving, or responding to a pleading, double check the language used to regulate the time in which to perform the act and verify that FAX service will constitute hand service. This will avoid problems of untimeliness, and more importantly preserve your client's rights if there are objections in responsive pleadings.

§ 1.25   Screening Clients

Interviews with potential clients begin with their first telephone contact to your office. In a small to medium law firm, a legal assistant may be called upon to screen potential clients to determine the specific nature of their legal problem before setting up an initial interview appointment. In speaking with a potential client, you need to learn the general nature of the legal problem which has led them to consult your law firm.

Questions based on the journalistic format of who, what, why, where, when and how will cover the key areas:

Who? Names of all potential defendants, names of all potential plaintiffs

What? The specific event which has caused the problem

Why? Reasons why the event occurred—specific actions or failure to take action that caused the problem

Where? Location of accident, signing of contract, act of negligence, and so forth, or the geographical location of event

When? Date of occurrence, dates of significant events leading up to the specific problem

How? Brief description of how the accident or act of negligence happened

In most cases, the prospective clients emotionally distraught and upset over the incident that has disrupted the normal routine of their life. Also they may have never have had an occasion to consult an attorney and they may not know how to explain their problem. You need to determine quickly whether the matter is a dissolution, personal injury, criminal arrest, business problem, civil rights problem, an alleged wrongful termination of employment, or some other problem. After determining the nature of the problem, advise the client whether or not your firm handles that particular area of law. Spend no more than five to ten minutes on the phone with a prospective client in an attempt to determine the basic problem and decide whether or not this is a case your firm would be interested in and/or qualified to handle.

§ 1.26   Checking for Conflict of Interest

The last step in screening a client is checking for a conflict of interest. If it is determined that a conflict exists, the client must be advised of this conflict and advised to seek other representation. Under the Code of Professional Responsibility and the Model Rules of Professional Conduct, a lawyer may not represent a potential client if such representation is or will be:

Adverse to the interests of an existing client, even when the matters are completely separate and distinct,

Adverse to the interests of a former client, or

Adverse to the interests of a party to the same matter who has already asked that the lawyer represent him.

Client consent may result in a law firm permissibly representing clients with essentially competing interests; however, this can only be done it the prospective client is advised in writing of the potential conflict and signs an agreement of waiver. The Code of Professional Responsibility and the Model Rules of Professional Conduct set forth three requirements for client waiver of a conflict:

1.   The lawyer must fully disclose to the client what the conflict is and how it may affect the lawyer's conduct;

2. The client must waive the conflict and give written consent to the lawyer's representation of both parties; and

3. A complete segregation of files and documents must be created within the structure of the law firm to protect the confidential nature of both clients' claims.

The most common situation for client waiver of potential or actual conflict occurs in situations where the matter may be adverse to the interests of a former client. It is extremely difficult to represent clients with competing interests when both cases are open files.

The legal assistant's responsibility in doing a conflict check is to review carefully the master case list and also the master list of expert witnesses and consultants routinely used by the attorneys in your office. This preliminary check will reveal immediate conflicts of interest, but unfortunately may not reveal potential conflicts of interest; for example, expert witnesses that have not yet been named, or consultants whose identities are only known to attorneys working on a particular case. A good method for flushing out these hidden potential conflicts is to circulate a memo to each attorney (not only the litigators, but each attorney) in your office stating the essential facts of the case as you have learned them from your initial screening telephone conversation with the client. Be sure to include the names of all parties, key players, and potential defendants with their business affiliations. This second check is a safeguard against embarrassing situations, such as agreeing to represent a plaintiff in an action against a particular doctor who is a member of a corporation or medical group which includes a doctor who has consulted on past cases for your office and may in the future be needed as an expert witness.

You can spot distinct conflicts of interest immediately, and a client may be referred to other counsel. Potential conflicts of interest may not be immediately recognizable. A client may come in for the initial interview, bringing documents which reveal a conflict situation. On the other hand, a client may come for the initial client interview without any documents, and the conflict situation may remain undetected until you have requested and received documents. The important thing in resolving a conflict of interest situation is to advise the client promptly and take immediate steps to either secure a written waiver or refer them to other counsel in a timely fashion to protect their rights under applicable statutes. Notification should be in writing. The sample letter (see **Form 1–6**) used for rejecting a case may be used with appropriate changes.

§ 1.27 —Computerized Conflict of Interest Systems

A computerized retrieval system for potential conflicts of interest is much more effective than a manual system. Many law firms now employ conflict of interest clerks, or calendar clerks, who, in addition to their basic calendaring duties, monitor conflict of interest data bases. In these recessionary times, law firms have merged, and many smaller or boutique law firms have been assimilated into full service law firms. This has created new job opportunities for legal assistants as "conflict clerks" whose job responsibilities include merging client lists from each firm into one overall master list that can be quickly checked for potential conflicts.

A computerized retrieval system checks a variety of data fields, such as proper names and organizations against existing client and matter information prior to the acceptance of any new client or new matter for an existing client. Law firms recognize the significance of checking against existing client matter information prior to the acceptance of new clients as of the utmost importance in preserving a client's confidences. The troublesome and often forgotten area of a potential conflict of interest arises when an existing client requests representation in a new matter. This problem can be addressed easily by reviewing existing data bases to determine any potential conflicts.

The benefits of a computerized retrieval system for a conflict of interest data base include:

Avoiding conflict situations by identifying prior client relationships as new matters are reviewed;

Insuring proper accounting and billing procedures;

Providing a tracking system of work by client and matter name; and

Insuring quality control in conflict checking by use of objective data.

§ 1.28 —Sample Data Fields for Computerized Systems

The most useful data fields (bases) in a computerized retrieval system are divided into two major categories: client data and matter data.

Client data should include the following fields:

1. Client number. The number assigned to each client by the firm for billing purposes.

2. Client name. Use an abbreviation, or phrase, which identifies the company, organization, agency, or other entity (that is, the responsible person for billing) to whom the firm provides service.

3. Principal contact. The full name of the person within your client's organization to whom general correspondence should be addressed.

4. Address. Include street address, building name, suite number, post office box of the company, organization, agency, or other entity. (The address should match the client name.)

5. City. The name of the city in which the company, organization, agency, or other entity or client is located.

6. State. Use two letter U.S. Post Office abbreviation for the state in which the company, agency, or entity, or individual client is located.

7. Zip Code. The five, or extended nine-digit, zip code number identifying the postal delivery area of the company, organization, agency, entity, or individual client. NOTE: If the zip code for the actual street address differs from the actual zip code used for the mailing address (usually a post office box) include both zip codes.

8. Country. The name or abbreviation for the country in which the company, organization, agency, entity, or individual client is located. Use accepted abbreviations such as U.S.A., ENG, and so forth.

9. Telephone number. The general telephone number (area code, number, and appropriate extension) of the company, organization, agency, entity, or individual client.

10. Comments/Notes. Narrative describing or summarizing anything requiring further explanation about the company, organization, agency, entity, or individual client.

11. Create/Edit Date. Indicate when the entry on the retrieval system was updated or edited last.

Matter Data should include the following:

1. Matter number. The number assigned by the firm to each case or unique project undertaken on behalf of a client. This number should coincide with accounting and billing records.

2. Matter name. The abbreviations, words, or phrases used to identify or describe the nature of the case or project undertaken on behalf of a client. Examples: PI (personal injury); MED. MAL. (medical malpractice); PL (product liability); and so forth.

3. Dates and events. Indicate the dates associated with the most pertinent events for the matter. Examples include: the date a file is opened, the date a file is closed, statute of limitations dates, and so forth.

4. Related/Friendly parties. The names of individuals and organizations, and how they are related to the matter. This should include the names of any persons or parties connected to the case or matter in a nonadversarial relationship such as, consultants, expert witnesses, members of corporate board of directors, and so forth. Also include organizations with which these persons are affiliated and the nature of their relationship to the client (co-defendant, co-counsel, and so forth).

5. Adverse parties. Include the names, organizations, and relationships of any person or parties connected to the case or matter as opponents, and the organizations with which they are affiliated and the nature of their relationship both to the client individually and to the client's organizations.

6. Partner opening matter. Identify the partner by initials responsible for opening the file. This information can be very important as a back-up quality control device. The partner responsible for opening the file is the best source of information about the client.

Additional data fields may be added to expand the computerized retrieval system so that it functions not only as a check for conflict of interest but also provides information for the billing and accounting departments. For example, data fields can be added identifying the billing partner, the billing frequency, and the taxpayer identification number. Other additional data fields for a corporate client might include officers and directors, subsidiaries, parents, affiliates, and so forth.

As the business of law becomes more complicated by lateral attorney and paralegal moves from one firm to another, merging small firms to create new larger firms, partnerships dissolving and corporations reorganizing, it becomes more and more complicated, time consuming, and dangerous to check for conflict of interest on a manual basis. An added benefit of such a conflict system is that it simplifies accounting and billing systems, which can be merged into the same system. It is essential to maintain an up-to-date and complete master client list. The most efficient manner of compiling and maintaining this list is with a computerized retrieval system which serves as a conflict of interest check and balance system and insures quality control.

§ 1.29   Initial Client Interview

If, after screening the potential client, you have determined that the problem falls within one of the areas of specialization of your firm and that the date(s) of the alleged wrong fall within the statute of limitations for that particular cause of action, you are ready to set up an appointment for the potential client.

Send a confirmation letter (**Form 1–24**) (see sample) to the client enclosing a client questionnaire. Explain to the prospective client that by filling out this questionnaire in advance they can save time by helping the attorney focus on the nature of the problem. Saving time and money are facts clients appreciate.

Two sample questionnaires are included. The first questionnaire (**Form 1–25**) is a sample of a form questionnaire that may be used for general as well as personal injury cases. The second questionnaire (**Form 1–26**) is a medical questionnaire and may be used in any case where injury has occurred, medical malpractice, personal injury, product liability, wrongful termination, and so forth. It is also useful for preparation of discovery responses and demand packages. It can be sent to the client any time within the first few months of work on a case.

FORM 1–24
SAMPLE LETTER CONFIRMING FIRST APPOINTMENT

Dear Client:

Thank you for contacting our office. We have scheduled an appointment for you with [attorney name], who is one of our associates specializing in wrongful termination.

Please bring the following documents with you to your interview:

1. All correspondence and memos from any of the proposed defendants.
2. Any photos, reports, personnel file, office manual, and so forth.
3. Any supporting documentation for damages (medical bills, invoices, leases, contracts, payroll stubs, and so forth).

Enclosed with this letter is our standard New Client Questionnaire. Please take some time before the interview to complete this form and bring it with you. Your appointment is set for [date] at [time] at the offices of [name of law firm], [address], [city, state].

If you are unable to keep this appointment, please call me at [telephone number] and I will reschedule your appointment.

We are looking forward to meeting you and hope that we can be of service to you.

Sincerely,

[name]
Legal Assistant

FORM 1–25
SAMPLE CLIENT QUESTIONNAIRE

NEW CLIENT INFORMATION SHEET

Interview Date: _____

Date of Accident/Incident: _____

Statute of Limitation Date: _____

Client's Name: _____

Name of Spouse: _____

Name of Parents: _____

Address: _____

_____

Date of Birth: _____

Social Security No.: _____

Driver's License: _____

Home Address:_____

_____

Home Phone: _____

Business Address: _____

_____

Business Phone: _____

Nearest Relative: _____

Address: _____

Phone: _____

Previous settlement offer received? _____

(Include date of offer, amount of offer, who made the offer, any responses to the offer, any documents supporting offer, letters, etc.)

_____

Adverse party (parties): _____

1. Name: _____

Address: _____
Phone: _____
2. Name: _____
Address: _____
Phone: _____
Add any other possible adverse parties: _____

Other facts and witnesses (include all additional facts giving rise to the incident including names and addresses of any witnesses and/or parties with information bearing upon the facts which gave rise to the incident):
_____
_____
_____

General Facts

Time: _____
Day of Week: _____
People present at time of incident or who have background information that is relevant to the events which caused this incident: _____
_____
_____

Location of incident, if applicable: _____
_____

Specific Facts Regarding Incident: _____
_____
_____

If you have consulted our office regarding a personal injury accident relating to an automobile, please fill out the following:
1. Location of accident scene, including direction of travel of all vehicles:
_____
_____

2. Diagram of accident scene: _____
3. Weather and road conditions: _____
4. Time: _____
5. Day of Week: _____
6. General facts of occurrence: _____
_____
_____

7. Driver's name, address and phone number: _____
_____
_____

8. Names and addresses of all passengers: _____
_____
_____
_____
_____

9. Was a police report made? If so, please furnish a copy or give all details necessary so that we may order a copy. _____

10. Were any photos taken of the vehicles involved in the incident? If so, where
can photos be obtained? _____

11. Name, address, phone number and name of insurance carrier of adverse
driver: _____
_____
_____

12. Repair estimate for vehicle: _____

13. Name, address, and phone number of your insurance carrier (include policy
number, and limits of liability coverage if known): _____
_____
_____

Personal Information

Please furnish the following employment information:

1. Place of employment, address, name of immediate supervisor: _____
_____
_____

2. Description of job responsibilities: _____
_____

3. Job title: _____

4. Wage: _____

5. Length of time at present job: _____

6. Please provide a brief employment history listing name, address and phone
number of your employers for the last 5 years: _____
_____
_____

7. If you lost time from work because of injuries you received in this incident,
please indicate dates and amount of money lost: _____
_____

8. Please provide medical information concerning significant previous illnesses,
doctors and hospitals whom you have treated with for the last 10 years: _____
_____
_____
_____
_____

FORM 1–26
SAMPLE MEDICAL QUESTIONNAIRE

GENERAL INFORMATION

1. What is your full name? _____
Date of Birth _____ Marital status _____
What is the name of your spouse? _____
Present address: _____

Present address of spouse: _____

Telephone no: (business) _____ (residence) _____

If a minor, full name of parent: _____

(His/her) relationship to you: _____

(His/her) address: _____

WORK BACKGOUND

The amount of your recovery in this case will be affected by your loss of earnings and earning capacity, so please outline carefully your work background.

1. Were you employed at the time of the occurrence? _____
If so, state name and address of your employer: _____
_____

2. What was your job title, or the type of work you were doing? _____
_____

3. What was your rate of pay? _____

4. How many hours per week were you working regularly immediately prior to the occurrence? _____
_____

5. When were you first employed by the company for which you were working at the time of the occurrence? _____

6. Have you remained in the same job since the occurrence? _____
If not, state the reason for the termination of your employment _____
_____

7. Have you missed any time from work as a result of your injury? _____
If so, list the inclusive dates you were unable to work: From: _____ To: _____
Before this occurrence, did you lose time from work due to any injury or for any other reason? _____
_____

If so, give details: _____
_____

8. Did you lose wages for the periods of time missed from work due to this occurrence? _____
If so, state the total wages lost to date and the dates: _____
_____

9. Have you had any increases or decreases in your pay since the occurrence? ___
If so, explain: _____

10. If you have changed jobs since the occurrence, give a summary of your present job, showing name and address of employer, rate of pay, hours, type of work, etc. __
_____
_____

11. Have you filed federal or state income tax returns for the last three years? ____

ADDITIONAL BACKGROUND INFORMATION

We must know about your background because your educational background and physical history will have an important bearing upon your case.

1. Education: What education have you had, including any special employment training or training in skills? _____

_____

2. Physical Examinations: List here every physical examination you have had during the last ten years, for example, promotion, insurance, selective service, armed forces, etc. State the date, name of the doctor and result, as fully as you recall.

Date: _____ Place: _____

Name of Doctor: _____

Purpose of Examination: _____

Result: _____

3. Other Accident and Injuries: Failure to mention other accidents or injuries can undermine your lawsuit, no matter how trivial they may seem. List here every such accident whether it resulted in a claim for damages or not, stating the date, place, nature of the accident, and extent of your injuries. If none, so state.

Date: _____ Place: _____

Nature of accident or injury: _____

_____

Extent of injury: _____

4. Activities Since this Occurrence: If you suffered a serious injury in the occurrence, it is possible the opposing side already has taken or will in the future take motion pictures of you. This is done with a telescopic lens, so that you never know it has been done until the pictures are presented in court to show that you are able to do something which you have either denied or neglected to mention that you are able to do. List here all your usual activities which you have not been able to perform since the occurrence, such as cutting grass, and so forth: _____

_____

5. Military Background: Have you ever been rejected for military service because of physical, mental, or other reasons? _____ If so, explain: _____

_____

Have you ever had military service? _____ If so, what branch? _____

Please state dates: _____

Type of discharge: _____

Any service-connected injuries? _____ If so, explain and give details: _____

_____

DAMAGES

The amount of recovery in this case will be affected by, among other things, the damages or expenses actually incurred as a direct result of the occurrence, such as hospital, doctor, and drug expenses; aggravation of your injuries by doctor's erroneous treatment; and loss of wages. These are items of special damage as contrasted with compensatory or general damages such as pain and suffering, loss of future earnings, impairment of your earning capacity, etc.

1. State in full detail all injuries recevied as a result of this occurrence: _____

_____

State your present physical condition, scars, deformities, headaches, pains, etc., due to injuries received in this occurrence: _____

_____

2. List here all of your usual activities which you have not been able to perform or can only perform with difficulty since the occurrence, such as climbing stairs, ironing, cutting grass, lifting children, etc.: _____

_____

3. Hospitalization: List all hospitals in which you were examined or treated or to which you were admitted as a patient as a result of the injuries sustained in the occurrence, the dates, and the costs:_____

Hospital: _____ Address: _____

From: _____ To: _____

Costs: _____

4. Physicians and Surgeons: List the full name, address and telephone number of each physician or surgeon who has examined or treated you for your injuries as a result of the occurrence, as well as the type, duration, and place of treatment or care:

Doctor's Name: _____ Address: _____

Telephone No: _____ Type of Treatment: _____

Place of Treatment: _____

Dates of Treatment: _____ Costs: _____

5. Drugs and Medicines: State the total cost to date of all drugs and medicines used and purchased by you as a result of the occurrence, and from whom purchased: _____

_____

6. X-Rays: Where taken, date, and by whom: _____

_____

7. Hire of Nurses (do not state lump sum, but itemize as to name of nurse, address, number of days or weeks, dates, and amount paid weekly):

Total amount spent for nursing care:

8. The cost of domestic help hired as a direct result of the occurrence constitutes an item of special damage. For example, in the case of an injured homemaker or mother, the cost of a baby sitter, the cost of washing, ironing, etc., which you have hired someone to do, should be listed. State here the full name and address of all domestic help hired as a result of the occurrence, the type of work done, the number of days or weeks employed, the dates, the amount paid weekly, and the total amount paid to date:

_____

9. Special Damages (other than medical) and source of proof (i.e. personal property which was damaged, lost or destroyed as a result of the occurrence and any items not previously listed, such as crutches, clothing, glasses, false teeth, aggravation of injuries by doctor's erroneous treatment, etc.). State the cost of the item:

_____

10. Convalescent Expense: In the event that you have been confined to a nursing home or other such place as a result of the occurrence, list here the full name of every such place, the address, the dates so confined and the total cost.

Convalescent Places: _____
Address: _____
From: _____ To: _____
Cost: _____

11. Loss of Earnings: State the length of time confined to bed as a result of the occurrence, including hospital confinement: _____

_____
Confinement thereafter to house: _____
State the time lost from work (in case of breadwinner or person employed outside of the home) _____
Time lost from work in case of homemaker or mother: _____

_____
State time partially lost or time partially disabled: _____
State time lost from school in case of pupil: _____

_____

§ 1.30   Client Narrative

Client questionnaire forms are most useful in simple cases, primarily personal injury and product liability cases. However, in commercial litigation it is better to have the client set forth the facts of the incident in narrative form. Advise the client to simply set forth the problem in a memorandum or narrative form to help you understand the nature of the problem. Essential points to be included are:

A chronological listing of the facts giving rise to the problems which have brought the client to your office.

A list of each and every individual whom the client feels has been a "player" in the scenario which has given rise to this incident, including a description of their role in the events.

A description of the client's role in the incident.

A discussion of any attempts made by either party to remedy the situation which has caused this incident.

An evaluation of the damage the client has suffered because of this incident, including lost business opportunities, commissions, customer referrals, actual cash lost, damaged goods or equipment, lost warehouse space, lost employee services, property damage, lost revenue to business, and so forth.

The names of each and every person that the client holds responsible for causing this problem, including a description of the actions which they may have taken to avoid or remedy the problem.

Copies of all documents which will prove the client's point of view and/or substantiate damage claims.

What results the client wishes to see—what will it take to make the client whole again?

What defenses will most likely be raised by the other side to defend the actions they took.

What allegations, if any, will be made against the client by the other side; could the client have prevented this incident?

Did the client act in good faith in dealing with business associates, independent contractors, employees, and other individuals?

It is important that you assure the client that this narrative will be considered confidential information which will either be used to assist in preparation of the case, or returned to the client if the firm decides not to undertake representation. In advising clients to write narrative descriptions, urge them to be concise and precise, leaving emotion out. It is helpful for a client to think of a narrative in outline form using the questions listed above as guidelines and organizing the narrative into five main headings:

1. Factual background
2. Injuries
3. Damages, monies lost, present and future damage
4. Liability exposure, yours and theirs
5. Relief sought, amount of money and/or equitable relief necessary to make whole again

§ 1.31   Preparations for Initial Client Interview

Once you have set an interview for a prospective client, immediately calendar the date on the master calendar, the attorney's calendar, and your calendar. Make a copy of the letter that you have sent to the prospective client for your attorney, and also prepare a new case memo briefly describing the problem as you have been able to ascertain it from your initial telephone interview. Assemble a new client packet which should include: (1) a retainer agreement (two copies); client authorization forms allowing release of investigative, wage, and medical record information (five to seven copies); and a new case memo. If the client has been referred by another law firm, indicate in the new case memo the name, address, and telephone number of the referring law firm. Also make arrangements through the client to obtain any records or files maintained by them. If the client does not bring the file to the interview, request it by letter immediately.

§ 1.32   Representing a Client Who Has Had Another Attorney

In the case of clients who have had another attorney, the most important thing to obtain is an executed, file-endorsed copy of a substitution of attorney. It is necessary to have this substitution of attorney on file before your office can officially represent the client and take any action on their behalf. The prior attorney may have substituted out and substituted in the client in pro per allowing the client to act as his own attorney until a new attorney can assume responsibility for the case. In that case, prepare a substitution of attorney form for the client to execute substituting the client out as pro per and substituting your firm in as attorneys of record.

If a client dismisses an attorney or law firm, it is the ethical responsibility of that attorney and/or law firm to return to the client each and every client document, file, or work paper that has been given to them in connection with the action. It is usually easiest for the client to contact their prior attorney and request their file. In most cases there are no problems, and the prior attorney is cooperative. When the parting of the ways is not friendly and the prior attorney is being replaced by a client who may have reason to believe that they were not properly represented, the relinquishment of a client's file is not as easy. The prior attorney knows that it is his ethical responsibility to release the file, but also must make every effort to protect himself against a legal malpractice action by copying the entire file and other materials which will document work on the file.

Send a friendly but firm letter to the prior attorney requesting the file. *See* **Form 1–27.**

FORM 1–27
SAMPLE LETTER REQUESTING A CLIENT FILE

Dear [former attorney]:

[Client], your previous client, has consulted our law firm regarding representation for injuries received in an accident which occurred on [date]. We understand that you were the attorney of record for [client] and that your firm handled [client]'s case from approximately [date] (date on client's copy of prior retainer agreement) until approximately [date], at which time [client] sent the enclosed letter to you (or caused and expressed clear intent to dismiss attorney), indicating the intention to seek new counsel and requesting the return of the original documents and client file.

We would like to arrange a specific date and time for [client] to come to your office and pick up [client]'s documents. Please contact our office within the next ten (10) days to set a time.

[Client] has retained our law firm and we have prepared a standard Substitution of Attorney form for your signature. Please execute this form and return it to us. We will be happy to send you a file-endorsed copy of the substitution for your records.

Your cooperation will be appreciated in expediting the transfer of [client]'s file so that we may file an appearance on [client]'s behalf and protect the interests in this lawsuit.

Thank you for your anticipated professional courtesy.

Sincerely,

[name of attorney named on

Substitution of Attorney who
will become attorney of record]

§ 1.33   The Legal Assistant's Role

Your role in preparation for the initial interview typically includes:

Telephone screening
Preparation of new client packet
Calendaring the interview date and time, and
Letter and questionnaire to client.

Your role at the interview typically includes:

1.   Greeting the client as soon as the client arrives for the interview. Offer the client a cup of coffee and sit with the client and chat briefly about everyday topics. This type of casual conversation will begin to ease tension, and as the client begins to relax, an atmosphere of congeniality and good rapport will be created. This is the first stepping-stone in building a good attorney-client relationship.

2.   Obtaining the client information sheet from the prospective client and immediately making two copies of it. Give one copy to the attorney and keep a copy for yourself.

3.   Introducing the client to the attorney and proceeding into the conference room or office where the interview is actually to take place. The legal assistant should be introduced by the attorney as part of the legal team. This is a good time for the attorney to inform the client of the cost-effectiveness of the utilization of legal assistants. The client should be encouraged to contact the legal assistant any time there is a problem or a question regarding the handling of their case. Most clients are only too happy to receive this information. It gives them an opportunity to communicate with someone in the law office other than the attorney, and receive timely and accurate information regarding the status of their case at a lower billing rate. Sophisticated clients are only too aware of the cost of legal services and appreciate the fact that this law firm can save them money.

4.   Asking questions regarding any items that have not been filled out. The actual interview will be conducted by the attorney based on the information on the client interview form. Clients will occasionally attempt to hide facts from their attorney such as prior accidents, claims, lawsuits, convictions, arrests, and so forth. It should be explained that the opposing attorneys and investigators will investigate thoroughly and discover any of these facts. The client must be convinced that it is to their benefit to disclose all of this information to their attorney, so that the attorney will know how to advise the client and will not be surprised. The client should be warned about the central information exchange about accidents and claims maintained by many insurance companies and that information about the client's former accidents and claims will probably be

known to the other side even if the prior injury or claim occurred in another state and even if it occurred many years ago. The client should also be told that the mere fact that there were prior accidents or claims does not diminish the value of this present claim, and that the attorney will know how to minimize the effect of prior claims on this case if the attorney has all pertinent information regarding those prior claims.

§ 1.34   —Ethical Considerations in Client Interviews

When conducting preliminary client interviews, a legal assistant must be careful not to violate the ethics of the unauthorized practice of law by doing any of the following:

1.   Quoting fee or financial arrangements between the law firm and the client. (It is permissible to explain what a contingency fee agreement means.)
2.   Giving legal advice of any kind to the client or answering legal questions. You may answer factual questions.
3.   Advising the client in any way as to the possible outcome of the case, or of the legal procedures or strategies that the attorney may choose to take in this particular case, such as filing a complaint, cross-complaint, demurrer, and so forth.
4.   Advising the client in any way of the possible duration of the matter or how long will it take for the case to settle.

As a legal assistant and client develop a close, trusting relationship, it becomes very difficult to dodge some client's questions such as, "How long will it take for my case to settle?" or "Do I have a chance of winning?" The best way to answer some of these questions is to draw comparisons from other cases. Tell the client that although you are not certain Attorney Smith will choose to take this particular tactic in their case, in a case similar to theirs Attorney Smith did the following . . . . A legal assistant must be careful when handling these types of questions, but must be prepared for the fact that they will come up. It is best to always compare the client's case with a similar case in the office when possible. In this way you are not telling the client that Attorney Smith will definitely choose a particular tactic or strategy in their case, but only that this particular tactic or strategy has been used before by Attorney Smith in a similar case.

Tell the client that it is the general procedure of Attorney Smith to attempt settlement negotiations with an insurance company and to conduct informal discovery before deciding whether or not to file a complaint. Advise the client of the statute of limitations for the filing of their complaint.

The famous question, "When will this all be over; when will my case settle?" is one that a legal assistant will hear frequently throughout the case. Again, a basic answer to this question can be given based on similar cases. It is also appropriate to tell the client that no meaningful settlement negotiations or discussions can be entered into until their physical injuries have stabilized and future medical treatment, if any, has been determined. In this case it would be appropriate to tell the client that

Attorney Smith has been communicating with the treating physician regarding the care and continuing treatment and is now waiting for a response from the doctor.

§ 1.35 Checklist for Client Interviews

_____ Always identify your status as a legal assistant and remind the client that you are part of the litigation team working on their case.

_____ Act professionally and compassionately, treating a client as you would like to be treated.

_____ Always return phone calls even when there is no new information on the case. Clients need to know that their attorney and paralegal are accessible by telephone when they need reassurance.

_____ Be a good listener. Remember communication is a two-way street. Listen to what your client is telling you even if you have heard it all before. Learn to listen to what your client is not saying as well as what they are saying.

_____ Keep control of the conversation by knowing how to steer the conversation in the right direction to elicit the information that you need.

_____ Develop skills in rewording legal questions into layman's terms. This saves confusion and helps focus your conversation.

_____ Develop ways to ask sensitive questions.

_____ Make file notations of all client contact by drafting short file memos as soon as possible after each and every telephone conversation with your client. Do not rely on your memory of what was discussed. Create a paper trail of all communications so that a case chronology can be prepared if needed.

_____ Be sensitive to special situations such as age and language problems. Elderly people, generally speaking, have short attention spans, and need to receive detailed information in written form rather than through a telephone conversation. People for whom English is not their first language present a difficult challenge. It is sometimes difficult to ascertain their level of understanding without appearing to be patronizing. It is important to treat these clients, and all clients, with compassion, friendliness, and concern. It is best to depend on the client or a family member to advise you of difficulty in understanding.

§ 1.36 Questioning Techniques For Interviews

Some clients and witnesses are very comfortable talking about themselves and the incident in question and they are eager to share problems and concerns. Questioning them is relatively easy. It is important to keep them on track and keep within the time frame allowed for the interview. A good technique is to use narrow or closed-ended questions. This allows you to control the subject matter and guide the client with specific questions geared to the specific information being sought. Narrow questions should be worded so that the answer is restricted to the desired topic. The advantage of this type of questioning is that you will get necessary information without wasting valuable time. However, the danger in using only that type of questions is that you receive direct answers, but do not learn the details and/or explanations surrounding those answers. There is a great possibility of losing valuable information. It is important to know how to steer the conversation in the right direction without controlling or limiting a client or witness' answers to such a degree that they appear artificial or out of context because of gaps left from missing background information.

Asking open-ended questions is an interviewing approach which works well with most clients. These types of questions afford the client a chance to unload their problems. It helps establish that all important close relationship between paralegal and client. Open-ended questions can be followed by quick follow-up questions (narrow and specific) to help elicit all of the background information needed to fill in time frame gaps or to explain an answer.

It is important to remember that you are in charge of the interview and that your goal is to steer the conversation in the right direction. A combination of open-ended and leading questions is frequently a good way to begin an interview. Switching to narrow and close-ended questions at the midpoint of the interview can control the flow of information and prevent the client from rambling away from the subject at hand.

§ 1.37 —Sample Client Interview

The following client interview is an example of many types of questioning combined to elicit relevant information by keeping the client on track.

PARALEGAL: Mary, I'd like you to tell me what happened just before the accident.

MARY: Well, the night before I was out with three girlfriends and we went to see a movie. My boyfriend found out about it and he was angry because he had wanted to take me to that movie . . .

PARALEGAL: Excuse me, Mary, I really don't think we need this information at this time unless you can explain why it is important. The accident happened at 8:00 p.m. on Thursday. Why don't you tell me what happened from about 5:00 p.m. on Thursday.

MARY: Well, I was only telling you about going to the movie with my girlfriends and my boyfriend being upset because if we hadn't have been fighting over the movie I had already seen, I would have gone out with him on Thursday night and not gotten into that car accident.

PARALEGAL: I understand all that, but you told me that your boyfriend was not with you at the time of the accident. As I understand it, you were alone in the car at the time, so I'm not sure that we need to talk about your boyfriend now. I need some other information such as where you were when the accident happened, and in what direction you were traveling.

In the above example, the paralegal has used a combination of questioning techniques with the client. The paralegal began the interview with an open-ended question, and after receiving an unfocused response, returned to closed-ended, narrow questioning to steer the client in the proper direction.

§ 1.38   Dealing with Difficult Clients

A paralegal is often the person who is most accessible to a client seeking information on their case. Many attorneys use their paralegals as buffers between themselves and difficult clients. Still other attorneys have discovered that because of their "nonattorney" status within the law firm, paralegals are in a unique position to gain client confidences and establish rapport. Most people are not as intimidated by paralegals as they are by attorneys. A skilled paralegal can use this to their advantage to help the client to be comfortable with them and ensure trust and confidence. Paralegals should always express an interest in the client, react sympathetically to the client's claim, and above all exhibit great patience while assuring the client that your firm will do the best to take care of their case.

Paralegals should always explain to a client that they are not an attorney. They should further explain that all of the work they do is under the supervising attorney's directive, and that they are not permitted to give legal advice. Interestingly enough, this does not matter to some individuals who will continue to ask you questions which call for legal advice. Legal assistants must be careful not to give legal advice, but may give a client factual and procedural information which will help them to understand the status of their case. Remember, as a paralegal you are a trained professional, able to give reliable advice and help as long as you do not give the client legal advice. To the client you are a real person, someone they can relate to without feeling intimidated. If you use this position of approachability as an asset, you will gain the confidence and respect of even the most difficult clients.

Frequently a client will simply want reassurance that things are manageable and not as bad as they seem. A paralegal can give the client a measure of reassurance without crossing the line into giving legal advice. Clients should receive direct answers to their questions, even if the direct answer is, "I'm not certain of that information, but I will relay your concern to the attorney and get an answer back to you tomorrow." Clients are not as concerned with receiving immediate answers to their questions as they are with being heard and having their questions taken seriously. However, it is important to keep promises to clients so that you do not lose credibility. If you are unable to get an answer for them within one or two days, a brief phone call to let them know that the attorney has been out of town and you have not been able to reach the attorney is important and appreciated.

Special situations may give rise to clients who appear to be difficult but in reality are just those which need special handling. Some clients are more demanding than others. Some want a weekly status report and insist that you tell them how much the case is worth. Other clients think they should call each and every time they go to the doctor or physical therapist to report on their progress. Others are disappointed when their attorney doesn't call frequently "just to see how I'm doing." Communicating with these more demanding clients can be time consuming, but manageable, by keeping lines of communication open through short letters and brief phone calls.

§ 1.39   A Client's Interview of the Law Firm

Prospective clients seldom are given the opportunity to interview the law firm and attorneys, rather the interview process is always one-sided. Most clients have had minimal exposure to attorneys and law offices and, therefore, have many questions which frequently go unanswered. You can anticipate some of these questions and volunteer basic information which will be greatly appreciated by the client and will allay some of their fears. The first and most obvious question a client needs to have answered is, "How much will this cost me?" If it is your firm's policy to handle certain cases such as personal injury, product liability, or medical malpractice on a contingent fee basis, tell the client exactly that and further explain exactly what is meant by a contingent fee basis. If it is your firm's policy to charge a modest amount for an initial interview, you must advise the client of that charge prior to setting up the interview.

Clients may also have questions regarding the reputation of the law firm, experience of the attorneys, and how the firm operates in general. If your firm has a firm brochure, include a copy of that brochure in your letter confirming the initial appointment.

Most clients are under strenuous pressure, and picking the right attorney is of great importance to them. Anything you can do to establish rapport with them will help to alleviate some of this pressure. The client should be told beforehand that everything discussed with the legal assistant and the attorney is protected and will be kept confidential. This also will allow the client to feel at ease and to be more candid in providing information.

If it is the practice of your firm to have a team (consisting of a partner, associate, and legal assistant) handle various cases, explain that to the client. Clients are usually pleased to learn that many tasks will be performed by a legal assistant, thus reducing the cost to them. Advise the client that you will be their liaison with the attorney and can always be contacted for case status information.

Many attorneys do not realize that an initial client interview is really a two-way interview. Although it is important to obtain all of the information necessary from a prospective client to determine whether or not your law firm will accept this case, it is equally important that the client be comfortable with the law firm's expertise and experience in handling cases of a similar nature. A client may be reluctant to question the attorney regarding his level of experience and expertise. It is up to the legal assistant to answer the unasked questions that may be of concern to a client. Clients who have never consulted an attorney before will have numerous questions. Most of their questions and concerns center around their desire to have an attorney who has the knowledge, resources, and motivation to win their case.

Subjects that should be addressed include:

Reputation of law firm, how long in practice in the community

Education and experience level of attorneys and legal assistants

Operation of firm—team concept, assignment of cases to areas of specialization of a particular attorney/legal assistant, and

Fee schedules

A firm brochure is very helpful in answering many of these questions and should be given to the client at the initial interview. However, a firm brochure is a cold, impersonal document. A legal assistant can personalize the brochure by speaking about the various attorneys, indicating their civic interests, number of children, participation and sponsorship of athletic events, youth activities, and so forth. As the client begins to think of the attorneys in your office on a personal level, the client will become more comfortable and cooperative and you will have a smooth working relationship.

§ 1.40   Rejecting a Case

If your law firm determines that a client's case should be rejected because of a conflict of interest, poor liability, minimal damages, or any other reason, it is your duty and obligation to notify the client as soon as possible and to return all documents that belong to the client. Rejection letters and documents should be sent certified mail, return receipt requested to guarantee delivery. The rejection letter in **Forms 1–28** and **1–29** are good samples. They are concise, nonjudgmental, and give the client proper warning regarding the time limits within which to bring an action.

FORM 1–28
SAMPLE CASE REJECTION LETTER

[name]
[address]

CERTIFIED MAIL

Dear [name]:

Thank you for contacting us regarding your potential action for damages. We appreciate your consideration of our law firm, and while we would be happy to represent you, it is not possible to do so at this time. Please be advised that this office is unable to undertake your representation concerning any claims you believe you have regarding [action client consulted you for] medical malpractice, breach of contract, etc.] because [reason].

If you wish to pursue any legal remedies you may have, you should immediately contact other counsel. I do not have enough information to be able to tell you what statutes of limitations may apply. This is another reason why you should contact another attorney if you wish to pursue the matter further.

If you need assistance in locating an attorney, contact the State Bar of [name of state] office lawyer referral services at [phone number]. They will be able to provide you with the name of an attorney who specializes in [type of action].

Thank you again for contacting us.

Very truly yours,

[name of attorney]

FORM 1–29
SAMPLE CASE REJECTION LETTER (CASE SPECIFIC)

VIA CERTIFIED MAIL
RETURN RECEIPT REQUESTED

[client name]
[address]

RE: Accident of [date]

Dear [client]:

After a careful review of the accident report, medical records, and documentation that you have provided regarding the above-referenced accident, we have determined that this case is most likely outside of the area of expertise of our law firm. We will, therefore, not be able to represent you in this matter.

You are free to consult with another attorney if you so desire. If you do not know of another attorney, you may contact the Bar Association of your town and ask for referrals to the Attorney's Reference Panel. They will be able to recommend an attorney who specializes in personal injury and product liability actions involving public entities.

If you wish to take action on this matter, a lawsuit must be filed within one (1) year of the date of this accident or it will be barred by the statute of limitations. If this case involves a public entity, and it appears this is so in your case, there are special time requirements that must be met. If they are not, your claim may be barred by the statute of limitations. If you wish to pursue a claim against a public entity, it is important to contact another attorney immediately.

I appreciate your consulting our firm, and I am sorry I could not be of further service to you at this time. If you have need of service for anything else in the future, please do not hesitate to contact me.

Thank you again, and good luck.

Sincerely,

[attorney name]

§ 1.41   Interview Follow-up

At the conclusion of the client interview, the attorney should take time to explain the general litigation process to the client and what the attorney feels is the appropriate first step. If documentation is needed, the client should be advised that you will obtain it through use of the authorizations they have executed.

At the conclusion of the interview, draft a memorandum for the file consisting of a to do list:

_____   Order medical records
_____   Order police report
_____   Order Department of Motor Vehicles search, other public records search
_____   Obtain contracts, insurance policies
_____   Locate and interview certain witnesses
_____   Hire private investigator, get photos
_____   Research applicable statutes
_____   Obtain product information from manufacturer

§ 1.42   Communication with Clients

In order to maintain rapport with the client, it is necessary to continue communicating with them, either verbally or through letters, even though nothing new may have happened in their case. This client "hand-holding" is extremely important and becomes almost exclusively the job of the legal assistant. Litigation is a new and frightening experience for most clients and your phone call every six to eight weeks advising them of case status, even if there have been no changes, will reassure them that someone is looking out for their best interests. Short telephone memos recording these conversations should become part of your file. Of course, a client should be advised to contact you whenever there is a change in their health, employment, address, or any matter that relates in any way to the case. A client should feel it is okay to contact the legal assistant at any time during the case if they feel uncomfortable in any way—whether it relates to a question regarding procedures or personal matters. The stress of a lawsuit will have a telling effect on a client and the client will simply have a need to unload their problems on someone. That someone is usually the legal assistant. By lending a sympathetic ear you are providing a valuable client service and at the same time saving the law firm attorney time and money. Be cautious, however, with clients who are eager to talk about themselves and their cases. Try to ask this type of client close-ended questions which will result in one or two word answers. Also inform them that while you would be very happy to discuss their case with them and are always available should there be a serious problem, you do have other clients and you can call them back at a more convenient time or they can send you a letter and you'll refer it to the attorney.

Communication is a two-way street, and the keys to handling clients who merely want someone to talk to are courtesy and a diplomatic expression of your own schedule. It is quite appropriate to tell a client that your work in the office involves cases for many other attorneys and that you have many assignments to complete and can only spend a few minutes with them at this time. Most clients are understanding of time demands and will appreciate being told at the beginning of a conversation that you can only spend five or ten minutes at this time. If the client has a contingency fee contract, they are aware that there is no extra charge for their phone conferences. However, if the case is being handled on an hourly basis, advise the client that you will be billing your time for their phone conference just as the attorney would bill his time.

§ 1.43 Insurance Defense Clients

There is often confusion in the mind of a client who has been referred to an attorney by their insurance company. It is important that the client understands the relationship between the insurance company and the law firm. They need to understand that you are representing their interests in this action, and will be working with them directly on their case.

Conduct an informational interview with the insurance adjuster who has been working on the case because they will have been in communication with opposing counsel. It is possible that plaintiff's counsel has served the insurance adjuster with a demand letter enclosing documentation of damages. This information with be helpful in evaluating damages and understanding the issues of the case.

New client packets in insurance defense firms differ from new client packets for plaintiff firms in the following respects:

> There may be no retainer agreement if your client is the insurance company and they are providing a defense for their insured.

> If your client has a small business and has provided insurance to the employees and is now being sued, there will be a need for a retainer agreement.

> You will need medical, investigative, and wage loss authorization forms if your client has been damaged, and, in addition to providing a defense, you will be filing a cross-complaint.

> A file is usually set up for claim investigation by the insurance company at the time they were first put on notice of the claim. That file, as well as any information obtained by the company from third parties as part of their claim investigation, should be part of your new client file.

> The most important document in the client packet is the actual insurance policy. Make certain that you have the entire policy and not just the endorsement pages. Also, be certain that you have the current policy (the policy that was in effect at the time of the incident) with all amendments and endorsements.

> Obtain a copy of any pleadings on file in the action and calendar all important dates affecting case status. Often there is some lag time in case referral and response times may need to be extended. Letters requesting extensions should be sent to opposing counsel as soon as possible.

§ 1.44 Communication with Insurance Carriers

As soon as a new client retains your firm to represent him, contact should be made with the defendant's insurance carrier. A letter of representation to the insurance (*see* **Form 1–30**) carrier puts them on notice that the client is no longer without legal representation, and that all further communications regarding the incident in question should be directed to your office. From the point that the insurance carrier receives your letter of representation, direct communications between the insurance company and the client should cease. It is unethical for the insurance carrier to attempt to deal directly with a client who has retained legal counsel.

FORM 1–30
SAMPLE LETTER OF REPRESENTATION
TO INSURANCE COMPANY

[insurance company name]
[address]

 RE: [client name]
 Date of Accident: [date]

Dear [insurance company]:

 Please be advised that this office has been retained by [client] with regard to personal injuries sustained on [date], when [client] slipped and fell in the lobby area of a building at [address]. We have been informed by the building supervisor, [name], that the appropriate insurance carrier to contact is [insurance company] with reference to the building's insurance coverage for premises liability.

 The floor where [client] slipped was unreasonably slippery, not covered by area rugs, and the cause of numerous other slip and fall accidents.

 [Client] reported the incident to a security guard stationed in the lobby, who made a report of the incident.

 [Client] has been under constant treatment for a fracture of [client]'s right leg, and we are attempting to contact medical care providers to obtain records and billing information.

 I would appreciate your having a claims representative contact our office.

     Sincerely,

     [name of attorney]

§ 1.45   Letter to Defendant When Name of Liability Carrier Is Unknown

If you do not know the name of the insurance company representing the defendant, you will need to send the defendant a letter (*see* **Form 1–31**) asking for this information. If a police report was made, you may be able to acquire the information from it. If, in reviewing the police report, it seems likely there will be more than one defendant, letters should be sent to each possible defendant with instructions to forward them on to their respective liability carriers.

FORM 1–31
SAMPLE LETTER TO DEFENDANT WHEN NAME OF LIABILITY CARRIER IS UNKNOWN

[defendant name]
[address]

   RE: [client]
   Date of Accident: [date]

Dear [defendant]:

   Please be advised that this office represents [client] for personal injuries sustained in an automobile accident with your vehicle in [city] on [date]. Please route this letter to your liability insurance carrier immediately so that we may discuss settlement with them.

   All communications regarding this matter should be directed to our office and not to [client].

Thank you for your cooperation in this matter.

                         Sincerely,

                         [name of attorney]

   In a situation where an incident (such as a slip and fall) occurs at or near a piece of real property, you may locate the name of the owner through your city and county tax collector or assessor's office. By researching the property address, you will be able to determine the responsible party for property taxes. A letter should be directed to that responsible party with instructions to forward it on to their liability carrier. (*See* **Form 1–32**.) After you receive a response which identifies the name of the insurance company, an official letter of representation should immediately be sent. (*See* **Form 1–30**.)

FORM 1–32
SAMPLE LETTER TO PROPERTY OWNER
REQUESTING INSURANCE INFORMATION

[property owner]
[address]

RE: [client]
Date of Accident: [date]

Dear [property owner]:

Please be advised that this office represents [client] for injuries received when [client] slipped and fell in the lobby of the building located at [address]. According to records which were available for inspection at the [city name] City and County Assessor's Office, the property listed at that address is owned by you. Accordingly, we are routing this letter to your attention with the request that you give it to your liability insurance carrier and ask them to contact us immediately so that we may discuss settlement of this action.

All communications regarding this matter should be directed to our office and not to [client].

Sincerely,

[name of attorney]

When you receive a response to your letter of representation from the insurance carrier, it will reference a particular claim or file number as well as identify the adjuster who will be handling that claim. An acknowledgement letter should be sent immediately to the insurance adjuster confirming the liability coverage and policy limits if they are known. This letter (*see* **Form 1–33**) is an important first step in establishing communications with the insurance adjuster and opening the doors for possible settlement.

At the same time that a letter of representation is sent to the insurance carrier, a letter should be sent to your new client acknowledging your representation of them. This letter (*see* **Form 1–34**) is an important first step in establishing rapport with the client and insuring cooperation. It is important that the client understand that from this point on they should not be dealing directly with the insurance carrier, and that all communications from the insurance company will be sent directly to your office.

FORM 1–33
SAMPLE LETTER TO INSURANCE ADJUSTER

[insurance adjuster]
[insurance company]
[address]

RE: Our Client: [client]
Claim No. [claim number]
Your Insured: [insured]
Date of Accident: [date]

Dear [insurance adjuster]:

Thank you very much for speaking with me on [date]. This will confirm that [insured] has liability coverage through [insurance company] and that the policy limits are $15,000/$30,000. [Client] is still under care and treatment for the injuries received in this accident. Records have been requested from medical care providers. As soon as we are advised that [client] has been released from care and have obtained records from all treating medical care providers as well as bills, we will forward them to you in a settlement demand package. We will also forward any other material that you desire. We look forward to working with you to settle this matter in an expedient and equitable fashion.

Sincerely,

[name of attorney]

FORM 1–34
SAMPLE LETTER TO NEW CLIENT AFTER
CASE HAS BEEN ACCEPTED

[client]
[address]

Dear [client]:

It was a pleasure meeting with you on [date], and we are pleased to be given the opportunity to represent you in this action.

As we discussed in our meeting, my legal assistant, [name], will be contacting you periodically so that we can be updated on your medical care and treatment. It is important that you keep copies of all medical bills which are mailed to you as well as any correspondence you may receive from the defendant or defendant's insurance company.

We have written a letter of representation to [insurance company], the defendant's insurer, a copy of which is enclosed for your records. You will note that we have requested all communications regarding this incident be directed to us rather than to you. It is important that you do not discuss your case with anyone outside of your immediate friends and family, treating physicians, and, of course, this office. It might be helpful for you to keep a journal in which you could jot down the dates of all doctor's appointments and your recollection of medical advice given at each appointment. You might also wish to include in the journal any pains, aches, or other symptoms which you are feeling at the moment. This is a useful way of charting your recovery, which we hope will be prompt.

We will advise you as soon as we have been contacted by an [insurance company] representative. It is our intention to gather your medical records and bills, wage loss verification, and other items of special damage to present to the adjustor in the form of a settlement package within the next 60 to 90 days. We are hopeful that upon receipt of this settlement package, the insurance adjustor will enter into meaningful negotiations with our office. Should we fail to achieve a satisfactory settlement offer from the insurance company, we will, of course, proceed to file an action on your behalf. We have one year from the date of your accident to do so, and we will keep you advised as that time approaches.

If you have any questions at all, please do not hesitate to contact my legal assistant, [name], or myself. We look forward to working with you in this action. Best wishes for a prompt and complete recovery.

Sincerely,

[name of attorney]

§ 1.46   Letter to Witness

Potential witnesses, who are either identified by the client at the initial client interview or those who gave statements to the police investigating the scene of the accident, should be contacted immediately because witnesses have been known frequently to experience a change of heart when they are called upon to give statements. Advise the client that the client should not contact potential witnesses directly (even though they may be the client's best friends), but rather the client should tell potential witnesses to expect that they will be contacted by your office. Anything your client can do to insure the cooperation of potential witnesses is beneficial. It is important to safeguard independent witnesses' recollections by contacting them as soon as possible to obtain an interview and/or statement. *(See* **Form 1–35.***)*

FORM 1–35
SAMPLE LETTER TO WITNESS

[witness]
[address]

    RE: Accident of [date]
    [location of accident]

Our Client: [client]

Dear [witness]:

This office represents [client] who was injured on [date] in an accident at the intersection of [location] in [city]. According to the police report, this accident occurred when a [vehicle type] operated by [name] hit the brown [vehicle type] operated by [client], causing it to strike a lamp pole and come to rest on the southwest corner of [location]. According to the police report, you gave a statement to the investigating officers.

I would like to have an opportunity to discuss this matter with you. Please contact our office so that we can make an appointment for a convenient time to discuss this further. If it is inconvenient for you to come into our office, please call [area code] [phone number] between the hours of 9:30 to 5:30, and we can have a discussion over the phone.

On behalf of [client], thank you very much for your anticipated cooperation.

Sincerely,

[name], Legal Assistant

§ 1.47   Initial Pleadings

If your firm decides not to represent a client, it is your obligation to notify the client of that fact promptly so that they may seek other counsel. A rejection letter should be sent certified mail, return receipt requested, enclosing any documents that belong to the client. Failure to notify a client promptly of your rejection of their claim and to return all of their personal documents may result in a potential malpractice claim against your firm. Many prospective clients operate on the false assumption that a law firm is representing them when in fact they are merely reviewing the case to decide whether or not to accept the client. Until a formal rejection letter is sent, the law firm is not off-the-hook and runs the risk of a malpractice action.

The initial pleading for a plaintiff is the Complaint, preceded when necessary by a notice of claim against a governmental agency, a certificate of merit for filing malpractice actions against professionals, a creditor's claim, or other necessary preliminary documents. The initial pleading filed by the defendant can be either an Answer or a Demurrer. Often a defendant will additionally file a Cross-Complaint at the same time as their initial pleading. Other initial documents include injunctions, requests for temporary restraining orders, lis pendens, mechanic's liens, or attacks on service of the Summons and Complaint. Procedural attacks on the service of a Summons and Complaint include: error in naming the defendant, the wrong person was served, an individual was served rather than a corporation, a business was not named correctly, and so forth.

A defendant may file moving papers designed to attack the Complaint rather than advance the litigation. Defendants may attack a Complaint in many ways. The most common way is to demur or to move to quash service of the Summons. Other less common but equally effective ways of attacking a Complaint are: a motion to strike a cause of action, or certain language, from the Complaint, or a motion to change venue. Strategically, all of these attacks on a Complaint help a defendant stall the proceedings by keeping the litigation at the initial stage. Until the defendant has responded by making an appearance in the action through moving papers, the litigation may not go forward (unless the statutory time for responding has expired and plaintiff elects to seek a default judgment).

The first stage of litigation begins after the Complaint has been filed, the Summons has been issued, the Complaint has been properly served upon all defendants, and defendants have answered.

The second, most important, and certainly longest stage of litigation is discovery. Formal discovery begins after defendants have answered the plaintiff's Complaint. In most states, discovery devices such as Depositions, Interrogatories, Requests for Admission of Truth of Facts and Genuineness of Documents, and Demands for Inspection of Documents and Tangible Items can all be served on opposing party without leave of court.

§ 1.48   Defendant Checklist

If you are representing the defendant in an action and have been served with a Summons and Complaint, the following checklist should be used at the initial stage of litigation.

_____   Check the Summons to make certain there are no procedural errors and that the defendant has been named correctly as an individual or a business entity. Check that the business has been named correctly (DBA, joint venture, limited partnership, or corporation).

_____   Prepare a motion to quash service of Summons if the Summons is defective in any procedural manner or material facts.

_____   Calendar the date of service of the Complaint and prepare a tickler date fifteen days in advance of the last day to respond. The tickler notation should be a reminder to counsel to consider whether or not there are grounds for a General or Special Demurrer to any of the causes of action.

_____   Forward a copy of the Summons and Complaint immediately to your client, and set a date for an initial case strategy meeting.

_____   Consider cross-complaining against any other individual or entity involved in the dispute.

_____   Serve Cross-Complaints at the same time if an Answer is to be filed rather than a demurrer.

_____   Initiate discovery immediately. Serve a first set of Judicial Council Form Interrogatories and a Request for Statement of Damages along with your

Answer. Remember as defendant you have the right to proceed first in discovery, and should do so. Taking the initiative in discovery forces the plaintiff to immediately be on the defense.

_____ Begin investigation by hiring a private investigator, researching applicable public records, and obtaining all pertinent documentation from your client.

_____ Notice plaintiff's deposition to take place on the day after you receive plaintiff's interrogatory responses.

It is important for defendants to initiate discovery early to obtain information necessary to formulate their case strategy and defense. Initiating discovery at the same time as the defendant files responsive pleadings places a burden on plaintiff to provide factual information to support the allegations raised in the Complaint on file. Continuances are generally commonplace in discovery proceedings, and the defendant may well be called upon to grant plaintiff a continuance to respond to written discovery. Granting such a continuance is contingent upon defendant's case strategy and overall litigation plan. Forcing plaintiff either to respond quickly with the requested information, or request a continuance places defendant in a somewhat superior initial bargaining position in the ensuing litigation.

CHAPTER 2

INFORMAL DISCOVERY AND INVESTIGATION

§ 2.1   Introduction

Informal discovery begins at the initial client interview and continues throughout the prelitigation stage of the case. Formal discovery devices such as depositions, interrogatories, requests for admissions, and demands for inspection of documents are usually reserved by statute or leave of court, for cases in active litigation. Special circumstances are necessary to obtain permission for conducting formal discovery before an action is filed. In every case, it is important to learn as much as possible about the facts, legal theories, and availability of supporting documentation and witnesses prior to filing an action. This early investigation and informal discovery provides the groundwork for later specific formal discovery inquiries.

§ 2.2   Purposes of Discovery

All discovery, whether it is informal prelitigation discovery or formal discovery, should be prepared with the goal of proving your client's case at trial. The main purposes of discovery are:

Uncovering evidence
Encouraging settlement
Emphasising main issues
Preserving evidence
Investigating
Economizing

Exploring Opponent's Perception of the Facts and Case

Documenting Testimony and Preserving Documents

Exploring opposition's factual and legal contentions, issues, supporting documentation, and so forth.

Pinpointing weaknesses in opponent's position on disputed facts, unsupported legal contentions, and so forth.

Recognizing strengths in opponent's position on disputed factual issues and legal theories, and planning research and investigation for rebuttal of opponent's strong points.

Establishing knowledge, or lack of knowledge, of a witness and/or party.

Locating and identifying tangible evidence (objects, machines, vehicles, defective products, and so forth) and preserving them in their original state for use at time of trial.

It is important to gather and preserve all physical evidence relating to the case such as defective products, photographs of damage to property and/or motor vehicles, and photographs of injuries in personal injury cases. Investigation of all neutral third-party sources of information will provide leads for further discovery and help with case evaluation. Documents should be obtained with client authorizations and through public records as soon as possible.

An assessment of the facts educates the attorney at an early stage as to the value of the case, and the amount of damages, and/or defenses that can be raised by the other side. Meaningful settlement demand packages can be submitted to insurance adjustors before discovery intensifies. Settlement prospects are at an optimum when costs are at a minimum and your client can be assured that the net recovery will not be diminished by a high cost bill. Insurance adjustors authorized by their principals to settle a particular case within certain limits will be in a position to offer more money if it has not yet been spent in costly discovery.

A claim may involve several issues. Some will be major and others will be minor but they may relate back to the major area of controversy. Facts on which there is no material controversy can be stipulated to between attorneys and removed from a claim. Issues can then be simplified and narrowed to the main points of controversy. As this happens, claims and defenses that require more investigation become highlighted, enabling attorneys to focus discovery in a more economical and productive fashion than "fishing-type" discovery where inquiries are broad-based and ask for "any and all information" without a sense of direction. That type of discovery invites objections from the responding party, whereas narrow, focused discovery can be propounded in a manner designed to be "objection proof." Avoiding possible objections also avoids the need for motions to compel and saves both attorney time and client money.

Physical evidence, such as damaged machinery and defective products, needs to be immediately preserved. Review local newspapers immediately after a major incident for press clippings and photographs. Statements should also be taken from witnesses who are either nonresidents of the area or aged and/or infirmed witnesses whose physical health may prevent them from testifying later when the case comes to trial. Take photographs of automobile damage, crop damage, property damage, physical injuries, and so forth. These photographs should be dated and identified with the location and the name of the photographer.

Begin investigation early and continue it throughout the case. The extent and nature of investigation at the initial stages of litigation, as well as who performs the investigation, depends on the nature of the action, time and expenses involved, and the financial means of the client. It is more economical and efficient to have early investigation done by the legal assistant than it is to hire an outside investigator.

Informal interviews of potential witnesses should be done shortly after an accident or occurrence while facts are still fresh in their minds. This interview need not be a formal statement-taking interview, but it can be an information gathering interview. Premature statement-taking can present problems in formal discovery regarding production of statements. A legal assistant's notes taken at an information gathering interview put in memo form to the attorney will be protected in the discovery process by the work product privilege.

Information obtained through a search of public records, client's authorization, and neutral, third parties can be obtained at minimal cost to your client. That information can then be evaluated by the attorney in deciding how to proceed. Informal investigation may indicate that the case should be settled without the investment of further costs by initiating a lawsuit. A demand package detailing a claim and anticipating and responding to possible claim defenses, can be presented to an insurance adjustor before expenses have mounted to the point where there is no alternative but full scale litigation.

§ 2.3   Limits on Discovery

Discovery statutes vary from state to state. Many are patterned on the Federal Rules of Civil Procedure for discovery which allow broad disclosure of facts to help educate attorneys before trial and prevent surprises and undisclosed information which may prejudice their case. The purpose of broad-based discovery is to expedite litigation and insure dispensation of justice by the courts by eliminating false or fraudulent claims and by placing litigants on an equal footing. This desire to place litigants on an equal footing has given rise to the broad discretionary powers of discovery sanctioned by most courts.

The scope of discovery is limited by the discretion of the trial court based on a good cause showing of relevancy and privilege. In other words, litigants may discover, or request, any information that is either relevant to the subject matter of the action at hand or reasonably calculated to lead to the admissibility of information relevant to the subject matter, as long as that information is not safeguarded from discovery through a statutory privilege.

§ 2.4   Preparing a Discovery Plan

The purpose of a discovery plan is to discover the relevant facts and contentions needed to prove your client's case, pin down your opponent, and achieve a cost-efficient, expedient result favorable to your client's interests. Discovery begins at the initial client interview which offers you the first opportunity to gain information and documents, and continues throughout the pretrial stage of the action. The discovery phase of litigation is the most critical and can be the most expensive of the entire case. The scope of permissible discovery in civil litigation is so broad that, if your client has enough time and money, you can be entrenched in discovery for years.

You must develop a discovery master plan to obtain the needed information at a minimum cost of attorney time and client money. An organized approach to discovery which integrates informal investigation with formal discovery devices such as depositions, interrogatories, requests for admission, and requests for production of documents will accomplish your objectives expediently and effectively. A master plan for discovery begins with:

1.   An analysis and careful review of all documentation provided by your client
2.   A listing of all legal theories applicable to the situation
3.   An identification of the elements of each cause of action or defense compatible with your client's objectives
4.   A listing of information needed to generate evidence that will prove your case
5.   An identification of information sources which need to be used to establish each element of the legal theories used in your causes of action or defenses
6.   A listing of your client's objectives and priorities. Sometimes these may be unrealistic or incompatible; however, you should list them as the client expresses them. It is the job of the attorney to explain why certain objectives may be inconsistent with the available legal theories and facts of the situation. It is the job of the legal assistant to note carefully a client's needs and report them in an opening memo so the attorney assigned to handle the case can review them.
7.   A determination of a maximum discovery budget—how much does the client have to finance the litigation, and how much is the client prepared to spend to achieve his objectives? Will the result justify the expense?

§ 2.5   Formalizing a Discovery Plan

A discovery plan using the devices identified as the principal devices for discovery per statute—depositions, interrogatories, requests for admissions, and demand for inspection and production of documents and other tangible items—should be formulated early after a meeting and discussion between all members of the litigation team. The best discovery procedures are those which provide you with the information required without educating the opposition.

The most frequently overlooked aspect is failing to investigate your opponent's side of the issue. It is necessary to play devil's advocate early in the case in order to discover those claims or defenses your adversary will most likely assert. Contention interrogatories, requests for production of documents, and requests for admissions are the best discovery tools to pin down your opponent's theories.

In most cases, there are some acts that are not really in dispute, such as dates, places, persons present at meetings, contracts, ownership interests in personal property, and so forth; however, this does not mean that you can safely regard these facts as proven. An early set of requests for admissions can nail down these uncontested facts in a manner that can be used as a foundation for evidence at the time of trial. Failing to nail down these uncontested matters early in litigation may result in unhappy surprises at the time of trial when your adversary's memory becomes clouded as to actually what it was that you agreed was uncontested. Do not rely on the good graces of the opposing counsel. Document through an early set of requests for admissions or interrogatories those facts which, although they may appear to be uncontested, are essential to proving your case at trial.

Considerations as to the timing and sequence of discovery devices depend upon many factors unique to each case, each client's budget, and each attorney's discretion. Consider carefully the rules of civil procedure for your state so that, as either defendant or plaintiff, you initiate discovery at the earliest possible time pursuant to statute. A defendant who follows the statutory preference given to defendants to initiate discovery may gain a tactical advantage by serving their answer accompanied by a request for a statement of damages and a first set of interrogatories. This forces the plaintiff to immediately assume a defensive position, which is the less desirable of the two possible positions a party may assume during the course of discovery.

The complexity of a discovery plan varies with the complexity of the action. Committing a discovery plan to writing early in an action saves time, expense, and duplication of efforts. The goal of discovery is to collect all useful information as expeditiously and economically as possible, to assist the supervising attorney in understanding opposing counsel's commitment to the litigation, and to assess the potential settlement value of the action. In complicated actions where discovery proceeds in waves, such as a wave of interrogatories to identify witnesses, documents, physical evidences, and so forth in order that subpoenas and requests for production of documents may be properly prepared with specific information, it is reasonable to expect that mutual extensions of time will become necessary and will delay responses. By formulating a written discovery plan and beginning early in an action, you can minimize the disadvantage of these unavoidable delays.

§ 2.6   Choice of a Discovery Plan

A factor influencing the formulation of a discovery plan is to determine whether your action is a people case or a document case. In cases where there is no paper trail that can be followed, the most effective means of obtaining information is through the key players, witnesses, peripheral witnesses, and other individuals with knowledge of the facts of the case. Other situations have paper trails from the start, such as commercial litigation, contract actions, and so forth. In cases where the known document population is numerous, be prepared to discover that the unknown document population may turn out to be even more voluminous. Documents may prove to be the best source of educating the attorney as to what critical issues to cover in depositions of the key players. In this type of a case, it is important to obtain the needed documents through subpoenas to third parties and the custodians of record prior to depositions. There is no rule of thumb which sets the sequence of discovery devices in a discovery plan. The disputed issues, legal theories, known document population, and key players must all be considered before an effective discovery plan listing the sequence of discovery can be formulated.

Each of the formal discovery tools has its own strengths and limitations. Consequently, choosing the proper tool to do the job requires weighing the advantages and disadvantages of each specific discovery device. Effective discovery requires a coordinated use of discovery devices, for example, using one device to flush out certain information, such as interrogatories to ascertain identifying information on relevant documents, and another device, such as a request for identification and production of documents, to follow up on the information obtained in order to request the specific documents. Other examples of coordinated use of discovery devices are depositions coordinated with document production and request for admissions coordinated with interrogatories. A deposition coordinated with document production is discussed in **Chapter 3.** Requests for admissions coordinated with interrogatories are discussed in **Chapter 5.**

§ 2.7   Discovery Plan Checklist

This checklist is a good way to help organize your approach to forming a discovery plan.

_____   1.   List each item of information, evidence, and other proof furnished by your client, including in your listing the name of the document, author of the document, date of the document, and a one- or two-sentence summary of the importance of the facts contained in the document. Include in your list a follow-up column for other sources of information mentioned in or linked in some way to the document.

EXAMPLE: Police report, February 23, 19__, Author of document: investigating officer, Joe S., Badge No. 3456. Supplemental report with diagram drawn by Officer Jane M., Badge No. 2345, same date. Conclusions of investigating officer place blame for accident on adverse driver citing violation of Vehicle Code 2356(a). FOLLOW-UP INFORMATION: Obtain copies of police photos; witnesses named in police report are: Jane T., Bob G., Joe W., and Susan B. Contact??

_____   2.   List the persons and entities who might be a source of evidence or proof for each document or item reviewed, such as the witnesses identified in a police report, police photos, record of citation, and so forth.

_____   3.   Request public records immediately so that you will have them early in discovery. These may include marriage certificates, birth certificates, transfers of title to real property, weather reports, building inspection reports, Cal-Osha report forms, and so forth. Ask for all the documents you need to obtain through a Federal Freedom of Information Act Request at the earliest possible date, keeping in mind that these requests are not necessarily processed in the most expedient fashion.

_____   4.   Do an initial screening for privilege as part of your initial review of the documents you have obtained from your client. This is particularly important when dealing with a business client. Certain documents will immediately be identifiable as privileged and should be set aside as soon as they are discovered. Privileges may have attached themselves to otherwise neutral documents pursuant to discussions between the client and attorney or legal assistant during the initial client interview. Particularly safeguard these documents by segregating them into a separate file folder and clearly labeling the folder: CLIENT DOCUMENTS FOR ATTORNEY USE IN PREPARATION OF LITIGATION— PRIVILEGED DOCUMENTS NOT TO BE CIRCULATED OR PRODUCED TO INDIVIDUALS OUTSIDE THIS OFFICE.

_____ 5. Consider carefully what information is needed to prove your case by analyzing the legal elements required to establish your client's cause of action or affirmative defense. A good source of information is the <u>Book of Approved Jury Instructions</u> pertaining to the causes of action or affirmative defenses you seek to establish. This will serve as a checklist of the elements needed to prove that particular claim or defense. For example, in order to prove a breach of the duty of due care of a driver on the public roadway, you need to establish inattentiveness, a cause of distraction, or some other reason which caused the adverse driver to breach his duty of due care to other drivers on the road.

_____ 6. Select that discovery device most likely to yield the required information.

§ 2.8   Sample Discovery Plan (Personal Injury Action)

In a typical personal injury action, informal discovery plays a large part in obtaining preliminary information to supply the factual basis for the plaintiff's allegation as to how the accident occurred. This discovery plan is for a personal injury suit resulting from a car accident. Informal discovery devices include:

Police report—complete with supplementary report, sketch of accident scene, and photographs.

Newspaper articles on the accident.

Vehicle storage report (if the vehicle was impounded by the investigating officers).

Records of the towing company (if the vehicle was towed from the scene of the accident).

Ambulance and paramedic reports.

Photographs taken by client of the damaged vehicle and the client's injuries.

Photographs taken by client's insurance adjustor.

Vehicle repair estimates. Rental car contracts can be obtained from your client.

Verification of adverse party's insurance policy and coverage as listed on police report.

Witness contact—an investigator should contact all witnesses listed on the police report, verify their addresses, and statements as given to investigating officers. The investigator should take additional statements from those witnesses favorable to your client.

Medical records and bills—Obtain these with the client's authorization.

Wage loss verification—Obtain these with the client's authorization.

Any and all records of out-of-pocket expenses, and any nonmedical, special expenses incurred as a result of the accident should be obtained.

Demand letter—After all this information has been gathered, and your client's condition has stabilized, send a demand letter to the insurance carrier in an attempt to settle the case at a prelitigation stage (*see* sample demand letters in **Chapter 1**).

Formal discovery in a personal injury case includes:

Interrogatories to identify witnesses, documents, objects, and evidence that the opponent contends supports their claim or defense (version of accident).

Demands for identification and production of documents and things based on information obtained from interrogatory responses.

Deposition of the adverse party.

Deposition of nonparties, party-related witnesses, and peripheral figures who may have knowledge of the incident.

Requests for admissions of facts and genuineness of documents, if applicable.

Depositions of expert witnesses.

Discovery in a personal injury action usually proceeds in waves. The first wave includes informal discovery and attempts to settle based on a settlement demand letter and further negotiations. The second wave includes interrogatories to identify witnesses, documents, custodians of record, transactions on which claims are based, as well as documentation of damages claimed, and so forth. The third wave includes depositions designed to narrow issues and resolve preliminary matters, and may also include depositions of experts, further legal research, motions in limine to limit testimony to opposition's experts, and so forth.

This is a typical discovery plan for simple personal injury cases and must be varied to fit more complicated cases. Informal discovery generally works as a catalyst and generates useful information at an early stage, which can be pursued with formal discovery devices such as depositions, interrogatories, requests for admissions, and demands for document production. Written discovery devices are often interdependent. For example, well-framed interrogatories can be used to identify documents by name, author, and date so that specifically tailored requests for production of documents can be drafted to avoid the standard objections raised during document production.

§ 2.9   Sample Discovery Plan (Contract Action)

In this sample, a Complaint has been filed by your office alleging a cause of action for breach of contract. Your attorney has asked you to prepare a discovery plan combining both formal and informal discovery devices. **Form 2–1** illustrates this discovery plan.

FORM 2–1
SAMPLE CONTRACT ACTION DISCOVERY PLAN

ALLEGATIONS IN COMPLAINT	PROPOSED DISCOVERY

First Cause of Action

Form of business and principal place of business correct as stated?	Obtain Articles of Incorporation or partnership documents from Secretary of State or Commissions of Corporations.
	Request production of documents to include articles of incorporation, corporate minute book, corporate seal, etc.
Contract signed in [city], [state].	Request production of documents of all draft contracts.
	Interrogatories to ask where contract was signed, where it was to be performed, any witnesses to the signing of the contract, any oral agreements attempting to modify or alter the terms of the contract.
Contract to be performed in [city], [state].	Interrogatories to party asking where contract was to be performed, all witnesses to any conversations about actual work to be performed, depositions of any individuals hired to perform the work in [city], [state].
	Informal discovery: search public records, department of public works, applicable building permits, etc.
Oral agreement re: financing to include [dollar amount] loan to be repaid with interest from the sale of out-of-state home. Condition precedent for construction contract.	Identification of listing agent for sale of home, deposition with production of documents to include all documents involved in listing and marketing home (multiple listing agreement, original listing contract, lists of comparable homes in area sold within 60 days of listing, etc.)
	Request for production of documents to include notes, memos, etc. on terms of loan.

Request for admissions requiring admissions of oral agreement from all parties.

Research background information on condition of economy and real estate market in state where home is listed.

Request for production to include documents such as canceled checks, ledger pages, all business records of real estate broker.

Breach of contract, failure to sell home, notice of rescission of construction contract.

Request for production of documents such as memos, phone messages, investigative reports, correspondence, etc. regarding removing home from multiple listing agreement with real estate agent.

Investigation re: parties who may have made offer to purchase home, subpoena documents from other real estate agents who may have made offers of purchase.

Interrogatories to trace paper trail on sales transaction asking for identification of any individuals with knowledge of withdrawal of home from real estate market.

Damages plus interest for contracts with subcontractors, building materials, supplies, etc.

Interrogatories asking for any and all calculations for interest and damages, all documents as referencing contracts with subcontractors, purchase of supplies, building materials, building permits, etc.

Request for production of documents to obtain those documents identified in interrogatories.

§ 2.10   Relevancy

Relevancy has been described as being in the eye of the beholder. That is, what is relevant and essential to the subject matter in the eyes of the plaintiff's attorney will most certainly be irrelevant and not calculated to lead to the discovery of any relevant facts pertaining to the subject matter by the defense counsel. To deal with questions of relevancy, the facts and issues of a particular case must be thoroughly investigated to prove that the information sought is relevant to the factual and/or legal issues of the case; and that they will support the particularized showing of good cause necessary to overcome an objection that the information sought is not relevant to the subject matter at hand.

Requirements for good cause differ from state to state and can either be found in the discovery statutes for your particular state, or in the Federal Rules of Civil Procedure. For example, in California a good cause showing requires that the party seeking discovery show not only specific facts justifying that discovery, but also that the information sought is either relevant to the subject matter of the action or reasonably calculated to lead to the discovery of admissible evidence and cannot reasonably be obtained through any other source. The fact that the testimony or information sought would be inadmissible if offered at trial is not grounds for objection. The test for relevancy requires that the testimony or information sought is relevant to the subject matter of the case rather than the specific issues of the case. Even if the information sought is inadmissible at the time of trial, discovery of that information may lead to the discovery of other information which will be admissible.

§ 2.11   Objections to Relevancy—Protective Orders

The procedure for objecting to information on the basis of relevancy is a motion for a protective order. If the objection is to a formal discovery proceeding (deposition, interrogatories, document request), the motion for a protective order must be accompanied by formal opposition points and authorities such as opposition to motions to compel further interrogatory answers, opposition to motions to compel production of documents, opposition to motions to compel answers to questions certified at deposition, and so forth. Procedures for protective orders vary from state to state, but usually consist of the following documents:

Notice of Motion
Motion
Points and Authorities in Support of the Protective Order
Declaration by Attorney in support of the protective order with exhibits
Proposed Order which specifically sets out that information which should fall within the protective order.

Information which does not fall under any of the statutory privileges, but which is not only irrelevant to the subject manner at hand, but also possibly highly prejudicial to your client, can be safeguarded through a protective order. For example, in a medical malpractice action the plaintiff may have reason to believe that the doctor and/or hospital named in the action has a track record of being sued, or at least being investigated for possible mistakes. Informal discovery can direct a request to the Bureau of Medical Quality Assurance in your state capital and an inquiry can be made as to the status of the license of the doctor in question. For a small fee, they will search their computer files and inform you of any actions brought before the Board against that doctor, including voluntary or involuntary suspensions of license.

If you find that the doctor has had a license suspension, it is important to know the date of that suspension and compare it with the date that the doctor treated your client to establish a critical time period. The closer in time that the suspension or misconduct is to the treatment, the greater the argument for the relevancy of information concerning the facts behind that suspension. Once formal discovery is initiated, interrogatories and requests to produce documents can be directed to the doctor and treating hospital to uncover further information regarding the suspension or misconduct.

An argument for irrelevancy of this information would be based upon the fact that the suspension or misconduct was too remote in time to influence the doctor's conduct in treating your client. Another argument that can be made against the relevancy of this type of information is that it is prejudicial in nature, and serves no useful purpose in furthering the action at hand. The counterargument for relevancy is that it is relevant to know the history of the doctor's course of treatment of patients with complaints similar to your client's. It is also relevant to learn any facts which might cast doubt upon the doctor's credibility as a physician, and the possibility that the doctor rendered services to your client which fell below the standard of care which should reasonably be expected of a physician with the same amount of skill and degree of training.

§ 2.12   Burden of Proof in Relevancy Disputes

The burden of proof in relevancy disputes rests with the party who desires the information. It is up to the propounding party to prove that the information sought is either directly relevant to the issues at hand or will reasonably lead to the discovery of directly relevant information. This burden of proof, or showing good cause, must be supported by both factual arguments and legal research set forth in points and authorities in a motion to compel.

One argument that can be advanced to gain access to information that you feel is relevant to your case, but as in the case of the physician may be highly prejudicial to the defendant on a personal level, is to ask in your motion to compel for an *in camera* inspection as an alternative to actual production of sensitive documents. *In camera* inspections are frequently used at the federal level pursuant to Federal Rule of Civil Procedure § 26(c) which provides the court with the discretion to shape an *in camera* order limiting the disclosure of the privileged information to serve best the compelling interests of all parties and the public. The court then weighs the arguments for relevancy against the interests of justice. The judge must decide if the value of the information sought will outweigh the burden the discovery places on the responding party. In the case of personal or confidential records which represent a potential invasion of privacy, the judge must consider the interests of the public versus the individual and reach a decision that best serves the interests of justice.

Arguments against relevancy are exactly the opposite of the arguments for relevancy. Arguments against relevancy can be a lack of good cause, the prejudice to the client will outweigh the value of the information, the information sought will not further the interests of justice, and finally that there is an alternative way of obtaining the information.

Example: Business Litigation—In a business litigation scenario where you are suing a parent corporation acting as a holding company for several subsidiaries, you may have an alter ego cause of action of attempting to pierce the corporate veil and establishing that subsidiaries really do not exist as separate entities. You would call the Secretary of State as part of your initial investigation to determine:

1.   The status of the corporation, and each of the subsidiaries,
2.   The names of all of the officers,
3.   The availability of certificate of domestic stock, and
4.   The agent for service of process.

After doing this research, you may notice names and/or addresses appearing on several lists leading to the suspicion that either the same person holds offices in both the parent corporation and one or two subsidiaries, or that the same mailing address is being used. You would then call the Commissioner of Corporations to see if any stock certificates had been issued by any of the subsidiaries and to see if corporate taxes had been paid.

In formal discovery, the critical documents to obtain would include corporate minutes for each entity. This would help to establish whether separate board meetings were held for each subsidiary, whether the business of the subsidiaries was discussed at one board meeting held by the parent corporation board of directors, or whether separate boards of directors exists for the subsidiaries. A relevancy objection would probably be raised as to the validity of requesting board meeting minutes from subsidiaries who are not named as defendants in your action. The argument would be that you are entitled to obtain corporate minutes from the parent corporation, a named defendant, but would need to show the relevancy of the need to obtain corporate minutes from the various subsidiaries. A good cause argument could be made for relevancy based on information found from the Secretary of State listing the names of the officers of the parent corporation and each subsidiary, duplication of address, failure to list separate boards of directors, and from the Commissioner of Corporations regarding stock issuance and tax status.

§ 2.13   Privileged Information

Information which is privileged is protected from discovery. This simple statement foreshadows discovery wars more than any other discovery restriction. It is important to understand privilege and its application to discovery so that you can not only protect valuable information for your clients, but also overcome privilege claims by the opposition to gain information needed to further the interests of your client. The privileges that most commonly effect discovery are (1) attorney/client privilege, (2) work product privilege, (3) medical information privilege, (4) official record privilege, and (5) confidential documents (invasion of privacy issues).

Federal Rule of Procedure 26(b)(1) explicitly declares privileged information to be nondiscoverable. On the state court level, there are comparable statutes safeguarding privileged information, as well as case law doctrines specific to certain privileges such as attorney work product and confidential medical information. There is no general principle securing a person from providing information in general, but the statutes have established specific privileges that permit the withholding of information in certain reasonably well-defined circumstances. What is and what is not privileged for discovery purposes is defined by constitutional provisions, statutory law, common law, the rules of evidence, and cases interpreting specific privileges.

The existence of privilege is one claim that will legitimately delay discovery inquiries. Becoming familiar with the limits of privilege helps to determine just what information can properly be sought and when objections and refusals to respond can properly be stated. The importance of claiming privilege early in discovery proceedings cannot be overemphasized. Often, by not claiming a privilege in a timely fashion, it can be deemed waived by the opposition, and information that properly would have been protected by a particular privilege becomes discoverable because of the waiver.

§ 2.14   The Elements Necessary to Establish Privilege

Privilege applies to communications occurring in confidential relationships. Several elements need to be present to create this privilege:

1. A communication, written or oral, must originate in confidence with an understanding that the information will not be disclosed;

2. The element of confidentiality must be essential to a full and satisfactory maintenance of a relationship between individuals (attorney/client, patient/ physician, husband/wife), or it must serve a vital, governmental, or public need (official records); and

3. The injury that would occur to the individual or entity by disclosure of this information must outweigh any benefit gained by the disposition of the litigation based upon the information. This is the balancing test which must be applied in ruling on motions concerning privileged information.

When deciding whether to uphold or overturn a privilege and release information, the court generally reviews each of the above-mentioned elements. The basic rationale for privilege is the need to retain the confidential character of the information. In deciding whether the information was intended to be a confidential communication, the court will look at how many people were present during a conversation or received copies of a written document. In corporate settings, the need to know is very important in establishing a privileged business communication. A business communication which is stamped TOP SECRET and then has a carbon copy list of 35 people is difficult to view as a confidential communication. On the other hand, a business communication stamped TOP SECRET which is circulated only to the chairman of the board and various members of the board of directors, with no carbon copies beyond the board of directors, may be viewed as a confidential communication.

Privilege must be properly asserted in a timely fashion. When the first inquiry into a sensitive area forces you to reveal the existence of a privileged document, a formal objection and privilege claim must be stated in written form for the record. Deposition questions regarding sensitive areas should not be answered on instruction of counsel. Deposition questions regarding the existence of privileged materials should be answered based on available information. The existence of privileged documents cannot be denied or the documents will not be allowed into evidence at the time of trial. When an interrogatory is propounded asking for specific information, an objection must be made and the privilege asserted. If that interrogatory is answered with the substance of the document in question, it may constitute a waiver of privilege and will make it difficult to claim that document as a privileged document should the opposition (based on the interrogatory answer) request that document specifically in a document production.

§ 2.15   Claiming Privilege in Diversity Actions

When you represent a client in an action that, but for the diversity of jurisdiction, would have or could have been filed in state court, establishing privilege can be confusing. Case law to support privilege claims can be problematic, especially in situations where there is a conflict between federal and state statutes and case law. After discovery has begun and you are reviewing documents in preparation for interrogatory responses and document production, you must make decisions as to specific privilege claims. In cases where the sole basis for filing in federal district court is due to the diversity of defendants, the specific privilege statutes and case law decisions of your state govern discovery proceedings. If the allegations of your complaint do not raise federal questions or allege legal theories or defenses based upon federal statutes, you may use state statutes and cases as arguments in discovery disputes. You may, of course, also use federal statutes where applicable and federal law will prevail should there be a conflict between federal and state statutes.

§ 2.16   Attorney-Client Privilege

All written and oral communications between clients and attorneys are privileged. This privilege extends to all agents of the attorney (such as investigators, legal assistants, and secretaries) and to any agents of the client who are necessary to transmit information to the attorney for the purposes of furthering the litigation. This includes guardians ad litem, spouses, adult children of elderly clients, and so forth. When clients are asked to prepare documents specifically for their case at the request of their attorney or legal assistant (such as time lines, narratives, journals of their medical treatment, or chronologies of business meetings), these are considered privileged written communications. When a client communicates with their attorney or an agent of the law office, the client presumes that the communication is confidential. The intent of confidentiality is always present and all information received from the client should be treated in a privileged manner.

The attorney-client privilege also applies to documents from former attorneys. For example, when a client comes to your office with a file from a former attorney, that file may contain many privileged documents. Any documents prepared for that case by the former attorney or any of his agents are privileged documents. The privilege does not automatically end because the attorney/client relationship has ceased. Communications between your attorney, written and oral, with the former attorney concerning the case are also privileged. This privilege is a conditional attorney-client/attorney work product privilege rather than an absolute privilege and portions of a former attorney's file may not be covered by the privilege. Materials which have been communicated to third parties who were not necessary to the litigation may be subject to discovery.

§ 2.17   Privilege Protection Checklist

The attorney-client privilege and work product privilege are the most frequently used privileges in litigation. These two privileges overlap frequently and simultaneously protect communications and documentation. In most states and jurisdictions, the attorney-client privilege is statutory and the work product privilege is a case law doctrine. *Work product privilege* is, in the strictest sense of the meaning, work product protection supported by case law decisions which define its scope and application to fact patterns.

Taking these actions at the very beginning of your case will help protect the client from inadvertent disclosure of privileged information and/or documents:

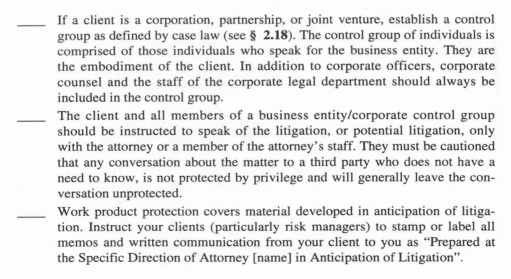

_____ If a client is a corporation, partnership, or joint venture, establish a control group as defined by case law (see § **2.18**). The control group of individuals is comprised of those individuals who speak for the business entity. They are the embodiment of the client. In addition to corporate officers, corporate counsel and the staff of the corporate legal department should always be included in the control group.

_____ The client and all members of a business entity/corporate control group should be instructed to speak of the litigation, or potential litigation, only with the attorney or a member of the attorney's staff. They must be cautioned that any conversation about the matter to a third party who does not have a need to know, is not protected by privilege and will generally leave the conversation unprotected.

_____ Work product protection covers material developed in anticipation of litigation. Instruct your clients (particularly risk managers) to stamp or label all memos and written communication from your client to you as "Prepared at the Specific Direction of Attorney [name] in Anticipation of Litigation".

_____ Caution your client and the client's staff on a regular basis that overuse of the work product label will render it meaningless. It is difficult to break many corporate executives and businessmen of the need to attach large distribution lists to all memos and if an opposing counsel can prove that a privileged stamp or cautionary words are used on all materials, especially those with large distribution lists, they can easily gain access to even the most confidential documents.

_____ Have all members of the litigation team, including the litigation support staff, sign confidentiality agreements. First, this makes sure they know how important it is not to divulge information accidentally that can then be discovered by the opposition. Second, these agreements can be used to demonstrate confidential intent.

§ 2.18   Corporate Clients

A corporation is not accorded privileges greater than those given to a natural person. However, a corporation as an artificial entity speaks through its individual agents and employees, making the application of the attorney-client privilege on a corporate level more broad-based than it is for a natural person. The definition of *client* on the corporate level includes all those individuals within the corporate control group. Examples of those in a corporate control group include

Members of a Board of Directors

Officers of a corporation

Individuals directly responsible for a particular function or department of the corporation

Administrative assistants and private secretaries to corporate officers

Corporate counsel

Corporate counsel's staff, which may include legal assistants, administrative assistants, secretaries, bookkeepers, risk management investigators, and so forth.

Identify all individuals who fall within a corporate control group as early as possible in litigation to protect the confidential nature of information which legitimately falls within the privilege. Distribution of communications received from, or sent to, legal counsel must be confined to those individuals within the control group on a need-to-know basis to preserve the attorney-client privilege.

The United States Supreme Court in *Upjohn Co v. United States*[1] discussed Federal Rules of Evidence § 501 (attorney-client privilege), and expanded the scope of a corporation's right to assert the attorney-client privilege. *Upjohn* discussed the corporate control group and expanded on previous federal cases which had limited the control group to those individuals "in a position to control or substantially participate in a decision about any action the corporation might take on advice of counsel." *Upjohn* stated that the privilege applied to all confidential communications

---

[1] 449 U.S. 383 (1981).

between those employees of a corporation and attorney which are "necessary in the course of investigation and/or litigation of an action."

On occasion the attorney-client privilege may be overused in a business relationship by attempting to encompass communications which are not strictly confidential. Only those communications deemed necessary within "the course and scope of the professional legal relationship" may truly be considered confidential communications. The test for applying the attorney-client communication privilege is the presumption of confidentiality as well as the relevancy of the communication to the subject matter of the legal issues.

Communications by, or between, an attorney and personnel of a wholly owned subsidiary or affiliated company made in the presence of, or to, personnel of the parent company or to another affiliated company needing to know the information to perform their duties properly are considered confidential and are protected by the attorney-client privilege even though the attorney may be employed by the parent corporation. Courts have consistently held that the attorney-client privilege applies to all communications between a corporation (including wholly owned subsidiaries or affiliated companies) and those employees that are necessary to carry out "the attorney's investigatory counseling and litigating functions."

§ 2.19   Corporate Employees

An issue directly related to the attorney-client privilege is the extent to which an attorney may privately interview present or former employees of a corporation or business. This was addressed in *Upjohn v. United States*[2] when the United States Supreme Court held that when the opposing party is a corporation, counsel may not communicate ex parte with any of the corporation's present employees. This leaves open the question of former employees, a question which has been addressed by various states, including California. In *Mills Land & Water Co. v. Golden West Refining Co.,*[3] the court ruled that an attorney could not interview a former employee who was still a corporate director. The former employee, as a member of the corporation's control group, was potentially privy to privileged information, thus the court ruled that an ex parte communication with the former employee was inappropriate and prejudicial to the action at hand.

Ex parte communications, or private interviews, with former employees of a corporate client can be a powerful discovery tool. Case law in California has held that a party can communicate ex parte with former employees of a corporate client, whether or not they were managerial employees or members of the corporate control group if the inquiry is made about relevant facts but not about privileged communications concerning those facts. A corporate client can seek a protective order regarding any former employees who the client knows or suspects may be privy to privileged information if they can demonstrate a real danger that the information might be disclosed if the employee is interviewed ex parte. If the former employee worked on a confidential project, and if all communications surrounding that project

---

[2] *Id.*

[3] 186 Cal. 3d 116, 230 Cal. Rptr. 461 (1986).

were protected by privilege, the privilege remains even after the employment terminates. Many corporations require their employees to sign confidentiality agreements when they begin employment in anticipation of this type of problem.

Upjohn v. United States[4] extended the corporate client-attorney privilege to former as well as current employees on the theory that either may possess or have access to confidential information. A party seeking the testimony of a former employee has the option of noticing the deposition of that person. Objections regarding questions concerning privileged matters may then be raised at the deposition in the normal course and scope of the testimony. Distinctions must be made carefully in questions about the subject matter and relevant facts of a transaction or contract dispute to avoid objections.

§ 2.20   Limits of Corporate Confidentiality

Corporations frequently have in their possession "dangerous, hot copy" that lasts forever and they face increasingly acute pressure to make at least partial disclosures of the results of internal investigations, risk analysis, and so forth. Astute corporate counsel take great care to plan and conduct corporate internal investigations protecting the hot copy, the attorney-client privilege, and work product doctrines. For example, in a voluntary disclosure program, the Department of Defense has promised to consider a voluntary disclosure in determining whether to suspend or prosecute a contractor. For a government contractor, suspension may mean going out of business. Participation in the voluntary disclosure program is then clearly advisable. The SEC offers lenient treatment under its own voluntary disclosure program. Partly as a result of these governmental entities participating in voluntary disclosure programs, it has become common practice for attorneys representing a corporate client to offer to disclose at least portions of a client's internal investigation in settlement attempts.

Auditors for a corporation involved in litigation will ask to be apprised of the status and merits of a case in order to protect the integrity of financial statements. Corporate insurers may request information developed during an internal investigation. Underwriters of securities offerings may also seek disclosure. Intense pressure to publicly disclose the result of an internal investigation arises also when a client's business conduct and integrity has been publicly questioned through media exposure.

The purpose of the attorney-client privilege is to foster candor within the attorney-client relationship by shielding confidential communications occurring at any time between an attorney and client. Disclosures to third parties are inconsistent with that confidentiality and can result in a waiver of the privilege. The work product doctrine, however, is not limited to confidential communications. It also covers any material obtained or prepared by counsel; however, this must be done in anticipation of litigation.

Some courts have carved out a special exception to waiver rules concerning work product and have adopted a limited waiver theory which allows selected disclosures

---

[4] 449 U.S. 383 (1981).

of internal investigation to selected third parties. An example is when a confidentiality agreement exists between the disclosing party and the selected third party. Courts have suggested in recent decisions that an express, agreed upon confidentiality agreement may prevent the waiver. Paralegals need to be aware of basic drafting techniques for corporate confidentiality agreements.

The scope of a waiver is uncertain and depends on case law as well as individual case facts which further complicates the question of whether to disclose portions of internal investigations. As a general rule, disclosure of a communication waives the attorney-client privilege not only regarding the communication actually disclosed, but also regarding other related communications. Because the issue has been determined by the courts fundamentally "as one of fairness", the courts have exercised considerable discretion regarding full subject matter waivers, and have often declined to impose them when the third-party disclosures are not inconsistent with the purposes of the privilege asserted. This prevents legal prejudice to the party and a distortion of the fact finding process through selected disclosure of otherwise protected information. Selected disclosures taken out of context are often misleading and may be used as favorable inferences of fact by your opponent.

The leading cases addressing the issues of selective disclosure and the limits of confidentiality agreements are *In Re Sealed Case*[5] and *United States v. Nobles*.[6] *United States v. Nobles* is a classic example of selected disclosure concerning an investigator who was called upon to testify about certain witness statements he had taken.

Limits of corporate confidentiality continue to be tested at the federal and state level. Waiver claims and limits of scope of waiver are issues that must be determined by a court given the facts of each individual case. Confidentiality agreements are becoming the norm rather than the exception, as corporations seek ways to prevent waiver of the all important attorney/client and work product privileges, particularly in the area of internal investigations.

§ 2.21   Work Product Privilege

Attorney-client communications and attorneys', law clerks', and legal assistants' work products are all closely-related privileges and overlap in particular documents. The work product privilege is specifically set forth in Federal Rule of Evidence 501. Case law in various states extends and further clarifies the work product privilege by applying it to that material prepared in anticipation of litigation and all material prepared during litigation by attorneys, law clerks, investigators, and legal assistants. This material can consist of legal research, factual research, case status memo, medical record review, business record review, narratives, and memos to the file.

In business litigation, work product may also include memoranda or reports received from corporate officers. A corporate client functions differently than an individual client, and this fact effects communications, memoranda, and confidentiality. In a corporation, there may be many individuals with relevant information

---

[5] 676 F.2d 793, 801–09 (D.C. Cir. 1982).

[6] 422 U.S. 325 (1975).

about the case involving both business and legal concerns. Many of these individuals will be corporate officers and agents as well as employees. Communications with them, both written and oral, and memoranda or status reports received from them prepared at the direction of the attorney, or in anticipation of litigation, qualify as work product. Examples of these privileged documents include preliminary claims investigation and risk analysis reports prepared by corporate officers, or agents, at the direction of their superiors in anticipation of litigation. As litigation commences and through the pendency of the case, corporate officers may be asked to provide critical information regarding their area of specialization. This consultant type of information may be presented in the form of a written or oral report. All of these communications are protected by both the attorney-client and the work product privileges. Legal assistant communications with employees of the corporate client are similarly protected.

§ 2.22   Absolute and Conditional Work Product

The attorney work product doctrine is designed to protect attorney-prepared trial materials from discovery. The work product doctrine was first articulated clearly by the Supreme Court in *Hickman v. Taylor*,[7] which was incorporated in Rule 26(b)(3) of the Federal Rules of Civil Procedure and defined work product as "documents and tangible things prepared in anticipation of litigation, or for trial or for another party, or by or for another party's representative." Absolute work product differs from qualified work product in that absolute work product refers to opinion work product defined at Federal Rule of Civil Procedure 26(b)(c) as "the mental impressions, conclusions, opinions, or legal theories of an attorney or their representative or the representative of a party concerning the litigation." The more a document reflects opinion, conclusion, and analysis rather than a mere recitation of facts, the more likely it is to qualify for absolute work product protection.

The majority of discovery disputes involving work product privilege are concerned with those materials which are considered qualified work product. Qualified, or ordinary, work product refers to all material prepared in anticipation of litigation "which does not reflect an attorney's opinions or mental impressions." Examples are those factual materials, even if compiled by an attorney, which do not contain the attorney's impressions, opinions, or conclusions including witness statements, site inspections, photographs, and so on. Case law is inconsistent as to a precise definition of what is, and what is not, qualified, or conditional, work product. The facts and issues of each case will most often be the determining factor as to whether the privilege is applicable. Federal and state cases are not always in agreement. Materials which may be protected as qualified work product on the federal level may be discoverable if the action was pending in state court. Materials which may qualify for protection pursuant to case law in state court may be discoverable in federal court.

Materials for which qualified work product privilege is claimed on the basis that they were prepared in anticipation of litigation cause the greatest number of discovery disputes. Federal Rule of Civil Procedure 26(b)(3) considers "anticipation of

---

[7] 329 U.S. 495 (1947).

litigation" to be something greater than the mere "possibility of litigation." It is not necessary for an action to have been filed; however, specific claims or parties should be identifiable at the time the materials were prepared. For example, in the case of an investigation of a wiring failure which results in an accidental fire and injury on a construction site, an in-house risk manager for the construction company will most likely order an investigative report in anticipation of litigation. An employee's investigation and accident report made at the request of his employer is considered privileged. Generally speaking, any employee's statement which is required in the ordinary course and scope of business becomes the statement of that business or corporation and is considered confidential and privileged.

A practical means of securing qualified work product protection for materials prepared in anticipation of litigation is to stamp them or label them "Attorney Work Product Prepared for Litigation." Such labeling or stamping at the time that the document is created conveys the intent that the document is confidential. This procedure facilitates the protection of documents and saves both the client and the attorney the hassle and expense of protracted discovery disputes.

§ 2.23   Legal Assistant Work Product

Legal assistant work done at an attorney's direction or under an attorney's supervision qualifies for conditional work product privilege protection. Whenever a legal assistant is acting in the course and scope of their agency relationship with the attorney, or working on behalf of the client, trial preparation materials, notes, memoranda, diagrams, charts, graphs, other demonstrative evidence, and factual analysis or documentation are all considered work product. As a safeguard, it is a good practice to stamp sensitive memos "Prepared at the Direction of [name], Attorney." Work product protection is not waived by the transmittal of a legal assistant product to the client (such as, deposition summaries, site inspection reports, minutes, notes taken at key meetings, and so forth). These work product documents are given to a client with the expectation that they will remain in confidence and be circulated only to the client or those members of the corporate control group on a need-to-know basis. Discretion in copying and distributing these materials is absolutely necessary to protect the intent of confidentiality. The work product doctrine assumes that the legal assistant, or any agent of the attorney, needs to communicate with the client in the normal course and scope of the professional relationship existing between the client and attorney in preparation for litigation, corporate business transactions, or any other professional or personal matter for which a client hires an attorney.

The federal court first addressed the issue of whether the work product of non-lawyers was protected under the work product doctrine in *United States v. Nobles.*[8] In that case, it was the work product of an investigator employed by an attorney in preparation for the defense that was at issue. In writing the majority opinion, Justice Louis F. Powell, Jr. stated:

---

[8] 422 U.S. 325 (1975).

. . . the work product doctrine is an intensely practical one, grounded in the realities of litigation in our adversary system. One of those realities is that attorneys often must rely on the assistance of investigators and other agents in the compilation of materials in preparation for trial. It is, therefore, necessary that the doctrine protect materials prepared by agents for the attorney as well as those prepared by the attorney himself.[9]

Extending the work product privilege directly to legal assistants has become necessary as attorneys and the courts have increased their awareness of the benefits to be achieved through the use of paralegals. The work of a paralegal, normally performed under the supervision of an attorney, is now entitled to the same protections as the broad spectrum of agents who have been previously covered by the protective umbrella of the work product doctrine. Public policy considerations clearly dictate that a paralegal's work product should be protected from discovery just as an attorney's work product is protected. The frightening complexity and sheer volume of documents involved in business litigation mandates the use of legal assistants as a cost-efficient method of providing legal services to the public. Federal cases extending the work product privilege specifically to legal assistants include *Dabney v. Investment Corp. of America*[10] and *United States v. Cabra.*[11]

Common sense, public policy, and case law all dictate the necessity that legal assistant work product be protected from discovery; however, specific examples of paralegal work product include:

Interoffice memoranda

Memoranda of telephone conversations and/or interviews with client

Notes from meetings with clients in preparation of discovery responses such as interrogatories, responses to documents production, and so forth

Memoranda of document screening or site inspections

Informal investigation memoranda

Document production notes

Factual or legal research memoranda

Opening case memos

§ 2.24   Protected Matter Examples

The work product protection is usually decided on a case-by-case basis depending upon the facts, both evidentiary and procedural. Federal Rule of Civil Procedure Rule 26(b) sets forth basic criteria for establishing the work product privilege and protecting documents; however, the language of the statute leaves a lot of room for interpretation by the courts. State statutes define work product privilege with the same degree of latitude, leaving room for interpretation of the privilege on a case-by-case basis. Occasionally there will be inconsistency between federal and state

---

[9] *Id.*

[10] 82 F.R.D. 464 (E.D. Pa. 1979).

[11] 622 F.2d 182 (5th Cir. 1980).

statutes and case law. This inconsistency can work to your advantage in attempting either to protect or to discover documents. If your case is within federal jurisdiction, federal statutes and cases may govern work product privilege decisions. (see § 2.15.) If your case has been filed in state court, use state statutes and case law, but you may reference federal statutes and case law in legal arguments made to protect documents or obtain privileged information. Work product protection generally applies in the following contexts:

Consultant.   The identity of an expert consulted, retained, or specifically employed by an attorney, or by the client at the direction of an attorney, is not discoverable until or unless it is reasonably certain that the expert will testify at the time of trial. The reports, opinions, and knowledge of a consultant are not discoverable unless the consultant is named as an expert and designated to testify. The identity of an expert may be learned during discovery (interrogatory or document request), or at the time of a mutual exchange of expert disclosures. Written reports, opinions, and test results create work product problems. If such reports exist, authored by a consultant who, for one reason or another, was not designated as an expert witness, a qualified work product privilege attaches to these documents and they are usually protected from disclosure. In a situation where a consultant has conducted tests, taken air samples, soil samples, or performed product testing which cannot be duplicated, a good argument may be advanced for obtaining this privileged information.

Nonexpert witnesses.   These are lay witnesses who may be called at trial. Although the identity of all persons with knowledge of relevant facts is discoverable, the identity of nonexpert witnesses intended to be called as trial witnesses is protected by a qualified work product privilege. The identity of persons with knowledge of relevant facts is a topic almost always addressed in early interrogatories. However, a decision as to whether all persons with relevant information will be called as witnesses at time of trial is rarely made until late in discovery close to the time of trial. It is a strategic decision made by the attorney who will try the case. Interrogatories seeking to discover the nature and extent of anticipated testimony by nonexpert witnesses are improper. The information sought is absolutely protected by the work product rule. There are other means for discovering the anticipated testimony of persons with knowledge of relevant facts. The most obvious and direct method is through depositions.

Law firm interoffice memos.   Interoffice memos almost always contain the thought process of an attorney, investigator, or legal assistant and as such qualify for protection under the work product privilege. Even mundane interoffice memos consisting of assignments or things to do qualify for protection as they relate to trial preparation and could reveal legal strategies or theories.

Attorney writings.   Writings reflecting thought processes of an attorney acting in a nonlitigation legal capacity as a business negotiator for a client are also protected. Frequently an attorney will act as a business negotiator in contracts, leases, mergers, and acquisitions in the course of the attorney's relationship with a client. It has been consistently held by state courts in California, and many other states, that an attorney in a nonlitigating capacity, is working within the scope of the professional relationship with a business client, and as such the work product is protected from disclosure. For example, California Code of Civil Procedure 2016(b) does not limit the work product privilege to litigation. Leading cases have interpreted the rationale of the work product privilege as a means of providing an incentive for an attorney to maintain the highest professional competence. Courts have held that protecting attorney's work product when they act in a nonlitigation legal capacity furthers the important goal of reducing the likelihood of litigation.

Investigator's notes.   Notes of an investigator containing comments on witness statements is protected. The problematic area of witness statements is unresolved and case law decisions are often inconsistent. There are situations when witness statements may be protected, and there are situations when they must be produced. There is, however, precedent for protecting the notes of an investigator. Problems arise when the investigator incorporates their notes into a witness statement, opening the door for a request for production of a redacted document. Notes of an investigator, prepared at the direction of an attorney in anticipation of litigation are protected pursuant to the work product privilege. Professional investigators should never intertwine their editorial comments with a witness statement. The preferred method is discussed at § 2.41. A professional investigator should provide you with a separate witness statement and a separate report. If that method is used, there is no question as to which is the protected document. The investigator's report will automatically qualify for work product privilege, whereas the statement may or may not qualify for protection depending upon the facts and circumstances of the particular case.

§ 2.25   Unprotected Matter Examples

Conservatively speaking, battles over whether information is protected by the work product privilege account for approximately 80 percent of all discovery disputes. Case law decisions should be carefully monitored and shepardized, especially on the state level, for changes, exceptions, examples of waiver of privilege, and so on. The basic argument which must be advanced by a party wishing to show that certain information does not qualify for the work product privilege must demonstrate the following:

1.   The requested information was not meant to be confidential (no confidential intent at the time the document was originated);
2.   The requested documents were not prepared in anticipation of litigation or as part of trial preparation;
3.   The information sought is directly relevant to the issues of the action, or calculated to lead to the discovery of information which is directly relevant to the issues;
4.   There is no other means by which this information may be discovered; or
5.   The probative value of the information sought is greater than the potential harm that may result from the release of confidential information.

All of this criteria must be set forth in the points and authorities accompanying a motion to compel production of documents withheld pursuant to privilege. Procedural facts and case history should be addressed in the attorney declaration accompanying the memorandum. A good cause showing, or a demonstration of waiver of privilege, must be set forth before the court will overrule a work product privilege claim.

Examples of situations in which courts have found the work product rule inapplicable include the following:

1. Attorney notes made during contract negotiations when the attorney is performing no legal work but is acting merely as a business agent or interested party (that is, member of board of directors) for a client. The difference in this situation is that the attorney is not acting in a negotiating capacity, but is acting only as a business agent for the client. Problems could arise when contract negotiations fall through and litigation becomes imminent. In order to have work product privilege revert back to notes made at a business meeting, contract negotiations, or board of directors meeting, it would be necessary to prove that the notes were of a confidential nature and reflected that attorney's thought processes in connection with the deal even though the attorney's presence at the meeting was not necessary to the negotiations.

2. Information gathered by an investigator or insurance adjuster before an attorney has been retained may not qualify for work product protection. The test of the privilege in this situation is the likelihood of, or anticipation of, litigation as well as the identity of the person who hired the investigator or insurance adjuster, and the instructions given to the investigator or adjuster.

3. Generally speaking, reports of accounting firms, appraisals and audit reports may be discoverable.

4. Information and opinions of an expert contained in a written report that was prepared for earlier litigation relating to a subject matter about which the expert had been designated to testify at trial may be discoverable. This situation usually arises when an expert's name is set forth in an interrogatory response in related litigation involving the same subject matter. The fact that the expert may not yet have been officially disclosed in the pending litigation does not preclude a party from gathering the information contained in reports prepared for earlier litigation. The test of relevancy is satisfied by the fact that the subject matter of the earlier report is identical, or similar, to the subject matter of the present litigation.

5. In a malpractice action, the attorney's work product must be provided upon request to the former client who has now become a plaintiff in an action against the former attorney. To deny access to attorney work papers prepared during the course of the litigation which has become the very subject of the malpractice action would be unjust and deny a malpractice plaintiff the very proof needed to support the plaintiff's allegations. Documents which reflect an attorney's impressions or conclusions remain protected even though the attorney's work files must be turned over upon request by the former client. In malpractice actions, the client puts the actions of the former attorney at issue and in doing so waives the privilege. The work product privilege is held by both the attorney and the client and can be waived by either. It is obviously in the best interests of the client to waive the privilege in this instance.

6. In criminal, fraud, or attorney disciplinary proceedings, the work product privilege does not protect work files of an attorney.

Examples of situations when courts have found the work product inapplicable are numerous and not always consistent. It cannot be stressed enough that the facts, circumstances, evidentiary issues, and procedural history of each case governs the applicability of the privilege. To uphold a claim for work product privilege or to order disclosure of the requested information or documents is completely within the discretion of the courts. All claims of privilege, including work product, are carefully scrutinized and balanced against the need for discovery versus the need to protect the best interests of the client.

§ 2.26 Are Witness Statements Protected?

Witness statements are perhaps the most sought after documents in litigation because they generally provide firsthand knowledge about the facts of a given situation. Witness statements have been generally protected by both the attorney-client privilege and work product protection. Work product in and of itself is not a privilege, but rather it is a protection which goes hand in hand with the attorney-client privilege. Sections **2.24** and **2.25** offer many examples of protected and unprotected matters.

Some courts have found that witness statements are only evidentiary in nature. Thus they are not considered "derivative or interpretative materials created by the attorney," and, therefore, do not qualify for work product protection.

Even though some cases hold that witness statements do not qualify for work product protection, they are still difficult to obtain from opposing counsel unless the requesting party is able to meet the burden of proof required for a good cause showing. Good cause requirements are often articulated in state statutes. For example, California Code of Civil Procedure § 2031(1) states that good cause is found "when the party seeking discovery is able to show a special need for the discovery, such as to refresh the witnesses memory, or the inability to obtain a similar statement or deposition testimony because the witness cannot be located". In order to support the theory that a witness cannot be located, an attorney declaration is necessary listing each and every diligent attempt made to locate the person. The court in most cases will not reward a lazy attorney with the fruits of another attorney's resourcefulness by giving them access to a witness statement. If the witness can be located and a statement can be obtained by opposing counsel, the court in its discretion uses a balancing test and protects the earlier statement from disclosure.

§ 2.27 Electronic Work Product Problems

Today's electronic age presents new challenges for safeguarding work product materials. Overuse of fax machines, hard disks, floppy disks, word processing files, and computer systems present a gold mine of information simply waiting to be discovered by a clever opponent. Presently there are no statutes or case law clearly setting forth examples of protected and unprotected electronic work product. Electronic work product is frequently case development work and contains early investigative material. Discovering these materials can frequently prove that a corporation or business entity had prior notice of a defect or problem in sufficient time to correct the deficiency.

Legal departments and law offices in general have become increasingly dependent on computers for everything from word processing to litigation budgets. Work product protection is no longer just a matter of stamping appropriate paper, correspondence, and memos. Data files stored in computer systems must also be labeled for protection.

The following checklist suggests ways in which you can prevent your opponent from gaining access to electronic work product.

_____ Include in all documents, including electronic documents and data base printouts, the statement, "Attorney Work Product, Prepared at the Direction of Attorney [name] in Anticipation of Litigation."

_____ Be certain that your attorney, or in-house legal counsel, communicates the facts and issues analysis and discovery plan only to members of the litigation support staff, and gives them input on the computerized document management system. This protects the litigation support data base from discovery giving it the status of attorney work product.

_____ Be sure that all members of the litigation support team sign confidentiality agreements. Include all members of the litigation support team, including temporary staff who may be hired to key in documents.

_____ Have the maintenance personnel sign confidentiality agreements to protect the contents of hard disk data in the machine if your computer must be sent out for repair.

_____ Include, in the event of a settlement of the litigation, a promise by your opponent to destroy the litigation support data base material as a means of protection for your client.

_____ Do not show the witnesses the data base reports when preparing them for depositions or trial testimony. Although the list of documents may be an aid to their memory, the witness could then be questioned regarding the contents of all documents reviewed. Depending on the questions and responses, the result could be a waiver of privilege for the entire litigation support data base.

§ 2.28   Preserving the Confidentiality of Fax Communication

It frequently becomes necessary to send confidential information via fax transmittal from an attorney to a business client and vice versa. Fax terminals are located throughout offices and faxes are retrieved by many individuals. In a business environment, an individual retrieving a fax transmittal could easily be a third-person, nonmember of the corporate control group. A practice pointer to attempt to preserve the confidentiality of fax transmittals is to include on the cover page the following caveat:

CONFIDENTIAL—ATTORNEY-CLIENT PRIVILEGE

THIS FAX COMMUNICATION IS INTENDED ONLY FOR THE INDIVIDUAL OR ENTITY TO WHOM IT IS ADDRESSED. IT MAY CONTAIN INFORMATION THAT IS PRIVILEGED, CONFIDENTIAL AND/OR PROTECTED FROM DISCLOSURE BY STATUTE AND/OR CASE LAW. IF YOU ARE NOT THE RECIPIENT TO WHOM THIS COMMUNICATION IS DIRECTED, YOU ARE HEREBY NOTIFIED THAT ANY DISSEMINATION, DISTRIBUTION, OR COPYING OF THIS COMMUNICATION IS STRICTLY PROHIBITED. IF YOU RECEIVE THIS COMMUNICATION IN ERROR, PLEASE NOTIFY US IMMEDIATELY BY TELEPHONE AND RETURN THE ORIGINAL FAX COMMUNICATION TO US AT THE ABOVE ADDRESS BY CERTIFIED U.S. MAIL.

Placing this caveat on your fax transmittal establishes the *intent of confidentiality* even though it may not totally protect the document from being retrieved or read by a person who is not in the privileged group. Whenever possible, it is preferable to send documents by Federal Express or messenger to avoid the problem of inadvertent disclosure of privileged information through fax transmittals. If your only option is to fax sensitive material to your client, the best procedure is to notify them in advance by contacting an administrative assistant or other member of the corporate control group. That individual should then proceed immediately to the fax machine and await the transmittal.

§ 2.29 Medical and Psychological Information Privilege

A general physician-patient privilege has been created by statute as well as by case law both on the federal level and on most individual state levels. It is presumed that those communications between a patient and any health care provider are meant to be confidential. The definition of *health care provider* extends to those persons from whom a patient may seek counseling, guidance, or medical attention. This broad-based definition includes lay counselors, social workers, marital counselors, school psychologists, licensed and unlicensed therapists, and case workers, as well as acupuncturists, biofeedback therapists, and all other practitioners of the healing arts. The presumption is that the patient, in expressing the need for treatment, reveals confidential information necessary for successful treatment to that person whom the patient perceives to be a health care professional. The test for the privilege here is the intent of the patient. If the patient intends that information to be confidential, a privilege exists. The intent of the patient, who is the holder of this privilege, operates as a safeguard against the disclosure of medical information except on a need-to-know basis such as consulting physicians.

§ 2.30 Physician-Patient Privilege Exceptions

There are exceptions to the physician-patient privilege per statute and case law. For example, in some states a patient litigant exception exists when a patient tenders their physical condition as the basis for a claim against the defendant. Limited disclosure of medical information is permitted, in, for example, personal injury, medical malpractice, and product liability damage claims, when the physical injury received by the plaintiff is alleged to have been caused by the actions of the defendant. Medical and psychological treatment which may have been received by the plaintiff for the injuries which are a part of the damage claim become discoverable records. On the other hand, by seeking recovery for a particular injury, the plaintiff does not open the plaintiff's lifetime medical history, and continues to be entitled to retain the confidentiality of all unrelated medical or psychotherapeutic or psychological treatment that the plaintiff may have undergone in the past. This is a very important distinction which is part of case law in many states, including California, as a safeguard for plaintiffs. Plaintiffs would be deterred from ever filing a lawsuit if they felt that they would have to open up their entire lifetime medical background. This loss of confidentiality for medical, psychotherapeutic, or psychological records would constitute an intrusion into their privacy completely out of proportion to the damage claim in any lawsuit.

§ 2.31   Psychotherapist-Patient Privilege Exceptions

The privilege laws against revealing psychotherapist and psychological records are construed very strictly. A personal injury, medical malpractice, or product liability action which simply claims emotional distress, humiliation, embarrassment, and nervousness does not usually qualify for the patient litigant exception. If a plaintiff claims extended mental distress interfering with their recovery from physical injuries and requiring further or extended treatment, or permanent limitations in their mental abilities, then the patient litigant exception will apply and psychological and psychotherapist records must be disclosed.

In actions when a client has suffered sexual harassment, assault, or rape, the physical injuries might be limited and resolved more quickly than the emotional traumas. In these cases, the bulk of the treatment might be with rape counselors, guidance counselors, and psychotherapists, and these records would be pertinent to the claim of severe emotional trauma. The privilege then would be considered waived falling under the patient litigant exception. Physician-patient and psychotherapist-patient privileges may be asserted by the patient, a guardian or conservator of the patient, or the personal representative of the patient if the patient is deceased. Privilege may also be asserted by a person who is authorized to claim the privilege by the holder, or by any person who is the physician or psychotherapist at the time of the confidential communication.

The patient litigant exception as discussed in relation to physician-patient records also applies to psychotherapist-patient records when a litigant has placed his mental state at issue. An exception to the psychotherapist-patient privilege is when the psychotherapist believes the patient is dangerous. This places the decision of whether to disclose confidential information on the health care provider as holder of the privilege. Federal statutes and many state statutes, as well as case law, have established a duty to warn holding that a psychotherapist may be found negligent for failure to disclose information regarding a dangerous patient. Several criteria have been established in duty to warn cases, especially in California. A psychotherapist must be convinced that the patient is dangerous and has a specific intent to do harm to a specific person. Failure to disclose this information can be found to be negligent and is considered malpractice on the part of the psychotherapist. The duty to warn has created an affirmative duty for persons employed in the mental health field, including psychologists, psychotherapists, licensed clinical social workers, school psychologists, and licensed marriage, family, and child counselors, to communicate threats made by a patient in order to prevent a potential danger.

§ 2.32   Official Record Privilege

Official information is information acquired in confidence by a public employee in the course and scope of their duties and not open, or officially exposed, to the public prior to the time of the communication. Public entities such as governmental entities may exercise a privilege not to disclose official information and to prevent another from disclosing such information. This privilege is a conditional one requiring a balancing process. The determining factor is whether the necessity for preserving the confidentiality of the information outweighs the necessity for disclosure in the interests of justice. This privilege operates in the discovery process to protect governmental entities from the disclosure of materials contained in their official records. For example, an official records privilege can be claimed by a city to protect their employees in negligence actions. The burden of proof in overcoming this privilege is that the public interest will be served best by making the record available for inspection. Litigation involving claims against governmental entities on the local or federal level almost always involves records that fall under the official records privilege. In many cases the court will order an *in camera* inspection permitting partial disclosure of those portions of the records necessary to further the interests of justice in that particular litigation.

§ 2.33   Confidential Records

Many records are classified as confidential such as tax returns, election results, property owners' statements to tax assessors, unemployment insurance returns, bank records, and so forth. It is considered an invasion of privacy to require the production of any of these records unless they are directly relevant to the instant litigation.

Even highly relevant, nonprivileged information may be shielded from discovery if its disclosure would impair a person's inalienable right of privacy. This protection is qualified, not absolute, and in each case the court must carefully balance the right of privacy against the need for discovery. The privacy protected may be either that of one of the parties to the action or of some third person (nonparty). An example of protection of a third party occurs when bank records and deposit information pertaining to other parties having accounts at the same bank as a plaintiff or defendant are privileged from discovery. It is the obligation of the bank or financial institution to remove all identification of third party accounts and materials related to other bank customers before allowing documents to be released. On the other hand, the bank is obligated to produce requested records concerning plaintiff's or defendant's accounts both personal and commercial.

The right of privacy may also limit the scope of discovery on matters directly relevant to the lawsuit. This occurs most often in combination with other privileged information such as medical, psychiatric, or financial information. Disclosure of a defendant's total net worth is usually considered confidential information and is usually limited to actions where punitive damages are sought and a prima facie case can be submitted to the court to prove that the prevailing party will succeed in proving malicious intent, thus obtaining punitive damages. Disclosure of a plaintiff's net worth is usually considered confidential financial information and is also protected from disclosure. The plaintiff in an action in which wage loss is claimed as part of damages does *not* tender the issue of the plaintiff's net worth.

§ 2.34 Confidential Personnel Files

Confidential personnel files maintained at a person's place of employment are usually considered to be within a zone of privacy and are protected from discovery. Personnel files present unique problems in that they may contain information regarding third persons who are not parties to a lawsuit. For example, a personnel file may contain confidential letters regarding the employee written by outsiders. Disclosure would violate the confidentiality those writers expected would be accorded to their communications at the time they were written. Personnel files may also include performance evaluations or in-house memoranda regarding specific projects that the employee has successfully completed or failed to complete. The in-house memoranda may discuss other employees who worked on the same project and comment on their job performance.

When personnel files are requested as they relate to a wage claim, the only information that should be released is the name of the employee, the date their employment began, the rate of pay, the fringe benefit compensation package, the job title, and the responsibilities. Any information in a personnel file that goes beyond the scope of this basic information should be considered privileged and should not be produced. There are exceptions to the right of privacy for an employee's personnel file similar to those for a patient litigant in regard to medical and psychiatric records. In cases of sexual harassment, wrongful termination, or any liability claim against an employer, the entire personnel file becomes relevant and must be produced.

Specific procedures for raising the right of privacy for a confidential record objection are similar to the procedures for raising other privilege objections. The claim of privilege must be asserted promptly either by an objection and refusal to answer a specific interrogatory, deposition question, or request for document, or, if there is time, by obtaining a protective order excusing the duty to answer. The most practical approach is simply to object and refuse to provide the information. This shifts the burden of proof to the party seeking discovery, and they must file a motion to compel answers to deposition questions, interrogatory answers, or requested documents. Responsive papers would then include opposition to the motion to compel and a motion for a protective order.

§ 2.35   Burden of Proof

The burden of proof in privilege claims rests upon the party seeking discovery. That party must show a particularized need to obtain the confidential information which is being sought. The fact that it may be relevant to the subject matter at hand is not enough proof to overcome a privilege claim. Good cause must be demonstrated to the court that the information is directly relevant and essential to determining the truth of a particular cause of action or defense. Additionally, it must be affirmatively demonstrated that there is no alternative means of obtaining this information. If it can be demonstrated that the information sought is available from other sources or less intrusive means, the court is likely to uphold the privilege. The court always carefully balances the right of privacy versus the public interest. If competing interests can be accommodated by allowing partial disclosure of the privileged information, the court will be inclined to limit its order accordingly. In the case of protecting the rights of third persons, the court may order their names deleted from documents disclosed, as in the case of bank records. *In camera* inspections and protective orders are frequently used by the court when performing this delicate balancing act.

§ 2.36   Screening Documents

As a legal assistant, you will be handling a great deal of privileged information as you work with a client. Care must be taken from the onset of the case to protect the confidential nature of records and guard against a waiver of privileges. Particular care should be paid to any handwritten memos, letters, or private journals. If there is any doubt as to the author of a particular document, that document should be segregated immediately from your working file and held for further review. Once privileged documents have been inadvertently produced in the discovery process, it is extremely difficult and frequently impossible to reclaim a privilege. As a rule of thumb, it is better to withhold any documents that could possibly be considered confidential. Discovery responses can be supplemented and those documents withheld at an early stage can always be produced later.

When representing a client involved in a personal injury, medical malpractice, or product liability action, you will be reviewing medical records in preparation for damage calculations. When providing copies of these medical records either to defense counsel or for a demand letter to an insurance adjustor, carefully screen them for treatment directly related to the accident. A common mistake in releasing medical records for an injured plaintiff is to release their lifetime of medical history simply because that is what you received from a family physician or treating hospital. These records may include 10 or 15 years of treatment. Records of this nature should be carefully reviewed and screened before they are copied for document production. For example, a family physician treating a female patient for a broken ankle, which may be the subject of this particular lawsuit, may have also acted as her gynecologist and provided treatment of a sensitive nature which should not be disclosed in a simple personal injury accident when the damage claim is limited to a broken ankle.

§ 2.37   Computer Screening of Documents

Privileged documents can sometimes be thought of as loose cannons. If they are inadvertently disclosed, the privilege is almost certainly waived. Courts have the power of discretion to find the privilege either waived or not. A showing of reasonable precaution taken during document screening is a prerequisite for the suppression of inadvertently produced documents. Today's technology not only provides a computerized means of protecting privileged documents against inadvertent disclosure but also meeting the reasonable precaution test for those that do slip through. Most client documents are produced and stored in a word processing system. Litigation data bases are also set up. Corporate documents can immediately be transferred to litigation data bases. Those documents that are only available on hard copy can be converted readily by using an optical scanning system.

§ 2.38   Checklist for Computerized Screening

When setting up a computerized screening system, the following checklist may help establish important criteria:

_____   An attorney or senior paralegal should write screening instructions.

_____   Establish a labeling system such as PRIVILEGED AND CONFIDENTIAL FOR ATTORNEY-CLIENT COMMUNICATIONS.

_____   Prepare an all encompassing list of all in-house and external counsel's names, administrative assistants, legal assistants, and investigators.

_____   Prepare a list of all crucial dates of meetings, contracts, interviews, and so forth.

_____   Initiate a quality control system of checklists on the screening process, including a means of document numbering.

_____   Review each document to be produced, selecting for further review by an attorney or senior paralegal every document that meets the following criteria:

(a) Contains PRIVILEGED label.

(b) Authored by, sent to, or copied to an attorney or member of corporate control group (refer to attached list of names).

(c) Contains the word legal followed by the word counsel or advice.

(d) Contains descriptions of certain meetings or actions known to be work product related based on date or subject matter discussed.

Second level screening can be done on the computer. For example, consider that all of the documents have now been screened for privilege, and those which have been preliminarily selected for withholding have been identified. Now you can go back through all of the documents to see whether other documents pertaining to a subject matter discussed in the documents designated privileged might have been prepared on or about the same date by nonlawyers. You can reexamine the document data base for documents meeting the second level criteria in a relatively straight forward manner using selected terms and key words. Not all of the documents located in this second level search may ultimately be designated privileged; however, locating them and withholding them for attorney review is most valuable and could save many hot documents from slipping through the cracks.

§ 2.39   Identification of Privileged Documents

Many times a request for production of documents will seek documents that, for various reasons, should be protected from the possibility of general distribution. For example, documents that contain trade secrets of a client, confidential business information, or confidential research should be protected through a protective order. Without a protective order, the opposing counsel and his client could disseminate the information to anyone, which could be harmful to your client if your client and the opposing party are competitors.

Upon review of a request for production, a determination should be made as to which of the documents requested are confidential. A protective order should be prepared, or at least considered. Alternatively, appropriate objections could be made to those requests seeking the confidential information on the grounds the documents are protected from disclosure because they are trade secrets or other confidential research, development, or commercial information. Language in the statute states "a protective order may require that a trade secret or other confidential research, development, or commercial information need not be disclosed or be disclosed only to specified persons or in a specified way." California Code of Civil Procedure § 2031(e)(5).

There are at least two levels of confidentiality available. The first is "Confidential"—the information is available only to counsel, their staff, and the parties, and cannot be used for any purpose other than the instant litigation. A second level of confidentiality is "Confidential-Attorneys Only"—only counsel and their staff may have access to the information, not the parties themselves. This type of designation is used in a situation where the parties are competitors and an adversary would benefit from the information.

The best way to keep track of documents which have been designated confidential or confidential—attorney only is to stamp each page of the document with that designation. This will eliminate any confusion over which documents are to be produced and to whom. Documents that have been withheld from discovery and for which privilege has been claimed must be identified in a privileged list. You should prepare two versions of a privileged document list. The first version will be the list that will accompany your discovery responses. This list (see **Form 2–2**) will contain the bare bones information required by statute.

FORM 2–2
SAMPLE PRIVILEGED DOCUMENT LIST
(DISCOVERY RESPONSE)

Name of document	Letter, memo, invoice, bill of lading, receipt
Date of document	The exact date that appears on the document. If there is no date, simply put "undated."
Length of document	2 pages, 3 pages, and so forth, 2 page letter, with 3 page enclosure.

Author of document   Signature that appears at the bottom of the letter, invoice, receipt, and so forth, along with any identifying information such as a title, vice president of marketing, secretary, bookkeeper, and so forth.

This identification is necessary for each document which, although it is responsive to a discovery request, will be withheld from discovery based on a privilege claim. A response to an interrogatory or document request would state:

> Plaintiff objects to the production of those documents requested in this interrogatory on the grounds that it is violative of the attorney-client and attorney work product privilege to require production. Those documents being withheld are:
>
> 1. Letter, 3 pages, dated [date], signed by [name], Chief Financial Officer, ABC Corporation.

The privileged list for your file (**Form 2–3**) will contain all of the basic information plus the following:

FORM 2–3
SAMPLE PRIVILEGE DOCUMENT LIST (ATTORNEY FILE)

Summary of document   1 or 2 paragraph summary of the document itself
Notes on document   This will include any handwritten notes that may be on a typed letter, any indication of who received the document, cc: Jim Jones, bcc: Mary Smith, and so forth.
                              Any other notations on the document such as "Received Loading Dock, 5/10/__";
                              "Reviewed by Jane Smith for meeting of 5/9/__," and so forth.

Whereas **Forms 2–2** and **2–3** illustrate not only the elements involved in a privileged document list but also a definition of those elements, **Form 2–4** is an actual sample of a privileged list that is paralegal work product prepared specially for litigation.

FORM 2–4
SAMPLE PRIVILEGED LIST

Document
Letter, 3 pages, dated [date], signed by [name], Chief Financial Officer, [name] Corporation.

Summary of Document
[name] summarizes financial activity for the first quarter including a discussion of the pros and cons of acquiring the warehouse space at the [city]. Includes cost analysis. CC: Board of Directors and attorney.

Document Requested
Requested by defendant [name] in First Set of Interrogatories, Interrogatory
No. 5, served [date], objection attorney-client and work product privileges.

Copies of Document (7)
Copies are located in witness files for each member of the Board of Directors,
[name of chief financial officer], and attorney's memo file.

Also note on your copy of the privileged list the number of copies of this particular privileged document and their location (whose file). This will be a reminder to
you when you are screening documents for document production to pull each copy
of a document for which you are claiming privilege. An important letter addressed to
the chairman of the board of directors at a savings and loan institution may have
been carbon copied to each member of that board. It does not do your client any
good to pull the original letter to the chairman of the board, and produce copies of
the very same letter when files of documents from individual board members are
produced. If you suspect there is more than one copy of a sensitive document, ask
your client and locate all copies immediately. A separate file should be set up for
privileged documents, and that file should be maintained completely separate from
the working files in the action. An annotated copy of the privileged list should be
part of the correspondence section of your working file.

§ 2.40   Investigation

When considering the proper person to conduct an investigation, be aware that legal
assistants may act as unlicensed investigators and perform many of the same tasks
that professional investigators perform. There is no magic touch to being a professional investigator. They do not have access to secret records, nor do they all lead
the charmed life that has been portrayed successfully on television by James Garner
as Rockford. They do, however, have more contacts and sources of information than
unlicensed investigators.

In determining what to investigate and how to do it, consider the nature of what
you are trying to prove, the assets available, and the demands of your client. The
decision as to when to hire a professional investigator should be based upon the following factors:

The budget of the case (can the client afford a professional investigator?)

Liability exposure of the client

Technical issues

Location of evidence and/or missing witnesses (Is travel involved?)

Will it be necessary for the investigator to testify at trial? When it appears that the
facts of the case will dictate that the investigator may have to testify about the
findings of the investigation at trial, it is best to use a professional investigator
who may appear to be a disinterested party because the investigator is not an
employee of the law firm.

§ 2.41   Using Professional Investigators

Professional investigators bring to the field an expertise that enables them frequently to shorten the investigative process. The tricks of the trade in investigation are simple and clear cut. Paralegals, professional investigators, and the general public have access to public records and documents. A professional investigator, however, may have more than just access to those public records and documents, the investigator may have contacts in certain public offices enabling him to retrieve information more efficiently. Many investigators are members of the National Association of Investigative Specialists and through that association they have access to national and international networks of information through computer data bases. The data available from governmental agencies and private companies allows them to find information on financial assets and other data which may be unavailable to an unlicensed investigator.

The corporate world is increasingly turning to professional investigators to dig up information on takeover suspects, employee theft, or preemployment screening. Evidence hidden in foreign countries, little known lawsuits in rural counties, and damaging information filed by obscure agencies is all within the reach of the professional investigator tapping into various computer data bases. Companies may be saved from takeovers by private investigators who collect damaging information on corporate raiders. Assets can be located of multinational companies in virtually any noncommunist country by a professional private investigator tapping into a myriad of computer data bases through the New York Times data bank and the Wall Street Journal data bank. Professional private investigators function as information brokers and through their contacts and computer data base exchange can supply answers to questions, locate witnesses and evidence, and provide background information necessary to evaluate a case properly, assist in trial preparation, and help obtain a favorable result for the client. The decision as to whether to use a private investigator must be made by the attorney and should be discussed with the client.

§ 2.42   Legal Assistants as Investigators

The facts surrounding a transaction or occurrence will determine the legal issues. The issues will determine the evidence material to a case. All evidence, whether helpful or detrimental to your client's cause, must be searched out and collected. Investigation is the backbone of pretrial preparation and begins at the first meeting with a client. Informal investigation precedes and leads into formal discovery and also continues as discovery progresses and new information becomes known. Conscientious investigation forms the basis for evidence used at trial. Whether your client wins or loses their case may very well depend on the thoroughness of the case investigation. Your client will have a substantial part of the information concerning the transaction or occurrence in controversy within their control. Usually the client is not only able to identify other persons who should be contacted but also is aware of other sources of evidence such as supporting documentation and records.

The legal assistant's role in investigation of the facts should begin as soon as possible. Your objectives are to:

1.   Identify the pertinent facts
2.   Locate the evidence
3.   Identify the sources of evidence
4.   Preserve the evidence in its original state
5.   Organize the evidence to make it useable at trial, and
6.   Be prompt and accurate in investigation of the facts.

Promptness is essential to good investigation. Evidence tends to vanish like smoke with the passage of time. Physical evidence gets lost; records are altered or shredded. Witnesses quickly forget the facts which they observed. Some witnesses try to forget. Some witnesses try not to be found. Former friendly and cooperative witnesses suddenly change their tune and become reluctant witnesses.

§ 2.43   Locating Witnesses

Locating witnesses is a major part of the paralegal's job in their continuing function as fact manager. Factual investigation must be controlled from the initial client interview through obtaining relevant records and basic research on factual issues. The paralegal functions as a fact manager and an investigator verifies the gathered information and uses it as a lead to other areas of investigation, including the names of other potential witnesses. Locating witnesses becomes difficult when a witness is not necessarily where the medical record, hospital record, police report, or your client says they should be. In today's mobile society with changing family styles, changing employment, and relocation of families, it is common to have to go through several addresses before locating particular witnesses. Good investigation techniques can help you find any identified person who is not purposely hiding through a series of logical steps including a thorough search of public records. Before beginning an intense search of public records, begin with the telephone book, reverse street directory, and by canvassing the neighborhood and interviewing known friends and relatives of the missing witness.

If you have time, drive to the last known address to find out who is living there and how long they have lived there. They may know the person you are looking for and be willing to provide you with helpful information, such as the place of employment, type of work they do, type of vehicle they drive, other persons who lived with them, names of close friends or relatives, whether they had out-of-state license plates on their vehicles and if so, what states.

The basic procedure of contacting the post office for a forwarding office is often forgotten. For a reasonable amount, usually a $1 search fee, the post office of the zip code for the last known address of the missing witness will process a mail forwarding request. **Form 2–5** is an example of a mail forwarding request. If the witness has left a forwarding address with the post office, this search will turn it up. Usually forwarding requests submitted to post offices are good for 90 days. After 90 days the post office does not forward mail and returns it to the sender; however, expired forwarding requests are occasionally maintained in the post office files. It is helpful to examine an expired forwarding request to obtain the last known address. You can then attempt to locate the person at that address, and if that fails fill out a new forwarding request and submit it to the post office of the zip code of the address you obtained from the expired request.

Before beginning an intense search of public records, start with the most obvious, the telephone book, and the reverse street directory which lists addresses and matches them to names. A reverse street directory is available in most public libraries and at some Board of Realtors offices. The two best known directories are the Cole Directory and the Polk Directory. It is best to search them both to obtain the most current information. Many telephone companies provide a special listing service where subscribers can telephone for statewide searches by name only.

If you know the social security number of the witness you are attempting to locate, charts can be obtained from your local Social Security office matching the first three digits of all Social Security numbers to the state in which they were issued. This may lead you to the person's home state, since it will usually be the state in which your missing witness held the first job. It can also help you to locate the birth state, because some parents apply for a Social Security number for the child as soon as the child is born. Obtaining the state of application for your missing witnesses' Social Security number is also helpful when the witness has an unusual last name. You may be able to locate other persons with that same last name in the home state who may turn out to be relatives of the missing witness.

Social Security numbers are also military identification numbers and are helpful if you contact the Veterans Administration. A Federal Freedom of Information Request may be completed to find out if your missing witness is a veteran, has a federal Veterans Administration loan, or receives some sort of disability benefits. In cases when the missing witness is receiving disability benefits, it is probable that you will be able to obtain a current address, or at least the address to which disability checks have been sent. The Veterans Administration has a required printed form that must be submitted before any information will be released. Contact the Veterans Administration agency directly and request the Federal Freedom of Information Act form.

FORM 2–5
SAMPLE LETTER TO POSTMASTER

Postmaster
[City, State, Zip]

  RE: Address Search, [name]

Dear Sir or Madam:

  In accordance with § 262.7, U.S. Postal Service Manual, I have enclosed our check in the amount of $1.00 to cover reasonable search and copy charges. I request, pursuant to the Federal Freedom of Information Act, the forwarding address of [name] who was last known to have resided at [street address], [city], [state], [zip code].

A stamped, self-addressed envelope is provided for your convenience, and a space is left at the bottom of this letter for your reply. Thank you for your courtesy and cooperation in this matter.

Sincerely,

[legal assistant]

FOR POST OFFICE USE ONLY
(   ) Address unchanged, still receiving mail.
(   ) Forwarding address filed on [Date]
        Address: [address]

Remember to send letter to the zip code of the last known address. Use the national zip code directory to make certain you have the zip code correct.

NOTE: Postmasters are required to keep forwarding addresses active for eighteen months when a patron fills out a request for forwarding. After eighteen months, the requests for change of address are stored in the post office archives which may or may not be located at the main building. Check with the postmaster for the procedure needed to search the archives. Should you encounter a new address through other investigation, do a second (or sometimes third) letter to the postmaster of the new zip code requesting forwarding information.

§ 2.44   Locating Military Personnel

If you learn through your investigation that it is likely that your missing witness joined a branch of the military service, you may write directly to the appropriate locator service for that branch of the military for information regarding active status and current military address. Military identification numbers are the same as social security numbers, and although it is not necessary to include a military identification number in your request, it does speed up the search process.

The following addresses and phone numbers are current as of the writing of this chapter; however, they should be verified before use.

United States Army.   Letters should be sent to: World Wide Locator Service, U.S. Army Personnel Service Support Center, Fort Benjamin Harrison, IN, 46249, (317) 542-4211.

United States Air Force.   Letters should be sent to: Air Force Military Personnel Center, Attention: World Wide Locator, Randolph Air Force Base, San Antonio, TX, 78150, (512) 652-5774 or (512) 652-5775.

United States Navy.   Letters should be sent to: Navy Locator Service, Washington, D.C. 20370, (202) 694-3155. Reference the following: #21, if request is from a private party or law firm, #36 if request is from a government agency, #38(c) if the request pertains to a Navy retiree. The Navy is the only branch of the military service which will provide information through their locator service regarding retired as well as active duty military personnel.

United States Marine Corps.   Letters should be sent to: Commandant of the Marine Corps, Headquarters, Marine Corps, Attention: Locator Service, Washington, D.C., 20380. The Marine Corps phone numbers depends on the first letter of the last name of the missing person:

(A - E)—(202) 694-1624
(F - L)—(202) 694-1861
(M - R)—(202) 694-1610
(S - Z)—(202) 694-1913

United States Coast Guard.   Coast Guard Locator Service, Room 4502, for enlisted personnel, Room 42(b) for officers, 2100 Second Street S.W., Washington, D.C., 20593, (202) 426-8898. The Coast Guard also provides information regarding retired civil service members who receive retirement benefits, contact: Office of Personnel Management, 1900 E Street N.W., Washington, D.C., 20415.

§ 2.45   Checklist for Locating Witnesses

_____ Check with the post office. Postmasters are required to keep forwarding addresses on file for 18 months. After that time, the request expires and is routed to postal archives. Information from archives is extremely difficult, but not impossible, to obtain.

_____ Send a letter to the last known address of the witness you are attempting to locate and write on the outside of the envelope "FORWARDING ADDRESS REQUESTED." You may get lucky because the person living at that address may respond with the requested information.

_____ Request that the post office furnish you with the name and address of the person who pays rent on that post office box if the last address you are able to determine for your missing witness is a post office box. This request must be made on an official form (No. A6) which is available at all post offices.

_____ Use old telephone books to get prior addresses for your missing witness and fill out a request for forwarding for each of the old addresses.

_____ Use a reverse street directory on the last two or three old addresses for your missing witness to get names of neighbors who may have knowledge as to where your witness has moved.

_____ Check Department of Motor Vehicle records for mobile homes and Department of Housing records for stationary trailers because your missing witness may have moved into a mobile home or a stationary trailer located in a trailer park.

_____ Talk to the local postmaster because, in a small town or rural area, word of mouth is the best source of information. This type of investigation is best done in person.

§ 2.46   Interviewing Witnesses

Interview known witnesses immediately. Information to be obtained from a witness includes their identity, background, observations, contacts with the parties, and any pertinent conclusions they may have. Ask whether they have been interviewed by anyone else or have given a recorded statement to anyone else. If prior statements do exist, obtain copies of them. Frequently, a witness will not be aware of the fact that they are entitled to receive a copy of any statement they have given to an investigator, insurance adjuster, or claims examiner. All they have to do is request a copy for their own use.

Often witnesses are reluctant to give statements because they do not understand the procedures and they want to avoid being involved in a controversy. You should approach the witness in a manner calculated to gain their confidence. Identify yourself and explain the purpose of the interview. The witness should be told and assured that there is nothing improper in talking to one side or the other, or in giving statements. They should be encouraged to sign the statement to guarantee its authenticity.

A reluctant witness may be a little more cooperative if he or she is told it may well be over a year before the case reaches trial and a written statement will help refresh his or her recollection. The assurance of its authenticity is his or her signature on the statement. If the witness still remains uncooperative, they may be told that they are already involved and their lack of cooperation will not help to avoid their involvement. The alternative to an informal statement is a deposition, which requires a response to a subpoena and testimony under oath. Most witnesses will eventually give statements when faced with this alternative.

A good statement should commit the witness to his or her version of the occurrence or transaction by clearly setting forth the facts known by the witness and establishing the basis and sources of his knowledge. Before interviewing witnesses, prepare a list of questions you want to ask so all important areas will be covered. There are many standard witness questionnaire forms available, which can be modified to suit specific cases. A sample witness questionnaire and preparation checklist follow.

Before interviewing witnesses, prepare a list of questions you wish to ask so all important areas will be covered. There are many standard witness questionnaire forms available, which can be modified to suit specific cases. A sample witness questionnaire form and preparation checklist follow.

§ 2.47   Preparing for Witness Interviews

Once you are familiar with the case background, and have had an opportunity to interview your client, you are ready to begin preparing for interviews of percipient witnesses, background witnesses, and other persons with relevant information regarding the incident. To effectively prepare for an interview you should:

Prepare a handwritten list of questions, or at least brief notes, of points to be covered in key areas.

Prepare interview questions avoiding all red flag words which will make the interviewee angry and perhaps end the interview before it is even started.

Word the questions so that the specific interviewee will understand them, work at the experience level of the interviewee, rather than asking questions in legalese.

Avoid closed-end questions, complex or compound questions, rhetorical questions, and questions which imply blame or fault.

Create a friendly atmosphere. Assume that the interviewee will be intimidated by your presence. Do not take notes at the start of an interview.

Let the interviewee give their version of the facts forming the basis of their opinion before launching into your questions.

LISTEN to what your interviewee is saying. Few people really listen. They are too busy thinking of the next question.

Never put words in the witnesses mouth. Do not rephrase their answers. Accept the answers as you hear them, unless you truly do not understand the answer.

Expect that the witness will digress. Remember that you must remain in control of the interview, and firmly but gently get the conversation back on track.

Never appear to be in a hurry, no matter how pressured you are. You must relax so that the interviewee will relax.

Meet the witness in their own surroundings, if possible, so that they will be more comfortable. If you are meeting a witness in their own surroundings, dress the part. For example, if you are investigating an accident at a manufacturing plant and need to discuss the mechanics of an assembly line with the foreman, do not go to the interview in a tailored silk suit. Dress down, but remain formal.

Precondition your witness to the taking of a formal statement by having them run through their entire story first as an ice breaker. You can then go back and tell them that you would like to take notes for their own protection. Explain that you do not want to misquote the witness and that you are expected to provide a record of this interview for your attorney.

Do not cut off answers. Encourage input from the interviewee and you may learn more information than you originally expected. The witness may have more information regarding the specific incident than you were aware of, and may provide answers to questions that you had not thought to ask. Remember, you might hear something that will give you leads to new witnesses or new information. As long as you remain in control of the interview, you can ask spontaneous questions based on this new information.

Maintain a neutral demeanor. You are there to obtain the facts of the incident and you are not necessarily on anyone's side. Of course, you must identify yourself as a legal assistant working for Beverly Smith, attorney for Jane Jones. Beyond that, do not lean towards one position over another. Be a factual observer and information recorder.

Failure to approach the interview with a neutral attitude can produce disastrous results. Most witnesses really wish to please, and their testimony will be colored by that effort if you allow it. You will end up with witnesses slanting information more favorably towards your position than they really perceive it even if it differs.

The result may be an inaccurate statement which may come back later to haunt you after other statements have been taken.

Chat with your interviewee before you begin to take a formal statement. In the course of chatting, much information can be obtained including the name and address of a previously unknown witness, the existence of documents, background information, and so forth.

Obtain information regarding an individual who will always know how to contact the witness. In today's society, witnesses tend to move around, change jobs, change geographical locations, and can be extremely difficult to find when a case is ready to go to trial. A good contact person is usually a relative, and the best relative is the witnesses' mother.

Identify yourself, the law firm, the client, the date of the incident, the incident under discussion, and the identity of the potential adverse parties. This identification should always be made at the onset of any contact with the witness. It is extremely important that, before the witness begins to answer your questions, the witness is fully aware of who you are and why you are talking to them.

Remember that the first person to interview a witness tends to mold the witness and firm up the story in the witness' mind, and that is the information that the second person who interviews the witness will get. It is an advantage to be the first person to interview the witness. If you are not, be sure to ask the witness whom they have spoken to, and if they gave a statement. Occasionally, a witness will tell you they have previously given a statement, and the statement was to an insurance agent or a representative of the adverse party, so they would rather not talk to you. Try to convince the witness that even though they have given this statement, you would still like to talk to them to obtain a second statement because you do not have the first statement. Try to obtain enough information regarding the prior statement so that you can request a copy.

§ 2.48   Special Pointers for Witness Interviews

Most of the suggestions included in **Chapter 1** regarding client interviews are useful for witness interviews. Although there is usually more time to prepare for interviewing clients if they come in at a scheduled appointment time, you do not always know you will be interviewing a witness until the last minute when your attorney may give you the name of someone who has just been located who "might know something that will help our case" and asks you to contact him and "find out what he knows." This type of all too common surprise witness interview requires a factual investigative technique that will help provide you with the most crucial information in the shortest amount of time. The following checklist can be used as a starting point:

_____   Focus on the end result of your interview.

_____   Understand the witness' role in key events and the extent of their knowledge.

_____   Establish the credibility of the witness.

_____ Define limits of witness' knowledge (areas outside of their personal knowledge).

_____ Establish extent of witnesses personal knowledge of client.

_____ Confirm lack of knowledge of witness on specific issues.

_____ Establish a strategy that is flexible and can be changed on a moment's notice depending upon answers received.

_____ Cover each of these areas:

    _____ Factual investigation.

    _____ Chronology of events.

    _____ Opinions.

    _____ Interpretation of the event.

    _____ Knowledge of documents or written material.

    _____ Conversations or admissions overheard by any of the key players.

_____ Ask a combination of leading questions, open-ended questions and focused questions, but do not forget the most important type of questioning is follow-up questioning.

_____ Conclude your interview by asking the all important catchall question to assure yourself that nothing has been overlooked.

During questioning it is important to be aware of the difference in statements of fact versus inferences of fact. For example, if your witness reaches a conclusion that is absolute with no conditions or opinions attached, it is a statement of fact, and may be useful or damaging to your client. Examples of statment of fact are:

I saw her left turn signal flashing as she approached the intersection.

Mary Jones was taken from the scene of the accident in an ambulance.

Mary Jones had surgery at St. Martin's Hospital.

Inferences of fact, on the other hand, are statments that may include conditions, opinions or conclusions such as:

Mary Jones was hospitalized at the best hospital in the country, St. Martin's. (In whose opinion is it the best hospital?)

You could tell Mary Jones was in tremendous pain at the accident scene. (How could you tell she was in pain?)

You cannot count on the witness to volunteer information unless you ask specific questions. Catchall questions can provide a great deal of information that might have been missed otherwise. Sample catchall questions are:

Is there anything else you remember about this incident?

Is there anyone else you think I should talk to about this incident who might have additional information?

Do you have any opinions about the incident that you have not already expressed?

As you think back on the incident and everything we have spoken about today, what is the most important impression that stands out in your mind?

It can be very damaging at trial to have a witness on the stand suddenly remember events that were not a part of his witness statement, and volunteer information on topics that were not addressed. Attempts to impeach this type of witness are difficult. An attack on their sudden change of memory of selected events is usually answered by "you did not ask me that question" or "you did not ask me if there was anything else I remembered about the incident."

§ 2.49   Sample Witness Questionnaire

Form 2–6 is an example of a witness questionnaire form which may also be used to get witness information in a personal injury case.

FORM 2–6
SAMPLE WITNESS QUESTIONNAIRE FORM

Please state your full name, address, and telephone number. _____

Please state your occupation, name and address of your employer, name and address of direct supervisor, and business phone number. _____

If you are married, please state the name of your spouse, and the name, address, and phone number of their employer if employed outside the home. _____

Please describe all events you observed prior to the accident. _____

Where were you when you first observed the accident or other event? _____

Where was [name] when you first saw them? _____

Where was the other vehicle when you first saw it? _____

Please describe the accident location, road description and markings, weather conditions, speed limit, traffic controls. _____

Please describe the accident chain of events as you observed it, including the speed of the vehicles before the accident, position of other cars when you first saw them, position of other cars when danger was first realized, evasive actions, if any, taken to avoid the accident, the position of cars at the time of the impact.

Immediately after the accident did you have conversations with any of the persons involved? _____

Did you observe any damages? _____

Did you observe any injuries? _____

Are you acquainted with any of the parties involved in this accident? If so, with whom? _____

Are you related to any of the parties in this accident? If so, whom? _____

Do you have any other information you feel might be helpful? _____

§ 2.50   Sample Questions for a Witness Interview

In addition to using a general questionnaire, it is important to develop specific questions focusing on the key issues of the case as they relate to elements of causes of action and affirmative defenses. For example, in negligence cases, the following questions would be appropriate when questioning a percipient witness:

Example 1

ELEMENT.   Duty (defined by plaintiff in Complaint on file, further defined by conditions of roadway at time of accident).

ISSUE.   Was the inclement weather, rain and fog, a factor in determining the degree of caution required by a normal person using the roadway under normal driving conditions?

WITNESS QUESTIONS.   Was the road wet the morning of the accident? How much of the road near the scene and at the scene of the accident was wet? Were there spots of the road where fog was particularly thick? Had you experienced any difficulty driving that same stretch of road yourself? Did you have control problems with your vehicle? Did you have your head lights on? Were you using low beams or high beams? Were your windshield wipers working? Was the speed of your windshield wipers sufficient to clear the windshield? Do you have adjustable speeds in your windshield wipers?

Example 2

ELEMENT.   Breach of duty.

ISSUE.   Was Ms. Smith driving too fast, given the conditions of the road due to inclement weather, at the time of the accident?

QUESTIONS.   How fast were you driving? How fast do you normally drive? How fast was Ms. Smith driving? From your observations, how did the rain affect or enter into your choice of driving speeds? In your opinion, was Ms. Smith driving too fast for the road conditions? Explain the basis for your answer. Did Ms. Smith have her headlights on? Were they low beams or high beams? Did you observe any other cars in the vicinity? What speed were they traveling at? How far behind Ms. Smith's car were you at the time of the accident?

Example 3

ELEMENT.   Breach as proximate cause of injury to plaintiff.

ISSUE.   Was Ms. Smith's speed under the wet and foggy road conditions the cause of Ms. Brown's injuries.

QUESTIONS.   In your opinion, what was the primary cause of the accident? Explain. Do you feel there were any other contributing causes? If so, what were they? Explain. What cause was the most significant? Explain. Was Ms. Smith's speed greater than other cars in the general flow of traffic? Did Ms. Forester, in your opinion, do anything to cause this accident?

This series of examples illustrates linking questions to initial pleadings in an action—complaint and answer. It is important to use follow-up questions for any issues which come up in your interview. Other factors in this example would include speed related to obstructions in the roadway, inattentiveness of drivers, reaction time of drivers, evidence of mechanical failure, automotive defects, and so forth. Questions need to be planned to gather information on the key points of contentions for each of the elements in plaintiff's complaint and each of the elements of affirmative defenses in defendant's answer. This preparation helps clarify the objectives of your interview and makes your interview much more valuable to the outcome of the case.

Some examples of follow-up questions regarding road conditions follow:

Please describe in detail what you mean by slippery?

How far did you travel on the road to where you observed the accident?

Were there other slippery spots on that quarter mile of road?

What percentage of the road was slippery?

Did you notice other cars slowing down?

Did you observe puddles of standing water or areas of flooding on the road?

What was the weather like that morning before you left your home?

Had it rained the night before?

Was it raining at the time of the accident?

Do you usually travel that road when you commute to work?

How often do you travel that road?

§ 2.51   Negative and Hostile Statements

A telephone interview will occasionally reveal that a witness is not a percipient witness and has little information which will help your client. You may also be surprised and find out through a telephone interview with a friendly witness that your client's perception of this witness was incorrect and that, in reality, this is a hostile witness who is biased against your client and has many unfavorable things to say. In this case, a memo to the file will suffice. It is not to your client's advantage to take a statement from a witness who has a bias. Negative statements are tricky and should be taken by professional investigators. It is too easy for a biased or negative witness to manipulate an interview resulting in a statement which is not factually based, but is rather an interpretation of those facts as seen through the eyes of the biased witness.

The only advantage to taking a negative statement is that it serves as a denial of knowledge. It should be brief and to the point so that the person who has been interviewed cannot come back later with any remembered information.

In considering whether to take a statement from a hostile or adverse witness, several factors must be considered. If it appears that the witness' statement will be adverse or hostile, then no written or recorded statement should be taken because this statement would be discoverable and harm your client. On the other hand, a skillful legal assistant may be able to turn a hostile witness into a friendly witness, by being friendly and cooperative with the witness and suggesting alternative views and interpretations of the facts. Generally speaking, however, adverse or hostile witnesses should be interviewed by a professional investigator who prepares a memorandum to the attorney labeled "confidential work product" but refrains from taking a statement. In the memorandum to the file, the professional investigator assesses the credibility of the witness and provides input as to whether the witness is adverse because of misinterpretation of facts, or truly hostile because of a bias towards your client. The adverse witness who is relying upon facts which the witness has misinterpreted can sometimes be turned into a friendly witness in a second interview if your client's version of the facts is carefully explained and documented by a disinterested, unbiased professional investigator. Be aware that this is a risky assignment to give an investigator and it could backfire on your client, especially if the adverse witness has a closed mind.

The following example (**Form 2–7**) is a negative statement of a witness in a motor vehicle accident. The value of this negative statement is that it precludes the witness from remembering later who was at fault for the accident. It also establishes that, although the witness was in the vicinity of the accident and almost a percipient witness, the witness really did not see the accident happen and cannot offer an opinion as to who caused the collision.

FORM 2–7
SAMPLE NEGATIVE STATEMENT

Statement of [witness]

My name is [witness]. I live at [address], [city, state], phone number [number]. My daughter [name] (who was [number] years of age at the time) and I were traveling south on [name] Street and I witnessed an accident between a [vehicle model] and an [vehicle model] car. I was about mid-way between [location] when the accident occurred. My daughter and I were talking about her new pet canary. I was watching the road, but honestly I was not paying much attention to the traffic. I really did not actually see either vehicle until they crashed. The first thing that I realized, I saw two vehicles look like they had jumped up into the air. I do not know how fast either one was going and I do not know which entered the intersection first, and I do not know who had the right of way, and I do not know who was at fault. I do know that they hit somewhere near the center of the intersection, I did hear the loud bang. I do not know exactly what part of the intersection they were in when they first hit. I have talked with my daughter and she says that she did not see the collision. The first thing that called her attention to the collision was the loud crash. She heard the crash and looked up and the two vehicles had stopped. That is what she told me.

I have read the foregoing statement and it is true and correct.

Dated: [date]

[signature]

Although this example of a negative statement focuses on a motor vehicle accident, it is not meant to preclude the value of taking negative statements in other actions. Percipient eye witnesses identified in reports, or by your client, occasionally turn out to be less than eye witnesses having missed the main event.

§ 2.52   Taking Witness Statements

In taking witness statements, remember it is a first person statement and should include only those facts the witness will testify to at trial. You are not writing a narrative. Save editorializing and comments for a cover report to accompany the interview which will become confidential legal assistant work product and will not be discoverable. A witness statement should be concise and precise, setting forth only those facts which the witness observed. and/or has personal knowledge of, and expects to testify to at time of trial.

The basic parts of a witness statement are:

1. Identification of the witness: name, address, phone number, date of birth, social security number, and employment.
2. Events before the incident, events leading up to the incident. Include why they were there, what their role was, what happened, what they saw or heard from any witness or bystander. What actions they took.
3. Postevent happenings: what happened, their observations, their conversations, any reports made, and any statements made.
4. What the witness did after the incident. Did they go home, go to work, were they alone or with someone else? Did they discuss this incident with anyone else? If so, get the name of that person.

A good witness statement should:

Be legible
Follow a chronological, factual pattern
Be written in the witness' words using their language
Be clear and concise and contain only those evidentiary facts perceived by the witness.

The statement can be handwritten or typed and should be in the words and language style of the witness, not legalese. The witness should have an opportunity to read the completed statement. Ask the witness to sign or initial each page of the statement to guard against missing pages.

At the conclusion of the statement, the following paragraph should be inserted:

I, [witness name], do hereby declare under penalty of perjury and of the laws of the State of [state name] that I have read the foregoing statement consisting of [number] pages, and I hereby certify that it is true and correct to the best of my belief. I further state that this statement was written by [name], whom I know to be a legal assistant for [attorney name], attorney representing plaintiff in this action. I further declare that this statement was executed on the [date] day of [month], [year], and that I have given it of my own free will.

Avoid giving the witness a copy of the statement. If a witness asks for a copy, explain that if you give the witness a copy, it removes the protective shield of the attorney work product privilege and that it is in the witness' best interests that the statement remains in your custody. If you have a situation where the witness insists on having a copy of the statement, refer the matter to your supervising attorney.

§ 2.53   Witness Interview Report

Witness statements should be accompanied by a memorandum written by the legal assistant editorializing, offering opinions regarding the witnesses' credibility, and containing any extraneous information that may be important to the case. This memorandum is confidential work product and is protected from discovery. Items to include are:

1. Extended biographical information on the witness, name of spouse, name and ages of children, employment background, union membership, type of work done by the witness, date of birth.

2. Information on their home state, how long they have lived in the area, whether they have any plans to relocate either because of a job relocation or a desire to move back to see relatives, and so forth.

3. Basic physical description of the witness including your impression of them regarding their credibility and what type of impact they will have on the jury.

4. Their attitude towards both your client and attitude towards the adverse party.

5. Information they have given you on other witnesses, existence of other documents, people to interview, investigation leads, and so forth.

6. Any information learned while chatting.

7. Your personal opinion of the witness—were they truthful? Were they holding back information? Can they be swayed easily by an overzealous opposing counsel? Do they have anything to gain or lose by testifying in this incident?

8. Any technical knowledge or expertise that the witness has which could be useful in interpretation of documentary evidence.

9. The witnesses' social security number and driver's license number. Explain to them that you will not be using these numbers to obtain any personal information about them or their family. These numbers are like an insurance policy to help you locate them when the case comes to trial which may take several years.

§ 2.54   Factual Investigation

Factual investigation, in its broadest sense, is literally nonlegal research, that is, research dealing with information about people, facts, and places. Quite often people think of investigation solely as locating, interviewing, and taking statements from witnesses. Although that is a major part of factual investigation, it is only the tip of the iceberg. Factual investigation includes site inspections, obtaining photographs, and obtaining documents such as medical, employment, business, court, and government agency records. It also includes investigating and testing products, obtaining diagrams, blueprints, and tracing grant deeds to properties through the grantor/grantee indexes in city records.

It is important to locate and collect evidence supporting your client's claim and/or defense, but it is equally important to locate evidence that may be used by your adversary to disprove your claim and/or defense. A civil action usually centers upon disputed facts. The party who has done the best job of collecting, preserving, and presenting evidence concerning the disputed facts generally prevails at trial or secures the most advantageous settlement.

Investigation of facts should begin as soon as possible. An investigator should:

1. Identify pertinent facts supporting the client's claim and/or defense
2. Locate all discoverable evidence and sources of evidence
3. Preserve the evidence in its original state for presentation at trial
4. Organize the evidence to make it useful at the trial
5. Be prompt and accurate—evidence tends to vanish with the passage of time
6. Obtain photographs immediately. Multiple photographs should be taken and time and date stamped on them. This is important in order to preserve the accident site, or item in dispute, as it was on the day of the occurrence.

Factual investigation is not all research, and definitely not all paperwork or reading. Factual research frequently involves interviewing and telephone inquiry. It also involves observing and using common sense and reasoning based on facts you have learned by other means.

An example of a factual research investigation project a paralegal might be given regarding damages is to establish future wage loss when records are not available. For example, in a wrongful death action concerning a Navy test pilot, it was important to know how that person would have been employed after leaving the military. Options for an ex-Navy test pilot going into civilian life might include the following: pilot for commercial airline, charter plane pilot, business owner—flight school, trainer or flight instructor for aviation based business, ground work (nonflight) for governmental agencies and/or private business in the field of aviation. These are but a few of the options considered when researching wage loss in a wrongful death action of a Navy test pilot. This research began by consulting the Dictionary of Occupational Titles to determine the most likely occupations for an ex-Navy test pilot. Then the commercial airlines were contacted to inquire about opportunities for employment, salary ranges, benefits, and so forth. The next step was to contact flight schools again to determine possibility for employment, salary, benefits, and so forth. After all this information was gathered, it was possible to predict with reasonable accuracy potential employ-ment possibilities for the client had the client survived the crash, as well as the client's future earnings. This information allowed us to present a future wage loss package as part of damages at our settlement conference in this action.

Another example of factual nonlegal research of an investigative nature is to deter-mine the present company, or successor in interest, of a company or manufacturer you wish to bring into a lawsuit as a potential defendant. You must trace the record of acquisitions of that company and their successor in interest in order to name them as a defendant in your action. Research is generally done at trade libraries and business libraries, or through data bases containing successor interest information. Consult your information broker regarding availability of data bases that can do on-line searches for successors in interest by tracing the record of acquisition of a company that is no longer in business. Another good source of information on companies that have gone out of business is State Board of Equalization records.

There is no doubt that public records form the background of any factual investi-gation. There is equally no doubt that obtaining them from custodians of those records is a long, difficult process. Understanding that the custodian of public records is usually a government employee whose job it is to maintain and retrieve records and learning to work patiently with that person will go a long way towards obtaining the results needed. The job of a records custodian is not exactly exciting. Each day is made up of dealing with hundreds of confused, impatient, and often demanding customers. The best approach in dealing with a records custodian is to view them as knowledgeable professionals, treating them as experts in their field. You will find that the old axiom "you can catch more flies with honey than with vinegar" truly works when dealing with custodians of public records.

§ 2.55   Library Resources

The secret in getting results through library searches is to know the right library to go to. There are many different types of libraries and some will certainly serve needs better than others. In addition to the public library system, and city, county or state libraries, consider college and university libraries, school libraries, business libraries, and special libraries which are devoted to collections of limited subjects. Many spe-cial libraries are run by private organizations such as historical societies, corpora-tions, social agencies, and even museums. There are thousands of special libraries and special subject collections within those libraries which may provide exactly the information you need to complete your investigation. The most important book to consult in determining which library will fulfill your needs is *The American Library Directory,* published by R.R. Bowker Company. This is a massive reference work and is usually found at the reference desk of most public libraries. This book lists more than 30,000 libraries in the United States and 3,000 in Canada. Listings are arranged geographically by state and city with enough detail to advise you whether it is worth consulting any given library.

A second valuable resource tool is the book *American Subject Collections,* edited by Lee Ash, also published by R.R. Bowker Company. The most recent edition was published in 1978 (Fifth Edition). It is organized by subject, and within the subject category there are alphabetical arrangements in geographical order. Listings include special libraries devoted entirely to one subject and special collections of books within general libraries.

Another valuable book to consult if you are searching for a special library is *Directory of Special Libraries and Information Centers,* published by Gale Research Company. This book has nearly 14,000 entries and serves a useful cross-check to those listed in the other two reference books mentioned. Organization is alphabetical and by subject in the first volume of the directory. The second volume of the directory has a geographical breakdown with the name of state, city, and town.

Access to private, special libraries, especially those in corporations, is sometimes difficult. These libraries are not open to the general public, but usually the librarian in charge will extend the courtesy of its use to an outsider who approaches them with a specific, focused intent. The key to gaining access to private libraries is to be courteous, sincere, and respectful of library privileges.

A prime example of a private library that is most useful in locating missing persons is the Genealogical Library maintained by the Church of the Latter Day Saints (LDS). All LDS Family History Libraries are a great source of information on family surnames and family trees. Although you may not be interested in the family tree, and are looking specifically for a crucial witness, learning about other members of the family may prove useful. The best method of gaining access to an LDS Family History Library is by labeling your search a genealogical search of the family history of the "Brown Family," rather than a search for a specific person, Mary Brown. Other genealogical libraries are maintained by the Immigrant Genealogical Society, the Claremont School of Theology, the German Genealogical Society of America, the Sons of the Revolution, and various historical societies such as the California Historical Society. LDS Family History Libraries are extremely comprehensive for doing a genealogical search. However, the main purpose of LDS Family History Libraries is to assist those persons interested in compiling their family tree.

A final note regarding the use of special libraries. Many of them are maintained by nonprofit foundations and permission for use is contingent on payment of a slight fee which is considered a contribution to that foundation. This contribution may place you on a list of contributors and you may receive annual mailings requesting donations. This is a small inconvenience that should not deter you from seeking out and using private collections and special libraries.

§ 2.56   Information Brokers

Information brokers, also known as independent researchers, are invaluable for many of the same reasons listed in § 2.39 regarding the use of professional investigators. The universe of information accessible on data bases is phenomenal: however, it is not always prudent or necessary to search each and every data base to locate a particular individual or a particular piece of information. It is necessary to have access to many different data bases and sources of information to conduct a proper and thorough search. It would be prohibitively expensive for all law firms and libraries to subscribe to all of the data bases available. Most information brokers are members of the Association of Independent Information Professionals. This membership gives them access to multiple data bases without the necessary subscription requirements because the Association of Independent Information Professionals is the subscriber. Information brokers also have training in conventional library research techniques, and many are former librarians. Information brokers have a specific expertise in researching specialized directories and trade publications that just might hold the key to finding elusive private company information or locating an expert witness on an obscure subject.

Information brokers with initiative will use whatever sources are appropriate to make headway with a particular assignment. Often it is a combination of on-line data bases, library research, and telephone contacts. Because they realize that their work will most often be used in current or potential litigation, good information brokers will, upon request, furnish you with a complete paper audit trail telling you exactly what data bases they checked and how far back they went, who they spoke with at which particular agency, and what publication they used to gather the information they supplied. Information brokers generally charge by the hour and bill back computer fees and other direct costs. You can control the fee charged by an information broker by asking for costs up front, and/or by limiting their search to specific time parameters, or by using other restrictions depending on the specifics of your search.

Information brokers are also known as search companies and document retrieval services. You will find listings of these public vendors in most bar association directories and legal newspapers. Contact them directly and they will be only too happy to send you information about their services and fee schedules. Always ask for local law firm references.

§ 2.57   Private Organizations for Information

Many private organizations are in business to collect and market information about people. It has become very big business to supply creditors or advertisers with consumer information. It can be useful to tap into this information when you are attempting to locate a reluctant witness. We are a nation of consumers and consumer information is useful not only to collection agencies and merchandisers, but also to those of us in the legal profession. The following private organizations are the most widely known information marketers:

DIRECT MARKETING BROKERS. Polk, Donnelley Marketing, Metro Mail Corporation, and Data Base America. There are also many other smaller marketing brokers but these are the major brokers in the nation. They sell consumers' names, addresses, and phone numbers to businesses who compile mailing lists. They also publish and sell several assorted directories.

NATIONAL DEMOGRAPHIC AND LIFESTYLES (NDL). This is the company to which you send warranty cards when you buy specific electronic and household goods. In order to validate the warranty on a particular product, you must fill out the product information card within a certain number of days and send it to NDL. NDL keeps on file your name, address, phone number and other valuable consumer information that you have checked on the card. Language on the warranty card reads as follows: "To help us understand our consumers lifestyles, please indicate the activities in which you enjoy participating on a regular basis." Unwary consumers often check many boxes here, and then are amazed by the flurry of mail they receive from merchandising companies. Consult an information broker to find out how you can access the NDL data base for name, address, and phone number information only. It is a valuable source of consumer information geared and marketed specifically to businesses; however, it can be useful for investigative purposes.

CREDIT BUREAUS. Consumer information from credit bureaus is most often requested by prospective creditors including landlords, employers, insurance companies, and banks. As was discussed in § 2.62, you may obtain credit header information which is extremely useful because it provides a social security number on an individual.

MEDICAL INFORMATION BUREAU. They compile physical, medical, and other information including data showing hazardous working conditions. This information is usually sold to insurance companies who use it to discover false or incomplete information on insurance applications. The usefulness for investigators of information compiled by the Medical Information Bureau (MIB) relates to hazardous working conditions. In product liability actions, when a client may have been working under hazardous conditions, it is useful to request their file. An individual person may request a disclosure form directly from the Medical Information Bureau at P.O. Box 105, Essex Station, Boston, MA, 02112. You may contact the MIB at (617) 426-3660 regarding disclosure of information for investigative purposes. An authorized form used by your firm for disclosure of medical record information is needed before an individual's file can be released.

DOCTORS AND HOSPITALS. Medical information is available directly to patients. If your client signs an authorization allowing the release of their medical records, you will be successful in obtaining them in the following states: California, Colorado, Connecticut, Florida, Hawaii, Idaho, Indiana, Louisiana, Massachusetts, Minnesota, Nevada, New York, Ohio, Oregon, Rhode Island, Tennessee, Utah, Virginia and Wisconsin. Other states have yet to enact legislation guaranteeing a patient's right to access to their individual medical records.

Federal law allows patients to obtain hospital records from public health service facilities, military hospitals, and Veterans Administration hospitals. A client authorization form is needed for release of records to any third person.

BANKS/FINANCIAL INSTITUTIONS. Records regarding deposits, withdrawals, and check writing are gathered by banks and financial institutions and are accessible to the FBI and IRS. There are laws in most states prohibiting banks from disclosing that information to anyone other than a governmental agency, account holder, or a person named in a court order. Your client who is the account holder or a person named in a court order may request account information. Third persons (law firms) can access information only through a properly executed subpoena.

VIDEO RENTAL STORES. It is amazing but true that video rental stores accumulate a great deal of personal information about video renters. This news first came to light in the televised hearings regarding the nomination of Clarence Thomas to the Supreme Court of the United States. Senate members had obtained a list of the movies he had rented from his local video shop. If Clarence Thomas had lived in California, Connecticut, Delaware, Iowa, Maryland, and/or Rhode

Island, the video store would not have been able to disclose that information. In other states, third persons (law firms) can access this information via subpoenas.

A federal law, the Video Privacy Protection Act, allows a video store to sell lists of customer names and addresses if the list does not contain the titles or descriptions of tapes rented and if it allows customers the option of not being included. Unfortunately, most customers are not only unaware of the amount of information contained in the data bases of their local video store, but also further unaware that they can opt not to be included in a list of customers that the video store might be required to produce pursuant to subpoena. It is a long shot to subpoena such a list from a video store; however, if you are looking for a witness and have learned that the witness is a movie buff, lives in a certain neighborhood, and rents a lot of videos, it might not be a bad idea.

§ 2.58   Public Record Investigation

Basic information may be obtained from public records detailing vital statistics on a person such as birth, death, and marriage. Licensing and regulatory activities are fertile fields of data searches. Government documents and publications offer a wealth of information that can provide you with personal facts including the subject's professional background and past and present employment. State and county licensing and regulatory agencies should also be checked along with city and county tax collectors. This is especially important when attempting to locate a witness who may be in business for themselves using a fictitious name.

The Department of Motor Vehicles is the first public agency that comes to mind when attempting to locate a witness. Given the fact that the majority of citizens of the United States over the age of 16 are licensed drivers, it is a logical step to begin the search for a missing witness by consulting the Department of Motor Vehicles. For a standardized fee, the Department of Motor Vehicles will process your request for current record information relating to a licensed driver. A request for information on a driver's license number may not always turn up the most recent address because not everyone reports changes of addresses to the Department of Motor Vehicles. However, vehicle registrations must be renewed on the average of every two years depending upon the requirements in each state. If you happen to have the license number of a vehicle, in addition to the driver's license number of the person you are attempting to locate, it is wise to run a search on both numbers. It is likely that you will turn up information more quickly based on current vehicle registration than on licensed driver information.

In addition to obtaining the name and address of the registered owner of a vehicle, the Department of Motor Vehicles can also furnish the name and address of the legal owner of the vehicle. Contact should be made with the legal owner (which is usually a financial institution) to see if they have a current address or any information on locating the missing registered owner. If the legal owner refuses to give you a current address claiming that they are protecting the privacy rights of their customer, you may be successful in writing a letter and asking that it be forwarded. Banks zealously protect confidential information and will not release information about customers. You will never be able to find out if your person has an account unless you reach a person who does not know the bank rules. The worst thing that can happen is that you will be told that the information is unavailable, but this should not prevent you from asking. If you do not go after certain information, you will not obtain it. You may be fortunate enough to reach a person with a sympathetic ear who will agree to forward your letter to the person you are attempting to locate.

Public records are valuable for many reasons, not just to locate individuals who may be important to your case as witnesses. Searching public records is particularly useful in motor vehicle accidents when you are attempting to determine basic information about a particular street or highway.

The letter in **Form 2–8** illustrates an attempt to determine the timing of traffic signals which was a major issue in this particular case. It is safe to say that there will frequently be a dispute between two drivers as to whether the traffic light facing them at the time of the accident was red or green. If there is a genuine dispute, and the plaintiff, defendant, and the percipient witnesses are credible, it is possible that there is a defect in the traffic signal itself. This letter seeks information to support the theory that the traffic signal at the intersection in question was defective and not operating properly on the day of the accident.

FORM 2–8
SAMPLE PUBLIC RECORDS REQUEST LETTER

Department of Public Works
Traffic Engineering and
Operations Division
City Hall
[street address]
[city, state, zip code]

RE: Accident of [date]
      Intersection of [street names]
      Our Client: [client name]

Dear Sir or Ms:

This office represents [client], who was injured on [date] at approximately [time] in an accident which occurred at the intersection of [street names] in [city]. We would appreciate receiving information regarding the traffic signals at that intersection. Specifically, please advise us of the following:

1. The timing of the signals at this intersection;

2. The maintenance schedule for inspecting traffic signals, including the last maintenance inspection for this intersection; and

3. Any existing reports of defects with this signaling device before or after the date of this accident, please furnish those reports.

Our office will be happy to reimburse you for any copy costs incurred in preparing this documentation for us. I would also be willing to research this information at your offices if that is permissible and the records are open for inspection.

Please contact our office if you have any questions or problems with this request. Thank you for your anticipated cooperation.

Sincerely,

[name], Legal Assistant

§ 2.59   Searching Public Records for Individuals

Many public records are available to use for searching for individuals. For information regarding individual witnesses, the following records should be consulted:

The Secretary of State. (Check for information regarding whether an individual is a corporation or a limited partnership. Also do a Uniform Commercial Code (UCC) search to see if the individual has ever filed a UCC Form 3.)

Voter registration

Various city and county departments and agencies requiring business licenses (The person you are seeking may be operating a small business which requires that the person obtain a business license and pay city and/or county taxes in order to operate that business.)

Fictitious business name statements

The local bar association

Insurance commissioner

Corporation commissioner

Public utilites commission

Auditor

City and county tax collector

Civil and criminal court indexes and documents, including bankruptcy court

Probate court

City and county clerk or recorder

County or city tax assessor

Armed Service World Wide Locator (There are also individual phone numbers for the various branches of the military, army, navy, marines, and so forth. *See* § **2.44**)

Newspaper articles

The newspaper morgue of the major newspaper in the city where the individual was last known to have lived and/or done business

The Dictionary of Trade Associations (A good reference book to locate information on professional associations relating to particular industries. This is useful information if you are aware of the occupation of the witness you are attempting to locate.)

Unions such as electricians, plumbers, machinists, and so forth should also be checked if the person you are seeking has ever worked in any trade, even if the last employment was several years ago.)

Licensing agencies (If the person you are seeking is employed in a profession which requires licensing or some form of regulation by the state, this avenue of information is frequently overlooked except for the most obvious professions which require licensing such as nurses, pharmacists, doctors, and beauticians.)

Check your state statutes and local and city ordinances for a complete listing of those professions in your state requiring registration or licensing. For example, a partial list of those professionals required to be licensed in many states includes:

Aircraft mechanics
Alarm installers
Alcohol sales
Auctioneers
Auto inspectors and wreckers
Bankers
Barbers
Bill collectors
Building contractors
Carpenters
Carpet cleaners
Certified Public Accountants
Child care/day care operators
Dentists
Meat packers
Meat storage
Mechanics
Notary Publics
Nursing home owners
Nurses
Painters
Pawn brokers
Pet groomers
Pest controllers
Pilots
X-ray technicians
Restaurant owners
Scrap dealers
Security guards
Taxi drivers

Insurance agents
Garment cleaners
Process servers

§ 2.60   Bureau of Vital Statistics

The Bureau of Vital Statistics keeps all official records for births, marriages, divorces and voter registration information as well as other records. This information can be extremely helpful.

Birth certificates.   These are especially helpful documents if the witness you are looking for is under 30 years of age. Many people in their early 20's move around a great deal, and you will have a better opportunity locating them by learning the names of their parents, locating them, and asking them for information.

Marriage certificates.   These also are also useful documents. In addition to the name of the bride and the groom, they will frequently list the parents of the bride and groom and the names of the witnesses to the marriage ceremony. Frequently the witnesses will be best friends of the bride or the groom and may be useful sources of information. At the very least, a marriage certificate will list a woman's maiden name, which is a valuable piece of information in attempting to locate her.

Divorce records.   Divorce records provide a great deal of useful information regarding a person's finances, charge accounts, bank accounts, and so forth. They also provide information on vehicles owned by a husband or wife (including license plate numbers and vehicle registration numbers), and social security numbers, all of which is helpful in attempting to locate a witness.

Voter's registration records.   These are most valuable for authenticating signatures. The person you are attempting to locate may have changed their name, reclaimed a maiden name, or dropped a middle name; however, if the signatures match, you will know you have located the correct person. Remember, the same name can often be spelled many different ways. Be certain in checking records that you check every possible spelling of a witness's name.

§ 2.61   The Public Library

The reference librarian is one of the most valuable persons you can enlist to assist you in investigating practically any person, place, or topic. The business section is an excellent place to begin when searching for information regarding public entities. General reference information which can be accessed includes the following:

National and state directories for scholarly and professional associations
Census reports

The National Directory of State Agencies, Wright & Allen (Information Resource Press, 1983) Information on headquarters for various manufacturing associations

Information on toy safety associations

Information on product standards as set forth by the American National Standard Institution

Medical literature detailing injuries, medicines, side effects, prognosis, and discussions of particular diseases from a layperson's point of view

University and college information

Small business administration information

The Readers Guide to Periodical Literature, a comprehensive yearly subject index to numerous periodicals

The Readers Guide to Legal Periodicals, index by subject to articles in legal magazines and journals

Out-of-state telephone books and publications of the telephone company such as The National Directory of Names and Addresses for the Business Customer, High Tech Business Directory, and The Book of Lists for Business Customers

Subject indexes for major newspapers such as the New York Times, Wall Street Journal, Christian Science Monitor, as well as to your local newspaper

Access to on-line searches for specialized data bases, many libraries subscribe to various data bases and will allow you to search after paying a basic user fee

The Encyclopedia of Associations, by Mary Wilson Pair, one of the most valuable reference books in the library, associations (national and state) listed by subject and alphabetically

University libraries, if the topic you are investigating is technical or specialized

§ 2.62 Data Bases for Searching for Individuals

The data bases described in § 2.64 provide information regarding both individuals and business entities. However, certain data bases have been proven to be most useful when your search is confined to locating one specific person. They are as follows:

1. NATIONAL IDENTIFIER DATA BASE. Provides information on a particular individual if you have a full name and any address. The address does not have to be a current address. A Social Security number is not needed to access this data base.

2. METRO NET. This data base pulls information from magazine subscriptions and post office changes of address. Additionally Metro Net receives some information from the census. It is unlikely that any individual is not listed in Metro Net.

3. NATIONAL CHANGE OF ADDRESS FILE DATA BASE. Post offices send change of address cards to the National Change of Address Data Base after they have expired (36 months). Names and addresses are held in the National Change of Address Data Base for several years. They are then sent on to the Metro Net data base.

4. CREDIT HEADER DATA BASE—TRW. Credit information that is contained in TRW reports is confidential, and generally cannot be accessed through an information broker with the exception of special circumstances such as collection actions. However, you can access credit header information from the TRW data base. Almost everyone is included in this data base, because most of the nation has purchased something on credit at some point in their lifetime. Information you will receive from the Credit Header Data Base includes a name, present address, and, most importantly, a social security number. The social security number then allows you to run searches on other data bases.

When attempting to locate an individual, the most logical place to begin your search is with the post office of the last known zip code. In many situations, the person filling out a change of address form may list a post office box instead of a street address. Do not think your search has ended when faced with a post office box mailing address. The postmaster must honor a subpoena and provide a street address to match a listed post office box if you can prove good cause exists for locating that person. An individual applying for a post office box as a mailing address must fill out a form with the postmaster indicating an agent for delivery of service. That form must include a street address for that person designated as the agent for delivery of service. Those are the forms to request in a subpoena which will enable you to translate a post office box into a street address. The agent for delivery of service may not be the person you are looking for, but it is highly likely that the agent is a relative or close friend of that person.

Access to Department of Motor Vehicle information has been limited in many states by recent legislation. In most states, the Department of Motor Vehicles demands a social security number before it will grant a driver's license and uses the social security number as an aid in tracking down those persons who are delinquent in child support payments.

In California, privacy is guaranteed by Vehicle Code § 1808.22. You may furnish the Department of Motor Vehicles with a mailing address which is not your residence address and frequently the mailing address chosen is a post office box. However, you must provide residence address information to the Department of Motor Vehicles, which is held in confidence and given only to those individuals with authorized requests. Check with an information broker regarding requirements to be an authorized requestor. Requirements vary from state to state just as the Vehicle Code requirements and statutes vary from state to state. It is worthwhile to spend time pursuing information from the Department of Motor Vehicles because most individuals obtain driver's licenses in the state where they plan to reside and drive a vehicle.

§ 2.63   Investigating Business Entities

When dealing with a business entity, the most important thing to find out is how they do business. Are they a corporation, a limited partnership, an individual doing business under a dba or fictitious business name, and so forth. This information may be obtained from the Secretary of State, city and county tax collector, and/or Department of Business Licenses. Once this basic information is obtained, the task of investigation turns to a different level. That is, how much information can we find out about how this business is conducted, the assets of the business, and the key individuals involved in the business.

Corporations buy or form smaller companies, divisions, or subsidiaries at a rapid rate. To find out if the company you are investigating is a parent corporation or a subsidiary corporation, consult the public library business section and review the following books:

> *Directory of Companies Required to File Annual Reports* (U.S. Government Printing Office publication). (This publication lists companies alphabetically and by industry classification. If the corporation that you are interested in is listed in here, they are required to file an annual report and you may write to the SEC headquarters for information about that company. Securities and Exchange Commission, 500 North Capital Street, Washington, D.C., 20549.)
>
> *Who Owns Whom, Directory of Corporate Affiliations* (Roskill & Company, England)
>
> *Standard and Poors Registry of Corporations*
>
> *The Dunn and Bradstreet Directory of Corporate Families*
>
> *Moody's Business and Industry Manual*

§ 2.64   SEC Documents and Stock Information

If the corporation you are investigating is a publicly held corporation, a wealth of information is available through the SEC. This information will enable you to construct a profile of the corporation, including history, assets, business activities, and principal officers. This information is available from many of the following documents which corporations are required to file.

1. Quarterly reports (10Q) are required for the first three years of existence before they are required to file an annual 10K.

2. 10K annual reports are required 90 days after the close of the fiscal year for corporations.

3. 10K Exhibits which are listed separately and must be filed at the same time as the annual 10K. In investigating a corporation, you may order copies of a 10K and index to exhibits without ordering the actual exhibits, which could be voluminous, not relevant, and expensive for your client. By ordering the index first, you can order copies of only those exhibits which are relevant.

4. 8K Forms are filed by a corporation when unusual circumstances occur within a fiscal year such as a merger, bankruptcy, or a change in board of directors and/or corporate officers.

5. No action letters from SEC to the corporation. A corporation considering an idea for business expansion, or anything that would have a financial impact on the shareholders of that corporation, is required to advise the SEC of the proposal. The SEC then reviews the proposal and responds with a no action letter stating that they will await the outcome before taking any action.

To obtain information on corporate stock, consult:

Standard and Poors Stock Reports
New York Stock Exchange Reports
Commissioner of Corporations
Nilson's Directory of Wall Street Research
Annual Reports for Corporations (available at most public libraries).

§ 2.65   UCC Filings as an Investigative Tool

In the field of business law, one of the most important statutes is the Uniform Commercial Code (UCC). The UCC provides a system of filing and storage of documents that occur at a state level (Secretary of State) and the county or town level. The UCC is a compilation of laws regulating interstate commerce that have been adopted in every state except Louisiana. The basic premise of the UCC is to protect the creditor and the debtor equally, although the regulation tilts toward the protection of and rights of the creditor. The basic objectives of the UCC are to promote uniformity among the various jurisdictions, facilitate continued expansion of commerce practice, regulate, standardize, enforce the law governing commercial transactions, and provide a standard location for filing liens.

UCC filings can be used as an investigative trail of financial dealings involving a particular witness, potential defendant, or business client. It has been conservatively estimated by public records search firms that 40 percent of all adults in the United States have filled out a UCC form at one time or another in the course of their financial dealings, which means that it is extremely likely that a search will yield information which could be useful in your case.

Article 9 of the UCC applies to all types of contractual security agreements for personal property, both tangible and intangible, fixtures, and other related assets. Article 9 deals with secured transactions and effects most businesses. UCC filings are alphabetical by a person's last name and also by the name of a business. Name variations as to spelling and form are frequent, making a UCC search a bit more complex than it appears at first. For example, Jack Jones may be listed individually. Jack Jones' business may be listed as Jack Jones Construction Company, Jack Jones Development Company, Jack Jones Home Builders, Jack Jones Building Supplies, and so on. You can conduct a search by the name of a debtor, a secured party or by the security instrument. To do a complete search, use all three methods.

Collateral is classified in many different ways and can vary in its classification from county to state. Some general categories of classifications of collateral at the county level are liens, fixture filings, consumer goods, farm products, oil, timber, judgments, and businesses. In addition to listing and describing the collateral, an address must be listed on the form for its location. Frequently this address is different from the address given for the person filing the UCC statement. This second address information can be useful when attempting to locate a missing witness.

Contractual security agreements for personal property create a security interest. Perfecting a security and filing a UCC statement is a form of creditor insurance. In order to perfect the security interest, UCC filing requirements must be satisfied in accordance with state regulations. This is usually accomplished by filing a financial statement which contains the names and addresses of the debtor and the creditor, the signatures of the debtors, and a complete description and classification of the collateral. The mailing address listed for the debtor must be that of the chief executive officer or the residence of an individual debtor. Physical address versus mailing address is a variable in each jurisdiction and index. In some states and counties it is acceptable, and in others it is not. The place for filing of a UCC statement is determined by state jurisdiction. Some states require dual filings, with both the state and the county.

Using UCC filings as an investigative tool can provide access to valuable information in many areas, such as:

1. Verifying the reliability of a payment pattern on existing promissory notes or loans (information from the UCC statement will enable you to contact secured parties);

2. Asset searching (determination of financial worth of potential defendant or profit line of a business or small corporation);

3. Obtaining information regarding fictitious business names, vehicles, property, and bankruptcy filings;

4. Skip-tracing for finding missing witnesses;

5. Avoiding conflict of interest in taking on representation of new clients (particularly useful in business litigation where multiple interests may be represented by an individual corporation); and

6. Locating the proper entity for service of process (particularly helpful for naming a business plaintiff or defendant correctly).

UCC searches are most economical and expedient when done by a professional service. UCC searches can be time-consuming and complicated for a legal assistant. On-line data base access to UCC information is available in certain states from the Secretary of State's office, and can be obtained through a public records search firm for a fee which will be substantially less than legal assistant time and billing for the same task. The advantages of using a professional investigator should be considered before a legal assistant decides to conduct an extensive UCC search without the use of computerized data base support. Public record search firms function as information brokers. Through their contacts with and subscriptions to data base networks, they can shorten a UCC search, providing the information sought cost-efficiently and expeditiously.

§ 2.66 Data Bases

Data bases contain a wealth of information which may be accessed through a computer search. If your law firm does not have a variety of data bases on line, you will find a great selection of data bases available at the public library. These bases can usually be accessed for a basic user fee and on-line time charge.

Some of the more common and most useful data bases include the following:

LEXIS and WESTLAW—full text information on case decisions, statutes, and administrative regulations.

LEGAL RESOURCE INDEX—provides indexing of law journals and legal newspapers.

LABOR LAW—provides decision summaries on labor relations, fair employment, wage and hours, and occupational health and safety relations (1930 to present).

TRADEMARKSCAN—provides records on currently active trademark applicants and negotiations.

NEXIS—provides full text coverage of national and international newspapers, magazines, and wire services.

NATIONAL NEWSPAPER INDEX—provides indexing of the Christian Science Monitor, the New York Times, and the Wall Street Journal (1979 to present).

NEWSSEARCH—provides textual coverage of prominent newspapers.

PUBLIC AFFAIRS INFORMATION—contains all bills and enactments for the current legislative session for each of the 50 states.

CONGRESSIONAL RECORD ABSTRACTS—provides abstracts of the congressional record.

CONGRESSIONAL INFORMATION SERVICE—provides abstracts of all congressional office of technology, assessment, and congressional budget office publications.

DUNN & BRADSTREET'S MILLION DOLLAR DIRECTORY—contains business information such as corporate credit and financial profiles on U.S. companies worth $5 million or more.

DUNN'S MARKET IDENTIFIERS—provides information on U.S. business establishments that have 10 or more employees.

PTS, FNS INDEXES and PTS PROMPT—provides information on products, mergers, forecasts, and so forth for domestic and international companies.

DISCLOSURE II—contains extracts of SEC reports filed by publicly owned corporations.

DOW JONES SPECTRUM PROFILES—offers extracts of SEC reports on institutional holdings, investment company holdings, beneficial ownership, tender offers, and insider trading.

SECURTIES DATA CORP—contains information on offerings of stocks and bonds.

PHARMACEUTICAL NEWS INDEX—offers current news on drugs, cosmetics, medical devices, and related health fields.

CHEMICAL EXPOSURE—provides information on chemicals found in the human body and food chain.

MEDLINE—indexes and abstracts articles from the major medical journals of the world (1966 to present).

AMERICAN STATISTICS INDEX—offers a thorough index of statistical publications from U.S. government agencies, population and economic censuses, CPI reports, unemployment and vital statistics.

ENVIRON RHINE—offers abstracts of publications on the world environment.

DIALOG—common data base owned by Lockheed containing hundreds of information systems, including many cross-indexes to the previously mentioned data bases.

PEOPLE FINDER—helpful in locating people and information in all 50 states, search of addresses, cities, phone numbers, access to 111 million names. Helpful to find witnesses, shareholders, beneficiaries, to skip-trace, or to do a background check. This data base includes many usually hard-to-find sources of information including subscription and marketing lists, along with the more common voter registration lists and Department of Motor Vehicle records.

DUNN'S BUSINESS RECORDS PLUS—more general business index than other Dunn & Bradstreet data bases. This index includes historical and operational data as well as financial information on each business listed. The unique feature of this data base is its ability to search by an executive's name. This is especially important when you are attempting to locate an important party or witness in business litigation who may have resigned from one corporation and joined another. This base covers all 50 states, any type or size of company, public or private. It is extremely helpful for obtaining background information regarding parties involved in litigation or mergers and acquisitions, such as the financial assets or health of the company, the background biography of the adverse party, a list of companies with whom an individual may be involved, or any potential conflicts of interest. The source of information for this data base is Dunn & Bradstreet Corporation, and it is their most comprehensive data base.

REAL PROPERTY REPORTS—search can be done by owner name or property address to find out what a specific party owns, who owns a specific piece of property, or the value of the property. This data base is available in California and will search the entire state. It is not available nationwide; however, it is useful for other states seeking information on individuals or property in California.

§ 2.67   Public Records Resources for Financial Institutions

In commercial litigation, breach of contract, and business tort actions, it is important to access information about financial institutions who may be involved as defendants or third parties. This section is a resource guide to public records which can be requested.

Bank holding companies are companies that hold banks as their primary business as opposed to offering common banking teller, deposit, withdrawal, and loan services. These companies are regulated by the Federal Reserve Board (FRB) and are required to disclose information to the public via the Federal Reserve Board on an annual and quarterly basis. The annual financial filings are called Y-6f and quarterly filings are called Y-9f. These filings are not as extensive as SEC filings; however, if a bank holding company is publicly held, it is also required to make certain SEC filings. Bank holding companies which are not publicly held are still required by the FRB to file quarterly and annual financial filings.

Federally chartered commercial banks are required to file with the Office of the Comptroller of the Currency. These banks are distinguished by the word national or the suffix "N.A." in the full name of the bank. State chartered commercial banks that are publicly held must file with the Federal Deposit Insurance Corporation (FDIC). They are then required to file annual F-2 and quarterly F-4 financial statements in addition to periodic transactional reports similar to SEC filings. A few state chartered banks are members of the Federal Reserve System and must file required disclosure documents with the federal banks.

All banks whether publicly or privately held are required to file CALL (Statement of Condition and Income) reports that can be accessed on-line directly from the FDIC. This type of search is best arranged through an information broker who has access to FDIC filings.

Savings and loan institutions are regulated by the Office of Thrift Supervision (OTS). Filings required by the Office of Thrift Supervision (OTS) mirror filings made at the Federal Communications Commission (FCC) in both name and format. The annual reports are 10K's, and the quarterly reports are 10Q's, and so forth.

If a savings and loan institution is under a conservatorship, it is under the control of the Resolution Trust Corporation (RTC), and, even though they do not continue their filings, considerable information is available from the Resolution Trust Corporation concerning the disposal of the assets of a savings and loan institution.

§ 2.68   Public Records Resources for Other Financial Information

Energy, oil, gas, and electric companies/entities are required to file financial and operating data with the Federal Energy Regulatory Commission (FERC). Accessing information about these entities is particularly important for environmental and real estate litigation. Electric companies must file a Form 1 with the FERC annually. They are required to report information which includes the cost and type of fuel they use monthly (Form 423). Natural gas companies file a Form 2 annually and report a monthly disclosure (Form 11) of the amount of gas sold and revenue generated. Oil pipeline companies make annual filings on a Form 6 and must also file rate schedules and tariff information with the FERC.

If the company is not involved in interstate transfer of energy sources and is not transporting energy across state lines, it may still be required to file within the state in which its principal business headquarters is located. Check with the local Public Service Commission or Public Utilities Commission. These agencies require forms very similar to those required by FERC.

Airline companies are regulated by the U.S. Department of Transportation and are required to file quarterly reports known as a Form 41. These reports include a breakdown of revenues by the type of operation and they contain route and seat information as well. Form 6-100 includes traffic information and is filed monthly by all major airlines. A very informative publication, the Air Travel Consumer Report, is available monthly for 29 of the busiest airports in the nation, who are required to report on the operation of those major airlines servicing that airport.

Rail and trucking companies over a specified size involved in interstate shipment of goods are required to disclose financial and operating statistics to the Interstate Commerce Commission (ICC). If a trucking company has more than $10 million in annual revenues, it is required to report financial and operational information on Form M-1. It also reports assets and liabilities quarterly on Form QFR and reports charges for carrying goods on tariff filings. Major railroads file an annual report called Form R-1. The quarterly commodities statement is required to report commodities shipped. The consolidated balance sheet contains asset and liability information. Form REI reports revenue earnings and income.

If you are attempting to collect a judgment against a rail or trucking company, a lien against the property may be filed with the ICC. If a railcar or locomotive has been used by the company as collateral to secure a loan, a lien will be on file at the ICC, and pertinent information about that loan is accessible to anyone by request to the ICC citing the Federal Freedom of Information Act.

Insurance companies are not regulated by any federal agency, although there have been many discussions regarding their regulation. State Insurance Commissioners require that each company licensed to do business in that state file detailed financial information in an Annual Statement (sometimes called a Convention Statement or Statutory Blank.) These filings can be requested from the State Insurance Commissioner's Office. Information on these filings include information regarding stock and bond holdings, real estate, and assets of the insurance company.

If you are attempting to locate information regarding a company that has filed for reorganization or liquidation, your first stop should be the Federal Bankruptcy Court. Documents with the most valuable information will include the Petition and Schedule of Assets and Liabilities which is required to be filed directly with the court. A company that is attempting to reorganize and stay in business is also required to file a monthly operating report outlining its incoming and outgoing cash.

§ 2.69   Sources of Information on Privately Held Companies

Although it is more of a challenge to locate financial information on privately held companies, it is not impossible. Before contacting an information broker or professional investigator, try these sources of information:

—Run on-line searches for articles that report on the company's activities accessing local newspaper data bases and other data bases such as the New York Times, Washington Post, and so forth.

—Call the local library to see if clippings or articles of the company are available in their periodical section.

—Obtain a business credit report by an on-line search through the Dunn & Bradstreet information data base.

—Call the company directly and ask to speak to the public relations department. You may find this to be the most valuable source of information, particularly if you give the impression that you are interested in investing in the company.

The following books are particularly helpful in attempting to locate information about privately held companies, sole proprietorships, closely held companies, and family entities:

Dunn's Million Dollar Directory.
Ward's Business Directory.
Thomas Register of American Manufacturers.

All these publications are most likely at your public library.

Directories such as the *Corporate Yellow Book* or the *Directory of Corporate Affiliations* will also give you information about smaller corporations and particularly about individual corporate players.

As small and medium-sized companies grow and become prominent Wall Street players, it becomes easier to access information about their assets. Standard and Poor's is known for their investment information and recently published a new Standard & Poor's Mid-Cap Index to measure the stock performance of 400 medium-sized companies. The index accompanies the popular Standard & Poor's 500 Index which tracks large companies. Both of these indexes, as well as all Standard and Poor's investment information, are generally available through Information America and/or the Dunn & Bradstreet data bases.

§ 2.70   Government Documents

In 1966, Congress passed the Federal Freedom of Information Act (FOIA) opening up to the public several important avenues of investigation. This act prescribes that public records must be open to inspection at all times during the normal office hours of the federal agency in custody of the records and that every citizen has the right to inspect any public records within certain exceptions set forth in the Government Code. FOIA applies to documents held by the administrative agencies of the executive branch of the federal government. It does not apply to information maintained by the legislative and judicial branches. The executive branch includes executive departments and offices, military departments, government-controlled corporations, and independent regulatory agencies. All records in possession of these entities must be released upon request unless the information falls within one of the exceptions. The government sources of information are so vast and widely spread, it is useful to think of the information you need in generic terms. To obtain information, first determine which agency is most likely to have it. The United States Government Manual lists all federal agencies and describes their functions. In addition, it usually lists their local and regional office addresses and telephone numbers. This manual is found in most public libraries or may be purchased by writing directly to the Superintendent of Documents, U.S. Government Printing Office, Washington, D.C., 20402.

In addition to the United States Government Manual, there are publications that include information on public information offices and federal agencies. The *Official Congressional Directory* (U.S. Government Printing Office—published annually) is a publication which contains information and phone numbers for Congress, members, committees, and an interesting section on staff history and traditions.

Non-official publications, or commercially produced material, regarding U.S. Government resources are frequently narrower in scope but can be more useful. They may give the background and an in-depth description of various departments and agencies, but many of them contain more names, paths for contact of an individual, telephone numbers, and more thorough indexes with better subject access. Commercially produced publications draw their information from official manuals as well as telephone directories. Their greatest value is that they are updated much more frequently than official U.S. Government published directories. Three of the best are the *Federal Yellow Book,* the *Congressional Yellow Book,* and the *Congressional Staff Directory.*

The *Federal Yellow Book* (Monitor Publishing Company, updated quarterly) is a publication that takes its information from federal telephone directories as well as the U.S. Government Manual. It provides easy access to agencies and staff in the executive branch not only through various indexes but also the table of contents. The *Federal Yellow Book* contains more names and phone numbers than the official publication. At the beginning of the federal department and the larger agency section is a list of helpful numbers such as public information hotlines and so forth.

The *Congressional Yellow Book* (Monitor Publishing Company, updated quarterly) provides a more comprehensive listing than the official publication of *Who's Who in Congress.* It includes committees and key staff members. Member listings include name, address, telephone number, committee assignment, and brief facts about key staff and congressional aides. The best feature of this book is a "Useful Telephone Numbers" list, which is helpful in tracking the progress of a particular congressional bill, resolution, and so forth.

The *Congressional Staff Directory* (Staff Directories Limited Publishers) is a basic handbook on the staff and structure of Congress with information on congressional districts, phone numbers, staff, committees, subcommittees, biographical briefs of members, and indexes by subject and individual names. The book is color coded for easy access.

Dealing with the government, either federal or state, takes perseverance, time, creativity, and preparation. Getting to the right individual with the right access to the information you need is not always easy, but the rewards can be great and the information obtained is frequently unrebuttable trial evidence.

§ 2.71   Locating the Correct Government Agency

The listings of major federal agencies and state agencies in §§ **2.69** and **2.70** are annotated to allow you to locate that agency most suited to answer your investigative query. However, if you simply do not know where to start, and reading about the agencies continues to leave you clueless, you might need to consult a guide to federal information such as:

Who Knows: A Guide to Washington Experts (Washington Researchers, 1992)— This publication lists approximately 12,000 experts from all parts of the federal government. It is indexed by over 14,000 subject headings. Experts are matched to subject.

Information U.S.A. by Matthew Lesko (Viking Press)—This book is a treasure trove of agency information with detailed topic index and subject access.

The U.S. Government runs a referral service to assist you in determining the correct agency. The Commerce Department's Office of Business Liaison offers the Road Map Program. They refer your questions concerning business to the appropriate office. Federal information centers, located in major cities, refer you to other government agencies. These sources are listed in any federal directory. Good sources of information regarding government agencies can also be obtained from the United States Government Book Store which is usually located in the federal court complex in most major cities.

Two publishing companies offer particularly useful catalogs to assist you in factual research and investigative work. They are Gale Publishing Company and Bowker Publishing Company. You may contact either company at 1-800-521-8110. Gale Research Company, a division of Gale Publishing Company, provides technical consultation on the accuracy of questions and answers on Jeopardy.

Public interest groups accumulate information regarding various products and companies. This information is particularly useful when you are investigating a particular manufacturer or product in the context of a potential product liability action. *The Encyclopedia of Public Affairs Organizations* published by Gale Publishing Company is a very comprehensive source for locating public interest groups.

§ 2.72 Major Federal Agencies

A complete listing of federal agencies may be obtained free of charge from the Office of Consumer Affairs, Consumer Information Center, Pueblo, Colorado, 81009. Request the booklet entitled *A Directory of Federal Consumer Offices.* Among the federal agencies listed in this directory are the following:

1. Federal Aviation Agency (FAA), 800 Independence Avenue, S.W., Washington, D.C. 20591, (202) 462-4000. This agency provides reports and information regarding airplane accidents, airplane safety standards, airplane schedules, and designated routes.

2. Department of Transportation, Urban Mass Transportation Administration, 400 7th Street S.W., Washington, D.C. 20590, (202) 426-4043. This department maintains information regarding automobile safety and highways including the safety standards of trucking companies, public transit, policies, and procedures for safe driver practices such as necessity for regular rest periods, physical exams for drivers, and so forth.

3. National Oceanic and Atmospheric Administration, 6010 Executive Boulevard, Rockville, MD, 20852, (301) 655-4000. This agency is useful if you need to obtain a certified copy of the weather report for any given date in any city or state. A certified copy of a weather report from the National Oceanic and Atmospheric Administration may be offered as proof at trial asking that judicial notice be taken of the contents of the report.

4. Department of Agricultural Soil Conservation Service, 14th Street and Independence Avenue S.W., Washington, D.C., 20250, (202) 655-4000. This department will send you (for a fee) aerial photographs of any area of the United States provided that you have an address, legal description, lot and block number, parcel location, or other identification.

5. The Department of the Interior Geological Survey National Center, 12201 Sunrise Valley Drive, Reston, VA, 22092. You may request from this department topographic maps which include roads, railroads, and buildings. Maps of all 50 states are available at a nominal cost.

6. Internal Revenue Service, 111 Constitution Avenue N.W., Washington, D.C., 20224, (202) 366-4021. The IRS can locate tax rates and schedules from prior years going back as far as 20 to 30 years. There is, of course, a fee for this service based on the number of years of tax rates and schedules requested.

7. Department of Agriculture, 14th Street and Independence Avenue S.W., Washington, D.C., 20250, (202) 655-4000. This department will provide you with literature regarding poisonous plants, animals, insects, and crops. Toxic tort, product liability, public nuisance, and condemnation actions may all benefit from the source materials provided by this department.

8. Department of Commerce Census Bureau, 14th Street between Constitution Avenue and E Street, N.W., Washington, D.C., 20230, (202) 377-2000. You can acquire statistics and miscellaneous information regarding the populations of cities, states, and towns in the United States from this department. The Census Bureau also has other miscellaneous statistics regarding ages, employments, number of persons in households, national average wages, cost of living increase, inflation factors, and so forth. The Census Bureau is the custodian of numerous miscellaneous statistics, and can answer questions that no other governmental agency can answer.

9. Consumer Product Safety Commission, 1111 18th Street N.W., Washington, D.C., 20207, (202) 634-7700. If you are involved in a product liability action, this is the department from which you can obtain information regarding safety standards set by the government for thousands of products. You can also obtain information regarding any other complaints or actions which have been filed against a particular product or manufacturer.

10. Employment Standards Administration, Department of Labor, 200 Constitution Avenue N.W., Washington, D.C., 20210, (202) 737-8165. You can request information regarding wages and working conditions as well as future outlooks for jobs in particular professions which is useful information in damage claims for lost wages and loss of future earnings.

11. Justice Department-Antitrust Division, Constitution Avenue and 10th Street N.W., Washington, D.C., 20530, (202) 737-8200. This department can assist you with inquiries regarding antitrust practices.

12. Federal Trade Commission Bureau of Consumer Protection, Pennsylvania Avenue at 6th N.W., Washington, D.C., 20580, (202) 523-3625. This agency offers assistance regarding credit discrimination practices and fraud.

13. Department of Commerce, Commissioner of Patents and Trademarks, Washington, D.C., 20231, or Central Office, 2021 Jefferson Davis Highway,

Arlington, VA. Patent and trademark infringement information and communications should be coordinated through this office.

14. Occupational Safety and Health Administration (OSHA), 200 Constitution Avenue N.W., Washington, D.C., 20201, (202) 523-8165. This department provides general information regarding job safety standards. This is a good department to start with if you are investigating an accident or other incident which took place at a job site.

This information is taken from *A Directory of Federal Consumer Offices* published by the Office of Consumer Affairs. It is a good source book of federal agencies, as is the *United States Government Manual.* Both of these publications are in most major public libraries.

§ 2.73   Federal Agency Information Example

The major federal agencies listed in the preceding section include the U.S. Department of Transportation, which has many divisions. The National Highway Traffic Safety Administration (NHTSA) is a division of the U.S. Department of Transportation and is an excellent source of information regarding either motor vehicles or items of motor vehicle equipment. Within the NHTSA, there are several departments including the Office of Defect Investigation and the Technical Reference Division. These two divisions are most useful when researching a particular automobile manufacturer for purposes of filing a product liability action. The NHTSA is authorized to order manufacturers to recall and repair vehicles or items of motor vehicle equipment when their investigations indicate they contain serious safety related defects. The NHTSA acts when defects appear in a group of vehicles and the defects represent an unreasonable risk of potential harm. Therefore, because they are interested in receiving information, they have established an Auto Safety Hotline at 1-800-424-9393 in Washington, D.C. An owner of a vehicle in which a defect is suspected (frequently your client) can contact the Auto Safety Hotline and request a vehicle owner's questionnaire. Vehicle owner's questionnaires are used by the NHTSA Office of Defect Investigation to determine whether certain defects appear in a group of vehicles from the same manufacturer, same model, same year, and so forth. If you complete a vehicle owner's questionnaire, you are entitled to request information from the NHTSA regarding whether other vehicle owner's questionnaires have reported similar problems. The privacy act prohibits the NHTSA from identifying by name those owners who have reported similar problems; however, they will provide information concerning the specific problem as well as the frequency of reported incidents. You may obtain a list of these consumer complaints from:

NHTSA Technical Reference Section (NAD-52)
400 7th Street, S.W., Room 5108
Washington, D.C. 20590
(202) 366-2768

When you write to the Technical Reference Division, you need to specify the make, model, model year, and type of problem. There is a nominal charge for providing the list, and you may contact the technical reference division directly to obtain copy charges before ordering.

In addition to vehicle owner reports, the NHTSA also maintains a data base of manufacturer service bulletins which are issued by the NHTSA when they have received consumer complaints which they deem to reflect a significant safety defect trend. If a significant safety defect trend has been noted, an investigation and a defect investigation file is set up concerning that specific model vehicle or item of motor vehicle equipment such as tires, clutches, and so forth.

The Federal Trade Commission (FTC) has jurisdiction over nonsafety defects and warranty matters regarding motor vehicles and motor vehicle equipment. The FTC can be reached by writing to:

Office of the Secretary
Correspondence Section, Room 701
Federal Trade Commission
Washington, D.C. 20580

Investigating a potential product liability action involving motor vehicles or items of motor vehicle equipment should start with letters to both the NHTSA Office of Defect Investigation and Enforcement and the Federal Trade Commission. The information you receive not only will help provide factual background regarding a particular vehicle but also will help establish prior notice by that manufacturer of a potential defect. It is best to request this information as soon as possible to allow time for your request to be processed.

§ 2.74   State Agencies and Publications

Most state agencies provide information on the same basis as federal agencies and have laws similar to the Federal Freedom of Information Act (FOIA). Check your state administrative codes and statutes to determine if your state has freedom of information legislation. Whether or not there is specific legislation, certain public records are available for inspection from various state and local agencies if a formal request is made. The following agencies can provide information useful in beginning investigation and evaluation of issues in many types of litigation:

1.   Department of Streets and Highways, Public Works Department—Provides blueprints of state highways, tunnels, and bridges. You can also get information regarding speed limits, timing of traffic signals, signs, street lights, and condition of roadways.

2.   Department of Motor Vehicles—Useful for obtaining driver's license information, car ownership and registration information, and records of moving violations.

3. Department of Labor and Industry—Useful for obtaining pamphlets with rules and regulations concerning industrial accident and safety standards in various industries. A request for this information should precede an OSHA request.

4. Geology Department—Geological surveys of various areas in a state can be obtained at nominal charges.

5. Department of Corporations—Possible defendant and/or plaintiff corporations, limited partnerships, and some joint ventures can be researched by a call to the Department of Corporations. You can request general information regarding domestic and foreign corporations qualified to do business in a particular state such as the registered agent, an address for service of process, principal place of business in your state, names of officers, date of incorporation, information regarding annual reports, and so forth. For a nominal fee you can obtain a certificate of good standing from the Department of Corporations.

6. Department of Vocational Rehabilitation—This department provides useful information as to the potential ability of a disabled person to become rehabilitated. Personal injury, product liability, and medical malpractice actions often require this type of information in compiling and evaluating damages.

7. Department of Employment—The information you can obtain from this department regards possible employment opportunities for a particular skill or trade based on the qualification of an individual. This is also useful in computing future earnings potential, damage claims for lost earnings, and so forth. You can also obtain information regarding wages for any given occupation.

8. Department of Insurance—This department provides useful information regarding your state's requirements for individual insurance coverage and general information regarding requirements of insurance companies doing business in that state. You may also be able to learn if complaints have been filed against a particular insurance company. You may also be able to learn if an insurance company has become insolvent and/or has been acquired by another insurance company. The Department of Insurance can provide you with information on the requirements for filing claims against insolvent insurance companies for reimbursement under your state's insurance guaranty program.

9. Department of Business and Professions—General information can be requested regarding licensing requirements of particular trades and businesses.

10. Department of the State Revenue Commissioner—This department maintains records of state taxes paid by individuals on personal property. In most states this information is considered confidential and will not be provided. However, in some states, for a nominal fee, this department will provide you basic information regarding an individual's ownership of personal property such as automobiles, boats, trailers, campers, and mobile homes. This information includes year, make, and model, legal owner, registered owner, information regarding any liens on the property including name of lienholder, amount of lien, date of lien, type of loan, and the last date any action was taken on the property.

11. County Tax Assessor's Office—You can research public records in this department on property ownership which includes the title in which the property is held, lot and block number, street address, tax assessment number, and the rate at which the property is assessed.

12. Local Chamber of Commerce—This is a forgotten office which retains a storehouse of information regarding local businesses and their products and services. You can also obtain various maps, charts, and brochures free of charge.

13. Better Business Bureau—This is a reliable source for inquiring into the business reputation of local businesses, because this office receives complaints directly from the public, previous customers, consumers of local businesses. Most reputable local businesses are members of this organization. The Better Business Bureau usually can provide you with information regarding complaints received and action taken by name of business or business owner.

14. City Department of Public Works and City Traffic Department—Information you can receive from these departments includes blueprints or diagrams to scale of city streets, roads and highways, local routes of public transportation, sequence and timing of traffic lights at any location in the city, and street maintenance and repair. All of this information is useful when you are reconstructing an accident.

In addition to the listing of state agencies, the following publications are helpful when you need to locate a specific government official at the state level.

1. *Book of the States* (Council of State Government). This book parallels the official federal publication in its scope with backgrounds about organizational structure and a listing of major officials at most state agencies.

2. *State Administrative Officials Classified by Function* (Council of State Government). This book provides an alphabetical listing of functional categories of state government, with the name, title, address, and phone number of the chief official in each area.

3. *State Executive Directory* (Carroll Publishing Company). This book has up-to-date listings of state agencies, their offices, divisions, and officials.

4. *Lawyer's Almanac* (Prentice Hall Publishing Company). This book includes a section devoted to federal and state governmental departments, agencies, and officials. It also lists independent establishments and government corporations.

5. *West's Legal Desk Reference* (West Publishing Company). This reference includes a compilation of names, addresses, and telephone numbers of state departments and state agencies. It has an expanded section titled "Useful Addresses."

§ 2.75   Choosing a Vendor for Public Record Searches

Documents may be obtained from each of the federal agencies listed in § 2.72 and each of the state agencies listed in § 2.74 through a request made pursuant to the Federal Freedom of Information Act (FOIA). However, even at its best, this is a cumbersome and time-consuming process. In the real world of litigation, there frequently is a time crunch and documents need to be obtained yesterday. It is then best to rely on the services of a professional vendor to obtain documents. In choosing a particular vendor or service, ask specific background questions regarding:

Their track record—get a list of those law firms, corporations, or businesses for whom they have provided services and a contact person (which will frequently be a legal assistant) for each reference. Follow through by calling the references to check on their level of satisfaction with the service.

Speed—(quick turnaround), accuracy (mistake-free), reliability (the ability to deliver on promises), and finally, flexibility (ability to deliver a finished product in a wide variety of formats to meet specialized needs of the requestor) are the main criteria you should consider.

Affordability—Measure the affordability of a service against quotes obtained from other services, and more importantly against the cost of legal assistant and support staff time on the same project. The lowest quote you receive will not necessarily always be the most reasonable quote. Frequently hidden costs are built into a quote. Ask specific questions regarding pick up and delivery, extra charges for collating, stapling, handling charges for federal express, and so forth. When you are given cost estimates, determine whether these are preliminary estimates or final estimates.

Cost estimate—Once you have received a final cost estimate, confirm that estimate in writing by sending a brief "confirmation of our telephone conversation" letter to the representative who has given you that cost figure.

Information sources—Ask if the vendor will rely on a single source for retrieval of information, for example, as an information broker, do they have subscriptions or access to the various computer data bases needed to provide you with the requested information, or will they be subcontracting part of the service to another agency with access to a specific data base? If the vendor you choose needs to subcontract part of your search, there may be additional charges you should be apprised of at the time you order the search.

UCC search—You may be ordering a specific search such as Uniform Commercial Code (UCC) filings. However, there are many aspects to a UCC search. Make certain that the vendor you are choosing has access to all UCC data bases—UCC 1 Financing Statements, UCC 2 Change Statements, UCC 3 Request for Information, and UCC Microfiche.

Data base searches—You may be searching for specific information, but not be aware of all of the public records you should search to retrieve that information. Ask your vendor to list those specific data bases that are included in their regular routine search. (See listing of the most common data bases at § **2.66.**)

Depending upon the nature of your request, a minimum search should include:

_____ Department of Motor Vehicle records relating to driving records, vehicle registration, and history of vehicle, accident reports, financial responsibility reports, and motor vehicle dealership division search

_____ Secretary of State corporation records, corporate name reservation records, status certificates, merger and reinstatement document search, limited partnership records relating to name reservations, status, and abandonment of name

_____ Franchise Tax Board search for letter of status and tax clearance certificates

_____ Commissioner of Corporation for issuance of stock statements

_____ Department of Housing for motor vehicle ownership

_____ Department of Consumer Affairs for those occupations requiring licenses. (See § 2.57 for a partial listing of those professionals required to be licensed.)

_____ Department of Real Estate for license status and history

_____ Department of Vital Statistics for birth, death, and marriage certificates. (See § 2.58.)

_____ SEC documents. (See § 2.62 for listing of documents.)

_____ State Board of Equalization for information on business sales and use tax paid by a particular entity

Selection of a vendor is frequently based on rapport between the legal assistant and client representative. You need to work with a client representative who understands your need for information. You need to know that searches will be performed expeditiously and cost-efficiently. You need to have a client representative who will keep you informed at each step of a search with a time and billing figure, so that you can understand the process and also decide when to discontinue a search when the expense incurred outweighs the value you will receive from the information.

Many services offer a courtesy fax of results without additional charge. This is an important selling point for public records service agencies, and one which is extremely popular with those attorneys who wanted their results yesterday. Ask what you will be receiving if you request rush service. Compare the time difference between rush service and routine service. You will be amazed at how little difference there may be. If you request rush service, expect that you will be charged extra, and ask precisely what that charge is before agreeing to the service. Remember, you are dealing with public agencies who observe all state and national holidays. It is not cost-efficient or wise to request rush service close to a weekend or a holiday. Your vendor may be ready and willing to perform the search but be unable to do so because of closed offices.

Official paper at all levels of the government has become more cumbersome and complex as we have progressed into the information age. The money spent hiring a public records search agency may well be the wisest investment made by a law firm for investigation and discovery. A reputable public service record search agency can provide you with the most comprehensive information most expediently, saving attorney and legal assistant time and client money. An additional benefit of using a vendor is protection against costly discovery mistakes, or incomplete investigation which may lead to potential malpractice claims or dismissal of your case.

§ 2.76 Requesting Documents under the FOIA

Information available under the FOIA applies only to documents held by the administrative agencies of the executive branch of the federal government. It does not apply to information maintained by the legislative or judicial branches. The executive branch of the government includes executive departments and offices, military

INFORMAL DISCOVERY

departments, government corporations, government controlled corporations, and independent regulatory agencies. All records in possession of these entities must be released upon proper formal request unless the information falls within one of the specifically and narrowly drawn exceptions.

The FOIA grants public access to final opinions and orders of agencies, policy statements and interpretations that are not published in the federal register, administrative staff manuals, and government records that may effect the public.

The records requested should be identified as accurately as possible. Although it is not required under FOIA that a document be specified by name or a title, requests must reasonably describe the information sought. The more specific and limited the request, the greater the likelihood it will be processed expeditiously resulting in a savings of cost and search fees.

When requesting documents under FOIA, it is not necessary that the individual seeking information demonstrate a need, or even a reason, for wanting the information, although in some instances the probability of getting the desired information may be enhanced by explaining the reason for requesting it. Agency officials have discretionary power to release files even when the law does not require it, and they may be more inclined to disclose information that could be withheld if they understand the use to which it is to be put.

Before formally requesting records under FOIA in a written form, it is useful to call the agency directly and make personal contact. Most public libraries have copies of the Washington, D.C. telephone book and more importantly a copy of the *Federal Yellow Book*. The *Federal Yellow Book* lists phone numbers for each governmental agency. By telephoning the federal agency directly, you can obtain information as to exactly what records are maintained in that agency and how to properly request them. Certain agencies are less busy than others, and you may be pleasantly surprised by the amount of information you are able to obtain by telephone contact; however, a telephone call should always be followed up with an official FOIA request letter. A sample FOIA request letter is illustrated in **Form 2–9.**

FORM 2–9
SAMPLE FOIA REQUEST LETTER

Custodian of Records
[bank name] Bank
[address]

RE: Freedom of Information Act Request

Dear Custodian of Records:

We hereby request disclosure of copies of materials available from your agency under the Freedom of Information Act 5, U.S.C. § 552 et. seq., described as follows:

1. Each document which relates to [bank] docket number [number].

2. Each document which evidences, refers, constitutes, or relates to form [number] filed with [bank name] Board, [city] office, by [name] Savings & Loan Association for the years [years involved].

We believe that all of the described documents will be found in your [city] office and/or your [city] office.

Under applicable law pertaining to the Freedom of Information Act, we believe that these documents are available to us and other members of the public. If any portion of this request is denied, we request a detailed statement of the reasons for the withholding and an index or similar statement of the nature of the documents withheld pursuant to the Freedom of Information Act. In accordance with the Act, we agree to pay reasonable charges incurred for the copying of these documents, upon presentation of an invoice, along with the finished documents. (If search and copying fees exceed $200.00, please telephone in advance at [telephone number].)

I look forward to hearing from you within the ten (10) days statutory period within which your agency must respond to this request.

Thank you for your anticipated cooperation in this matter.

Very truly yours,

[name of attorney]

§ 2.77   Availability of Government Documents

There are many types of government documents that may be of interest to you depending upon the factual and legal issues in your particular case. The following list exemplifies some of the available documents.

1. Reports are compiled by the Department of Health and Human Services concerning conditions of federally supported nursing homes as well as all federally supported health care facilities.
2. Data is collected by the Agricultural Department regarding the purity and quality of meat and poultry products and the harmful effects of pesticides and other toxics.
3. Records are available from regulatory agencies concerning such matters as air pollution control programs, safety records of airlines, safety investigation reports, and so forth.
4. Test results are maintained by departments and agencies on those products and services which fall into their specific category and can be quite useful. Examples include the nutritional content of processed foods, the effectiveness of drugs, the safety and efficiency of all makes of automobiles, television sets, and so forth.

5. The Bureau of Consumer Affairs and the Federal Trade Commission are good sources for consumer complaints regarding corporate marketing practices, interstate moving companies, faulty products, and so forth.

6. The General Accounting Office (GAO) is a highly valuable and underutilized source. The GAO submits reports to Congress and acts as a general clearing house for material received from other federal regulatory agencies. There is a monthly list of GAO reports available in most public libraries and business and trade libraries. By consulting the monthly list of GAO reports, you may discover that a report has been made on a particular issue directly relevant to the factual or legal issues of your case. You may then request that specific GAO report by date, report number, number of pages, and so forth. Samples of GAO reports include tests on safety standards for aircraft, defects in bridge construction leading to bridge collapses, and alcohol and drug abuse in the transportation industry.

§ 2.78   Denial of FOIA Requests

Government agencies can refuse to disclose information that falls within one of the nine specified exception categories. The legislative history of the FOIA makes it clear that Congress did not intend for agencies to use these exempt categories to justify the automatic withholding of information. Rather, these exceptions are intended to designate those areas in which, under certain circumstances, information may be withheld. The general exceptions are as follows:

1. Classified documents concerning national defense and foreign policy. This refers to information that is classified as confidential, secret, and top secret under terms and procedures of a presidential order for classified documents.

2. Internal personnel rules and practices such as agency rules concerning employee behavior.

3. Information exemption under other laws permits the government to withhold information where other laws clearly require that it be withheld. Examples of this type of information include patent applications, income tax returns, and records regarding nuclear testing.

4. Confidential business information and trade secrets. Includes trade secret data, formulas, manufacturing plans, chemical compositions, corporate sales data, salaries and bonuses of industry personnel, and bids received by corporations in the course of acquisitions.

5. Internal communications applies to intraagency or interagency memoranda or letters which would not be available by law to a party other than the agency in litigation. The concern here is to protect communications of staff assistants and agency personnel during claim investigation and/or litigation.

6. Protection of privacy is an exemption which covers personnel and medical files and relates to records that contain details about the private lives of individuals. This is the only exception under the FOIA that allows the balancing of

interests between disclosure and nondisclosure and operates in much the same way as the state statutes dealing with confidential records.

7.   Investigatory files refers directly to investigatory records compiled for law enforcement purposes.

8.   Information concerning financial institutions is an exception which applies directly to those matters dealing with the examination, operation, or condition reports prepared by, on behalf of, or for the use of an agency responsible for the regulation and supervision of financial institutions. Specific records covered by this exception include investigatory reports of the federal reserve board concerning federal banks and documents prepared by the SEC commission regarding the New York Stock Exchange.

9.   Information concerning wells applies to geological and geophysical information and data including maps concerning wells.

All of these exceptions are referenced at 5 U.S.C. § 552 (b)(1) through (b)(9).

§ 2.79   Appeal Procedure

If a request for information is denied, a letter of appeal (see **Form 2–10**) should be sent to the person or office specified in the agency's reply. If for some reason this information is not provided, an appeal should be filed with the head of the agency. Enclose a copy of the rejection letter along with a copy of your original request and state as strong a case as possible for the right of the requester to obtain this information. Most agency regulations require that appeals be made within thirty (30) days after notification that a request is denied.

Federal agencies are required to respond to all requests for information within 10 working days after receipt of the request. If an agency runs into difficulty meeting the 10-day time requirement due to unusual circumstances or volume of information requested, it must inform the requester in writing that an extension not to exceed 10 more working days will be required. If an agency denies your request, that agency must set forth the reasons for the denial and advise to whom an appeal should be made within the agency. It also must give you the names, addresses, and job titles of those responsible for denying your request.

Agencies are required to publish annually in the federal register the existence and characteristics of their record keeping systems, including all records that have been exempted from access to the public. Agencies are also required to release records in a form that is comprehensible. This means that all computer codes and unintelligible notes must be translated into understandable language. All code systems must be disclosed to the extent necessary to decipher the documents. Records which are disclosed through FOIA requests must be accurate, relevant, up-to-date, and complete. Records withheld from a request must be identified by name, author, and date.

Responses from the federal agency that they "just do not have the time to gather this information for you and just do not have the personnel" are in most cases attempts to intimidate you. If the documents requested are public records and do not fall under one of the listed exceptions, you can look at them and you can request copies. If you are denied access to certain records, an appeal letter should be sent within the statutory time period. If your appeal is denied, an action can be filed in the U.S. District Court.

FORM 2–10
SAMPLE FOIA APPEAL LETTER

CERTIFIED MAIL
RETURN RECEIPT REQUESTED

Custodian of Records
[bank name] Bank Board
[address]

ATTENTION: [name]
                        Chief Department Head

Dear [name of department head]:

   This is to advise you I have been denied access to the records contained in your office, specifically those documents which relate to [bank] docket number [number] and those documents which relate to form [number] filed with the [bank] in [city] by [name] Savings & Loan Association for the years [years involved].

   Attached hereto is a copy of the letter which we have received from [name] of your office. We can see no reason why our request was denied. You will note that [name] cites no reasons in the letter. I have also included a copy of our original Federal Freedom of Information Act request letter, and call your attention to the third paragraph wherein we state "if any portion of this request is denied, we request a detailed statement of the reasons for the withholding and an index or similar statement of the nature of the documents withheld . . . ."

   I trust that upon your investigation of this matter you will conclude that the information I am seeking should be disclosed.

   As provided for in the Federal Freedom of Information Act, I will expect a reply from your office within twenty (20) days. Please be advised that if this appeal is not answered or if the information is not released, we will file an action in the U.S. District Court. We hope this legal action can be avoided.

   If you have any further questions in this connection or wish to discuss the matter, please feel free to contact our office.

                                        Very truly yours,

                                        [name of attorney]

Enclosures

Note: Enclosures include the original Federal Freedom of Information Act request letter and the denial letter.

§ 2.80   Commercial or Personal FOIA Requests

A FOIA request may be either commercial or personal. A commercial request which deals with general information on a particular topic is the most frequent. A personal request deals with a specific person or a specific piece of property. It is similar to a request for consumer records. There is no charge to the requesting party for obtaining personal records if the request is accompanied with a proper release. The sample case study in **Chapter 4** deals with a situation where personal FOIA requests were extremely useful. A sample release for personal FOIA information, tailored to the specific facts outlined in the flood case in **Chapter 4** would read as follows:

FORM 2–11
SAMPLE RELEASE

I, [name], hereby authorize the Federal Emergency Management Act to release any and all documents regarding flood insurance issues relating to the property located at [address], [city], [state], to my attorney at law, [name].

Executed on the [date] day of [month], [year] , in [city], [state].

_____

[name], Authorized Person,
Property Owner of the Parcel
Described Herein

§ 2.81   Product Recalls

In litigation involving causes of action for product liability, breach of express or implied warranty or design defect, information on product recalls is extremely useful as a tool for investigating a manufacturer, company, and product. Information on recalls by specific companies is usually published in newspapers of general circulation and occasionally broadcast by the radio and television media. To obtain more precise information on product recalls, contact the following agencies:

1.   Consumer Product Safety Commission (CPSC), (800) 683-CPSC.
2.   National Highway Traffic Safety Administration (NHTSA), (800) 424-9393.
3.   Food and Drug Administration (FDA), (301) 443-3170.

These agencies can provide you with information regarding consumer complaints on specific products in addition to recall information. Information regarding a recall (total recall or partial recall, involving only certain models) will be sent upon written request. Frequently, the NHTSA announces a recall of a particular vehicle that does not affect all models. For example, a recall was announced by the NHTSA of the 1984 to 1988 Pontiac Fiero due to defective engine design. This recall did not affect any other vehicles manufactured by Pontiac for the same years.

CHAPTER 3

DEPOSITIONS

§ 3.1   Introduction

A deposition is sworn testimony given by a party in an action or a witness to an action as a means of preserving that testimony prior to trial. Of all the major discovery devices, depositions are the only ones to provide a face-to-face encounter between the parties and their counsel. Depositions have become such an important method for discovering facts, evidence, and legal contentions that not to take the deposition of a party in an action comes close to being a cause for legal malpractice. Depositions enable opposing counsel to meet and size up the client and/or opposing party before trial.

Unlike other discovery devices, which can only be directed to parties in an action, depositions can be taken of parties and nonparties including custodians of records of disinterested third parties, for example, banks, title companies, hospitals, medical laboratories, and so forth. Depositions enable you to gather information and facts including testimony to be offered at trial by the opposing party and hostile witnesses. Questioning at depositions will often reveal not only the nature of alleged claims but also sources of documentation to support those claims. Likewise, a deposition may reveal weaknesses in opposing parties' claims or defenses enabling a defendant or a plaintiff to successfully negotiate an early settlement.

Depositions may force the adversary to better prepare. They can also trigger counterdepositions. Depositions educate witnesses because they learn about the process of testifying as well as what to say or not say at time of trial. Information obtained through an oral deposition is limited to the knowledge of the witness as opposed to interrogatories, which require information that is also known to the attorney.

The primary disadvantage of depositions is that they are expensive, both in terms of out-of-pocket expense and attorney time spent preparing for and taking a deposition. Depositions scheduled too early in the case may also be disadvantageous because other discovery has not been conducted to obtain as much information as possible prior to depositions. For instance, interrogatories or document productions should be considered for purposes of accumulating as much information as you can prior to depositions. The attorney will then be better prepared with background information with which to depose a particular party or percipient witness.

Depositions can be categorized into several major types. Reviewing the pleadings, documents, photographs, and all prior discovery will help you not only to determine what kind of deposition will be the most useful, but also to design questions which will elicit the needed information without raising objections as to form and content from the opposing counsel. The major types of depositions are discovery, evidence, document, expert, admissions, and assessment.

§ 3.2   Discovery Depositions

This is the most common type of deposition and consists of carefully designed, rambling, open-ended questions to find out everything a given witness may know about any of the underlying facts and/or evidence in a case. Preparation of questions for this type of deposition requires a thorough knowledge of all documents and facts in a case, so the deponent may be questioned on any documents that they may have authored, been copied on, or mentioned in context, as well as any facts that may be within their personal knowledge.

In a discovery deposition it is important to ask the deponent personal background questions, such as name, address, whether they have given previous depositions, and whether they have given a statement before in connection with this lawsuit. In a personal injury case, ask the deponent questions such as:

1. Describe your activities immediately before the accident, and at the time of the accident.
2. Where were you at the time of the accident?
3. When did you first come upon the accident scene?
4. What did you immediately see?
5. Who did you speak to at the accident scene?
6. Who did you observe at the accident scene?
7. What time of day was it?
8. What was the weather condition?
9. When did you leave the scene of the accident?
10. Where did you go immediately after leaving the scene of the accident? and
11. When did you first communicate with any of the parties involved in the accident?

If the witness authored any documents, ask all standard investigative questions regarding these documents using the guidelines of investigative news reporters—who, what, why, when, where, and how. For example:

1. Who authored the final document and each draft?
2. When was the document authored? (This does not necessarily mean the date that appears on the document.)
3. Where were you when the document was created?
4. Why was the document created?
5. What was the purpose of the document?
6. How was the document created?
7. Was the document created after a series of conversations, conferences, discussions, brainstorming sessions, and so forth?
8. What is the content of the document?
9. How many drafts were created before the document was finalized? and
10. Who approved the final document?

This type of a deposition should conclude with open-ended questions asking the witness to tell you anything else the witness feels is important about this accident or lawsuit; anything they observed that you failed to ask questions about, but they feel would have a bearing on the facts of the accident. Questioning along these lines is often objected to as being irrelevant, that you are going on a fishing expedition. Strategically, the way around a fishing expedition objection is to ask the witness follow-up questions which will encourage them to go on past your answer, giving you other pertinent facts. Encourage the witness to continue a lengthy answer by commenting, "And what else do you know about that fact?"

§ 3.3   Evidence Depositions

This type of deposition consists of very tight questioning designed to elicit testimony that can be used at trial. Most often, an evidence deposition is taken of a percipient witness, or a hostile witness, in an attempt to perpetuate testimony and tie the deponent to one story or one set of facts. Questions for this type of deposition should be prepared in such a way that the same information can be obtained through alternative wording of the basic questions or through a series of questions on the same topic. Reframing the question at the deposition will be possible if sample questions are prepared in advance on sensitive issues. Foundation questions will prevent many relevancy objections.

As an example, consider this scenario. In a breach of contract action which was brought by an aunt and uncle who had leased farm land to their nephew and his wife for the purpose of growing Christmas trees, a dispute arose. The contract called for the nephew and his wife to plant Christmas trees, tend them, and have them ready for the selling season. In return for providing the services of planting and nurturing the growth of the Christmas trees, the nephew and his wife received free room and board in the ranch house which was attached to the Christmas tree farm. In addition to raising Christmas trees as they agreed to do under the terms of the contract, the nephew and his wife also grew marijuana. Once the aunt and the uncle learned of this deception they attempted to force the nephew and his wife off the property. A lawsuit ensued. Questioning in the deposition of the nephew and his wife centered on obtaining the evidence that they had breached the contract by planting marijuana along with the Christmas trees, thus using the land for an illegal purpose as well as not fulfilling their contractual obligations. See the following sample questions:

1. At any time prior to December 23, 19__, did you inform your aunt and uncle that Christmas trees had been planted and were growing?
2. At any time prior to that date, did you inform your aunt and uncle that in addition to the Christmas trees, a second substance was growing on the farm?
3. Were you at all times aware that growing marijuana was and is illegal?
4. Were you at all times aware that your aunt and uncle are personally opposed to the use of controlled substances?
5. Do you deny that marijuana grew on Joe's Christmas Tree Farm?
6. Did you plant marijuana along with Christmas trees on Joe's Christmas Tree Farm?
7. Do you know if anyone else planted marijuana on Joe's Christmas Tree Farm?
8. Were you at all times aware of the provisions of the contract?
9. Did you ever invite your aunt and uncle to visit the tree farm?
10. Did you ever offer any financial contribution to your aunt and uncle to compensate them for your use of the property?

11. Describe each crop you planted (all specifics of crops).

12. Who did the planting?

13. How many plantings were done? (All specifics.) and

14. Were you aware at any time that something other than Christmas trees was growing on the land?

Most questions on sensitive issues will not be answered upon instruction of counsel. It is important, however, that the questions are asked so that a record can be made by the reporter and the questions certified. Certified questions can later become the subject of a motion to compel answers to certified questions, which is discussed at a later point in this chapter. Any unanswered questions may be certified if a request is made by the attorney at the time the question is asked. Certification of unanswered deposition questions must be done by the court reporter at the time the deposition is taken so that it can become a part of the deposition transcript.

§ 3.4 Document Depositions

This type of deposition usually involves many exhibits which may consist of documents the deponent has authored, reviewed, been copied on, or transmitted to other parties in the action. The focus of this type of deposition is the documents, especially those the deponent has authored. Your involvement in a document deposition begins with organization of those documents to be considered as possible deposition exhibits. Documents that may be selected would include:

1. Any documents authored by the deponent

2. All handwritten notes or memos

3. Key documents (contracts, addenda, notices of acknowledgment, and so forth)

4. Logs (phone logs, job diaries, work-related logs, job site reports, and so forth)

In regard to handwritten notes or memos, sometimes you are not familiar with handwriting and it is difficult to select those handwritten notes and memos that have been authored by the deponent. If a handwritten note or memo is selected as a deposition exhibit for a documents deposition, and it turns out that the deponent has not authored that particular document, it may still be useful because they may be able to identify the handwriting. Once the handwriting has been identified, that particular handwritten note or memo can become an exhibit in the documents deposition of the person identified as the writer. Key documents such as those mentioned in the list should always be included when the deponent is a key party or corporate officer. Even though they may not have authored the particular document, in the chain of command of that particular business or corporation, they should be, and usually are, familiar with the contents of the document and may be responsible for the policy contained therein. Phone logs should be chosen as deposition exhibits when the phone messages are directed to or from a party or key player. The guidelines for selection of documents in a document deposition should always be the main issues of the case. As a legal assistant, you can familiarize yourself with the issues in the case by reading the pleadings on file as well as checking the file of client documents, and through conversations with the client.

§ 3.5   —Organization and Selection of Exhibits

Organization of documents for a documents deposition should always be chronological. This gives you a time line which will be valuable throughout the entire course of the pending action. Documents may be organized by specific issue, allegations, or affirmative defense, maintaining chronological order within each subsection.

Once deposition exhibits have been selected, prepare the appropriate number of clean copies of each exhibit, and one extra copy of each exhibit that will be marked up with all important sections highlighted and annotated for use by the attorney conducting the deposition. Clean copies of each exhibit will go to the opposing counsel, the court reporter, and the deponent. Preparing these in advance will enable the deposition to move along smoothly and will also ensure that documents are not misplaced, overlooked, or taken out of sequence. Documents to be used as exhibits at a deposition should also be marked with an identification number such as a Bates stamp, so that the document will acquire a unique identity of its own and not be confused with any similar documents.

In a case when there will be numerous document depositions, it is advisable to number the exhibits sequentially throughout the course of all depositions. For example: Mary Smith, Deposition Exhibits 1 through 51; John Smith, Deposition Exhibits 52 through 85; Susie Smith, Deposition Exhibits 86 through 120, etc. Sequential numbers in this fashion will eliminate the problem of two deposition exhibits numbered 21, or 42. Exhibits from depositions taken early in the case can be used in later depositions and are then identified as Exhibit 14—Mary Smith, and so forth. This type of document control of deposition exhibits enables you to follow a corporate chain of command as well as a chronological time line of issues in the case. Important issues always leave a document trail and that type of evidence is best presented in court through carefully marked deposition exhibits.

§ 3.6   Expert Depositions

This type of deposition can be combined with an evidence a a document deposition; however, the main purpose of an expert deposition is to have the expert explain the documents they have reviewed, the hypotheticals they have used, and all materials they have relied on in preparing their report, as well as the conclusions they have reached in the area upon which they will testify at trial. Ask questions of the expert which will clarify the opinions and/or conclusions that the expert has reached as well as the results of any tests or experiments the expert has performed. Have the expert explain all technical terms in common language so that there can be no misunderstanding as to the expert's opinion. The expert should always be asked if the witness plans to conduct any further investigation or modify the report in any way between the time of deposition and trial. If the expert states that the report is only preliminary and the expert does anticipate further work before trial, stipulations between counsel to redepose the expert should be placed on the transcript to prevent surprises at trial.

Shortly after noticing the deposition of an expert, contact opposing counsel and ask for a copy of the expert's resume or curriculum vitae. Obtaining this information beforehand will enable your attorney to plan questioning at the expert's deposition. It should also reduce the number of deposition questions designed to elicit qualifying information such as educational and work experience, prior expert testimony, and so forth. All of this background information is usually contained in the resume enabling the attorney to focus the expert deposition on the key points of the case and of the expert's testimony and avoiding the unnecessary delay and expense of questioning about background, education, and so forth.

An additional value in obtaining a resume prior to an expert deposition is that it provides material such as a publications list which enables you to research the expert prior to the deposition. Valuable information can be obtained by reviewing articles written by the expert on issues that relate to your case. Experts can also be questioned about articles they have written. This is often the most advantageous method of questioning an expert who usually is more than willing to discuss and explain opinions expressed in articles that the expert has written.

§ 3.7 Admissions Depositions

An admissions deposition is similar to an evidence deposition, but it usually has a narrower focus. It is primarily used when the facts and evidence in a given case have pointed to the likelihood of an admission of liability. Because admissions depositions are often used at summary judgment hearings, the questioning is extremely tight and restricted to a single subject. This type of deposition is generally very brief. Effective uses of an admissions deposition are in collection cases, breach of promissory notes, unlawful detainers, breach of leases (equipment, commercial space, and so forth) to name a few.

§ 3.8 Assessment Depositions

This type of deposition is usually taken as a discovery-type deposition to find out exactly how much a witness knows about a given subject. For example, someone may have been a witness to an accident and given a statement to the investigating officer at the time of the accident indicating that they could contribute a specific point of evidence. A deposition of this type of witness will attempt to elicit exactly what that person does know. Another use of the assessment-type deposition is in business litigation where all members of a board of directors attend various meetings and sign various letters and key business documents. In this particular instance, an assessment deposition will attempt to pinpoint those members of the board of directors with the most involvement in a particular issue. It will also explain how information is disseminated in a business or corporation—if it is on a need-to-know basis or if all members of a board of directors have equal access to information.

§ 3.9 Procedural Checklist for Depositions

This checklist can help you plan how to approach depositions.

1. Oral deposition of party or party-related witness:

Deposing Party

_____ Serve deposition notice on all parties (Include notice of intent to audio or video tape)

Party Served

_____ Serve written objections to notice

_____ Serve notice of intent to video or audio tape

_____ Move to quash notice or for protective order

_____ Attend and testify or examine witness

Any Other Affected Person

_____ Move for protective order

2. Oral deposition of nonparty (see also Item 4):

Deposing Party

_____ Serve on deponent: copy of subpoena, witness fees, and mileage

_____ Serve on all parties: copy of deposition notice and subpoena

_____ Retain original subpoena and proof of service

Nonparty Deponent

_____ Move to quash subpoena or for protective order

_____ Attend and testify, collect unpaid fees, and demand payment for any records

Other Party

_____ Move to quash subpoena or notice or for protective order

_____ Serve objections to notice

_____ Serve notice of any intent to video or audio tape

_____ Move for protective order

_____ Attend and examine witness

Any Other Affected Person

_____ Move for protective order

3. Deposition for production of business records (no appearance required) (see also Item 4):

Deposing Party

_____ Serve deposition subpoena on custodian of records and on all parties

Deponent

_____ Move to quash subpoena or for protective order

_____ Deliver to deposition officer: copies or originals of records, custodian's declaration, and statement of any copying or retrieval cost, or

_____ Deliver to attorney or attorney's representative: originals for copying, declaration, if required, and statement of any costs paid to third person for retrieval off-site or of microfilm

Other Party

_____ Move to quash subpoena or for protective order

_____ Request copies of records from deposition officer

Other Affected Person

_____ Move for protective order

4. Deposition for production of consumer records:

Deposing Party

_____ Serve on consumer: copy of subpoena, notice of privacy rights, and deposition notice

_____ Serve on witness: proof that consumer served with privacy notice or consumer's written records' release; subpoena (see Items 2 and 3)

Consumer

_____ Move to quash or modify subpoena or for protective order

Other Party

_____ Move to quash or modify subpoena or for protective order

Deponent

_____ Move to quash or modify subpoena or for protective order

_____ Comply with subpoena: produce records and testify, if required

§ 3.10 Deposition Notices

A deposition may be noticed by any party in an action without leave of court. Notice requirements differ slightly for state and federal courts. In federal court, according to Federal Rule of Civil Procedure § 45(d), reasonable notice must be given in writing to every other party in the action. There is no definition of reasonable notice, so the number of days required for notice is left up to the attorneys of record and parties in the action. In some state courts (for example, California), ten days formal written notice must be given plus additional time for distance according to local statutes. In both state and federal courts, depositions can also be taken by stipulation between counsel. The requirement of reasonable time and/or ten days is not a consideration.

Depositions can be scheduled and set by notice for parties and by subpoena for nonparties. In California, a deposition notice must be served upon a party to an action 10 days by hand and 15 days by mail before the date you wish to take the deposition. The dates and times of depositions may be continued once notice has been served. This continuance is usually by attorney stipulation or agreement. All continuances of depositions should be memorialized in a letter, just as all discovery continuances should be. This preserves the attorney's right to take that deposition in the order and sequence which the attorney has determined is most beneficial to the client's case. (See sample letter following § 3.15.)

A deposition of a nonparty requires a deposition subpoena and has different procedural requirements than a deposition of a party. A party may be deposed on notice only, and may also be required to bring documents with them to the deposition; however, a nonparty being deposed must be subpoenaed. In federal court, a subpoena must be issued by the court, and not by the attorney of record.

§ 3.11   Procedure for Issuance of a Federal Court Subpoena

If you need a federal court subpoena, you must:

1. Use the proper form—a deposition subpoena;
2. Have a notice of deposition, with proof of service attached, accompanying the deposition subpoena before the court will issue the subpoena; and
3. Serve the deponent personally once the deposition subpoena is issued. You have a choice of hand or mail service for all other parties in the action.

 ## § 3.12   Preparation of a Federal Court Deposition Notice

If the deposition notice requires a subpoena (as in the case of a nonparty witness), follow the steps outlined in § 3.11 and obtain a form deposition subpoena from the U.S. District Court in your jurisdiction. Prepare the subpoena along with a deposition notice and proof of service. Take the notice and proof of service to the court so that the court will issue the subpoena.

After the subpoena is issued, send it to a process server for service. Prepare instructions for the process server which include:

full name of deponent (also nicknames)

home and business address

home and business phone numbers

phone numbers, addresses, and names of neighbors and businesses located next to deponent's residence and business location.

It is also helpful to include any other information you may have. For example, if the witness is hostile, the process server should be forewarned. If any other information is known about the witness which will enable the process server to identify the person being served, it is wise to include that information. For example, you may have a physical description of the deponent (which you have obtained from your client) or a photograph. You may know other information about the witness such as the license plate of the vehicle, the witness' work hours, or information on the witness' personal habits. All of this information should be given to the process server to enable the process server to effect service quickly and efficiently.

Once the process server returns the original proof of service to your office, file the original subpoena and original proof of service with the court. Unlike state courts, which differ in their filing requirements, federal courts require the return of an original subpoena and original proof of service for filing. Once you have filed it with the court, retain a conformed copy in your files.

Preparation of a federal court subpoena for a nonparty whose residence, or place of business, is not within the federal district where the case is pending, is a bit more complicated. For the preparation of this type of a subpoena, follow the same procedural steps as outlined in § **3.11** with the following additions:

1. Fill in the name of the district court where the deponent resides in your preparation of the subpoena. For example, if you have a case pending in Nevada but the person to be subpoenaed lives in Seattle, the subpoena must be prepared for issuance out of the U.S. District Court in Washington, because that is where personal jurisdiction for the deponent flows.

2. Prepare and file a notice of deposition and a proof of service noting that the deposition will take place in Reno, Nevada. The original notice of deposition and proof of service will be filed in the jurisdiction where the case is pending.

3. Certify the notice of deposition and proof of service because the court issuing the subpoena may require a certified rather than a conformed copy. For example, the District Court of Nevada will certify your deposition notice and original proof of service for a fee. Check fee schedules.

4. Send the conformed copy of the notice of deposition and proof of service, plus the original subpoena to the district where the witness is located.

The prepared subpoena will be issued by the district court with jurisdiction over the witness. That subpoena may then be served following the same procedures for preparation of a federal court subpoena.

§ 3.13   Preparation of a Deposition Notice for State Court

When preparing a deposition notice for state court, it is important to:

1. Obtain the full name and address of the witness, and of the witness' attorney if the witness is not a party. Your attorney should also furnish you with work and home phone numbers whenever possible to facilitate service on the deponent. Note that you need a street address and not a post office box, since it is impossible to effect personal service on a post office box.

2. Determine the date, time, and location of the deposition. Secure a room for the deposition, and a court reporter.

3. Calendar not only the date of the deposition, but several other important dates such as the date the subpoena is sent out for service to the process server, the date the conformed process of of service is returned to your office, and the date you send the original subpoena with original proof of service to the court. Note that some state courts will no longer accept a subpoena for filing. Check local rules before sending an original subpoena and original proof of service to the court.

4.   Note on the deposition notice whether it is a videotaped deposition. In some states, a videotaped deposition must be noted as such on the deposition notice. The party being deposed must be forewarned that their deposition will be videotaped to allow them time to object within the statutory time period prior to the deposition. If no objection to videotaping is filed within a reasonable time after service of the deposition notice, you may proceed with the videotaping. Check local rules governing videotaped depositions before preparing the deposition notice.

Preparation of a deposition notice for federal and/or state court is a procedure done frequently by legal assistants. If you are unfamiliar with preparing deposition notices, you will find the clerks in most courts will be helpful in assisting you with procedural guidelines and steps. **Forms 3–1** and **3–2** illustrate two different types of deposition notices for state court purposes.

§ 3.14   Sample State Court Deposition Notices

FORM 3–1
SAMPLE STATE COURT DEPOSITION NOTICE

[attorney for plaintiff]
[address]
[telephone number]

Attorneys for Plaintiff
[plaintiff]

SUPERIOR COURT OF THE STATE OF [state name]

IN AND FOR THE COUNTY OF [county name]

[plaintiff],	No. [case number]
Plaintiff,	NOTICE OF
	TAKING DEPOSITION
vs.	
[defendant A] and [defendant B],	
Defendants.	

_____/

TO: DEFENDANT, [A], AND TO THE ATTORNEY OF RECORD:

PLEASE TAKE NOTICE that at [time] on the [date] day of [month], [year], at the Offices of [plaintiff's attorney], [address], [city, state], Plaintiff, [name], will take the deposition of Defendant, [A], whose address is known to [defendant A]'s attorneys, upon oral examination before a Notary Public authorized to administer oaths in the State of [state name] pursuant to [code section] of the [state] Code of Civil Procedure. Said deposition shall continue from time-to-time, and day-to-day (exception Sundays and Holidays), until completed.

Dated: [date].

LAW OFFICES OF [attorney for plaintiff]

By: _____

[name]
Attorney for Plaintiff
[plaintiff name]

Be certain to check your local state court rules of Codes of Civil Procedure regarding time requirements for hand service and service by mail for a Notice of Taking Deposition. Also be aware that should your Notice of Deposition include the production of documents, **Form 3–1** will not suffice. Additional time is required when documents are requested to be produced at a deposition.

As an example, the Notice of Taking Deposition and Production of Records is authorized by statute in California pursuant to Code of Civil Procedure § 2025(d)(4). (Check your local state statutes and local court rules for applicable statutes governing this procedure.) California Code of Civil Procedure § 2025(d) is an example of the coordinated use of discovery use. This procedure allows a party to notice a deposition of any other party or witness, and at the same time require the deponent to produce documents at the deposition. This procedure enables the attorney taking the deposition to ask the deponent questions regarding the documents, eliciting explanation of their contents at the time of the deposition.

The Sample Notice of Taking Deposition and Production of Records in **Form 3–2** was used in a situation where defendants were corporations and small businesses. When the deponent named is not a natural person, it is permissible pursuant to statute in California (as well as in many other states) to place the burden upon defendant to designate that person most knowledgeable and qualified to testify regarding a specific subject matter. The burden is on the party noticing the deposition to describe those matters on which the deposition examination will be based with as much particularity as possible. The noticed party must then designate and produce those persons within their organization or business most qualified to testify on their behalf based on the extent of information known or reasonably available on those matters designated in the deposition notice.

The sample Notice of Taking Deposition and Production of Records in **Form 3–2** was used in a personal injury action which occurred on a stairway in a shopping mall.

FORM 3–2
SAMPLE STATE COURT DEPOSITION NOTICE
REQUESTING DOCUMENTS

[attorney for plaintiff]
[address]
[telephone number]

Attorneys for Plaintiff
[plaintiff name]

IN THE SUPERIOR COURT OF THE STATE OF [state name]

IN THE CITY AND COUNTY OF [name]

[name],
 	
          Plaintiff,
 	
vs.
 	
[name] SHOPPING MALL, A
LIMITED PARTNERSHIP,
[defendant A] and
[defendant B], as limited partners
of [name] SHOPPING MALL,
[defendant C], individually
and (dba) [business D],
and (dba) [business E],
and DOES 1 through 30,
inclusive,
 	
          Defendants.
_____/
	No. [case number]
	
	NOTICE OF TAKING
	DEPOSITION AND
	PRODUCTION OF RECORDS
	[state code]

TO: DEFENDANT, [name] SHOPPING MALL, A LIMITED PARTNERSHIP, AND TO ITS ATTORNEYS AND TO ALL OTHER PARTIES HEREIN:

PLEASE TAKE NOTICE that, pursuant to [state] Code of Civil Procedure [code section], Plaintiff [name] will take the following depositions on the dates designated at the Office of [plaintiff's attorney], [address], [city], [state], before a duly qualified Notary Public.

Pursuant to [state] Code of Civil Procedure [state code], defendant [name] SHOPPING MALL, a limited partnership, is requested to designate that person "most qualified" to testify on its having knowledge of the matters inquired of in the following categories:

(1) That person most knowledgeable regarding the construction and design of the steps where the accident complained of in this action occurred on [day], [date], [year], at [time].

(2) That person most knowledgeable regarding the maintenance and repair of the stairs at [name] SHOPPING MALL where the accident complained of in this action occurred on [day], [date], [year], at [time].

(3) That person designated by defendant as the individual responsible for safety practices, policies, and procedures for [name] SHOPPING MALL that were in effect on [date], on [day], [date], [year], at [time].

Pursuant to the provisions of [state] Code of Civil Procedure [code section], defendant is requested to produce the records described in Attachment A at the time of these noticed depositions.

Dated: [date].

LAW OFFICES OF [plaintiff's attorney]

By: _____
[name]
Attorney for Plaintiff
[plaintiff's name]

ATTACHMENT A

1. Each writing pertaining to maintenance of the stairway at [name] SHOPPING MALL in [city], [state], where plaintiff [name] fell on [date].

2. Each writing pertaining to safety inspections authored by any person who had safety or maintenance responsibility for the stairway at the [name] Shopping Mall.

3. Each writing pertaining to any deficiency and/or unsafe condition noted by any individual conducting a safety inspection on behalf of defendant [name] SHOPPING MALL for the stairways at [name] SHOPPING MALL in [city], [state].

4. Each writing setting forth change(s), modification(s), or corrective measure(s) taken by defendant [name] SHOPPING MALL to remedy any deficiency or unsafe condition noted on the stairways at [name] SHOPPING MALL in [city], [state], including the stairway wherein plaintiff [name] fell on [date].

5. Each writing setting forth the maintenance duties of each person employed by defendant [name] SHOPPING MALL who was responsible for the maintenance of the stairways.

6. Each writing pertaining to the investigation of the accident of [date], including, but not limited to, Report Number [number], prepared by an [name] SHOPPING MALL security guard at approximately [time] on [date].

7. Each and every statement and/or other writing taken by any representative of defendant [name] SHOPPING MALL from plaintiff [name].

Federal Rules of Civil Procedure 30(6) also require a corporate or business defendant to identify and produce that person most knowledgeable to testify on particular matters. To notice a deposition with documents in federal court, notice must be served pursuant to Federal Rule of Civil Procedure 30(5) coordinated with Federal Rule of Civil Procedure 34, document production procedures. A party noticing a deposition in federal court and joining a request for production of documents to that notice must give a minimum of 30 days notice and must cite Rule 34(b).

§ 3.15 Sample State Court Deposition Notice to a Nonparty

Deposition notices to nonparties always require a subpoena. The Judicial Council for the State of California has prepared a form deposition subpoena which includes the options of personal appearance alone or personal appearance with production of documents and things. Your state most likely has a comparable form. In order to subpoena the deposition of a nonparty with a subpoena combined with the production of documents, **Form 3–3,** tailored for use in California, may be modified for use in your state.

FORM 3–3
SAMPLE STATE COURT DEPOSITION NOTICE TO A NONPARTY

[attorney for defendant]
[address]
[phone number]

Attorneys for Defendant
[name] SHOPPING MALL

SUPERIOR COURT OF THE STATE OF [state]

IN THE CITY AND COUNTY OF [city]

[name],	No. [case number]
Plaintiff,	NOTICE OF TAKING DEPOSITIONS
vs.	
[name] SHOPPING MALL, A LIMITED PARTNERSHIP,	

[defendant A] and
[defendant B], as limited partners
of [name] SHOPPING MALL,
[defendant C], individually
and (dba) [business D],
and (dba) [business E],
and DOES 1 through 30,
inclusive,

     Defendants.

_____/

    TO ALL PARTIES AND THEIR ATTORNEYS OF RECORD:

    PLEASE TAKE NOTICE that, pursuant to [state] Code of Civil Procedure [code section], defendant [name] SHOPPING MALL will take the following listed depositions. The depositions will take place at the Offices of [plaintiff's attorney], [address], [city], [state], on the dates and times listed below:

Deponent	Date	Time
[name]	[date]	[time]

    The depositions will be taken on oral examination before a Notary Public authorized to administer oaths in the State of [state name] pursuant to [code section] of the [state] Code of Civil Procedure. Further, the depositions may be videotaped.

    Please take further notice that all the witnesses are required, under [state] Code of Civil Procedure [code sections], to bring all documents including notes, run reports, reports, evaluations, photographs and any other such items of tangible evidence concerning their response to the accident that occurred on [date] involving plaintiff [name].

    Dated: [date]

                        LAW OFFICES OF [attorney for defendant]

                        By: _____
                           [name]
                           Attorney for Defendant
                           [name] SHOPPING MALL

§ 3.16   Preparation of a California Judicial Council Deposition Subpoena Form

The California Judicial Council has prepared three official subpoena forms. One subpoena form is used exclusively for personal appearance at trial. The second subpoena form is a business records subpoena (no appearance necessary). The third form is the most commonly used deposition subpoena as it allows for both personal appearances and production of documents and things. That form (**Form 3–4**) is included for your easy reference.

The following guidelines will assist you in preparation of a deposition subpoena form:

1. 1(a) through (d) gives you several choices. If you wish documents along with the deponent, check box (b). If the deposition will be videotaped, check box (d). Thus, if you are requesting the deponent to appear with documents and the deposition will be videotaped, you will have checked both boxes (b) and (d).
2. Check box number 2 and box number 3 if you are requesting documents to be produced at the time of the deposition. Under number 3, itemize those documents that you wish. A list of documents may also be prepared separately as an Exhibit A to the subpoena. In that case you would check box number 3 and include the following language: "See attached Exhibit A for description of documents to be produced at the deposition of [name]."

§ 3.17   Depositions Taken Pursuant to Stipulation

A great majority of depositions are taken by stipulation rather than notice. Frequently, however, a friendly agreement to stipulate to the deposition of a particular person will become unfriendly as litigation proceeds. It is highly recommended that if counsel for both sides enter into a stipulation for taking a particular person's deposition (usually a party), that it be set down in written form and formalized. **Form 3–5** is an example of such a stipulation.

FORM 3–4
CALIFORNIA JUDICIAL COUNCIL DEPOSITION
SUBPOENA FORM

ATTORNEY OR PARTY WITHOUT ATTORNEY *(Name and Address):*	TELEPHONE NO.:	FOR COURT USE ONLY

NAME OF COURT:
STREET ADDRESS:
MAILING ADDRESS:
CITY AND ZIP CODE:
BRANCH NAME:

PLAINTIFF/PETITIONER:

DEFENDANT/RESPONDENT:

DEPOSITION SUBPENA **For Personal Appearance** ☐ **and Production of Documents and Things**	CASE NUMBER:

THE PEOPLE OF THE STATE OF CALIFORNIA, TO *(name, address, and telephone number of deponent, if known):*

1. **YOU ARE ORDERED TO APPEAR IN PERSON TO TESTIFY AS A WITNESS** in this action at the following time and place:

Date: Time: Address:

    a. ☐ As a deponent who is not a natural person, you are ordered to designate one or more persons to testify on your behalf as to the matters described in item 3. (Code of Civil Procedure section 2025(d)(6).)

    b. ☐ You are ordered to produce the documents and things described in item 3.

    c. ☐ This deposition will be recorded stenographically   and by ☐ audiotape ☐ videotape.

    d. ☐ This videotape deposition is intended for possible use at trial under Code of Civil Procedure section 2025(u)(4).

2. ☐ The **personal attendance** of the custodian of records or other qualified witness ☐ and the **production of the original documents** are required by this deposition subpena. The procedure authorized by Evidence Code sections 1560(b), 1561, and 1562 will not be deemed sufficient compliance with this subpena.

3. ☐ The **documents and things to be produced and any testing or sampling being sought are described as follows:**

    ☐ Continued on attachment 3.

4. *A deposition permits an attorney to ask questions of a witness who is sworn to tell the truth. An attorney for other parties may then ask questions also. Questions and answers are recorded stenographically at the deposition; later they are transcribed for possible use at trial. A witness may read the written record and change any incorrect answers before signing the deposition. The witness is entitled to receive witness fees and mileage actually traveled both ways. The money must be paid, at the option of the party giving notice of the deposition, either with service of this subpena or at the time of the deposition.*

DISOBEDIENCE OF THIS SUBPENA MAY BE PUNISHED AS CONTEMPT BY THIS COURT. YOU WILL ALSO BE LIABLE FOR THE SUM OF FIVE HUNDRED DOLLARS AND ALL DAMAGES RESULTING FROM YOUR FAILURE TO OBEY.

Date issued:

    ....
             (TYPE OR PRINT NAME)

▶

    _____
      (SIGNATURE OF PERSON ISSUING SUBPENA)

    _____
                (TITLE)

(See reverse for proof of service)

Form Adopted by Rule 982
Judicial Council of California
982(a)(15.1) [Rev. January 1, 1993]

DEPOSITION SUBPENA – PERSONAL APPEARANCE

Code of Civil Procedure, §§ 2020, 2025
Government Code § 68097.1

FORM 3–4 (continued)

PLAINTIFF/PETITIONER:	CASE NUMBER:
DEFENDANT/RESPONDENT:	

PROOF OF SERVICE OF DEPOSITION SUBPENA -- PERSONAL APPEARANCE

1. I served this Deposition Subpena — Personal Appearance by personally delivering a copy to the person served as follows:

   a. Person served *(name)*:

   b. Address where served:

   c. Date of delivery:

   d. Time of delivery:

   e. Witness fees and mileage both ways *(check one)*:
      (1) ☐ were paid. Amount: .... $ _____
      (2) ☐ were not paid.
      (3) ☐ were tendered to the witness's
           public entity employer as re-
           quired by Government Code
           section 68097.2. The amount
           tendered was (specify): .....$ _____

   f. Fee for service .... $ _____

2. I received this subpena for service on *(date)*:

3. Person serving:
   a. ☐ Not a registered California process server.
   b. ☐ California sheriff, marshal, or constable.
   c. ☐ Registered California process server.
   d. ☐ Employee or independent contractor of a registered California process server.
   e. ☐ Exempt from registration under Bus. & Prof. Code section 22350(b).
   f. ☐ Registered professional photocopier.
   g. ☐ Exempt from registration under Bus. & Prof. Code section 22451.
   h. Name, address, and telephone number and, if applicable, county of registration and number:

I declare under penalty of perjury under the laws of the State of California that the foregoing is true and correct.

Date:

▶ _____
(SIGNATURE)

(For California sheriff, marshal, or constable use only)
I certify that the foregoing is true and correct.

Date:

▶ _____
(SIGNATURE)

FORM 3–5
SAMPLE DEPOSITION STIPULATION

[attorney for plaintiff]
[address]
[telephone number]

Attorneys for Plaintiff
[plaintiff name]

SUPERIOR COURT OF THE STATE OF [state]
IN AND FOR THE CITY AND COUNTY OF [city]

[name],
 	
      Plaintiff,
 	
vs.
 	
[name] SHOPPING MALL, A
LIMITED PARTNERSHIP,
[defendant A] and [defendant B],
as limited partners of
[name] SHOPPING MALL,
[defendant C], individually
and (dba) [business D],
and (dba) [business E],
and DOES 1 through 30,
inclusive,
 	
      Defendants.
_____/
	Case No. [case number]
	
	STIPULATION FOR
	TAKING DEPOSITION

   IT IS HEREBY STIPULATED by the parties through their counsel, under [state] Code of Civil Procedure [code section], that [plaintiff/defendant], [name], will take the deposition on oral examination of [name of deponent] on [date(s) of deposition] at [time of deposition], at [address], and that further notice of the taking of the deposition and service thereof is waived.

   Dated: [date]

                             _____

                             [name]
                             Attorney for Plaintiff
                             [plaintiff name]

Dated: [date]

[name]
Attorney for Defendant
[name] SHOPPING MALL

§ 3.18   Witness Fees

Witness fees must always be offered to a nonparty deponent at the time a subpoena is served. A subpoena served without a witness fee may be invalid. Some deponents may refuse the fee, but cannot avoid honoring the subpoena if fees have been offered. The amount of witness fees varies from state court to federal court and must also include expenses for travel. The amount per mile again differs from state to federal court. A process server is the most knowledgeable person in the area of witness fees. If you are unsure of calculating witness fee mileage, remember that you must pay mileage from the witness' home to the place of the deposition, not round trip. Mileage figures are given out by the travel department of the American Automobile Association (AAA) to all members. If you or someone in your office is a member of AAA, simply phone them for information.

§ 3.19   Videotaped Depositions

Federal Rule of Civil Procedure 30(b)(4) provides that the recording of deposition testimony may be made by other than stenographic means such as mechanical, electronic, or photographic. Provision is made for parties to stipulate in writing, or indicate on the deposition notice, that the testimony shall be recorded "by other than stenographic means." Some state statutes, for example, California Civil Code of Procedure §§ 2025(l)(1)–(2) state that all depositions must be recorded stenographically, unless the parties agree by stipulation, or the court orders, otherwise. They do, however, provide for a simultaneous videotape or audiotape recording of a deposition in addition to the stenographic record. Before a videotaped deposition can proceed, a notice of deposition must be served on all parties to the action clearly stating the intention to record the testimony by audio or videotape. (See **Forms 3–6** through **3–8.**) The most common reason for a videotaped deposition is the deponent's expected unavailability at trial. (For example, when a deponent is seriously ill, or when an expert whose testimony is crucial to the action may not be available at time of trial.) It is difficult to hold a jury's attention while a deposition transcript is read at trial. A videotaped deposition is much more interesting for a jury and permits them not only to hear the actual testimony and the deponent's voice, but also to examine the demeanor of the deponent, which is an important factor in weighing credibility. In the case of experts, it is frequently impossible to arrange professional schedules to accommodate courtroom appearances. The fees charged by experts for courtroom appearances may be higher than fees for a videotaped deposition. (See **Chapter 7** at **§ 7.36** for a discussion of expert witness videotaped depositions.)

FORM 3–6
SAMPLE VIDEOTAPED DEPOSITION NOTICE

SUPERIOR COURT OF [state]
IN AND FOR THE COUNTY OF [county name]

[plaintiff name]	No. [case number]
Plaintiff,	NOTICE OF TAKING VIDEOTAPED DEPOSITION
-vs-	
[defendant name],	
Defendant.	
_____/	

TO: [name], attorney for [opposing party]:

NOTICE IS HEREBY GIVEN that on [date], at [time], in the law offices of [name of law firm], located at [address], [name of party] will take the deposition of [name of deponent] upon oral examination before a deposition reporter authorized by law to administer oaths, and such deposition to continue from time to time, and day to day until completed.

TAKE FURTHER NOTICE that this deposition will also be videotaped.

Dated: [date]

_____
Attorney for [name of party]

FORM 3–7
SAMPLE VIDEOTAPED DEPOSITION NOTICE (TRIAL EXPERT)

SUPERIOR COURT OF THE STATE OF [state]
IN AND FOR THE COUNTY OF [county]

[plaintiff name]	Case No. [case number]
Plaintiff,	NOTICE OF VIDEOTAPED DEPOSITION
-vs-	
[defendant name],	
Defendant.	
_____/	

To each party and to the attorney of record for each party in this action:

PLEASE TAKE NOTICE that on [date], at [time], at the offices of [name of law firm], located at [address], [plaintiff/defendant] will take the oral deposition of [deponent's name], whose address is [address], and whose telephone number is [telephone number]. This deposition will be taken before [name], a notary public, or other officer authorized to administer oaths, and will continue from day-to-day until completed.

The above-named deponent is [expert witness/treating physician/consulting physician]. The testimony taken during this deposition will be recorded both stenographically and by videotape. The deposing party reserves the right under (Federal Rule of Civil Procedure 30(B)(4), or [state code section], or any other state statute) to offer in evidence at the trial of this action the videotape of this deposition testimony in lieu of presenting the live testimony of the deponent expert.

Dated: [date]

_____
[name of attorney]
Attorney for [plaintiff/defendant]

FORM 3–8
SAMPLE VIDEOTAPED DEPOSITION NOTICE (WITH DOCUMENTS)

IN THE UNITED STATES DISTRICT COURT
FOR THE [judicial district] DISTRICT OF [state]
[name] DIVISION

[plaintiff]	§	
-vs.-	§	CIVIL ACTION NO. [case number]
[defendant]	§	

NOTICE OF ORAL DEPOSITION
(VIDEOTAPED)

TO: [name of attorney]
       [address of attorney]

Please take notice that at [time], on the [date] day of [month], [year], at the offices of [name of company] Court Reporters, [city], California, plaintiff in the above-styled and numbered cause will take the deposition of [name of deponent], defendant, and the witness is advised to bring with the witness at such deposition the following documents:

1. Any and all documents, papers, photographs, drawings, records, log books, memoranda, or other material relating to the aircraft which crashed on [date].

Please take notice that the deposition will be recorded by videotape in addition to the stenographic recording.

Dated: [date]

[attorney for plaintiff]

§ 3.20   Videotaped Deposition Procedures Checklist

The following procedures must be observed if a deposition is to be videotaped:

_____   1.   Testimony must also be recorded stenographically, unless the court orders otherwise.

_____   2.   The location for recording the deponent's oral testimony must be large, adequately lit, and reasonably quiet.

_____   3.   The video operator must be competent to set up, operate, and monitor the recording equipment, and must not use any camera or sound recording techniques that distort the appearance or demeanor of the participants.

_____   4.   The deposition must begin with a statement on the tape that includes the following:

      _____   The operator's name and address

      _____   The name and business address of the operator's employer

      _____   The date, time, and place of the deposition

      _____   The caption of the case

      _____   The name of the deponent

      _____   The name of the party taking the deposition

      _____   Any stipulations

      _____   A statement that this videotaped deposition is going forward with the permission and consent of all present

_____   5.   Counsel for each party must identify themselves on camera.

_____   6.   The oath must be administered to the deponent on camera or on audiotape.

_____   7.   If the deposition requires more than one unit of tape, the end of each unit and the beginning of each succeeding unit must be announced on camera. At that time the actual time must be stated for the record and memorialized through a camera shot of a clock on the wall or of someone's watch.

_____   8.   A statement must be made on camera that the deposition is ended, or that the unit of tape has ended, and that the deposition will be continuing on a second unit of tape.

_____ 9.   At the conclusion of the deposition, a statement must be made setting forth any stipulations concerning custody of the videotape recording, the exhibits, or all other pertinent matters.

_____ 10.   The videotape operator shall retain custody of the tape and store it under conditions that will protect it against loss, destruction, or tampering and preserve as far as practicable the quality of the tape and the integrity of the testimony and images it contains.

_____ 11.   The operator who has custody of a videotape record of deposition testimony shall retain custody of it until six months after final disposition of the action. At that time, the videotape may be destroyed or erased, unless the court, on motion of any party and for good cause shown, orders that the tape be preserved for a longer period of time.

_____ 12.   Videotaped depositions of experts may be used at trial even though the deponent may be available to testify, if the deposition notice reserves the right to use the deposition at trial in place of the live testimony of that expert.

The notice of deposition must explicitly state that the party noticing the deposition is reserving the right to use the videotaped testimony in lieu of the live testimony of the expert. The parties to whom the notice is given may seek a protective order postponing the videotaped deposition to allow time for a discovery deposition prior to the video or precluding the use of the videotaped deposition at trial. Taking a videotaped deposition of an expert does not preclude the noticing party from calling that expert at trial to give live testimony. The deposition notice merely forewarns other parties that the use of the deposition at trial is contemplated. Without that wording on a deposition notice, the videotape will not be admissible at time of trial. The notice serves the intention of the noticing party to reserve the right to use at trial a videotape deposition of an expert in lieu of live testimony.

At the request of any party to the action, including a party who did not attend the taking of the deposition testimony, or at the request of the deponent, the videotape operator shall promptly permit the person making the request to hear or to view the tape on receipt of payment of a reasonable charge for providing the facilities for hearing or viewing the tape, and furnish a copy of the videotape recording to the one making the request on receipt of payment of the reasonable cost of making that copy of the tape.

§ 3.21   Telephone Depositions

Federal Rule of Civil Procedure 30(b)(7), which became effective August 1, 1980, provides that "the parties may stipulate in writing or the court may upon motion order that a deposition be taken by telephone." It further provides that "the deposition taken by telephone is taken in the district and at the place where the deponent is to answer questions propounded to him." Taking a deposition by telephone is obviously a convenience and money-saver in many pretrial and trial situations. See Notice of Taking Deposition by Telephone (**Form 3–9**). With a proper written stipulation (**Form 3–10**), and no dispute between counsel, a telephone deposition may be taken under either federal or state rules. Absent a written stipulation or general agreement between counsel, but with no indication of an attack of the procedure, the court reporter can be located with the attorneys, or even at another location on a conference call. The preferred method is to have whoever is to swear the witness be at the same location as the witness for positive-identification purposes. If the court reporter is located on the witness' end of the telephone call, it is easier to swear in the witness and record the testimony by stenographic means. The court reporter should include on the transcript how the witness was identified. Identification may be through questions asked by the attorney and answered under oath. The court reporter may personally view such items as the witness's address verified from a telephone directory or any other address directory in general use, a telephone bill with the telephone number, name, and address of the witness, a driver's license, a social security card, a military identification card, or any other proper form of identification. In some cases, the witness might be personally known to the court reporter. Identification of the witness is the weak link in the telephone deposition process, and if precautions are not taken at the time the deposition is taken, problems with admissibility of the deposition transcript may surface at the time of trial.

A conference telephone call is the generally accepted method for telephone depositions so that counsel from both sides may participate in the questioning and hear all of the answers. Recent electronic advances will soon enable each attorney to see the person on the other end of the telephone through use of the new picture phones. This technical innovation may create a need for a new set of rules and procedures.

The obvious disadvantage of a telephone deposition is the lack of spontaneity and confrontation between deponent and opposing counsel. The main advantage of a telephone deposition is the cost. Travelling to remote cities and paying travel expenses for witnesses can become extremely expensive, and in some small or medium cases, the ends do not justify the means. For example, you may need to take a deposition of a person who has particular knowledge on one aspect needed to establish specific special damages in your case. This limited knowledge may be essential to proving that damage claim, and it may be the type of testimony that may be elicited through a telephone deposition. In situations when a deposition needs to be taken of a peripheral witness who has a small but important contribution to make to the case, a telephone deposition may be the most expedient and least expensive method of obtaining the testimony.

In the event that counsel refuses to stipulate to the use of a telephone deposition, a motion may be made pursuant to Federal Rule of Civil Procedure 30(b)(7), and a memorandum of points and authorities in opposition of the motion may be filed by the person challenging the telephone deposition (**Form 3–11**). **Form 3–12** is a sample order allowing the telephone deposition.

FORM 3–9
SAMPLE TELEPHONE DEPOSITION NOTICE

SUPERIOR COURT OF [state]
IN AND FOR COUNTY OF [county name]

[name]　　　　　　　　　　　　　　No. [case number]

Plaintiff,   NOTICE OF TAKING
                                        DEPOSITION BY TELEPHONE
-vs-

[name],

Defendant.
_____/

TO: [name of attorney], attorney for [opposing party]:

NOTICE IS HEREBY GIVEN that on [date], the deposition of [name of witness] will be taken by telephone with the witness located at [location] at [time], upon oral examination before a deposition reporter authorized by law to administer oaths, which reporter will be located at [location of witness/attorney] and such deposition will continue from time to time, and day-to-day, until completed.

Dated: [date]

_____
Attorney for [name of party]

FORM 3–10
SAMPLE TELEPHONE DEPOSITION STIPULATION

SUPERIOR COURT OF [state],
IN AND FOR COUNTY OF [county]

[name]   No. [case number]

Plaintiff,

-vs-   STIPULATION

[name],

Defendant.
_____/

STIPULATION FOR TAKING TELEPHONE DEPOSITIONS

Now come the plaintiffs and defendants and agree to take the depositions of the following by telephone:

(1) [deponent A]   (2) [deponent B]
     c/o [company A]   [company B]

[city, state]   [city, state]
[telephone number]   [telephone number]

The court reporter who will take such depositions will be [name], and said court reporter will be present in the offices of [company/law firm], where the attorneys will be present for the taking of such depositions.

The depositions will begin at [time] and [time]. [Name], the attorney for plaintiffs, will be responsible for having made arrangements with the witnesses to be present at such time at the addresses and telephone numbers listed herein. The plaintiffs' attorney will make arrangements for a court reporter to be present. It is further agreed that the witnesses may be sworn by telephone by such court reporter.

A speaker phone in the offices of [company/law firm] will be used so that all attorneys may speak to the witness.

The parties agree to waiver of the witnesses' signatures, provided the witnesses agree to waive said signatures. Otherwise, the court reporter will follow the Rules of Procedure with regard to the signatures of such witnesses.

STIPULATED AND AGREED to this [date]

_____
[attorney for plaintiff]

_____
[attorney for defendant]

FORM 3–11
SAMPLE TELEPHONE DEPOSITION MOTION

IN THE UNITED STATES DISTRICT COURT
FOR THE [judicial district] DISTRICT OF [state]
[division number] DIVISION

[plaintiff]	§	
-vs-	§	CIVIL ACTION NO. [case number]
[defendant]	§	

MOTION TO TAKE TELEPHONE DEPOSITIONS PURSUANT TO
RULE 30(b)(7) OF THE FEDERAL RULES OF CIVIL PROCEDURE

TO THE HONORABLE JUDGE OF SAID COURT:

Now come the plaintiffs and move the Court for leave to take certain depositions by telephone, after having conferred with opposing counsel pursuant to Local Rule [rule number] and having been unsuccessful in securing the agreement of counsel to take said depositions by telephone.

1. This is a product liability suit in which a wheel came off the vehicle being driven by the plaintiff, causing an accident which resulted in the destruction of the vehicle and injuries to the plaintiff. The vehicle being driven was a one-ton 1980 [vehicle model] pickup, which was almost new. Plaintiffs have had the wheel assembly examined following the accident and determined that it was apparently produced and sold without a cotter pin being placed on the right front wheel spindle which thereafter resulted in a wheel coming off. The vehicle was almost new, having less than 1,500 miles on it, and the persons who had custody of the vehicle from the time of sale by the manufacturer to the time of the accident are readily identifiable, and it is these people whose depositions are sought to be taken by telephone.

2. The witnesses sought to be deposed for the purposes set forth above live out-of-state, and the substance of their testimony is very simple and uncomplicated. This deposition's purpose is to perpetuate that testimony in a form which shall be deemed admissible at time of trial pursuant to Federal Rule of Civil Procedure 30(b)(7) as valid deposition testimony.

3. Plaintiffs have arranged to have said telephone deposition take place on [date] at [address], and further have made arrangements for [name of court reporter] to be present at the time of the deposition to swear in the witness and record the transcript stenographically. A speaker phone in the offices of [name of law firm], attorneys at law, will be used and a conference call will be set up in such a fashion so that all attorneys and the court reporter may simultaneously hear the witness speak, and so that each of the attorneys present may question the witness.

4. Proper notice will be given to all parties to the action of the date, time, and place of said telephone deposition, and copies of the transcript will be provided to all attorneys of record upon request.

In conclusion, no injustice to the interests of any parties in this action will result in the taking of this telephone deposition. Plaintiffs agree that this telephone deposition transcript shall not be used at the time of trial in lieu of live testimony of the witness. Plaintiffs respectfully seek the court's permission to depose [name] by telephone in the above-entitled action.

Dated: [date]

_____

Attorney for [name of party]

FORM 3–12
SAMPLE TELEPHONE DEPOSITION ORDER

IN THE UNITED STATES DISTRICT COURT
FOR THE [judicial district] DISTRICT OF [state]
[division number] DIVISION

[plaintiff]	§	
-vs-	§	CIVIL ACTION NO. [case number]
[defendant]	§	

ORDER

There came on to be considered plaintiff's motion to take certain depositions by telephone and it appearing to the court that the witnesses sought to be deposed by telephone deposition are proper subjects for a Rule 30(b)(7) telephone deposition and that good cause exists for taking said depositions by telephone:

IT IS, ACCORDINGLY, ORDERED that said depositions be taken by telephone at a time to be agreed upon between counsel or upon reasonable notice by plaintiff of a date, time, and place for the taking of such deposition.

IT IS FURTHER ORDERED that the Court Reporter in [city] who will transcribe said testimony may swear the witness by telephone.

SIGNED this [date].

[name]_____
United States District Judge

§ 3.22 Objections to Deposition Notices

A Notice of Deposition served pursuant to Federal Rules of Civil Procedure Rule 30 requires only that "reasonable notice in writing" be given to all parties in order to initiate a deposition. This requirement differs from the minimum notice required by many states. The distance limitation on a party's deposition in state court actions does not exist in federal court actions. Under federal law, generally, a plaintiff or party to the action must be available for a deposition in the district where the action is pending regardless of how far this may be from the plaintiff's residence. Defendants may be forced to travel in accordance with those limitations set forth at Federal Rule of Civil Procedure 45(d) (Deposition Subpoenas). The party receiving a subpoena duces tecum pursuant to Rule 45(d) may serve written objections (see **Form 3–13**) to the deposition and/or to the inspection or copying of any or all of the designated materials contained in the subpoena within ten days after service. After the objections have been made, the burden is placed on the party serving the subpoena to file a motion to require the deponent not only to appear at the deposition but also to produce the requested items (Rule 45(d)). The most common objections to deposition notices are not procedural, but rather deal with documents requested to be produced at the time of the deposition.

Federal Rule of Civil Procedure 30(5) provides that "notice to a party deponent may be accompanied by a request for documents made in compliance with Rule 34 for the production of documents and tangible things at the taking of the deposition." The amount of notice required when a request for production of documents is joined with a deposition in a federal court action is 30 days (Federal Rule of Civil Procedure 34(b)(5)).

The procedure for objecting to a deposition notice joined with a request for document production is identical to the procedure required for objecting to a request for identification and production of documents pursuant to Rule 34 served as a document request and not as a request to produce documents at time of deposition. For a discussion of objections, **Chapter 6** sets forth acceptable grounds for objecting to the production of documents. The responding party may object to any item or category requested in whole or in part. An effective objection must not only identify the specific document but also set forth the reason for the objection including any claim of privilege or work product in accordance with Rule 34(b). The objections that are the most likely to be sustained include the following:

1. The document requested exceeds the permissible scope of discovery, that it is not relevant to the subject matter of this action or likely to lead to the discovery of admissible evidence;

2. Statutory privilege, work product privilege, right of privacy, and so forth; and

3. The requested document creates an unreasonable and oppressive burden on responding party, that compliance would be unreasonably difficult and unduly expensive (Federal Rule of Civil Procedure 26(b)).

Objecting to a notice of deposition requiring the production of documents must be timely. In state court, the time for filing objections is significantly less than it is in federal court. For example, in California (see **Form 3–14**), objections to a notice of deposition requiring production of documents must be filed in accordance with California Code of Civil Procedure § 2025(g). Objections must be served promptly and in no event less than three calendar days before the date scheduled for the deposition. Failure to file a notice of objection within this time frame renders objections invalid and the requested documents must be produced. Filing a notice of objection to a deposition notice requiring the production of documents in either state or federal court does not relieve the person noticed from appearing at the deposition. Objecting to a notice usually is done in those cases when the objection is to the documents themselves and not to the deposition. It is presumed by the person receiving a notice of objection to a deposition notice requiring production of documents that the person will appear for the deposition with those documents to which no objections have been filed. Even if objections have been filed for each category of documents requested, the deponent must appear and testify on the date scheduled for the deposition. Filing a notice of objection does not take the deposition off calendar.

In addition to serving written objections to a deposition notice requiring production of documents, a party objecting to the deposition itself may move for an order staying the taking of the deposition and quashing the deposition notice. Filing a motion requesting a stay will automatically take the deposition off calendar until the court rules on the motion.

FORM 3–13
SAMPLE NOTICE OF DEPOSITION OBJECTION (FEDERAL)

UNITED STATES DISTRICT COURT
[judicial district] DISTRICT OF [state]

[plaintiff A] and [plaintiff B]

         Plaintiffs,

-vs-

[company C],
and [company D]

         Defendants.
_____/

No. [case number]

OBJECTIONS TO DEPOSITION
OF EXPERT [name of expert]

AND ALL RELATED CROSS-ACTIONS.
_____/

TO EACH PARTY AND THEIR ATTORNEY OF RECORD:

PLEASE TAKE NOTICE that pursuant to Rule 30(b)(5) of the Federal Rules of Civil Procedure, which states, "If the party noticing the deposition joins a Request for Production of Documents, Rule 34 Procedures apply. . . ." plaintiff serves notice of the following objections to those documents requested in Schedule A of the amended notice of taking deposition of expert [name] duces tecum served on them by defendant on [date].

OBJECTIONS TO DOCUMENTS REQUESTED

REQUEST NUMBER 7:
     Plaintiffs object to this request on the grounds that it is oppressive and burdensome and a compilation would be unreasonably difficult and expensive (F.R.C.P. 26(b)). Without waiving that objection, plaintiff states that this information is equally available to defendant through those public records available in a docket search.

REQUEST NUMBER 8:
     Plaintiffs object to this request on the grounds that it exceeds the scope of permissible discovery and is not relevant to the subject matter of this action nor

likely to lead to the discovery of admissible evidence. Plaintiff further objects on the grounds that this request is oppressive and burdensome and a compilation would be unreasonably difficult and expensive (F.R.C.P. 26(b)).

REQUEST NUMBER 9:
Objection; see objection to Request Number 8.

REQUEST NUMBER 10:
Plaintiffs object to this request on the grounds that it exceeds the scope of permissible discovery and is not relevant to the subject matter of this action nor likely to lead to the discovery of admissible evidence at time of trial. Without waiver of such objection, plaintiff will produce such documents to the extent the witness relied on them in formulating his opinion.

REQUEST NUMBER 11:
Plaintiffs object to this request on the grounds that it is overbroad, ambiguous, vague, and unlimited in time and scope in its reference to "any ski area at which said expert has been employed or retained as a correction in any fashion."

REQUEST NUMBER 12:
Plaintiffs object to this request on the same grounds as stated in their objection to Request Number 11. Plaintiffs further object to the vague and ambiguous nature of "the duties of accomplishments of said expert for any ski resort or ski lift operator. . . ." This request clearly exceeds the permissible scope of discovery.

REQUEST NUMBER 13:
Plaintiffs object to this request on the same grounds as are stated in their objections to Requests Number 9, 10, 11 and 12. These requests clearly exceed the permissible scope of discovery by inquiring into matters which are not relevant to the subject matter of this action. Without waiver of said objection, plaintiffs will produce such documents to the extent the witness relied on them in formulating his opinion.

Those documents responsive to defendant's request to which no objection has been made will be produced at the time set for the deposition, [date].

Dated: [date]

[name]
Attorney for Plaintiffs

FORM 3–14
SAMPLE NOTICE OF DEPOSITION OBJECTION (CALIFORNIA)

SUPERIOR COURT OF THE STATE OF [state]
IN AND FOR THE COUNTY OF [county name]

[company A] et al.,	No. [case number]
Plaintiffs,	OBJECTIONS TO
-vs-	NOTICE OF
	DEPOSITION
[name], et al.,	California Code of Civil Procedure § 2025(g)
Defendants.	
_____/	_____

AND ALL RELATED CROSS ACTIONS.
_____/

TO THE PARTIES HEREIN AND THEIR ATTORNEYS OF RECORD:

Plaintiff hereby objects to the Notice of Deposition served upon him by defendant [name] on the grounds that the writings designated in the Notice are duplicative of documents previously requested in defendant [name]'s 53 prior requested categories of documents. Plaintiff has responded to each and every request for document production propounded to plaintiff by defendant [name] and has produced all responsive documents in plaintiff's possession. It is burdensome, harassing, and oppressive to require plaintiff to produce documents in 20 different categories when these documents have, for the most part, been produced in prior discovery, or are in the possession of defendants.

<u>GENERAL OBJECTIONS</u>

Plaintiff objects to any request herein which seeks documents protected from discovery by the attorney-client privilege or the attorney work product doctrine, basing its objection on the grounds of such privilege or such doctrine.

Plaintiff's specific objections are as follows:

Documents requested in Nos. 1, 2, 3 and 4 have already been produced. Each of these items was requested by defendant [name] in their First and Second Request for Production of Documents to plaintiff. Plaintiff further objects on the grounds that the Articles of Incorporation and By-Laws, in addition to having been previously produced by plaintiff, are equally available to all defendants through the Office of the Secretary of State. Plaintiff further objects to No. 3 on the grounds that all Resolutions of the Board of Directors authorizing the opening of accounts at [bank A], [bank B], and [bank C] are in the possession of those named financial institutions, as plaintiff has stated repeatedly in verified responses to document requests requesting those identical documents.

Plaintiff's objection to No. 4 is based upon the fact that these documents were requested in [name]'s First and Second Request for Production of Documents to plaintiff, and plaintiff has repeatedly stated under oath that the only Resolutions of the Board of Directors have already been produced. There are no other documents responsive to this request.

With regard to the requested corporate seal, Request No. 5, an imprint of that seal appears on documents which have been previously produced to defendants. However, in the spirit of cooperation with discovery, plaintiff will bring to his deposition the original corporate seal.

Plaintiff objects to requested items Nos. 6 and 7, bank statements and deposit tickets. All bank statements for [bank A], [bank B], and [bank C] have already been produced in response to requests for production of documents served upon plaintiff by defense counsel representing [defendant] and [bank A]. Further, bank statements are most certainly in the possession of the financial institutions involved in the creation of these statements. Further, plaintiff wishes to point out that bank statements for [bank C] were subpoenaed by defendant [name] on [date]. Records were produced by the Custodian of Records of [bank C] on [date]. On [date], plaintiff sent, under separate cover, statements from [defendant] for the time period [date] through [date], which had been inadvertently excluded from the deposition subpoena response of [bank C]. These statements were sent to all counsel as part of plaintiff's response to [defendant]'s Third Request for Production of Documents, No. 52.

Plaintiff's objection to Category No. 7, deposit tickets, is based upon the fact that plaintiff has no separate deposit tickets in this possession. Deposits were recorded in plaintiff's passbook, a copy of which has already been produced to defendants. Plaintiff further points out that deposit tickets, if any exist, would be in possession of those financial institutions where plaintiff maintained accounts, because in the usual course of business a deposit ticket is filled out and left with the bank. Plaintiff was not given a separate copy of a deposit ticket; rather the amount of deposit was entered into the passbook.

Plaintiff objects to those documents requested in Categories 8 and 9 relating to checks draw or deposited on the grounds that it is burdensome, harassing, and annoying to require plaintiff to produce documents which are in the possession of defendants. Plaintiff further points out that all documents relating to [bank C] were produced as part of their response to the deposition subpoena of [date]. Checks drawn and deposited at [bank A] and [defendant] are in possession of those defendants.

Regarding Category No. 10, plaintiff has previously produced, pursuant to Request No. 25 of [defendant]'s First Request for Production of Documents an imprint of the rubber stamp endorsement for [bank B]. Plaintiff will bring to the deposition rubber stamp endorsements for [bank A] and [bank C].

With regard to Category No. 11, plaintiff has previously produced check registers for the six accounts at [bank B], all information on [bank C] has been copied to all counsel as it was provided on [date] by [bank C] in response to the deposition subpoena served upon it by [defendant]. Plaintiff will produce at plaintiff's deposition any other documents in plaintiff's possession which correspond to those requested in this category.

Plaintiff objects to Nos. 12, 13, 14, 15, and 16 on the grounds that to ask again for documents which have already been produced in discovery and/or are available to defendants is burdensome, harassing, and annoying.

Plaintiff objects to Category No. 17, all documents used to open all deposit accounts, on the grounds that these documents have already been produced, or are not in plaintiff's possession. Documents used to open deposit accounts are in the possession of those financial institutions where plaintiff established accounts. On [date], plaintiff propounded a First Request for Production of Documents to [bank A] asking for documents used to open the account. Documents used to open the [bank C] account were part of their subpoena response of [date]. Documents used to open accounts at [defendant] were obtained by plaintiff from [defendant].

Plaintiff objects to Nos. 18 and 19, on the grounds that these are identical requests to Nos. 40, 41, and 46 of defendant [name]'s Second Request for Document Production. Plaintiff has already produced documents responsive to Request No. 46, and to require him to produce them again at his deposition is burdensome, harassing, and annoying.

Plaintiff will produce Item No. 20, "the ledger book" which [deponent] referred to in [deponent]'s deposition.

Dated: [date]

[name]_____
Attorney for Plaintiff

§ 3.23   Objections to Deposition Notices (Notice Priority)

Ordinarily depositions proceed in whatever order they have been noticed by the parties in spite of the fact that dates may be continued. Questions of priority arise when a later-served notice sets a deposition before the date set in the first-served notice. State and local court rules are not uniform regarding deposition priority policy, and your state Code of Civil Procedure may provide statutory priority protection for deposition scheduling. For example, the California Discovery Act does not recognize priority based on notice alone.

In the absence of statutory authority, an Objection to Notice of Taking Deposition should be filed along with a motion for a protective order. Judges usually prefer to have depositions taken and completed in the order originally noticed and may grant a protective order to stop discovery abuse and prevent a party from playing games with the deposition sequence.

Form 3–15 is a sample Objection to Notice of Taking Deposition. It is specifically for use in California, but it may be modified for use in any state by citing appropriate authorities (statutes and/or local court rules).

FORM 3–15
SAMPLE NOTICE OF DEPOSITION OBJECTION
(NOTICE PRIORITY)

[attorney for plaintiff]
[address]
[phone number]

Attorneys for Plaintiff
[plaintiff name]

IN THE SUPERIOR COURT OF THE STATE OF [state name]

IN THE CITY AND COUNTY OF [city name]

[name],	Case No. [case number]
Plaintiff,	OBJECTION TO NOTICE OF TAKING DEPOSITION
vs.	(California Code of Civil Procedure § 2025(g))
[name] SHOPPING MALL, A LIMITED PARTNERSHIP, [defendant A], and [defendant B], as limited partners of [name] SHOPPING MALL, [defendant C], individually and (dba) [business D], and (dba) [business E], and DOES 1 through 50, inclusive,	
Defendants.	
_____/	

TO ALL PARTIES HEREIN AND TO THEIR ATTORNEYS OF RECORD:

Plaintiff [name] hereby objects to the Notice of Deposition served upon plaintiff by defendant [name] SHOPPING MALL on the grounds that depositions should be taken and completed in the order originally noticed. Plaintiff noticed depositions of defendant [name] SHOPPING MALL'S most knowledgeable employees regarding the relevant issues in this action on [date]. Defendant [name] SHOPPING MALL objected to plaintiff's Deposition Notice on [date]. As of this date, defendant [name] SHOPPING MALL has failed to designate those persons most knowledgeable regarding the matters set forth in plaintiff's Deposition Notice. Defendant now seeks unilaterally to alter the sequence of depositions by noticing the deposition of plaintiff [name] prior to producing [name] SHOPPING MALL employees for the previously-noticed depositions. Plaintiffs have agreed to depose [name] SHOPPING MALL employees at their home office in [city] should that location be warranted. Rather than working with plaintiff to reschedule depositions at a mutually convenient time and place, defendant [name] SHOPPING MALL has chosen to notice the deposition of plaintiff [name] and establish the sequence and timing of depositions for their convenience.

For good cause shown, the court may establish the sequence and timing of discovery for the convenience of parties and witnesses and in the interests of justice (California Code of Civil Procedure § 2019(c)).

Because discovery proceedings can seldom, if ever, be conducted simultaneously, it is inherent in such proceedings that the party who secures discovery first may derive advantages by securing information from their adversary before they are required to reciprocate by divulging information.

In conclusion, plaintiff seeks to establish a reasonable deposition schedule allowing for depositions to proceed in the order noticed. If defendant [name] SHOPPING MALL fails to operate by establishing mutually convenient deposition dates, plaintiff will be forced to seek a protective order asking the court to set the deposition schedule in the order required to protect the interests of all parties to this action.

Dated: [date].

_____
[name]
Attorney for Plaintiff

§ 3.24   Deposition Scheduling Strategy

The timing and scheduling of depositions are very important strategically and should be part of your discovery plan (see **Chapter 2**). For example, in business litigation it can be advantageous to move up the corporate ladder saving the deposition of the

Chief Executive Officer (CEO) until the end of the deposition schedule. This enables you to determine the duties of each officer or member of that corporation, how business is conducted, who reports to whom, and exactly what duties fall on the CEO's shoulders. This information can then be used to prepare questions for the CEO and to cover each area of the CEO's responsibility and involvement.

In other types of business litigation, the attorney may wish to move down the corporate ladder beginning with the CEO. This is often the case when there are many documents that have been authored by the president of a corporation. A CEO who authors many documents is often the most knowledgeable person in that corporation, and in fact may be the sole officer of the corporation with the other officers acting in name only. This is particularly true in a family-owned business where the entire corporation follows the dictates of the CEO who authors all of the documents for incorporation, corporate policy, corporate minutes, corporate stock options, and so forth. In this case, deposition taking may begin and perhaps end with the CEO, and all information needed may be obtained by one deposition.

In some states, the defendant retains deposition priority, which means that the defendant may notice plaintiff's deposition first, before plaintiff may notice defendant's deposition. Whether to exercise this deposition priority is a strategic decision made by the attorney on the case.

A deposition may need to be continued or rescheduled for a variety of reasons. In any event, a letter should be sent to confirm any rescheduling of a Noticed deposition as a precautionary measure to avoid discovery disputes. **Form 3–16** is a sample letter confirming the rescheduling of a deposition.

FORM 3–16
SAMPLE LETTER CONTINUING OR RESCHEDULING A DEPOSITION

Re: [plaintiff] vs. [defendant]

Deposition of [plaintiff]

Dear Opposing Counsel:

This will confirm my conversation with your secretary, [name], today, [date], at which time arrangements were made to continue the deposition of our client, plaintiff [name], from [date] to [date]. We appreciate your cooperation in agreeing to this continuance which has been necessitated by serious illness in the family forcing our client to travel out of town to care for our client's mother. We will notify you when our client returns and confirm at that time that this deposition date is firm.

Thank you for your courtesy in agreeing to this continuance. This office will make arrangements for a court reporter and the deposition will go forward at [time] on [date] at the law offices of [name of law firm], [address], [city], [state].

Thank you again for your courtesy and cooperation.

Sincerely,

[name]_____
Legal Assistant

§ 3.25   Depositions Requiring a Court Order

Depositions are generally available to litigants as a matter of right, that is, without leave of court, after an action has commenced pursuant to those rules set forth at Federal Rules of Civil Procedure 30(a). Deposition testimony is governed by Federal Rules of Civil Procedure 30 to 32. Deposition notices are routinely sent out in federal and state actions by either plaintiff or defendant. Depositions may be arranged by stipulation, which should always be memorialized in writing, or by subpoena pursuant to the rules set forth for subpoena of nonparty witnesses at Federal Rule of Civil Procedure 45(d) and applicable state statutes. There are, however, certain situations where depositions may not be taken without a court order.

A court order (based on a showing of special need) is required for taking depositions in the following instances:

1.   Prelawsuit,
2.   After judgment while appeal is pending
3.   During a discovery hold or after a discovery cutoff
4.   A prisoner incarcerated in a state or federal institution.

Although these situations may be considered uncommon rather than usual, a fact of life in a law firm is that they do occur, and when they do, the legal assistant is usually required to do the factual research relating to the procedure required to obtain a court order which will permit the taking of the deposition.

§ 3.26   Prelawsuit Depositions

Prelawsuit depositions may be sought to perpetuate testimony that might otherwise be lost. Petitions may be brought pursuant to Federal Rule of Civil Procedure 27(a) stating that the moving party is presently unable to bring an action, or cause it to be brought, and that the deposition is necessary to perpetuate the testimony and prevent a failure or delay of justice. To state a special need in this situation, the moving party must clearly show why the lawsuit cannot be filed before the deposition. When the moving party is the potential defendant, it is very easy to fulfill this requirement because a defendant cannot commence litigation. When the moving party is the plaintiff, it is somewhat more difficult to demonstrate a special need for a deposition and at the same time prove to the court's satisfaction that the moving party is presently unable to file an action.

A prospective plaintiff can attempt to demonstrate a special need based on insufficient information presently available to support the action at hand, a key witness who is about to leave the country (for example, on an extended European or Mideastern assignment), or the need to take a prelawsuit deposition of an aged or gravely ill witness or party who may not be available to testify at a later date. A petition must be presented to the court in accordance with Rule 27(a). In state court actions in California, a petition may be presented in accordance with Code of Civil Procedure § 2035(b). The courts have held that a petition may not be used by parties as "a method of obtaining discovery to ascertain whether a cause of action or a viable defense exists or to identify persons who might be parties to an action not yet filed," and further states that an attempt to misuse the prelawsuit deposition can result in sanctions. Depositions taken pursuant to court order (Rule 27) may be used in an action "involving the same subject matter" subsequently brought in a federal district court.

§ 3.27   The Burden of Proof for a Prelawsuit Deposition

In bringing a petition not only for the perpetuation of evidence but also the taking of depositions before the filing of an action, the defendant has the decided advantage. The two areas that require the most in the way of judicial interpretation and leave the most room for judicial discretion are the requirements for a showing of why the anticipated lawsuit has not yet been filed, and of why it is necessary in advance of such a filing to perpetuate the evidence described in the petition. The requirement of a showing why the petitioner is presently unable to either bring that action or cause it to be brought takes care of itself when the one seeking the perpetuation of testimony can show a realistic fear that a lawsuit will be filed in which it expects to be made a defendant. It is statutorily impossible for a defendant to initiate an action. In a 1961 federal case, *Martin v. Reynolds Metal Corp.*,[1] the owner of an aluminum plant fulfilled the requirement of why it was necessary to perpetuate the evidence described in his petition by alleging that a ranch owner, known to him who had previously sued him on three occasions, had made claims that the operations of the aluminum plant were polluting his ranch and killing his cattle. The court reasonably concluded that defendant had demonstrated a realistic fear that the ranch owner would file a fourth action, and granted the petition.

In a 1942 probate matter, *Petition of Ernst*,[2] an executrix was permitted to perpetuate testimony concerning the circumstances of a gift in anticipation of a possible claim by the Internal Revenue Service that the gift was made in contemplation of death. It was necessary to perpetuate the testimony of an elderly individual who was not suffering from any illness, mental or physical, which would have lead to the contemplation of death at the time the gift was made.

It is far more difficult for a plaintiff to fulfill the requirements which must be addressed in a petition to perpetuate evidence than it is for the defendant. Courts are generally suspicious of would-be plaintiffs and fear that a plaintiff s motive is more likely to be discovery of evidence rather than perpetuation of evidence. Federal courts have consistently held that Federal Rule of Civil Procedure 27(a) was not intended to

---

[1] 297 F.2d 49 (9th Cir. 1961).

[2] 2 F.R.D 447 (S.D. Cal. 1942).

be used as a discovery statute, and "its purpose was not to enable a prospective litigant to discover facts upon which to frame a complaint." Further interpretation of Rule 27(a) by the courts has unequivocally stated, "One shall not employ the procedures of this section for the purpose either of ascertaining the possible existence of a cause of action or a defense to it, or of identifying those who might be parties to an action not yet filed. . . ." Common sense and public policy dictate the interpretation of the statute in this manner in that it is fundamentally unfair to subject someone to discovery when that person is at the distinct disadvantage of not knowing even the rough outlines of the lawsuit which may be prompting the discovery.

Plaintiffs can most easily satisfy the requirement of the perpetuation procedures by pointing to a legal impediment to the present institution of a lawsuit This situation may arise where petitioners have been victims of a tort committed by a public entity. Prospective plaintiffs are not permitted to file an action until a claim for the injury has been presented to the entity and the entity has been allowed 45 days to accept or reject the claim. If an emergency arises during that 45-day interval (for example, the scheduled demolition of the building or destruction of the property where the injury occurred), the injured party (prospective plaintiff) would certainly be in a position to demonstrate to the satisfaction of the court the need to perpetuate testimony by way of deposition. Examples of federal cases wherein this situation occurred include *Mosseller v. United States*[3] and *DeWagenknecht v. Stinnes*.[4]

Another method for a potential plaintiff to qualify for the use of the perpetuation procedure would be to show that defendant is presently engaging in actions which may in the future result in a cause of action, but that those actions have not yet crossed the line and ripened into a justifiable cause of action. This situation occurs most frequently in contract disputes and unfair competition actions when a continuing cause of action or pattern of behavior by the defendant can be identified as that which may ripen into a cause of action.

Once the prospective plaintiff or defendant has made an adequate showing to the court of why the anticipated action has not yet been filed, it is usually not too difficult to fulfill the additional requirement of a sufficient reason for acting now to preserve the evidence and to perpetuate the testimony. When the evidence to be preserved is the testimony of an individual, showing that the person is gravely ill or well advanced in years is sufficient reason in and of itself. When it can be demonstrated that there will be a considerable passage of time before the expected suit may be filed, the mere danger that memories will fade, or that witnesses will move away, or just disappear is usually sufficient to warrant the taking of a deposition to preserve the testimony. In *Petition of Ernst,*[5] the court held that, "It is common knowledge that the lapse of time is replete with hazards and unexpected events. This is so regardless of the age, health or general status of an individual. . . ." The main criterion for satisfying the requirement for acting now to preserve the evidence is to demonstrate to the court that there is a valid reason why conditions will have so changed by the time a lawsuit is filed that subsequent perpetuation of testimony will be impossible or substantially less effective.

---

[3] 158 F.2d 380 (2d Cir. 1946).

[4] 250 F.2d 414 (D.C. Cir. 1957).

[5] 2 F.R.D. 447 (S.D. Cal. 1942).

§ 3.28   Petition Requirements

The petition must be titled in the name of the person who desires either to perpetuate testimony or preserve the evidence. The petition must be filed in the district of the residence of any expected adverse party. The petitioner's residence and the residence of the person to be deposed are immaterial. The contents of a petition for use in federal court are set forth at Federal Rule of Civil Procedure 27(a)(1). The petition must be verified and must set forth the following information:

1. A plaintiff filing a petition must set forth the specific reasons why a lawsuit cannot be filed at the present time when the petitioner expects to be a party in an action over which there is federal jurisdiction but is presently unable to bring the action (usually because petitioner expects to be sued as a defendant).
2. The subject matter of the expected action and the petitioner's interest in the action.
3. The facts desired to be established by the proposed testimony and the reasons for desiring to perpetuate it and the identity, including addresses, of persons expected to be adverse parties.
4. The identity, including addresses, of the persons to be examined and the substance of the testimony expected to be elicited from each proposed examinee.

The petition (see **Form 3–17**) must then ask the court to enter an order (**Form 3–18**) authorizing the petitioner to take a deposition (or several depositions, or use any other proposed discovery method) for the purpose of perpetuating testimony or preserving the evidence described in the petition. A memorandum of points and authorities and declarations supporting the factual basis for the petition should be filed with the petition. The petition must be accompanied by a notice of petition stating that the petitioner will apply to the court at a specified time and place for the order requested in the petition.

Copies of the petition and the notice specifying the time and date of the hearing must be served on each expected adverse party in accordance with the rules set forth at Rule 27(a)(2) and Rule 4(d). The usual time requirement for notice is 20 days; however, be certain to check local rules for your state or district before preparing the notice. In special circumstances where it appears that the witness will not survive the 20-day notice period due to extreme illness or other critical factors, a party may file a lawsuit and seek immediate leave of court for a deposition pursuant to Rule 30(a), *Petition of Jacobs.*[6]

In the event that an expected adverse party cannot be located and served, the petitioner may apply to the court for an order for service by publication. At the hearing on the petition, the court must appoint counsel to represent any prospective party served by publication who does not appear, and must order that reasonable attorney's fees and expenses be paid by the petitioner. Check your state statutes and local court rules for requirements for notice, filing, and service. For example, in California, this procedure is governed by California Code of Civil Procedure § 2035(c) to (f). These documents must be accompanied by a Notice of Petition,

---

[6] 110 F.R.D. 422 (N.D. Ind. 1986).

Memorandum of Points and Authorities, and Declaration of Attorney setting forth those items described in the list of requirements.

FORM 3–17
SAMPLE FEDERAL COURT PETITION AUTHORIZING
PRELAWSUIT DEPOSITION

UNITED STATES DISTRICT COURT
[judicial district] DISTRICT OF [state]

[plaintiff name],	Case No. [case number]
Plaintiff,	PETITION TO PERPETUATE TESTIMONY
-vs-	
[defendant name],	
Defendant.	

Petitioner, [name] , respectfully states:

1. Petitioner is a citizen of the State of [state name], and resides in [city], and within the jurisdiction of this Court. [prospective defendant] is a citizen of [State] and is subject to the jurisdiction of this Court.

2. Petitioner intends to file a complaint in this Court against [prospective defendant] to [state nature of action].

3. [description of basic facts giving rise to liability].

4. [reason(s) why immediate deposition is necessary]

5. Petitioner desires to perpetuate the testimony of [name]. The substance of his testimony is expected to be as follows: [nature of expected testimony].

WHEREFORE, petitioner prays the Court for an order authorizing them to take the deposition of [name] upon oral examination for the purpose of perpetuating testimony pursuant to Rule 27 of the Federal Rules of Civil Procedure.

Dated: [date]

[name]_____
Attorney for Petitioner

FORM 3–18
SAMPLE ORDER AUTHORIZING PRELAWSUIT DEPOSITION

ORDER

Having considered the foregoing petition and the matters stated therein, IT IS HEREBY ORDERED that petitioner be permitted to take the deposition of [name] upon oral examination pursuant to Fed. R. Civ. P. 27.

Dated: [date]

> [name]_____
> United States District Judge

According to statute in California, the Notice of Hearing (**Form 3–19**), accompanied by a copy of the petition to perpetuate testimony or preserve evidence (**Form 3–20**), must be served on the named expected adverse parties in the same manner as a summons. Check local court rules and statutory requirements for your state for manner of service and time requirements. **Form 3–21** illustrates an Order Authorizing the Perpetuation of Testimony for the State of California. These California forms may be adapted for use in all state courts by consulting local rules and citations. Requirements may vary as to timing and filing; however, the content requirements will be fairly consistent from state to state.

FORM 3–19
SAMPLE NOTICE OF HEARING PETITION (CALIFORNIA)

SUPERIOR COURT OF THE STATE OF [state name]
IN AND FOR THE COUNTY OF [county name]

Petition of   No. [case number]

[name of prospective litigant]   NOTICE OF HEARING OF
                                           PETITION TO PERPETUATE
                                           EVIDENCE BEFORE ACTION

TO: [names of expected adverse parties]

PLEASE TAKE NOTICE that on [date], [year], at [time] (a.m. or p.m.), or as soon thereafter as the matter can be heard, in Department [name] of the above-entitled Court, located at [address], petitioner, [name], will apply to the Court for an order authorizing perpetuation of evidence in accordance with the petition served on you with this Notice of Hearing.

Dated: [date]

> [name]_____
> Attorney for Petitioner

FORM 3–20
SAMPLE PETITION TO PERPETUATE TESTIMONY (CALIFORNIA)

SUPERIOR COURT OF THE STATE OF [state name]
IN AND FOR THE COUNTY OF [county name]

Petition of   No. [case number]

[name of prospective litigant]   PETITION TO PERPETUATE
                                         TESTIMONY BEFORE ACTION

Petitioner, [name], states:

1. Petitioner expects to be a [defendant/plaintiff] in an action in a court of this state, namely, [specify details of expected action].

2. The parties adverse to petitioner when the anticipated action is filed, so far as petitioner knows, will be [names of expected adverse parties].

*(Use the following if petitioner is prospective PLAINTIFF.)

3. Petitioner is presently unable to bring that action because [specify reasons].

*(Use the following if petitioner is prospective DEFENDANT.)

3. Petitioner is unable to cause that action to be brought because [specify reasons such as: petitioner expects to be made a defendant to the action, and statute of limitations will not bar the filing of the action against petitioner until [date]].

4. Petitioner desires to perpetuate the testimony of [name of prospective deponent], whose address is [address].

5. The substance of the testimony that petitioner expects to obtain from [name of prospective deponent] is [specify substance of expected testimony].

6. Petitioner desires to perpetuate the testimony of [name of prospective deponent] because [specify reasons].

WHEREFORE, petitioner prays the Court for an order authorizing [petitioner] to take the deposition of [name of prospective deponent], on [oral/written] examination for the purpose of perpetuating [name of prospective deponent]'s testimony.

Dated: [date]

                                         [name]
                                         Attorney for Petitioner

VERIFICATION

I declare under penalty of perjury that the statements in the foregoing Petition to Perpetuate Testimony are true of my own knowledge, except the matters that are stated on my information and belief, and as to those matters, I believe them to be true.

Dated: [date]

[name of petitioner]

Executed at [city], [state]

FORM 3–21
SAMPLE ORDER AUTHORIZING THE
PERPETUATION OF TESTIMONY (CALIFORNIA)

SUPERIOR COURT OF THE STATE OF [state name]
IN AND FOR THE COUNTY OF [county name]

Petition of	No. [case number]
[name of prospective litigant]	ORDER AUTHORIZING PERPETUATION OF TESTIMONY

The Petition of [name] for an order authorizing the taking of the deposition(s) of [name of prospective deponent] for the purpose of perpetuating [name of prospective deponent]'s testimony under California Code of Civil Procedure § 2035 was heard on [date], [year], [attorney A] appeared as counsel for Petitioner, and [attorney B] appeared as counsel for the expected adverse parties named in the Petition. It appearing to the Court that the perpetuation of testimony requested may prevent a failure or delay of justice,

IT IS ORDERED that:

1. Petitioner, [name], is granted leave to take the deposition(s) of [name] via [oral examination/written questions] regarding [specify nature of expected testimony].

*(Optional: 2. Petitioner shall furnish at Petitioner's expense a copy of these depositions to counsel appearing for the adverse parties.)

Dated: [date]

[name]
Judge

§ 3.29   Depositions after Discovery Cutoff

Discovery cutoffs are established by the Code of Civil Procedure for your state and the local court rules where the action is venued. Discovery cutoffs are generally thirty days prior to trial for nonexpert witnesses and fifteen days prior to trial for expert witness depositions. These cutoffs are measured from the first date set for trial of the case. As all experienced litigation paralegals know, a trial seldom, if ever, goes out on the first date for which it is set. Continuances and postponements of trial dates are axiomatic in a busy litigation office. A continuance of the trial date does not operate to reopen discovery proceedings. Many attorneys presume that simply because a trial has been set over for a second or third time and many months have transpired, they may notice depositions. This is not the case. For example, in California, California Code of Civil Procedure § 2024(e) measures the discovery cutoff from the date initially set for trial. All parties to the action may, however, stipulate to extend the time to complete discovery proceedings (specifically depositions) and/or to reopen discovery after a trial date has been continued. Such a stipulation must be in writing and does not become effective unless all parties to the action have consented. It may be an informal stipulation, but it must state in writing the specific extended date for discovery including discovery motions. The stipulation should be signed by all parties, but need not be filed with the Court unless it becomes relevant in a motion to compel.

On motion of any party, the Court may allow discovery proceedings to continue after a cutoff date or after the trial has been continued to a new date. Consult your Code of Civil Procedure for the requirements of such a motion. Generally, the motion should be accompanied by declarations stating the facts giving rise to the need for depositions or other discovery to continue after a cutoff date. A copy of the proposed discovery (deposition notices or subpoenas) should be attached to the motion. In ruling on such a motion, the court will consider the necessity and reasons for the additional discovery, the length of time elapsed between any date previously set for trial, and the date presently set for trial.

§ 3.30   Depositions after Judgment

After a lawsuit has been concluded and the judgment has been entered, the possibility of a successful appeal that will reserve the judgment or remand it for retrial makes it desirable to have a procedure for the perpetuation of testimony and the preservation of evidence pending the outcome of the appeal. Federal Rules of Civil Procedure 27(b) provides the mechanism for posttrial perpetuation of evidence. The right to perpetuate testimony pursuant to Rule 27 is discussed in detail in American Law Reports.[7] A motion for leave to engage in the process must be made to the court that entered the judgment, not the appellate court, and it must be made in the same manner as a discovery motion during the pendency of the action.

The motion shall set forth the following:

---

[7] 60 A.L.R. Fed. 924.

1. The names and addresses of persons to be examined and the substance of the testimony expected to be elicited from each person; and

2. A statement of the reasons for resorting to the perpetuation of testimony or the preservation of evidence pending the outcome of the appeal.

If the court determines that the perpetuation of evidence sought "is proper and may avoid a failure or delay of justice, it may make an order allowing the depositions to be taken." The depositions may then be taken pursuant to Rules 34 and 35 of the Federal Rules of Civil Procedure and the depositions may be used in the same manner and under the same conditions as are prescribed in the rules for depositions taken in actions pending in the district court wherein the motion has been made.

Good cause must be demonstrated to the satisfaction of the court as to the value of this witness (eyewitness, percipient witness, and so forth) and as to the fact that the identity and whereabouts of this person did not become known until after the trial of this matter had concluded. The possibility that this new witness will have new evidence that could alter the outcome of the action, and the unavailability of the witness to testify at a later date is the strongest argument that can be made to the court.

Circumstances requiring the use of this motion (**Form 3–22**) are rare, but do occur. For example, a new witness may have been discovered whose testimony would be relevant upon retrial (success of appeal), but who is ill, in the military, or for some other reason may not be able to testify at a later date. The motion must be accompanied by a notice of motion, a memorandum of points and authorities, and an attorney declaration. The attorney declaration should be evidentiary in nature and discuss the specific facts behind the grounds for the motion.

FORM 3–22
SAMPLE MOTION TO PERPETUATE TESTIMONY
PENDING APPEAL

SUPERIOR COURT OF THE STATE OF [state name]
IN AND FOR THE COUNTY OF [county name]

[plaintiff name], et al.,	No. [case number]
Plaintiffs,	MOTION TO PERPETUATE TESTIMONY PENDING APPEAL
-vs-	
[defendant name], et al.,	
Defendants.	

_____/

TO: [defendant/plaintiff], [name], and their attorney, to each other party, and to the attorney of record for each other party in this action:

PLEASE TAKE NOTICE that on [date], at [time] (a.m. or p.m.), or as soon thereafter as the matter can be heard, in Department [name] of the above-entitled Court, located at [address], [plaintiff/defendant] will move the Court under [specific statute] for an order allowing the taking of the deposition of [name of prospective deponent], whose address is [address], and whose telephone number is [telephone number].

The grounds for this motion are as follows:

1. The identity and whereabouts of [name of prospective deponent] as a person knowledgeable about the subject matter of this action did not become known to [plaintiff/defendant] until after the trial of this case had concluded.

2. [Name of prospective deponent] was [specify reason of unavailability].

3. Although [name of prospective deponent] is presently a resident of [city], [state], it is anticipated that [name of prospective deponent] will soon be leaving this jurisdiction and moving several hundred miles to [location].

4. [Defendant/plaintiff] has taken an appeal from the judgment for [plaintiff/defendant] that was entered on the jury's verdict in this case, and this creates the possibility of a retrial of this action, at which the testimony of [name of prospective deponent] will be useful to prevent a failure or delay of justice.

This motion is based on the attached memorandum of points and authorities, and [specify documents, exhibits, or declarations that accompany the motion].

Dated: [date].

[name of attorney]_____

§ 3.31 Depositions of Prisoners

Depositions of prisoners for use in civil actions may be taken only by leave of court and on such terms as the court prescribes. Statutory authority may be found at Federal Rule of Civil Procedure 30(a) or applicable state statutes. For example in California, statutory authority for taking the deposition of a prisoner in state prison is discussed at Penal Code § 2623 and California Code of Civil Procedure §§ 1995 to 1997. A motion for an order for the prisoner to be examined in prison must be made to the court in which the action is pending. The motion must be made on an affidavit or declaration under penalty of perjury showing the nature of the action, the testimony expected from the witness, and its direct relevancy to the action.

A notice of motion for order authorizing the deposition of a prisoner (see **Form 3–23**), or an application for an ex parte order, may be used. The motion must be accompanied by a memorandum of points and authorities setting forth the statutory basis for the motion and discussing the specific relevant facts and information known by the prisoner.

The first step in arranging such a deposition is to contact the warden's office where the prisoner is incarcerated. The secretary to the prison warden will assist you in arranging for a court reporter and arranging a conference room. Arrangements with the prison warden should be documented in a letter which can then be attached to your motion or application for ex parte order. Once the order is granted, the deposition may proceed in the same manner as any other deposition, observing all statutory requirements and local rules for the jurisdiction in which the action is pending. The deposition may be used in court subject to the same provisions as any other deposition.

If you represent a plaintiff who has unfortunately been incarcerated for an action totally unrelated to the action at hand, it is to your advantage to make arrangements for the deposition by working with the warden's office and proceeding to obtain an ex parte order. Requiring the defendant to prepare a noticed motion and attend a court hearing to take the deposition of plaintiff prisoner is not good strategy. Although these situations are rare, they do occur, and if handled correctly, damage to your client's credibility can be minimized. For example, you may represent a plaintiff involved in a motor vehicle accident where the plaintiff was rear-ended by a vehicle traveling at an excessive rate of speed, which has been documented in a police report. Your plaintiff, unfortunately, may have also forged checks for which the plaintiff has been caught and placed in prison. Whether the plaintiff has plead guilty to the charge of forgery is not relevant in the personal injury action at hand. The facts of the criminal case may not be used at the time of deposition to attack the credibility of your client.

FORM 3–23
SAMPLE NOTICE OF MOTION FOR ORDER
AUTHORIZING DEPOSITION OF PRISONER

SUPERIOR COURT OF THE STATE OF [state name]
AND FOR THE COUNTY OF [county name]

[plaintiff name],   No. [case number]

           Plaintiff,   NOTICE OF MOTION FOR
                                               ORDER AUTHORIZING DEPOSITION
                                               OF PRISONER

-vs-

[defendant name],

           Defendant.
                                               Date: [date]
                                               Time: [time]
                                               Location: [location]
                                               (Trial Date): [trial date]

TO: [noticed party] and to the attorney of record:

NOTICE IS HEREBY GIVEN that on [date], at [time] (a.m. or p.m.), or as soon thereafter as the matter may be heard, in Department [name] of this court, located at [address], [moving party] will move for an order that [name of prisoner] a prisoner in [name and location of jail/prison], be produced for the taking of their deposition on [oral examination/written questions], to be conducted at this [jail/prison] at [location] on [date], commencing at [time] (a.m. or p.m.) or at such other time as the court may designate. The motion will be made on the grounds that [name of prisoner] has knowledge of matters relevant and material to this action, and that their testimony as to such matters is necessary to [moving party] in preparing for and proceedings to the trial of this action.

The motion will be based on this notice of motion, on the declaration(s) of [names] and the memorandum of points and authorities served and filed herewith, on the records and file herein, and on such evidence as may be presented at the hearing of the motion.

Dated: [date]

[name]_____
Attorney for Moving Party

§ 3.32   Out-of-State Depositions

Taking the deposition of a third party who resides outside of the state in which the action is pending, or whose principal place of business is out of the state in which the action is pending, can require a more complex procedure than noticing in-state parties. (Check Civil Procedure Codes and local court rules for your state for specific procedural guidelines.) The place of deposition depends on whether the entity you wish to depose is a party to the action, and whether the party has an in-state office or place of business. The deposition of a corporation, partnership, or association that is not a party to the action, but has designated a principal place of business or executive office in your state, can be noticed pursuant to your state deposition notice. Mileage requirements as to distance from place of business to deposition site are stated in local codes and must be observed unless stipulated to otherwise by all counsel.

If a corporation does not have a designated office or principal place of business in your state, the deposition may be taken at the option of the deposing party either at the location of the corporation's home office (or principal place of business in another state) or in the state where the action is pending.

Procedures for taking a deposition in another state usually involve obtaining a court order that the deposition should take place at a location which is most convenient for the deponent. The court can also order the party seeking the depositions to pay the deponent's travel costs.

Many states, including California, authorize the courts to subpoena local residents to appear for depositions when it can be shown by an affidavit that their testimony is required in a lawsuit pending in another state. Such states issue deposition subpoenas upon proper procedural application for out-of-state depositions and require the party to appear. Other states require a showing of relevancy and good cause regarding the testimony to be obtained from a local resident. An application to that court must be made before the court will issue a deposition subpoena. Consult local rules for your state regarding good cause requirements. Still other states require a commission from the court where the action is pending. This requirement includes the issuance of a deposition subpoena in the court where the action is pending and the appointment of an officer to administer oaths and take the deposition. The forms for an issuance of a commission can be found in the Code of Civil Procedure for your state.

Practically speaking, if it becomes necessary to take depositions in another state, the most economical and expedient way to arrange them is through association of local counsel. Local counsel are familiar with local court procedures, admitted to practice in that state, and will be able to work with the local courts to obtain whatever orders are necessary for the deposition to go forward. If your attorney is a member of American Trial Lawyer's Association (ATLA), it is easy to locate an attorney practicing in the city or town where the deposition must be taken. This is a routine procedure and a professional courtesy that ATLA members extend to one another. It cuts through the red tape procedural nightmare of making certain the deposition notice meets the requirements of the local court.

If you wish to take the deposition of a third-party custodian of records, and are seeking only records and not a personal deposition, your local process server is your best resource person. A process server from your state can prepare a records only deposition subpoena and send it to a court reporter in the state where the custodian of records resides. That process server then reissues the subpoena making it state specific, and obtains the records. To insure that the records return to your office, designate your attorney and law firm as deposition officer on the face of the subpoena. This procedure is very straightforward, but it does require a longer time span than noticing an instate custodian of records deposition. An example of where this procedure is most useful includes corporations whose principal place of business is in another state. For example, in product liability actions when General Motors is a defendant, their principal place of business is not necessarily where the action may be filed because General Motors has been admitted as a foreign corporation licensed to do business in many states.

§ 3.33   Depositions of Nonparty Witnesses

Depositions are unique as discovery devices because they are the only discovery device that permits you to take the testimony and/or obtain the records of an individual who is not a party to the action. Depositions of nonparties are usually depositions of Custodians of Records of an entity such as a hospital, bank, title company, or other business. Preparation of a nonparty Deposition Subpoena Duces Tecum, which requires the production of business records on a specified date and at a specific time, is a procedure that can and should be accomplished by the legal assistant. The following procedural outline will serve as a guideline.

Procedural Outline for Subpoena Duces Tecum
for Custodian of Records Deposition in State Court

1. Prepare a "Dear Custodian of Records" letter in cases where you desire only records and do not require the personal appearance of the custodian of records. (See **Form 3–24** for a sample letter.) This letter should explain that a personal appearance can be avoided if the records are prepared in the proper fashion and a declaration of the Custodian of Records is executed stating that the designated custodian has made a due and diligent search for all records responsive to the subpoena, and has included them in the response. The declaration may also state that after a due and diligent search no records have been found which are responsive to the subpoena request. (See **Form 3–25** for a sample Declaration of Custodian Records.)

2. No letter of explanation or declaration is needed if the personal appearance of a Custodian of Records is required.   The advantage in having the personal appearance of a Custodian of Records is that, if properly noticed, you will have someone who has knowledge of the contents of the records and is able to explain the significance of various entries, technical abbreviations, and other business jargon unique to those records. Be sure to specify that the personal appearance of the "person most knowledgeable regarding the contents of the documents" is required. This may be someone other than the custodian of records. If this is not done, you could end up with the personal appearance of a clerical person whose only function was to assemble the required documents.

3. Prepare the subpoena.   Preparation of the subpoena itself is very straightforward. Check with your local court for a copy of their standard judicial council subpoena. Note that the deposition officer portion of the subpoena must be filled in with the name of a professional photocopying service and/or court reporter. The deposition officer must be a disinterested third party.

4. Attach Exhibit A.   Exhibit A to the Subpoena Duces Tecum is the most important part of the subpoena; it sets forth item by item those records which you are interested in obtaining. Requested records in Exhibit A to the subpoena should be set forth in categories with specific subheadings so that records can be clearly identified. See **Form 3–26** for a sample Exhibit A suitable for sending to a bank or savings and loan. Note that in the language of the Exhibit A, bank terminology and designation of records are very specific. To prepare an Exhibit A properly, you must become familiar with the exact names of those records you wish to obtain as well as what other records are generated in that particular industry which would be useful. The biggest mistake that can be made in requesting records on Exhibit A to a Subpoena Duces Tecum is misidentification of requested records. Another mistake is not asking for all the records relative to the issues of your case that the particular type of business might maintain in the daily course and scope of their business activities. To avoid this lapse in preparation of requested documents simply ask for "any and all documents which refer, relate, evidence, or constitute any references to the issues of this action as set forth in the pleadings on file in this action, specifically plaintiff's complaint filed on (Date) in (Name of Court)."

5. Prepare an attorney declaration of good cause which sets forth the identity of the attorney, the fact that they are the attorney of record for the party they are representing, and that good cause exists for the production or the requested records. The declaration of good cause is the most important part of the Attorney Declaration and it must state the specific relevance of the records; that no alternative means of discovering the information exists; and that the information sought is either admissible at trial or reasonably designed to lead to evidence admissible at the time of trial. See **Form 3–27** for a sample attorney declaration.

6. Prepare Notice to Consumer.   When requesting records of a personal nature (this includes phone records, hospital records, bank records, savings and loan records, real estate transaction records, and so forth), it is necessary to send a Notice to Consumer informing them that certain records have been requested regarding certain personal business activities. The consumer must be given ample warning, to file an objection to the production of those records which takes the form of a Motion to Quash service of Subpoena or Protective Order. A Notice to Consumer can usually be sent to the named consumer in care of their attorney of record. If the consumer is representing himself, the Notice to Consumer must be sent directly to him at his last known address. See **Form 3–28** for a sample Notice to Consumer.

Check the Codes of Civil Procedure for your state definition of consumer records. Many records which are not commonly thought of as consumer records have now been defined as consumer records. See **Chapter 6** definition of a consumer.

7. Prepare a Certificate of Compliance to be executed by the attorney of record. The Certificate of Compliance (**Form 3–29**) is attached to the Notice to Consumer which is attached to the Attorney's Declaration, Subpoena, and Exhibit A to the Subpoena. The entire Deposition of Custodian of Records packet must then either be served by hand or mailed to all attorneys who have appeared in the action.

8. Serve the subpoena on the custodian of records.   Service of the subpoena on the custodian of records must be by personal service. This can be accomplished by a process server who will advance witness fees if they are demanded. The amount of witness fees varies from jurisdiction to jurisdiction and should always be checked with the superior court in your county. The process server will execute a Proof of Service indicating the name of the person served. It is important to serve the person authorized to accept service on behalf of the business, or you will have a potential invalid service claim. Provide the name of that person to the process server at the time you request service. Because process servers follow your instructions, make every effort to give clear, concise, nonlegalese instructions.

FORM 3–24
SAMPLE LETTER TO CUSTODIAN OF RECORDS

[bank A]

Dear Custodian of Records:

   Enclosed is the subpoena served upon [name] Bank for the records pertaining to accounts of [defendant A] and [defendant B], as well as various business entities of which [defendant A] is an officer, director, partner, or controlling person. Please note that you do not need to make a personal appearance to satisfy the requirements of this subpoena. You may choose to execute the enclosed Declaration in compliance with Evidence Code § [code section].

To comply with the Subpoena Duces Tecum for business records copies of the records designated in Exhibit A should be separately enclosed in an inner envelope sealed with the title and number of the action (Case No: [case number], [bank B v. [defendant A], [defendant B, et al.] inscribed upon the envelope. That sealed envelope shall then be enclosed in an outer envelope sealed and mailed to:

[name of deposition officer]
[address]

You must mail the records requested within fifteen days after your receipt of this subpoena.

The enclosed check is the witness fee authorized by Evidence Code § [code section]. If there are additional photocopying or reproduction charges, you may claim reimbursement for reasonable fees by submitting an invoice directly to the deposition officer.

If you have any questions regarding compliance with this subpoena or execution of the enclosed declaration, please do not hesitate to call me.

Sincerely,

_____

[name]
Legal Assistant

FORM 3–25
SAMPLE DECLARATION OF CUSTODIAN OF RECORDS

SUPERIOR COURT OF THE STATE OF [state name]
IN AND FOR THE COUNTY OF [county name]

[bank B],   No. [case number]

      Plaintiff,   DECLARATION OF [name of custodian of records]
                            RE BANK RECORDS
-vs-   ([code section])

[defendant A], [defendant B],
et al.,

      Defendants.

I, [name], declare:

1. I am [name], the duly authorized custodian of records of [bank A], and have authority to certify such records.

2. [date], I was served with a Subpoena Duces Tecum and supporting declaration issued by the Superior Court of the State of [state name] for the County of [county name] in an action entitled [bank B] v. [defendant A], [defendant B], et al., calling for certain business and banking records more specifically described in Exhibit A to the Subpoena Duces Tecum relating to accounts held by [defendant A], [defendant B], and various business entities.

3. The accompanying copies are true copies of all records described in the subpoena that are in my possession and custody as custodian of records of [bank A]. These records were prepared by the personnel of [bank A], and other persons acting under the control of said personnel, in the ordinary course of business, at or near the times of the acts, conditions, or events recorded therein.

4. Of the records described in the Subpoena Duces Tecum, [bank A] does not have the following:

[list of unavailable records] _____

_____

_____

I declare under penalty of perjury under the laws of the State of [state name] that the foregoing is true and correct.

[date] and [location]

                              [signature] [title of custodian of records] _____

FORM 3–26
SAMPLE EXHIBIT A TO SUBPOENA DUCES TECUM

INSTRUCTIONS AND DEFINITIONS

(See instructions and definitions in **Chapter 6**)

Plaintiff requests that all documents be produced in the form in which they were found in their normal filing places, including in the production the file folders or other bindings in which such documents have been so found.

Unless otherwise specified, the time period covered by this subpoena extends from [date] to the present.

DOCUMENTS TO BE PRODUCED

1. Any documents relating to any applications or requests by defendants and any of the defendants' companies and other entities for credit or funding, and any inquiries relating to such credit or funding.

2. Any documents provided by defendants or any of defendants' companies and other entities to you relating to credit and funding, and to requests and applications therefor.

3. Any documents received, created, or reviewed by you to evaluate and analyze any applications of, or the creditworthiness or credit of, defendants or any of the defendants' companies and other entities, including, but not limited to:

(a) Any credit or funding applications and all backup material, work papers, and support information therefor;

(b) Any credit or funding approval packages and reports, and all backup material, work papers, and support information therefor;

(c) Any backup material and work papers relating to any credit or credit application;

(d) Any documents relating to any analysis of credit, creditworthiness, and credit applications;

(e) Any financial statements, spread sheets, balance sheets, income statements, funds flow statements, business plans, forecasts, budgets, projections, and appraisals;

(f) Any credit reports, trade credit reports, trade checking, and any documents relating to any credit investigation;

(g) Any lease or rental agreements, loan agreements, and contracts;

(h) Any documents analyzing or reviewing credit or creditworthiness, and any documents relating to any meetings regarding the approval, denial, or provision of credit, including but not limited to any minutes and notes of such meetings, and officer write-ups;

(i) Any documents relating to any communications between you and other lenders, banks, savings and loans, insurance companies, pension funds, and any other providers of credit;

(j) Any documents relating to any denial of credit;

(k) Any call reports, business development reports, relationship plan reports, comment sheets, and any documents relating to the supervision of credit and funding.

4. Any documents relating to any communications between you and plaintiff relating to defendants or to any of the defendants' companies and other entities.

5. Any documents relating to any communications between you and defendants or any of defendants' companies and other entities.

6. Any documents relating to any communications between you and the defendants or any of the defendants' companies and other entities relating to credit, creditworthiness, or funding.

7. Any documents relating to any payments, delinquencies, defaults, late payments, or defaults of defendants, any of defendants' companies, and other entities, and any documents relating to any workouts or negotiations relating to any credit or funding of defendants or any of defendants' companies and other entities.

FORM 3–27
SAMPLE DECLARATION SUPPORTING ISSUANCE OF SUBPOENA DUCES TECUM

SUPERIOR COURT OF THE STATE OF [state name]
IN AND FOR THE COUNTY OF [county name]

[bank B],   No. [case number]

      Plaintiff,   DECLARATION SUPPORTING
                                           ISSUANCE OF SUBPOENA DUCES
-vs-   TECUM RE DEPOSITION

[defendant A], [defendant B],
et al.,

      Defendants.

I, [name of attorney], declare:

1. I am a member of the law firm of [name], attorneys of record for plaintiff [bank B].

2. [bank A] has, in its possession or under its control, the following described documents, records and/or physical evidence described in Exhibit A attached hereto.

3. Said documents, records, and/or physical evidence are material to the issues in this case because plaintiff has alleged that the defendants have transferred funds between other defendants, breached agreements with plaintiff and failed to make payments on a specific Letter of Credit No. [number] in the amount of [dollar amount] funded by plaintiff [bank B], at defendants' express request.

4. The requested documents will set out the economic relations between defendants and various business entities, joint ventures, corporations, subsidiaries, and companies; and will reflect defendants' creditworthiness. As such, the requested documents will provide essential evidence on defendants' financial holding and ability to satisfy the terms of the outstanding amounts owed to [bank B] on promissory notes, and a letter of credit.

5. Good cause exists to require [bank B] to produce the documents, records and/or physical evidence described in Exhibit A, in that it is necessary that we inspect and/or copy the same in order to prepare this case effectively for trial, to prevent surprises at trial, and there is no alternative source for such information and no alternative means to obtain inspection and copying thereof.

I declare under penalty of perjury of the laws of the State of [state name] that the foregoing is true and correct.

Executed this [date] day of [month], [year], at [city], [state].

[name of attorney]

FORM 3–28
SAMPLE NOTICE TO CONSUMERS

SUPERIOR COURT OF THE STATE OF [state name]
IN AND FOR THE COUNTY OF [county name]

[bank B],	No. [case number]
Plaintiff,	NOTICE TO CONSUMERS PURSUANT TO SECTION [code section] OF THE CODE OF CIVIL PROCEDURE
-vs-	
[defendant A], [defendant B], et al.,	
Defendants.	

TO: [defendant A] and [defendant B], individually and dba [company A] and [company B]; [company C] and its subsidiaries, [company D]; [company E], a corporation; [company F], a corporation; [company G], a corporation; [company B], a corporation; [company H], a corporation; and [company I], a limited partnership.

PLEASE TAKE NOTICE that pursuant to Section [code section] of the Code of Civil Procedure:

1. RECORDS ABOUT YOU ARE BEING SOUGHT by plaintiffs [bank B] from the witnesses listed below, as set forth in the Subpoena Duces Tecum and Declarations attached hereto:

Witnesses	Date Witness is to Produce Documents Regarding You
Custodian of Records of [bank A]	[date], [time]

2. IF YOU WISH TO OBJECT to this witness furnishing the records, you must file papers with the Court prior to the data listed above when that witness is to produce documents regarding you.

3. YOU OR YOUR ATTORNEY MAY CONTACT THE UNDERSIGNED, as the attorney for the parties seeking to examine such records, to determine whether the undersigned is willing to agree in writing to cancel or limit the Subpoena Duces Tecum. If no such agreement is reached, YOU SHOULD CONSULT AN ATTORNEY about your interest in protecting your right of privacy.

Dated: [date]

Respectfully submitted,

[attorney for plaintiff]

FORM 3–29
SAMPLE CERTIFICATE OF COMPLIANCE

SUPERIOR COURT OF THE STATE OF [state name]
IN AND FOR THE COUNTY OF [county name]

[bank B],	No. [case number]
Plaintiff,	CERTIFICATE OF COMPLIANCE WITH SECTION _____ OF THE CODE OF CIVIL PROCEDURE

-vs-

[defendant A], [defendant B]
et al.,

       Defendants.

NOTICE IS HEREBY GIVEN that the individuals and entities listed below have been given the notice required by section [code section] of the Code of Civil Procedure:

[defendant A] and [defendant B], individually and dba [company A] and [company B]
[company C], and its subsidiary, [company D]
[company E], a corporation
[company F], a corporation
[company B], a corporation
[company H], a corporation
[company I], a limited partnership

Dated: [date]

                        Respectfully submitted,

                        [attorney for plaintiff]

§ 3.34 Grounds for Challenge on Service Requirements

Service requirements for consumer notices, deposition notices, and subpoenas vary from county to county, and from state to state, and should always be checked with the county clerk before preparation. All rules of service must be strictly followed to prevent a motion to quash service of subpoena based on a claim of invalid service. Internal consistency is also extremely important in the preparation of all the documents for subpoenas. Double check names of business officers, key personnel, and so forth to prevent giving the opposition grounds for challenging the validity of the subpoena service. Challenges give away valuable time and could upset the strategy of your discovery plan. On the other hand, if a subpoena has been served and you wish to challenge it, look carefully at the following areas where mistakes are most commonly made:

1. Lack of proper timely notice to consumer,
2. Lack of notice to second consumer (for example, the spouse of a party) where joint records (financial or property) are sought,
3. Service of certificate of compliance in an untimely manner,

4. Incorrect name of business entity, and

5. Incorrect identification of account numbers or property description.

§ 3.35 Deposition Question Preparation

You can help an attorney who is preparing to take a deposition by reviewing the pleadings, documents, photographs, and other reports in the file and compiling a list of possible deposition questions. A useful tool in compiling an outline of possible deposition questions is your state's jury instructions. Jury instructions set forth those elements necessary to prove a prima facie case for your client. By tailoring deposition questions along the lines of jury instructions, the attorney will be able to elicit information that can be used at the time of trial to prove or disprove the causes of action of a particular complaint.

Reviewing prior discovery, such as other depositions or interrogatories, often yields useful information for preparing deposition questions. For example, in a personal injury action, the deponent might state that the deponent returned to work on a particular date but complained regularly to the supervisor of pain and stiffness in the deponent's back. The deponent might further state that there was a discussion with the deponent's supervisor regarding reassignment or lighter duties.

A basic outline of topics suggesting the questions to be used in a deposition should be prepared based around key background topics. The outline must be tailored to the facts of your case; however, certain general topics will usually be explored in any deposition. The outline of topics should refer to the exhibits which will be used with the deposition such as letters authored by the deponent, medical records, statistical reports, and other documents either authored by the deponent or of which the deponent has personal knowledge. The following topical outline is helpful for beginning a draft of deposition questions:

1. Background
    a. Name and address
    b. Personal and family history
    c. Education
    d. Job history
2. Claims History
    a. Any prior claims or lawsuit
    b. When, where, parties involved, and results
    c. Prior depositions
    d. Prior court testimony
3. Educational Background
    a. Formal training, college
    b. Special job training/experience
    c. Military job training/experience
4. Work History

    a.   Present employer—job title, listing of duties and responsibilities, name of immediate supervisor

    b.   Past employment history for 5–10 years and reasons for job changes

5.   Current Professional Involvement

    a.   Membership in professional societies, offices held

    b.   Trade or professional journals subscribed to/read on regular basis

    c.   Lectures, published articles

6.   Relationship with Defendant/Plaintiff

    a.   Length of time known

    b.   Work relationship

    c.   Social relationship

7.   Documents and Records

    a.   Motion to produce/subpoena for deposition

    b.   Method of record keeping

    c.   Records search

    d.   Identify and produce records

    e.   Names and addresses of other persons and entities who may have records related to this case

8.   Identity of Business for Corporate Deponent

    a.   Officers, directors, employees, agents

    b.   Parent corporation and subsidiary licensees

    c.   Incorporation and place of business

    d.   Places where licensed to do business

    e.   Names used in business

9.   Witnesses

    a.   Names and addresses of persons witnessing events and transactions

    b.   Names and addresses of persons deponent has communicated with

    c.   Names and addresses of persons who may know something about the case

10.   Discovery

    a.   Interrogatory responses

    b.   Investigative reports, investigation of incident

    c.   Preparation for this deposition, meetings with attorney, documents reviewed, and so forth

This outline of background topics is by no means complete, rather it should assist you in the organization of basic preliminary areas of questioning. The legal and factual issues, and the deponent's relationship to them, is the most crucial part of the deposition. The key to preparing deposition questions is to be detailed. All topics should be logically organized in a chronological sequence. All pertinent documents which will be used as deposition exhibits should be copied for use at the deposition. Deposition exhibits need to be prepared so that you have a clean copy for all opposing counsel, the court reporter, and the deponent. The copy that goes to your attorney should be highlighted to point out key areas for deposition questions. Prepare foundation questions to lead into the introduction of each particular document as an exhibit. If interrogatory responses are to be used at the deposition, prepare a blue-lined or highlighted copy of the responses for your attorney indicating those answers which are nonresponsive or need further explanation.

§ 3.36   Sample Deposition Questions

The questions on a deposition should be tailored not only to the position of the deponent but also to the nature of the litigation. Questions for the deposition of a Chief Executive Officer (CEO) regarding documents could include:

1.   Did you consult with any other corporate officer before authoring the document, "Corporate Hiring Policies," "Corporate Stock Options," "Corporate Retirement Plan," and so forth?

2.   Are there any officers or members of the board of directors responsible for preparation of drafts of corporate policy and procedure documents?

3.   Is it your policy to draft proposed corporate policy for review by other corporate officers before finalizing?

4.   What is the procedure for reviewing drafts of corporate policy and procedure documents?

5.   Do any of your other corporate officers have input of any kind into formal corporate documents?

6.   Are corrections or revisions made to corporate policy documents at corporate meetings prior to their finalization?

These questions focus on corporate documents because policy and procedure are the lifeblood of a corporation. Other questions regarding the personal and educational background of the CEO and each corporate officer as well as criteria for board member selection should not be overlooked.

If the deposition was of a plaintiff's supervisor in a personal injury case the questions would be quite different and would need to be tailored to address plaintiff's wage loss claim. Some of the questions that should be prepared for the deposition of a plaintiff's supervisor include the following:

1.   When did Joe return to work?

2.   How often did you see Joe while he was at work?

3.   Did you speak to Joe on a regular basis?

4.   Did Joe ever complain to you of stiffness and soreness in his back?

5.   How often did Joe complain to you? (Dates, times, any documentation?)

6.   Did Joe ever indicate to you that he was having difficulty performing his job duties because of pain in his back? (Dates, times, anyone present at the time of complaints, and so forth?)

7. Do you recall any discussions with Joe regarding a change of assignment?

8. How long has Joe worked for you?

9. Have you always been Joe's supervisor?

10. Does anyone else supervise Joe's work?

11. Have you had occasion to evaluate Joe's job performance?

12. What specifically were Joe's job duties before the accident and what are his duties now that he has resumed work?

13. What are the names of Joe's co-workers? What are their duties?

These sample questions could be expanded depending on the issues of the case, the amount of damages at issue, and other information gained. Discovery is never static, and good discovery serves as a catalyst for new information, new liability theories or defenses, and so forth. These questions are appropriate for an information gathering deposition of a witness who has been identified in prior discovery, and whose main importance to the case at issue is limited to the issue of damages and job performance. From the answers you receive you will be able to learn:

1. If Joe continued to have subjective symptoms relating to his back injury;

2. If Joe reported these complaints to his supervisor;

3. If Joe made any effort to mitigate his damages (wage loss), by returning to work prior to full recovery;

4. If Joe requested a change in job assignment;

5. If Joe was a "good" employee—on time, good job performance, and so forth; and

6. You will also learn names of Joe's co-workers, and other supervisors, who you might want to question later.

§ 3.37   Preparing the Client for Deposition

Once a deposition notice is received in your office, it should be forwarded to the client with a letter of explanation. Although deposition schedules are frequently changed to suit the convenience of attorneys, a client's convenience must also be considered and the date selected may not be appropriate for your client; therefore, the deposition may need to be continued to a date mutually agreeable.

The letter in **Form 3–30**, or a variation of it, should become part of your office exemplar file so that as soon as a deposition notice is received in your office it can be routed directly to the client.

FORM 3–30
SAMPLE LETTER NOTIFYING CLIENT OF A DEPOSITION

[date]

[client name]
[address]

   RE: [client] v. [name] Shopping Mall

Dear [client]:

   The attorneys for the [plaintiff/defendant], [name of firm], have scheduled your oral deposition for [date], at the offices of [name of offices], at [time]. You will be questioned under oath by an attorney in my presence. A deposition reporter will record everything that is said. As you know, this procedure is commonly used by attorneys in preparing a case.

   Although a deposition is an informal proceeding, it has important consequences for the outcome of our case. Therefore, please arrange to be in my office on [date] at [time] so that I can explain the proceedings to you in advance, answer your questions, and review your testimony.

If the deposition notice also requests documents, include this paragraph:

   The deposition notice, a copy of which is enclosed, also requests you to produce certain documents and objects. Please carefully review the items listed and bring with you any you have in your possession, or have access to at the time of our appointment. Many of the items requested are in our file, and we will assist you in locating those items and documents. However, it is important that you make a careful search for the items requested, so that if asked at your deposition whether you have made a due and diligent effort to obtain the requested items, you can truthfully say that you have done so.

   I look forward to meeting with you on [date] at [time].

                         Sincerely,

                         [attorney name]

   This letter is prepared for signature by an attorney, but it can be authored and signed by a legal assistant with modifications as to the predeposition meeting without a violation of ethics because it does not give legal advice, but is merely an informational type letter.
   Preparation of the client for deposition is a process that should be done by both the attorney and the legal assistant. An attorney will personally want to review not only the facts of the case with the client before the deposition, but also the files for statements taken, photographs of an accident, medical records, if there are any, employment records, contracts that the client has executed, and so forth. Further preparation of the client for a deposition can be accomplished in many ways. Some major law firms have purchased video cassettes which simulate a deposition and have their clients watch them to understand the deposition process. Other law firms play tape

recordings for a client which simulate deposition questions. The client listening to the tape recording of simulated deposition questions is then instructed to give proper answers. Often a legal assistant will sit with a client to monitor the question and answer process and report to the attorney on areas that need further attention.

The best preparation of a client for a deposition comes from a two part meeting. The first part of the meeting is with the attorney and the second part is with the legal assistant. At the first part of the meeting, the client and attorney go over the facts of the case, questions, and issues that will come up during the deposition, and prepare for different approaches to answering. For example, a client is always instructed to tell the truth. However, many times a client will be ashamed to admit that they either do not know or do not remember a particular fact and will want to try to guess at an answer. The client needs to be reassured that it is okay not to remember everything. There are many questions a client will have about the deposition process in general which deal simply with the procedural aspects of a court reporter taking down sworn testimony. These questions and many others can be answered in part two of the client's preparation which should be handled by the legal assistant. **Form 3–31** is a sample letter to a client regarding deposition preparation.

FORM 3–31
SAMPLE LETTER TO CLIENT
REGARDING DEPOSITION PREPARATION

Re: Preparation for Deposition
[plaintiff A] v. [defendant B]

Dear [name of client]:

This is to advise you that your oral deposition is scheduled for [time] at [location] and your presence is necessary. This is an important step in the handling of your case. A deposition involves questioning of you under oath before a court reporter by the lawyer for the other side about the facts of your case, your injuries, complaints, elements of your damages, as well as background information about you personally.

Because your deposition is one of the most important parts of your case and because we know that you are not familiar with this procedure, it is absolutely necessary for you to meet with me to discuss the deposition procedure. In fact, the oral deposition may require our talking to you on more than one occasion.

I have scheduled an appointment for you to be in my office on [date] at [time], so that we can prepare for your deposition.

Please bring with you to our meeting any medical bills, invoices, or other bills relating to your injuries or damages that you have not previously furnished to our office. Also, if you have lost wages and have any evidence to prove this, such as check stubs before and after the accident, please bring these along.

Please sign and date the enclosed postcard cofirming that you will be present at the time and place specified. Please plan on this meeting taking several hours. It is best that you come without your spouse or children so that we can focus on the deposition preparation without distractions. It is also possible that opposing counsel may wish to depose your spouse at a later date which is another reason why your spouse should be excluded from this preparation, so that your spouse's deposition testimony will be independent recollection.

I am looking forward to seeing you at our meeting.

Sincerely,

[name]
Legal Assistant

The letter in **Form 3–32** illustrates a combination of informing the client regarding the time, date, and place of the deposition and including many of the items discussed in **§§ 3.38** through **3.41.** Sending this letter to a client does not replace the predeposition conference; however, it does provide a great deal of useful information for the client in advance of the predeposition meeting and may be useful depending upon the individual circumstances of your case.

FORM 3–32
SAMPLE LETTER NOTIFYING CLIENT
OF A DEPOSITION (NARRATIVE FORM)

[date]

[plaintiff name]
[address]

RE: [plaintiff] v. [name] Shopping Mall

Dear [plaintiff]:

Please be advised that the defendants have noticed your deposition for [date] at [time] at the offices of [name of offices].

At the deposition, the attorneys for the defendants will have the opportunity to ask you questions while you are under oath. At this time, they will have the opportunity to hear your side of the story as well as to size you up as to the type of witness you will make at trial. If your case does not go to trial, and is settled, this is the only opportunity the defense attorney will have to meet you and to form an impression of you.

Accordingly, the deposition is probably the most important pretrial proceeding in your case. Due to the importance of the deposition, I would like to meet with you at my office on [date] at [time] to review the facts of your case and to answer any questions concerning the deposition which you may have.

There is no reason to be apprehensive about your deposition. However, we have found that many of our clients feel more relaxed and better prepared if they have some written suggestions to review prior to their deposition. Therefore, we enclose the following list of suggestions.

Please look them over and bring them with you when you come for your pre-deposition conference. At that time, if you have any questions or concerns, we can go over them together. Your attention to these matters will make you a more effective witness and will enhance our position regarding either settlement or trial.

SUGGESTIONS

1. RECALL AND REVIEW THE FACTS SURROUNDING THE PRESENT CLAIM: Concentrate and reflect upon the facts surrounding the incident leading up to, evolving around, and occurring subsequent to this claim. If you maintain a diary, review all aspects of the matter prior to our meeting and bring the diary with you. We will review all facts prior to the deposition with you.

2. AT THE DEPOSITION, LISTEN TO THE QUESTIONS ASKED AND BE SURE YOU UNDERSTAND THE QUESTION BEFORE YOU ANSWER: All too often, a witness will assume they know what the next question is going to be and will therefore answer without really hearing the question. DO NOT DO THIS. An inaccurate answer will result.

Also, if you do not understand a question asked by the opposing lawyer, do not try to answer it. Tell the questioner that you do not understand the question. The questioner will then rephrase it. It is your right to insist on a question that you can comprehend before making your answer.

3. IF NEEDED, ALLOW YOURSELF TIME TO REFLECT BEFORE BEGINNING YOUR ANSWER: Do not allow the opposing lawyer to pressure you into hurried answers. Remember, no jury is present here; in the deposition transcript, a 30-second pause looks the same as a one-second pause.

4. ANSWER THE QUESTION AS BRIEFLY AS POSSIBLE:

   (a) If possible, answer the question with a "yes" or "no";

   (b) <u>Do not volunteer</u> any additional information;

   (c) Answer only the question asked; and

(d) Do not guess or speculate.

5. MAINTAIN A PLEASANT DEMEANOR:

(a) In answering questions of the opposing attorney, maintain a polite and cooperative attitude.

(b) Only in rare instances do opposing attorneys get belligerent or try to take advantage of a witness. Should this occur, do not display annoyance. We will take the necessary and appropriate actions on your behalf.

6. AVOID EXAGGERATION:

(a) Do not try to improve upon the facts of your case because this conduct is invariably recognized by the opposition who could later exploit any inaccuracy to its advantage.

(b) If, at a subsequent time, the judge or jury feel that you have exaggerated on one point, they may well surmise that you have exaggerated on other points. Undesirable results have been known to occur because of an unfortunate tendency to exaggerate.

7. MAKE AN EFFORT TO ENUNCIATE CLEARLY: The court reporter is recording everything you say which may be used in court later. If you speak audibly and clearly, a more precise record will result. This includes avoiding nods or shakes of the head, as well as "uh-uhs" and "uh-huhs".

8. PRESENT YOUR BEST APPEARANCE: For your deposition we suggest that you dress in your usual work clothes or whatever is comfortable for you, as long as it is neat and relatively conventional. You should know that the opposing lawyer will be appraising you and making some tentative evaluations about how you will impress a jury. Also, it helps to appear interested in the case and project a sincere, candid demeanor.

9. CONSIDER CAREFULLY TIME:

(a) Very often, witnesses are careless with respect to time. An inaccurate answer usually is the result of not giving the subject of the question sufficient consideration. It would be well to review this point until you are reasonably certain you have a clear comprehension of it, and if necessary, your answers to such questions should be couched in terms of estimate or opinion.

(b) Do not be forced into a guessing game with the opposing attorney. If the opposing attorney indicates to you that they want only your best judgment with respect to facts concerning time, but you are unable to make a reliable judgment, indicate that you cannot make a reasonable estimate and would only be guessing.

10. CAREFULLY SCRUTINIZE PHOTOGRAPHS, DOCUMENTS, AND SO FORTH: If photographs are displayed by opposing counsel and you are asked if they correctly portray the scene as it appeared at a specific time, carefully examine the photographs before you answer. If you cannot be certain, then you should so indicate. Should you be asked to examine documents and answer questions concerning them, take as much time as you need.

11. DO NOT QUALIFY FAVORABLE FACTS: Answer questions concerning favorable details as definitely as possible. Avoid expressions such as "I think" or "I guess".

12. SUGGESTED BEHAVIOR WHEN YOUR COUNSEL OBJECTS: If during the deposition I object to a question or line of questioning, suspend your answer immediately, and say nothing further until the matter has been resolved. I will then direct you as to whether your answer is required.

Also, do not be concerned if, during the deposition, I occasionally caution you to avoid speculation or to listen to the question before answering. Witnesses frequently forget these things, and the record does need to be kept clear.

13. QUESTIONS POSED AT THE DEPOSITION: The following questions are frequently asked at depositions. If you reflect on these things prior to your appointment with us, this will expedite our conference:

(a) Date, time, and places of meetings with the various parties;

(b) Your residence addresses for the past ten years; and

(c) Your employers (including addresses) for the past ten years.

We will be telephoning you a day or two before the deposition to confirm that it is actually going. (Frequently deposition dates must be changed at the last minute because of trial attorneys' scheduling conflicts.)

If you have any questions to ask between now and the time of your predeposition conference, do not hesitate to call.

Very truly yours,

[attorney name]

§ 3.38 Tips for Client Preparation for a Deposition

The following tips can be used by a legal assistant in preparing the client for a deposition:

1. Tell the client exactly what a deposition is procedurally, what will happen, the function of the court reporter, how the testimony will be used later on at the time of trial, and the importance of being accurate and not guessing at answers.

2. Assure the client that they will have an opportunity to read and review their testimony in transcript form before it becomes final. Many clients are not aware of the fact that they are entitled to see a copy of the transcript of their deposition testimony and have 30 days to review it, make corrections, and return it. Clients, however, must be cautioned that if there are major corrections to a deposition transcript it could seriously undermine their credibility. It is best to counsel them to avoid the need for later changes by correcting testimony on the spot. For example, if it occurs to a client during the deposition that they have made a mistake in their testimony, they should immediately inform the attorney questioning them that they wish to back up to have a question reread to them. A question can be reread, and a corrected answer can be given on the spot. This will then appear in the transcript as a correction in testimony and will establish the witness' credibility.

3. Clients need to be told how to dress for the deposition. It needs to be emphasized to the client that their dress, demeanor, and total appearance will affect the other side's evaluation of them as a witness and in turn influence their credibility. It is best to tell the client to dress as though they were going to church, an important meeting, or a job interview. It is also wise to counsel the client not to dress in anything that is brand new or uncomfortable. A client who works at a blue collar job will not feel comfortable attending a deposition dressed in a shirt and tie. Though the client may feel the need to dress in a shirt, tie, and jacket to impress the opposing counsel, the reality of it is that he will probably feel so uncomfortable and nervous that his credibility will be destroyed by his wiggling and general sense of uneasiness. It would be better for a client who rarely wears a suit and tie to appear at a deposition dressed in casual clothes.

The biggest problem in dressing for deposition occurs with women clients who may tend to overdress. Women clients should be cautioned to dress down for a deposition, underplaying makeup, perfume, and most of all jewelry. Clients should avoid bright neon colors, revealing garments, and especially t-shirts with favorite sayings. The general rule for both men and women can be stated in one word—conservative. This does not mean that only black, navy blue, and white can be worn. Any color can be worn as long as it is a subtle understated color. The psychology of color is an often overlooked aspect in preparing a witness. Certain colors, such as blue, have connotations of honesty and sincerity. Black and white have connotations of power and authority. Red is a color that works strong emotions such as anger, and it should be worn only as an accessory color. Warm shades such as rust, gold, yellow, and peach tend to portray a person who is open and friendly. Whatever colors are chosen should be flattering to the witness so that the most pleasant, sincere, and credible image is portrayed.

4. Other general tips for clients include telling them to:

Sit up straight and do not slouch
Avoid unnecessary gesturing

Avoid chewing gum or smoking

Be courteous at all times

Say yes or no distinctly instead of nodding your head

Do not joke or wisecrack

Consider the seriousness of the occasion and avoid getting chummy with the opposing counsel.

Be aware that the opposing counsel may try to be very charming to disarm them, but they must remember he is not their attorney, and may have ulterior motives.

5. Clients will frequently ask if they can be accompanied to their deposition by their spouse. This decision should be made by the attorney, but in general it is not wise to appear at the deposition with anyone except your attorney and legal assistant.

6. The client will wonder about the length of the deposition, and what will happen if, during the deposition, they need to confer with their attorney. They should be told that many breaks will be taken during the course of the deposition. These breaks are usually taken to give the court reporter a chance to change paper on the transcript machine or just to relax. The client may, however, request a break at any time it is necessary to have a conference with his counsel. Clients also have a right to ask for a break at any time they do not understand a question being asked. Clients need to know that it is perfectly acceptable to ask opposing counsel to ask the question again, rephrase it, or define the words being used in a particular question. It is a grave mistake for a client to attempt to answer a question that they do not understand. Most clients will, however, attempt to answer all questions, even the ones they are not certain of or do not understand for fear of appearing stupid or embarrassing the opposing counsel.

7. Clients will have many questions about depositions and almost always will address these questions to the legal assistant. A client will frequently say, "I don't want my attorney to think I'm really stupid, but is it okay if I ask you these questions?" The moral support that a legal assistant can provide for a client at this time is invaluable. The legal assistant truly becomes the hand holder for the client.

8. There are two important points to emphasize to your client when preparing the client for a deposition. The first is to be courteous at all times. Never become angry, antagonistic, hostile, or sarcastic. The even-tempered. serious client who answers all questions in a matter-of-fact manner, and treats the deposition proceedings as a serious part of their cause, does much to establish their credibility. The second most important rule to stress to the client is not to volunteer extra information. An over-anxious client will answer questions in a rambling fashion, giving more information than was originally asked for, and may seriously damage his case. It is natural for clients to want to volunteer information. They feel they are helping their case. They feel they are providing the information that is necessary for the opposing counsel to understand just how seriously they were injured.

§ 3.39   Deposition Preparation Test for Clients

After you have prepared a client for their deposition and cautioned them on all of the items in **§ 3.38,** including not volunteering extra information, try this simple test. Ask the client, "Do you have a watch?" The standard answer from the client probably will be, "Yes, it's 2:30." You should then explain, "I did not ask you what time it was, I merely asked you if you had a watch." This example illustrates for the client how easy it is to fall into the trap of adding information to an answer. This will illustrate that some information is so automatic in our minds that we answer unasked questions. The question, "Do you have a watch?" implies the second unasked question, "What time is it?" The point of this little exercise is to illustrate to the client that only one question was asked and not a second question. Many times in the deposition one question will be asked and a second obvious follow-up question will not be asked. It is not the job of the client to supply answers to both questions, but to answer only the question that has been asked. It is up to the opposing counsel to ask the correct follow-up questions. It is not the fault of the client that the opposing counsel is not proficient in questioning.

At the conclusion of the meeting to prepare a client for their deposition, the client should be given a letter stating the time, date, and location of the deposition. It should state whether the client is to meet their attorney at the opposing counsel's office or whether they will meet and go over to the deposition together. At this time a client may also be given a brief handout for pointers on depositions. Your local bar association should have pamphlets available free of charge which can be given to your client. **Section 3.40** contains a list which is designed as a client handout and may be given to clients who need positive reinforcement of pointers covered in their predeposition meeting.

§ 3.40   The Twelve Commandments of Deposition Preparation

1. Tell the truth, do not guess. Honesty is the best policy. If you always tell the truth, and tell it accurately, no one will be able to cross you up.
2. Take your time in answering questions. Give the question thought, as much as it requires to understand it. Formulate your answer in your mind before giving the answer. By hesitating you will also give your attorney time to lodge an objection. If you answer a question too quickly when an objection should have been made, you can damage your case.
3. Never volunteer information beyond the scope of the actual question.
4. Request clarification or explanation for a question or its phraseology if it is not clear or understandable. Never answer ambiguous questions. You cannot possibly give a truthful and accurate answer unless you understand the question.
5. Talk loud enough so everyone can hear you. Keep your hands away from your mouth, do not chew gum, and do not nod your head when you mean yes or no.
6. Answer questions concisely. Do not give narrative answers. Make the attorney who is questioning you ask you a series of questions to get detailed information. Do not do the work for the attorney.

7. Do not look at your attorney for help every time you are asked a question. Determine before the deposition how to interact with your counsel. Do not pass notes, kick them under the table, nudge them, and so forth.

8. Beware of questions involving distances, dates, and times. If you can make an accurate estimate, it is okay to go ahead and do so. If you are uncomfortable in making an estimate and will truly be guessing, admit that you do not know.

9. Be wary of trick questions, especially those questions asked in the negative, such as, "When did you stop beating your wife?" or, "Is it true you never use seat belts when driving?"

10. Do not be afraid to look the opposing counsel in the eye when you answer questions and to maintain eye contact throughout the deposition. This will lend credibility to your testimony.

11. Give a positive answer whenever you can. If you are certain of a fact, you are certain of it. Do not be afraid to swear to a set of facts as being true and accurate, if you truly know they are. In a deposition you are sworn to tell the truth, and you are expected to do so.

12. Relax. A deposition is not final until the transcript has been prepared and delivered to you for corrections, and those corrections, if any, have been made in the original transcript. (See sample letter in **Form 3–33**).

FORM 3–33
SAMPLE LETTER TO CLIENT
REGARDING DEPOSITION CORRECTIONS

Re: [plaintiff A] v. [defendant B]

Dear Client:

Your deposition in the above-entitled action which was taken on [date] has now arrived in our office for your review and corrections, which must be accomplished within thirty (30) days or by [date]. We are sending you a copy of the transcript which you can mark up with pencil and return to us. We will then have corrections typed on a separate piece of paper and send it to the court reporter to be attached to your deposition. It would be helpful to us, if in addition to correcting the deposition transcript itself, you prepared a list on a separate piece of paper listing your corrections by page and line and incorrect word along with correct word or phrase.

Please remember that you may not rewrite or change any portion of your deposition transcript. You are merely to check it for accuracy as you recall your testimony. You may wish to correct spelling of certain names or places. You may also wish to correct matters of fact. If you have a serious problem with the way the transcript has recorded your answers, please contact our office immediately so that we can call it to the attention of the court reporter. The court reporter will then compare the transcript with the tape and make the necessary corrections. Occasionally there are mistakes made in the transcript which can be corrected by the court reporter by referring back to the original tape.

It is important that we have your corrections within the statutory time period or we will lose the opportunity to make corrections in the transcript, and inconsistencies or inaccuracies will remain part of the record.

If you have any questions regarding this procedure or need assistance, please do not hesitate to contact our office. Thank you for your cooperation and prompt attention to this request.

> Sincerely,
>
> [name]_____
> Legal Assistant

§ 3.41   Common Sense Deposition Rules

Although it is extremely important to prepare a client for a deposition, overpreparation can backfire on you causing problems at the actual deposition. Clients want to do well and they frequently believe, despite what they have been told by their attorneys, that they have the power to win their case by performing well at a deposition. After lengthy predeposition meetings, clients are frequently nervous and need to be told to remember basic common sense rules, such as:

> Get a good night's sleep the night before your deposition;
> Eat moderately, but DO NOT FORGET TO EAT BEFORE THE DEPOSITION; and
> Do not bring notes or papers of any kind with you into the deposition.

If your client has taken notes during the predeposition conference, it is logical for them to think it is appropriate to bring these notes to the deposition so they will not forget anything they have been told. Remind them that any notes or other papers brought with them into the deposition can be requested by the opposing counsel.

It is important for the client to know that the predeposition meeting was meant to be a rehearsal and that they are not expected to memorize the right answers. The following five step plan is a quick summary of basic predeposition preparation. Tell your client before each question to do the following:

1. Make sure you hear the entire question;
2. Repeat the question silently to yourself;
3. Say the answer quietly to yourself;
4. Formulate the answer the way you want to phrase it; and
5. Take a deep breath and say the answer while looking opposing counsel directly in the eye.

By applying these simple rules, your client will not blurt out information, and will be able to remain calm during the deposition.

§ 3.42 Deposition Summaries

Summarizing, or digesting, deposition transcripts is a typical duty of the legal assistant. The summary is a tool for an attorney to use when reviewing the important principles of law, facts of the case, and evidentiary matters contained in the transcript. One of the primary benefits of a deposition summary is the ability it gives the attorney to cross-reference testimony from a given party with that of another witness in the action, thus enabling the attorney to spot inconsistencies or variations on facts presented.

The complexity of a summary, or digest, depends entirely upon the complexity of the case. Some cases involving antitrust litigation, trademark infringement, or complex commercial litigation, can be so involved that only a computer digest system will be adequate.

Before beginning to summarize a deposition transcript, it is important to understand that deposition summaries have the following objectives:

1. To create order out of hundreds or thousands of pages of data;
2. To provide ready access to selected topics, categories or points of law, and so forth;
3. To provide a way of comparing testimony between parties and/or witnesses which will enable the attorney to spot inconsistencies and identify evidentiary holes in testimony that will need to be filled in by further investigation and/or discovery; and
4. To assist the attorney in organizing for trial by indicating which important documents should go into a witness file. The witness file will assist the attorney in preparing questions for direct and cross-examination. Some of the deposition questions and responses may be entered into testimony at trial and/or used for impeachment or direct examination.

§ 3.43 Use of Deposition Summaries

The first major objective to keep in mind when summarizing depositions is that the ultimate purpose of the summary is to focus directly on the information being sought. Keeping this focus in mind will enable you to eliminate the wordiness and irrelevancy of many responses. The second major objective is that the finished product, the summary, must stand alone. That is, it must be complete enough so that the attorney does not need to refer to the deposition transcript in order to understand the summary.

Before summarizing a deposition, consider who will use the summary and for what purpose it will be used. In major law firms, the attorney who takes a deposition may not be the attorney who ends up taking the case to trial; it would then be necessary to prepare a more lengthy, detailed deposition summary because the ultimate user of the summary will be the attorney who prepares the case for trial and not the attorney who took the deposition. In a small to medium-sized law firm, when the attorney who originally took the deposition will most likely be the attorney who will try the case, a deposition summary may be more concise and keyed to the points selected by that attorney for summarization. In most cases, the attorney will have taken their own notes at the deposition and those notes will be used to supplement the deposition summary.

Another consideration is whether the deposition summary will be strictly an in-house document, or whether it will be sent to your client. Corporate clients and insurance companies are occasionally sent deposition summaries as part of litigation status reports. The style of the deposition summary will differ whether it is to be an in-house document, or whether it is to be sent to the client or another person outside of the office. Generally speaking, a deposition summary that is kept as an in-house document will tend to use more abbreviations, jargon, comments on further discovery, attorney's notes, and so forth. A deposition summary that is sent out of the office will tend to be a narrative summary which will speak to the main points of the testimony, but will not contain attorney's comments on that testimony. It is important to mark the summary "Confidential—Attorney-Client Communication" to safeguard it as a privileged document so that it will not be subject to production in discovery.

§ 3.44   Language Techniques

It is crucial to follow the language of the witness exactly as it appears in the testimony. For example, if the witness uses the term "think," "recall," "remember," "assume," or "believe," be exact so that the flavor of the testimony remains intact. There is a great tendency while summarizing a deposition to editorialize or comment on the testimony. This must be avoided in the actual context of the summary, but can be included in a separate column entitled "Notes." When summarizing a deposition, use fragments and clauses, rather than complete sentences. Fragments of subjects and verbs without connecting prepositional phrases are the most effective way to quickly focus on major ideas in a summary.

Distinguish between testimony regarding what the witness recalls from the witness' own independent recollection and that which the witness testifies to with the assistance of a letter, or memorandum, or other deposition exhibit. For example, a doctor may recall treating a patient from the doctor's own independent recollection and testify regarding that treatment; however, the doctor may be more specific about the care and treatment rendered after consulting the medical records. Those medical records will then become a deposition exhibit, and the doctor can testify more specifically on the treatment of the patient based on reading those records. Testimony of this type will be a mixture of independent recollection and recollection aided by reviewing notes and medical records.

When summarizing a deposition, look for flag or key words that relate to the facts of the case such as lease, contract, spine, back injury, real property, and so forth. Your understanding of the case will enable you to quickly spot certain key or flag words. Always read a deposition transcript all the way through once before beginning your summary. Having read it through once, and perhaps circling or underlining key words, will enable you to summarize more efficiently and rapidly.

§ 3.45 Common Errors

The first question that will come to your mind when faced with hundreds of pages of deposition transcript is what can be eliminated? Must I include every single item of information that is mentioned in this transcript in my summary? The answer is no. Not only should you not include every bit of information that appears in the deposition transcript, but also you should make every effort to exclude irrelevant, self-serving, repetitive, and nonresponsive information. The following items should always be excluded from your deposition summary:

1. Basic procedural discussions between attorney and deponent such as: Do you understand the deposition process? Are you comfortable? If you do not understand a question, please ask me to repeat it. Is there any reason why your deposition should not be taken today?

2. Excess verbiage that is repetitive and gives no new information. Be careful of instances when the same question is asked a second time and the witness gives a different answer. This is important to include for its contradictory nature. Excess verbiage that can be excluded refers to introductory comments made by a witness before a direct response is given to a question.

3. Nonessential statements of opinion, or of a self-serving nature. For example, in a personal injury case when a witness is asked the direct question, "Were you wearing a seat belt at the time of the accident?," the only answer that needs to be recorded is a yes or a no. A response such as, "No, because several of my friends have worn seat belts in accidents and received serious injuries; as a matter of fact, one of them even died because they were wearing a seat belt at the time of the accident," is an example of excess verbiage that is self-serving, nonrelevant and serves no useful purpose. It should be eliminated from the deposition summary.

4. Questions, unless they are certified questions. Remember, questions are not part of the testimony. The testimony comes from the witness, not from the attorney who is taking the deposition.

5. It is not necessary to continue to repeat the word deponent or witness, or use the witness' last name such as Smith or Jones. It is better to use pronouns whenever necessary such as he or she. In most cases this will not be necessary because the subject will be understood.

6. Be careful to use the correct verb tense as it appears in the deposition transcript. That is, use past when the witness is discussing events that happened in the past and use present when you are dealing with present tense events. Do not put everything in the same verb tense as this will distort the testimony.

§ 3.46   Basic Information to Include

Certain information must be included in all deposition summaries regardless of the format chosen to digest the deposition. Always include:

1. Date of the deposition and name of the attorney taking the deposition;

2. Name of the opposing counsel and name and telephone number of the court reporter (including the name and telephone number of the court reporter will be useful as trial approaches and you need to obtain original depositions to be lodged with the court);

3. All names and addresses included in the deposition transcript;

4. All dates mentioned in the deposition transcript exactly as they are mentioned, even if you have documents which disprove those dates;

5. Identification of all exhibits in a deposition. Indicate Exhibit 1, name of exhibit, and so forth within the summary or attach to your deposition summary a numerical identification list of exhibits indicating the page of the transcript where the exhibit is first identified; and

6. Certified questions must always be noted in the deposition summary and identified with a page and line reference and the exact question. They are questions that have not been answered on advice of counsel and have been certified at the request of the attorney who has asked the question. (Your deposition summary can then be used as an aid in preparing motions to compel answers to questions certified at deposition.)

§ 3.47   Types of Deposition Summaries

When an attorney requests a deposition summary, the attorney usually has only one kind in mind: the traditional page and line chronological summary. Although this format is very useful, and in most cases preferable (especially for a deposition involving complex issues), there are other types of deposition summaries. Make your attorney aware of other methods of deposition summary so that an appropriate method may be selected to meet the particular needs of the case, attorney, and client. The most popular formats for deposition summaries are:

Chronological (page and line)
Categorical
Narrative
Index
Abstract

Frequently, a hybrid type of deposition summary will evolve which contains particular elements from one or more of the major types. For example, a chronological type of deposition summary may include headings of major categories within the chronology. Similarly, a narrative summary may include chronological references at certain key points in the narrative. An index method of summarizing a deposition can stand on its own or be combined with any of the other types. A frequent combination is an index to a lengthy chronological deposition summary. In this case the index is of the deposition summary rather than of the deposition itself. This type of an index serves as a super summary.

The most important consideration in choosing a type of deposition summary is that the summary is an independent document; that is, it must stand on its own and be understood by anyone who reads it without the necessity of referring to the deposition transcript itself to explain the summary. This point cannot be stressed enough, because frequently attorneys will wish to take only deposition summaries with them when they go out of town to prepare for another deposition in the sequence of the case. This enables them to leave the lengthy and bulky deposition transcripts in the office for associates and legal assistants to continue their work on the case, and also allows them the briefcase space to take other important documents. Given that fact, the attorney relies completely on the deposition summary for the details of the transcript and needs to be able to read the summary as an independent document.

§ 3.48   The Chronological Deposition Summary

This is the type of deposition summary that is the most common, known, and favored by attorneys. The chronological deposition summary covers subjects page by page in the order they appear in the transcript. Accurate citations are to page and line, and very little is left out. The most important point to remember in preparing this type of a summary is to be faithful to the chronology. If a subject is discussed two or three times and the same answer is given, each answer must be recorded in chronological fashion.

Extended attorney colloquy, or objections, over a particular question can be briefly summarized as: "Attorney colloquy re objection raised to questions regarding plaintiff's involvement in prior litigation." It should also be noted whether the attorney colloquy results in the certification of a deposition question, withdrawal of the question by the deposing attorney, or an arrangement between counsel to provide the information at a later date or in another form. That information should be recorded in the notes column (see in § 3.54).

When summarizing a deposition transcript, focus on the witness' responses rather than the questions. The actual questions asked in a deposition are rarely included in a deposition summary, because the summary is meant to focus on the witness' testimony. One exception is a certified question. Certified questions and answers should always be recorded verbatim in a deposition summary. Certified questions are explained and discussed in § 3.3 on evidence depositions. Motions to compel answers to certified questions are discussed later in this chapter at § 3.58.

The basic problem legal assistants face in digesting hundreds of pages of deposition transcript in a chronological fashion is wordiness. It is sometimes difficult to cut through extended wordy descriptions to focus on the essence of the testimony. The following example in **Forms 3–34** and **3–35** illustrate that point:

FORM 3–34
SAMPLE DEPOSITION TRANSCRIPT

Deposition Transcript of [deponent]

Page/Line
Pg. 10,

1	Q.	Could you please tell me how long after the accident
2		you first felt the pain in your neck?
3	A.	Well, it's hard to say precisely because everything
4		happened so fast and I was very shook up. I really
5		did not even realize what had happened. My daughter
6		was with me at the time and was also very upset.
7	Q.	Was it an hour, a day, a week, exactly when did you
8		first feel the pain?
9	A.	Well, no it wasn't quite that long. I'd say the pain
10		started about 10 minutes after the collision. I was
11		in so much pain that I really could not get out of my
12		car and approach the other driver until I had rested
13		a bit, and calmed my daughter down. The accident was
14		such a shock to both of us. We had no idea, no fore-
15		warning.

FORM 3–35
SAMPLE DEPOSITION SUMMARY

Deposition Summary of [deponent]

Pg/L	Heading/ Category	Content	Attorney/ Paralegal Notes
P 10 L 1-15	Injury	Began feeling pain about 10 minutes after collision, daughter was with her and was also upset.	Interview daughter.

The chronological deposition summary is probably the most accurate record of the deposition transcript and frequently can be used verbatim at trial to impeach a witness. A chronological deposition summary can include elements of the categorical deposition summary which will provide access to information. For example, subject headings can be used prior to the actual content of any given entry, key words can be underlined for easier visual reference, and asterisks can be used to signal important statements, inconsistencies, admissions, and so forth. The format for chronological deposition summary (see **Form 3–36**) is as follows:

FORM 3–36
SAMPLE HEADINGS FOR CHRONOLOGICAL
DEPOSITION SUMMARY

DEPOSITION OF [deponent]

Pg/L	Heading/Category	Content	Attorney/ Paralegal Notes

Forms 3–37 and **3–38** are further examples of chronological deposition summaries.

FORM 3-37
SAMPLE CHRONOLOGICAL
DEPOSITION SUMMARY (DEPONENT A)

Deposition of [deponent A]

Deposition Taken July 13, 19__

Pg/L	Heading/Category	Content	*Attorney/ Paralegal Notes
P3, L15-19	Biographical Information	[address] [city, state]	
P4, L19-25	Education/ Military	BA political science, Univ. of [state]; JD Univ. of [university name], 19__, passed [state] Bar 19__. Military-Army, 19__–19__, Vietnam; started law practice, 19__.	
P5, L8-20	Present Occupation	Practices trial law, corporation counsel, [city] City Atty. Office, does primarily defense work.	Any trial experience? Primary emphasis defense.

Pg/L	Heading/Category	Content	*Attorney/ Paralegal Notes
			Sophisticated deponent.

*This column is used for follow-up discovery and opinions.

FORM 3–38
SAMPLE CHRONOLOGICAL
DEPOSITION SUMMARY (DEPONENT B)

Deposition of [deponent B]

Pg/L	Heading/ Category	Content	*Attorney/ Paralegal Notes
	Medical Treatment		
P3, L1-5	Immediate:	Accident resulted in injuries to neck, right shoulder, back, and right leg. [hospital name] emergency on day of accident, no x-rays were taken, blood pressure, various tests, released and told to consult with family doctor if [deponent] had not improved by the next day.	
P3, L8-15	Follow-up Treatment:	[date], [time] appoint-ment with family doctor, Dr. [name]. X-rays ordered, traction for neck for 1/2 hour, hot pack, massage, and ultra-sound treatments, pre-scription for therapy to begin immediately.	

Pg/L	Heading/ Category	Content	*Attorney/ Paralegal Notes
P3, L16-18	Therapy:	Therapy with Dr. [name], prescribed neck brace, continued hot packs, ultrasound, adjustments, and prescribed thermofax heading pad.	Have we ordered records from all treating physicians? Do we have a bill for the heating pad?

§ 3.49   The Categorical Deposition Summary

The categorical deposition summary is the most detailed and time-consuming method of summarizing. Its main objective is to place all statements in the transcript regarding a given subject together in the summary. It becomes especially valuable when a deposition is lengthy and complex, and other depositions are scheduled which will cover that witness' preception of the same major categories or events. There are several ways to prepare a categorical summary. Choose the method most compatible with the word processing and computer capabilities of the support staff. For example, key words may have to be set up in a particular fashion in order to be input in a way that information can be retrieved and cross-referenced. If you are preparing a categorical summary, first determine the categories. This can be done in many fashions. Perhaps your attorney reviewed the file and/or took the deposition and has some categories in mind. For example, you might have "medical treatment," "color of light," and "location of pedestrian" as categories. The list of topics can be expanded as you go through the deposition transcript and note other categories. Compile a list of major categories with subheadings for a more detailed overview of the relationship of main issues in the case. The advantage of subheadings is that they provide a more detailed analysis of each category and allow room for expansion of ideas.

A good categorical deposition summary can be extremely helpful in a case because it brings together statements from several volumes of testimony and makes inconsistencies easier to spot. A categorical deposition summary of a key witness may be useful for comparison purposes with a deposition summary of another key witness to compare crucial testimony and key issues.

After a main list of categories, including headings and subheadings, has been prepared, read through the deposition page by page noting which sections fall under which category. Have a copy of the deposition transcript handy which you can mark up or tag in some fashion, so that you can go back and dictate the deposition summary easily, referring to those pages you have designated to each category. The categorical summary can take the same format as the chronological summary with just a few minor changes. (See **Form 3–39.**)

FORM 3–39
SAMPLE CATEGORICAL DEPOSITION SUMMARY

DEPOSITION OF [deponent]

Category	Content	Attorney/ Paralegal Notes
Medical Treatment		
P3, L1-5 Immediate treatment, Dr. [name], family doctor.	Saw Dr. [name] on D/A, [date], for x-rays and exam.	Get records

In this case the main category should be set out in boldface, italics, and subheadings should be capitalized or underlined. An index should be prepared along with the summary which lists all categories and subheadings for easy access. The actual content of the summary is not included in the index.

§ 3.50   The Narrative Deposition Summary

The narrative deposition summary (see **Form 3–40**) is different from the other forms of deposition summaries discussed, in that the writing style of a narrative summary is full sentences with very few fragments or abbreviations. A narrative summary is usually used for minor witnesses or as an enclosure in a case status report to an insurance company or corporate client.

The narrative deposition summary can, and should, include page and line references to the actual deposition text. Although actual page and line references to the deposition text are not essential, when the main purpose of the summary is to keep the corporate client informed of case status, they can be invaluable when you need to go back and retrieve specific information from the deposition transcript. A minor witness can become a more important witness as discovery continues and more is learned about the involvement of that person. Without page and line references, the narrative summary becomes merely an overview of the deposition and is not a useful discovery tool. Remember that in doing a narrative deposition summary, you are looking at the actual testimony. Do not fall into the trap of paraphrasing or you will have a deposition report rather than a deposition summary.

Occasionally, a narrative deposition summary will be the second deposition summary done on a particular deponent. For example, although a detailed chronological page and line summary of the deposition of an important witness may have already been prepared, you may still be asked to prepare a narrative overview of that deposition summary to send to the corporate or insurance company client. In that case your narrative will be taken off the chronological deposition summary and will not need to include page and line references. Its purpose at that point is an overview of the deposition rather than a deposition summary.

When preparing a narrative deposition summary, it is important to read the deposition all the way through to understand the chronology of events, flavor of testimony, and important categories covered in the transcript. You can then dictate your narrative deposition summary with categorical or subject headings. Examples of some of the headings that might prove useful in preparing a narrative or categorical deposition summary in a personal injury case would include the following:

Background information;

Education;

Past employment;

Present employment; and

Prior litigation exposure (including prior depositions).

FORM 3–40
SAMPLE NARRATIVE DEPOSITION SUMMARY

DEPOSITION OF DEFENDANT [name]

Deposition Taken [date]

Biographical Information
Defendant resides at [street address], [city], [state]. [name] is an attorney for the City of [city], [state], and has been licensed to practice since 1975. Defense attorney for the City of [city name]. Defendant has a B.A. in political science from the University of [state], law degree from the University of [university name] School of Law, has worked primarily in the defense area for the past eleven years.

Date and Location of Accident
D/A Friday, [date], [time], Interstate 80 in [city], [state], near [street name] Street off-ramp.

Activities Prior to the Accident
Defendant had a business appointment at [time] on the date of the accident. [name] borrowed a car from defendant's sister-in-law, [name], with her permission. He had borrowed this car on other occasions in the [location] and is very familiar with the car and Interstate 80 where the accident occurred. [defendant] left for the appointment at [time], allowing time for the morning commuter traffic.

Description of Accident
Defendant states [defendant] was driving about 45 miles an hour and was about 30–40 feet behind plaintiff when [defendant] hit the rear of plaintiff's car. [defendant] does not recall whether plaintiff's car was stopped or still moving at

the time of impact, but remembers wondering why plaintiff slammed on the brakes. Police were called to the scene and [defendant] gave a statement to them at the time of the accident. Police report was introduced into the deposition and marked Exhibit 1. Witness generally agrees with the facts as contained in the police report.

§ 3.51   The Index Deposition Summary

This is the easiest to prepare and the least detailed of all deposition summary methods; however, it is seldom useful by itself and is often combined with other deposition summaries such as a chronological or categorical deposition summary. This method could be used for a deposition of a minor witness, or for an attorney who has taken extensive notes on the deposition and wishes to have only a brief outline as a reminder to where certain topics were discussed. To prepare for the index method, read through the deposition transcript and note the major topics covered and page references. Next, go back and group topics under major headings. This would be the same method used if you were preparing an index deposition summary as a supplement to a page and line chronological deposition summary. The form that this type of deposition summary (**Form 3–41**) would take is as follows.

FORM 3–41
SAMPLE INDEX DEPOSITION SUMMARY

INDEX TO DEPOSITION OF [deponent name]

Deposition taken [date].

Subject	Page
Circumstances of Injury	
Accident scene and location	4, 5, 26, 32
Accident report as exhibit	6, 7, 8
How accident occurred	9, 10, 11
Force of impact	11, 12
Injury	
Description	3, 4, 5
Immediate medical treatment	14, 19, 20
Medical care provided	15, 20, 21
Specific nature of treatment	22, 23, 24
Specific complaints	24, 25, 27
Residual injuries	32, 34

§ 3.52 Deposition Abstracts and Extracts

In addition to the major types of deposition summaries, there are other methods of summarizing a deposition transcript which, although they are not complete summaries, may often prove to be useful depending upon the circumstances of the case. Two such methods are abstracts and extracts. The abstract of a deposition is a very brief overview of the key elements of the transcript. The entire deposition transcript must be considered in the preparation of an abstract. However, the actual testimony may be reduced to one sentence per page of transcript. This particular method is good for noneyewitnesses, or parties with minor involvement in the case. This differs from a deposition summary in the sense that you are not summarizing the deposition, but paraphrasing the content of the deposition. Should the facts in the case change and this testimony become crucial in discovery, a deposition summary would have to be prepared.

An extract differs from an abstract in that it does not focus on the entire deposition transcript, but rather on one isolated issue of fact, liability or damage. In preparing the extract, you must have tunnel vision rather than peripheral vision since you are looking at the testimony for only one particular issue or fact. Extracts are frequently done when witnesses have testified with differing stories regarding a key element in a case. For example, in a case involving potential liability for a hotel in a lawsuit arising after an injury of a college youth following a fraternity party, the hotel was interested in proving a cause of action on a cross-complaint for contributory negligence based on the fact that the college youth who dove into the hotel swimming pool (when there was no water in the pool) was acting under the influence of a controlled substance. The assignment was to read depositions taken of 18 people who had attended the fraternity party, extracting from each deposition only that testimony concerning the amount of substance abuse that had gone on prior to the time of the accident, with a particular focus on the amount of substance that had been ingested by the injured plaintiff. Given this narrow focus it was possible to go through 18 depositions and extract testimony on that one key issue in a brief amount of time. This is not to say that other issues were not of importance in the 18 depositions; however, in order to substantiate the cross-complaint, that was the issue the legal assistant needed to focus on to complete the assignment.

§ 3.53 Summarizing a Custodian of Records Deposition

The deposition of a custodian of records, or a corporate officer designated to identify documents, is extremely difficult to summarize because the focus of the testimony is on the documents which become exhibits to the deposition transcript. In summarizing this type of a deposition, first make sure that all the exhibits have arrived, have been properly numbered, and have been referenced in the deposition transcript exactly as they are numbered. The deposition summary can then be prepared utilizing any of the methods discussed in **Chapter 3.** The best method would be the chronological page and line detailed summary. Each time an exhibit is mentioned in the transcript and identified as exhibit A, B, and so forth, it should be identified as such in the deposition summary. **Form 3–42** illustrates this technique.

FORM 3–42
SAMPLE CUSTODIAN OF RECORDS
DEPOSITION SUMMARY

DEPOSITION OF [deponent]
CUSTODIAN OF RECORDS OF [name] CORPORATION

Deposition taken [date].

Pg/L	Summary	Attorney's Notes
P3, L1-10	Exhibit A-Corporate minutes of [date]. Document is identified by witness as a correct copy of the corporate minutes of [name] Corporation Board of Directors meeting of [date]. Acknowledgment of [name] and verification of the signature as corporate secretary on page 5 of the minutes. Reference is made to item 7(a) on page 3 of the minutes discussing the [name] Joint Venture Agreement. Acknowledgment that the proposal was presented to the Board and discussed by those directors present.	Note names of directors present at this meeting. Have their depositions been taken?

§ 3.54   The Notes Column of Deposition Summaries

This column is extremely important and should be used as you are preparing the deposition summary as well as later when you have learned more facts through later discovery. Initial entries in this column include references to contradictory statements. For example, "See testimony at page 6, line 7; contradicts present testimony." A note can also be made to testimony that, although it is not necessarily contradictory, it simply does not make sense and bears further investigation.

Notes should be made regarding further discovery such as references made to a prior lawsuit or prior statement given about the present incident. The discovery reminder note would read: "Get copies of prior accident report" or "Do docket search to retrieve name of case and get pleadings in prior litigation." Other comments regarding further discovery may relate to the discovery of a new witness. For example if a plaintiff refers in the deposition to having complained to the plaintiff's supervisor of persistent pain in plaintiff's back and shoulder area after returning to work, the deposition note would read: "Interview [name], the supervisor. Get statement re date and specific nature of complaints. Were they recorded in any form?"

If during the course of the deposition, transcript reference is made to records that the opposing counsel agrees to make available to your attorney, such as supplemental invoices or medical bills, note this. Your deposition note would read: "Call to arrange to get copies of documents" or "Have we received these documents?" If the existence of documents is discovered through deposition questions (internal memos, meeting notes, phone logs), your deposition note would state "Remember to prepare subpoena for records."

The notes column also becomes your commentary column on the deposition transcript, and may include comments relating to the elements of the case. For example, in a sample real estate breach of contract situation, plaintiffs allege they would not have purchased a particular house if they had known the escrow instructions did not include payment for repair work on the front porch, and further claim that they did not understand the escrow instructions. In this case, indicate in your notes column that the deposition transcript reveals that the plaintiff has bought and sold several pieces of real property in the past five years. Give page and line references to that background testimony. Your commentary in the notes column might indicate that someone with that much expertise in the buying and selling of real property could be reasonably expected as an informed buyer to have studied the escrow instructions for specifics on payments for repair, and so forth prior to finalizing this particular contract.

If you have summarized several depositions in a particular case and you note that there are inconsistent or contradictory statements on a key point in other deposition transcripts, use your notes column to refer to those particular depositions. For example, indicate after the key testimony, "See Jane Doe's deposition at page 5, line 20 for comparison."

An additional use of the notes column can be to update your deposition summary. After you have completed your deposition summary, other facts may become known through further discovery such as interrogatory answers or documents produced pursuant to request, all of which may relate to the deposition testimony. Supplement your deposition summary in the notes column with this new information and note the date and method of discovery of this new information. For example, "See 2/15/__ interrogatory answer #6 for contradiction." This type of updating of a deposition summary is very useful at time of trial since it serves to coordinate all discovery into one easily accessible digest.

The notes column can also be used by an attorney preparing for trial referencing certain sections for direct examination or cross-examination. Depending upon the use of the attorney/paralegal notes column, the digest may have to be reformatted to allow ample room for inclusion of the specific notes.

§ 3.55 Compelling Discovery Relating to Depositions

The main areas relating to depositions that require motions to compel and counter motions to oppose are:

1. Compelling the attendance of a deponent at a deposition;
2. Opposing a subsequent deposition of the same deponent;
3. Compelling a subsequent deposition of the same deponent;
4. Compelling answers to certified questions at deposition; and
5. Opposing answers to certified questions and upholding those privileges stated in deposition transcript.

§ 3.56 Motion to Compel Attendance

A motion to compel attendance at a deposition should be prepared when a proposed deponent will not voluntarily appear for a deposition. For instance, a proposed deponent may argue that they are not within the jurisdiction of the court and, therefore, cannot be compelled to attend the deposition. The points and authorities to accompany a motion to compel attendance of this particular person would include research aimed at establishing that particular person's residence and/or place of business in the jurisdiction where the action is pending. If that fails, arrangements must then be made for a commission to take that person's deposition in another state. That person would be served with a subpoena issued by the court having personal jurisdiction on the deponent requiring the deponent's attendance at a deposition in another jurisdiction.

Another situation where a motion to compel attendance at a deposition will be necessary is the reluctant deponent. This person simply refuses to be deposed, claiming that they have no information relevant to the pending action, did not witness the accident, did not sign the contract or negotiate any part of it, resigned from the board of directors or the employ of the particular company prior to the times mentioned in the complaint, and so forth.

Points and authorities to support a motion to compel attendance of a reluctant deponent would include careful research of all documents in the file to document the times the person worked for the defendant, was on the board of directors of the defendant corporation, or was mentioned in a key piece of correspondence or received a carbon copy of a relevant document, and so forth. This documentation is then attached as an exhibit to the points and authorities compelling the attendance of the reluctant deponent.

§ 3.57 Opposing and Compelling
Subsequent Depositions

Motions to compel attendance and motions to oppose attendance at subsequent depositions are often governed by the same fact patterns. You may have deposed a key player early in the discovery plan, only to find out from subsequent depositions that this particular deponent was involved in other business transactions and deals that have a direct bearing on the instant litigation. In this situation you would want to redepose this person and question him regarding the new evidence.

Points and authorities supporting a motion to compel attendance at a subsequent deposition would include (as exhibits) those portions of deposition transcripts from subsequent deponents indicating the involvement of this key player, in particular business transactions or this key player's personal knowledge of key issues such as attendance at meetings, negotiations, and so forth. It would be necessary to establish not that this information was not available before the first deposition of the key player and has only been learned through subsequent depositions. In order to persevere on such a motion, it must be shown that there were no alternative means of finding out this information prior to taking the first deposition, and that there are no alternative means of obtaining this information without redeposing this person.

An argument may be made to compel a subsequent deposition by an attorney who has just substituted in to a particular action. The basis of the points and authorities in that particular motion would be that the attorney who has just substituted in has not had an opportunity to question this particular witness along the lines and strategies that the new attorney has developed in the new discovery plan. Although the opposing argument will be made that the deposition transcript is readily available for the new attorney, and that the former attorney did indeed ask pertinent questions representing that particular client's liability exposure and/or interests, an argument can still be made that this particular attorney has a different approach and needs to requestion the deponent. This is a difficult argument to sustain but one that is frequently used in an action where a client has fired or dismissed the client's former attorney for not representing the client properly. An affidavit from the client attached to the points and authorities stating that the attorney had been fired or dismissed from the case for failing to represent the client adequately and that the client has now engaged another attorney, who is mounting a completely different defense strategy which requires the subsequent deposition of a witness would be helpful. Occasionally, the new areas of questioning are included in an attorney declaration to accompany the points and authorities. The actual deposition questions do not have to be listed, only suggested as areas of inquiry.

In opposing a motion to compel subsequent depositions of the same deponent, the most important element of proof to stress in the points and authorities is that the purpose of this subsequent deposition is harassment and not information gathering, because all of the information was readily available prior to the first deposition, and that it was simply a manner of lack of preparation on the part of opposing counsel for the first deposition. Another argument may be made that the same information can be obtained through alternate discovery methods such as interrogatories, requests for production of documents, or depositions of other officers in the business or corporation. The argument that a second or third deposition would be unduly harassing or burdensome to the deponent can also be based on the content of the first deposition, particularly if that deposition went for several days with all attorneys present with ample opportunity to ask questions.

§ 3.58   Motions to Compel Answers
to Certified Questions

Motions to compel answers to certified questions at depositions are the most common type of motions to compel. For this motion, you will need to obtain the deposition transcript and to attach sections of certified questions and responses as exhibits to the points and authorities accompanying the motion to compel answers. The points and authorities for this particular type of motion must address each question that the deponent has refused to answer as well as each privilege claimed by the opposing counsel in instructing the witness not to answer. An argument must be made showing that the privilege claimed is invalid and that the question should be answered. An alternative showing could be made that although the privilege is valid, it is not totally inclusive and certain portions of the question can be answered. An argument might be made that the privilege involved for this particular question was waived when a question subsequently asked in the deposition was answered. In this case, an exhibit to the points and authorities would include both the question that was certified and the question that was subsequently answered which you claim has waived the privilege. Other arguments can be made against privilege along the lines that the burden of proof of establishing the privilege has not been met by the opposing counsel. Another argument frequently made is that although the information is privileged, it is directly relevant to the lawsuit and the greater ends of justice will be served if the question is answered. In all of these examples, the burden of proof that the privilege is valid and has not been waived is on the holder of the privilege and their counsel.

§ 3.59   Motions to Oppose Compelling
Answers to Certified Questions

Motions to oppose answers to certified questions and to claim the privilege asserted in a deposition transcript will include those certified questions and responses citing the privileges claimed as exhibits. Points and authorities in this particular instance will focus directly on the privilege with an argument as to why certain information is privileged. Points and authorities will frequently point out that there are alternate methods of obtaining the same information through nonprivileged channels. Of course, an argument will have been made by the person who wants an answer to this question that there is no alternative method for getting this information. The court makes the final decision on privileges. The burden of proof in a privilege claim rests with the side that has asserted the privilege. In asserting the privilege, proof must be made to the satisfaction of the court that this particular requested information falls within the privilege claimed. On the other hand, the person who desires the information must prove to the satisfaction of the court that the requested information does not fall within the scope of the privilege claimed, or that the privilege is invalid.

§ 3.60   Meet and Confer Requirements

In most states, motions prepared to compel discovery relating to depositions can be made only after a good faith attempt has been made by the moving party to meet and confer with opposing counsel. This meet and confer requirement can be satisfied by phone contact followed by a letter explaining counsel's arguments for the discovery sought. Opposing counsel must be given reasonable time to respond and/or enter into a stipulation for limited discovery before motions to compel can be set for a court hearing. **Form 3–43** illustrates a sample meet and confer letter.

FORM 3–43
SAMPLE MEET AND CONFER LETTER

Re: [plaintiff] v. [defendant]

Dear [attorney A]:

As a follow up to our conversation of [date], wherein I indicated new information has come to light regarding your client's involvement in prior business dealings which has direct impact on the present litigation concerning [name] Corporation, I am enclosing with this letter pages from deposition transcripts of three witnesses who are members of the [name] Corporation Board of Directors. You will note from the pages enclosed from the depositions of [deponent A], [deponent B], and [deponent C] that your client is a member of several other board of directors and has been involved in putting together joint ventures for several other projects similar in nature to [name] Joint Venture, which is the subject of this litigation.

Prior to taking depositions of these witnesses, we had taken the deposition of your client, [plaintiff]. It is our desire to redepose [plaintiff] so that we may have the opportunity to question [plaintiff] regarding plaintiff's involvement with other business dealings which we feel are directly relevant to the instant litigation.

You have indicated to me that you feel [plaintiff], having been deposed on [date] for two full days of testimony, has contributed all of the information within [plaintiff's] own personal knowledge that has a direct bearing on the instant litigation. You further indicated to me that you would not make [plaintiff] available for further depositions and intend to oppose a motion to compel attendance of [plaintiff] at a second deposition. I am hopeful that we can come to an agreement prior to the necessity of my making a motion to compel. I propose that you allow your client, [plaintiff], to be redeposed for no more than three hours during which time [plaintiff] will be asked questions limited to the following areas:

1. [Plaintiff]'s membership on the board of directors of [name] Corporation and the joint venture agreements entered into by [name] Corporation.

2. [Plaintiff]'s membership on [name] Corporation's Board of Directors and [plaintiff]'s participation in joint venture agreements while on that board.

Please contact my office within the next ten (10) days, or by [date], if you are willing to enter into a stipulation for a second deposition of [plaintiff], which will not exceed three hours and which will focus on the limited areas discussed above. If I do not hear from you within the prescribed time, I will be forced to move the court for a motion to compel attendance of [plaintiff] at a second deposition.

Sincerely,

[attorney for plaintiff]

§ 3.61   Use of Depositions at Trial

The use of depositions at trial in federal court is governed by Federal Rules of Civil Procedure 32(a) to (d). The procedure for introducing deposition testimony varies from state to state. Local statutes as well as the particular rules of each superior court should be checked well in advance of the time of trial. In all cases, it is necessary to lodge the original deposition transcripts with the court prior to the beginning of trial. Original deposition transcripts may be ordered from the court reporter who took the depositions. Usually court reporters will deliver transcripts to the presiding judge in a sealed envelope, if you request them in a timely fashion with an accompanying letter of instruction. In some states, court reporters no longer keep original transcripts, but return them to the attorney who noticed the deposition at the time they deliver a copy of the transcript. If this is the practice in your state, you will receive sealed original transcripts for all the depositions noticed by your law firm well in advance of time of trial. Under no circumstances should these sealed original transcripts be opened prior to trial.

Depositions are used at trial for the following reasons:

1. **Witness impeachment.** This is the most common use of depositions at trial and it invites comparison of the deposition transcript with a witness' trial testimony to impeach that witness on cross-examination. Impeachment is accomplished by reading selected portions of the deposition into the trial transcript for comparison. Caveat, if you offer into evidence selected portions of a deposition, any other party may introduce any other part of a deposition. Review the deposition transcript to weigh the risks of introducing only those portions which support your case against the introduction by the adverse party of those portions of the deposition which may damage your case.

2. **Admissions, substantive evidence, impeachment and cross-examination.** The deposition of a party or corporate, governmental or other organizational party may be used by the adverse party for any reason. A deposition may be used even if the deponent party or agent is available to testify, or has already testified. If a witness was an officer, director, or managing agent of a party, or

a person designated under Rule 30(b)(6) or Rule 31(a) of the Federal Rules of Civil Procedure, to testify on behalf of the public or private corporation, partnership, association, or governmental agency which is a party to the action, their entire testimony (as long as it constitutes admissible evidence) can be introduced by an opposing party. If the deponent qualifies as one of those persons pursuant to Rule 30(b)(6) or Rule 31(a), the deposition can be used in the same manner and fashion as if the deponent had been a party to the action. In deciding what weight to give deposition testimony of a corporate agent, the courts generally consider whether the interests of the individual agent are similar to that of the principal, and whether the individual has functions, responsibilities, and authority regarding the subject matter of the litigation. Objection to this type of deposition testimony being offered at trial may be raised if there is a person of higher authority than the deponent responsible for the particular matters testified to in the deposition, and that person is ready, willing, and able to testify.

3. **Deponent Unavailability.** The deposition of anyone may be used by any party for any reason if one of the following conditions exists: the deponent is dead, the deponent is more than 100 miles from the courthouse, the deponent cannot testify because of age, sickness, infirmity, or imprisonment, the deponent cannot be subpoenaed, and upon a showing of any other exceptional circumstances.

4. **Similar Parties/Action.** A deposition from another lawsuit may be used in a common action if there was a substitution of parties or if the former action involved the same subject matter and parties. Depositions may also be used in other cases if one or more of the adversaries have the same motivation to examine or cross-examine the deponent in the prior action.

5. **Noticed Videotape Deposition.** Videotaped depositions of expert witnesses may be introduced at trial if at the time the deposition was noticed it was so stated on the notice that the deposition would be used at trial in lieu of live testimony.

The value of using depositions at trial is that they often serve as efficient, economical, and effective techniques in establishing substantive evidence in lieu of live testimony, refresh the recollection of a witness during trial, and serve as impeachment tools for cross-examination purposes.

A deposition may be presented to the jury in various ways. The manner chosen usually depends upon the circumstances, lawyer's preference, and economics. The simplest and most economic method is for the lawyer to read the pertinent parts of the deposition to the jury after making an introductory statement telling the jury what the lawyer is going to do, and why the deposition is being read in the absence of the witness. This method frequently puts the judge and jury to sleep and should be used only when short excerpts of a deposition need to be read.

Another method of presenting a deposition to a jury is to role-play the deposition. This can be accomplished by the trial attorney asking questions, and the role-player acting as the deponent sitting in the witness' chair answering the questions by reading the answers from the deposition transcript. Frequently legal assistants are chosen to role-play the witness. This method is much more lively and usually holds a jury's attention. A legal assistant role-playing the witness should read slowly and precisely with emphasis where the intention is to show the conflict in the testimony. The purpose of reading the deposition testimony is to point out to the jury that there is a conflict in the evidence, or a contradiction of prior testimony, and they must reflect on what they are hearing. Therefore, the reading of deposition testimony must be slow, distinct, and purposeful or the value will be diminished.

The last method of presenting deposition testimony at trial is to have the witness read his own deposition. After a witness has been examined and given certain testimony, the cross-examination begins with the deposition testimony to impeach the witness. In this instance, the lawyer reads the questions as stated in the deposition asking the witness to read the responses given in the deposition exactly as they were given at the time the deposition was taken. It is very effective for a jury to hear the contradictions from the witness' own lips as they read testimony from their deposition which contradicts testimony given in their direct examination.

Remember, if the deponent is a party to the litigation, the deponent's entire testimony (as long as it constitutes admissible testimony) can be introduced by an opposing party even though the deponent is present in court. This right to introduce deposition testimony is extended to all parties in litigation and all opposing counsel, and provides the greatest opportunity for witness impeachment.

§ 3.62   Depositions in Large Cases

In multiparty actions, when there are several plaintiffs and defendants, there are sure to be many depositions taken, or at least noticed. The organizational task of coordinating the schedule of depositions usually falls to the legal assistant. Keep your priority list of depositions in mind when offering to schedule depositions for other parties in the action. It may be important in your overall discovery plan and strategy to have certain depositions precede others, and they should be noticed accordingly. In scheduling depositions when many players are involved, it is important to notice depositions early to have priority in scheduling. In approximately 98 percent of all large cases, the depositions are not taken on the date they have been originally noticed. Renoticing of depositions is very common; however, renoticed depositions automatically take priority in scheduling over a deposition that has been noticed for the first time.

In cases when there are several plaintiffs, defendants, cross-complainants or cross-defendants, it may not be necessary for your attorney to attend all of the depositions, especially the ones the attorney has not noticed. If a deposition is set for a minor player, or a witness who will be furnishing information about aspects of the case, allegations of the complaint, or defenses that do not apply directly to your client, it may be unnecessary for the attorney to appear. In this instance, it is more time- and cost-efficient for a legal assistant to attend the deposition and take notes. A legal assistant attending a deposition and taking notes on behalf of an attorney may not ask any questions or participate in the deposition in any fashion other than as an observer. It is not necessary to order a copy of the deposition transcript at the time of the deposition. You should obtain the name and address of the court reporting firm and the individual court reporter (they usually have a business card) so that a copy of the transcript can be ordered later after your attorney reviews your deposition notes and decides whether to order a copy. If exhibits have been introduced at the deposition, a copy of those exhibits may be ordered from the court reporter in addition to, or in lieu of, the transcript. Your deposition notes should be completed and given to your attorney as soon as possible after the deposition.

All deposition notices should be maintained in a separate discovery file titled "Deposition Notices." An index to this file should be set up with the following headings:

Date of deposition notice

Noticed by (name of law firm, representing plaintiff/defendant, and so forth.)

Renoticed (date)

Date deposition was taken

Attorneys and/or legal assistants present

Name of court reporter/service

Repository of transcript and exhibits (either court reporter or attorney who noticed the deposition)

Copy of transcript and/or exhibits ordered/received/date

This organizational system will allow you to identify quickly those people who have been deposed and the location of their transcripts and exhibits. In a multiparty case, there could be 100 to 200 parties deposed over the course of discovery, and copies of transcripts which seemed unimportant at the beginning of discovery may take on crucial importance after other depositions have been taken. With this type of indexing, you will be able to identify immediately the name of the court reporter who took a particular deposition and order a copy.

§ 3.63   Handling Deposition Exhibits in Large Cases

In large cases when many depositions will be taken and hundreds of exhibits may be used, it is best to coordinate the numbering of deposition exhibits so that they will run consecutively from deposition to deposition. For example, if the first deposition in a particular case is of M. Jones, CEO of ABC Corporation, the exhibits would be numbered Jones #1, Jones #2, Jones #3, Jones #4, and so forth. If the next deposition to be taken is of J. Smith, CFO of ABC Corporation, they would begin with the next number consecutively in sequence. For example, if M.'s last number was 10, J.'s first number would be 11, Smith #11, Smith #12, and so forth. Deposition exhibits introduced in one person's deposition may be used as exhibits in another person's deposition. In this case, it is best not to renumber. The deposition exhibit already has a number and an identity. It can be used in another person's deposition and be referred to by that number, for example, Smith #10. The system of numbering deposition exhibits consecutively works very well if all parties agree at the first deposition to implement the system. It avoids duplication of exhibits and creates a system so that missing exhibits are easily identifiable. This organizational plan of numbering deposition exhibits consecutively works best in cases where no more than 30 to

35 depositions are taken. As depositions progress, each attorney should have a deposition exhibit binder with the exhibits arranged numerically by deponent, and indexed (see **Form 3–44**). This deposition binder then goes with the attorney to each deposition so that new exhibits may be added. In addition to the index, the binder should have numbered tabs for easy retrieval of exhibits.

An index of deposition exhibits should be placed in the front of the binder of deposition exhibits. The deposition exhibits themselves should be separated by colored paper and numbered tabs.

FORM 3–44
SAMPLE DEPOSITION EXHIBIT INDEX

[name], Vol. 1
Deposition
Exhibits

Exhibit No.	Description of Exhibit
Exhibit # 1	Copy of letter to [name] from M. Smith [date].
Exhibit #2	Memo to J. Powers from S. Carter dated [date].
Exhibit #3	Handwritten note to S. from [name] dated [date].
Exhibit #4	Handwritten document to S. from M. dated [date].
Exhibit #5	[name] Deposition, 41-page document, dated [date], stating restrictions for subdivision.
Exhibit #6	Copy of document entitled [document name] recorded in [name] County on [date].

In addition to a numbered deposition exhibit index, a second index should be prepared listing the same deposition exhibits in a chronological sequence. It is important to keep the time line of a case intact so that critical time periods can be keyed to documents generated during that period. Deposition exhibits are introduced into the transcript as questions are asked regarding those exhibits and they are numbered accordingly. This does not always coincide with chronological sequence. A chronological index of deposition exhibits provides an overall time line and helps tell the story of the case. Because the deposition exhibit index contains dates of documents, a chronological index of documents can be pulled from the same information without the necessity of redoing an index. Both indexes are invaluable in keeping track of the number of documents introduced at the various depositions as the case progresses. These indexes will also be useful as the time of trial draws near, and trial exhibits are selected.

CHAPTER 4

INTERROGATORIES

§ 4.1   Introduction

Interrogatories are written questions which may be served upon any adverse party who has made an appearance in an action through filing a complaint, cross-complaint, or answer. Interrogatories, unlike depositions, are limited in their use in that they may be served only on parties, not nonparties. Interrogatories arc specific questions propounded to a party which the party must answer under oath within a certain statutory time limit. Interrogatories are usually served soon after an action is commenced as an opening inquiry. They are the most economical discovery device available for obtaining basic information about the opposing party, the party's version of the transaction or occurrence, and the existence of items of evidence to support their version of the transaction or occurrence.

§ 4.2   The Purpose of Interrogatories

Legal professionals are well versed in the advantages and disadvantages of interrogatories and view them as a necessary discovery tool. Legal assistant responsibilities relating to interrogatories include drafting, responding, and preparing discovery motions to compel and counter motions to oppose. The most common paralegal task is responding to interrogatories. Clients are always amazed, bewildered, and annoyed when they receive opposing counsel's set of 127 or more specially prepared interrogatories. They do not understand why they must respond to so many personal and not even relevant questions. In order to obtain your client's cooperation, you must tactfully explain the purpose and function of interrogatories. It is essential that clients understand that they cannot avoid responding to interrogatories. Preparing answers to specially prepared interrogatories is a big job, and can not be completed successfully without full client cooperation.

Black's Law Dictionary defines interrogatories as, "A set or series of written questions drawn up for the purpose of being propounded to a party, witness, or other person having information of interest in the case." This definition implies that answers to interrogatories therefore supply information of interest to the case, or at least information of interest to the party asking questions. The opposing party may propound numerous specific interrogatories, and always asks interrogatories which are objectionable.

The following list of reasons for using interrogatories is helpful when you are explaining the importance of interrogatories to clients. Interrogatories are essential to preparation of a case for trial because they help:

1. To particularize the basis of the Complaint, Answer, Cross-Complaint, initial pleading, and the opponent's case
2. To probe the merits of a claim or defense
3. To establish the extent of the responding party's personal information
4. To identify additional parties who may have helpful information
5. To circumvent the corporate bureaucratic maze
6. To substantiate a party's prior litigation history
7. To formulate better questions for depositions
8. To assist in formulating specific document requests
9. To further investigation
10. To document the extent of insurance coverage and/or reservation of rights claims
11. To establish the extent of injury or harm, whether it is physical or nonphysical, claimed by plaintiff
12. To establish the monetary value of the case
13. To identify percipient witnesses
14. To elicit lay and expert opinion
15. To act as a tool at trial for the purpose of witness impeachment
16. To secure admissions
17. To obtain statements
18. To use as support for summary judgment motions
19. To narrow triable issues
20. To hasten settlement
21. To identify and locate specific pieces of evidence
22. To assist in settlement negotiations
23. To identify all relevant records with sufficient particularity as required by the subpoenas
24. To substantiate preexisting injuries and conditions (in personal injury, product liability, and medical malpractice cases).

All of these reasons for interrogatories can be reworded in simple English and used as a basis for explaining why your client must take numerous burdensome interrogatories seriously and assist in providing responses.

As a final note, it is always good to mention to the client that you have prepared a similar set of 150 or more burdensome interrogatories and served them upon the opposing party. Clients are more than willing to help work on their own case and provide responses to interrogatories if they know that opposing party is undergoing the same type of torture.

§ 4.3   The Advantages and Disadvantages of Interrogatories

As a preliminary discovery device, interrogatories have the following advantages over other more complex and costly discovery devices:

1.   They are economical. Form sets of basic interrogatory questions can be developed for the types of actions in which your firm specializes, so that an introductory set of interrogatories can be quickly assembled from your basic set with a few changes to tailor them to the specific facts.

2.   They are a fast and efficient method of obtaining information.

3.   They force the opposing side to furnish basic information which will enable you to plan further discovery and develop further areas of inquiry.

4.   They are flexible; different questions can be asked in different sets at different times during the pendency of a particular case.

5.   They complement other methods of discovery because answers received can be used to determine the best person for later depositions, or the appropriate documents for later requests for production of documents.

6.   They reveal information that will put the parties in realistic and informed positions from which to negotiate a settlement or stipulate to agreed facts and remove them from controversy.

7.   Interrogatories call for the collective knowledge of the recipient. This requirement may compel a certain person's participation in the preparation of answers, whether that person is specifically addressed or not. This use of interrogatories is similar to a homing device in that it finds and locates the proper spokesperson who must reveal correct and complete information.

8.   It is the intended method to particularize the factual and legal basis for pleadings in that it enables you to gather specific factual information in far greater detail than in depositions.

9.   Nothing is considered sacred. Interrogatory responses draw from the collective knowledge of the answering party and its agents which may include every corporate officer in a corporation, their investigators, and their attorneys.

10. They can be used as a follow-up device after other discovery. For example, interrogatories can be used to follow up on questions that have not been completely answered at depositions or to request more particulars about documents obtained through document production. Interrogatories may also be used in a supplementary fashion to elicit later acquired information. This particular form of interrogatory, the supplemental interrogatory, is extremely important in trial preparation because it requires the responding party to update previous discovery responses.

Interrogatories also have certain limitations, weaknesses and risks including the following:

1. They may be directed only to parties in the action, and not to nonparties.
2. They are slow. There is usually a thirty-day wait between the time the interrogatories are propounded and the answers are received. This often is extended by stipulation between counsel. (In depositions the answers are immediate.)
3. There is no spontaneity in interrogatory answers because they are usually prepared by or with the assistance of legal assistants and counsel. There is little likelihood of spontaneity or unguarded revelations as the client's answers are carefully screened before they are finalized.
4. There is no chance for follow-up questions as there is in a deposition. If the answer you receive fails to respond precisely to the question asked, your alternative is to send out a new set of interrogatories or make a motion to compel further answers. At a deposition, immediate follow-up questions are possible.
5. They provide no assistance in sizing up your adversary or the client in terms of their credibility or their witness potential. Depositions are face-to-face encounters which enable you to assess witness potential.
6. They actually can assist the opposing counsel by forcing him to conduct investigation, do research, and prepare their case thoroughly in order to respond to your interrogatories; something they may not as yet have undertaken.

The use of interrogatories as a discovery device has both advantages and disadvantages which should be considered before they are served. The timing of interrogatories should also be considered. Many attorneys prefer to take a deposition first and then send out specific interrogatories to eliminate evasive answers and to follow up on avenues opened in deposition testimony. Other attorneys send interrogatories out as a first discovery device, timing the interrogatory responses to be received before the deposition. Deposition questioning can then be directed to interrogatory answers eliminating one interrogatory disadvantage, the lack of follow-up questions. It is proper at a deposition to ask a client to review their answer to interrogatory number 4 where they stated that they attended monthly board meetings in January, February and March of 19__, but did not attend board meetings for the balance of the year. Deposition questions could then be asked to flush out the missing information, such as:

1. Why didn't you attend board meetings the balance of the year?
2. Were board meetings held in any other months of the year?
3. Was the presence of every board member required at each and every board meeting?

An advantage of having received interrogatory responses prior to a deposition is that it affords you an opportunity for follow-up questioning. It is also very embarrassing for the deponent who has not reviewed their interrogatory answers, but has signed the verification that accompanied those responses, to be confronted with answers that they may never have seen. Legal assistants who prepare final versions of interrogatory answers for clients should always send a copy of the finalized answers to the client and urge them to read them to avoid such embarrassing situations.

§ 4.4 The Subject Matter of Interrogatories

Interrogatories may relate to any matters which are relevant and not privileged. The subject matter of interrogatories may include:

The identity of witnesses and experts including their names, addresses, and last known phone numbers

The subject matter, opinions, and basis for opinions of experts

Pictures, graphs, charts, and other physical evidence

Any claim or defense, allegation and complaint, and so forth, including factual basis behind each claim

The existence and contents of any correspondence or documents relevant to the action

Opinions or contentions that relate to the factual basis of legal theories

The extent of any investigation done, including persons who have been interviewed or have provided statements

Summary explanations of technical data and statistics, manuals, reports, studies, and materials containing technical information

Other contracts or transactions between, or relating to, the parties before or after the events of the particular case

Similar incidents, problems, or complaints encountered by third persons and related to the subject matter of the case

Business and corporate information concerning the nature, extent, principal place of business, initial date of incorporation, and so forth regarding the business

Financial information, including the existence of reports, balance sheets, and financial status of business, as well as income, assets, and liabilities

Government licenses that authorize or regulate a party's conduct

The existence and coverage limits of liability or other insurance

Information concerning letters, memoranda, notes, and other materials that a party or a witness has composed, signed, or read and reviewed

The financial status and net worth of a defendant who is defending a claim for punitive damages

The identity of all persons that may have information regarding the subject matter of this case.

§ 4.5 What Is Discoverable?

Any material which can be shown to be relevant to the action at hand and which is not privileged is discoverable. A partial listing of information which is discoverable includes:

Factual information about a business client, usually 5 to 10 years' worth of corporate records, board of directors minutes, annual meeting reports, profit and loss statements, and corporate housekeeping documents

Medical history including records of treatment and all identification required to subpoena records of health care providers for 5 to 10 years of a litigant's medical history

Existence of liability insurance coverage including policy limits

Documents and records used by a deponent to refresh the deponent's memory prior to a deposition

The names, addresses, and other statistical known information concerning potential expert witnesses

The names, addresses and last known phone numbers of percipient witnesses

The financial condition of a party if punitive damages are sought

The report of an accountant prepared at the request of one partner, if it is based on that accountant's examination of partnership books, which are not in themselves privileged

Pictures taken of the plaintiff by the defendant's investigator

Any and all photographs of damage

A piece of defective equipment

Statement of the plaintiff to the defendant's investigator and observations of the investigator

Knowledge obtained by an investigator hired by the insurance carrier, but not by the defense counsel

Statements of independent witnesses taken on behalf of the adverse party if it can be shown that there is no alternative means for obtaining those statements

All facts forming the basis of any allegation, affirmative defense, or counterclaim in the pleadings

Previous accident reports filed with the Department of Motor Vehicles

Information on prior litigation

Information relating to a client's personal background such as former marriages, educational background, military background, and criminal record, if any.

This is a partial list of discoverable materials which is by no means meant to be exhaustive. Generally speaking, it is a good rule of thumb to ask each interrogatory or deposition question, and request each document which you feel will benefit your case. It is up to the opposition to claim and maintain a privilege to keep you from discovering the material.

§ 4.6   What Is Generally Not Discoverable?

There are materials which are considered to be generally not discoverable. A partial listing of those materials follows:

Tax returns unless they are particularly relevant to the litigation at hand such as an investigation by the IRS into tax evasion, family law situations when tax records directly relate to income and expense declarations, or claims of business fraud, breach of fiduciary duty, and so forth;

Information imparted by a party, or their attorneys, to potential expert witnesses while preparing to defend the action;

Reports of any consultants who have been retained by an attorney to investigate the underlying facts of the case; consultants' materials are protected by the work product privilege until they are named as expert witnesses;

The identity, location, and opinion regarding the valuation of damages made by an appraiser;

Opinions of medical members of a committee formed to consult with defense counsel in a medical malpractice action, and reports of hospital committees who regularly review their peers for purposes of disciplinary action, and almost all internal investigations by corporate entities;

The financial condition of a party if there is no punitive damage claim;

A person's lifetime medical or psychiatric history;

Property owners statements to tax assessors;

Unemployment insurance returns;

Trade secrets;

Bank statements;

Any information relating to the religious or ethnic background or belief of the party; and

Materials which are usually privileged can be generally grouped into categories of personal/confidential records, official records, and attorney-client and work product materials.

§ 4.7   Requesting Privileged Information

Attorney work product information can be requested as well as the existence of documents to which privilege may be claimed. Requesting them in interrogatories will force the responding party to identify the particulars of a document, for example, the parties who attended a meeting, the parties to a conversation, and so forth. The responding party will undoubtedly claim that the information is privileged and provide nothing further; however, you will have learned the existence of the document, meeting, or conversation, and can plan alternate methods for obtaining the information sought. In drafting interrogatories, it is a mistake to exclude interrogatories which you feel will not be answered because of a privilege claim. It is important to know the existence of all witnesses, supporting documentation, and physical evidence that exists to support the opposition's claim, even if it is privileged. An unasked question affords the responding party the opportunity to withhold key information. The responding party is not under a duty to disclose any item of information that is not specifically requested.

The responses to interrogatories may affect the way you establish that the opponent lacks certain evidence or information. For example, when a defendant serves interrogatories requiring the plaintiff to disclose the identity of witnesses to an accident, a negative response by the plaintiff tells the defendant that he does not have to spend time countering evidence by the plaintiff in that area. If the responding party, plaintiff or defendant, attempts to produce surprise witnesses at trial after stating that they have no witnesses, the court may preclude the witnesses from testifying. A party's negative responses to interrogatories indicating that they are not aware of any relevant documents, photographs, charts, graphs, or other evidence, may also give the surprised party grounds for keeping nondisclosed items out of evidence. Responses to interrogatories must be accurate in light of the information available to the party, the party's agents, employees, and attorneys at the time they are responding. Failure to disclose witnesses, documents, or other physical evidence, if known, precludes its exclusion at time of trial.

Remember that the information provided in interrogatory responses may be accurate at that time, but as investigation and discovery continue, the information may change. Responding parties are always under an ethical duty to supplement interrogatory responses, but in many states, unlike Federal Rule of Civil Procedure 26(e), there is no statutory duty to supplement interrogatory responses. Supplementary interrogatories should always be sent out to prevent surprises at time of trial. (See § **4.55** for further discussion and forms.)

§ 4.8   Drafting Interrogatories

In order for an interrogatory to be of value, it is necessary that the language of the interrogatory gives the answering party no leeway in responding to the question. The answer must give exactly the information that the propounding party desires. Interrogatories need to reflect the tightest possible language and be worded so that they stand alone. Interrogatories should neither be vague, too broad, nor overly exclusive. The interrogatory should be open to one interpretation only, the interpretation of the drafting party. When drafting interrogatories, keep in mind that interrogatories and their responses may be introduced at trial in the same fashion that depositions are admissible. The language used in drafting must be chosen to maximize the potential evidentiary effect. Questions should be worded in simple, nonlegal terms so that they can be understood by a jury when they are read aloud. In drafting interrogatories, it is wise to remember what you learned in high school English classes pertaining to sentence structure, grammar, and verb tense. Be extremely careful about the verb tense used in interrogatory questions. Present tense is always used to determine facts that are still current. Past tense is used to determine events that are over. If your interrogatory relates to both past and present events, it is best to break the question down into several questions to avoid the objection of ambiguity. If your interrogatory contains vague, ambiguous, and conclusionary words, it is certain to be objectionable. Choose words that are factually descriptive to avoid nonresponsive answers.

Interrogatories should be drafted to produce as much information as possible; however, care must be taken not to draft fishing expedition questions. The scope of an interrogatory must be limited by parameters of time and/or definition as to the information sought to avoid the objection of being "overbroad, ambiguous, unintelligible, and so forth." Drafting interrogatories to imply fault on the other side is a technique that should be handled very carefully through narrowly drafted contention and liability interrogatories (see § **4.34** for sample contention interrogatories). Requests for admissions lend themselves more easily to asking a question that will imply fault on the other side; however, carefully drafted interrogatories may reveal fault by omission and/or failure to act. For example, in a premises liability action regarding a slip and fall accident on a stairway in an apartment building, the following interrogatory was used:

Please state the time and date of each and every inspection performed by an employee, agent, or servant of [name] Corporation, of the stairway located on the east side of the apartment building located at [address], [city], [state]. (You may limit your response to the last five years.)

If through other discovery you have already established that a defect existed in the steps, broken concrete, missing railing, torn carpet, and so forth, and that such defect was reported by your client to the property manager by written report on a particular date, the dates in this response regarding various inspections are crucial. If the response indicates that inspections were performed subsequent to the notice of the defect, but no repairs were done, you will have established that defendants knew of the defect prior to the accident and were, therefore, under a duty to repair or remedy the situation.

§ 4.9   Checklist for Drafting Interrogatories

The following checklist can be helpful in drafting clear and concise interrogatories:

_____   1.   Know the case on which you are working inside and out before you begin drafting your interrogatories. Read all the pleadings filed to date, all the correspondence in the file, the client intake memo, and the client documents. Many ideas for questions will come from this information. It is also necessary to know the legal issues of the case to ask about the facts upon which those issues are based.

_____   2.   Determine what you do know. Once you have learned the issues of the case, match them with the facts as you know them from your client's point of view and from all that you have gained from any investigation or informal discovery.

_____   3.   Determine what you need to know to particularize the areas of inquiry about which you need more information. Frame your questions along the investigative questions: who, what, where, when, why, and how.

_____   4.   Examine the pleadings in the file and break the causes of action and defenses into the elements necessary to prove those causes of actions, claims, and defenses. Each of these elements then becomes a checklist for you. Questions can be framed that seek the facts that can potentially be used to support each of these elements. A good reference for determining elements necessary to prove a particular claim or defense is the jury instruction used in your state. For example, by reviewing the jury instructions for negligence, design defect, or constructive fraud, you will be able to spot the elements necessary for a jury to make that finding and draft your questions accordingly.

_____   5.   Ask interrogatories in a way that the story of the facts comes out chronologically. The development of a case story is important in selling your case to a jury. Your client will have their version, or story, of the case and the opposition will have a different version, or story, to tell. Developing a factual basis in a chronological sequence of events is the most accurate method of presenting a case story. All good stories should have a beginning, middle, and end without gaps in the middle. The specific information you can obtain in interrogatory responses can assist you in filling in the gaps of information in your case story, so that a jury can see the total picture of your case.

_____   6.   Use simple words and short sentences whenever possible. An answer to a complex or lengthy interrogatory is not likely to prove useful for evidentiary purposes particularly in a jury trial. A verbose interrogatory may provide an excuse for the responding party to avoid an answer or be equally verbose and ambiguous in their response.

_____   7.   Avoid questions that call for simple yes or no answers unless you are able to follow up these questions immediately with subparts asking for specific details, names, addresses of witnesses, documents, and so forth.

_____   8.   Phrase interrogatories so the person answering them will have to indicate whether the person is talking from firsthand knowledge, secondhand knowledge, or relying on documents so that you can learn the original source of critical information.

_____   9.   Avoid poorly drafted interrogatories which allow your opponent wiggle room and produce evasive answers. One method of avoiding this is to play devil's advocate. After drafting your interrogatories, attempt to answer them yourself. For example, consider whether the questions can be redrafted in a simpler, less complex fashion; decide whether some interrogatories can be eliminated or consolidated; and finally consider all ways that the responses to your interrogatories can be fudged.

_____   10.   Use the "ladder" approach as an effective drafting technique for interrogatories suitable for use in federal court, or in those state courts which allow questions to refer back to previous answers. This approach asks a broad question which usually elicits a yes or no answer, and then follows with specific questions relating to one or more of the possible responses. For example:

State whether the defendant is a corporation or a partnership;

If the defendant is a corporation, identify the members of the board of directors by name, address and phone number;

If the defendant is a partnership, identify all the partners by name, address and phone number;

If the defendant is a corporation, state the date of incorporation and the principal place of business;

If the defendant is a partnership, identify all the limited partners.

The ladder approach of drafting interrogatories is effective, but uses a lot of questions. It is more efficient if you know, or are fairly certain of, some of the responses to avoid questions which can be answered with a yes or a no. It is best to ask questions which require a more detailed answer. The following question is a proper interrogatory; it would not be considered overbroad, and it combines several ladder steps:

State the date and state of defendant's incorporation, its principal place of business, and all members of the board of directors by name, address, and telephone number.

Summary of procedures for drafting interrogatories is:

- Make an outline of the information you are seeking;
- Use form interrogatories as a source of standard questions;
- Review jury instructions for the elements of each legal theory in your pleadings. (See sample.)
- Consult your office exemplar file for interrogatories which have been drafted in similar cases, rewording them as necessary.
- Draft additional interrogatories necessary and specific to the particular case.
- The final step is to review all your questions, arranging them in a logical sequence. Each response to build upon the previous response so that when questions and answers are read to a jury, your client's version of the story line of the case will become apparent.

§ 4.10   Sample Use of Jury Instructions in Drafting Interrogatories

A review of jury instructions for specific causes of action sets forth the elements necessary to prove that allegation at time of trial. The following jury instruction is an approved California Civil Jury Instruction (BAJI 6.20). It is used as an illustration of the elements necessary to prove the cause of action of negligent selection, training, and retention of hospital personnel. This cause of action frequently appears in medical malpractice cases when the plaintiff is suing not only the treating physicians but also the hospital and other medical personnel.

Duty of a Hospital

It is the duty of a hospital such as the defendant to use reasonable care in furnishing a patient the care, attention and protection reasonably required by the plaintiff's mental and physical condition.

It is also the duty of the hospital such as the defendant to use reasonable care in selecting a competent medical staff and periodically reviewing the competency of its medical staff.

The amount of caution, attention and protection required in the exercise of reasonable care depends upon the known condition of the patient and his or her needs, and must be appropriate to that condition and those needs.

The standard of reasonable care required of a hospital is the care, selection and diligence ordinarily used by hospitals generally in the same or a similar locality and under similar circumstances. A failure to fulfill any such duties is negligence.[1]

The key words in this jury instruction are ". . . reasonable care in selecting a competent medical staff, periodically reviewing the competency of its medical staff. . . ." Specific interrogatories designed to determine the criteria for hiring, specific duties of medical personnel, training and evaluation procedures, personnel policies, and so forth of a hospital will provide the information that the plaintiff needs in order to prove this particular allegation to a jury. **Form 4–1** illustrates the interrogatories written with these jury instructions in mind.

FORM 4–1
SAMPLE INTERROGATORIES
INCORPORATING JURY INSTRUCTION ELEMENTS

SPECIAL INTERROGATORY NO. 1:
State the name, address, phone number, and job title of each and every person responsible for creating, reviewing, revising or editing any policy and procedure guidelines or operations manuals for [name] Hospital from 19__ to the present. (Suggested permissible time frame, 5 years.)

SPECIAL INTERROGATORY NO. 2:
State the name, address, phone number, and job title of each and every person responsible for recruiting, screening and hiring employees for [name] Hospital from 19__ to the present.

SPECIAL INTERROGATORY NO. 3:
State in specific detail the hiring criteria, selection process, and specific job descriptions for medical personnel at [name] Hospital from 19__ to the present.

SPECIAL INTERROGATORY NO. 4:
State the name, address, phone number, and job title of each and every person responsible for training new employees, including interns and nurses, at [name] Hospital from 19__ to the present.

SPECIAL INTERROGATORY NO. 5:
Identify by name, address, phone number, and job title each and every [name] Hospital personnel supervisor from 19__ to the present.

---

[1] Book of Approved Jury Instructions (7th ed. 1986) § 6.20.

SPECIAL INTERROGATORY NO. 6:

Identify by name, address, phone number, and job title each and every person responsible for oral or written evaluations of hospital personnel employed at [name] Hospital from 19__ to the present.

SPECIAL INTERROGATORY NO. 7:

Please set forth the schedule of performance evaluations for interns, residents, and nurses that was in effect for [name] Hospital from January through December, 19__. (To safeguard this interrogatory from being overbroad, limit your time frame to the 12 months immediately preceding the incident.)

SPECIAL INTERROGATORY NO. 8:

Please state in specific detail the procedure supervisory personnel at [name] Hospital utilized to inform their employees of the content of personnel policies, procedures, manuals, or other special hospital rules from 19__ to the present.

SPECIAL INTERROGATORY NO. 9:

State in specific detail the duties and responsibilities of the personnel manager from 19__ to the present.

Note: This same interrogatory can be reworded to apply to specific supervisors as the case warrants. For example, charge nurse of the surgical team, chief of residents, neurology unit, chief of interns, and so forth.

Contemporaneous with service of these interrogatories, a request for identification, production, and inspection of documents and tangible things should be served on the custodian of records for the hospital. Documents to be requested are illustrated in **Form 4–2:**

FORM 4–2
SAMPLE REQUEST FOR PRODUCTION
TO ACCOMPANY INTERROGATORIES

REQUEST NO. 1:

The [name] Hospital staff bylaws that were in effect on [date of incident].

REQUEST NO. 2:

Each writing which refers, relates, or pertains to staff privileges at [name] Hospital, including but not limited to applications, reapplications, appointments, letters of recommendation, evaluations, and so forth pertaining to Dr. [name].

REQUEST NO. 3:

The personnel file maintained by [name] Hospital for [name], M.D.

REQUEST NO. 4:

Each writing which refers, evidences, or pertains to any duties or responsibilities of a surgeon performing any type of orthopedic surgery.

REQUEST NO. 5:

Each writing pertaining to Dr. [name] by any hospital administrator not derived from any investigation into the quality or care of evaluation thereof by a medical staff committee at [name] Hospital.

REQUEST NO. 6:

Each writing pertaining to evaluation of Dr. [name] that is not preceding, nor the record of any organized committee having the responsibility of evaluation or improvement of the quality of the care rendered at [name] Hospital.

REQUEST NO. 7:

Any organizational chart detailing the organization of the hospital administration, chain of command, duties, rules, and responsibilities of each of the named defendants in this action.

REQUEST NO. 8:

Each writing of any committee having responsibility for evaluation or improvement of quality of care rendered at [name] Hospital pertaining to the care provided to [name of client].

The general cause of action of negligent selection, retention and supervision has been broadened by case law in many states to include various principal-agency relationships, not only hospitals. For example, title companies, brokerage houses, accounting firms, department stores, large chain stores of any variety (grocery, drug, auto parts), cruise ships, recreation centers, health clubs, and many other situations where a principal-agency relationship exists.

§ 4.11 Topic Checklist

If you have thought through your discovery strategy, you should know what information can best be obtained through interrogatories. Also consider what information you want now so that you can use subsequent discovery methods to develop information more fully, realizing that the responding party has a duty to investigate facts before answering and cannot merely state that the information is not available. Interrogatories give the propounding party an opportunity to learn about the specifics of the opposition's case in an early stage of the litigation. The initial information you will wish to obtain varies from case to case, but it can be grouped into the following categories of topics which should be included in each and every initial set of interrogatories:

_____ **1. Identity of parties, agents, and employees**—In commercial litigation, this will include the proper formal names and corporate titles of parties, parent corporations, subsidiaries, individuals who are licensed to do business, (DBA), and so forth. You need to know this basic information as well as the interrelationships between parties to frame further meaningful discovery. Identity in commercial litigation means business identity, which will include corporation information, business licenses, basic information on the type of business, principal place of business, identification of logo, trademark, and so forth.

_____ **2. Identity of Witnesses**—Almost every lawsuit will have witnesses to the events and transactions on which the claims are based. Interrogatories are the best method for obtaining the witnesses' identities, locations, and relationship to the parties. Interrogatories can also be used to obtain specifics about conversations and meetings that a party has with another person, or conversations between others that the party overheard. Interrogatories can ask for the exact wording or request the substance of what was said by each person present at a particular meeting.

_____ **3. Identity of Documents and Tangible Objects**—Almost every lawsuit will have some documents, records, and other tangible things or items of physical evidence upon which the claim is based. Interrogatories are the best method for identifying and locating these, and for determining who has custody and control of them. Information gained in interrogatories can be used to prepare a concise document request requesting specific documents by name and author. A good standard interrogatory that can be used to flush out documents and physical evidence is:

> Please identify by name, date, and author each and every document which you referred to or reviewed in order to obtain the information provided in your responses to plaintiff Jane S.'s First Set of Interrogatories, questions numbered 1 through 35, served on you on January 9, 19__. Please include in your identification the name, address and phone number of those persons who have custody or control of the documents identified.

_____ **4. Identity of Experts, Facts, and Opinions**—Federal Rule of Civil Procedure 26(b)(4) designates interrogatories as the required method for discovering the identity of experts expected to be witnesses at trial along with the subject matter of their testimony, their opinions, and a summary of the grounds for their opinions. Civil procedure in each state varies to some extent; however, most states permit the use of interrogatories for discovery of experts and their opinions. If interrogatories are served in an early stage of the litigation, the answering party may not have selected the experts who will ultimately be witnesses at trial. However, questions concerning experts should still be asked, especially in federal litigation because Federal Rule of Civil Procedure 26(e) requires reasonably prompt supplementation of responses. A party would therefore be required to supplement an answer regarding expert witnesses as soon as they had been selected and designated to testify at trial. Undesignated experts are considered consultants. There is no duty to disclose any information regarding consultants who may have been asked to review records, perform tests, or otherwise offer opinions to an attorney who is preparing a case for trial. It is only when that consultant is designated as an expert that the consultant's early tests, opinions and reports become discoverable.

_____ **5. Details and Sequences of Events and Transactions**—Interrogatories are a useful method for obtaining concrete facts underlying vague or generalized claims. They are particularly useful in commercial litigation when lawsuits are frequently based on a series of events and transactions spread out over a period of time, but not detailed in the pleadings. In breach of contract, wrongful termination, business fraud, and misrepresentation, there is frequently a series of events that create a continuing claim. Specific interrogatories can be asked to establish a time line which can include key meetings, conversations, check transfers, delivery of various goods, performance of various services, and so forth, all of which may interrelate and form the background of the present claim.

_____ **6. Damage Information and the Ability to Pay**—Damage interrogatories sent to the plaintiff are essential for drawing out the specific legal theories of recovery that the plaintiff is asserting, the exact dollar amount claimed for each element of damages, and the basis for each damage claim. It is equally important for a plaintiff to determine the defendant's ability to pay a judgment. A standard interrogatory should always be served asking about the existence of insurance policies that may cover the events or transactions on which the lawsuit is based. It is permissible to ask for details of coverage and to obtain the endorsement page of insurance policies. If a punitive damage claim is asserted in the pleadings, the defendant's financial condition becomes relevant and information can be obtained regarding their net worth, balance sheet, assets, liabilities, and so forth. The discovery of net worth and confidential financial records (for example, tax returns), which in ordinary circumstances are privileged, is permissible in a punitive damage claim when the plaintiff is able to show the basis for their claim and a prima facie showing of evidence that the plaintiff will prevail at trial.

_____ **7. Identity of Persons Who Prepared the Answers and Sources Used**—This is particularly useful when interrogatories are served upon a corporation or business entity. The identity of the person or persons who participated in preparing the answers opens up an entirely new avenue of discovery because you may not have known that that person, or their department, existed. The sources used in preparation of the answers to interrogatories should correspond with the identity of the documents and tangible items asked for in the interrogatories; however, you may learn of the existence of other documents which were used as reference or background data by the responding party. By asking this question: "to identify each and every document used by the person(s) who assisted in preparing the interrogatory responses," later document requests can be propounded requesting specific documents identified in the response.

_____ **8. Positions on Issues and Opinions of Fact**—Interrogatories that ask for opinions, contentions relating to the facts, or application of the law to the facts are usually considered proper and objection proof. If the pleading is vague, this interrogatory can prove to be useful. For example, it is proper in a negligence action to ask what specific conduct the plaintiff claims constituted the negligence, just as in a contract action it is proper to ask what conduct the plaintiff claims constituted a breach. The plaintiff must then respond with specific allegations such as unlawful speed, failure to yield the right of way, driving on the wrong side of the roadway, failure to signal a left-hand turn, or failure to keep a proper lookout, all of which would support a negligence claim. In a breach of contract claim, the plaintiff must respond with specifics such as: failure to deliver goods ordered, goods received in a defective condition, failure to perform certain services agreed upon in the contract, lack of specific performance, late performance, substitution of goods or services without prior approval, and so forth.

Of course, the plaintiff may pose the same type of interrogatory to the defendant concerning affirmative defenses and counterclaims. Interrogatories framed this way are useful to assist both parties in focusing on specific issues by obtaining more detail and specific information about any claim or defense, whether it be contract, tort, or statutory.

§ 4.12   Use of Form Interrogatories

The biggest advantage in using judicial council form interrogatories is that they are usually considered "objection proof" as to form and content as long as the case is of the type covered by that specific form. General form interrogatories are available as judicial council forms in most states. Because general form interrogatories have been officially approved and adopted by the courts, objections are usually not upheld. Only in rare instances will a discovery commissioner, or a judge, uphold an objection to a standard form interrogatory unless it can clearly be demonstrated that the case simply does not fit the question. For example, standard form interrogatories dealing with personal injury cases which are sent in business litigation give rise to many objections which have been upheld by discovery commissioners simply because some questions are not relevant. In choosing standard form interrogatories, review each set available and select the set that fits your action. The use of standard form interrogatories is optional and does not restrict the right of a plaintiff or defendant to serve additional specially prepared interrogatories. Form interrogatories are especially helpful for complex cases where many subparts are required to cover each and every aspect of the information requested fully.

The wording of form interrogatories is helpful when you are beginning to draft specific interrogatories in areas where technical knowledge is necessary. There are many form books of interrogatories dealing specifically with swimming pools, escalators, elevators, ski lifts, farm machinery accidents, sales transactions involving real estate, equipment leases, and so forth. If you are drafting interrogatories in an area that is unfamiliar to you, it is a good practice to consult the form book of interrogatories for preliminary questions and ideas.

The important thing to remember when using form interrogatories is not to fall into the boiler plate interrogatory trap. That is, do not use excessive subparts or subquestions which require the responder to refer back and forth to make certain that they have not overlooked the impact of the previous question. This type of questioning provides the responding party with an opportunity to claim objection on the grounds of burdensome, harassing, and oppressive.

Form interrogatories are useful in achieving economy and efficiency in discovery practice, if you are aware of their limitations. Form interrogatories do not fit every case. The more unique your case, the less help you will get from form interrogatories. Moreover, even in routine cases, you cannot use form interrogatories indiscriminately. The questions need to be edited to fit your case. Failure to edit gives the responding party ample room for objection. It is embarrassing to send an individual a set of form interrogatories which asks such questions as:

When were you incorporated?

Name all the officers of your corporation or

List each state in which you are licensed to do business.

The danger in using preprinted form interrogatories is mechanically propounding them without an effort to tailor them to the facts of the individual lawsuit. Ideally, form questions should be used selectively, must be germane to the issues of the case, and must be of a reasonable number, given the nature of the case. If a multitude of preprinted form interrogatories which have no relevance to the subject matter of the action are served upon a party, they constitute an abuse of the discovery procedure and are objectionable. An objection can be based upon the grounds of oppression and harassment. Courts have held that indiscriminate use of form interrogatories is " . . . an imposition upon the witness being interrogated and an unprofessional practice."

Form interrogatories can be useful, if judiciously used. Reviewing form interrogatories before drafting specific interrogatories is helpful in almost all cases for language, content, and style of questioning. It is economical, and in the best interests of your client, to use form interrogatories in cases where damages are minimal, and there is a form set designed for your particular case (such as an unlawful detainer action, money had and received, breach of promissory note, and many municipal court actions). Many of the questions placed in form books are there because they are pertinent to most cases of the type involved, and because the questions are ones that the courts have repeatedly approved for use in more common types of litigation such as personal injury, wrongful death, breach of contract, and unlawful detainer.

§ 4.13   Standard Introductory Paragraphs

A common practice, in specially prepared interrogatories, is to have the actual interrogatories proceeded by a section with definitions and instructions. Terms used repeatedly in the interrogatories can be defined making the interrogatories easier to follow and also effectively deterring evasive answers. Terms commonly defined in interrogatories include record, document, communication, witness, participant, transaction, occurrence, collision, state, describe, identify, writings, and so forth. Definitions should also be used for terms particular to a case which will be used repeatedly. For example, the "Valley West Condominium Complex Project" could be defined as "Project." Writings such as contracts, addenda, invoices, and other key documents can also be shortened. If more than one contract is referred to in a set of interrogatories, care should be taken to keep the dates of the contracts distinct. For example, "contract between Jane S. and Melvin S. of January 19, 19__" can be shortened to "Contract 1." If in the same set you wish to refer to the "contract entered into between Jane S. and Melvin S. on August 10, 19__"; that contract would become "Contract 2."

Definitions for basic terms such as communication, witness, document, occurrence, and so forth can be found in pleading and practice form books. Definitions for words which are not found in the form books can be found by consulting a good legal dictionary such as *Black's Law Dictionary*, or simply *Webster's Dictionary*.

The instructions which follow the definitions may refer to statutory authority which sets forth the requirements for answers. For example:

Plaintiff requests that the defendant answer the following interrogatories in writing and under oath pursuant to Rule 33 of the Federal Rules of Civil Procedure and that the answers be served on plaintiff within 30 days after service of these interrogatories. (More detailed instructions can be included if desired.)

Common variations include the following:

Plaintiff requests that in answering each interrogatory state:

(a) Whether the answer is within the personal knowledge of the person answering the interrogatory and if not, the identity of each person known to have personal knowledge of the facts contained in the answer.

(b) Identify each document that was used in any way to form the basis of your interrogatory answer.

In cases where a series of events or transactions is involved, it is useful to state the time frame the interrogatories are intended to cover. For example:

Unless expressly stated otherwise, each interrogatory relates to the time period beginning January 1, 19__ through and including the date on which answers to these interrogatories are verified under oath.

§ 4.14   Sample Introductory Paragraphs (California)

Civil procedure, as it relates to discovery, has recently changed in California. Introductory paragraphs and definitions are no longer allowed in interrogatories. If a definition is needed in interrogatories because the term is particular to the case, the definition must be set forth in the first interrogatory within the context of the question. For example:

1. Please identify by name, address, and job title each and every employee of [name] Construction Company who worked on the [name] Condominium Apartment Complex, hereinafter known as "Apartments," during the months of January–December, 19__.

The only instructions which may be given in a set of interrogatories must be taken directly from California Code of Civil Procedure § 2030, and may be set forth as illustrated in **Form 4–3**:

FORM 4–3
SAMPLE INTERROGATORY INSTRUCTIONS (CALIFORNIA)

Pursuant to California Code of Civil Procedure § 2030, plaintiff [name] hereby requests that defendant [name] answer separately and truthfully, in writing, under oath, within 30 days of service hereof, each of the interrogatories set forth below in accordance with the instructions contained in California Code of Civil Procedure § 2030(f)(1) through § 2030(f)(3) which require that each answer shall be as complete and straightforward as the information reasonably available to the responding party permits. If an interrogatory cannot be answered completely, it shall be answered to the extent possible. If the responding party does not have personal knowledge sufficient to respond fully to an interrogatory, that party shall so state, but shall make a reasonable and good faith effort to obtain the information by inquiry to other natural persons or organizations, except when the information is equally available to the propounding party.

Each interrogatory shall be answered fully unless it is, in good faith, objected to, in which event the reason for the objection shall be stated in detail. If only part of the interrogatory is objectionable, the remainder of the interrogatory shall be answered. If an objection is made to an interrogatory, or part of the interrogatory, the specific grounds for the objection shall be set forth clearly in the response. If an objection is based on a claim of privilege, the particular privilege invoked shall be clearly stated. If an objection is based on a claim that the information sought is protected under the work product doctrine under California Civil Code § 2018, that claim shall be expressly asserted.

§ 4.15   Sample Interrogatory Format

Form 4–4 is a sample of the format that can be used for interrogatories in the district courts.

FORM 4–4
SAMPLE INTERROGATORY FORMAT

UNITED STATES DISTRICT COURT
[judicial district] DISTRICT OF [state]

[name]   No. [case number]

    Plaintiff,   PLAINTIFF'S INTERROGATORIES
                                                TO DEFENDANT

-vs-

[name],

    Defendant.

PROPOUNDING PARTY: Plaintiff, [name]
RESPONDING PARTY: Defendant, [name]
SET NUMBER: [set number]

Plaintiff requests that the defendant answer the following interrogatories in writing under oath pursuant to Rule 33 of the Federal Rules of Civil Procedure and that the answers be served on plaintiff within thirty (30) days after service of these interrogatories.

In answering these interrogatories, furnish all information, however obtained, that is available to you and information known by or in the possession of yourself, your agents, and your attorneys or appearing in your records.

If you cannot answer the following interrogatories in full after exercising due diligence to secure the full information to do so, so state and answer to the extent possible, specifying your inability to answer the remainder, stating whatever information or knowledge you have concerning the unanswered portion and detailing what you did in attempting to secure the unknown information.

In addition to these instructions, various other instructions may be given. Additionally, definitions may be given in federal court and some state courts. Check local rules governing inclusion of instructions and definitions with a preface to interrogatories.

After the preface, interrogatories should begin as Interrogatory No. 1, Interrogatory No. 2, Interrogatory No. 3, and so forth, with consecutive numbering. At the end of the interrogatories, there should be a signature and date line. The interrogatories must be signed by the attorney of record for the party (plaintiff or defendant) propounding the interrogatories. Interrogatories can be served by hand or by mail and must be accompanied by the applicable proof of service.

§ 4.16   Limitations and Restrictions

Interrogatories may be used for many purposes. They are the most frequently used discovery device by attorneys, from sole practitioners to large firms. Irrespective of the distinct disadvantages to the use of interrogatories, detailed in § 4.3, the advantage of their expediency and cost-effectiveness makes them the discovery device used most frequently to acquire the most information for the least expense. This great advantage of interrogatories has lead to many discovery abuses. Interrogatories in some states may be sent out at any time during the pendency of an action in consecutive sets without prior court approval, and with little to no restrictions on the scope (subparts) and number. The popularity of interrogatories and the lack of restriction on their use has lead many a party to attempt to bury their adversary in mountains of paper. A set of interrogatories with 100 to 120 separate questions with subparts ranging from (a) to (z) was commonplace in litigation until discovery reform acts were enacted by various state legislatures. For example, in 1987 in California, interrogatories were restricted to 35 specially prepared interrogatories without subparts which may be served in addition to a set of form interrogatories. No further special interrogatories may be served unless a declaration stating the need for additional discovery signed by the attorney of record is attached to those interrogatories. (See § **4.19.**)

In federal jurisdictions, the overuse of interrogatories by zealous adversaries has also caused federal courts to adopt local rules limiting the number of interrogatories which may be propounded without leave of court. For example, in the Central District of California, Central District Court Rule 6.2.1 requires a court order based on good cause for service of more than 30 interrogatories—including all subparts—on any other party. A motion for such an order must also have notice of at least seven days provided.

In Southern District Courts, a court order based on good cause is required for service of more than 25 interrogatories or requests for admissions. Subparts of any interrogatory must "relate directly to the subject matter" of the interrogatory (Southern District Court Rule 230-1).

In the Northern District the number and scope of interrogatories is limited to 35. Interrogatories are mandated to be "brief, simple, neutral, particularized and capable of being understood by jurors when read in conjunction with the answer" (Northern District Local Rule 230-1(b)). Northern District's rule on the number and scope of interrogatories further restricts the subject matter of interrogatories and refers to the limitations stated in FRCP 26(b)(1) which mandates that interrogatories should be "limited to requesting objective facts, such as identification of persons or documents, dates, places, transactions and amounts. Argumentative interrogatories, attempts to cross-examine, multiple repetitive interrogatories (such as state all facts on which an allegation or denial is based) are deemed objectionable. Standard interrogatories generated by word processors should also be avoided.

Subparts are permissible on interrogatories served in Northern, Central, and Southern District Courts, but even though the courts do not restrict the form of interrogatories, they strongly advise against subparts "which are designed to gain new information, thereby extending the number of interrogatories counting against the numerical limit by disguising the question as a subpart." Central District Courts expressly state that subparts will count against the 30 interrogatory limit. Southern District Court speaks sternly to subparts by ordering them to "relate directly to the subject matter." The relation to subject matter is a matter of court discretion. Arguably, one receiving a set of interrogatories in Southern District Court jurisdiction with multiple subparts requiring extended answers and documentation, could move for a protective order based on the language of local court rule in Southern District.

Northern District Court rules for the scope, number, and service of interrogatories closely mirror California discovery rules as modified by the Discovery Act of 1987. The major difference in civil procedure for interrogatories in California between state and federal jurisdictions is not the number (35 is the maximum in each court), but the use of subparts which are still allowed in Federal District Court but are *not* allowed in state court actions.

§ 4.17 Prefaces, Instructions, and Definitions

Another restriction imposed by both state and federal district courts to insure against the misuse of interrogatories relates to the prefaces, instructions and definitions which accompany a set of interrogatories. To insure that the limitations on the number of interrogatories established by state statutes, local rules, and federal district court rules are not cleverly circumvented by counsel using lengthy prefaces or instructions that might amount in themselves to subparts, courts have consistently held that each interrogatory "must be full and complete in and of itself." For example, in California, prefaces and instructions are not allowed in state court actions unless they have been approved by the Judicial Council pursuant to California Code of Civil Procedure § 2033.5. The Northern District Federal Court cautions parties to " . . . avoid lengthy preambles and complex and all-inclusive definitions."[2] The Central District and Southern District of California do not have local rules directly addressing the use of introductions, instructions, and definitions, but they caution counsel to adhere to the limitations imposed by Federal Rule of Civil Procedure 26(b), which require that interrogatories as a whole must not be " . . . unreasonably cumulative or duplicative, obtainable from some other source that is more convenient, unduly burdensome or expensive taking into account the needs of the case, the amounts in controversy, the limitations on the parties' resources, and the importance of the issues at stake in the litigation."

In ruling on protective orders in accordance with Rule 26(c) of the Federal Rules of Civil Procedure, district courts have considered the preamble, instructions, and definitions accompanying interrogatories to be "an integral part of the document." Protective orders granted by district courts to prevent abusive discovery frequently address the issue of lengthy definitions and instructions which are "designed in a manner to render the interrogatories ambiguous and unintelligible."

A standard introductory paragraph specific to California is discussed in § 4.14. As more and more states adopt not only a limit of 30 to 35 interrogatories but also restrictions on the use of lengthy prefaces and preambles, such a sample introductory paragraph may be useful (if adopted for use in compliance with local court rules) for your specific jurisdiction.

Definitions may be used in a set of interrogatories if defined words are capitalized whenever they appear in the interrogatories. The preferable manner for defining terms is to capitalize them the first time they are used in an interrogatory. Definitions are helpful in avoiding repetition in drafting interrogatories and in avoiding an objection to a specific vague, ambiguous, uncertain, and unintelligible interrogatory. In some instances, definitions are a necessity; for example, in construction cases involving a general contractor, numerous subcontractors, and numerous suppliers, all of whom have been named parties to a contract dispute or a construction defect action it is important to define the terms to avoid confusion. In such cases the use of definitions to show differentiation between phases of construction, specific work orders, specific contracts, specific invoices, and other crucial documents is mandatory to insure the clarity of interrogatories propounded to any of the parties in the action.

Using definitions to clarify interrogatories by defining common usage terminology such as IDENTIFY is extremely helpful in tailoring an interrogatory to be uncluttered, and thus avoiding a complex, compound or disjunctive objection. The following example illustrates this point:

---

[2] Local Rule 230-1(b)–(c).

IDENTIFY by name, address, phone number, and job title, each individual employed by you who was present on the **JOB SITE** hereinafter known as that construction for the subdivision commonly known as [name] Hills located in the City of [city name], State of [state name], on the date of the accident which is the basis of this litigation, [date].

This interrogatory properly defines **JOB SITE,** so that in subsequent interrogatories you merely need to use the words **JOB SITE** whenever necessary. An argument may still be made that the interrogatory is compound, conjunctive, and disjunctive simply because it is too wordy and could be construed as being confusing. In order to avoid this mistake, define the word IDENTIFY. For example:

IDENTIFY, by providing the name, address, phone number, job title, and work responsibilities, each individual employed by defendant from the date defendant entered into a contract with [name] Corporation to the date of the accident which is the subject of this litigation.

Subsequent interrogatories may simply use the words **IDENTIFY** and **JOB SITE** to address specific areas of inquiry. Tailoring interrogatories with definitions of terms, both case-specific and common usage, helps make interrogatories separate and complete of themselves as is required by local statute. Tailoring interrogatories by eliminating extra words gives the responding party less wiggle room and less room to raise an objection claiming that the interrogatory is compound, conjunctive and disjunctive.

§ 4.18   Sample Instructions and Definitions

Certain state courts, including California, and most federal district courts have ruled that it is no longer appropriate to include instructions and definitions when propounding interrogatories. In the event that your particular state or jurisdiction allows instructions and definitions, **Form 4–5** may prove to be useful. Be certain to include your specific Code of Civil Procedure, or local rule, authorizing the inclusion of instructions and definitions at (b) in the following form.

FORM 4–5
SAMPLE INSTRUCTIONS AND DEFINITIONS
FOR INTERROGATORIES

[attorney for the plaintiff]
[address]
[telephone number]

Attorneys for Plaintiff
[name]

IN THE SUPERIOR COURT OF THE STATE OF [state name]
IN THE CITY AND COUNTY OF [city/county name]

[name]	Case No. [case number]
Plaintiff,	
	SPECIAL INTERROGATORIES
vs.	
[name] SHOPPING MALL, A LIMITED PARTNERSHIP, [defendant A] and [defendant B], as limited partners of [name] SHOPPING MALL, [defendant C], individually and (dba) [company D], and (dba) [company E], and DOES 1 through 30, inclusive,	
Defendants.	

PROPOUNDING PARTY: Defendant [name] SHOPPING MALL

RESPONDING PARTY: Plaintiff [name]

SET NUMBER: [set number]

INSTRUCTIONS

(a) In Superior Court actions, an answer or other appropriate response must be given to each interrogatory requested by the asking party.

(b) As a general rule, within 30 days after you are served with these interrogatories, you must serve your responses on the asking party and serve copies of your responses on all other parties to the action who have appeared. See Code of Civil Procedure Section [code section] for details.

(c) Each answer must be as complete and straightforward as the information reasonably available to you permits. If an interrogatory cannot be answered completely, answer it to the extent possible.

(d) If you do not have enough personal knowledge to answer an interrogatory fully, say so, but make a reasonable and good faith effort to get the information by asking other persons or organizations, unless the information is equally available to the asking party.

(e) Whenever an interrogatory may be answered by referring to a document, the document may be attached as an exhibit to the response and referred to in the response. If the document has more than one page, refer to the page and section where the answer to the interrogatory can be found.

(f) Whenever an address and telephone number for the same person are requested in more than one interrogatory, you are required to furnish them in answering only the first interrogatory asking for that information.

<u>DEFINITIONS</u>

Words in **BOLDFACE CAPITALS** in these interrogatories are defined as follows:

(a)   **YOU**—means your agents, employees, attorneys, and anyone else acting on your behalf.

(b)   **WRITING**—means handwriting, typewriting, printing, photostating, photographing, and every other means of recording upon any tangible thing, any form of communication or representation including letters, words, pictures, sounds, symbols, signs or signals, or combinations thereof.

(c)   **IDENTIFY EACH WRITING**—means you are required to state:

     1. The name, date and subject matter of each such writing;

     2. The person or persons who composed, dictated, or directed the making of such writing;

     3. The person or persons currently in custody of the original writing and each copy thereof;

     4. Whether without a court order to do so, you will produce such writing. If you will produce, please attach a copy of each such writing to your answers to these interrogatories.

(d)   **IDENTIFY EACH PERSON**—means you are required to state:

     1. The full name of each person;

     2. The last known residential address and telephone number of such person;

     3. The last known business address and telephone number of each such person;

     4. The job title and job description of such person.

(e)   **PERSON**—includes the natural person, firm, association, organization, partnership, business trust, corporation, public entity, and governmental agency.

(f)   **INCIDENT**—includes the circumstances and events surrounding the alleged accident, injury, or other occurrence or breach of contract giving rise to this action or proceeding.

§ 4.19   Declarations for Additional Discovery

Any party who is propounding, or has propounded, more than the allowable number of specially prepared interrogatories must file a declaration for additional discovery. In the Central and Southern Districts of federal court in California, a court order based on good cause is required for interrogatories exceeding the court's imposed limit. The Northern District Court in California is silent upon the requirement of an order. Local rules for the Northern District indicate that "good cause must be demonstrated." Whether you are required by your court to prepare a motion for permission to exceed the limit set for the number of interrogatories, or whether you are simply preparing a declaration to attach to additional interrogatories, the most important part of your documents will be an attorney declaration which clearly sets forth good cause for exceeding the limit.

A declaration for additional discovery demonstrates good cause by setting forth specific facts and arguments which address the following issues:

1. The complexity and/or quantity of existing and potential issues of controversy and/or fact in the particular case;

2. The financial burden on the parties entailed in conducting discovery by oral deposition (as opposed to using interrogatories); and

3. The economic value of using interrogatories to provide a means for inquiry and investigation to obtain the information sought because a contrast must be demonstrated between discovering this information via interrogatories as opposed to depositions, business record subpoenas, production of documents, and so forth.

Once a declaration demonstrating the necessity for additional discovery has been completed, it should be attached to the proper moving documents and served on all parties, not only the party from whom you are seeking the additional discovery.

A fact often overlooked by attorneys seeking to exceed the numerical limit of interrogatories is the fact that such a declaration is reciprocal and opens the door for the other side to propound an equal number of interrogatories to your client using the information in your declaration to establish the need for additional discovery. Unless you are prepared to respond to additional interrogatories on behalf of your client, and unless the facts and issues of the case are truly complex, it is wiser to draft interrogatories carefully in a manner which will allow you to obtain the desired information while remaining within the numerical limit set forth by the court.

Motions seeking additional discovery (leave of court to exceed the numerical limit) or an additional discovery declaration may be opposed by filing an opposition to such a motion or declaration, whichever is appropriate in your local jurisdiction. In opposing such a declaration, the moving party needs to demonstrate that the issues in the case are not complex and that information may be obtained within the limit of 35 interrogatories. Moreover, an argument may be made that additional interrogatories are repetitive, burdensome, and oppressive, as well as nonrelevant, and so forth. In addition to opposing the motion or declaration for additional discovery, the opposing party may make a motion for a protective order (see § **4.63**).

Form 4–6 is a sample Declaration for Additional Discovery for the State of California.

FORM 4–6
SAMPLE DECLARATION FOR ADDITIONAL DISCOVERY
(CALIFORNIA)

CALIFORNIA SUPERIOR COURT
COUNTY OF [county name]

[plaintiff A] and [plaintiff B] by and through their Guardian Ad Litem, [plaintiff C]; [plaintiff C], individually, [plaintiff D], [plaintiff E]　　　Plaintiffs,	Case No. [case number] DECLARATION FOR ADDITIONAL DISCOVERY

-vs-

[defendant F],
[defendant G],
[defendant H], [defendant I],
and DOES ONE through THIRTY, inclusive
　　　Defendants.
_____/

I, [attorney for the plaintiff], declare:

1. I am one of the attorneys of record for [C], [D], [E], [A] and [B], the plaintiffs in the above-referenced action. All of the matters set forth below are personally known to me, and if called as a witness, I could testify competently thereto.

2. I am propounding to [defendant I], one of the defendants in the above-referenced action, the attached set of Interrogatories.

3. This set of Interrogatories will cause the total number of Interrogatories propounded to the party to whom they are directed to exceed the number of

Interrogatories permitted by paragraph (2) of subdivision (c) of § 2030 of the Code of Civil Procedure.

4. I have not previously propounded any Interrogatories.

5. This set of Interrogatories contains a total of 43 (forty-three) Interrogatories.

6. I am familiar with the issues and the previous discovery conducted by all of the parties in the case.

7. I have personally examined each of the Interrogatories.

8. This number of Interrogatories is warranted under paragraph (2) of subdivision (c) of § 2030 of the Code of Civil Procedure because of the complexity and quantity of the existing and potential issues in the particular case. Plaintiff must determine the factual basis for the allegations and contentions of defendant in this action. The information sought by each question is necessary for the proper preparation of this case and reasonably requires this number of questions.

9. None of the Interrogatories is being propounded for any improper purpose, such as to harass the party, or the attorney for the party, to whom it is directed, or cause unnecessary delay or needless increase in the litigation.

I declare under penalty of perjury under the laws of California that the foregoing is true and correct, and that this declaration was executed on [date].

[attorney for the plaintiff]

§ 4.20   Compound and Complex Interrogatories

Statute and case law dictates an interrogatory must be ". . . separately set forth and full and complete in and of itself." Attorneys who began their practice under the old discovery rules find this part of the statute the most troublesome. Indeed, it is difficult to draft an interrogatory carefully discussing a factual issue without running the risk of drafting a compound, complex, conjunctive, and disjunctive interrogatory. It is safest, when drafting specially prepared interrogatories, to stay away from questions that branch into the famous who, what, when, why, how syndrome. Interrogatories of such a nature are almost always objectionable due to their compound complex nature. Instead, try drafting interrogatories which require narrative or descriptive answers using words like state, identify, describe, and so on. (Using the word "identify" is illustrated in § 4.17.) Using the word "describe" accompanied by a definition appearing the first time the word is used in an interrogatory can eliminate a subpart objection and may furnish you with who, what, when, why, and how information within the context of the response. For example:

DESCRIBE the documents, by stating their title, date, author, and general subject matter, that were discussed at the homeowners meeting held on November 5, 19__.

By defining the word "DESCRIBE" in this interrogatory, you have built document identification into the question. Each subsequent interrogatory relating to a document can use the general description of the word "DESCRIBE."

The purpose behind the "no compound, conjunctive or disjunctive rule" is to prevent questions worded so as to require more information than could be obtained by separate interrogatories falling within the numerical limit. How strictly this rule is enforced depends upon your state and local rules and case law. Arguably, any question containing an "and" or "or" is compound and conjunctive. In reality, the rule should only apply where more than a single subject is covered by the question. Questions regarding the same subject should be allowed even if they include an "and" or "or." For example, "State your first name, middle name, last name, and your current address and telephone number" can hardly be considered a compound conjunctive question because only one subject is involved—the identity of the responding party. This question should clearly not be objectionable because of the use of an "and."

The rule against subparts disguised in compound, conjunctive or disjunctive interrogatories usually applies only when two discrete matters are covered by the same question; that is, when there are really two separate questions linked together by a conjunction. A safe test for determining whether an interrogatory is truly compound, conjunctive, or disjunctive is to apply basics of grammatical sentence construction to determine whether there are two sentences contained in one single interrogatory. Apply the single subject test to all interrogatories which are suspect. Clearly, when a second subject is addressed in the same interrogatory, even though it may be closely related to the main subject, it may be compound and conjunctive.

A good, general all-purpose rule to avoid drafting compound, conjunctive and complex interrogatories is to keep them brief. Any interrogatory that is more than five lines on pleading paper (with certain exemptions for contention interrogatories quoting directly from pleadings) should be suspect for complexity. The following nine-line interrogatory purports to relate to a single subject, but in reality is compound, complex, and conjunctive. For example:

Have you made a claim against any insurance carrier or filed a lawsuit regarding the incident of August 8, 19___? If so, please state the name, address, and telephone number of the insurance representative you are dealing with, or have dealt with, and the name, address and telephone number of the carrier. In the event that you failed to settle with the insurance carrier and filed suit, please state the title of the action, the court number, county in which the action was filed, status of action, and the names, addresses and telephone numbers of each defendant and each attorney.

An argument could be made that this interrogatory seeks information about claims made for a single accident, and is therefore relating to a single subject. In reality, it contradicts several grammatical principles for sentence construction and seeks to discover information on several subjects. Several complete sentences are contained within this one interrogatory which could easily be redrafted into at least five separate interrogatories as illustrated below:

1.   Have you made a claim against any insurance carrier or filed a lawsuit regarding the incident of August 8, 19__?

2.   If so, please state the name, address, and telephone number of the insurance representative you are dealing with, or have dealt with,

3.   The name, address and telephone number of the carrier.

4.   In the event that you failed to settle with the insurance carrier and filed suit, please state the title of the action, the court number, county in which the action was filed, status of action, and

5.   The names, addresses and telephone numbers of each defendant and each attorney.

§ 4.21   Drafting Mistakes to Avoid

When drafting interrogatories, use tight, precise language and eliminate any terms that can lend ambiguity to the questions. Any loophole in an interrogatory leaves room for the responding party to lodge an objection to that question in the form of "vague, ambiguous, unintelligible, impossible to respond to in the format in which it is written." The following examples are poorly drafted interrogatories:

Example 1.   Were there any road conditions that may have contributed to this accident?

   The problem with this interrogatory is vagueness in the terminology "road conditions." It calls upon the responding party to speculate as to the intent of the question and define "road conditions" for themselves. A better way to phrase this question would be:

Describe the road conditions at the time of the accident including in your answer the lighting, traffic signals, shrubbery, other vehicles, and so forth.

Example 2.   Identify each and every document which refers or relates to the relationship regarding all circumstances surrounding the accident with the defendant.

   The intent of this question is to discover each and every writing which could in any way be evidence and/or relate to any of the causes of action alleged in the plaintiff's complaint. This question is simply poorly written and ambiguous. This information can be retrieved by specifically asking for each writing that supports the factual basis of each cause of action, or each affirmative defense in the action. The wording "refers or relates to the relationship regarding all circumstances" is so vague, ambiguous, confusing, overbroad, and burdensome that the question simply cannot be answered in the format in which it is written.

Example 3.   Describe each disruptive occurrence between you and any other person which may have occurred at the time of the accident.

   This is a question that is also vague and ambiguous. Specifically, the terminology "disruptive occurrence" requires definition. It places an unfair burden upon the responding party to speculate as to the precise meaning of "disruptive occurrence." The intent of the question is unclear to the responding party. It assumes facts not in evidence—that there were disruptive occurrences. Responding to this interrogatory, as it is phrased, would be falling into propounding party's trap. (See example #6 for further discussion.)

Example 4.   List the name, address and phone number of each and every person who has been a passenger in your 1983 Datsun in the last year.

This is one of those questions that is so overbroad, vague, and ambiguous that it simply cannot be rewritten to achieve any semblance of clarity. The intent of this question is to gather information about passengers in the Datsun in hopes that they will be able to provide information on the driving ability of the responding party. It is a typical fishing expedition question which hopes to gain information which may lead to the discovery of witnesses. There are several possible objections to this question, such as invasion of privacy and irrelevance to the subject matter of the action. Perhaps the owner of this Datsun has had passengers who should not have been either passengers or seen with the owner. Further, it is unlikely that any one of us could sit down and compile a name, address, and phone number list of each and every person who has been a passenger in our vehicle in the past year.

Example 5.   State the legal basis for your contention that plaintiff was negligent in plaintiff's operation of a motor vehicle, and that that negligence was the sole cause of the accident referred to in the complaint on file in this action.

This question is a good question in its intent, that is, to discover the basis for the contention of negligence in the complaint. The problem is with its phraseology. It calls for a legal conclusion, or at the very least an expert opinion which cannot be offered by a lay witness. A lay witness, who has alleged negligence in their complaint, can only be questioned on the factual basis for their contention. A better way to phrase this question, and one which will get the information desired without objection is:

State the factual basis for your allegation in the first cause of action in the complaint on file in this action that plaintiff was negligent in plaintiff's operation of a motor vehicle at the time of the accident; or, state each and every fact upon which you base the allegation in the first cause of action of your complaint on file in this action which states as follows: ". . . ". The quotes, of course, are to be filled in with the exact language of the complaint.

Example 6.   Another common mistake in drafting interrogatories is the "when did you stop beating your wife?" syndrome, that is, interrogatories which assume facts not in evidence and proceed to attempt to build upon those invisible facts. An example of a liability question which falls into this category is:

Do you contend that any entity other than this answering defendant was in any way responsible for the occurrence at issue in this case?

By answering this interrogatory a defendant would concede that the defendant believes that they were in some way legally responsible for the occurrence. The interrogatory will undoubtedly be objected to by stating that the interrogatory calls for a legal conclusion and assumes facts not in evidence, as well as calls for an admission of liability on the part of the defendant. You can obtain the same information by rephrasing this interrogatory as follows:

Do you contend that any entity or person is responsible in any way for the occurrence at issue?

Because this interrogatory would elicit a yes or no answer, it would need to be followed up with specific interrogatories designed to obtain the necessary information such as:

If your answer to the previous interrogatory was in the affirmative, please state the name, address, and phone number of each entity or person whom you identified as being responsible in any way for this occurrence.

Example 7. Interrogatories which ask why a party did or did not do something, or could or could not have established something, are proper and appropriate interrogatories; however, they do not yield much useful information because they are seeking the opinion, or value judgment, of the responding party. For example:

What prompted you to drive the front of your car into the left rear of the 1984 Mercury on the evening of February 4, 19__?

The response to this question should be "nothing," accompanied by a qualifying statement that they did not drive the front of their vehicle into the left rear of defendant's vehicle. Even if there is a damaging document such as a police report which clearly indicates that this is the manner in which the collision happened, the responding party would be wise not to add to the damage and simply state "nothing."

§ 4.22 Avoiding Inclusive Language

Inclusive language such as "any and all" and "each and every" is standard legalese for many attorneys. The all-inclusiveness of these terms seems to assure the drafter of interrogatories that nothing can be withheld in a response. In reality, overuse of these terms gives responding party wiggle room upon which to base an objection of ". . . overbroad, ambiguous, lacking specifics, and so forth." In order to avoid this trap, try substituting the pronouns "that" or "those" for "each and every".

For example, the following interrogatory leaves room for defendant to object on the grounds that it is overbroad as written:

State the name, address, and job title of each [name] Corporation employee or agent who has knowledge of the automatic shift mechanism as it was included in certain models of the 1992 [car model].

Presumably, the defendant would argue that the vehicle was worked on by hundreds of individuals from its design concept through the assembly and manufacture process until it finally left the custody and control of [name] Corporation. A rewrite of this interrogatory to circumvent the objection is as follows:

State the name, address, and job title of those two or three [name] Corporation employees or agents with the most personal knowledge of the . . . .

By using the words "that" or "those", and by limiting the interrogatory by the number of individuals with "personal knowledge", "direct participation", or "sole responsibility", the plaintiff can avoid the all-inclusive trap and demonstrate to the defendant a spirit of cooperation with the discovery process. This is particularly important when the plaintiff has brought suit against a defendant corporate entity with hundreds of employees and officers in many locations. It is important from a financial standpoint (expense of discovery motions) because it streamlines the discovery process and avoids needless depositions around the fringes of corporate knowledge.

§ 4.23   Avoid Drafting Objectionable Interrogatories

The checklist for drafting interrogatories in § 4.9 sets forth some general principles for drafting effective interrogatories. The main objective in drafting interrogatories is to draft objection proof interrogatories which will force your opponent to provide that information needed to allow you to preview their case effectively. Interrogatories are the least expensive form of discovery and the use of them can be cost-efficient and time-efficient for your client. Interrogatories may be propounded quickly after the commencement of an action, and they are not limited to a single set. Pay particular attention to your state or local rules governing the number of interrogatories per set and their form. For example, many jurisdictions do not allow the use of subparts in interrogatories. However, the number of sets of interrogatories is usually not limited by local rule. Successive sets of interrogatories may need to be accompanied by a declaration for additional discovery demonstrating the need for the information sought in the questions. It is extremely important in follow-up sets of interrogatories to draft precisely by taking dead aim at the issues in dispute. Try to eliminate lengthy, run-on sentences, and use plain English.

Remember that the scope of relevance for discovery purposes is much broader than for evidentiary purposes. The information sought in interrogatories does not necessarily need to be relevant if it is reasonably calculated to lead to the discovery of admissible evidence.

The test for a "burdensome, harassing, and objectionable" response to interrogatories is weighing the value of the information sought against the hardship imposed upon the respondent. Generally speaking, burdensome interrogatories are those in which the value or content of the information sought is disproportionate to the scope of the action and is merely intended to create an unreasonable burden. An example of this type of objectionable interrogatory includes the argumentative interrogatory (see Example 6 in § 4.21) which refers to the "when did you stop beating your wife syndrome." The argumentative interrogatory is one which characterizes the facts, issues, and events rather than discloses the facts, issues, and events. Characterization of facts, issues, or events from the plaintiff's point of view will tend to be argumentative to a responding defendant. The language of interrogatories should be neutral and unemotional.

A prime example of interrogatories which are often considered overbroad includes those interrogatories seeking information about documents. To avoid an overbroad, harassing, and burdensome objection, give the opposing party an opportunity to attach documents instead of describing them by tendering access to the records (see § 4.50).

By giving the opposing party an opportunity to attach documents, instead of describing them, you have not only saved time and money but also alleviated the necessity of filing a formal demand or subpoena for production of documents.

In drafting contention interrogatories, look for the who, what, when, where, why and how of each allegation or response. By focusing on the individual elements of a cause of action or affirmative defense, and addressing separate interrogatories to each individual element, you will avoid the most commonly raised objection that the interrogatory is "overbroad and further seeks to invade the attorney-client and work product privileges." Although the ordinary rules of privilege apply to interrogatories, specific fact-based interrogatories zeroing in on each element of an issue of dispute can hardly be considered objectionable.

§ 4.24   Sample Problem Interrogatories

The following problem interrogatories are examples illustrating common drafting problems. In the case given to paralegal students, the plaintiff's parents brought an action for damages against a preschool owner and instructor. Their child was bitten by a dog during an unsupervised noon recess. The dog, owned by an instructor and was on the grounds of the preschool with the knowledge and consent of the owner/director of the preschool. Accompanying each interrogatory is an explanation of its deficiencies and a rewrite.

Example 1

Interrogatory No. 1.   Identify any and all inquiries you made to [name of teacher] previous employees regarding the teacher's behavior with children at the preschools, including date of your inquiry, name, address, and phone number of person you contacted, and results of the inquiry.

The main problem with this interrogatory is that it is compound, complex, and contains enough material for several separate questions. A rewrite follows:

(1) Identify each inquiry you made to [teacher]'s previous employees regarding the teacher's behavior with children at their preschools by indicating the date of that inquiry.

(2) Identify each person by name, business address, and telephone number to whom you addressed an inquiry regarding [teacher]'s prior employment.

(3) State the results of each inquiry you made regarding [teacher]'s prior employment by furnishing the information you were given by the teacher's prior employer.

Example 2

Interrogatory No. 2.   State your written policy for employees in detail regarding the presence of animals at your preschool.

The problem with this interrogatory is a dangling modifier (misplaced preposi-tional phrase). A rewrite of this interrogatory requires moving the modifying prepo-sitional phrase to its grammatically correct position as follows:

State in detail your written policy for employees regarding the presence of ani-mals at your preschool.

Example 3

Interrogatory No. 3.   Please state your reasons why you chose to enroll your child at [name] preschool after visiting many children's centers and interviewing owners and instructors, and knowing that [name] preschool permitted animals to be present on the playground.

The problem with this interrogatory is the long unnecessary explanation following the question which is conclusionary and assumes facts not in evidence. Correcting this interrogatory can be done by simply eliminating the last part of the question as follows:

Please state your reasons for choosing to enroll your child at [name]'s preschool.

The extra material in the question can be used to draft other questions establishing as fact that the parents did indeed visit other preschools and interview owners before deciding to enroll their child in that particular preschool. Other questions could be asked to discover the names of other preschools and their owners. Depending upon the interrogatory answer received, avenues of discovery many be opened up, includ-ing sending an investigator to obtain witness statements from other preschool direc-tors interviewed by the parents, follow-up questions for depositions of the plaintiffs and so forth.

Example 4

Interrogatory No. 4.   Knowing that your child, [name], had displayed disruptive behavior, temper tantrums, and impatience with other students at prior preschools, didn't you think you owed a duty to inform the staff of [name] Preschool of these problems before you enrolled the child at the school.

This interrogatory is argumentative, characterizes facts which are not in evidence, and cannot be placed in evidence without a proper foundation. The second problem with this interrogatory is that it attempts to shift the duty owed to the parents (who are the plaintiffs in this action) away from the preschool (the defendant in this action). It is a reasonable assumption that parents who enroll their child in a preschool believe their child will be adequately supervised and cared for during the time spent at the school, irrespective of any behavior problem their child might have had in other environments/situations.

A rewrite of this question needs to focus on the information sought and to estab-lish a factual foundation for the information sought. For example:

(1) Please describe any behavior problems that you were aware of that occurred at [name]'s prior preschool, [name]'s Preschool.

(2) Please describe how you learned of the behavior problems referred to in the previous interrogatory.

(3) Please describe each and every step you took to remedy the behavior problems referenced in the prior interrogatory.

Example 5

Interrogatory No. 5.   Is it your opinion that [name of child] has had sufficient experience with animals to be aware of the possibility of their violent propensities in a preschool environment.

There are many problems with this interrogatory. First, it seeks and requires a professional opinion from a lay witness. We can assume that the child's parents are not child psychologists or experts on animal behavior. Second, it assumes facts not in evidence (that animals in preschools display a propensity for violence.) Last of all, it is a wasted interrogatory that will not establish any facts that will further the plaintiff's cause of action. Because the interrogatory deals only with a characterization of facts that can be interpreted as being argumentative, it is of no value to the case. There is no rewrite possible for this question.

Example 6

Interrogatory No. 6.   State whether any other animals have been allowed on the premises of [name]'s Preschool during the past five years, and if so, the owner's name and last known address.

The problem with this interrogatory is that it is overbroad and inquires about all animals allowed on the premises of the preschool, which would include animals visiting for show-and-tell, stray cats and dogs who might wander onto the grounds of the preschool, and all other animals which could include goldfish, turtles, rabbits, gerbils, and other animals that small children might bring to their preschool. It is unlikely that the school has kept a record of each and every animal and it is not relevant to the subject matter of the action (a dog bite case).

Rewriting this interrogatory requires narrowing the scope of the question by shortening the time span (five years is too long), and defining the type of animal. The animal specific to the case scenario for which this interrogatory was written was a dog. A narrowly-focused interrogatory inquiring about dogs over the past year would be more appropriate.

Example 7

Interrogatory No. 7.   State the provisions that insure the protection and safety of the children at [name]'s Preschool.

The subject matter of this interrogatory is relevant to the action, and the content of the question is appropriate. The problem is a poor choice of the word "provision." This interrogatory can be corrected by rewording and substituting specific language for the ambiguous terminology. The following rewrite broadens the scope of the question while retaining the specific intent:

Identify by author and date each rule and/or procedural guideline for safety that was in effect at [name]'s Preschool on the date of the incident complained of herein.

The problem interrogatories referenced in this section illustrate the main challenge in drafting interrogatories. It is necessary to strike a balance between the structural framework of the rules of procedure and your own creativity. Achieving this balance will allow you to draft interrogatories that will elicit helpful information for your attorney's use in preparing a case for trial. Remember, when drafting interrogatories, to stick to the basic areas of dispute in the action. Attack the crucial areas of dispute from all aspects to make your interrogatories comprehensive. In drafting interrogatories, focus on ideas, and, in a second draft, go back through to rework wordy, overbroad interrogatories into the narrow, tailored, focused language necessary for procedural accuracy.

§ 4.25   Sample Interrogatories (General Liability)

Basic liability questions are designed to discover the circumstances and conditions of the plaintiff or the defendant's conduct at the time of the occurrence. **Form 4–7** is a good sample of interrogatories directly related to the circumstance and conditions surrounding the date of the accident or occurrence in a general liability situation.

FORM 4–7
SAMPLE INTERROGATORIES (GENERAL LIABILITY)

1. Please state when the alleged occurrence happened, giving the date, hour, and minute as nearly as possible.

2. If a series of occurrences are the basis of your claim in this action please state in chronological fashion each and every occurrence, or chain of events, which you feel in any way contributed to, or gave rise to, your allegation that the defendant acted "in a fraudulent manner." *

* Modification of interrogatory to individual action.

3. Please identify and describe the appearance of each and every person who observed, or was present in the vicinity of, plaintiff's alleged occurrence, giving the name and address of each such person known to you.

4. If any of the persons listed in your previous answer are agents or employees of the defendant, please:

(a) Describe in as much detail as you can everything that was seen or noticed by each such agent or employee.

(b) State where in relation to the point of the occurrence each such agent was at the time of any such witnessing of the occurrence.

5. Did you or any agent, employee or other representative of the defendant ever take or receive any statement, either in oral or in writing, from any person, including parties who had any information or knowledge relating to the alleged occurrence?

6. If your answer to the preceding interrogatory is in the affirmative, please state as to each person:

(a) Their identity, including name, address and phone number.

(b) The date of any such statement.

(c) The name, address, phone number, and job title of the person taking the statement.

(d) The substance, as best you can give it, of any such statement.

(e) If such statement was in writing, either attach a copy hereto or indicate where and when such statement may be examined by counsel.

7. If any of the defendant's agents or employees came to plaintiff's assistance immediately following the alleged incident, please state:

(a) A complete description of any such agent or employee.

(b) The name, address, phone number, and job title of any such agent or employee of the defendant.

(c) Specifically what type of assistance was rendered.

(d) If this assistance or any other action was reduced to a written report, either attach a copy hereto or indicate where or when such report may be examined by counsel.

§ 4.26 Sample Interrogatories (Damages)

It is extremely important to learn in detail about the costs and expenses which have been, or will be, incurred by all parties to an action. Claims can be made for medical costs and expenses, including doctors and hospitals, loss of earning capacity, personal property damages, costs of repairs or remodeling, loss of business, loss of good name, emotional damage, and so forth. In summary, losses can be claimed for any damage incurred by any party that is deemed necessary to restore that party to the state the party was in prior to the accident, incident, or occurrence. This general rule of damages is based on the theory of making the person whole again.

Sample general interrogatories designed to be broad enough to encompass most damage claims are exemplified in **Form 4–8.**

FORM 4–8
SAMPLE INTERROGATORIES (DAMAGES)

1. Please give an account, itemized as fully and as carefully as you can, of all losses and expenses which you claim were incurred by you or on your behalf as a result of the alleged occurrence, stating in your answer those losses or expenses which are attributable to hospitals, doctors, medicines, medical appliances, and any health care provider.

2. If you have suffered any financial loss as a result of the alleged occurrence, please state each item, itemizing as fully as possible any and all nonmedical losses including wages, salary, loss of earning capacity, or business expenses.

3. Please give an itemized statement of all monetary loss incurred by you or on your behalf as a result of the alleged occurrence. Include in your answer the method by which you have computed these losses.

4. What is an itemized amount of each and every financial obligation incurred by you or on your behalf on account of the alleged occurrence?

5. If you received any injury or damage to your feelings, including distress, anguish, embarrassment, and humiliation, please state:

(a) The nature, extent, and duration of such injury or damage.

(b) Specific examples of special damages incurred due to such injury or damage.

(c) Full details on how, wherein, and in what manner you received such injury or damage.

(d) Any and all financial losses relating in any way to such injury or damage.

6. If you received any injury or damage to your good name and/or business or personal reputation, please state:

(a) The nature, extent, and duration of such injury or damage.

(b) Specific examples of special damages due to such injury or damage.

(c) Full details of how, wherein, and in what manner you received such injury or damage.

(d) Any and all financial losses relating in any way to such injury or damage.

7. If you suffered any loss of earning capacity as a result of the alleged occurrence, please state:

(a) The amount or amounts of any such loss of earning capacity.

(b) The time period or duration of such alleged loss of earning capacity.

8. If you have received any raises in wages, salary, or income since the alleged occurrence, please state:

(a) The date of such raises.

(b) The weekly amount of such raises.

9. If you are claiming any loss of earning capacity, please state:

(a) The full name and address of your employer or your place of business.

(b) Specific details of your job duties and responsibilities.

(c) The name, address, and phone number of your immediate supervisor.

(d) The inclusive dates during which you were unable to work as a result of the alleged occurrence.

(e) The total amount of earnings which you lost as a result of your absence.

(f) Your earning basis on a weekly, monthly, or annual basis including commissions, bonuses, and other pay incentives.

10. If you continue to be employed by the same employer you had on or about the date of the alleged occurrence, please state:

(a) The date on which you returned to your position.

(b) Whether your duties or responsibilities are less, the same, or greater than before the incident.

(c) Describe in detail how, wherein, and in what manner your duties and responsibilities on your job declined or expanded, or changed, after the date referred to above.

(d) Your average weekly or monthly wages for each week or month for one year following the date referred to above.

(e) Your average weekly or monthly wages at the present time.

11. If you were self-employed at the time of the occurrence, state the name under which and the address at which you conducted such business, profession,

or trade, the nature thereof, and the period of time during which you have been so engaged.

12. Do you claim that, as a result of the alleged occurrence, you have sustained or will sustain any loss of income from any source other than wages, salary, or income of any kind?

13. If the answer to the previous interrogatory was in the affirmative, please describe fully each such source, the amount of your claim of loss as to each, and your annual net income from each source during the five-year time period immediately preceding the alleged occurrence.

14. Please give an account, itemized as fully and as carefully as you can, of all losses and expenses which you claim were incurred by you or on your behalf other than those referred to in answers to interrogatories above, as a result of the alleged occurrence.

15. Please give an account, itemized as fully and as carefully as you can, of all losses and expenses which you claim you will incur in the future as a result of the alleged occurrence.

§ 4.27   Sample Interrogatories
(Identification of Corporate Officers)

A corporate entity has an obligation to seek answers to interrogatories from its agents or employees. The corporation acts through its agents and employees acting in the course and scope of their employment. If a remark made by an employee, or document authored by an employee, is anticipated to contain vital information that will further your client's action, it is likely that opposing counsel acting on behalf of the corporation will resist being bound by that admission or document on the grounds that the employee did not have the authority to bind the corporation.

Specific interrogatories, as exemplified in **Form 4–9,** which require a detailed identification of corporate officers is recommended in all actions where a corporation is a party.

FORM 4–9
SAMPLE INTERROGATORIES
(IDENTIFICATION OF CORPORATE OFFICERS)

1. Please identify yourself, including as part of your answer your name, residence, office you hold in [name] Corporation, business address, and telephone number of said corporation.

2. Please state the name, address, and official capacity in the [name] Corporation of the person responding to these interrogatories.

3. Prior to answering these interrogatories, have you made a due and diligent search of your books, records, and papers, and a due and diligent inquiry of your agents and employees, with a view to eliciting all present information available in this action?

4. Please identify the state in which [name] Corporation was incorporated, giving its date of incorporation and present corporate status.

5. Please identify the state in which [name] Corporation has its principal place of business, including its business address, telephone number, and the name of chief executive officer.

6. Please identify the duties and responsibilities of your position with [name] Corporation, including the name of your immediate supervisor, if applicable.

7. Please list your dates of employment with [name] Corporation, including job titles and responsibilities from the beginning of your employment to the present time.

8. If you are a member of the board of directors of [name] Corporation, please state your position on the board of directors and the dates for which you held that position.

9. If you are a shareholder in [name] Corporation, please list the number of shares which you hold, and the dates on which you acquired those shares.

§ 4.28   Sample Interrogatories (Defendant)

If plaintiff alleges that the defendant or any agent or employee of the defendant contributed in any way to the alleged occurrence or incident by some act or activity, or omission to act, the interrogatories in **Form 4–10** will force the plaintiff to be more specific:

FORM 4–10
SAMPLE INTERROGATORIES (DEFENDANT)

1. Please state everything you saw the defendant do up to the moment of the alleged occurrence, describing the defendant's entire conduct and action in detail.

2. Please describe the actions and activities of the defendant from the time of the occurrence until the defendant was completely out of your view.

3. Please state everything you saw any agent or employee of the defendant do which had any bearing or relation on the happening of your alleged occurrence.

4. Do you claim or contend that the defendant or any agent or employee of the defendant engaged in any action or activity or failed to act in any manner causing or contributing to this alleged occurrence.

5. If your answer to the preceding interrogatory is in the affirmative, please state:

(a) A full description of the defendant and each such agent or employee, giving names, phone numbers, addresses, or other means of identification.

(b) A full description of each such action or activity.

(c) A full description of each omission of action or activity, including the specific action or activity which the plaintiff contends the defendant should have taken.

(d) A full explanation of how or in what manner each action or activity, or failure to act, caused or contributed to your alleged occurrence.

§ 4.29   Sample Interrogatories
(Government Entity—California)

Form 4–11 illustrates questions sent by the plaintiff to the State of California regarding a motor vehicle accident which occurred on a flooded section of state highway. Contentions in this action included prior knowledge of a dangerous condition (flooding), inadequate warnings to motorists, and failure to correct an existing dangerous condition on a public highway.

Although these interrogatories are specifically directed to the State of California, they can be modified for use in your state for any action involving design defect, lack of maintenance of state-controlled roadways, failure to protect motorists from hidden traps, and so forth. This example of interrogatories also illustrates the use of follow-up questions (nos. 3, 14, 25, 26, and 27 are particularly good examples of following up on each element of a contention using the who, what, why, where, when, and how approach).

FORM 4–11
SAMPLE INTERROGATORIES
(GOVERNMENT ENTITY—CALIFORNIA)

[attorney for the defendant]
[address]
[telephone number]

Attorney for Defendant
[name] Corporation

SUPERIOR COURT OF THE STATE OF CALIFORNIA

FOR THE CITY AND COUNTY OF [city/county name]

[plaintiff A] and [plaintiff B],	Case No. [case number]
Plaintiffs,	DEFENDANT [name] CORPORATION'S SPECIAL INTERROGATORIES TO DEFENDANT STATE OF CALIFORNIA
vs.	
[defendant C], [name] CORPORATION, STATE OF CALIFORNIA, and DOES 1 to 100,	
Defendant. _____/	

PROPOUNDING PARTY: [name] CORPORATION

RESPONDING PARTY: STATE OF CALIFORNIA

SET NUMBER: [set number]

Interrogatory No. 1: Please state the date of construction of the portion of California State Route [number] where the accident occurred that is the subject of this lawsuit.

Interrogatory No. 2: Please describe and state the date of each modification to California State Route [number] within ten miles of the accident that is the subject of this lawsuit.

Interrogatory No. 3: Please state the reasons for each modification described in your response to Interrogatory No. 2.

Interrogatory No. 4: Please describe how you designed the portion of California State Route [number] within five miles in either direction of the site of the accident that is the subject of this lawsuit in order to prevent flooding of that portion of California State Route [number].

Interrogatory No. 5: Please describe how for the past ten years, you maintained the portion of California State Route [number] to prevent flooding within one mile in either direction of the site of the accident that is the subject of this lawsuit.

Interrogatory No. 6: Please describe how for the past ten years, you maintained any easements you have to land abutting the portion of California State Route [number] within one mile in either direction of the site of the accident that is the subject of this lawsuit to prevent flooding of California State Route [number].

Interrogatory No. 7: Please describe how for the past ten years, you maintained any culverts under California State Route [number] for five miles in either direction of the site of the accident that is the subject of this lawsuit.

Interrogatory No. 8: Please list by date and report number for the past ten years, all motor vehicle accidents which have occurred on California State Route [number] within five miles in either direction of the accident site that is the subject of this lawsuit.

Interrogatory No. 9: Please describe all drainage easements within five miles in any direction of the site of the accident that is the subject of this lawsuit.

Interrogatory No. 10: Please describe any evidence you have showing that you attempted to make any alterations within the last 10 years, to land owned by [name] Corporation abutting California State Route [number] within five miles of the site of the accident that is the subject of this lawsuit.

Interrogatory No. 11: Have you ever considered condemning or other acquiring land owned by [name] Corporation within five miles of the site of the accident that is the subject of this lawsuit?

Interrogatory No. 12: If your answer to Interrogatory No. 11 is yes, identify all persons who have information concerning considerations by the State of California for the condemning of land owned by [name] Corporation within five miles of the accident site.

Interrogatory No. 13: Please describe all documents relating to your responses to Interrogatories No. 11 and No. 12.

Interrogatory No. 14: Please identify all persons who prepared drainage calculations relating to California State Route [number] or its surrounding area within five miles of the site of the accident that is the subject of this lawsuit.

Interrogatory No. 15: Please identify all documents relating to drainage calculations concerning that portion of California State Route [number] and its surrounding area within five miles of the site of the accident that is the subject of this lawsuit.

Interrogatory No. 16: Please identify all equipment available at the time of the accident that is the subject of this lawsuit for use on California State Route [number] to designated maintenance patrol personnel for establishing road closures such as but not limited to signs, barricades, trailers, and beacons.

Interrogatory No. 17: Please identify any employees of any Division or Department of the State of California responsible in the last ten years for land management within five miles of the site of the accident that is the subject of this lawsuit.

Interrogatory No. 18: Please describe all techniques and procedures available to employees of any Division or Department of the State of California to reduce flooding within five miles of the site of the accident that is the subject of this lawsuit.

Interrogatory No. 19: Please identify each employee of any Division or Department of the State of California who was in the last five years responsible for the inspection of California State Route [number] within ten miles of the site of the accident that is the subject of this lawsuit.

Interrogatory No. 20: Please identify all inspection reports prepared by any employees of any Division or Department of the State of California within the last five years concerning California State Route [number] within ten miles of the site of the accident that is the subject of this lawsuit.

Interrogatory No. 21: Please state if the State of California ever received notice from any person of the occurrence of flooding or the potential of flooding of California State Route [number] within five miles in either direction of the site of the accident that is the subject of this lawsuit.

Interrogatory No. 22: If your response to Interrogatory No. 21 is yes, please describe each such notice received by the State of California.

Interrogatory No. 23: If your response to Interrogatory No. 21 is yes, please state the name of each person who has knowledge of each such notice received by the State of California.

Interrogatory No. 24: If your response to Interrogatory No. 21 is yes, please state the date of each such notice received by the State of California.

Interrogatory No. 25: Please state if any employees of any Division or Department of the State of California had any conversations with any persons concerning the flooding or potential flooding of the portions of California State Route [number] within ten miles in either direction of the site of the accident that is the subject of this lawsuit.

Interrogatory No. 26: If your answer to Interrogatory No. 25 is yes, state the date and the participants of each such conversation.

Interrogatory No. 27: Identify all acts of [name] Corporation which you contend caused the accident that is the subject of this lawsuit.

Interrogatory No. 28: Identify any persons with knowledge of the facts listed in your response to Interrogatory No. 27.

Interrogatory No. 29: Identify any and all writings which refer or relate to the facts listed in your response to Interrogatory No. 27.

Interrogatory No. 30: Please state the date that the State of California acquired each parcel of property on which California State Route [number] was constructed within one mile in either direction from the site of the accident which is the subject of this lawsuit.

Interrogatory No. 31: Please state the manner (for example, by purchase, condemnation, or other method) in which the State of California acquired each parcel of property on which California State Route [number] was constructed within one mile in either direction from the site of the accident which is the subject of this lawsuit.

Interrogatory No. 32: Please state from whom the State of California acquired each parcel of property on which California State Route [number] was constructed within one mile in either direction from the site of the accident which is the subject of this lawsuit.

Interrogatory No. 33: Please identify each person with knowledge concerning the acquisition by the State of California of any parcels or property on which California State Route [number] was constructed within one mile in either direction from the site of the accident which is the subject of this lawsuit.

Interrogatory No. 34: Identify by date and title each document relied on by defendant State of California in preparation of its responses to this set of interrogatories.

Dated: [date].

[attorney for defendant] _____

§ 4.30   Drafting Contention Interrogatories

Interrogatories are a valuable tool for discovering the facts behind legal contentions and theories. Care must be taken in drafting these interrogatories to inquire as to the factual basis for each contention rather than the legal theory behind these contentions. A party may be asked to state not only their contentions but also each and every fact supporting such claim or contention; however, they may not be asked their contentions as to legal issues such as whether a contract has been performed or breached. A party is not required to disclose the legal theories or reasons supporting their claims; however, a party may be asked to state their contentions, opinions, and conclusions as to any matter of fact, rather than law.

Sample questions to ask regarding allegations in pleadings are exemplified in **Form 4–12.**

FORM 4–12
SAMPLE CONTENTION INTERROGATORIES

1. State each and every fact upon which you base the allegation that plaintiff, [name], was solely responsible for the termination of this contract.

2. Identify each and every document upon which you base this allegation and in this regard, please state with particularity sufficient to support a request for production of documents:

   (a) The name or title of the documents.

   (b) The name, business address, and business telephone number of the sender or preparer of the documents.

   (c) The name, business address, and business telephone number of the addressee or receiver of these documents.

   (d) The name, business address, and business telephone number of all persons possessing or in control of the original or a copy of any of the identified documents.

3. State each fact known or believed by you to exist which may support your allegation.

4. Identify the name and street address of each person known or believed by you to have information which may support your allegation.

5. State the identity, location, and custodian of each document, item, or thing which contains, or which you believe contains, information which may support or tend to negate your allegation; and whether, with respect to each document, item or thing, you will attach a copy thereof to your answers to these interrogatories without the necessity of a separate request for document production.

The important thing to remember in attempting to determine the factual basis of contentions and allegations in pleadings is to cover all of the bases for each contention:

1. Persons with knowledge,
2. Identity of documents which support the given allegation or contention, and
3. Physical evidence such as photographs, charts, or graphs which tend to lend support to the contention or allegation.

§ 4.31   The Form and Content of
Contention Interrogatories

Contention interrogatories are a broad reaching device designed to investigate your opponent's case at an early stage of discovery. They should be directed toward denials, allegations, and affirmative defenses in answers, complaints, cross-complaints, and other pleadings on file in the action. Their use takes on a more narrow focus in the late stages of discovery, and they can then be addressed to discovery, interrogatories, admissions, denials, depositions, and document responses. A basic format for contention interrogatories is:

1. Refer to the first affirmative defense in paragraph 8 in your answer to the complaint and the contentions set forth therein and state:

(a) Each and every fact upon which such contentions are based;

(b) The name and current address of every witness you know of to any such facts; and

(c) With sufficient particularity to permit the issuance of a subpoena or request to produce documents, the identity of each and every document or other writing upon which such contentions are based.

When an opponent's allegations, contentions, documents, or other evidence are wordy, complex, seemingly ambiguous, or otherwise voluminous, you may wish to pin him down to particular and specific facts. For example:

1. Refer to lines 2 to 4 of paragraph 8 of your complaint which states that "cross-defendants, and each of them, with malice aforethought did the things herein before alleged and the contentions set forth herein" and state:

(a) Each and every fact upon which such contentions are based;

(b) The name and current address of every witness you know of to any such facts; and

(c) With sufficient particularity to permit the issuance of a subpoena or request to produce documents, the identity of each and every document or other writing upon which such contentions are based.

Variations on contention interrogatories are numerous, and with minor revisions they can be tailored to fit almost any contention that has been made by an opponent in any document, pleading, or piece of evidence relevant to the action.

§ 4.32   The Advantages of Contention Interrogatories

Contention interrogatories are particularly useful in the early stages of litigation for the following reasons:

1. They make your opponent's case a matter of record.   Factual data, witnesses, and documents supporting an opponent's case are not known until well into a lawsuit following time-consuming discovery including depositions, interrogatories, requests to produce documents, subpoenas, and so forth. Contention interrogatories directly address your opponent's case and ask them to lay it out up front so you know what you are facing and can plan further discovery accordingly.

2. They make your opponent take a fixed position.   Occasionally pleadings will be filed that are generally protective, that is, you may face a defendant who is blanket defending by listing each and every possible denial and affirmative defense the defendant can think of. This buys time for them. Contention interrogatories will make this opponent take a position at the beginning of the litigation and help alleviate the problem of an opponent who has blanket-defended hoping that the discovery of later facts will validate their defenses.

3. They keep "information and belief" pleadings honest and straightforward. Information and belief pleadings are often devices to protect the litigant when the litigant does not know the facts personally. Contention interrogatories require identification of sources of information and belief.

4. They guide you in later discovery.   The basic picture laid out in the answers to contention interrogatories guides you in subsequent discovery. You may propound particularized interrogatories on information received in the contention interrogatories. You may determine if there are either newly identified witnesses whose depositions are essential or newly discovered documents which must be subpoenaed or requested through a request to produce documents. Contention interrogatories can enable you to structure a systematic approach to further discovery which saves both time and money.

5. Contention interrogatories guide the attorney as to a course of law and motion.   Based on facts revealed in the answers to contention interrogatories, the attorney may decide to bring a motion to file amended pleadings. Answers to contention interrogatories also immediately uncover the real areas of dispute, and may be useful in the preparation and drafting of a motion for summary judgment and summary adjudication of issues.

6. They identify liability and exposure at an early stage of the litigation.   The basis and support for a claimant's allegations, or a defendant's opposition, is the key to liability and damage exposure. Early contention interrogatories advise both the plaintiff and the defendant as to the major issues of liability, potential for damage awards, and measure of exposure.

The basic elements of contention interrogatories have been well-tested by various appellate courts. Propounding them should not lead to substantial objections. They are not considered "shotgun" as each interrogatory has subparts which do not require the answering party to relate back to their own pleadings. They are also not boiler plate as they are directed specifically to ascertain the facts of the case in question and are drafted directly from the opponent's pleadings.

§ 4.33   Sample Contention Interrogatories (Discovery Responses)

Contention interrogatories served after depositions, document production, and other discovery can be specifically directed to facts making up the basis of your opponent's allegations. For example, in an action involving misrepresentation and fraud in the sale of property, allegations would have been made that the sellers of the property failed to disclose certain material defects or deficiencies in the property to their real estate agent in the original listing agreement. It would be further alleged that certain material defects and deficiencies were fraudulently concealed by the sellers, and did not become apparent to the buyers of the property until after a close of escrow when they took up occupancy.

The course of discovery in this type of action could have included depositions of the key individuals, buyers, sellers, real estate agents for both, brokerage firm, and any individual hired by either the plaintiff or the defendant to inspect the property prior to the close of escrow. Sample interrogatories from defendant to plaintiff after this type of discovery could include:

1. Please state each and every fact upon which you based your decision not to obtain the services of a soil or structural engineer as described in page 10 of the report of [name] Inspection Services dated [date]. (Exhibit 101 to the Deposition of [name].)

2. Please state each and every fact upon which you based your decision not to obtain, prior to the close of escrow, the services of a licensed drainage contractor, as described on page 2 of the standard inspection report of [name]'s Termite Control dated [date]. (Exhibit 25, Deposition of [name].)

§ 4.34   Sample Contention Interrogatories (Real Estate Misrepresentation and Fraud)

The following interrogatories may be propounded by defendants, sellers of the property, real estate brokers and agents named by the plaintiff in an action regarding misrepresentation and fraud in the concealment of defects in property sold and/or transferred.

1. Please state all facts upon which you base your contention that the [defendant] knew that the subject property contained those material defects and deficiencies as alleged in paragraph 13 of your complaint on file in this action.

2. Please state all facts upon which you base your contention that the [defendant]'s misrepresentations were not "obviously false" as alleged in paragraph 14 of your complaint on file in this action.

3. Please state all facts upon which you base your contention that the [defendant] negligently failed to reasonably inspect the property to ascertain deficiencies and defects therein and/or to disclose the same to the [plaintiff].

In this same action, the plaintiff can turn these contention interrogatories around into questions for the sellers, the defendants, as follows:

1. Please state each and every representation you made about the property located at [address] to your listing agent, Martha J., and to [name] Realty when you initially contacted them about placing the subject property on the market.

2. Please state the name, address, and job title of the person who made the last inspection of your property prior to the date of the listing agreement with [name] Realty.

3. Please state the substance of the inspection report referred to in your previous interrogatory response and attach a copy of said report.

§ 4.35   Sample Contention Interrogatories
(Construction Defect)

Form 4–13 illustrates questions that a design professional, sued in a construction defect action, could pose to the developer suing them to elicit information concerning breach of the standard of care, breach of contract, and so forth.

FORM 4–13
SAMPLE CONTENTION INTERROGATORIES
(CONSTRUCTION DEFECT)

1. Do you contend in this case that the [name] Soils Engineer owed a duty to you? (As used in these interrogatories, YOU or YOUR includes you, your agents, your employees, your insurance companies, their agents, their employees, your attorneys, your accountants, your investigators, and anyone else acting on your behalf.)

2. If you contend [name] Soils Engineer owed a duty to you in this case, please state all facts upon which you base your contention.

3. Please identify all WRITINGS that support your contention that [name] Soils Engineer owed a duty to you in this case. (As used in these interrogatories, WRITINGS means handwriting, typewriting, printing, photostating, photographing, and every other means of recording upon any tangible thing including any

form of communication or representation, including letters, words, pictures, sounds, symbols, or combinations thereof. [state] Evidence Code § [section].)

4. Please state the name, address, and telephone number of each PERSON with knowledge of your contention [name] Soils Engineer owed a duty to you in this case. (As used in these interrogatories, PERSON includes a natural person, firm, association, organization, partnership, business, trust, corporation, or public entity.)

5. Do you contend in this case that [name] Soils Engineer breached a duty owed to you?

6. If you contend [name] Soils Engineer breached a duty owed to you in this case, please state all facts upon which you base your contention.

7. Please identify all writings that support your contention [name] Soils Engineer breached a duty owed to you in this case.

8. Please state the name, address, and telephone number of each person with knowledge of your contention [name] Soils Engineer breached a duty owed to you in this case.

9. Do you contend in this case that [name] Soils Engineer owed a duty to any other person?

10. If you contend [name] Soils Engineer owed a duty to any other person in this case, please state all facts upon which you base your contention.

11. Please identify all writings that support your contention that [name] Soils Engineer owed a duty to any other person in this case.

12. Please state the name, address, and telephone number of each person with knowledge of your contention [name] Soils Engineer owed a duty to any other person in this case.

13. Do you contend in this case that [name] Soils Engineer breached a duty owed to any other person?

14. If you contend [name] Soils Engineer breached a duty owed to any other person in this case, please state all facts upon which you base your answer.

15. Please identify all writings which support your contention [name] Soils Engineer breached a duty owed to any other person in this case.

16. Please state the name, address, and telephone number of each person with knowledge of your contention [name] Soils Engineer breached a duty owed to any other person in this case.

17. Do you contend in this case that [name] Soils Engineer entered into a contract with you?

18. If you contend [name] Soils Engineer entered into a contract with you, please state all facts upon which you base your contention.

19. Please identify all writings that support your contention [name] Soils Engineer entered into a contract with you.

20. Please state the name, address, and telephone number of each person with knowledge of your contention [name] Soils Engineer entered into a contract with you.

21. Do you contend in this case that [name] Soils Engineer breached a contract entered into with you?

22. If you contend [name] Soils Engineer breached a contract entered into with you, please state all facts upon which you base your contention.

23. Please identify all writings that support your contention that [name] Soils Engineer breached a contract entered into with you.

24. Please state the name, address, and telephone number of each person with knowledge of your contention that [name] Soils Engineer breached a contract entered into with you.

25. Do you contend in this case that [name] Soils Engineer entered into a contract with any other person?

26. If you contend [name] Soils Engineer entered into a contract with any other person in this case, please state all facts upon which you base your contention.

27. Please identify all writings that support your contention [name] Soils Engineer entered into a contract with any other person in this case.

28. Please state the name, address, and telephone number of each person with knowledge of your contention [name] Soils Engineer entered into a contract with any other person in this case.

29. Do you contend in this case that [name] Soils Engineer breached a contract entered into with any other person?

30. If you contend [name] Soils Engineer breached a contract entered into with any other person in this case, please state all facts upon which you base your answer.

31. Please identify all writings that support your contention [name] Soils Engineer breached a contract entered into with any other person in this case.

32. Please state the name, address, and telephone number of each person with knowledge of your contention [name] Soils Engineer breached a contract entered into with any other person in this case.

§ 4.36 Sample Contention Interrogatories (Defamation)

Form 4–14 illustrates contention interrogatories in a defamation action.

FORM 4–14
SAMPLE CONTENTION INTERROGATORIES
(DEFAMATION)

1. State the name, address, and telephone number of each person you contend witnessed the defamatory statements allegedly being made.

2. State the name, address, and telephone number of each person you contend heard any alleged defamatory statements made by any individual at the scene.

3. State in detail each defamatory statement that you contend defendant allegedly made.

4. Identify each writing submitted by you to the Department of Industrial Relations (Labor Board).

5. Identify each place of employment at which you have been employed since the subject incident.

6. Identify each location at which an application for employment was submitted by you since the date of the subject incident.

7. If you contend you were fired, discharged, or terminated from your position at [name] Corporation, state all facts upon which you base such contention.

8. If you contend you were fired, discharged, or terminated from your position at [name] Corporation, state the name, address, and telephone number of each person having knowledge of such facts.

9. State the name of your immediate supervisor at [name] Corporation.

10. State the name, address, and telephone number of each person you contend heard, read, or had knowledge of the defamatory statements or writings alleged in your complaint.

11. State each and every instance on which you contend publication was made of the alleged defamatory statements (material).

12. State the name and address of each person you know received a copy of the alleged defamatory material.

13. State the date or dates you contend the publication was made of the alleged defamatory material.

§ 4.37 Sample Contention Interrogatories (Damages)

The interrogatories in **Form 4–15** were used by the plaintiff in an action for damages against a contractor hired for remodeling. The plaintiff alleged that the work done by the contractor was substandard. The plaintiff further alleged that it was necessary to bring in a second contractor to remedy the mistakes made by the first contractor, thus incurring monetary damages for the replacement as well as general damages.

FORM 4–15
SAMPLE CONTENTION INTERROGATORIES (DAMAGES)

Interrogatory No. 1: Please state the factual basis of your contention that [name] Contractors "failed, refused and neglected" to perform labor and deliver materials necessary to complete the contracted work at [address], [city], [state].

Interrogatory No. 2: Please state with particularity what labor was to be performed, and what materials were necessary to be delivered to complete the contracted work at [address], [city], [state].

Interrogatory No. 3: State with particularity the cost of labor and cost of materials was necessary to complete the work that you allege was left unfinished and/or substandard by [name] Contractor.

Interrogatory No. 4: Identify by name, business address, and phone number each person who submitted a written estimate, including the breakdown of labor and materials necessary to complete the work contracted for between the plaintiff and [name] Contractor.

Interrogatory No. 5: State with particularity and describe specifically all work done, and by whom, including the cost of all such labor provided and materials furnished to complete the work you allege was unfinished and/or substandard by [name] Contractor.

Interrogatory No. 6: Please state the factual basis of your contention that you demanded that defendant [name] Contractor, "repair or replace the defective modifications and remodeling and perform such other repairs as are necessary to comply with the agreement".

Interrogatory No. 7: State each and every fact, as opposed to conclusions of law or references to general allegations in the Complaint, upon which you base your claim, if any, of negligence against defendant contractor.

Note: The magic words in this contention interrogatory ". . . as opposed to conclusions of law or references to general allegations in your complaint . . ." are essential to avoid the responding party wiggling out of a specific answer by quoting general language for pleadings on file. These contention interrogatories seek factual information to support the plaintiff's damage claim that it was necessary for a new contractor to repair and/or finish the work contracted for with the original contractor. Frequently damage interrogatories are combined within a set of contention interrogatories to flush out all of the elements of damage allegations.

§ 4.38   Sample Contention Interrogatories (Government Entity—California)

The contention interrogatories in **Form 4–16** are appropriate to send if you are representing a defendant government entity. In this example, the State of California is involved in an action in which the plaintiff has alleged improper maintenance of a state highway and prior knowledge of a dangerous condition.

Compare these contention interrogatories to the general forms in § **4.33.** These interrogatories combine those general principles outlined in § **4.33** and add case-specific information based on the Complaint filed by the plaintiff in this particular action.

FORM 4–16
SAMPLE CONTENTION INTERROGATORIES
(GOVERNMENT ENTITY—CALIFORNIA)

<u>Interrogatory No. 1:</u> Identify all acts of the State of California which you contend caused the accident complained of herein.

<u>Interrogatory No. 2:</u> Identify any persons with knowledge of the facts listed in your response to Interrogatory No. 1.

<u>Interrogatory No. 3:</u> Identify any and all writings which refer or relate to the facts enumerated in your response to Interrogatory No. 1.

<u>Interrogatory No. 4:</u> Identify all acts of the State of California which you contend were performed negligently, or without due care, and caused or contributed to the accident complained of herein.

<u>Interrogatory No. 5:</u> Identify any person with knowledge of the facts listed in your response to Interrogatory No. 4.

<u>Interrogatory No. 6:</u> Identify any and all writings which refer or relate to the facts enumerated in your response to Interrogatory No. 4.

<u>Interrogatory No. 7:</u> Identify all acts which you contend the State of California could have taken to prevent the accident complained of herein.

Interrogatory No. 8: Identify any person with knowledge of any facts listed in your response to Interrogatory No. 7.

Interrogatory No. 9: Identify any and all writings which refer or relate to the facts enumerated in your response to Interrogatory No. 7.

Interrogatory No. 10: Identify all acts which had they been taken by the State of California would have prevented the accident complained of herein.

Interrogatory No. 11: Identify all persons with knowledge of the facts listed in your response to Interrogatory No. 10.

Interrogatory No. 12: Identify all writings which refer or relate to the facts enumerated in your response to Interrogatory No. 10.

Interrogatory No. 13: Identify all facts supporting your contention on page [number] of the Complaint on file in this action that "the State of California did negligently maintain . . . its property on State Route [number] so as to allow State Route [number] to be regularly flooded with water, mud, silt and other substances . . . ."

Interrogatory No. 14: Identify all persons with knowledge of any facts enumerated in your response to Interrogatory No. 13.

Interrogatory No. 15: Identify all writings which refer or relate to the facts listed in your response to Interrogatory No. 13.

Interrogatory No. 16: Do you contend that the State of California changed its State Route [number] in such a manner as to change the quality or manner in which the water flowed across the State Route [number]?

Interrogatory No. 17: If the answer to the preceding interrogatory is in the affirmative, please identify any person with knowledge of any facts supporting this contention.

Interrogatory No. 18: If your answer to Interrogatory No. 16 was in the affirmative, please identify any writings which contain information supporting this contention.

Interrogatory No. 19: Do you contend that the State of California had notice prior to the date of the accident complained of herein that water and mud ever flowed onto State Route [number] at the site of the accident?

Interrogatory No. 20: If your answer to the preceding interrogatory is in the affirmative, please identify all persons with knowledge of any of the facts supporting this contention.

Interrogatory No. 21: If your answer to Interrogatory No. 19 was in the affirmative, please identify all writings which contain information supporting this contention.

<u>Interrogatory No. 22:</u> Other than on the date of the accident, do you contend that mud or water ever flowed onto State Route [number] at the site of this accident?

<u>Interrogatory No. 23:</u> If your answer to the preceding interrogatory is in the affirmative, please identify any persons with knowledge of any of the facts supporting this contention.

<u>Interrogatory No. 24:</u> If your answer to Interrogatory No. 22 was affirmative, please identify all writings which contain information supporting this contention.

§ 4.39   Responding to Interrogatories

Interrogatories should be carefully scrutinized before they are answered. Your goal in responding to interrogatories is to provide only the information which will satisfy the question. Interrogatories should be construed by the responding party in their narrowest possible focus. Just as your goal in drafting interrogatories is to use tight, precise language making the interrogatories objection proof; your goal in responding to interrogatories is to also use tight, precise language construing the question in its narrowest possible light and giving only that information which has been specifically requested. This approach to answering is similar to the military query demanding name, rank, and serial number. Responses should state facts, and just the facts without amplification.

§ 4.40   The Preliminary Steps in Preparing Responses

When a set of interrogatories arrives in your office, it should be read very carefully and scrutinized for drafting errors, sloppy construction, and objectional requests. Interrogatory answers require a substantial amount of work, and a large part of the information necessary to prepare the answers must be obtained reasonably quickly from your client. If a client is out of town or unavailable, or if the interrogatories are extremely lengthy or detailed, contact opposing counsel promptly and request additional time to respond. When contacting opposing counsel to request an extension of time, ask for time to respond, rather than answer, which leaves the door open for objections rather than direct answers to the interrogatories. Once you have obtained this extension, a confirming letter (see **Form 4–17**) should be sent immediately to opposing counsel confirming the extension of the statutory time limit in which to respond. This is important to protect your client's right and not waive privileges.

Extensions must be requested prior to the date responses are due. Failure to seek an extension in a timely fashion can result in waiving objections. Extensions for interrogatory responses are routinely given by agreement of counsel on the state court level. On the federal level, it is necessary to prepare a stipulation for the extension and file that stipulation with the court (see **Form 4–18**). If a stipulated agreement cannot be reached with opposing counsel regarding an extension of time within which to submit interrogatory responses, a motion must be made. A form motion for extension of time to respond to requests for admissions is included in **Chapter 5.** This same form may be used for seeking an extension of time within which to respond to interrogatories.

The procedure for obtaining an extension to respond to interrogatories by stipulation is to contact the opposing counsel and/or his legal assistant or secretary by telephone requesting such an extension. Once the extension has been granted, confirm it immediately by letter. You may send a letter which simply thanks the opposing counsel for the extension and repeats the date now considered the due date for responses, or you may send a more formal letter which requires the signature of opposing counsel confirming the extension in writing with a copy to be returned to your office. Depending upon the strategy of the lawsuit, and, more importantly, the relationship between counsel and opposing counsel, a formal written document documenting the extension may be advisable.

FORM 4–17
SAMPLE INTERROGATORY EXTENSION LETTER

[attorney name]
[law firm]
[address]

   RE: [plaintiff] v. [defendant]

Dear [attorney name]:

This will confirm my conversation today with your secretary, [name], at which time you granted this office a two week extension within which to answer or otherwise plead to the first set of interrogatories propounded by defendant, [name] Construction Company, to plaintiff. The due date for plaintiff's responses is now [date].

Your courtesy and cooperation in granting this extension is greatly appreciated.

                Sincerely,

                _____
                [name], Legal Assistant to
                [name of attorney]

FORM 4–18
SAMPLE STIPULATION EXTENDING TIME

[attorney for plaintiff]
[law firm]
[address]

Attorney for Plaintiff
[name]

UNITED STATES DISTRICT COURT
[judicial district] DISTRICT OF [state]

[name],	No. [case number]
Plaintiff,	STIPULATION EXTENDING TIME TO ANSWER INTERROGATORIES
-vs-	
[name],	
Defendant.	

The defendant, [name], served defendant's Interrogatories to Plaintiff—Set No. One on [date]. Plaintiff has requested an extension of time to respond to these interrogatories to and including [date], a period not in excess of sixty (60) days. This extension is sought as the plaintiff needs further time to provide full, complete, good faith answers. There have been no prior extensions of time regarding these interrogatories.

Defendant, in an attempt to facilitate the discovery process and to allow plaintiff ample time to provide full, complete and meaningful good faith answers, is willing to grant an extension of time regarding these interrogatories. This stipulation is entered into with the understanding that plaintiff will undertake no discovery against the defendant until this office receives good faith answers to these interrogatories.

THEREFORE, IT IS HEREBY STIPULATED between the plaintiff and the defendant that plaintiff has to and including [date] to respond to these interrogatories to plaintiff - set no. one.

Dated: [date]

_____
[attorney for plaintiff]

Dated: [date]

_____
[attorney for plaintiff]

§ 4.41 Preparing an Interrogatory Transmittal Letter

Assuming your client will be at the least slightly intimidated and/or annoyed when they receive 100 or more interrogatories, it is important to communicate to them that you are relying upon their assistance in providing thorough answers to these interrogatories. It may be necessary to help your client through this burdensome discovery process by translating unfamiliar legalese into understandable English. It is not a violation of unauthorized practice of law statutes for a legal assistant to translate certain interrogatories or terms used throughout the interrogatories into understandable English, and to communicate that translation in written or oral form to a client. Be careful when translating contention interrogatories. You need to explain the meaning of the legalese without interpreting the legal significance of the question.

Be certain that your transmittal letter emphasizes you are ready and willing to assist the client in responding to this burdensome discovery. Remember the following:

1. Send out the interrogatories quickly. The sooner the interrogatories are sent to the client, the better. The more time they have to prepare their answers, the more helpful they will be.

2. Provide the client with a highlighted set of interrogatories, marking those which require the client's special attention. In this way you can limit the number of questions upon which they must focus. Clients usually do not provide the information needed to respond to contention interrogatories.

3. Note specific dates in your letter, rather than referring to "ten days from now" or that your answers are "due in final thirty days after our receipt of them."

4. Remind the client of their duty to answer. Helpful language which can be modified depending upon the complexity of your case and sophistication of the client is as follows:

We have a duty to answer these questions as long as the questions are relevant to the subject matter of this lawsuit, appear reasonably calculated to the discovery of admissible evidence, and do not involve privileged communications and discussions of legal strategy. We can and will object and not respond to those questions which are unreasonably repetitive, unduly burdensome, or when the information can be obtained from some other less burdensome source. We can also seek a protective order from the court and not respond to questions which appear designed to harass and embarrass you and/or those questions which seek confidential information.

5. Remind your client that a certain amount of latitude is allowed regarding background questions even though the client may feel that the question is not relevant to the lawsuit and it is an invasion of privacy.

6. Remind the client that opposing counsel has the right to gather information which may lead to the discovery of admissible evidence even though the relevance of a particular question may not be readily apparent. It is best to describe the efforts that "a reasonable person" would put forth in responding to the questions, explaining that the client must act as a reasonable person and diligently search out information with which to provide responses.

7. Remind your client of the potential legal consequences of not providing thorough responses. The following language may be modified for use in your letter:

Failure to cooperate with the discovery process by providing thorough answers based on all information presently known and/or within your custody or control can result in consequences such as expensive and lengthy discovery motions and sanctions. A further consequence may be that the trial court will exclude certain evidence at the time of trial, or even dismiss our lawsuit.

8. Mark your calendar for a follow-up letter or phone call to the client approximately seven to ten days after your original letter of transmittal with interrogatories has been mailed. Always call the client and remind them that you are waiting for a first draft of their answers. This gentle reminder frequently generates questions regarding certain interrogatories and opens the door for a discussion about the client's duties in this process. It is helpful to tell the client that, by taking the necessary steps to gather the information and provide thorough and complete answers to these interrogatories, you are organizing the case and defining the issues in dispute. You are also preparing for the client's deposition and later trial testimony.

9. Be certain that your client receives a copy of the response after the interrogatory answers have been finalized and sent to opposing counsel. It is important that the client realizes that if circumstances change and/or new information is discovered which makes a prior answer incorrect, they have a duty to advise you of the changed circumstances so that amended interrogatory answers can be filed on their behalf.

§ 4.42   Interrogatory Transmittal Letter

When answering interrogatories, it is a common procedure to send the interrogatories to the client and ask them to respond to the requests for information from their records and from personal recall. **Form 4–19** is a sample cover letter to be used when sending interrogatories to a client. Many clients, upon receiving your cover letter and interrogatories, will telephone the office asking for an appointment to go over their interrogatory answers. Meeting with a client to discuss interrogatory answers is an excellent method for establishing greater client rapport. It also provides you with an opportunity to obtain information that, although it has not been requested in the interrogatories, may be relevant to the case. In a meeting with you, clients should be encouraged to discuss the fullest possible answer to each interrogatory. They should also be told that not all of the information they have given you will appear in the final version of their interrogatory answers, but that it is important for you to have complete answers for your file and that you are fully apprised of all of the facts of the case. This meeting with the client to prepare draft interrogatory answers is a confidential meeting fully protected by the work product privilege. Only that information which is included in final interrogatory answers is divulged. Any extra information furnished by the client in the draft answers or at the meeting with you becomes part of the file and remains privileged information.

FORM 4-19
SAMPLE LETTER ENCLOSING INTERROGATORIES

Dear [client]:

Enclosed are the interrogatories recently received from the attorneys for the defendants in your case. Would you please read carefully through each interrogatory and answer each question to the best of your ability on a separate sheet of paper? You should return your answers to me in the envelope provided by _____ [date]. You must take great care to make your answers accurate and complete. Some of the requested information will be supplied from that contained in our file, and those questions which address legal contentions or theories will be answered by [name], your attorney.

Some of these interrogatories may be confusing to you because of the language and style in which they are written. This is due to the fact that interrogatories are a formal legal document and are not drafted in everyday language. Please contact our office and we will be happy to assist you in interpreting the questions. I would also be happy to meet with you, if you prefer, to answer the questions in an interview session.

We are enclosing a verification form which you must sign, but do not date, and return along with your answers. The verification form is a legal requirement and it is necessary to attach it to the final version of your interrogatory answers.

We must submit final answers to the defendants no later than [date]. If you find that you are unable to provide your answers to our office by _____ [date], please contact me immediately so that I can attempt to arrange an extension of time within which to respond.

Thank you for your cooperation in this matter.

Sincerely,

_____

[name], Legal assistant

§ 4.43   Preparing Responses for Corporate Clients

Interrogatories directed to a corporation do not designate who is to answer on behalf of the corporation. That designation must be done by the corporation. Ordinarily, a corporate officer who has personal knowledge of the transactions or claims involved, or who has knowledge of corporate record keeping systems, is an appropriate choice. Whoever answers on behalf of the corporation is under a duty to provide whatever information is known to any of the corporate officers or agents of the corporation. A corporate answer is imputed to and binding on the corporate body.

The person answering on behalf of the corporation has an obligation to investigate files that are in the possession or control of the corporation, to collect the requested information from those files, and to put it into the response. Records are considered to be in a party's possession or control if they are records that are kept at the corporate offices including the home office and all of its branches. Records are also considered to be in a party's possession or control if they are physically in the possession of an agent of the corporation, such as an accountant or storage company, and the corporation has the power to retrieve those records. The corporation's duty to investigate is limited to the extent of its own records; there is no duty to conduct an independent outside investigation.

A corporate party cannot avoid answering a proper interrogatory through the device of selecting someone to answer the interrogatories who lacks personal knowledge of relevant facts. It is their duty to select the person most knowledgeable to provide the responses. Interrogatories should be sent to your corporate client with a cover letter requesting that the corporate client select the proper person or persons to prepare the responses. A sample letter for transmitting interrogatories to a corporate client follows in **Form 4–20.**

FORM 4–20
SAMPLE LETTER TRANSMITTING INTERROGATORIES
TO A CORPORATE CLIENT

[name]
Chief Executive Officer
[name] Corporation
[address]

    RE: [plaintiff] v. [name] Corporation

Dear [name]:

    Enclosed are the interrogatories recently received from the attorney for the plaintiff in this action. Please go through and answer each question to the best of your ability on a separate sheet of paper, returning your answers to me in the envelope provided by _____ [date].

    You will note that the interrogatories are addressed to the [name] Corporation as a corporate entity. It is the obligation of [name] Corporation, and you as its chief executive officer, to make a thorough investigation of all files maintained not only at this office but at corporate headquarters to obtain the information requested in the interrogatories. It is also your obligation to contact any officer, agent or employee of [name] Corporation who is within your control and may have information relating to any of the interrogatories.

Some of the requested information can be supplied from that which is contained in our files or in documents you have previously provided to our office. Those interrogatories directly addressed to pleadings on file in this action and legal contentions will be answered in that fashion.

A copy of these interrogatories has been sent to [name], corporate counsel for [name] Corporation, and we suggest that you coordinate your information gathering and preparation of responses with [corporate counsel]'s office.

Enclosed is a verification form which must be signed by yourself, or any other corporate officer who has the power to bind the corporation to the responses provided.

If you have any questions or problems, please give my office a call. Thank you for your prompt cooperation in this matter. I look forward to receiving your responses within the next ten days. If you anticipate there will be a delay in the retrieval of information from corporate files, please contact me immediately and I will request an extension of time from opposing counsel. It is necessary that we request our extension of time prior to the expiration of the statutory time to provide responses, so that we may preserve our rights to enter objections to any of the interrogatories.

Sincerely,

[name]
Legal Assistant

§ 4.44   Drafting Responses

Before drafting responses to interrogatories, carefully review each specific interrogatory, and check to see if it is:

1. Appropriate discovery, whether it is relevant or clearly outside of the scope of issues in this lawsuit;
2. Relevant and reasonably calculated to lead to admissible evidence, or just a fishing expedition;
3. Calling for privileged information;
4. Asking for identity of experts prior to expert witness disclosure (Remember that in state superior court actions, experts retained early in a case are considered consultants whose identity is protected pursuant to the work product privilege. Their identities are only relevant after the procedural deadline has passed for disclosure of trial experts.); and
5. Reasonable and limited as to the scope of time, or is it overbroad? (Pay particular attention to an interrogatory which calls for compilation of information over a five- or ten-year span.)

The cardinal rules in responding to interrogatories are to:

1. Provide only the information asked for and do not volunteer any information that is not directly responsive to the question;
2. Read the definitions carefully, if they have been used in the interrogatories, so the buzz words are understood;
3. Answer the interrogatories in the same format as the question has been posed; and
4. Pay particular attention to internal consistency in interrogatories because an interrogatory which combines tenses or time periods lacks internal consistency which makes it vague and ambiguous.

§ 4.45 Practical Tips for Drafting Responses

The following checklist provides practical tips for the working legal assistant:

_____ Familiarize yourself with the Code of Civil Procedure and Evidence Code in your jurisdiction as well as local court rules governing response time and requirements for written discovery.

_____ Study your attorney's style by reviewing finalized answers submitted in cases other than the one you are working on. Be particularly sensitive to your attorney's method and choice of objections. Many attorneys will customarily object first, and decide later on whether to provide supplementary responses. Still other attorneys believe in providing as much information as possible in the opening set of interrogatories to avoid what they deem unnecessary discovery motions.

_____ Contact your client shortly after they receive the interrogatories from your office to be certain that they understand the importance of providing responses. Check to see if you will need to ask for an extension of time to prepare responses.

_____ Review every piece of paper in your file including phone messages, scribbles by your attorney, memos, and research. Pay particular attention to any documents you have received from your client. It is embarrassing to ask a client for information which they have already provided. Clients believe that all documents they have given their attorney have been placed carefully in their file.

_____ Read the interrogatories thoroughly for internal consistency and procedural mistakes and bring these to the attention of your attorney immediately.

_____ Do not leave any numbered questions blank, even if you do not have adequate information with which to respond to a particular interrogatory. Make a notation "to be supplied later", and include the specific information needed in order to respond properly.

_____ Do not make the determination yourself that you might be providing more client information than necessary. Do not exclude questionable information. Prepare answers and, in a separate column, note the questionable information.

This type of notation alerts the attorney that certain documentation or information exists or can be acquired by the client, but there are concerns about the appropriateness of submitting it in formal answers to opposing counsel.

_____ Be certain to find out the names of those people who have access to the information regarding bills, invoices, or other damage confirmation and write to them with your client's authorization requesting copies of the documentation if the client does not have copies of this information.

_____ Remember that every answer to an interrogatory has the potential of being read aloud to a judge and jury, and may be used to discredit or impeach your witness at a crucial point in trial. Always draft answers in appropriate language even though style varies with particular attorneys. Some attorneys prefer first person responses and others prefer third person. It is important to personalize responses. For example, a name is better than the word plaintiff.

_____ Rely on information contained in the pleadings on file, if you are responding to contention interrogatories regarding allegations and/or defenses. For example, if the plaintiff is asked to substantiate the factual basis for a particular contention, refer to the complaint on file and quote the appropriate language from that cause of action. Remember that most answers to contention interrogatories involve information that may have been learned from a consultant or potential expert witness and, as such, it is protected under the attorney-client and work product privilege.

_____ Take every precaution to ascertain that your responses are consistent with responses which may have been provided to other parties in written discovery and/or prior deposition testimony. Also, be vigilant about internal consistency between form interrogatories, special interrogatories, requests for admissions, and written responses to a demand for production of documents. Lack of consistency in discovery responses is a fertile source for impeachment at trial.

_____ Use medical records to answer all questions regarding injuries in personal injury actions. In some cases, it is acceptable, and preferable to quote a doctor's diagnosis rather than explaining the basis of the plaintiff's injury in lay terms.

_____ Compare your firm's initial intake notes, or the insurance company's original incident report, or the police report, or any other initial reports of injury with the client's recollection while you are preparing interrogatory responses and review discrepancies with the client immediately. In a separate memo, make sure your attorney knows of any discrepancies between the client's current recollection and the initial incident report.

_____ Send the final interrogatory responses to the client for review and signature before they are sent to opposing counsel. This avoids the risk of misinterpreting something the client related to you during your interview or your translation of the client's draft answers into legal language. Be prepared, when sending final answers to the client, for the inevitable question as to why the final response is so brief and concise, leaving out so much information.

_____ Never limit an answer with an absolute! Interrogatory responses should always include the following language: "Investigation, discovery, and pretrial preparation are continuing, plaintiff (or defendant) reserves the right to supplement this response up to and during trial." If the question concerns documents confirming damages, always include in your response the following: "Plaintiff (or defendant) responds to this interrogatory by providing that information presently in their custody and control. Should further information and/or documents become known through discovery, plaintiff (or defendant) reserves the right to supplement and/or amend this response accordingly."

§ 4.46   Response Checklist

Prior to responding to a set of interrogatories, consider the following:

_____   1.   What information is needed to answer the questions? Consider the amount of investigation necessary to answer the interrogatories. This frequently depends on how much discovery has preceded their service. Many interrogatories can be answered from information which you already have in your file. Some interrogatories will require obtaining records from third parties (medical records, wage records, accounting records, sales records, ledgers, and so forth).

_____   2.   How will you obtain the necessary information? Sources of information will include your in-house legal files, client documents, and interviews with the client, corporate employees, and any other persons with knowledge of the case.

_____   3.   Are any of the interrogatories objectionable? Objections may either be simple statements as to why the question is objectionable or a lengthy statement including supporting facts needed to claim a particular privilege. Interrogatories must be objected to within the proper time frame, or the right to object to that interrogatory is waived.

_____   4.   Are there any interrogatory answers which will be damaging to your client? Interrogatories must be answered truthfully and, in some cases, telling the truth is damaging to your case. Responses to damaging interrogatories should be concise, straightforward, and phrased in neutral language to mitigate their damaging effect.

_____   5.   Does the interrogatory seek identification of documents? If so, make certain that you ask your client to provide these documents in sufficient time for review prior to responding to the interrogatories.

_____   6.   Are there contention interrogatories? Advise the client that contention interrogatories are primarily directed to the attorney and that the client need not be concerned with answering them. It is more important that the client devote their attention to obtaining necessary background information in order to respond fully, completely, and truthfully to all of the other questions than it is for him to worry over contention interrogatories.

§ 4.47   Sample Format for Interrogatory Responses

Form 4–21 illustrates the format, with introduction, of proper interrogatory responses.

FORM 4–21
SAMPLE FORMAT FOR INTERROGATORY RESPONSES

PROPOUNDING PARTY: Defendant, [name]
RESPONDING PARTY: Plaintiff, [name] Hospital

INTRODUCTION

Because discovery, pretrial preparation, and investigation are continuing, plaintiff is unable to fully and completely answer all the interrogatories contained herein; and, therefore, reserves the right to supplement or amend said answers prior to or during trial. Plaintiff generally objects to those interrogatories which request information privileged under the client and/or work product doctrine. Partial response to any interrogatories, including the disclosure of any information which might be privileged, is not intended as a waiver of any privilege as to any other item of information.

Without waiving these objections, plaintiff will respond based on such information and documents as are presently available. The following interrogatory responses are given without prejudice to plaintiff's, [name] Hospital, right to produce evidence of any subsequently discovered facts. Plaintiff accordingly reserves the right, upon request, to change any and all responses (as additional facts are ascertained and analyses are made). The following responses are made without waiver of objections previously stated in a good faith effort to supply factual information which should be in no way to the prejudice of plaintiff in relation to further discovery or analysis.

RESPONSE TO INTERROGATORY NO. 1:

Each interrogatory must then be answered separately and completely. If a claim of privilege is made to a specific interrogatory, it should be set forth in the response to that specific numbered interrogatory. Use of this introduction does not relieve responding party of the duty to claim specific privileges as they relate to specific questions, rather it sets forth general objections and reinforces claims of privilege, and the plaintiff's right to supplement answers as information becomes available.

§ 4.48 Responding to Contention Interrogatories

Contention interrogatories are more difficult than factual interrogatories and require carefully worded responses. Before preparing draft responses, remember to:

Review the allegations of the complaint or answer, quote directly, and use the form language in your response;

Read all available consultant and investigation reports and paraphrase the conclusions, incorporating them into your response;

Review other files with similar causes of action to see how contentions were answered and adopt the answers to your case specifics;

Use extreme caution to avoid language that limits any allegations or defenses. The focus of a case is rarely cast in cement during discovery. It is extremely important to use the "discovery is continuing . . . " response in formulating a response to a contention, negligence, or defense interrogatory.

The usual response to contention interrogatories propounded in the early stages of litigation will be,

Investigation, discovery, and trial preparation have just begun, and plaintiff does not have sufficient knowledge of the facts underlying these contentions to respond at this time. Accordingly, plaintiff reserves the right to supplement this answer up to and during time of trial as discovery continues and depositions are taken and interrogatories are propounded.

Receiving this answer is not the end of the line for the propounding party. A motion to compel further answers can be made citing plaintiff's own statement that plaintiff "reserves the right to supplement this answer as discovery progresses." An alternative means of acquiring this information is to propound the identical contention interrogatories 90 days before trial at which point the plaintiff will have to come up with specific answers. Contention interrogatories propounded after substantial discovery has been conducted focus on evidentiary issues rather than initial pleadings, and require an answer based on information learned through discovery.

§ 4.49   Objections to Interrogatories

An interrogatory not objected to must be answered. A party who receives an interrogatory that is objectionable is not required to answer it, however, they must respond by, clearly and promptly, stating an objection. Proper objections may be made to interrogatories dealing with privileged information interrogatories exceeding the legitimate bounds of discovery and which are burdensome, harassing and oppressive.

In framing objections, keep in mind that the objection may become an exhibit at a later motion to compel responses and should be complete as to specific grounds. It is not permissible to respond to an interrogatory with the single word "objection." The specific grounds for the objection must clearly be set forth in the response. If an objection is based on the privileged nature of the matter covered by the interrogatory, it is not sufficient to state "objection, privileged." The particular privilege involved must be identified and set forth. If there is case law which supports your privilege claim, it should be cited as further proof that the information requested is privileged.

The strategy of objecting to interrogatories differs with each case and with each attorney. Some attorneys, as a matter of course will object to every interrogatory, especially if they have a bad relationship with opposing counsel. Other attorneys rarely object and feel that it is their duty to provide full and complete information in interrogatory responses to promote settlement of their case. Most attorneys choose a middle ground, objecting when necessary, but not to excess, and furnishing relevant damages and defense information to promote honest claim evaluation. You have a duty to your client to object to improper interrogatories and to raise those privilege claims necessary to protect the client's best interests. Decisions as to whether to object to a neutral interrogatory as a means of forcing a motion to compel to buy time to get the answer, or merely to throw a road block into the discovery plan of opposing counsel, is a game playing technique employed by many attorneys. Proper objections should always be made, and what seems proper to you and protects the interests of your client will most certainly seem improper and unjustified to the opposing counsel. There are times in the course of discovery of most cases when objections will be made to a discovery request simply because case strategy dictates that an objection be made in order to buy time. An objection may then be made by counsel with the full knowledge that it is not made meritoriously, and that the information will have to be provided at a later date. This type of game playing is considered by many counsel to be effective case strategy. It is a safe bet that 99 percent of all attorneys practicing in the United States have resorted to this type of case strategy at one time or another in their litigation careers.

§ 4.50   Sample Objections to Interrogatories

The major grounds for objecting to interrogatories include:

1. Basic relevance—The interrogatory calls for information that is simply not relevant to the subject matter of this action. The standard for relevancy in discovery is quite broad; therefore, the courts generally do not look favorably upon this objection. The court generally measures relevancy not only on whether the information sought bears on one of the material issues in the case, but also by the much broader discovery criteria of relevance to the general subject matter of the entire lawsuit and to the discovery of admissible evidence. It has been said many times that relevancy is in the eye of the beholder; what is relevant to the plaintiff will never be relevant to defendant and vice versa. Relevancy objections are frequently raised, and they are always difficult to substantiate.

2. Broad and remote—This objection is frequently used when the question is overly broad without a limiting time factor and deals with issues remote in time to the critical time period of the occurrence.

3. Right of privacy—This objection can be used for any inquiry that deals with matters of a sensitive, confidential nature such as an entire history of medical records, tax returns, financial information, drug and alcohol rehabilitation treatment, and so forth.

4. Annoyance, embarrassment, oppression, unduly burdensome, and so forth—This is a frequently raised objection and one that has generated a substantial body of case law in most states. Often, when this objection is raised, the responding party also moves for a protective order under Federal Rule of Civil Procedure 26(c) (or comparable state statutes). This objection is especially useful when an interrogatory asks for information contained in public records or information that can be obtained via subpoena from third parties. This information is equally available to the propounding party and, therefore, the responding party is not obligated to do opposing counsel's homework.

5. Form of question is argumentative—An objection can be made based on the form of the question if it is phrased in an argumentative manner and cannot be answered in the form in which it is presented such as the classic "when did you stop beating your wife" type question. This objection can also be used when the interrogatory is not really a question, but is a statement, or declaration, to which the responding party can only agree or disagree.

6. Uncertain, ambiguous, and unintelligible—The answering party is under no obligation to rewrite and then answer a poorly drafted interrogatory. Neither are they required to speculate as to the meaning or intent of the propounding party before preparing their response. If responding party chooses to answer this type of question, they can interpret it to their advantage, and object and then state, "assuming that the intent of this interrogatory is . . . ."

7. Continuing interrogatories—Interrogatories requiring a continuing duty upon the responding party to supplement are not allowed. Federal Rule of Civil Procedure 26(e) impose a statutory duty for supplementing interrogatory responses, and some states have comparable statutes. An interrogatory cannot require the responding party to provide supplemental information. To do so within the format of an interrogatory is considered burdensome and oppressive.

8. Asked and answered—This objection can be used when the requested information has been provided and the question has been asked and answered in prior discovery, such as depositions, interrogatories, or document production. In making this objection, it is not enough to simply say "asked and answered." You must identify specifically when the question was previously asked and answered, and restate the answer.

9. Ineffective objections to interrogatories are those objections which are generally stated without a specific reference—For example, a privilege claim that is stated simply as "attorney-client privilege" without specific reference as to why that particular privilege claim has been raised is ineffective. Suggestions in this section at numbers 1 through 6 can all become ineffective objections merely by stating them generally. For example, an objection that the question is unintelligible, ambiguous, and so forth, will be ineffective without a specific reference to that portion of the question which is objectionable and ambiguous. A proper statement of this objection should directly quote from the interrogatory those words found to be ambiguous.

Effective objections are those objections which are stated and then illustrated either by quoting an example directly from the interrogatory, by citing case law, or by reference to other documents (pleadings, prior discovery, and so forth). It is never enough simply to state a bare bones objection without explanation.

§ 4.51   Sample Interrogatories with Responses

Form 4–22 is a good example of sample interrogatories with responses.

FORM 4–22
SAMPLE INTERROGATORIES WITH RESPONSES

Interrogatory No. 1: Identify each person who was present during the execution of the contract that forms the basis of count 1 of plaintiff's complaint.

Response: John S., James B., Robert R., Betty J., and Larry B.

Interrogatory No. 2: Identify each person who participated in or was present during any of the negotiations leading up to the contract executed by plaintiff and defendant on [date].

Response: James B., Robert R., and Betty J.

Interrogatory No. 3: Identify all conversations between defendant's employees and defendant's corporate counsel between [date] and the present date. Include in your identification the substance of each communication as it relates to this contract or any of the negotiations leading up to the contract.

Response: Objection is made to this interrogatory on the grounds that the substance of any statements or conversations made by defendant's employees to defendant's corporate counsel are protected by the attorney client privilege.

Interrogatory No. 4: Please identify each and every church or religious organization of which you are a member, or at which you attended services for a period of two years prior to [date].

Response: Plaintiff objects to this interrogatory in that it seeks confidential information and it is a violation of privacy. Further objection, this interrogatory is irrelevant to the subject matter of this action in that it seeks disclosure of plaintiff's religious affiliation, if any, which has no bearing on the subject matter of this action.

Interrogatory No. 5: Please identify each and every social or fraternal organization of which you were a member or otherwise attended functions for a period of two years prior to [date].

Response: Please see response to previous interrogatory. Plaintiff objects to this interrogatory on the grounds that it seeks confidential information and is an invasion of privacy. It is also irrelevant to the subject matter of this action.

Interrogatory No. 6: Please identify each and every one of your friends or acquaintances who can testify to your physical condition and well-being for a period of two years prior to [date].

Response: Plaintiff objects to this interrogatory on the grounds that it is overbroad. There are many friends and acquaintances whom plaintiff sees on a regular basis, and plaintiff presumes that they could testify to plaintiff's physical condition and well-being based on activities which they have participated in together such as bowling, water skiing, and golf. Prior to the injuries plaintiff suffered in this accident, plaintiff regularly participated in those activities with Harry J., Robert W., Bill P., Jim R., and Roger H.

Interrogatory No. 7: Please identify by name, address, and phone number each person with whom you socialized on at least a monthly basis for a period of two years prior to [date].

Response: Plaintiff objects to this interrogatory on the grounds that it is uncertain and ambiguous in its use of the term "socialized." A response is impossible without speculation as to the meaning of this question. Plaintiff further objects on the grounds that this interrogatory is overbroad and could require the listing of hundreds of names depending on defendant's definition of "socialized."

§ 4.52   Responding by Tendering Access to Records

A great deal of information that is relevant to the subject matter of a lawsuit exists in files and records of both parties. When an opposing party wants to examine these records himself, the proper discovery method is a request for demand for inspection of records. In some situations, however, the opposing party is not interested in obtaining access to the records themselves, but simply wants the benefit of certain portions of information that the records happen to contain. As long as this information is simple and the records containing it are readily accessible, the proper method of discovery is by way of interrogatory rather than a demand for inspection of documents. This method is more expedient and cost-efficient for the client.

Requesting information in this fashion may sometimes put an unreasonable demand upon the responding party, and force the party to sort through their records making a compilation, or summary, of some aspect of their contents. A proper objection to this type of interrogatory is that the interrogatory calls for, "a compilation or summary that has not yet been undertaken." The responding party, in addition to entering this objection, can make a motion for a protective order based on the undue burden and expense connected with furnishing the response.

An example of this type of interrogatory is *West Pico Furniture Co. v. Superior Court*.[3] In this particular action, West Pico Furniture Company filed against the finance company to which it had been assigning its conditional sales contracts with its customers. The plaintiff then proceeded to serve an interrogatory on the finance company seeking the names and addresses of all employees of the finance company who had participated in certain transactions. In order to furnish an answer to this interrogatory, the finance company would have had to search records located in over 75 branch offices to make a summary and compilation for the plaintiff. The defendant objected on the grounds that such a request placed an undue burden and expense on the responding party, and tendered access to records to plaintiff as an

---

[3] 56 Cal. 2d 407, 364 P.2d 295, 15 Cal. Rptr. 119 (1961).

alternative means of obtaining the requested information. The defendant was required to furnish the names, addresses, and custodians of records for each of the branch managers in their 75 branch offices in order to allow plaintiff to serve a demand for inspection of records on each branch office, thus shifting the burden and expense of obtaining and analyzing the records on to plaintiff.

Another example of this type of interrogatory can be found in *Adelman v. Nordberg Manufacturing Co.*[4] In this case, approximately 100 factory workers sued to recover portal-to-portal pay for a six-year period. They served an interrogatory requesting information from their employer regarding the hours each had worked every day during this six-year time frame. An answer to this interrogatory would have required first, a sorting out of their clock times from those of other employees on approximately 60,000 clock tapes, each containing 150,000 entries, and then an analysis of each of the 1/4 million entries that would pertain to the plaintiffs involved in this action. In this instance, the response by defendant was to tender access to the records to the plaintiff.

By tendering access to records to the propounding party, responding party avoids the expenditure of time, energy, and money that such a response would entail. It permits the responding party to tell the propounding party to "find the information yourself." It may also be used when the answer to the interrogatory would necessitate the preparation of a compilation, abstract, audit, or summary.

The proper format for setting forth a tender of access to records in an interrogatory response is:

An answer to this interrogatory would require a compilation of customer complaints (or employee records, or time records, or audit records, and so forth), which compilation does not presently exist. It would not be substantially less expensive for responding party to make this compilation than it would be for the party propounding the interrogatories to do so. Accordingly, the files in which these records may be found will be made available at the office of [name of attorney] at [time] on [date] or at any other mutually convenient time and place.

By using this option, the responding party shifts the burden of obtaining this information to the propounding party. The response must specify the records from which the information sought may be denied, and the specification must contain sufficient detail to enable the propounding party to locate and identify the pertinent records. Responding party cannot use this type of a response to send the propounding party on a search through a haystack of records and documents for a needle of information by stating that the information is available in a broad mass of documents. The correct documents must be specified. That is, before offering tendering of access to a certain set of documents, the responding party must go through those documents to ascertain that the information is indeed contained in them. The response then can truthfully state that the information is retrievable, and that responding party is willing to make those documents containing the requested information available to opposing counsel at a specified time and place.

---

[4] 6 F.R.D. 383 (D. Wis. 1947).

§ 4.53   Qualifying Interrogatory Responses

Interrogatory responses cannot be evasive, incomplete, or deceptive. Situations do arise, however, when the responding party cannot respond either in whole or in part to a question or may wish to qualify a response. Always promote the best interests of your client by phrasing answers in the best possible light. This type of a response should not be rambling or unnecessarily self-serving, however, you can describe the situation or circumstances in terms which will qualify your answer. **Form 4–23** exemplifies qualified responses.

FORM 4–23
SAMPLE QUALIFIED INTERROGATORY RESPONSES

1. If you are unable to answer an interrogatory because of lack of information or for other reasons, indicate the reasons. For example, in response to a question requiring you to list each and every item of special damages which you incurred in repairing rain damage to your roof, a response might be: Plaintiff has not yet received bids for the total repair job required by the damage to plaintiff's roof and at this time is unable to total the expenses. When this information is known, it will be provided to defendant.

2. If you do not know any answer at the time the responses are due, you may explain so in a response and provide the information later in a supplementary answer. For example: Plaintiff has not yet obtained any repair bids for the roof; as soon as these bids are received and a contractor is selected to do the work, plaintiff will supplement this answer.

3. If you base your response upon documents, records, or other sources of information, the response can be prefaced with an explanation such as: "According to records maintained by the defendant at its corporate office in Chicago . . ."

4. If a corporate, governmental, or other organizational body has difficulty determining who knows what about its internal structure, you may explain the scope of the inquiry with qualifying language such as: "All employees of the plaintiff involved in the [date] water test reviewed this interrogatory and supplied the following information: . . ."

5. You may answer one interrogatory by referring to a previous response. This is appropriate as long as the previous response (or prior discovery) really does answer this interrogatory. You must identify clearly where the response can be found.

6. If you disclose hearsay information, the nature of the information can be explained. For example: "I do not have personal, firsthand information concerning this question, however, I have been informed by [name]."

7. If you do not wish to vouch for the accuracy of some information, you can explain the source of the information or its uncertain status by prefacing the

response with wording such as: "The following information is provided in response to this interrogatory and was obtained from . . ." or you may say, "We do not know the answer to this question, but we have received information from . . . ."

Qualifying interrogatory responses does not relieve the responding party from their duty to make conscientious endeavors to make available all such information that does not require undue labor or expense. The responding party must reveal whatever information they, or their employees, officers, subsidiaries, and other agents:

Know,

Have learned through hearsay,

Believe to be true on information or belief,

Have in their records or documents,

Have in their possession, or

Have control over.

§ 4.54   Verification of Interrogatory Responses

Responses to interrogatories must be verified under oath and signed by the person making those responses. Interrogatory responses submitted without a verification are, technically speaking, no responses. The propounding party receiving interrogatory answers which are unverified may file a motion to compel answers and seek sanctions.

Send a verification form (**Form 4–24**) to the client along with the interrogatories in your initial transmittal letter. Request that the client signs, but does not date the verification form, and returns it along with their draft interrogatory responses. When the answers have been finalized, send a copy of the final answers along with the signed verification form back to the client for the client's records.

In dealing with a corporate client, follow the same procedure in sending a verification form (**Form 4–25**) along with interrogatory answers. Explain in your cover letter to the corporate client that the verification form must be signed by an officer of the corporation who has the authority to bind the corporate entity to the responses provided.

Under no circumstances should an attorney verify interrogatory responses for their client unless that attorney has been appointed the agent of the client for the purpose of responding to discovery. In such a case, the attorney should state in the verification that the attorney has been designated as the agent of the client to answer the interrogatories and is responding on information or belief.

FORM 4–24
SAMPLE VERIFICATION FORM

VERIFICATION

I, [name], declare:

That I am the plaintiff in the above-entitled action; I have read the foregoing responses to interrogatories, set [set number], and know the contents thereof; that the same is true of my own knowledge, except as to the matters which are therein stated on my information or belief, and as to those matters I believe them to be true.

I declare under penalty of perjury that the foregoing is true and correct.

Executed at [city], [state] this [date].

_____
[name]

FORM 4–25
SAMPLE VERIFICATION FORM (CORPORATIONS)

I, [name], declare:

That I am the defendant in the above-entitled action; I have read the foregoing responses to interrogatories, set [set number], and know the contents thereof; that the same is true of my own knowledge, except as to the matters which are therein stated on my information and belief, and as to those matters, I believe them to be true.

I am the chief executive officer of [name] Corporation, and submit these interrogatory responses in that capacity on behalf of [name] Corporation as a defendant in the above-entitled action.

I declare under penalty of perjury that the foregoing is true and correct.

Executed at [city], [state] this [date].

_____
[name]

§ 4.55   Supplementing Interrogatory Responses

Under Federal Rule of Civil Procedure 26(e), a party has a duty to supplement a response with late-acquired information as it relates to the identity and location of persons expected to be called as expert witnesses, as well as the anticipated substance of their testimony. A similar duty exists when the party responding to a discovery request subsequently obtains information which makes clear that the original response was incorrect, or, if correct at the time, is no longer true. Failure to amend the response when the information is known to be no longer correct amounts to a knowing concealment of the facts under Rule 26(e)(2). The duty to supplement under Rule 26(e) is limited specifically by statute leaving much to the discretion of the responding party. Supplementation of interrogatories and other discovery requests may be stipulated to between counsel. Motions for broader supplementation of interrogatory responses may be made by stating with particularity the grounds relied upon when setting forth the interrogatory response previously received and requesting that the responding party supplement their prior response with any additional information acquired after their previous answer.

In most state courts, there is no statutory authority requiring supplementing of interrogatory responses. In order to obtain supplemental answers, you may propound a supplemental interrogatory (**Form 4–26**) which requires the responding party to review all previous interrogatory responses and update them with any recently acquired information which, in any way, changes his original response. It is a good practice to serve a supplemental interrogatory at least 45 days before trial to allow time for compelling a response.

FORM 4–26
SAMPLE SUPPLEMENTAL INTERROGATORY FORM

[attorney for the plaintiff]
[address]
[telephone number]

Attorneys for Plaintiff
[name]

IN THE SUPERIOR COURT OF THE STATE OF [state name]

IN THE CITY AND COUNTY OF [city/county name]

[name],	Case No. [case number]
Plaintiff,	
	SUPPLEMENTAL
vs.	INTERROGATORY
[name] SHOPPING MALL, A LIMITED PARTNERSHIP, [defendant A] and [defendant B], as limited partners of [name] SHOPPING MALL, [defendant C], individually and (dba) [company D], and (dba) [company E], and DOES 1 through 30, inclusive,	
Defendants.	

_____/

PROPOUNDING PARTY: Plaintiff, [name]

RESPONDING PARTY: Defendant, [name] SHOPPING MALL

SET NUMBER: Supplemental Interrogatory

YOU ARE HEREBY REQUESTED, pursuant to [state] Code of Civil Procedure, §[code section], to answer under oath the following interrogatory:

SUPPLEMENTAL INTERROGATORY: Please review your answers and responses to all forms and special interrogatories propounded by you by plaintiff [name]. If, for any reason, any answer or response is no longer correct and complete, identify that answer or response by set and number and state whatever information is necessary to make it correct and complete as of the date this response to this supplemental interrogatory is due.

Dated: [date].

_____

[attorney for plaintiff]

§ 4.56 Amending Interrogatory Responses

Rule 26(e) of the Federal Rules of Civil Procedure sets forth statutory guidelines for the amending or supplementing of responses and clearly makes it a statutory obligation to amend or supplement discovery responses when the party who has made the original response becomes aware of information which changes or alters original responses. Rule 26(e) requires a party to amend a response upon learning "that the response was incorrect when made or that the response, though correct when made, is no longer true and the circumstances are such that a failure to amend the response is in substance a knowing concealment."

Although, in most state courts, there is no statutory duty requiring supplementing or amending interrogatory responses, it is to the advantage of a party obtaining additional information or discovering an error in an earlier response, to disclose the information by filing amended answers. The advantage of amending an answer is that, by doing so, the responding party avoids arguments at trial of surprise and concealment and prevents the possibility of the court granting a continuance at trial to allow discovery into the new information. Rule 26(e) controls the circumstances when answers need to be supplemented, but there is no statutory authority on the federal level resolving the issue of whether the responding party can voluntarily submit other written responses to amend a previous interrogatory answer. If a party wishes to change a response (amend it) rather than supplement it, present federal authority seems to require that the party obtain a court order permitting such amendment. It is the practice of many attorneys to stipulate to accept amended answers on a unilateral basis without requiring the party desiring to amend responses to make a motion and seek a court order. The reasoning is that the court would probably grant a motion and, in any event, the party seeking to amend would testify to the changed information at trial. Stipulating to exchange amended answers saves time and money.

In some states, for example California, there is statutory authority. California Code of Civil Procedure § 2030(m) allows for subsequent amendment of interrogatory responses without leave of court. In allowing the amendment of responses without leave of court, the propounding party, or any other party, may at the trial of the action, or at any hearing, use the initial response as well as the amended response.

A discussion of the amending of responses to requests for admissions in **Chapter 5** suggests methods which may also be used in seeking a motion to amend interrogatory responses.

§ 4.57   Compelling Interrogatory Responses

Interrogatory responses are generally due thirty days from the date they are propounded to opposing party. Local rules govern service by hand or by mail and generally give five days additional time to those interrogatories which are served by mail. If responses have not been mailed within the statutory time frame, and you have not been contacted by the opposing counsel asking for an extension of time within which to respond to the interrogatories you have propounded upon the client, begin the process of compelling responses. The obligation to provide interrogatory responses is clearly set forth in federal and state statutes. Failure to respond results in a waiver of all objections to the interrogatories and relieves the propounding party of an obligation to meet and confer with the delinquent party. Only in rare circumstances will there be a showing of substantial justification for the failure to provide timely responses. The court will order responses and impose sanctions in most cases. If the court order is not obeyed by the delinquent party, they face further sanctions for acting in contempt of court.

The time frame within which to make a motion to compel (see **Form 4–29**) interrogatory answers varies with local rules from jurisdiction to jurisdiction. When interrogatories are first propounded, calendar dates for responses to be received from opposing counsel as well as the date for a motion to compel responses if none have been received or further responses are desired.

Form 4–27 is a sample letter written to opposing counsel regarding the unanswered interrogatories and allowing counsel extra time to respond before filing a motion to compel. **Form 4–28** illustrates a sample Notice of Unanswered Interrogatories.

FORM 4–27
SAMPLE LETTER TO OPPOSING COUNSEL

Dear [opposing counsel]:

I would like to direct your attention to the fact that written interrogatories were served upon your client, [name], on [date]. To date we have not received any response to said interrogatories, nor have we been contacted by your office regarding an extension of time within which to respond.

Because more than 35 days since our service of these interrogatories has expired, it is our position that you and your client's time to object to any of the interrogatories has been waived. We are enclosing with this letter a notice of unanswered interrogatories requesting that you serve full and complete answers to the interrogatories propounded to you by plaintiff, [name], within 10 days of this request. Our office will withhold the filing of any motions to compel answers to interrogatories and request for sanctions out of professional courtesy for the next 10 days.

Thank you for your prompt attention to this matter.

Sincerely,

_____

[name of attorney]

Enclosure

FORM 4–28
SAMPLE NOTICE OF UNANSWERED INTERROGATORIES

Law Offices of
[name]
[address]

Attorneys for Plaintiff
[name]

SUPERIOR COURT OF THE STATE OF [state name]
IN AND FOR THE COUNTY OF [county name]

[name]	No. [case number]
Plaintiff,	NOTICE OF UNANSWERED INTERROGATORIES, WAIVER OF OBJECTIONS, REQUEST FOR ANSWERS
-vs-	
[name],	
Defendant	

TO: DEFENDANT, [name], AND DEFENDANT'S ATTORNEY OF RECORD:

PLEASE TAKE NOTICE that plaintiff, [name], served the first set of written interrogatories on the above-named defendant on [date]. Said interrogatories have not been answered within the time provided by [cite specific statute], and any objections to said interrogatories are thereby deemed to have been waived.

Defendant is hereby requested to serve answers to said interrogatories within ten (10) days of receipt of this request.

Dated: [date].

By: [attorney for plaintiff]

FORM 4–29
SAMPLE MOTION TO COMPEL RESPONSES

SUPERIOR COURT OF THE STATE OF [state name]
FOR THE COUNTY OF [county name]

[name], et al.,	No. [case number]
Plaintiff(s),	MOTION TO COMPEL RESPONSES TO INTERROGATORIES
-vs-	
[name], et al.,	
Defendant(s)	

TO: [defendant/plaintiff], [defendant's/plaintiff's] attorney, to each other party, and to the attorney of record for each other party in this action:

PLEASE TAKE NOTICE that on [date], at [time] [a.m./p.m.], or as soon thereafter as the matter can be heard, in Department [department name] of the above-entitled Court, located at [address], [city], [state], [plaintiff/defendant] will move the Court under [statute] for an order directing [defendant/plaintiff] to serve a response to the [plaintiff's/defendant's] interrogatories, Set. No. [set number]. The ground for this motion is that the period specified by [statute] has elapsed without the service of a response to this set of interrogatories.

PLEASE TAKE FURTHER NOTICE that if this motion to compel a response to interrogatories is opposed and substantial justification for that opposition is not shown, [plaintiff/defendant], and [plaintiff's/defendant's] attorney, shall request an amount equal to the attorney's fees incurred by the moving party, as shown by the attached declaration setting forth the attorney's hourly rate and the number of hours consumed in preparing and presenting this motion.

This motion is based on the attached memorandum of points and authorities, and [specify any documents, exhibits, or declarations that accompany the motion].

Dated: [date].

_____

[name of attorney]
Attorney for [plaintiff/defendant]

This motion must be accompanied by points and authorities which need only set forth the statute for interrogatories including the procedural time requirements, and a detailed attorney declaration including attempts, if any, to request responses.

§ 4.58 Sample Meet and Confer Letter

Form 4–30 illustrates a meet and confer letter which should be used when responses received are inadequate and further responses are required.

FORM 4–30
SAMPLE MEET AND CONFER LETTER

Law Offices of
[attorney name]
[address]

    RE: [plaintiff] v. [defendant]
    No. [case number]

Dear [attorney]:

I have had an opportunity to review the first set of responses provided by defendant to plaintiff's first set of interrogatories which were received by this office on [date]. We would appreciate further responses to several of the interrogatories.

In your response to interrogatory 3, you identify by name, address, and policy number your insurance carrier; however, you fail to state the limits of coverage for each category of coverage contained in the policy. Clearly the amount of available insurance, both primary and excess, is relevant and discoverable.

With regard to your response to interrogatory 18, it is respectfully submitted that your objection on the grounds of privilege and legal conclusion is improper. In your answer to the complaint on file you assert as affirmative defenses the allegation that the negligence that proximately caused the injury to the plaintiff was that of third parties. In your second affirmative defense, you allege that the injuries to the parties are the proximate result of independent third parties or their agents or employees. In your sixth affirmative defense, you allege that the co-defendants so negligently, carelessly and recklessly conducted and maintained themselves as to proximately cause this incident and the alleged injuries and damage. Interrogatory 18 asks for the necessary information on which you are basing your affirmative defenses. Clearly this is not privileged information, nor does it call for legal conclusions. We respectfully request that you file further responses stating the name, address, employer and job title of each person you contend is in any way legally responsible for the injuries to plaintiff. We also respectfully request that you state the factual basis of the contentions and any information pertaining to writings which will support the factual basis of these contentions.

With respect to interrogatory 20, it is well recognized that statements obtained by a party from nonparties are relevant and discoverable and not protected by attorney-client or work product privileges. Accordingly, a request is hereby made that you provide the information sought in interrogatory 20 and its subparts including the name, address, phone number, and job title of the custodians of such statements.

I would greatly appreciate your forwarding to this office further responses to the above interrogatories within twenty (20) days. If you are unable to do so in that period of time and wish more time, I would be happy to extend further time to file responses, provided that you extend plaintiff's time to file a motion to compel further responses. Please contact me at your earliest convenience to discuss these matters in an attempt to resolve them without court intervention.

Sincerely,

_____

[name of attorney]

§ 4.59   Sample Meet and Confer Letter
(Interrogatories and Request for Documents—California)

In a situation when specially prepared interrogatories have been served accompanied by specific tailored request for production of documents tied into the interrogatories, it is more appropriate to send one meet and confer letter discussing the inadequacies of both sets of written responses rather than sending them two separate letters. The argument made in a letter discussing inadequate interrogatory responses will overlap those arguments which need to be made in a letter addressing inadequate document responses.

The letter in **Form 4–31** illustrates exemplar language showing conformance to local civil procedure code requirements for meet and confer letters in California. With modification as to applicable Codes of Civil Procedure and local rules for your state or jurisdiction, this letter may be used as a basis for conformance with meet and confer requirements.

The letter addresses a common discovery problem for plaintiffs when dealing with a corporate defendant. Frequently, the plaintiff is at a loss as to knowing which persons within the corporation are appropriate for deposition and have sufficient knowledge of the critical issues of the action, and the plaintiff must rely upon defendants pursuant to California Code of Civil Procedure § 2025 to identify the "most knowledgeable" persons. A defendant corporation or business entity has an affirmative duty under California Code of Civil Procedure § 2025 to designate the person most knowledgeable regarding critical issues designated by plaintiff. A corporate entity has a duty not only to designate and produce the officers and employees most qualified to testify on its behalf with knowledge of specific matters but also that person so designated must testify to the extent of any information known or reasonably available to the deponent entity.

In the beginning stages of discovery, a defendant entity frequently employs a defense strategy and states that they have hundreds of employees and cannot possibly make the determination as to the most knowledgeable person regarding a particular topic. Defendants refer to this test of determining the most knowledgeable person as a subjective test rather than an objective test, and claim not to know exactly what plaintiff wishes to ask at a deposition, or what test the plaintiff would employ to determine the person most knowledgeable, and so forth.

The truth of the matter is that defendant corporate entity can identify their officers, directors, and employees by name and scope of job responsibilities. The defendant is in a superior position to access this information while the plaintiff is in an inferior position by not having access to employment records. The test suggested by the statute is an objective rather than subjective test. California case law has held that defendant may rely upon written job descriptions and scope of responsibilities to identify the most knowledgeable individual. Unfortunately for the plaintiff, the defendant may designate a person based upon their written job responsibilities and scope of responsibilities who in reality has little, if any, direct knowledge of the issues. Should this occur, the plaintiff should attempt in a deposition to elicit information such as names, job descriptions, and so forth which would enable them to depose the correct individual. This type of gamesmanship in discovery unfortunately adds a great deal of expense and time to the action which is exactly defendant's goal.

The meet and confer letter in **Form 4–31** is somewhat more strongly worded than the meet and confer letter in § **4.58.** It addresses deficiencies not only in interrogatories but also in the accompanying requests for production of documents. It is permissible to combine several discovery documents into one meet and confer letter, and it is appropriate to do so when the area of discussion of the basic questions in the interrogatories is the same as the area of dispute in document production.

The introductory paragraphs of this letter are strongly worded to imply that the plaintiff's patience is wearing thin and a motion to compel is eminent.

FORM 4–31
SAMPLE MEET AND CONFER LETTER (INTERROGATORIES AND REQUEST FOR DOCUMENTS—CALIFORNIA)

[attorney for the defendant]
[address]

    RE: [plaintiff] v. [name] Corporation

Dear [attorney for the defendant]:

I have carefully reviewed defendant [name] Corporation's responses to plaintiff [name]'s first set of specially prepared interrogatories and first request for identification and production of documents, and I find both deficient in several respects. The plaintiff requests that the defendant provide further responses to the following interrogatories.

This letter is sent pursuant to the meet and confer requirements of the California Code of Civil Procedure § 2030(1) in an attempt to inform you of these inadequacies and to request further written supplemental responses and/or the production of documents within the next week.

As of now, the plaintiff's last day to bring a motion to compel further responses and production of documents is [date]. Of course, plaintiff would prefer to resolve all of these issues extrajudicially without burdening the court with the prospect of resolving the matter for us. Therefore, please provide the defendants supplemental written responses by [date] or inform us as to whether you need additional time to comply.

Alternatively, if you need further time to review your files to obtain the necessary information to provide adequate responses and documents, the plaintiffs will be willing to defer bringing a motion to compel until a later date which is reasonable and mutually agreeable. If you will comply with the items discussed in this letter, please so inform the plaintiffs this week. If you require additional time to respond further and to provide the requested documents, the plaintiffs will provide [name] Corporation with an extension of time within which to do so, provided plaintiffs are afforded a commensurate period of time in which to review the responses and documents, so as to compel if necessary.

Nonetheless, please be advised that once you force a motion to compel, compliance with your discovery obligations while the motion is pending will not result in the withdrawal of the motion. Rather, once the plaintiffs are put through the expense of filing a motion to compel, they will see the motion through and seek reimbursement under the statute.

Interrogatory No. 4. Plaintiff agrees to limit this interrogatory to those individuals who directly participated in the design of the brake transaxle. Plaintiff requests that defendants respond with the name, last known address, and job title for those employees and/or agents of [name] Corporation who directly participated in the design of the brake transaxle on the 1992 vehicle.

Interrogatory No. 6. [Name] Corporation states they will identify a person who is knowledgeable regarding the brake transaxle mechanism, but then objects to the interrogatory to the extent that it requires [name] Corporation to make the determination as to "who is the most knowledgeable". Defendant goes on to that, "they do not know what tests plaintiff would employ to determine who is the most knowledgeable." Certainly, defendant would concede that they are in a superior position to plaintiff as to knowledge regarding specific employees and their employment experience. Plaintiff reminds defendant that California Code of Civil Procedure § 2025(d) places a duty on a corporate entity to designate and to produce the officers and employees most qualified to testify on its behalf having knowledge of specific matters. That person so designated by the entity must testify "to the extent of any information known or reasonably available to the deponent entity."

Plaintiff requests that defendant identify that employee or agent who is most knowledgeable regarding the brake transaxle mechanism as it was included in certain models of the 1992 vehicle. The purpose of this interrogatory is to seek names of those individuals who actively participated in some manner in the design of the mechanism, so that their depositions may be noticed in this action.

Note: Each interrogatory to which plaintiff desires a more complete answer is addressed in similar fashion by summarizing the content of the interrogatory, the answer provided by defendant, and the reasons why that answer does not meet defendant's obligation to provide a full and complete response. After each of the interrogatories have been addressed, the following transition paragraph should be used before beginning a discussion of the inadequacies in defendant's response to plaintiff's first request for documents.

Plaintiff's First Request for Documents

I have carefully reviewed defendant [name] Corporation's responses to the plaintiff's request for identification, inspection, and production of documents and find them evasive, incomplete, and deficient in several respects. Plaintiff requested documents in 26 specific categories, and received documents in only 3 categories. The only documents defendant produced for the plaintiff were the 1991 and 1992 owner's manuals for the vehicle in question, and copies of consumer complaints regarding the vehicle. The plaintiff requests that defendant review their responses and supplement them by producing all responsive documents in their custody, control, and possession responsive to the remaining 23 specific categories. Plaintiff reminds defendant that should documents no longer be available in any of these categories because they have been lost, misplaced, or destroyed, defendant is obligated to state that a due and diligent effort has been made to locate those documents and to the best of their knowledge, under oath, none exist.

In particular, the plaintiff requests that defendant review the following individual requests, withdraw their objections, and produce the responsive documents.

Request No. 2. This request specifically requests those documents relating to the incremental cost per car of adding the mechanism to the 1992 vehicle. Defendant's response that "cost was not the reason that the modified brake transaxle was not incorporated into the 1991 vehicle . . . ." is not responsive. Plaintiff requests that defendant provide those documents requested that specifically relate to the incremental cost per car of adding the mechanism to the 1992 vehicle.

Defendant's objection that this request "is therefore irrelevant and not calculated to lead to the discovery of admissible evidence" is without merit. California Code of Civil Procedure § 2017(a) holds that admissibility at trial is not a requirement in discovery. Rather, the test is whether the information sought might reasonably lead to other evidence that would be admissible at trial. The information sought in this request is critical to plaintiff's preparation of this case for trial.

Request No. 8. Defendant's response that "the lack of technical feasibility was not the reason [name] Corporation did not incorporate a mechanism in the 1991 vehicle . . . ." is unresponsive. Plaintiff has requested, "all memos, correspondence, notes or other documents that discuss adverse consequences, in particular, either prospectively or in retrospectively." Plaintiff requests that defendant respond directly to the specific request by producing relevant documents.

Note: Each individual request should then be addressed in the same fashion as the disputed interrogatories by first stating the substance of the request, defendant's response, and reasons why the response is inadequate.

In conclusion, plaintiff requests that defendant [name] Corporation review their responses to plaintiff's specially prepared interrogatories and request for identification and production of documents and provide supplemental information to these discovery responses so that plaintiff may proceed in this action without being prejudiced by defendant's refusal to respond in good faith to discovery.

This letter will serve as our compliance with California Code of Civil Procedure § 2030(1) and § 2030(m). Plaintiff requests that defendant provide supplementary responses to both plaintiff's specially prepared interrogatories and plaintiff's first request for identification and production of documents no later than [day], [date], or plaintiff will be forced to file a motion to compel further responses on or before the last day allowed for such a motion, [date]. I am hopeful that all of these discovery disputes may be resolved without the necessity of court intervention.

Sincerely,

[attorney for the plaintiff]

§ 4.60   Compelling Further Responses

Although timely responses to interrogatories may have been served, the propounding party may not be completely satisfied with the contents of the responses. Responses to particular interrogatories in the form of an objection may be viewed by the propounding party as being meritless objections, or stated with such generality that the particular privilege that the responding party is attempting to claim becomes unclear and may be viewed as waived. The provided answers may not be considered as complete and straightforward as the information reasonably available to the responding party allows and are, therefore, considered evasive or incomplete. The responding party may have tendered access to records instead of providing a response, and that tender of access may not provide enough particulars to allow the propounding party to obtain the requested information.

The procedural aspects of filing a motion to compel further interrogatory responses include:

1.	A notice of motion,
2.	A motion,
3.	The points and authorities in support of that motion,
4.	A declaration of counsel establishing the fact that efforts have been made at good faith resolution of the dispute, and
5.	The proposed order compelling further responses.

Motions to compel further interrogatory responses (**Form 4–32**), like all motions to compel further discovery responses, should always include a request for monetary sanctions to be assessed by the court on the losing party. General grounds for seeking monetary sanctions in connection with an order to compel further responses to interrogatories include:

1.	The responses are evasive or incomplete;
2.	The response includes objections that are too general, without merit, or completely frivolous; and
3.	The responding party has unjustifiably exercised the option to produce documents and tendered access to records inadequately specifying the documents.

When responses to interrogatories include objections to any particular interrogatory, the burden is on the propounding party to demonstrate through a particularized good cause showing that the objection:

1.	Is invalid as raised,
2.	Does not apply to the specific circumstances,
3.	Is without cause, or
4.	Has been waived through an untimely response.

Opposition to a motion to compel interrogatory responses places the burden upon the party who has provided the responses to show through specific information that the privilege claimed in the interrogatory response:

1.	Is valid,
2.	Does have merit, and
3.	Does apply to the particular circumstances addressed in the interrogatory.

There is also a burden on the responding party to show that the responses were made in a timely fashion and with a proper verification, thus preserving the right of responding party to enter objections.

FORM 4–32
SAMPLE MOTION TO COMPEL FURTHER RESPONSES

SUPERIOR COURT OF THE STATE OF [state name]
FOR THE COUNTY OF [county name]

[name], et al.,	No. [case number]
Plaintiff(s),	MOTION FOR FURTHER RESPONSES TO
vs.	INTERROGATORIES
[name], et al.,	
Defendant(s).	

TO: [defendant/plaintiff], [defendant/plaintiff]'s attorney, to each other party, and to the attorney of record for each party in this action:

PLEASE TAKE NOTICE that on [date], at [time] [a.m./p.m.], or as soon thereafter as the matter can be heard, in Department [department name] of the above-entitled Court, located at [address], [city], [state], [plaintiff/defendant] will move the court under [statutory authority] for an order directing [defendant/plaintiff] to provide further responses to Interrogatories, Nos. [interrogatory number(s)], in [plaintiff's/defendant's] Interrogatories, Set No. [set number]. The grounds for compelling further response to the enumerated interrogatories are [specify grounds].

PLEASE TAKE FURTHER NOTICE that if this motion for a further response to interrogatories is opposed and substantial justification for that opposition is not shown, [plaintiff/defendant] also moves for a monetary sanction against the [defendant/plaintiff], and [plaintiff's/defendant's] attorney, in an amount equal to the attorney's fees incurred by the moving party, as shown by the attached declaration setting forth the attorney's hourly rate and the number of hours consumed in preparing and presenting this motion.

This motion is based on the attached memorandum of points and authorities, and [specify any documents, exhibits, or declarations that accompany the motion].

Dated: [date].

_____
[name of attorney]
Attorney for [plaintiff/defendant]

§ 4.61   Points and Authorities Format

The most important part of a motion to compel further responses to interrogatories is the memorandum of points and authorities wherein the party desiring further responses presents its arguments and legal authority in a clear and concise manner. A general format is as follows:

Factual and procedural background—Two to three paragraphs should state in concise terms the factual background of the case including the procedural background relating specifically to discovery. For example:

On [date], plaintiff served on defendant, Robert L., a first set of interrogatories. On [date], defendant served his objections to plaintiff's first set of interrogatories. Defendant objected to each and every interrogatory on two grounds. First, that every interrogatory was irrelevant to the subject matter of the action. Second, that the requested information was protected by the attorney-client and work product privileges.

Interrogatory and response—Set forth each interrogatory in question with the response made to that interrogatory set forth directly under the interrogatory.

Factual and legal basis—The factual and legal basis for compelling further responses for each interrogatory must be set forth in a manner which demonstrates the defects in the response provided, and the arguments which constitute a good cause showing that further responses should be ordered by the court.

Conclusion—A general conclusion which states how the information requested is vital to plaintiff's preparation of this action for trial, how the information cannot be obtained through any alternative source, and how the information requested that is within the control and possession of defendant should be set forth concisely to conclude plaintiff's argument for the compelling of further interrogatory responses.

§ 4.62   Sample Attorney Declaration

A motion to compel interrogatory responses (when none have been provided) and a motion to compel further interrogatory responses must be accompanied by a supporting declaration of the attorney of record. The following sample in **Form 4–33** can be used (with proper variables) in both situations.

FORM 4–33
SAMPLE ATTORNEY DECLARATION

1. I, [name], declare that I am a partner in the firm of [name of law firm], [address], [city], [state], attorneys for plaintiff, [name], in the above-entitled action. I am admitted to practice before all of the courts of this state.

2. On [date], plaintiff served the first set of interrogatories on defendant, [name].

3. On [date] defendant, [name], served defendant's purported answers on [plaintiff].

NOTE: IF NO RESPONSES AT ALL HAVE BEEN RECEIVED—USE THIS VARIABLE.

3(a). Plaintiff, [name], has as of this date received no responses to these interrogatories, nor has [plaintiff] received any communication from defendant or defendant's attorney as to the reason for the lack of response.

NOTE: IF RESPONSES RECEIVED ARE UNSATISFACTORY—USE THIS VARIABLE.

3(b). Plaintiff [name], received responses to interrogatories on [date]. Those responses are attached as Exhibit "A" and made a part of this declaration. The responses received contained evasive and incomplete answers as well as generally stated, nonspecific and meritless objections.

4. On [date] I sent a letter to defendant's attorney, [name], requesting responses (or further responses). A copy of that letter is attached as Exhibit "B" and made a part of this declaration. To date, I have not received an answer to that letter, nor have my subsequent telephone calls to [attorney name] been returned.

NOTE: SPECIFY ANY OTHER ACTIONS TAKEN TO CONFER WITH THE OPPOSING PARTY IN A REASONABLE AND GOOD FAITH EFFORT TO INFORMALLY RESOLVE THE ISSUES COVERED BY THIS MOTION.

5. Plaintiff bases plaintiff's request for the imposition of a sanction in the amount of [dollar amount] on plaintiff's reasonable expenses in preparation of this motion [itemize and explain the basis of the computation of the monetary amount of sanction requested].

I declare under penalty of perjury under the laws of the State of [state name] that the foregoing is true and correct.

Dated: [date].

_____
[name of attorney]
Attorney for [name],
Plaintiff

§ 4.63 Protective Orders

The function of protective orders as they relate to interrogatories is to prevent the responding party from being annoyed, embarrassed, or suffering an undue burden or expense. Motions for protective orders are usually made in order to protect particular confidential or sensitive information such as trade secrets, confidential research, product development, or commercial information. Such information may be directly relevant to the issues of the case, and thus may not be protected by any specific privilege or work product protection. The use of a protective order in this instance enables the moving party to prevent, delay, or restrict access to information that, although relevant to the subject matter of the action, is extremely sensitive or confidential.

The relief available under a protective order includes:

1. Excusing answers to any or all interrogatories;
2. Setting specific terms and conditions upon which answers will be required; and
3. Protecting certain information from disclosure or ordering disclosure only in a certain way such as in sealed envelope or in camera inspection.

A motion for protective order (**Form 4–34**) must be made promptly, that is, before expiration of the statutory period within which interrogatory responses must be served, otherwise, the grounds for objections may be waived as well as the right to seek a protective order.

Motions for protective orders should not be made unless both parties have made a reasonable and good faith attempt to resolve the issues involved in an informal manner. Motions must be accompanied by a declaration (**Form 4–35**) detailing the steps that have been taken by each counsel in an effort to resolve these issues without court intervention. This requirement is frequently referred to as the meet and confer—good faith requirement.

§ 4.64 Procedure for Filing a Protective Order

The scope of discovery under the Federal Rules of Civil Procedure, as well as most state rules, is very broad. It may, however, be limited by court order. Limits may also be placed on the methods and frequency of discovery that a party uses. When confidential or highly sensitive information is sought in interrogatories or through other discovery requests, the party from whom discovery is sought may seek to limit the scope or method of discovery pursuant to Federal Rule of Civil Procedure 26(c). If good cause is demonstrated by the moving party, the court may grant a protective order or any order necessary to protect the party from annoyance, embarrassment, oppression, or undue burden or expense.

After filing objections to interrogatories pursuant to Federal Rule of Civil Procedure 33(a), the responding party may move for a protective order under Rule 26(c). The usual procedure is for the party seeking further responses to interrogatories to move to compel further responses pursuant to Rule 37(a). If that motion is denied in whole or in part, the court on its own recognizance may make any protective order it would have been empowered to make had a motion been made specifically for a protective order.

There is a difference in statutory requirements at the federal level and many state levels regarding motions for protective orders. For example, in California a party responding to interrogatories and filing objections may at the same time make a motion for a protective order. At the federal level, it is not necessary for a party who is served with interrogatories to move in the first instance for a protective order in order to limit the scope of discovery. The accepted procedure is to respond to the interrogatories stating objections to those interrogatories deemed to be outside the scope of discovery and/or privileged. It is then up to the party who has propounded the interrogatories to move the court for a motion to compel further responses and to determine the sufficiency of the objections lodged. It is not necessary for the responding party to seek a protective order immediately in order to avoid answering burdensome or oppressive interrogatories. The responding party can merely object, clearly stating the grounds for each objection. This shifts the burden to the propounding party to file a motion to compel responses. This approach saves time and money for your client that would have been otherwise required had you filed the pleadings necessary for the motions accompanied by declarations to obtain orders shortening time in order to notice a motion for a protective order.

§ 4.65   Grounds for a Protective Order

Protective orders are granted by the court only after a specific demonstration of facts establishes the necessity of the protective order. Good cause must be demonstrated with specific facts, and the burden is on the moving party to establish this good cause. It must be shown that the information sought is confidential, highly sensitive, or will cause undue annoyance, embarrassment, oppression, or unreasonable expense to the party from whom the information is sought.

A court being asked to issue a protective order will consider the purpose of the information sought, the effect that disclosure would have on the parties and the trial, and the nature of the objections urged by the party who resists disclosure. The court's decision is usually based on a balancing act between the values of mutual pretrial knowledge and the elements of annoyance, expense, embarrassment, or oppression.

Confidential records dealing with a party's financial affairs are often the subject of protective orders. Any disclosure of a party's financial information pursuant to a punitive damages claim must be limited to insure that the invasion into privacy is held within the limits required by the United States Constitution.

The scope of a protective order may limit the disclosure rather than strictly prohibit disclosure of confidential information. A protective order may state:

1.   That the parties simultaneously file specified interrogatory answers and requested documents in sealed envelopes to be opened only upon court order;

2.   That the scope of the interrogatory be limited to certain matters, books, documents, or other areas of inquiry;

3.   That the information need only be revealed to counsel for the discovering party or their representative, and that, once revealed, the information may only be used for the purposes of the lawsuit; and

4.   Any other disclosure that justice may require to avoid annoyance, embarrassment, or oppression.

§ 4.66   Sample Motion for a Protective Order

Form 4–34 is a sample notice of motion and motion for a protective order restricting discovery and imposing monetary sanctions, as well as a supporting declaration of the attorney of record when the moving party is seeking to protect confidential business information.

FORM 4–34
SAMPLE MOTION FOR A PROTECTIVE ORDER

SUPERIOR COURT OF THE STATE OF [state name]
FOR THE COUNTY OF [county name]

[name], et al.,	No. [case number]
Plaintiff(s),	MOTION FOR PROTECTIVE ORDER
vs.	
[name], et al.,	
Defendant(s).	

TO: [name], Plaintiff, and to Plaintiff's attorney of record:

NOTICE IS HEREBY GIVEN that on [date] at [time], or as soon thereafter as the matter may be heard in [department/division] of this court located at [street address], [city], [state], defendant will move for an order that interrogatories numbers 10 to 25 of the first set of interrogatories served by plaintiff, [name], on defendant, [name], are deemed not to be answered and further move this court for an order requiring plaintiff, [name], and plaintiff's attorney, [name], to pay a monetary sanction in the amount of [dollar amount] to the moving party, defendant. The motion will be made on the grounds that the interrogatories call for commercial information that could harm defendant's business if the information becomes public and that defendant has made a reasonable and good faith attempt at an informal resolution of the issues presented by this motion.

The motion will be based on this notice of motion, on the declaration of [attorney for the defendant], the memorandum of points and authorities set forth below, on the records and files herein, and on such other evidence as may be presented at the hearing of this motion.

Dated: [date].

_____
[name]
Attorney for Defendant [defendant name]

§ 4.67 Sample Supporting Declaration

FORM 4–35
SAMPLE SUPPORTING DECLARATION

SUPPORTING DECLARATION OF [attorney for the defendant]

1. I, [name], declare that I am a partner in the law firm of [name of law firm], [address], [city], [state], and have been admitted to the courts in this state.

2. On [date], plaintiff served plaintiff's first set of interrogatories on defendant, [name]. A copy of that first set of interrogatories is attached hereto as Exhibit "A" and made a part hereof.

3. There is good cause for the order sought by defendant in that interrogatories number 10 to 25 refer to secret, commercial information relating to licensing agreements entered into by defendant, including licensing fees. Defendant's business is highly competitive, and its competitors have systematically attempted to persuade defendant's customers to patronize them instead of defendant. Divulging the terms of defendant's licensing arrangements would enable defendant's competitors to offer better terms and thereby take away the defendant's customers.

4. On [date] I sent a letter to plaintiff's attorney asking that plaintiff withdraw the interrogatories which are the subject of this motion. A copy of the letter is attached as Exhibit "B" and made a part of this declaration. To date, I have not received an answer to that letter, nor have my subsequent telephone calls to plaintiff's attorney been returned.

5. Defendant bases this request for the imposition of a sanction in the amount of [dollar amount] on [itemize and explain the basis of the computation of the monetary amount of sanction requested].

I declare under penalty of perjury under the laws of the State of [state name] that the foregoing is true and correct.

Dated: [date].

_____
[attorney for defendant]

A memorandum of points and authorities must accompany this notice of motion and supporting attorney declaration. In this particular case, the memorandum of points and authorities should include information to support the fact that defendant's business is specialized and highly competitive, and that, by revealing licensing agreements and fees charged, the business will suffer economic detriment. The defendant must also show that there are specific competitors who have in the past, and are likely to in the future, attempted to lure away defendant's customers. Because defendant's business is of a specialized nature, the base of prospective customers is also specialized and somewhat smaller than the average base of customers, so a true economic hardship would exist if these responses were given. It is also possible to argue relevance issues and suggest alternative means of discovery.

§ 4.68 Preparing Interrogatory Responses for Use at Trial

A party's answers to interrogatories may be used at trial to the extent permitted by the rules of evidence. The most common basis for receiving answers to interrogatories into evidence is that they constitute admissions by a party. However, answers to interrogatories may be used for impeachment purposes to contradict a party's testimony at trial without being offered into evidence. Not all impeachment evidence is substantive evidence. Some impeachment evidence is heard by the jury only for the purpose of discrediting the witness, but it cannot be considered by the jury as proof of any facts in the main dispute between the parties.

Frequently interrogatory responses are given early in a case before the investigation has been completed and before a party has firmly decided on a particular legal theory or planned an overall strategy. The responding party is not bound to early responses that subsequently become incomplete or inaccurate if the party can show reasons for the changes. An interrogatory response does not automatically bar a party from taking a different position at trial. However, a party must respond as well as the party can in answering interrogatories, giving whatever information is available at the time of the responses. It is easier to amend or supplement interrogatory responses before trial to avoid appearing to be inconsistent at the time of trial. Any inconsistent testimony works against your client and is questioned by a jury.

The duty to supplement interrogatory responses in Rule 26(e) of the Federal Rules of Civil Procedure is statutory in federal litigation, and, although not mandatory, it is strongly suggested by statutes in many states. It is not a wise practice to neglect supplementing or updating answers, even if there is no specific rule or case requiring such disclosure. If there are changes presented at trial from previous interrogatory responses, the witness must present persuasive and legitimate reasons to explain not only the inconsistency, but why the supplemental information was not disclosed to the opposing party.

There are two methods of preparing interrogatory responses for use at trial, and often both are used and included in a trial binder. The first method is to take the interrogatories and the responses and through a cut-and-paste method prepare a document which when read provides question and answer, question and answer, and so forth. If the same question, or a closely related question, has been asked and answered at deposition testimony of the same witness, it is a good practice to indicate that in the margin next to the interrogatory question with a reference to those pages of the deposition. This is an excellent method of comparing testimony, and discovering inconsistencies which can be followed up at trial through direct and/or cross-examination questions. The second method of preparing interrogatory responses for use at trial is to prepare a summary of interrogatory responses and include that document in the trial binder.

§ 4.69   Summary of Interrogatory Responses

After interrogatory responses have been received from the opposing party, prepare a summary of the responses (see **Form 4–36**) concentrating on information provided regarding claims, contentions, and affirmative defenses. After this summary has been prepared, discuss it with your client so that they are aware of the information and the defenses raised in the responses. Your client may have rebuttal information that they can provide once they are aware of what has been claimed.

FORM 4–36
SAMPLE SUMMARY OF INTERROGATORY RESPONSES

Background information

Defendant, [name] Realty Company and [name] Broker, responded to plaintiff, Buyer [name]'s first set of interrogatories on [date].

They provided basic business identification. [name] Realty Company is incorporated with its principal place of business in [city], [state]. [name] has been an agent with [name] Realty Company for seven years and received the license as a real estate agent in [year] and has never been the subject of any disciplinary action before the Board of Realtors.

The listing agreement was taken by [name] on behalf of [name] Realty Company on [date]. The information in the listing agreement was provided to him by [name]s, the sellers of the property.

Legal contentions

Defendants deny any duty to inspect the property beyond a "reasonable and diligent visual inspection." They further contend a reasonable visual inspection was made on [date] and no unusual problems were discovered by defendants that would have required further investigation. They also contend that plaintiffs, (buyers), through numerous independent inspections made on the subject property prior to the close of escrow, would have become aware of any defects. Responding defendants have no knowledge of concealed problems on the property, or areas inaccessible to visual inspection. Defendants contend that they have not violated any statute, ordinance, or regulation. They further deny any misrepresentations or making any false statements to the buyers regarding the subject property.

Responding defendants deny inducing plaintiffs to make a bid on the subject property in any manner, including by making untrue representations and/or concealment of facts. They further deny that plaintiffs relied upon any representations made by buyers in making the bid on the subject property.

Defendants deny they had any duty to request or arrange for additional inspections regarding the subject property beyond which they felt diligent and reasonable.

They further assert that plaintiffs' purchase agreement called for numerous inspections of the subject property including a pest control, roof, and structural inspection. These inspections were performed on [date] and [date], and plaintiffs were provided with copies of those reports prior to the close of escrow on [date]. Plaintiff chose the individuals to perform the structural inspections, roof inspection, and heating inspection, and reports regarding all these inspections were accessible to all concerned parties prior to the close of escrow.

They further assert that plaintiffs' pest control report on the subject property noted damp substructure soil and indicated the need to consult a licensed drainage contractor.

Defendants further assert that plaintiffs' independently-prepared inspection report by [name] Inspection Services advised plaintiffs (prior to the close of escrow) that the roof was in a general worn condition and should be considered near the end of its useful life, and also that there appeared to be previous leakage in the bedroom area. Robert's report recommended that the roof be thoroughly inspected.

Responding defendants contend they had no knowledge of any latent defects on the subject property, and additionally, no knowledge of any defects which would have been discovered only by "expertise beyond that of a real estate agent and broker."

Documents and persons with knowledge of defendants' contentions

Defendants furnished the names of the sellers, [names], the broker, [name], [name] of [name] Inspection Service and [name] Roofing Company as all having knowledge of the facts contained in defendants' contentions and affirmative defenses.

The documents relied on include: inspection reports, termite reports, and roofing inspection reports as well as the escrow file on the property maintained by [name] Realty Company.

Basis of affirmative defenses

In addition to the previously addressed inspection reports, defendants claim that plaintiffs were aware of any and all problems based upon the various inspections and inspection recommendations. The inspection recommendations addressed the damages asserted in plaintiffs' complaint, and that not withstanding the knowledge of these problems and potential problems, plaintiffs removed the contingencies on the subject property, for a reduction in price, prior to the close of escrow.

§ 4.70 Sample Case Study

Approximately 35 vacation cabins situated along the Feather River suffered extensive water damage due to flooding. Each of the cabins was owned by an individual, or a husband and wife. All of the owners were members of the Feather River Homeowners' Association, and all of their insurance was placed through the same insurance broker, Nationwide Insurance Company. Each of the individuals filed claims with Nationwide Insurance Company for water damage based on a single occurrence, the flood. In some cases Nationwide Insurance Company sent a claims adjuster out to inspect the scene, take photographs, and prepare a written report of the flood damage. In some cases Nationwide Insurance Company failed to respond to the claims for an inordinate length of time (9 to 12 months). In some of the cases the damage was of such a nature that the owners advanced the fees themselves to have their cabins repaired, to prevent further damage, without waiting for settlement or determination of coverage from Nationwide Insurance Company. In other cases, the owners did nothing to repair their property and waited for Nationwide to contact them regarding coverage for the work.

A basic set of interrogatories to be propounded to each owner of a cabin in the Feather River should include:

1. Basic background information, identity and proof of ownership of each claimant. How title was held—joint tenants?

2. Questions regarding their use of the cabin—was it just a vacation home, how often did they use the cabin, did they rent the cabin to others or use it only for themselves, did they live in the cabin part of the year, how long have they owned the cabin? etc.

3. Basic insurance questions to include when they took out the Nationwide policy, the terms of the policy, coverage limits, length of time they had the policy, whether or not taking out a policy with Nationwide was an independent decision that they made, or whether the insurance was purchased as part of their homeowners' package, etc.

4. Basic questions regarding the claim procedure—when they first notified Nationwide that they had suffered flood damage, who they spoke to, any correspondence they received regarding their claim, any investigation of their claim by a representative of Nationwide, any photographs of the damage, site inspections, etc.

5. Complete description of each and every item of damage they have suffered, loss of earnings to investigate the damage, loss of rental income, loss of use of the cabin for planned vacations, actual damages suffered in repairing the flood damage, continuing damages, consequential damages, etc.

Many other basic questions along the lines of witnesses, physical evidence, and contacts with Nationwide Insurance Company should be asked. Also bids, repair costs, and other items of damage should be documented. Interrogatories can ask for copies of all writing(s) to be attached to the answers.

§ 4.71   Using Interrogatories in a Large Case

Interrogatories are especially useful as fact gathering discovery devices in large cases or cases involving multiple parties who have all suffered damage arising from the same set of circumstances. Propounding interrogatories is simpler than responding to interrogatories in these cases. In propounding, a sample set of basic questions can be drafted and then sent to each of the parties who filed claims against a particular defendant. Preparation of the responses for each individual claimant is a far more lengthy and tedious job.

§ 4.72   Responding to Interrogatories in a Large Case

Procedures for responding to interrogatories for any group of plaintiffs or claimants require a high level of organization, charts, and coordination with the word processor who will prepare the finalized version of the answers. Prior to sending these interrogatories out to the clients, read them through and segregate those questions which can be answered by material which you have in the client's file. Also segregate those questions dealing with contentions or legal theories that you, and not the client, will be answering. Responses to these questions should be prepared immediately. Once your draft of those answers has been reviewed by the attorney and is ready to be finalized, give it to the word processor so that it can be entered into the system and given a code number.

Next, look at the interrogatories to see if any of them are objectionable. All objections should be prepared, reviewed by your attorney, and also put into the word processing system. They, of course, will be given a different code number which should be identical to the number of the interrogatory for which they apply.

The interrogatories should be sent to the clients as soon as possible with a cover letter explaining that certain questions will be answered by you and they need not bother with them. It is useful to highlight with a marking pen those questions for which the client must prepare responses. Give a deadline for the receipt of responses in your cover letter, and also indicate that because there are many claimants for whom you will be preparing final responses, that you will attempt to seek an extension from opposing counsel.

It is easiest to serve responses in groups of 5 to 10 claimants to the opposing counsel rather than attempting to send all responses at the same time. By sending responses in this fashion you demonstrate a good faith attempt at meeting discovery deadlines, and you place yourself in a good position for requesting further extensions for the remaining responses. Because human nature and human error will play a factor in your receipt of the responses from 25 or 35 individuals, it is wise to seek an extension as soon as possible. Be realistic in your request for an extension, and do not ask for six months. It is realistic, however, to ask for an additional 30 to 60 days. Sending responses in groups comes in handy when you need to seek a second extension of time for those few individuals who have been on vacation, ill, or for some other reason have delayed preparing their responses.

When interrogatory responses come in from the individual claimants, read and review them immediately for deficiencies. Contact clients immediately if you spot deficiencies or missing information in the responses they have provided. This insures your getting complete answers in a timely fashion. Delays in contacting the client increase the likelihood of incomplete answers, and can cause many other problems.

§ 4.73   Sample Chart for Tracking Responses

The most efficient manner of keeping track of interrogatory responses in multiple party cases is to organize a chart which flags every step of the way. As each step is completed for each client, a check mark can be placed in the appropriate column. This chart, along with individual client folders, (draft responses, verification, letters to client) is your tool for organizing large case interrogatories.

To create a chart, choose a large piece of heavyweight paper and set up the name, address, and phone number of each plaintiff on the left-hand side. Then create columns for each of the following:

1.   Date interrogatories sent to client with letter
2.   Date responses and verifications received from client
3.   Information received complete
4.   Information supplemented, if needed
5.   If no responses by date in letter, first reminder to client
6.   If no responses, second reminder to client
7.   Client responses reviewed and finalized
8.   Legal assistant draft responses done
9.   Draft legal contention answers prepared/typed
10.   Draft objections prepared/typed
11.   Final responses typed and ready to mail

As each item is completed it should be checked off with the date of completion and the initials of the responsible party.

CHAPTER 5

REQUESTS FOR ADMISSIONS

§ 5.1   Introduction

A request for admission is the procedure whereby one party can force the other party to admit or deny the truth of any relevant fact, or the genuineness of any relevant document. This discovery device permits a litigant to ask the other party to concede that, for the purposes of the pending lawsuit, certain documents will be treated as genuine or certain matters will be considered as true.

A request for admission differs fundamentally from other discovery tools in that it is not used to discover new information. Depositions, interrogatories, inspection demands, medical examinations, and expert witness exchanges all have as their main thrust the uncovering of factual data that may be useful in proving matters at trial. On the other hand, requests for admissions seek to eliminate the need for proof in certain areas of a case. Requests for admissions are used to separate those facts that are not in dispute from those that are at issue. The main advantage of using requests for admissions is that they limit the triable issues in a particular action by forcing litigants to take fixed positions. Matters which are admitted are binding upon the responding party and may be used at trial or in motions for summary judgment.

§ 5.2   Scope and Subject Matter

The scope of requests for admissions and/or requests to admit genuineness of documents may relate to the truth of certain facts and the application of law to facts. The limitations on matters that can be included in a request for admissions, or request for genuineness of documents, are the same as the limitations which apply to all discovery devices such as depositions, interrogatories, and requests to produce documents. The scope of matters which may be addressed is any nonprivileged information that is either relevant to the subject matter at hand or reasonably designed to lead to the discovery of relevant matter. Privilege rules apply to requests for admissions in the same manner as they apply to all discovery devices. The most frequent privilege claims raised in response to requests for admissions are attorney-client privilege and work product claims.

Federal Rule of Civil Procedure 36 states that requests for admissions "should be used to obtain admissions of facts about which there is no real dispute and should deal with singular relevant facts which can be clearly admitted or denied rather than complicated situations involving many distinct and vital controversial issues of fact." Requests may deal with conclusions of fact, but not conclusions of law. This is what is meant by application of law to the facts. For example, it is proper to request the manner in which an accident occurred even though the responding party must make certain conclusions of facts in order to respond. (See § **5.10** for further discussion.)

Requests for admissions should not be directed to all the facts of the case, but only to those which are material to proving your claims and/or defenses. Depositions, interrogatories, and requests for document production are more appropriate discovery devices for detailed discovery regarding claims and/or defenses of your opponent. The most effective requests for admissions are based on your pleadings and evidence although the most effective interrogatories are based on their pleadings.

§ 5.3   The Question of Relevancy

The question of relevancy permeates all discovery. What is relevant to the plaintiff will never be relevant to the defendant and vice versa. Federal rules of discovery, as well as most state statutes concerning discovery, define relevancy in the broadest possible sense to allow discovery of any nonprivileged matters which are "subject to the matters involved in the pending action." Case law has further defined relevant information as "that which is relevant to the subject matter and helps a party prepare for trial or facilitates pre-trial settlement." Relevant information is that which uncovers the ultimate facts behind the pleadings. Subject matter has been further defined to include not only the acts that constitute the cause of action but also the circumstances and physical facts from which the action arises including the property, contract, individuals, or other items which are in dispute. Because discovery serves the function of testing the pleadings, the pleadings are especially important in the eyes of the court in making initial determinations of whether the particular information sought to be discovered is relevant to the subject matter of the action.

Relevant information relating to claims or defenses, generally speaking, is information that relates to a claim or defense of any party and is relevant to the subject matter of an action, and subject to discovery even though that information may be inadmissible at trial. This includes information relating to contentions made by other parties and factual information supporting allegations in the pleadings, including affirmative defenses and general denials. Information may be sought concerning potential as well as actual issues in a case. Discovery may be obtained with regard to damages even before a determination of liability has been made. Information on damages has been held to be relevant because it precipitates pretrial settlement in that it allows both sides an opportunity to evaluate the financial impact of the litigation.

Examples of relevant informational inquiries are discussed as follows:

Financial information.   When the financial condition of a party is at issue, as it is frequently in both business disputes and corporate matters, substantial discovery and analysis is relevant concerning the claimant's fiscal condition including the production of financial statements, projections of revenues and expenses, authentication of business documents, and other budgetary materials. Financial information is also relevant to alter ego issues, particularly in breach of contract cases. Information regarding the subsidiaries of a corporation including authentication of corporate documents and financial statements is also considered relevant.

Insurance information.   The existence and content of the insurance agreement or policy under which a carrier may be liable either to satisfy in whole, or in part, a potential judgment or to indemnify or reimburse payments needed to satisfy the judgment is discoverable. The existence of liability insurance may not be relevant to the underlying subject matter of the action and such information may not be admissible in evidence at the time of trial; however, the basic information is relevant, discoverable, and has been held to facilitate pretrial settlements.

Information on assets.   Unless the financial condition of a defendant or a plaintiff is itself an issue, it is usually not discoverable. The exception is when a party has been sued for punitive damages. The relevancy then becomes the party's ability to respond to the damages.

Plaintiff's compensation.   Discovery, such as interrogatories and requests for admission which seek information about compensation received by plaintiff for personal injuries or property damages, has been held to be relevant to make a determination as to whether a plaintiff is a professional litigant. Discovery may be conducted through interrogatories to ascertain whether any part of the plaintiff's damages have been paid by a third party. In requests for admissions, plaintiff may be asked to admit to the genuineness of insurance checks and/or insurance policies.

Factual and/or legal contentions.   Information that seeks to establish a party's contentions or to determine the facts that support those contentions is relevant. Contentions may be addressed in interrogatories or in requests for admissions. Requests for admissions may require that a party admit the genuineness of documents or the truth of specified matters of facts, opinions relating to facts, or the application of law to facts. Discovery of factual and legal contentions through requests for admissions is best addressed by referring directly to the pleadings which have been filed.

§ 5.4   Privileged Matters

The subject for a request for admission may relate to privileged materials. Although the subject matter of the request for admission may be relevant, it may be insulated from discovery by a particular privilege such as the attorney-client privilege, privilege for governmental secrets, taxpayer's privilege, or privilege against self-incrimination. However, there is a difference in requesting privileged materials through a request for admission as opposed to depositions and interrogatories. When the privilege involved protects only confidential communications, it is rarely asserted in responses to an admission request. This is because the admission or denial of the fact that the communication took place can be made without revealing the nature of the communication. The mere fact that the communication actually did take place is not privileged and would be revealed in a deposition or interrogatory answer. When the privileged matter relates to the genuineness of a document, such as a highly sensitive document which could possibly be privileged under the taxpayer's privilege, the best response is to invoke the best evidence rule stating that the document speaks for itself.

The assertion of the privilege against self-incrimination in response to a request for admission poses a unique problem. An admission made in response to a discovery request is considered to be made for the purposes of the pending action only, and it has been held that that admission cannot be used in any matter against that party in any other proceedings. Federal courts have been faced with the argument that this prohibition against the use of the admission in any other action means that a discovery admission could never incriminate the responding party, and that accordingly the privilege against self-incrimination cannot be validly asserted as an objection to a discovery admission request. Frequently civil actions and criminal actions will result from the same set of facts. For example, in *Gordon v. Federal Deposit Insurance Corp.,*[1] a federal agency requested that the defendant admit certain facts concerning the defendant's defaults in dealings with a federally insured bank. The defendant objected, claiming the privilege of self-incrimination on the grounds that the defendant's answers would be self-incriminating. The Federal Deposit Insurance Corporation (FDIC) fought to overturn this claim of privilege by relying on the prohibition of Federal Rule of Civil Procedure 36(b) against the use of a discovery admission against the defendant in any other proceedings. The court ruled in the *Gordon* case that:

> FRCP 36(b) does not prevent the use of facts set forth in the admission by the criminal prosecutor as a confirmation that facilitates preparation of the criminal case, or perhaps as a lead to other evidence, which is part of the protection of the constitutional privilege . . . .[2]

Of all of the privileges that can be claimed, the privilege against self-incrimination is the most problematic. There is case authority on the federal level, and in many states, regarding the use of this privilege. Frequently, complex business cases will have both civil and criminal causes of action pending simultaneously. This situation presents unique problems both for the propounder of requests for admissions and for the responding party. It is wise to make a claim for privilege and seek a protective order to protect the best interests of your client, and let the court make the decision as to whether the privilege claim is valid based on the individual facts of the pending action(s).

§ 5.5   Drafting Requests

The general rules for drafting requests for admissions are similar to the rules for drafting interrogatories. The cardinal rule in drafting is to keep it simple. A lengthy, complex, or compound request for admission of fact leaves the door open to qualified and unresponsive answers. A lengthy, complicated request begs to be either

---

[1] 427 F.2d 578 (D.C. Cir. 1970).

[2] *Id.* at 581.

objected to or responded to with a lengthy, equivocable answer. A request for admission should be short and contain a single, declarative statement of fact. Because the purpose of a request for admission is to narrow the legal and factual issues of a case, a request for admission should be narrowly drawn. A general and all-inclusive statement allows many points which give an opposing party grounds to deny the entire statement. Each request for admission should be able to stand alone and should not be vague, ambiguous, or unintelligible. The responding party is under no obligation to figure out the meaning of the request prior to responding. Pay particular attention to the syntax and grammatical structure of your request. An objection can be made that due to typographical and grammatical errors the request is unintelligible.

In preparing to draft requests for admissions, it is essential to review the pleadings to see what has been alleged. Examine all of the allegations, admissions, denials, affirmative defenses, counterclaims, cross-claims, and draft requests for admissions in language which sets forth as binding facts either those allegations set forth in your complaint or those affirmative defenses set forth in your answer.

§ 5.6   Timing and Strategy

Requests for admissions of facts are generally used early in a case to detect sham pleadings and to narrow the focus of issues. They are also useful once discovery has begun and each party has taken fixed positions on key issues through deposition and interrogatory responses and through requested and/or subpoenaed documents which have been received. By reviewing discovery to see what concessions or admissions have been made, you can draft requests for admissions to address those issues specifically. Facts conceded in interrogatory answers or depositions are admissions by the party but are not the same thing as conclusive binding admissions. A party who admits a fact in an interrogatory response, or at a deposition, can still present contrary evidence at trial. This can be avoided by focusing on matters the opposition has admitted in previous discovery and drafting requests for admissions and by seeking binding admissions in those areas. Matters which are admitted under Federal Rule of Civil Procedure 36 are deemed "conclusively established for the purposes of that pending action." Deposition questions and interrogatory responses are not necessarily admissible at trial under certain rules of evidence, but responses to requests for admissions are admissible. Admissions in interrogatories will be expressed in the language of one's opponent with all of the potential of ambiguity, hedging, qualifications, and equivocation that this implies. This is similarly true for deposition answers which may be filled with ambiguity and shading of the facts for your opponent's best advantage. However, the propounding party in requests for admissions has substantial control over the precise wording of the admission, and should the responding party admit without qualification, you will have a binding admission for evidentiary purposes phrased in your language rather than the language of your opponent.

The strategy of propounding requests for admissions which directly address liability and challenge the other party to deny fault is that, by doing so, you are forcing an admission or denial which may be used at time of trial. If you have an admission, the issue does not have to be addressed at time of trial. It is stipulated at court that defendant and/or plaintiff has admitted the liability; however, the more frequent case is a denial under oath. If you are successful at trial in presenting facts to prove that this was a false answer and liability is proven to the jury and and you win, you are entitled to those expenses incurred in proving those facts at trial which were denied under oath by the responding party.

The sample requests for admissions that follow at §§ **5.12** and **5.13,** relating to medical malpractice, are an example of liability admissions. They will most certainly be denied by both plaintiff and defendant because to admit would seriously weaken their case and perhaps give grounds for a motion for summary judgment. However, those sworn under oath denials may be used as items in a cost bill by the winning side to be reimbursed for the expenses of proof at trial.

§ 5.7   Checklist for Drafting Requests for Admissions

Before you begin drafting requests for admissions, you should know the case on which you are working inside and out. If you are drafting at the beginning of a case, draft from the pleadings on file. Requests for admissions differ from interrogatories in that you do not draft them based on information that you need to know about your opponent's case. Rather, you base requests for admissions on your pleadings and draft them in a manner that will obtain proof of your allegations, claims, or affirmative defenses. When drafting, it is important to keep in mind the following concepts:

1. Requests for admissions, like contention interrogatories, can quote directly from a complaint, answer, counterclaim or claim, and are most effective when they are based on the language of the pleadings that have been filed.

2. Requests for admissions must be simple and straightforward; each request for admission should be a simple, declarative statement that addresses a single issue and is not compound, complex, or ambiguous.

3. Requests for admissions should be arranged in a chronological sequence so that each admission is a building block that will help build your case. Requests for admissions should be thought of as bricks in a brick wall. By piling one brick (one admission) on top of the other you will build a brick wall that your opponent will not be able to scale, leaving him boxed into a fixed position. As each fact is admitted, the allegations of your complaint, or affirmative defenses, will be proven and may be used at trial as evidence of binding admissions.

§ 5.8   Drafting Mistakes to Avoid

The scope of requests for admissions is governed by the relevancy standard, that is, the scope must be relevant to the issues framed by the pleadings and the subject matter of the action. This standard of relevance is a very sweeping one, but it is still possible for particular admission requests to exceed this boundary. Objections can be made that the request is overbroad, burdensome, harassing, and so forth. For example, in a hypothetical product liability action brought after the tragic events of the

Tylenol poisonings, a request was propounded that defendant manufacturer conspired with the news media to suppress publicity concerning the lawsuit. An objection to this request could be made, and would probably be sustained, that the publicity or lack of publicity in the news media had nothing to do with the legitimate range of the product liability claim. The general subject of trial publicity by the media is not considered a triable issue in any action.

Federal Rule of Civil Procedure 36 does not clarify whether a request for admission can properly be directed to facts that are clearly in dispute between the parties. There is a line of case law that confines the request for admission mechanism to "essentially undisputed and peripheral issues of fact." However, requests for admissions that concern the major areas of dispute between the parties have been addressed in many federal cases and are frequently propounded. Such a request should be very carefully worded, and will probably be denied. A denial, however, can be useful to the propounding party if the facts which are denied are later conclusively proven to be true at time of trial. In this instance, the party who propounded the original request can obtain expenses incurred in proving those facts through a motion to recover expenses of proof made after trial.

Remember that a request for admission, or a request to admit the genuineness of a document, is a declarative statement and not a question. The only exception to this is when a request for admission is drafted as follows:

Do you admit that you hired John J. to paint the exterior of your residence located at 123 Main Street, Anytown, U.S.A.?

This is not an improper request for admissions however the preferred format is a declarative statement:

Admit that you hired John J. to paint your residence located at 123 Main Street, Anytown, U.S.A. as evidenced by the written contract attached as Exhibit A to this request for admissions and genuineness of documents.

In drafting requests for admissions and genuineness of documents, it is a good idea to combine both in the same pleading so that a reference to attached documents can be made to clear up any ambiguity that would exist without the document. There is a danger, however, of referring to documents which were not authored by, or which are not within the custody of the responding party. The following example illustrates this point:

Admit that Dr. B.'s office note of February 1, 19___ contains a complete description of what patient advised Dr. B. of at the patient's December 10, 19___ visit concerning the patient's physical condition and complaints on that date.

The response to this request for admission will be that plaintiff is unable to admit or deny this request because the specific nature of each and every description given by plaintiff patient to Dr. B. is not presently known. The plaintiff can only respond to the complaints and symptoms that the plaintiff complained of to Dr. B. Plaintiff lacks the medical expertise necessary to respond to the specific nature and description that may or may not have been recorded in Dr. B.'s office note. The plaintiff has no knowledge as to whether all such descriptions given by the plaintiff patient were accurately and completely recorded in the specific documents, because plaintiff is not in possession of Dr. B.'s office notes or typed consultations of those notes.

An alternate method of attempting to prove this point would be through a request for genuineness of documents by attaching the doctor's notes or typed consultations. However, such a request for genuineness of documents could still be objectionable in that the responding plaintiff, as a patient, would have no idea of the exact date on which these notes were written by Dr. B. or transcribed by the typist, or even that they were written by Dr. B. unless the responding patient is extremely familiar with Dr. B.'s handwriting. Obviously Dr. B. is the proper person to verify the genuineness of these documents.

The grammatical format of requests for admissions should be reviewed for proper verb tense, syntax, and placement of modifiers. One of the most common formatting errors is a misplaced or dangling modifier which makes the request ambiguous and unintelligible. For example:

Admit that you contend that Frank J. entered into a contract with Mary B. to paint the exterior of her house on February 23, 19__ at 1234 4th Avenue.

This request is unintelligible on several points. The modifying clause which includes the date and location of Mary B.'s house confuses the issue addressed in the request. It is possible to interpret the request to mean that the contract was either entered into on February 23, 19__ or that the painting was done on February 23, 19__. It is also possible that the contract was entered into at 1234 4th Avenue or that the residence is located at 1234 4th Avenue. The correct format for this request is:

Admit that on February 23, 19__, Frank J. entered into a contract with Mary B. to paint the exterior of her house, which is located at 1234 4th Avenue.

Requests for admissions should not be propounded for discovery purposes, but rather should be based on your pleadings and documents in an effort to establish as binding facts all of your allegations, affirmative defenses, and counterclaims set forth in the pleadings and documents on file in the action. Requests for admissions which are drafted as disguised attempts to discover new information are generally objectionable and can backfire on the propounding party who may receive surprise answers. Draft requests for admissions on known facts so that you can be fairly certain of the answers you will receive.

Requests for admissions which are propounded in the midst of discovery may refer to documents produced or answers given at depositions or in interrogatories. A request for admission which is drafted in the exact language of the discovery response is likely to result in an admission. Avoid the common mistake of rephrasing discovery responses and leaving room for the responding party to object on the basis that the rephrased response does not accurately reflect the meaning and intent of the original response.

Draft precise and direct requests for which a yes or no answer will provide you the admission or denial you seek. Do not draft a multiple choice type of request. For example, do not ask:

Admit that the color of the sky you saw falling was blue, green, yellow, orange, or some other color.

Rather ask:

Admit that the color of the sky you saw falling was blue.

Eliminate all unnecessary adjectives, adverbs and other qualifying words. Be certain that you have carefully reviewed the grammatical structure of a request for admissions. Dangling and misplaced modifiers can cause an admission to become unintelligible. For example, do not ask:

Admit that a large segmented portion of the upper thinner atmosphere landed with a shuddering thud upon the relatively small location you occupied which is considered the farmhouse.

Rather ask:

Admit that a one-foot square piece of sky hit the farmhouse.

Draft requests as simple, singular, separately numbered requests rather than attempting to combine many facts into one complex request. For example, do not ask:

Admit that the segment that fell from the sky, which you observed falling on February 5, 19__, hit the top of your head on February 5, 19__, causing you emergency and hospital room expenses of $2,400.00 and subsequent medical treatment with Dr. F.

This compound, complex, and multipart request for admission should be broken down into several individual requests as follows:

REQUEST NO. 1: Admit that you saw a piece of sky fall on February 5, 19__.

REQUEST NO. 2: Admit that a piece of sky fell on February 5, 19__ shattering through the roof of the farmhouse where you were working.

REQUEST NO. 3: Admit that the piece of sky that fell through the farmhouse on February 5, 19__ hit you on the top of the head.

REQUEST NO. 4: Admit that you were treated at [city]'s Hospital emergency room on February 5, 19__.

REQUEST NO. 5: Admit that you were billed $2,400.00 from [city]'s Emergency Services for treatment received on February 5, 19__.

REQUEST NO. 6: Admit that subsequent to February 5, 19__, you sought additional medical treatment for injuries received from the accident.

§ 5.9   Analysis of Problem Requests

The following requests for admissions of fact were written based on a fact scenario given to a class of paralegal students in investigation, discovery, and trial preparation. This section contains a discussion and critique of five of these requests for admissions. (The interrogatory samples in **Chapter 4** were also based on the same fact scenario.) In the fact scenario, a 5-year-old child enrolled at Miss Mary's Preschool was bitten by a dog. Plaintiffs alleged in their complaint lack of supervision of the playground area by Miss Mary's school personnel including, but not limited to, the child's teacher who had been assigned to be the noontime playground supervisor. The dog in question was owned by the teacher.

Example 1

1. Admit that you assumed neither Miss Mary nor Sally Teacher were not supervising the children during the noontime recess at Miss Mary's Preschool on the date the incident complained of herein occurred.

The main problem with this request is the double negative construction, neither and nor. The issue addressed in the request for an admission of fact is relevant to the cause of action of, negligence. Rewritten, this particular request for an admission of fact is particularly relevant for plaintiffs to direct to defendant and can be rewritten as follows:

Admit that neither Miss Mary *or* Sally Teacher were on duty supervising the children during noontime recess at the time the incident complained of herein occurred.

This request is an improvement, but may still raise an objection from defendant that it is compound and requires a response from two defendants. An alternate, and *preferred* method of drafting this request for admission would be to set out Miss Mary and Sally Teacher separately as follows:

1. Admit that Miss Mary was not on duty . . .

2. Admit that Sally Teacher was not on duty . . .

Example 2

2. Admit that Brutus the dog is very small in relation to the child, Angel, whom you claim was attacked by Brutus on the date complained of herein.

The main problem with this request is grammatical structure. Because of the placement of the clause ". . . whom you claim. . .", it is difficult to focus on the intent of the request.

Another problem with this request for an admission of fact is relevance. The size of the dog and the size of the child are not important issues. The fact that the dog attacked and bit the child is the focus of this lawsuit. Although, in some actions for negligence and product liability, it can be helpful not only to focus on the size of plaintiff in relation to the size of defendant but also to draw inferences regarding a particular course of conduct, this size comparison does not transfer to an action when children and dogs are the key players.

Example 3

3. Admit that you were not aware that the injury producing event was causing injury to the victim at the time it occurred.

The problem with this request is the total ambiguity of the request, making it difficult to understand what it is saying. The responding party may properly object to this request as being unintelligible. The ambiguity of the phrase "injury producing event" is linked to causation of injury. It is also inconsequential whether the responding party knew the event in question caused injury to the victim at the time it occurred or at a later time. Medical records and documentation of damage will be the best evidence as to causation and time of injury.

Another problem with this request is the use of the word victim. It is an emotional word favored by the plaintiffs which the defendant will always find objectionable.

There is no rewrite for this request because it does not deal with a relevant matter which is genuinely in dispute. Whether the plaintiff was injured by the incident will be documented by reliable, objective sources such as police reports, accident reports, medical records, x-rays, and so forth.

Example 4

4. Admit that you were not in visual contact with the dog during the incident involving Angel at Miss Mary's Preschool on the date complained of herein.

The problem with this request for admission is the ambiguity of the term visual contact. Instead of using legalese, use plain English: To say "admit that you did not see the incident" is more straightforward.

Example 5

5. Admit that on the date complained of herein, around lunch time at Miss Mary's Preschool, the dog, Brutus, belonging to Sally Teacher, was on the playground with the children with your permission when you were not in attendance.

This request for admission addresses several relevant issues pertaining to liability such as whether Miss Mary gave permission to Ms. Teacher to bring her dog onto the playground during a noontime recess where the dog would mingle with the children. It also addresses the issue of whether Mary, as director of Miss Mary's

Preschool, was in attendance during the noontime recess on the day in question. The main problems with this request for admission are misplaced modifiers and several compound, complex ideas presented in one single request for admission. To begin a rewrite of this request: (1) remove the misplaced, dangling modifying clauses, which occurs after the word "children"; and (2) separate the ideas in this request for admission and address them in separate requests. This is illustrated in the following example:

1. Admit that on the date and at the time in question, the dog belonging to Ms. Teacher was on the playground with the children.

2. Admit that on the date and at the time in question, the dog belonging to Ms. Teacher was on the school playground with your knowledge and consent.

3. Admit that you were not present on the playground on the date of the incident at the time the incident occurred.

§ 5.10   Sample Application of Requests for Admissions Law to Fact

The application of law to fact is treated in requests for admissions in common situations including issues of title, ownership, agency, and employment. For example:

Plaintiff, Ralph J., requests defendant, Mary S., to make the following admissions, within 30 days after service of this request, for the purposes of this action only:

Admit that each of the following facts is true:

1. Defendant was the legal title holder of a commercial lot commonly known as [address], [city], [state], on January 28, 19__.
2. On January 28, 19__, Barbara O. was an employee of ABC Corporation.
3. On January 28, 19__, Barbara O. was authorized to enter into any and all sales contracts on behalf of ABC Corporation.
4. On January 28, 19__, Barbara O., on behalf of ABC Corporation, entered into a sales contract with Ralph J. (Exhibit A.)

This request to admit facts can be accompanied by a request to admit genuineness of documents. For example:

Plaintiff, Ralph J., requests that defendant, Mary S., admit within 30 days after service of this request, for the purposes of this action only, that each of the following documents is genuine:

1. A contract, attached as Exhibit "A," is a true and correct copy of the contract signed by plaintiff and defendant on January 28, 19__.

2. The signature which appears at line 33 of the contract of Barbara O. on behalf of ABC Corporation is a true and valid signature.

3. A cashier's check, attached as Exhibit "B," is a true and accurate copy of the cashier's check signed by plaintiff, Ralph J., on January 28, 19__, and made payable to ABC Corporation.

4. The endorsement stamp, a copy of which is attached as Exhibit "C," is a true and accurate copy of the endorsement stamp appearing on the back of the cashier's check (Exhibit "B"), and is a true and accurate copy of the check endorsement stamp of ABC Corporation.

§ 5.11 Sample Requests for Admissions
(Commercial Case)

Requests for admissions are a very effective discovery device in commercial cases such as breach of promissory note, breach of contract, money had and received, and so forth. An effective combination for admissions of genuineness of documents and admissions of facts in the breach of an equipment lease would include:

Requests to admit genuineness of documents of the lease and all contracts, invoices, and billing documents.

The genuineness of the invoices as they relate to the leasing contract should be established. For example, do you admit that the invoice which you received on March 4, 19__ was for the equipment referred to at line 9 of the lease attached as Exhibit "A"?

The genuineness of all letters of warning for failure to pay amounts due. Letters should be accompanied by the certified mail return receipt and combined with a request for admission to verify the signature on the receipt.

Each item of the equipment lease forms the basis of a separate request for admission:

1. Admit that the terms of the lease are set forward in lines 5 through 7 of the document attached as Exhibit "A."

2. Admit that the delivery date of February 4, 19__ stated in line 12 of the attached lease (Exhibit "A") is a true and accurate date.

3. Admit that you received the equipment identified in line 12 of the equipment lease on February 4, 19__.

4. Admit that you received the billing invoice dated March 31, 19__.

Through this use of requests for admissions and genuineness of documents you can establish:

The genuineness of the documents, and the equipment lease;

The authenticity of the signature on the lease;

The certainty of terms regarding rental and description of equipment;

The fact that responding party has received invoices for the rental of that equipment;

The fact that responding party has received warning letters regarding nonpayment of invoices;

The fact that responding party still has the equipment in their possession; and

The fact that responding party has made no effort to pay for his use of the equipment.

Unless responding party intends to assert defenses such as oral modification of the lease, guaranteed free time of use of equipment, or some other setoff, this case should resolve quickly based on admissions and/or denials of the requests.

§ 5.12 Sample Requests for Admissions (Medical Malpractice Case—Plaintiff)

In a standard medical malpractice case, the plaintiff's allegations usually include lack of informed consent, negligence in care and treatment provided by the treating physician, failure to disclose risks of the proposed treatment, failure to consult with a specialist, and abandoning the patient. **Form 5–1** illustrates sample requests for admissions from plaintiff to defendant doctor:

FORM 5–1
SAMPLE MEDICAL MALPRACTICE REQUESTS
FOR ADMISSIONS (PLAINTIFF)

REQUEST NO. 1: Admit that at all times referred to in plaintiff's complaint on file herein, defendant [name of doctor], lacked that degree of knowledge and skill ordinarily possessed by reputable specialists practicing in the same field, and in the same or similar locality under similar circumstances, while caring for plaintiff, [name of patient].

REQUEST NO. 2: Admit that at all times referred to in plaintiff's complaint on file herein, defendant [name of doctor] failed to use and exercise that degree of care and skill ordinarily used and exercised by physicians and surgeons practicing in the same field under similar circumstances in the diagnosis, care, and treatment of plaintiff, [name of patient].

REQUEST NO. 3: Admit that at all times referred to in plaintiff's complaint on file herein, defendant [name of doctor] was required to refer the plaintiff to a specialist, or to recommend the assistance and consultation of a specialist, while participating in the diagnosis, care, and treatment of plaintiff, [name of patient].

REQUEST NO. 4: Admit that at all times referred to in plaintiff's complaint on file herein, defendant [name of doctor] abandoned plaintiff during the duration of the doctor's responsibility to provide care and treatment for plaintiff, [name of patient].

REQUEST NO. 5: Admit that at all times referred to in plaintiff's complaint on file herein, defendant [name of doctor] failed to fully advise plaintiff [name of patient] of each and every medical risk associated with the care and treatment provided by defendant.

REQUEST NO. 6: Admit that at all times referred to in plaintiff's complaint on file herein, defendant [name of doctor] failed to make reasonable disclosure to [name of patient] of all facts necessary to form the basis of an intelligent and informed consent to the treatment, care and attention provided to him by defendant.

REQUEST NO. 7: Admit that at all times referred to in plaintiff's complaint on file herein defendant [name of doctor] failed to disclose to plaintiff the exact nature and extent of [plaintiff]'s medical condition, or the risks of the proposed treatment of [name specific treatment, surgery, and so forth].

REQUEST NO. 8: Admit that at all times referred to in plaintiff's complaint herein defendant [name of doctor] failed to disclose to [name of plaintiff] the exact and specific nature of all risks associated with the surgery performed by defendant doctor on [date].

§ 5.13   Sample Requests for Admissions
(Medical Malpractice Case—Defendant)

In the same case, the defendant's requests for admissions, based on their pleadings, would seek to establish the exact opposite. **Form 5–2** is an example of the defendant's requests for admissions.

FORM 5–2
SAMPLE MEDICAL MALPRACTICE REQUESTS FOR ADMISSIONS
(DEFENDANT)

REQUEST NO. 1: Admit that at all times referred to in plaintiff's complaint on file herein defendant [name of doctor] possessed and had that degree of knowledge and skill ordinarily possessed by reputable specialists practicing in the same field and in the same or similar locality under similar circumstances while caring for the plaintiff [name of patient].

REQUEST NO. 2: Admit that at all times referred to in plaintiff's complaint referred to herein defendant [name of doctor] used and exercised that degree of care and skill ordinarily used and exercised by reputable physicians and surgeons practicing in the same field under similar circumstances in the diagnosis, care, and treatment of plaintiff [name of patient].

REQUEST NO. 3: Admit that at all times referred to in plaintiff's complaint on file herein defendant [name of doctor] was not required to refer the plaintiff to a specialist or to recommend the assistance of a specialist while participating in the diagnosis, care, and treatment of plaintiff [name of patient].

REQUEST NO. 4: Admit that at all times referred to in plaintiff's complaint on file herein defendant [name of doctor] did not abandon plaintiff during the duration of [name of doctor]'s responsibility to care and treat [name of patient].

REQUEST NO. 5: Admit that at all times referred to in plaintiff's complaint on file herein defendant [name of doctor] obtained the consent of [name of plaintiff] before treating or operating on the doctor's patient.

REQUEST NO. 6: Admit that at all times referred to in plaintiff's complaint on file herein the defendant [name of doctor] fully advised plaintiff [name of patient] of each and every medical risk associated with the care and treatment that defendant provided to patient.

REQUEST NO. 7: Admit that at all times referred to in plaintiff's complaint on file herein, defendant [name of doctor] made all reasonable disclosures to plaintiff [name of patient] of all facts necessary to allow plaintiff [name of patient] to form the basis of an intelligent and informed consent to the treatment, care, and attention provided to [plaintiff] by defendant [name of doctor].

REQUEST NO. 8: Admit that at all times referred to in plaintiff's complaint on file herein, [plaintiff] consented to the treatment, care, and attention that defendant [name of doctor] provided.

§ 5.14 Sample Requests for Admissions (Discovery Responses)

Requests for admissions as part of an overall discovery plan can be propounded based on discovery responses and documents produced in the course of discovery. For example, in a case when plaintiff alleges causes of action for negligence and negligent selection and retention of staff on a cruise ship, hotel, or child care center stemming from injuries which occurred to plaintiff while on the premises of the cruise ship, hotel, or at the child care center would most likely generate depositions, interrogatories, and requests to produce certain documents. The documents pertinent to the above causes of action would include copies of hiring policies, employee evaluation sheets, schedule of employee evaluations, personnel files, and disciplinary memoranda pertaining to that particular employee thought to be responsible for the injuries. If defendant produced such documents, a follow-up set of requests for admissions addressing each document might be propounded as follows in **Form 5–3:**

FORM 5–3
SAMPLE REQUESTS FOR ADMISSIONS
(DISCOVERY RESPONSES)

REQUEST FOR ADMISSION NO. 1: John S. was an employee of [name] Cruises, Inc. from December 16, 19__ to August 10, 19__.

REQUEST FOR ADMISSION NO. 2: John S. was on board the [name of ship] ship on its cruise from [port] to [port] on August 10, 19__.

REQUEST FOR ADMISSION NO. 3: John S. disembarked on September 10, 19__ for disciplinary reasons.

REQUEST FOR ADMISSION NO. 4: A performance appraisal for John S. was done on August 10, 19__.

REQUEST FOR ADMISSION NO. 5: John S. was rated "unsatisfactory" in "judgment" in the performance appraisal of August 10, 19__.

REQUEST FOR ADMISSION NO. 6: John S. was rated "unsatisfactory" in "enthusiasm" in the performance appraisal of August 10, 19__.

REQUEST FOR ADMISSION NO. 7: John S. was rated "unsatisfactory" in "flexibility" in the performance appraisal of August 10, 19__.

REQUEST FOR ADMISSION NO. 8: John S. was rated "unsatisfactory" in "contact with others" in the performance appraisal of August 10, 19__.

REQUEST FOR ADMISSION NO. 9: John S. was rated "unsatisfactory" in "adherence to company policy and procedures" in the performance appraisal of August 10, 19__.

REQUEST FOR ADMISSION NO. 10: John S. was rated "unsatisfactory" in "absence" in the performance appraisal of August 10, 19__.

REQUEST FOR ADMISSION NO. 11: John S. was rated "unsatisfactory" in "personal integrity" in the performance appraisal of August 10, 19__.

REQUEST FOR ADMISSION NO. 12: On July 31, 19__, John S. was provided with verbal employee counseling.

REQUEST FOR ADMISSION NO. 13: The reason for verbal employee counseling with John S. on July 31, 19__ was for his not complying with duties over and over, and repeatedly being warned of unsatisfactory results on his next performance evaluation.

REQUEST FOR ADMISSION NO. 14: Subsequent to August 10, 19__, John S. was "on report."

REQUEST FOR ADMISSION NO. 15: "On report" in the terminology of [name] Cruise Lines means that an employee has been place on probationary status.

These requests for admissions based on documents received relating to employee disciplinary memorandums and performance evaluations would be difficult for a defendant to deny, because the documents from which these requests for admissions are based were in defendant's possession and control and were produced in accordance with a request to produce documents in discovery. These requests for admissions should be combined with requests to admit genuineness of documents and a separate request to admit genuineness for each performance evaluation referred to in the requests. The effect of admissions by the defendant will not only further plaintiff's allegation of negligent selection and retention of an employee but also will establish that defendant employer had evaluated the employee and found him to be lacking in many key areas to the extent that he had been placed on probation prior to the date that he caused injury to plaintiff.

§ 5.15   Sample Requests for Admissions
(Interrogatory Follow-Up)

Requests for admissions of fact served after interrogatory responses have been received are most successful when they zero in on specific interrogatory answers relating to the liability claims. The following sample (**Form 5–4**) was used in a product liability case against a major automobile manufacturer. In responding to interrogatories, the defendant volunteered information which limited the defense of the action. This influenced the plaintiff's trial preparation by limiting investigation and discovery in those areas which defendants had voluntarily stated would not be part of their defense of the lawsuit. In order to protect the plaintiffs and prevent defendant from introducing evidence at the time of trial regarding the very issues they had stated would not be part of their defense, plaintiff propounded the following requests for admissions of fact:

FORM 5–4
SAMPLE REQUESTS FOR ADMISSIONS
(INTERROGATORY FOLLOW-UP)

[attorney for plaintiff]
[address]
[telephone number]

Attorneys for Plaintiff
[plaintiff name]

IN THE SUPERIOR COURT OF THE STATE OF [state name]
IN AND FOR THE COUNTY OF [county name]

[name], Plaintiff, vs. [defendant], et al. _____/	No. [case number] REQUEST FOR ADMISSIONS OF FACT

PROPOUNDING PARTY: Plaintiff, [name]

RESPONDING PARTY: Defendant, [name]

SET NUMBER: [reference to set number]

YOU ARE HEREBY REQUESTED to admit the truthfulness of each of the facts set forth below.

REQUEST NO. 1:
Admit the truth of the statement made by defendant in response to plaintiff's specially prepared Interrogatory no. 7 that "[Defendant] will not defend this lawsuit by claiming that technical feasibility or cost considerations prevented it from including a brake transaxle in the 1992 vehicle.

REQUEST NO. 2:
Admit the truth of the statement given in response to plaintiff's first request for identification and production of documents no. 8, "the lack of technical feasibility was not the reason [defendant] did not incorporate a brake transaxle in the 1992 vehicle.

REQUEST NO. 3:
Admit the truth of the statement given in response to plaintiff's first request for production of documents no. 8 that, "likewise neither cost or possible adverse consequences were the reason [defendant] did not incorporate a brake transaxle in the 1992 vehicle."

Dated [date]

[attorney for plaintiff]

_____

§ 5.16   Declaration for Additional Discovery

When a party in an action propounds more than the allowable number of requests for admissions of fact, the party must file a Declaration for Additional Discovery to accompany the request. (This is similar to a Declaration for Additional Discovery needed for interrogatories discussed in **Chapter 4.**) Several districts of the federal court such as the Central, Southern, and Northern also require a Declaration for Additional Discovery when the number of requests for admissions of fact exceeds 35. California, and many other states, also require an attorney declaration which states facts supporting the need for additional discovery. The grounds demonstrating good cause for additional discovery in **Chapter 4** for interrogatories are almost the same as those needed in a Declaration for Additional Discovery for admissions of fact.

The purpose of requests for admissions is to limit triable issues and promote settlement. The focus of requests for admissions of facts is each element of plaintiff's cause of action or defendant's affirmative defenses. Requests for admissions of facts should relate only to liability issues. A Declaration for Additional Discovery (see **Form 5–5**) is needed when you are propounding additional requests for admission of fact, but it is not needed (in most states and federal court districts) if you are seeking to have documents admitted as genuine. A request for admission seeking to establish genuineness of documents may contain an unlimited number of separately itemized requests as long as they are relevant and not "burdensome, harassing, and duplicative of prior discovery." Remember, when propounding a request for admission seeking genuineness of documents to always attach the document as an exhibit. Failure to attach the documents to your request makes it, "vague, ambiguous, and unintelligible", and leaves room for responding party to object claiming uncertainty because the document referenced is not attached to the request.

FORM 5–5
SAMPLE DECLARATION FOR ADDITIONAL DISCOVERY
(CALIFORNIA)

[attorney for plaintiff]
[address]
[telephone number]

Attorneys for Plaintiff
[plaintiff name]

IN THE SUPERIOR COURT OF THE STATE OF CALIFORNIA
IN THE CITY AND COUNTY OF [county name]

[name],	Case No.
Plaintiff,	DECLARATION OF [attorney for plaintiff] FOR ADDITIONAL DISCOVERY

vs.

[name] SHOPPING MALL, A
LIMITED PARTNERSHIP,
[defendant A] and [defendant B],
as limited partners of
[name] SHOPPING MALL,
[defendant C], individually
and (dba) [company D],
and (dba) [company E],
and DOES 1 through 30,
inclusive,

    Defendants.
_____/

I, [attorney for plaintiff], declare:

1. I am the attorney for plaintiff herein.

2. I am propounding to defendant [name] SHOPPING MALL the attached set of requests for admission of fact.

3. This set of requests for admissions of fact will cause the total number of requests for admissions of fact propounded to the responding parties to exceed the number of requests permitted by paragraph (1) of subdivision (c) of § 2033 of the Code of Civil Procedure.

4. This is our first set of requests for admissions of fact.

5. This set of requests for admissions of fact contains a total of 38 requests.

6. I am familiar with the issues in this case.

7. I have personally examined each of the requests for admissions of fact.

8. This number of requests for admissions of fact is warranted under paragraph (2) of subdivision (c) of § 2033 of the Code of Civil Procedure because of the complex nature of the litigation involving multiple building structures which requires plaintiff to seek discovery in excess of the statutory number of 35 requests for admission.

9. None of the requests in this set of requests for admission of fact is being propounded for any improper purpose, such as to harass the parties, or the attorney for the parties, to whom it is directed, or to cause unnecessary delay or needless increase in the cost of litigation.

I declare under the penalty of perjury under the laws of California that the foregoing is true and correct.

Executed this [date] day of [month], [year], at [city], [state].

[attorney for plaintiff]

---

§ 5.17   Combining Requests for
Admissions with Interrogatories

A discovery practice of combining requests for admissions with interrogatories in one document is very effective in getting detailed information behind denials and qualified responses. This procedure is, however, no longer allowed by statute and case law in many states. The reasoning behind the case law which disallowed the combination of requests for admissions and interrogatories was that it not only placed an unfair burden upon the responding party but also was confusing in terms of time limits for responses because a request for admission time limit was shorter than an interrogatory response time limit. The combination of interrogatories and requests in a single document is the crux of the problem. The combination can still be effective through using two separate discovery documents which are served simultaneously. The purpose of following up requests for admissions with interrogatories is to obtain information behind those responses which admit part and deny part of a request and those requests for admissions which are denied. California Code of Civil Procedure § 2033(c)(7) states that requests for admissions must be set forth in a *separate* document, and may not be combined with interrogatories or any other discovery.

Prior to this statute, it was a common discovery technique to combine requests for admissions and interrogatories in the same document. This was done so that if a request for admission was denied, the interrogatories would force the responding party to disclose the facts, witnesses, and documents upon which their denial was based. While this technique was a helpful discovery tool, it was often a trap for the unwary and confusing to the responding party.

If you have propounded a judicial council set of form interrogatories and a set of requests for admissions, this is accomplished by simply checking the question on the form which states:

Is your response to each request for admission served with these interrogatories an unqualified admission? If not, for each response that is not an unqualified admission:

(a) State all facts upon which you base your response.

(b) State the names, addresses, and telephone numbers of all persons who have knowledge of those facts.

(c) Identify all writings and other tangible things that support the response and state the name, address, and telephone number of the person who has the custody of each writing or thing.

The request for admissions, which is served concurrently with the set of form interrogatories, should then include an introductory paragraph which states as follows:

Plaintiff's attention is directed to that certain set of form interrogatories served contemporaneously with this set of requests for admissions, specifically question number (refer to number on form set of interrogatories) which directs responding party to respond with particularity and additional information to all those requests for admissions which have not been expressly admitted.

If you have not propounded a judicial council form set of interrogatories, but have propounded instead a set of specially prepared interrogatories, you may propound and serve contemporaneously with those interrogatories a set of requests for admissions. The method then of combining the two documents is to propound an additional interrogatory stating:

If you did not admit all of the matters stated in Request Nos. 1 through 10 of Plaintiff's First Set of Requests for Admissions served concurrently with Plaintiff's First Set of Interrogatories, please state for each such request:

(a) Each fact on which you based your denial of that numbered request.

(b) The identity of each person having knowledge of each fact stated in your response to each numbered request.

(c) A description of each document that supports the facts stated in each numbered request.

(d) The name, address, and phone number of each person having custody of all documents referred to in subsections (a) through (c) of this response.

Combining interrogatories with requests for admissions is a powerful discovery tool because it ties up loose ends and allows you to obtain more information than you will receive from simple responses to requests for admissions. Although requests for admissions have as their main purpose eliminating matters that are not in controversy and narrowing issues for trial, using them in tandem with interrogatories broadens their scope allowing propounding party access to information that would otherwise not be available through a simple response of "denial" to a request for admissions.

§ 5.18   Responding to Requests for Admissions

A party on whom requests for admissions have been served must respond under oath within 30 days of receiving the requests (unless an extension of time has been granted), or the matters in the request will be deemed admitted. These admissions are then treated as stipulations to the truthfulness of the matters set forth in the requests. They are binding and conclusive to the issue, and no other evidence is necessary to establish that point at trial. The evidentiary effect of requests for admissions which are "deemed admitted" is that the subject matter addressed in the request for admission is no longer considered a triable issue. Whether you intended to admit or deny the request for admission is no longer important. What is important is that by inattention, an important deadline has been allowed to expire and the result has been an automatic binding admission in favor of the propounding party. The automatic deemed admission portion of Federal Rule of Civil Procedure 36 makes requests for admissions a formidable weapon because inattentiveness on the part of the responding party can have an automatic and usually devastating consequence. Relief is possible from deemed admissions, however, it is a cumbersome and costly court process to seek this relief. There must be a good cause showing to the court demonstrating the compelling reasons why you did not respond in a timely fashion. Simply stating that the secretary forgot to calendar the date, or the client was on vacation and failed to return the proposed answers to your office in a timely fashion, is not sufficient. To avoid falling into the trap of deemed admissions, requests for admissions should be reviewed as soon as they come in to your office and sent to the client as soon as possible for his responses. A date to respond to the requests for admissions should be calendared, with a tickler date at least 10 days in advance of that due date. If an extension is needed, it must be sought promptly to protect your client's rights.

In responding to requests for admissions (see **Form 5–6**), five basic responses are permitted:

1.   You can object to a matter in the request, in which case you must state the reasons for the objection, which may include privilege.

2.   You may admit the matter. A responding party should admit whatever they do not in good faith intend to contest at trial.

3.   You can deny the matter. You may also admit part of a request for admission, and deny the second part of the same request.

4.   You may state that you cannot admit or deny the matter because the matter is genuinely in dispute, or because even after reasonable inquiry you do not have sufficient information to determine if the matter is true or not. In this instance, you must set forth the reasons which must include a detailed description of the efforts made to obtain the information necessary to frame a response.

5.   You may move for a protective order. Be certain you have substantial basis for each denial of a request for admission. If a responding party denies a fact in a request for admission without a substantial basis or knowledge upon which to base that denial, and that fact is later proved at trial, the party proving the fact can receive court costs for the reasonable expense of providing the denied fact at trial, including attorney's fees. Additionally, sanctions are available under Rule 37 of the Federal Rules of Civil Procedure for facts which are proved to be genuine at time of trial but were denied when requests for admissions regarding those same facts were propounded to the adverse party.

Objections have the effect of denials, qualified denials. Rule 36 states:

A denial shall fairly meet the substance of the requested admission, and when good faith requires that a party qualify his answer or deny only a part of the matter of which an admission is requested, he shall so specify so much of it as is true and qualify or deny the remainder.

The more specific and clearly drafted the request for admissions, the more difficult it is for the responding party to avoid making the admissions desired by the propounder. The burden is on the propounder of the request for admission to be accurate and specific. An objection can be raised stating that the request is ambiguous and unintelligible and cannot be answered in the form in which it is phrased.

Admissions must be as complete and straightforward as the information available to the responding party permits. The responding party is also under a duty to make a reasonable inquiry to obtain the information necessary to prepare a response. Requests for admissions served upon a corporation or public entity must be responded to by an officer of the corporation, or the director of the public entity who is in a position to bind the entity to the responses. The responding party for a corporation or public entity must respond not only with that knowledge which is their personal knowledge, but with the knowledge of the corporation, its agents, employees, and representatives.

Answers to individual requests for admissions may be partial or qualified in that they may admit the part that the responding party concedes is true, while denying the rest. They may also admit the truth "as reasonably and clearly qualified." For example, the responding party may restate the fact in slightly different terms than those used in the request. A request for admissions is always expressed in the language of one's opponent and supplies the wording for admitting the matter it covers. A responding party does not have to accept the wording of the request, and may choose to rephrase the request in a clear and reasonable manner that is more helpful or less damaging to your client. Example:

REQUEST FOR ADMISSION: Admit that as a result of the injuries plaintiff received in the accident which is the subject of this litigation, plaintiff missed time from his regular employment, a crossing guard for the City of [city name].

RESPONSE: Defendant admits that plaintiff received injuries in the accident which is the subject of this litigation, and further admits that plaintiff was off work for some period of time, but cannot either admit or deny that plaintiff missed time from work as a direct result of the injuries received in the subject accident.

Admissions may be made based on information and belief. For example, "I am informed and believe that the matter stated in Request No. 3 is true." This type of admission has the same effect as a direct admission. It is useful when the responding party lacks personal knowledge of the matters referred to in the request, and is basing the admission on hearsay or third-party information.

A responding party may answer all or part of a request for admission by stating that they have made a reasonable inquiry concerning the facts, or opinions, or other matters stated in the request, and that the information which is known or readily available to them is insufficient to enable them to either admit or deny the request. When this type of response is used, the responding party should state specifically the nature of his reasonable inquiry. For example:

<u>REQUEST FOR ADMISSION:</u> Admit that on May 1, 19__ Mary S. and Barbara B. entered into a written contract.

<u>RESPONSE:</u> Responding party lacks sufficient information or knowledge to admit that Mary S. and Barbara B. entered into a contract. Responding party has looked at the files of [name] Company under their names and found no document that purports to be an agreement between them. Responding party has never heard them exchange words which might amount to a contract or express the intent or desire to enter into a contract. Responding party has made a reasonable inquiry concerning this matter, and the information known to them or readily available to them is insufficient to enable them to either admit or deny the matters stated in this request.

This type of a response fulfills the duty of the responding party to go beyond direct personal knowledge and make a reasonable inquiry. Propounding party cannot compel the responding party to hire investigators or to bear the expense of preparing the case. In this particular example, the best evidence of the existence of a contract would be the document itself. Propounding party could request an admission as to the genuineness of documents and attach a copy of the contract.

FORM 5–6
SAMPLE REQUEST FOR ADMISSIONS RESPONSE FORM

SUPERIOR COURT OF THE STATE OF [state name]
COUNTY OF [county name]

[name], et al.,	Case No. [case number]
Plaintiff(s),	RESPONSE FOR REQUEST FOR ADMISSIONS
-vs-	
[name], et al.,	
Defendant(s).	

PROPOUNDING PARTY: Defendant, [name]

RESPONDING PARTY: Plaintiff, [name]

SET NUMBER: [set number]

INTRODUCTION

Since discovery, pretrial preparation and investigation are continuing, plaintiff is unable to fully and completely answer all of the requests for admissions propounded by defendant and, therefore, reserves the right to supplement or amend said answers prior to or during trial. All responses are based upon such information and documents that are presently available.

Plaintiff also generally objects to each and every request for admission to the extent that it requests information privileged under the attorney-client and/or work product doctrine. Partial responses to any request for admission, including the disclosure of any information which might be privileged, is not intended as a waiver of any other item of information.

These responses are given without prejudice to plaintiff's right to produce evidence of any subsequently discovered facts. Plaintiff accordingly reserves the right, upon request, to change any and all responses as additional facts are ascertained and analyses are made. Responses contained herein are made in a good faith effort to supply factual information and legal contentions as required, and further to confirm that a diligent search has been made to locate documents and materials which would enable plaintiff to make a full and complete response to each request.

Plaintiff, therefore, responds to the request for admissions served upon her by defendant on [date] as follows:

RESPONSE TO REQUEST NO. 1: [Specify the response; either express admission or denial, for example, plaintiff denies the genuineness of the document, a copy of which is attached.]

RESPONSE TO REQUEST NO. 2: Plaintiff denies the truth of the matter set forth in this request [state specifically the matter which is being denied, for example, that plaintiff was the registered owner of the vehicle described in this request].

RESPONSE TO REQUEST NO. 3: (Use this response if you are admitting in part and denying in part.) Plaintiff admits that [specify which part of the request you are admitting], but denies that [specify the part of the request which you are denying].

RESPONSE TO REQUEST NO. 4: (Use this response if you can neither admit nor deny the facts stated in the request for admission.) Plaintiff cannot truthfully admit or deny the matters set forth in this request because neither plaintiff nor plaintiff's employees, agents, attorneys, nor plaintiff's attorneys' agents or employees have any knowledge of these matters, nor have they been able, despite making a reasonable and diligent inquiry into the matter by [specify efforts made to obtain information from which the truth or falsity of the matter might have been learned] to ascertain the truth or falsity of the matters referred to in this request.

RESPONSE TO REQUEST NO. 5: Plaintiff objects to this request on the grounds that the subject matter of this request is not relevant to the subject matter of this action, nor reasonably calculated to lead to admissible evidence in that [specify why the subject matter of the request is irrelevant, or a particular privilege claim is being made, or the request is ambiguous, unintelligible].

§ 5.19 Extensions of Time

A response to a request for admissions is due 30 days after service. Local rules should be checked for additional time if service was made by mail. If responses cannot be prepared within the time provided by local rules, immediately seek an extension of time within which to submit responses. If there is no agreement from the propounding party allowing the responding party an extension of time, the responding party may still seek an extension of time through a motion to the court for an order granting more time (**Form 5–9**). A motion for extension of time in which to respond must be made before the time for answering the original requests for admissions expires. Usually the procedure for obtaining this extension is an application for an ex parte order.

Form 5–7 is an example of a letter confirming an agreed upon extension of time with the other party's attorney.

FORM 5–7
SAMPLE LETTER CONFIRMING EXTENSION OF TIME

[attorney name]
[law firm]
[address]

     RE: [plaintiff] v. [defendant]

Dear [attorney name]:

This will confirm my conversation today with your secretary, [name], at which time you granted this office a two-week extension within which to respond to the first set of requests for admissions propounded by defendant, [name] Company, to plaintiff. The due date for plaintiff's responses is now [date].

Enclosed with this letter is a form stipulation which I have prepared confirming the extension. Please execute the stipulation and return it to our office, and we will file the same with the court.

Your courtesy and cooperation in stipulating to this extension of time is greatly appreciated.

     Sincerely,

     [name]
     Legal Assistant to
     [name of attorney]

Enclosure

The enclosure is the following stipulation (**Form 5–8**), which may or may not be filed with the court depending on local rules. In the event it is not necessary to file such a stipulation with the court, prepare the stipulation and have it executed by opposing counsel, keeping the original in your files for use at time of trial should there be a question regarding timeliness of responses.

FORM 5–8
SAMPLE STIPULATION EXTENDING TIME

SUPERIOR COURT OF THE STATE OF [state name]
IN AND FOR THE COUNTY OF [county name]

[name], et al.,   No. [case number]

    Plaintiff(s),   STIPULATION EXTENDING
                                         TIME TO RESPOND TO
-vs-   REQUESTS FOR ADMISSIONS

[name], et al.,

    Defendant(s).

The undersigned attorneys agree, on behalf of [propounding party] and [responding party] that plaintiff shall have until [date] to respond to defendant's first set of requests for admissions.

Date: [date]

                              [attorney for plaintiff]

_____

Date: [date]

                              [attorney for defendant]

_____

A variable to this stipulation might include the terms of the agreed upon extension, such as "plaintiff may have an extension of time within which to respond to certain requests for admissions, as numbers 1, 2, 3, and the balance of the set of requests for admissions is still due on the original due date." Other modifications might include the fact that defendant has only granted this stipulation for time to respond based on the fact that plaintiff will either admit or deny, but not object to the requests.

FORM 5–9
SAMPLE APPLICATION FOR COURT ORDER EXTENDING TIME

SUPERIOR COURT OF THE STATE OF [state name]
IN AND FOR THE COUNTY OF [county name]

[name], et al.,   No. [case number]

    Plaintiff(s),   APPLICATION FOR ORDER
                                EXTENDING TIME TO RESPOND

-vs-   TO REQUESTS FOR ADMISSIONS

[name], et al.,

    Defendant(s).

[attorney for plaintiff] declares:

1. I am an attorney for plaintiff, [name], the responding party.

2. Defendant, the requesting party, served a First Set of Requests for Admissions on the responding party on [date].

3. The responding party cannot answer this First Set of Requests for Admissions before [date] because [statement of specific reasons for postponement such as the illness of either the responding party or the attorney, the attorney's trial schedule causing her to be out of town for an extended period of time, the necessity of ordering records from storage for a search, and so forth].

4. [Statement that "postponing the responses to this later date will not inconvenience the requesting party in that no procedures to which such responses would be relevant are scheduled in this case until _____, 19___," or any additional statements demonstrating that the postponement of these responses will not inconvenience the requesting party.]

5. I have notified [name], the attorney of record for the requesting party, of the time and place that this application would be made to the court.

6. [Name], defendant's attorney, has declined to agree to this extension of time, but has told me that [name] does not object to the seeking of this order by ex parte application and will not be sending the court a declaration in opposition to it.

I declare under penalty of perjury under the laws of the State of [state name] that the foregoing is true and correct, and that this declaration was executed on [date].

                       [attorney for plaintiff]

                 _____

Note: For Item Number 5, be sure to check local rules. In many instances the formal requirements of notice and a noticed motion must be met. In other jurisdictions this application for an ex parte order to extend the time to respond to requests for admissions is the proper procedure. Given the choice, an application for an ex parte order with notification to opposing counsel by telephone of the time set for the ruling of the ex parte order is more expedient. For Item Number 6, if there is opposition, an ex parte order will not be granted and a hearing will be necessary.

§ 5.20   Response Verification

Responses to requests for admissions of facts and requests to admit genuineness of documents must not only be verified under oath but also signed by the person making those responses and having knowledge of the facts contained in those responses. Unverified responses to requests for admissions and requests for genuineness of documents are treated as express admissions. The importance of a verification in responding to requests for admissions and requests for genuineness of documents cannot be stressed enough. It is a serious matter to submit unverified responses. Unverified interrogatory responses merely mean that the responding party has waived their right to object to certain interrogatories. The responding party in interrogatories may supplement their answers and may even, under certain circumstances, apply for relief from the waiver of privilege or right to make objections to certain interrogatories. Unverified responses to requests for admissions, however, are treated as binding admissions. Relief is possible through a notice of motion for leave to withdraw or amend responses to requests for admissions; however, this costs attorney and client time and money and is not always successful.

A verification form (**Form 5–10**) should be sent to the client along with the request for admissions as soon as they are received in your office. The client should be requested to sign, but not date the verification form, and return it along with the client's draft responses. When responses have been finalized, a copy should be sent to the client for the client's records.

FORM 5–10
SAMPLE VERIFICATION FORM

I, [name], am the president of defendant, [name] Corporation, in the above-entitled action. I have read the foregoing responses, which are true of my own knowledge, except as to those matters which are stated on information and belief, and as to those matters, I believe them to be true.

I declare under penalty of perjury under the laws of the State of [state name] that the foregoing is true and correct.

Executed on [date] at [location].

_____

[name], President
[name] Corporation

§ 5.21 Objecting to Requests for Admissions

Objections can be made to individual requests for admission or individual requests to admit the genuineness of a document by clearly setting forth the specific grounds for objecting to either all or part of each admission. Should the objection only address one part of a request for admission, the other part of the request for admission must be answered. It may be answered by an express admission, a denial, or a statement of lack of information. Objections may be made to any request which seeks admissions regarding facts that are in dispute, seeks information regarding privileged matters, or is deemed to be irrelevant to the subject matter at hand.

Objections to requests to admit the genuineness of documents may be made if the propounding party has failed to attach a copy of the document which they are seeking to have admitted as genuine, or if the responding party has attached an unclear photocopy or annotated copy of the document they are seeking to have admitted as genuine. Documents which are attached to requests to admit genuineness of documents should be the original document if it is in the custody of the propounding party, or a clean, unannotated, and clear photocopy of the document. Objections may also be made by the responding party to a request to admit the genuineness of a document if the party is not the author of that document, or for some other reason is unfamiliar with the document and unable to authenticate its genuineness.

Specific objections to requests for admissions are similar to those specific objections which may be raised at depositions and in responses to interrogatories. The strategy of raising objections in all discovery proceedings is to shift from a defensive position of responding to discovery to an offensive position of objecting to discovery, thereby forcing the propounding party to resume a defensive position and defend the relevance of the specific request. If the propounding party wishes an answer to the request for admission that the party has propounded, after an objection has been raised by the responding party, the party must take the initiative to seek further answers through a motion to compel.

Objections are generally always raised "for the record" even if they are withdrawn later in the discovery proceedings. It is important that objections are raised in a timely fashion so that they are not waived. Objections may always be withdrawn and supplemental answers provided as discovery progresses in an action. However, objections which are not raised in a timely fashion may not be raised later in the discovery proceedings after the statutory time within which to raise them has expired.

§ 5.22 Sample Objections to Requests for Admissions

This section discusses and evaluates many of the types of objections raised against requests for admissions.

Relevancy objections. The responding party may object to a request on the grounds that the admission seeks irrelevant material. Discovery through requests for admissions must be within the scope of discovery permitted by statute which permits a party to obtain discovery regarding any matter relevant to the subject matter involved in the pending action. Relevancy objections are difficult to substantiate given Federal Rules of Civil Procedure ground rules of broad-based discovery which require that requests for admissions be relevant only to the subject matter involved in the lawsuit, even if they are not directly relevant to the issues. Form language for stating a relevancy objection is as follows:

Plaintiff objects to Request No. 7 based on the fact that the statement in this request has no relation to the subject of the lawsuit; further, an admission or denial of the statement would neither prove nor disprove any matter of consequence in this action, nor lead to admissible evidence.

This form objection may be amended to object to admitting genuineness of a document as follows:

Plaintiff objects to Request for Genuineness of Documents No. 3 in that the document attached has no relation to the subject matter of this lawsuit. Whether the document is genuine would neither prove nor disprove any matter of consequence in this action.

Privilege objections.   Privilege objections must clearly state the privilege invoked by the responding party. It is not sufficient to claim an objection based only on privilege. A response citing the privilege and indicating the basis for its application to the request for admission is the proper form. Form objections based on privileges include the following:

Plaintiff objects to Request No. 1 and claims the attorney-client privilege. Admitting or denying this request would require plaintiff to disclose the contents of confidential conversations with the client's former attorney.

The attorney-client privilege is partially based upon the client's need for confidentiality and also upon the attorney's need for full disclosure of all information from the client in order to prepare an action for trial successfully. Communications with a former attorney usually are considered attorney-client communications, and remain privileged even though that attorney is no longer representing the client. There are, of course, exceptions to this rule depending on the nature of the action. For example, in legal malpractice or in actions where the former attorney is a percipient witness, this would not be a valid objection.

Work product privilege.   Objections to individual requests for admissions may assert that the matter or issue of the request is protected work product information. The format of this objection would be:

Plaintiff objects to Request for Admission No. 3 on the basis that the request calls for disclosure of the protected work product of Tom J., my attorney.

The basis of the work product objection is that an attorney has the right to prepare a case for trial, investigating thoroughly the favorable and unfavorable aspects of the case without fear that the information might be disclosed to the other side. The work product privilege also prevents lazy attorneys from taking advantage of more industrious ones. In claiming the work product privilege in a request for admission, explain in a general manner that the information is protected because it seeks the following information:

The identity of consultants;

The identity of nonexpert witnesses whom the attorney intends to call at time of trial;

Information contained in memoranda and notes of attorneys, law clerks, and legal assistants;

Information contained on interoffice memos or research memos;

Information which reflects the thought process of attorneys;

The notes of investigators; or

The notes of attorneys acting in nonlitigation capacity as claims investigators.

Request is unintelligible or ambiguous, and so forth.   Objections are permitted to requests based on the fact that they are ambiguous or unintelligible. Lengthy, complex, and compound requests for admissions such as requests that attempt to cover a variety of matters in a single question may be objectionable. Improper formatting of requests for admissions also leaves an avenue open for objections. Requests for admissions which are formulated as questions rather than declarative statements are frequently objectionable. A request for admission that seeks to uncover new evidence, as well as one that assumes facts that are not in evidence, may also be objectionable. Requests for admissions that have been rendered unintelligible through poor sentence structure, improper grammar, and even typographical errors changing the meaning of the request are also objectionable. A simple typographical error on the date of a contract leaves room for an objection and the responding party may choose to deny the request based on the fact that the date of the contract is wrong. This renders the question ambiguous. If there are several contracts at issue in a particular action all executed on different dates, it becomes extremely important that the wording of the request for admission refer specifically to a contract by its correct date to avoid confusion.

Burdensome, harassing, and oppressive.   This objection may be used in the same manner in which it is used in interrogatories. The responding party must show that the request for admission possesses an unfair burden and that, although the information may indeed be within the possession of the responding party so that an express admission and/or denial is possible, it is burdensome, harassing, and oppressive to force the responding party to go through the procedures necessary to respond to the request. For example:

REQUEST FOR ADMISSION NO. 4: Admit that during the years 19___, 19___ and 19 ___, [name] Corporation increased its profit margin by 75 percent over the years 19___, 19___ and 19___.

The information requested in this request for admission may indeed be relevant and concern itself with a critical three-year time period. It is possible that during these three years in question a new product was marketed by the corporation which was designed by the defendant, or that the defendant was the head of a particular division responsible for an increase in sales or marketing during that three-year time period and has now been unlawfully terminated. However, an objection may still be made to this request based on the fact that it is burdensome, harassing, and oppressive. For example:

RESPONSE TO REQUEST TO ADMISSION NO. 4: Objection. This request is improper because it would require defendant to read more than 30,000 pages of records which are now available only on microfilm, page by page and line by line, in order to admit or deny that these records truly reflect the financial status and profits of [name] Corporation for the years in question.

§ 5.23   Poor Objections

Some objections have been held by the courts to be lacking merit and frivolous. Making objections without merit places the issues open to a motion to compel further responses and possible sanctions. Some objections which have consistently been held to be without merit by the courts are:

1.   The request requires an analysis of complex facts;
2.   The request relates to matters which are in controversy between the parties;
3.   The request calls for an opinion by responding party; and
4.   The propounding party already knows the truth of the matters stated in the request for admission.

Certain requests for admissions are propounded strictly for evidentiary purposes and are used to establish facts necessary to lay a foundation for the admission of relevant evidence at trial. Requests may relate to matters upon which the responding party knows the truth or call for an opinion or an analysis of complex facts. All such requests have been held to be proper in the eyes of the court and objections to them have been held to be improper.

§ 5.24   Sample Requests for Admissions with Responses

REQUEST FOR ADMISSION NO. 1: On February 5, 19__, William S. was an employee of ABC Rental Cars, and was acting in the course and scope of that employment in driving the 19__ Pontiac Firebird on Third Avenue, Anytown, U.S.A.

RESPONSE TO REQUEST FOR ADMISSION NO. 1: Defendant admits that on February 5, 19__ William S. was an employee of ABC Rental Cars; however, defendant denies that William S. was acting in the course and scope of that employment in driving the 19__ Pontiac Firebird on Third Avenue, Anytown, U.S.A. on the date in question.

REQUEST FOR ADMISSION NO. 2: At all times relevant to this action, Mary S. was the sole title holder of a residential piece of property commonly known as 123 Seventh Avenue, Anytown, U.S.A.

RESPONSE TO REQUEST FOR ADMISSION NO. 2: Defendant can neither admit nor deny this request. Public records investigated by defendant neither confirm nor deny the existence of other title holders. The defendant has no access to any documents which could confirm or deny this request.

REQUEST FOR ADMISSION NO. 3: On February 5, 19__, John S. was authorized to enter into sales contracts on behalf of ABC Corporation.

RESPONSE TO REQUEST FOR ADMISSION NO. 3: Objection. Responding to this request would disclose the substance of conversations between John S., an attorney for ABC Corporation, and other individuals at ABC Corporation, which are protected from disclosure by the attorney-client privilege.

REQUEST FOR ADMISSION NO. 4: At certain times relevant to this action, particularly 1985, Barbara S. occupied certain real property commonly known as 123 Seventh Avenue, Anytown, U.S.A.

RESPONSE TO REQUEST FOR ADMISSION NO. 4: Barbara S. admits the facts stated in this request for admissions with the following qualifications: During the year 1985, Barbara S. did occupy that property, but only for the months of January, February, and March. Barbara S. denies occupying the property from April through December, 1985.

It is possible that Barbara S. occupied this property at other times than during the year 1985. However, in responding Miss S. is under no duty or obligation to furnish the dates or times of other occupancy. She merely needs to respond specific to the time frame of the request for admission, 1985. If propounding party wishes to discover the other dates that Miss S. may have occupied the property, the proper discovery device to use is an interrogatory. If, on the other hand, in prior discovery, such as depositions and interrogatories, propounding party has narrowed the critical time frame to 1985, this is a useful request for admission and will provide the information needed by propounding party.

§ 5.25   Use of Responses in Summary Judgment Motions

Look at Request for Admission No. 1 and the response in § **5.24.** ABC Rental Cars, having denied that William S. was acting in the course and scope of his employment at the time that he was driving the Pontiac Firebird on February 5, 19__, might well use that admission along with other carefully drafted requests for admission to support a motion for summary judgment. Assuming that William S., while driving this specific Pontiac Firebird, was involved in a motor vehicle accident. In this accident, plaintiff alleged that William S. entered a busy intersection failing to stop at a stop-light, thus causing the collision with plaintiff's vehicle. Plaintiff suffered serious injuries from this accident and is seeking reimbursement. ABC Rental Cars was named as a defendant, along with William S., based on the fact that William S. was employed at the time of the accident by ABC Rental Cars, and that the accident happened on a Wednesday afternoon during work hours. William S. would reasonably have been expected to be performing job-related responsibilities for ABC Rental Cars and acting within the course and scope of his employment at the time of the accident. In order for ABC Rental Cars to succeed in a motion for summary judgment, they must prove the following facts:

1. The Pontiac Firebird was registered to William S., and not to ABC Rental Cars;

2. William S. was driving the Pontiac Firebird on a personal errand, and not on company business; and

3. No one at ABC Rental Cars had asked William S. to do any errands, or perform any tasks which would have required him to be driving on February 5, 19__ along Third Avenue at the time of the accident.

It is permissible under statute for defendant ABC Rental Cars to propound requests for admissions to William S., who is also a defendant. Any party may propound requests for admissions to any other party in an action including coplaintiffs and codefendants. A sample set of requests for admissions which ABC Rental Cars would need to propound to William S. to establish the essential facts cited above and proceed with a motion for summary judgment would include:

REQUEST FOR ADMISSION NO. 1: Admit that at all times relevant to this action, you were the registered owner of the vehicle in question, a 19__ Pontiac Firebird.

REQUEST FOR ADMISSION NO. 2: Admit that on February 5, 19__, you left the office of ABC Rental Cars at 1:00 p.m. signing out for the day for a medical appointment.

REQUEST FOR ADMISSION NO. 3: Admit that on February 5, 19__ you were driving your Pontiac Firebird on Third Avenue on a personal errand.

REQUEST FOR ADMISSION NO. 4: Admit that on February 5, 19__, you had a 1:30 appointment with Dr. Paul B., whose office is located at 1846 Third Avenue, Anytown, U.S.A.

REQUEST FOR ADMISSION NO. 5: Admit that you had not been asked by any agent or employee of ABC Rental Cars to perform any job-related task on February 5, 19__ at the time of the accident.

Based on responses to these requests, ABC Rental Cars can make a motion for summary judgment stating that there are no substantial facts constituting a cause of action against defendant ABC Rental Cars, because these admissions have established that at the time of the accident William S. was not acting within the course and scope of his employment, that he was driving a car which he owned, and was on a personal errand, a doctor's appointment.

§ 5.26   Withdrawal and Amendment of Responses

Federal Rule of Civil Procedure 36 grants the court the power to convert an untimely response to a timely response by retroactively extending the time limit, and also allows untimely answers to be considered "amendments" to admissions. Rule 36(b) allows a party to "withdraw admissions and amend answers." A responding party who files untimely responses can seek to withdraw the admissions and substitute the later responses as amendments (see **Form 5–11**). The responding party is allowed this option unless "it adversely affects the presentation of the case or otherwise prejudices the requesting party." Factors considered by the court in permitting withdrawals or amendments to requests for admissions are expressly stated at Rule 36(b): "The court may permit withdrawal or amendment when the presentation of the merits of the action will be subserved thereby and the party who obtained the admissions fails to satisfy the court that withdrawal or amendment will prejudice him in maintaining his action or defense on the merits of the case."

A party seeking to persuade the court to allow amendments or withdrawal of admissions, and wishing to convince the court that the case will be subserved, needs to demonstrate that the omission was a genuine mistake, should not have been made, and distorts the merits of the case. Another reason for change might be that circumstances have changed, so that the admission, although true when originally made, is no longer true.

The party who originally requested the admissions may seek to persuade the court that the withdrawal or amendment being sought will prejudice their case by indicating that they relied on the admission to their detriment and stopped discovery on a particular issue because of their reliance on the admission. They may be able to show that some investigation was deferred, some discovery curtailed, or a bit of physical evidence which was being preserved was allowed to deteriorate because of their reliance on the admissions.

The court must weigh the degree of prejudice in determining whether to allow the withdrawal or amendment of an admission. A significant factor in influencing the degree of prejudice is the timing of the request for the withdrawal or amendment. The sooner the change is sought after the submission of the original admissions, the more likely it is that the court will grant the motion. The closer in time to trial the change is sought, the more likely it is that the court will deny it and agree that a withdrawal or amendment would unfairly prejudice the case.

The responding party who wishes to withdraw or amend an admission which was previously made in response to requests for admissions must demonstrate to the court that the admission was the result of mistake, inadvertence, or excusable neglect, and that the party that obtained the admission will not be substantially prejudiced in maintaining an action or a defense, on the merits of the case, by the amendment or withdrawal.

FORM 5–11
SAMPLE MOTION WITHDRAWING OR AMENDING RESPONSES

SUPERIOR COURT OF THE STATE OF [state name]
IN AND FOR THE COUNTY OF [county name]

[name], et al.,   No. [case number]

    Plaintiff(s),   NOTICE OF MOTION FOR
                                                   ORDER (WITHDRAWING OR
-vs-   AMENDING, OR WITHDRAWING
                                                   AND AMENDING).

[name], et al.,

    Defendant(s).

Requesting party: Plaintiff, [name].
Responding party: Defendant, [name].

TO: ALL PARTIES AND THEIR ATTORNEYS OF RECORD:

PLEASE TAKE NOTICE that plaintiff, [name], moves the court under [statutory authority] for an order [withdrawing/amending/withdrawing and amending] certain admissions previously made in response to requests for admissions propounded by defendant. The grounds for issuance of this order are that the admissions that are the subject of this motion were the result of plaintiff's mistake, inadvertence, or excusable neglect, and that the order will not substantially prejudice the defendant in maintaining their defense on the merits of this case.

This motion is based upon this notice, the pleadings, records, and files in this action, the attached memorandum of points and authorities, the attached supporting declaration of [name of attorney], attorney for plaintiff, and the attached documents and exhibits including [specify each document/exhibit attached to the motion], and such other oral or documentary evidence as may be presented at the hearing of the motion.

Dated: [date]

                                 [name of attorney]
                            _____

This motion must be accompanied by a memorandum of points and authorities which sets out the statutory authority and the particular circumstances which have arisen in this case to make it necessary for the moving party to seek amendments and/or withdrawals of original responses. Case law may also be cited if there are cases "on point," that is, with facts similar to your case.

A declaration of the moving party's attorney must also accompany the motion along with exhibits referred to in any of the moving papers. (See **Form 5–12.**) Exhibits should include the original requests for admissions, plaintiff's original responses to the requests for admissions, and any exchange of correspondence between the attorneys which prefaced the motion.

If the motion is to amend rather than withdraw responses, the specific request, specific original response, and amended response should be set forth in a separate document as a statement of proposed amended responses (see **Form 5–13**).

FORM 5–12
SAMPLE DECLARATION SUPPORTING THE MOTION

SUPERIOR COURT OF THE STATE OF [state name]
IN AND FOR THE COUNTY OF [county name]

[name], et al.,	No. [case number]
Plaintiff(s),	DECLARATION OF [name of attorney] SUPPORTING MOTION FOR ORDER
-vs-	OF WITHDRAWAL AND AMENDMENT OF REQUEST FOR ADMISSIONS
[name], et al.,	
Defendant(s).	

I, [name of attorney], declare:

1. I am attorney for plaintiff, the responding party.

2. The requesting party served her first set of requests for admissions on the responding party on [date]. A copy of that set is attached to this declaration marked Exhibit "A."

3. The responding party served a response to that set of requests on [date]. A copy of that response is attached to this declaration marked Exhibit "B."

4. The responding party now asks the court to allow withdrawal and amendment of certain admissions made in that response as follows: [admissions to be amended].

5. [Basis for amendment] [State facts here showing that the original admission resulted from the party's or the attorney's mistake, inadvertence or excusable neglect. These facts should be specific, giving the date of service of the original requests for admissions, other information such as illness of party or attorney, vacation of party or attorney, mistake in calendaring, and so forth.]

6. The requesting party is not prejudiced in that [state facts here showing that the proposed change will not substantially prejudice the requesting party in pursuing his action or defense. Such facts could include that it is still early in the discovery, that other depositions have been scheduled, that there are alternate methods available to obtain the same information, and so forth.].

I declare under penalty of perjury under the laws of the State of [state name] that the foregoing is true and correct and that this declaration was executed on [date].

[name of attorney]

_____

Note: For paragraph 4, set forth each admission that is to be amended or withdrawn using a format which sets forth the full text of the request, followed by the full text of the original response, and then followed by the proposed amended response.

This same declaration may be used for a party seeking the withdrawal of a request for admission. The first four paragraphs of the declaration would be the same. The change would occure at paragraph 5, which should state the basis for the withdrawal. The basis for the withdrawal must be set forth in particular with facts showing that the original admission resulted from the party or the attorney's mistake, inadvertence, or excusable neglect. Follow this with a paragraph showing that the requesting party is not prejudiced in that it is still early in the case; other discovery is being conducted, and so forth. Basically the same arguments used for amending can be used for withdrawing requests, the only difference is that when you are withdrawing a request you are not offering an amended answer. The moving party is seeking to wipe out the response so that the ultimate effect is that the request is stricken from the record.

FORM 5–13
SAMPLE STATEMENT OF PROPOSED AMENDED RESPONSES

SUPERIOR COURT OF THE STATE OF [state name]
IN AND FOR THE COUNTY OF [county name]

[name], et al.   No. [case number]

    Plaintiff(s),   STATEMENT OF PROPOSED
AMENDED RESPONSES

-vs-

[name], et al.,

> Defendant(s).

In support of this motion seeking amendment of previously provided responses by plaintiff to defendant's first set of requests for admissions, plaintiff herein lists those requests for admissions verbatim along with original responses and amended responses as follows:

REQUEST FOR ADMISSION: Admit that on [date] Mary S. and Barbara B. entered into a written contract.

ORIGINAL RESPONSE: Responding party lacks sufficient information or knowledge to admit that Mary S. and Barbara B. entered into a contract. Responding party has looked at the files of [name] Company under their names and found no document that purports to be an agreement between them. Responding party has never heard them exchange words which might amount to a contract or express the intent or desire to enter into a contract. Responding party has made a reasonable inquiry concerning this matter, and the information known to him or readily available to him is insufficient to enable him to either admit or deny the matters stated in this request.

AMENDED RESPONSE: Plaintiff admits that Mary S. and Barbara B. entered into a written contract on [date].

REASON FOR AMENDED RESPONSE: Plaintiff has located a copy of a document which appears to be the contract. At the time of plaintiff's original response, files relating to work contracted prior to [name] Company's acquisition of the [city] office had been placed in storage. Plaintiff only became aware of files in storage marked "preacquisition" when the storage facility notified them of overdue rental charges on [date].

Dated: [date].

> Respectfully submitted,
>
> [name of attorney]
>
> _____

§ 5.27   Motion to Oppose Withdrawal or Amendment of Responses

The original requesting party who has received responses, and then receives a motion to withdraw or amend those responses must prepare opposition papers. The opposition to a motion to allow amendment or withdrawal of admissions should focus upon the fact that the proposed withdrawal or amendment will severely prejudice the requesting party in pursuing their action or defense. The memorandum of points and authorities and declaration opposing the motion to amend or withdraw requests should focus on contradicting the facts stated in the moving papers, particularly the attorney declaration. Additionally, a good cause showing must be made demonstrating the substantial prejudice that would result if the motion were granted. Again, the timeliness of the motion to withdraw or amend responses is a critical factor. If discovery is about to close, there will be a substantial prejudice to the original requesting party who relied upon certain facts in preparing their case for trial. The party opposing a motion to withdraw or amend requests may also ask the court to impose certain conditions on any order that is made, such as allowing additional discovery beyond the discovery cutoff, and further allowing this discovery to be pursued at the responding party's expense. A basic argument can be advanced for asking the court to impose conditions on any order that it makes, based on the fact that the withdrawal or amendment forces additional trial preparation. A party who has relied upon responses which were given and considered those facts to be stipulated to, has accordingly narrowed his focus of trial preparation relying upon the admissions as conclusive. Now the party is faced with having to prove matters at trial which the party had not originally intended to address.

Courts are likely to grant motions to amend or withdraw admissions if they are made in a timely fashion, and if a good cause showing can be made that there were mistakes, neglect, or inadvertence on the part of the attorney. The key factor in success for such a motion is the timeliness of the request for amendment or withdrawal. A key factor in opposing such a motion is to show a delay between the time the party knew there was a need to amend or withdraw the response, and the time the actual motion was made.

A proposed order should be a part of opposition papers to a motion to amend or withdraw admissions. Preparation of a proposed order in advance of the motion allows the party to set forth the specific discovery that will be needed should the motion be granted. For example, a clause can be added stating:

The requesting party shall be entitled to take the deposition of BARBARA S. on [date] on the subject of [matter involved in the amended or withdrawn admission] and the responding party shall pay the costs of taking, recording, and transcribing that deposition not to exceed $[dollar amount].

§ 5.28   Motion That Requests Be Deemed Admitted

A requesting party who has not received timely written responses may move for an order that the truth of any matters and the genuineness of any document specified in their request be deemed admitted and also that sanctions be imposed on the party to whom the requests were directed. This motion (see **Form 5–14**) is usually granted unless the responding party serves the request before the date set for the hearing of the motion.

If the responding party serves a properly signed, verified written response containing denials and objections after having been served with a notice of motion that requests be deemed admitted, but has not obtained an order relieving them of waiver of objections for the untimely response, the requesting party may ask the court to order that any individual requests to which the responding party has objected be deemed admitted. Responses served after the requesting party has noticed a motion that requests be deemed admitted must be "in substantial compliance with the statutory authority governing admissions and denials." Requests for relief from waiver for failure to file timely objections and/or denials may be made under the statutory authority governing mistake, inadvertence, and inexcusable neglect.

The requesting party has the option of moving that all requests be deemed admitted, or asking the responding party to stipulate to the truth of all items saving both sides the time and expense of a formal motion.

Statutory authority, Rules 36 and 37 of the Federal Rules of Civil Procedure, states that for a motion for admissions to be deemed admitted it must be served and filed as early as the day after the response was due to be served. There is no statutory authority requiring the requesting party to contact the other party or to make any effort in good faith to obtain responses before moving that matters be deemed admitted. However, it is good strategy for the requesting party to ask the responding party to sign a stipulation admitting the truth of all of the matters specified in the request for admissions. If the stipulation is obtained, it serves the same purpose and may be entered as evidence at the time of trial. If, on the other hand, the other party refuses to stipulate, this fact may be cited in the formal motion as grounds for a greater monetary sanction.

FORM 5–14
SAMPLE MOTION THAT REQUESTS BE DEEMED ADMITTED

SUPERIOR COURT OF THE STATE OF [state name]
IN AND FOR THE COUNTY OF [county name]

[name], et al.,	No. [case number]
Plaintiff(s),	NOTICE OF MOTION FOR ORDER THAT REQUESTS FOR ADMISSIONS BE DEEMED ADMITTED AND FOR MONETARY SANCTIONS
-vs-	
[name], et al.,	(F.R.C.P. 36, F.R.C.P. 37)
Defendant(s).	Date: [date] Time: [time] Dept. [department name]

TO EACH PARTY AND THEIR ATTORNEYS OF RECORD:

PLEASE TAKE NOTICE THAT plaintiff, [name], moves the court under F.R.C.P. 36 and F.R.C.P. 37 for an order that the truth of the matters, and the genuineness of documents, specified in a set of requests for admissions served on defendant, [name], on [date] be deemed admitted and that a monetary sanction under F.R.C.P. 37 be imposed on [name], defendant. The grounds for this motion are that [name], defendant, has not responded to requests for admissions within the statutory time prescribed by F.R.C.P. 36 and further has not requested an extension of time within which to respond.

This motion is based on the attached documents and exhibits including declarations of [name] dated [date], a copy of the original requests for admissions and proof of service served on defendant [name] dated [date] and on all pleadings, papers, and records filed in this action, and such evidence as may be presented at the hearing.

Dated: [date].

[attorney for plaintiff]

_____

Form 5–15 is a sample declaration supporting the motion that requests for admissions be deemed admitted. This declaration must accompany the motion.

FORM 5–15
SAMPLE DECLARATION SUPPORTING THE MOTION

SUPERIOR COURT OF THE STATE OF [state name]
IN AND FOR THE COUNTY OF [county name]

[name], et al.,	No. [case number]
Plaintiff(s),	DECLARATION OF [attorney for plaintiff] SUPPORTING MOTION
-vs-	THAT REQUESTS FOR ADMISSIONS BE DEEMED ADMITTED
[name], et al.,	
Defendant(s).	

[Attorney for plaintiff] declares:

1. I am an attorney for [name], plaintiff, the requesting party.

2. The requesting party served the first set of requests for admissions and genuineness of documents on [name], defendant, the responding party, on [date], by mail.

3. The responding party did not serve a response to that certain set of requests for admissions and genuineness of documents by [date], the date on which response is required by F.R.C.P. 36.

4. On [date] I asked [name], attorney for responding party, to stipulate to the truth of these requests, but the attorney refused to do so.

5. As a result of the responding party's failure to serve a timely response, and further failure to stipulate to the truth of those requests, the requesting party has necessarily incurred reasonable expenses as follows: I have spent 7 hours at the rate of $150.00 per hour in attempting to obtain responses to the above-described requests for admissions and in preparing this motion. I expect to spend 10 more hours preparing and presenting the motion. In addition the following costs have been incurred: [specify each cost and amount].

I declare under penalty of perjury under the laws of the State of [state name] that the foregoing is true and correct, and that this declaration was executed on [date].

[attorney for plaintiff]

Service of this motion (**Form 5–14**) and declaration (**Form 5–15**) must be made in accordance with local court rules allowing responding party time to file opposition papers. The notice of motion, motion, and attorney declaration must be accompanied by a memorandum of points and authorities briefly setting forth the statutory authority and pertinent case law dealing with the propriety of the requests and their relevance to the action at hand. A proposed order may be submitted along with moving papers if local court rules permit. **Form 5–16** is an illustration of a motion that requests be deemed admitted with an attorney declaration and memorandum of points and authorities attached. **Form 5–17** is a sample proposed order.

FORM 5–16
SAMPLE MOTION THAT REQUESTS BE DEEMED
ADMITTED (CALIFORNIA)

[attorney for defendant]
[address]
[telephone number]

Attorneys for Defendant
[name] SHOPPING MALL

IN THE SUPERIOR COURT OF THE STATE OF CALIFORNIA
IN THE CITY AND COUNTY OF [city/county name]

[name],	Case No.
Plaintiff,	NOTICE OF MOTION FOR ORDER ESTABLISHING ADMISSIONS
vs.	AND FOR MONETARY SANCTIONS UNDER CALIFORNIA

[name] SHOPPING MALL, A LIMITED PARTNERSHIP, [defendant A] and [defendant B], as limited partners of [name] SHOPPING MALL, [defendant C], individually and (dba) [company D], and (dba) [company E], and DOES 1 through 30, inclusive,	CODE OF CIVIL PROCEDURE § 2033(k); DECLARATION OF [defense attorney] IN SUPPORT OF MOTION; POINTS AND AUTHORITIES IN SUPPORT OF MOTION DATE: [date] TIME: [time] PLACE: [judicial department]

        Defendants.

_____/

TO PLAINTIFF [name] and TO [plaintiff]'s ATTORNEY OF RECORD:

YOU ARE HEREBY NOTIFIED that at [time] on [date], or as soon thereafter as this matter can be heard in Department [judicial department] of this Court located at [address], [city], [state], defendant [name] SHOPPING MALL will move this Court for an order establishing the truth on each matter specified in the Request for Admissions served on plaintiff [name] on [date] (a true and correct copy of said Request for Admissions is attached to the Declaration of [defendant's attorney], served and filed concurrently herewith this motion) and also for an order that plaintiff [name], and their counsel, [plaintiff's attorney], pay monetary sanctions to the moving party in the sum of [dollar amount] for reasonable expenses and attorney's fees incurred by the moving party in connection with this proceeding.

Said motion will be made on the grounds that said Requests for Admissions are relevant to the subject matter of this action and do not relate to any privileged matters, and that the plaintiffs have failed to serve a timely response thereto.

Said motion will be based on this notice, the Points and Authorities attached herewith this motion; the attached Declaration of [defendant's attorney] and the complete files and records in this action, as well as any other relevant testimony or documentary evidence that this court deems property at the time of hearing.

Dated: [date]

                              [attorney for defendant]
                              _____

            DECLARATION OF [attorney for defendant]

    I, [attorney for defendant], declare as follows:

1. That I am an attorney at law duly licensed and admitted to practice law in the State of California, and before this court, and am the attorney of record for defendant, [name] SHOPPING MALL, in the above-entitled action.

2. That I am familiar with the facts set forth herein, and if called upon and sworn as a witness, I could and would testify competently from personal knowledge as to the following matters.

3. This declaration is offered in support of a motion for order establishing admissions and for monetary sanctions.

4. On [date], this declarant caused to be served on plaintiff [name] the following described Request for Admissions.

NAME OF PROPOUNDING PARTY: [name] SHOPPING MALL

RESPONDING PARTY: [plaintiff]

SET NO.   [set number]

5. A true and correct copy of said Request for Admissions is attached hereto as Exhibit "A" and incorporate herein by this reference.

6. The party to whom said Request for Admissions was directed, plaintiff [name], has not served any response thereto, and the time remaining for responses expired and has not been extended by agreement of the parties or court order.

7. As a result of said failure to respond, defendant [name] SHOPPING MALL has incurred reasonable costs and attorney's fees in connection with this motion and the hearing thereon, totaling [dollar amount] consisting of the following: two hours to draft and prepare this motion for filing and service, and six hours for travel from [city] to [city] Superior Court to hear this motion. This declarant's reasonable attorney's fees are $120 per hour.

I declare under penalty of perjury under the laws of the State of California that the foregoing is true and correct.

Executed this [date] day of [month], [year], at [city], California.

[attorney for defendant]

_____

Declarant

MEMORANDUM OF POINTS AND AUTHORITIES

1

Statement of Facts

Defendant [name] SHOPPING MALL, is a defendant in [plaintiff] v. [name] Shopping Mall, Case No. [case number] in the Superior Court of the State of California, in and for the City and County of [city/county name].

On [date], defendant [name] SHOPPING MALL served Request for Admissions, Set No. One, on plaintiffs. (See Exhibit "A" attached hereto).

Plaintiff, by and through plaintiff's counsel, has not responded whatsoever to the requested admissions.

Therefore, defendant [name] SHOPPING MALL moves this court for an order establishing the truth of each matter specified in the attached Request for Admissions and that plaintiff [name] and plaintiff's counsel, [attorney for plaintiff], pay jointly and severally, sanctions in the amount of [dollar amount] as reasonable attorney's fees necessitated by this motion.

2

Defendant is Entitled to a Court Order
that the Truth of Matters Specified in
Subject Request for Admissions be Admitted
and Defendant is Entitled to Monetary Sanctions
for Plaintiff's Failure to Respond
CCP Section 2033(k)

Moreover, California Code of Civil Procedure § 2033(k) provides that:

It is mandatory that the court impose sanction under Section 2033 on the party or attorney, or both, whose failure to serve a timely response to Request for Admissions necessitated this motion.

Therefore, defendant requests this court order the truth of the matters in the attached Request for Admissions be deemed admitted and this court order plaintiff's attorney to pay sanctions in the amount of [dollar amount] for reasonable attorney's fees necessitated by this motion. See Declaration of [attorney for defendant] attached hereto this motion for a statement of reasonable attorney's fees.

3

Conclusion

Based on the foregoing, this defendant requests this court to grant its motion and mandate that plaintiff and plaintiff's attorney pay sanctions in the amount of [dollar amount].

Dated: [date].

[attorney for defendant]

_____

NOTE: Exhibits attached to the declaration should include the request for admissions with a proof of service.

FORM 5–17
SAMPLE PROPOSED ORDER (CALIFORNIA)

[attorney for defendant]
[address]
[telephone number]

Attorneys for Defendant
[name] SHOPPING MALL

IN THE SUPERIOR COURT OF THE STATE OF CALIFORNIA
IN THE CITY AND COUNTY OF [city/county name]

[name],
 	
      Plaintiff,
vs.
 	
[name] SHOPPING MALL, A
LIMITED PARTNERSHIP,
[defendant A] and [defendant B],
as limited partners of
[name] SHOPPING MALL,
[defendant C], individually
and (dba) [company D],
and (dba) [company E], and
DOES 1 through 30,
inclusive,
 	
      Defendants.
	Case No. [case number]
	
	PROPOSED ORDER

_____/

The motion of defendant [name] SHOPPING MALL for an order that the truth of the matters specified in the Request for Admissions, Set No. One, propounded by defendant, [name] SHOPPING MALL to plaintiff, [name], and served on plaintiff [name] on [date] be deemed admitted and that monetary sanctions be imposed against plaintiff [name] and plaintiff's attorney of record, [attorney for plaintiff], and that they pay forthwith to defendant [name] SHOPPING MALL its reasonable expenses in making this motion including attorney's fees, in the amount of [dollar amount] on or before [date].

Dated: [date].

[name]

_____

Judge of the Superior Court

§ 5.29   Replying to a Motion That Requests Be Deemed Admitted

A responding party who has been served with a notice of motion that requests for admission be deemed admitted should proceed as follows:

1. Serve and file a sworn verified proposed response before the hearing date that is in substantial compliance with statutory authority.

2. Serve and file a notice of motion for an order relieving the party from waiver of objections for untimely response accompanied by a memorandum of points and authorities setting forth the specific reasons for the responding party's failure to serve the responses. Reference to the fact that the failure to serve the responses was the result of mistake, inadvertence, and excusable neglect must be explained by facts showing the reasons for your untimely response.

3. Serve and file the motion and supporting documents in opposition in an attempt to convince the court that justice requires denial of the motion and/or that the responding party be given additional time to serve a full response including objections.

If the responding party does nothing, the court must order that the matters referred to in the motion are deemed admitted and impose a monetary sanction. The sanction may be less if a proper response is filed or if the responding party concedes the truth of the request. If the responding party fails to seek relief from waiver, the court may simply ignore any objections in the response and issue an order that all requests are deemed admitted.

It is difficult to oppose a motion that requests be deemed admitted and, although it is possible to correct this mistake, it is costly and time consuming and places your client in a dangerous position. If matters are deemed admitted, those matters are considered conclusively proven for purposes of trial. It is a serious mistake to fail to serve a timely response to requests for admissions. Of all of the formal discovery devices, requests for admissions are the most dangerous. They must be taken seriously and answered promptly to avoid placing your client in a position of having to seek relief from waiver of the client's right to object.

§ 5.30   Protective Orders

A responding party has the right to seek a protective order, even after objections have been served, if responses to the requests would cause unwarranted annoyance, embarrassment, oppression, and undue burden or expense on the responding party. Protective orders may also be sought when the admission relates to highly sensitive, confidential, or privileged matters.

Federal Rule of Civil Procedure 26(c) governs protective orders and requires that the party who moves for a protective order must show good cause. Grounds for seeking protection are numerous. Among the most common grounds are that the discovery requested is so lengthy and detailed that it is unduly oppressive and expensive, for example, discovery involving lengthy or repetitive and overly detailed requests for admissions. Grounds for seeking a protective order when the information is highly sensitive or confidential usually seek to limit or prevent the disclosure of business secrets. Federal Rule of Civil Procedure 26(c) provides a variety of remedies that can protect a party from embarrassment, oppression, and undue burden or expense. The remedies must be specifically asked for in a motion for protective order and include:

Barring the requested discovery,

Regulating the terms, conditions, methods, and scope of the discovery,

Requiring the sealing of documents, and

Regulating or barring complete disclosure of trade secrets, confidential research and development, or other commercial information.

A motion for a protective order is most frequently used to assert a point that would have validity because the request deals with matters that are relevant to the subject and are not protected by any privilege, even the work product protection. It is generally not necessary to make a motion for a protective order when the only ground for doing so is that the requests for admissions call for matters which are irrelevant to the subject matter or privileged. In that case, objections filed in a timely fashion in response to those requests for admissions are the more appropriate procedural device. Motions for protective orders should be reserved for resistance to admission requests when the matters involved are arguably within the scope of allowable discovery, and can only remain undisclosed through court order.

For good cause shown by the moving party, the judge may make "any order that justice requires" the judge may:

Deny all or part of the protection sought by the motion;

Place "just and equitable" terms and conditions on the disclosure that the responding party must make;

Impose a monetary sanction on any party, person, or attorney who unsuccessfully makes or opposes a motion for protective order, unless the court finds the person acted with substantial justification;

Grant the protection sought, order the particular set of requests for admissions or not answer the particular specific request quoted in the moving papers;

Order that some or all of the requests be answered and those answers be sealed and opened only on court order.

§ 5.31   Notice of Motion for a Protective Order

A protective order is a noticed motion (**Form 5–18**) which must comply with the specific notice requirements in your state or the federal jurisdiction in which the action is set. Notice must be served in a timely fashion allowing time for the opposition to respond with formal opposition points and authorities. A motion for a protective order must include: a notice of motion, motion, memorandum of points and authorities, supporting declaration(s) (**Form 5–19**), and, in many jurisdictions, a proposed order.

FORM 5–18
SAMPLE NOTICE OF MOTION FOR A PROTECTIVE ORDER

SUPERIOR COURT OF THE STATE OF [state name]
IN AND FOR THE COUNTY OF [county name]

[name], et al.,	No. [case number]
Plaintiff(s),	NOTICE OF MOTION FOR PROTECTIVE ORDER
-vs-	RESTRICTING DISCOVERY AND IMPOSING MONETARY
[name], et al.,	SANCTIONS
Defendant(s).	

TO: [name], Defendant, and to [Defendant]'s attorney of record.

NOTICE IS HEREBY GIVEN that on [date], [year], at [time], or as soon thereafter as the matter may be heard in Department [name] of this court located at [street address], plaintiff will move for a protective order that Request No. 1 in Request for Admissions, Set 1, propounded by [name], plaintiff, and served on [name], defendant, on [date], need not be answered and an order imposing a monetary sanction against [name], defendant, and defendant's attorney in the amount of $[dollar amount]. The motion will be made on the grounds that the request relates to confidential research that plaintiff has been conducting in the course and scope of [plaintiff]'s business, and that plaintiff made a reasonable and good faith attempt to resolve informally the issues presented by this motion.

This motion will be based on this notice of motion, on the declaration of [name], attorney for plaintiff, and the memorandum of points and authorities set forth below, on the records and files herein, and on such other evidence as may be presented at the hearing of this motion.

Dated: [date].

[attorney for plaintiff]
_____

This notice of motion and motion must be accompanied by a memorandum of points and authorities which clearly sets out the particular circumstances which have arisen in this case forcing the plaintiff to seek a protective order. If a claim has been made that the matters inquired into in the requests for admissions relate to confidential product development, research, or trade secrets, set forth identification of the information sought as to the type of document and author of the document referred to in the request. Case law must also be cited in the memorandum of points and authorities to support the argument for the protection of trade secrets and confidential information.

Additionally, a declaration of the moving party's attorney must accompany this motion. Other declarations may also accompany the motion. In the case of a corporate defendant, this may include the president of the corporation, or head of the research and development unit, and so forth.

FORM 5–19
SAMPLE DECLARATION SUPPORTING A MOTION
FOR A PROTECTIVE ORDER

SUPERIOR COURT OF THE STATE OF [state name]
IN AND FOR THE COUNTY OF [county name]

[name], et al.,	No. [case number]
Plaintiff(s),	DECLARATION OF [name of attorney] SUPPORTING MOTION FOR
-vs-	PROTECTIVE ORDER, RESTRICTION OF
[name], et al.,	DISCOVERY AND IMPOSITION OF MONETARY SANCTIONS
Defendant(s).	

I, [name of attorney], declare:

1. I am an attorney-at-law duly admitted to practice before all of the courts of the state of [state name], and the attorney of record herein for [name], plaintiff in the above-entitled action.

2. Plaintiff, [name], is seeking a protective order from this court directing that the plaintiff not be required to answer Request No. 1 in Requests for Admissions, Set No. 1, which is attached to this declaration as Exhibit "A."

3. Good cause exists for the protective order sought by plaintiff in that the above-specified Request No. 1 relates to highly confidential research which plaintiff has been conducting in the course and scope of plaintiff's business and which is of marginal relevance to the issues involved in this litigation.

4. On [date], I sent a letter to defendant's attorney asking that defendant withdraw Request No. 1. A copy of that letter is attached as Exhibit "B" and made a part thereof. To date, I have not received an answer to this letter, nor have my subsequent telephone calls to defendant's attorney been returned.

5. Plaintiff bases plaintiff's request for the imposition of monetary sanctions in the amount of $[dollar amount] on [itemize and explain the basis of the computation of the monetary amounts of sanctions requested].

I declare under penalty of perjury under the laws of the State of [state name] that the foregoing is true and correct.

Date: [date].

[attorney for plaintiff]

_____

§ 5.32   Sample Protective Order

Depending upon local rules, a proposed order may or may not be required along with your moving papers. The advantage of submitting a proposed order, when it is permissible in a particular court or jurisdiction, is that the proposed order can be drawn up at the same time as the moving papers expressing exactly the relief sought in the terms of the moving party. This gives the moving party a certain amount of control in the precise wording and substance of the order. Of course, a judge granting the order may not accept the proposed order as it is written and may alter it even though the motion is granted. **Form 5–20** illustrates a sample protective order.

FORM 5–20
SAMPLE PROTECTIVE ORDER

SUPERIOR COURT OF THE STATE OF [state name]
IN AND FOR THE COUNTY OF [county name]

[name], et al.,   No. [case number]

Plaintiff(s),   ORDER

-vs-

[name], et al.,

Defendant(s).

The motion of plaintiff for a protective order directing that Request No. 1 of Request for Admissions, Set No. 1 propounded by defendant and served on plaintiff on [date] need not be answered and for monetary sanctions came on regularly for hearing by the court on [date]. Plaintiff appeared by counsel [name]; defendant appeared by counsel [name].

On good cause being shown and on proof made to the satisfaction of the court that the motion ought to be granted,

IT IS ORDERED that the motion be, and it hereby is, granted and Request No. 1 in Request for Admissions, Set No. 1, propounded by defendant, [name], and served on plaintiff, [name], on [date] need not be answered.

IT IS FURTHER ORDERED that defendant and defendant's attorney [name] pay forthwith to plaintiff the sum of $[dollar amount] as reasonable expenses and attorney's fees.

Dated: [date]

[name]

_____

Judge of the Superior Court

§ 5.33   Opposing Protective Orders

A party preparing opposition points and authorities to a motion for protective order may also submit a proposed order as part of their opposition papers. The form would be identical to the order in **§ 5.32** with the exception of the second paragraph, which would change as follows:

On proof made to the satisfaction of the court that the motion ought to be denied,

IT IS ORDERED that the motion be, and thereby is, denied, and that plaintiff serve a response to defendant's Request No. 1 of Set No. 1 within 15 days of this order.

On further proof made to the satisfaction of the court, it was found that defendant and defendant's attorney acted with substantial justification in propounding said requests for admission and in opposing plaintiff's motion for a protective order.

IT IS FURTHER ORDERED that no monetary sanction be imposed on defendant and defendant's attorney, [name].

Or if defendant has requested sanctions in opposition papers:

IT IS FURTHER ORDERED that monetary sanctions in the amount of $[dollar amount] be awarded to defendant.

The opposition to a protective order should include a memorandum of points and authorities which contradicts the motion. Opposition papers need to address each point made by the moving party and show that the original requests for admission should be answered, that the requests are relevant and not burdensome, and so forth. Case law should be cited if the facts are similar to your case.

In opposing a motion for a protective order, you may offer to modify your original request by limiting it, or you may argue that an in camera inspection is acceptable. By offering some type of compromise in your opposition papers, you are demonstrating a good will effort to resolve the dispute, which is always in the best interests of your client and pleasing to the court.

§ 5.34   Motions to Compel Further Responses

Upon receiving responses to requests for admissions, the requesting party should immediately review the responses as to the sufficiency of any answer that is not an express admission and the propriety of all objections raised. If the propounding party feels that the responses received are lacking in any way, or that the objections raised are without merit, a motion may be made to compel further responses. This motion must be made in a timely fashion. Local rules should be checked for the procedural requirements and time limits for moving to compel further responses. Federal Rule of Civil Procedure 37(a) governs motions to compel on the federal level. Motions to compel further responses may only be made after a good faith effort has been made to negotiate with the opposing party and obtain further responses without the necessity of court intervention. All such attempts at informal resolution must be made prior to the expiration of the statutory time frame within which the requesting party may move the court to compel further responses.

Partial or qualified admissions and statements that the responding party lacks sufficient information or knowledge to either admit or deny a request are likely targets for orders compelling further responses. Responses which admit part of the request without denying the rest may also be the subject of a motion. A motion to compel further responses may be directed to an entire set of written responses as well as to particular answers and objections. Motions to compel further responses may be directed to requests to admit genuineness of documents as well as to requests to admit facts. Unsigned and/or unverified responses to requests for admissions of facts and genuineness of documents may be the subject of a motion to compel further responses in the sense that such a response is treated the same as no response.

The decision as to whether to move to compel further responses when you have received unsigned and unverified responses is a matter of strategy. Technically speaking, unsigned and unverified responses are to be treated as express admissions. However, a party who has served unsigned or unverified responses may move the court for an order seeking relief from the mistake by claiming that the omission of a verification or signature was through mistake, inadvertence, or excusable neglect. Such a motion is usually successful based on the fact that the party intended to make the responses or they would not have served them.

A motion to compel further responses consists of the following documents:

1. A notice of motion (**Form 5–21**) and motion,
2. A document which sets forth in verbatim each original request and the response received,
3. A memorandum of points and authorities setting forth the factual and legal reasons for compelling further responses,
4. A declaration (**Form 5–22**) from the attorney of record for moving party setting forth those attempts at meeting and conferring in good faith to negotiate further responses without the intervention of the court,
5. The original requests for admissions with proof of service and original responses (**Form 5–23**) to the requests for admissions with proof of service must be attached as exhibits to the attorney's declaration, and
6. A proposed order (**Form 5–24**).

If a judge grants an order which is substantially different than the order sought, the successful party will be required to prepare a new proposed order.

FORM 5–21
SAMPLE NOTICE OF MOTION TO COMPEL FURTHER RESPONSES

SUPERIOR COURT OF THE STATE OF [state name]
IN AND FOR THE COUNTY OF [county name]

[name], et al.,	No.
Plaintiff(s),	NOTICE OF MOTION FOR ORDER REQUIRING FURTHER RESPONSES TO REQUESTS FOR ADMISSIONS AND IMPOSING MONETARY SANCTIONS
-vs-	
[name], et al.,	
Defendant(s).	

TO: Each party and to their attorney of record.

PLEASE TAKE NOTICE that on [date], at [time], or as soon thereafter as the matter may be heard in Department [name] of this court located at [address], plaintiff will move the court for an order pursuant to [statutory authority] that defendant serve further responses to Requests No. [number] (specify each numbered request to which a further response is being compelled) of plaintiff's first set of Requests for Admissions served on defendant on [date], and for an order imposing monetary sanctions against defendant and [defendant]'s attorney in the amount of $[dollar amount].

This motion will be made on the grounds that the matters of fact which are the subject of the requests for admissions specified above are relative to the subject matter of this action and are not privileged, and that the answers given to these requests for admissions are evasive and incomplete, and that the objections to them are without merit and too general. ([cite specific responses and the reasons why the responses are inadequate]. For example, the objection to Request No. 2 is improper in that the matter in question is not privileged under the attorney-client privilege. The response to Request No. 4 does not comply with statutory authority and is improper in that defendant refused to admit or deny the genuineness of the document in question, but gave no reason whatsoever for his purported inability to admit or deny the genuineness of the document in question.)

This motion will be based on this notice of motion, on the declaration of [name], attorney for plaintiff, copies of the requests for admissions and responses, and pertinent correspondence, as well as the memorandum of points and authorities set forth below, and the records and files herein, and on such evidence as may be presented at the hearing of this motion.

Dated: [date]

[attorney for plaintiff]

FORM 5–22
SAMPLE DECLARATION SUPPORTING THE MOTION

SUPERIOR COURT OF THE STATE OF [state name]
IN AND FOR THE COUNTY OF [county name]

[name], et al.,	No. [case number]
Plaintiff(s),	DECLARATION SUPPORTING MOTION
	TO COMPEL FURTHER RESPONSES
-vs-	TO REQUESTS FOR ADMISSIONS
	AND FOR IMPOSITION OF MONETARY
[name], et al.,	SANCTIONS
Defendant(s).	

I, [name], declare:

1. I am an attorney-at-law duly admitted to practice before all the courts of the State of [state name] and the attorney of record herein for plaintiff, the requesting party.

2. This is an action [specify the subject matter and issues of the action] (specifically referring to the pleadings and documents on file).

3. On [date], the requesting party served the First Set of Requests for Admissions on defendant, [name]. A copy of those requests for admissions is attached hereto as Exhibit "A" to this declaration and made a part thereof.

4. On [date], defendant [name] served defendant's purported responses to those requests for admissions on plaintiff, [name]. A copy of those responses is attached hereto as Exhibit "B" to this declaration and made a part thereof.

5. The answers in the purported responses to Request No. [list individual requests by number] were evasive and incomplete and the objections made to request No. [list individual requests] were without merit and too broad as more fully appears in the attached statement of requests and responses in dispute.

6. On [date], I [met with/telephoned/wrote to] counsel for the responding party, and attempted to resolve disputes concerning the adequacy of the responses to each of the requests for admissions stated in the preceding paragraph.

7. As a result of the refusal and failure of the responding party to properly respond to the requests and to agree to furnish further responses to them, the requesting party has necessarily incurred reasonable expenses as follows: [itemization of expenses].

I declare under penalty of perjury under the laws of the state of [state name] that the foregoing is true and correct.

Dated: [date].

[attorney for plaintiff]

Note: For paragraph 6, continue with as many paragraphs as is necessary to state facts that show that a reasonable and good faith attempt has been made to resolve the issues informally before making this motion. For example, as to each of the requests, present the argument and authorities supporting the propriety of further responses and in each case counsel for the responding party refused to change or add to the response previously given, or refused to withdraw the objection set forth.

FORM 5-23
SAMPLE STATEMENT OF REQUESTS AND RESPONSES IN DISPUTE

SUPERIOR COURT OF THE STATE OF [state name]
IN AND FOR THE COUNTY OF [county name]

[name], et al.,	No. [case number]
Plaintiff(s),	STATEMENT OF REQUESTS AND RESPONSES IN DISPUTE AND
-vs-	LIST OF REQUESTS FOR ADMISSIONS REQUIRING
[name], et al.,	FURTHER RESPONSE
Defendant(s).	

In support of the requesting party's motion for an order compelling defendant to make further responses to certain requests for admissions, the requesting party, plaintiff, herein lists those requests for admissions verbatim and the response, answer, or objection to each as given in the responses received from defendant dated [date], as well as the reasons and authorities compelling further responses.

[List each request separately, followed by the response, and finally by the legal authority for compelling a further response.]

REQUEST NO. 12: Admit that prior to [date], the date of [name]'s injury, [name] Corporation had received more than 50 reports of falls with injuries on the front stairs of the administration building located at [address], [city], [state].

RESPONSE TO REQUEST NO. 12: Defendant lacks sufficient information or knowledge to admit or deny the truth of this request.

REASONS WHY FURTHER RESPONSE SHOULD BE COMPELLED: This response gives no indication what inquiry, if any, was made to learn whether the facts stated in the request are true. Specifically, defendant [name] Corporation should be required to examine appropriate corporation records relating to reports of accidents in and around the administration building, and to count the number of those accidents specifically relating to the front stairs. The requested information appears to be readily obtainable by [name], Chief Executive Officer, who answered the requests as president of [name] Corporation. The responding partner has a duty to make a reasonable investigation of all available information within their custody or control, and further, even if the party does not have personal knowledge, the party must answer requests when it is reasonably within the party's power to obtain answers from outside sources. <u>E.H. Tate Co. v. Jiffy Enterprises, Inc.</u>, 16 F.R.D. 571 (___ 19___). Furthermore, the requested information relates directly to the knowledge of [name] Corporation regarding the defective condition of the front stairs of the administration building <u>prior</u> to the date of plaintiff's accident.

Dated: [date].

Respectfully submitted,

[attorney for plaintiff]

A memorandum of points and authorities must accompany this statement of request and responses. The memorandum of points and authorities should set forth the following:

1. A brief statement of the factual and procedural background of the action,
2. An argument as to why each of plaintiff's requests for admissions are relevant to the subject matter of the action,
3. Statements as to why each objection claimed by defendant is without merit, and each privilege claimed by defendant is inapplicable, and
4. A concluding section emphasizing why the information sought in the request for admissions is necessary to help prepare plaintiff's case for trial adequately.

FORM 5–24
SAMPLE ORDER COMPELLING FURTHER RESPONSES

SUPERIOR COURT OF THE STATE OF [state name]
IN AND FOR THE COUNTY OF [county name]

[name], et al.,   No. [case number]

    Plaintiff(s),

-vs-   ORDER

[name], et al.,

    Defendant(s).

The motion of plaintiff for an order compelling further responses to requests for admissions came on for regular hearing on [date]. Appearing as attorneys were [name], attorney for plaintiff, moving party, and [name], attorney for defendant, responding party.

Satisfactory proof having been made and good cause showing,

IT IS ORDERED that:

1. Defendant shall make further responses as follows: [list the requests and any instructions concerning required further response].

REQUEST NO. 12: Answer this request by admitting, denying or stating the basis for inability to admit or deny. Obtain copies of accident reports from company records and outside sources to determine the number of accidents on the front stairs of the administration building of [name] Corporation as well as the dates of those accidents and any injuries resulting from those accidents.

After obtaining those records, defendant is to make a full and complete response to that specific request. These responses are to be served upon plaintiff no later than 30 days of the date of this order.

2. Defendant shall pay a monetary sanction to plaintiff for the expenses of bringing this motion in the amount of $[dollar amount].

Dated: [date].

[name]

_____

Judge of the Superior Court

§ 5.35   Opposition to Motion to Compel Further Responses

A responding party who is served with a notice of a motion to compel further responses to requests for admissions has several options. The easiest course of action is simply to file supplemental responses prior to the date the motion is scheduled to be heard. If, after receiving these supplemental responses, the opposing party remains unsatisfied and refuses to take the motion off calendar, there is a great likelihood that the motion will be denied, or at the very least, if it is granted, there will be no sanctions awarded because supplemental responses were served in a good faith attempt to respond and avoid the expenses of the motion.

A second course of action is to file formal opposition points and authorities and a declaration in support of a motion to oppose compelling further responses in a timely fashion. Supporting declarations should set forth facts that show the attorney's reasonable and good faith efforts to resolve the issues informally. The responding party may have sent the requesting party a letter detailing the reasons why additional responses could not be given. If so, this letter should become an exhibit to the supporting declaration. The declaration should also contradict any false statements in the requesting party's declaration and provide the court with the factual basis for awarding monetary sanctions to the responding party if the motion to compel further responses is denied.

The responding party should set forth in the memorandum of points and authorities accompanying the opposition papers the factual and legal basis for each objection raised in the original responses. The responding party should also set forth that the answers given in those responses were as complete and straightforward as information available to the responding party permitted.

A statement of requests and responses in dispute should also be prepared and served along with the opposition papers. The format of this document should set forth each request and each response followed by an argument stating the reasons why further responses should not be compelled, and why the stated objections should be upheld. Finally, in opposing a motion to compel further responses to requests for admissions, a good strategy is to make a motion for a protective order calendared for the same time as the motion to compel. The arguments to restrict discovery will be very similar for both motions.

§ 5.36   Using Requests for Admissions at Trial

Any matter admitted in response to a request for admission, and not amended or withdrawn pursuant to noticed motion, is conclusively established in the action against the party who has made the admission. These admissions may be used for evidentiary purposes and laying foundation for testimony at trial. They may also be quoted verbatim by the party who has requested the admissions in support of the motions in limine part of the trial or any other motion in the action.

There is no prescribed statutory way of presenting admissions to the judge or jury at time of trial. A preamble to the reading of admissions to jurors is provided in standardized jury instructions; however, its inclusion among the jury instructions does not necessarily mean that admissions must be read for the first time at the close of the trial. Depending on the strategy of the attorney, it may be useful to have admissions read early in the case as a means of laying the foundation for other testimony. It is helpful to select those admissions that favor your client's case, arrange them in logical order (which may be different than the order in which the requests were originally made), and ask the judge to read the admissions to the jury at the point in the trial that seems the most advantageous to your case. They can be read at the beginning of a case, immediately after opening argument, at midpoint in the case prior to testimony by certain witnesses, and again at the final argument or instruction stage of the trial.

An additional use of requests for admissions at trial is as a basis for objecting to evidence that the other party wishes to introduce. One of the purposes of the request for admission procedure is to narrow the issues in the case. Those facts admitted through requests for admissions are conclusively established. Thus, it may be argued that a party is charged with having admitted such facts and, therefore, should not be permitted to present evidence to the contrary at time of trial.

§ 5.37   Use of Requests for Admissions in Large Cases

Requests for admissions and requests for genuineness of documents are useful in large cases to narrow the focus of triable issues. For example, in the flood damage case set out in **Chapter 4,** requests for genuineness of documents propounded early in the case would have included requests to admit the genuineness of insurance policies, claim forms, inspection reports, repair invoices, photographs, and so forth. Requests for admission served contemporaneously with interrogatories in the same case could address the pleadings on file, various claims and allegations made against the insurance company, and various affirmative defenses raised by the insurance company against the plaintiff.

Responding to requests for admissions in a large or multiparty case should follow the same procedures set forth in **Chapter 4.** Responding to any discovery request, interrogatories, requests for admissions and genuineness of documents, and requests for production of documents in large cases must be organized in a systematic approach that safeguards all discovery deadlines, preserves the client's right to enter objections as appropriate, and provides timely and complete responses. The organizational chart detailed in **Chapter 4** may also be adopted for use in preparing responses to requests for admissions and genuineness of documents.

CHAPTER 6

DOCUMENT PRODUCTION

451

§ 6.1   Introduction

Presentation of evidence at trial usually includes testimony of the parties and witnesses, and the introduction of documents and tangible items as exhibits. The discovery mechanism for gaining pretrial access to documents which might become exhibits is a request to produce and inspect documents and tangible items. Procedures for demanding and responding to requests for production and inspection of documents and other tangible objects, and for entry onto or inspection of real property are governed by Federal Rule of Civil Procedure 34. A request may be propounded under Rule 34 to any other party in the litigation. Requests for documents under Rule 34 may be propounded only upon parties. The only method by which documents can be obtained from a nonparty to the litigation process is through a subpoena. Federal Rule of Procedure 45 permits the discovery of tangible information and documents from nonparties. A request to permit the inspection and copying of documents and other tangible items may be propounded without leave of court. Motions to compel production of documents are noticed motions and may only be made after the use of the procedural requirements of a request to produce pursuant to Rule 34 have failed to produce documents.

The scope of a request to produce documents under Rule 34 is governed by Rule 26(b), which permits the discovery of any relevant matter that is not privileged. For a more complete discussion of relevancy and privilege, *see* **Chapter 4** on Interrogatories, and **Chapter 5** on Requests for Admissions. The standards for relevance and privilege as discussed in Rule 26(b) apply to all of the formal methods of discovery—depositions, interrogatories, requests for admissions, and requests for production of documents.

§ 6.2 Document Production Through Other Discovery

The specific discovery procedure set forth in Rule 34 of the Federal Rules of Civil Procedure allows inspection and production of documents; however, other discovery conducted as part of an overall discovery plan in an action can also be utilized to obtain documents. For example, Rule 33(c) allows a responding party to produce business records in lieu of interrogatory answers by tendering access to records (see **Chapter 4**). This is a voluntary procedure and a choice made by the responding party. Records received in this method do not necessarily negate the necessity of a formal request to produce documents especially when a more broad-based response is required. For example, a tendered access to business records offered in response to an interrogatory will generally have a narrow focus and permit inspection of only those records specifically asked for in the interrogatory. They may contain information that will lead to the identification of other key documents. After reviewing the records, a precise document request can then be drafted to retrieve those documents.

Deposition notices served on a party pursuant to Rule 26 and Rule 30(f)(1) allow the production of documents and things at a deposition. A deposition notice directed to an officer, director, or managing agent of a corporate defendant may include a specific listing of documents or categories of documents which must be produced at the deposition. This is an effective means of obtaining documents and is frequently used in discovery. The main advantage of having documents produced at a deposition is that the person producing them is available for questions and explanations of the documents (see **Chapter 3**).

Having documents produced at a deposition is an excellent starting point for drafting a request to produce documents. Documents produced and discussed at a deposition will provide detailed information which can be used to prepare a specific request to produce documents zeroing in on those documents immediately preceding, or immediately subsequent to, those produced at the deposition and also those documents referred to either in the deposition transcript or attachments to documents which were not included. A request to produce documents as a follow-up procedure can pick up all of these loose ends effectively, as well as address new issues which have arisen since the deposition was taken.

The main difference between a request to produce documents pursuant to Rule 34 and documents which are produced along with interrogatory answers or at depositions is that under Rule 34, in addition to the inspecting and copying of documents, you are permitted to obtain tangible items (products) and test them. You are also permitted to enter on land or real property for inspection and testing such as soil tests, water tests, and so forth. The inspection procedure under Rule 34 is the only formal discovery method that provides for gaining entry to an opponent's land, or other property, for discovery purposes.

§ 6.3   The Scope and Subject Matter of Document Requests

Federal Rule of Civil Procedure 34 permits inspection and production of:

1. Documents defined as papers, books, accounts, letters, photographs, graphs, charts, illustrations, phone records, as well as "every other means of recording upon any tangible thing, any form of communication or representation including, letters, words, pictures, sounds, symbols, or combinations thereof." Electronic data compilations and computer printouts in general have been held to be documents within the context of a request to produce.

2. Tangible things for inspections, copying, and testing including any product, piece of machinery or equipment, or any mechanical device which has become relevant in the litigation through claims or defenses raised regarding its use and/or misuse.

Most, if not all, cases involve locating and analyzing documents. A growing number of cases such as product liability, real property, and environmental actions, involve both tangible and real property. Pretrial access to property is becoming increasingly important in discovery. Cases involving real property and construction defects require access to property. Treatment facilities, in toxic waste cases and environmental litigation, need to be inspected relative to their safety conditions and procedure. Inspection tours of factories may be necessary to obtain evidence for product liability and/or employment discrimination cases. Rule 34 authorizes the broadest sweep of access, inspection, examination, testing, copying, and photographing of documents or objects in possession or control of another party.

§ 6.4   What Can Be Requested?

All documents, things, and property requested must be in the possession, control, and custody of the party to whom the request has been propounded. Possession and custody include both actual and constructive possession and custody, and have been interpreted to mean that the responding party has a legal right to obtain the documents. This obligates the responding party to produce all relevant documents, even those not in the party's actual possession, if the party has a lawful right to obtain them from another person or entity. The responding party cannot avoid production through the simple device of transferring the documents to another person or entity such as their attorney, accountant, insurance carrier, or a corporate subsidiary. If this avoidance device is used, the party is deemed to have retained control of the documents and is required to have them returned in order to comply with the production request.

The subject matter of a request to produce documents may include all of the items discussed in **Chapter 4.** Any document which has been used to prepare an interrogatory answer may be requested through a request for production of documents. Reviewing interrogatory answers is an excellent means of obtaining the information necessary to draft particularized requests for production of documents. Case law on federal and state levels has clarified (as well as confused) the discoverability of various items. The following items have generally been considered appropriate items and documents subject to inspection pursuant to Rule 34:

1. Nonparty witness statements on a good cause showing of substantial need and undue hardship upon the requesting party not to have a copy of the statement. A nonparty witness may always obtain their own statement through a request to the party who has the statement in their custody or control. Have a friendly witness who may be testifying for your client request a copy of their statement, which was taken by an investigator or representative of the opposing party at an early stage of the litigation. This is easier than requesting the same document through a formal Rule 34 request.

2. Documents of which a party does not have copies, but has a right or opportunity to obtain copies, must be produced. Examples of documents which fall under this category include profit and loss statements, accountant's records, inventory control sheets, and so forth.

3. Documents a party possesses, but which belong to a third person who is not a party need to be disclosed. For example: a party in real estate litigation may have in their custody copies of relevant documents concerning the history of a piece of property which they obtained when they purchased the property. The documents may have been given to them by prior owners who are not now parties to the instant litigation. However, because the property is the subject of litigation the documents are relevant and must be produced.

4. Documents prepared by, or under the direction or supervision of, an expert who will testify at time of trial must be produced. This differs from a consultant who may have prepared documents, reports, or tests while they were a consultant and not a designated expert. However, once an expert has been designated and is expected to testify at trial, the expert's reports, opinions, and conclusions are discoverable. These documents and reports may be requested at the time the deposition is taken of that expert, or they may be obtained through a Rule 34 request for production to the opposing party.

5. Documents and objects that a party possesses, controls, or has custody of are discoverable, even though such records and things may be beyond the territorial jurisdiction of the court. For example, documents and objects which have

been prepared in complex business litigation, real estate litigation, antitrust litigation, and other instances which involve documents prepared by a foreign entity or corporate subsidiary operating in another state are discoverable.

6. A corporate litigant is required to produce documents held by any of its subsidiaries. This is true even if the subsidiaries are not directly involved in the dispute.

Requesting privileged information in a document request should be handled in the same manner as discussed in **Chapter 4** and **Chapter 5.** Privileged information should be requested. The strategy of requesting information and/or documents which you anticipate will draw a privilege claim is that it forces the opposition to identify those documents. Garbage answers to requests to produce documents and meritless claims of privilege are also important in that they determine the existence of documents in a particular category. A party who has consistently responded to requested information at a deposition, through interrogatories, and a formal request to produce documents by stating that no such document exists will have a practically impossible task introducing that document or piece of information at the time of trial. Establishing that the opponent lacks certain evidence, information, or documents is vitally important in trial preparation.

§ 6.5 Protecting the Corporate Client

When representing a corporate client, precautions must be taken at every step of case preparation, investigation, and discovery to insure that the corporate client's work product and attorney-client privileges are protected. A corporate client, like any other artificial entity, can only receive communications from its attorney by means of human agency such as officers, agents, and employees of the corporation selected by the corporation's directors and officers to act on its behalf. A corporation, like a natural person, is entitled to the full benefit of the attorney-client privilege and work product privilege as it applies to all phases of discovery. As discussed in **Chapters 4 and 5,** special duties fall upon the corporate entity which go beyond that of an individual in preparing responses to requests for information through interrogatories and requests for admissions. They are bound to investigate and provide information that is not only within their own personal knowledge but also within the corporation's body of knowledge.

Care must be taken from the onset of any investigation or other corporate activity which could lead to an incident resulting in litigation to protect those communications, both written and oral, that flow between officers of the corporation, agents of the corporation, and attorneys for the corporation. Case law has held that communications, both written and oral, that occurred before an actual complaint was filed and litigation was commenced may be considered confidential if it can be shown that the intent of the communications was in anticipation of litigation and/or the communications were intended to be treated as confidential communications.

Generally speaking the two primary causes of waiver of privilege for a corporate entity are when there is either (1) a disclosure of privileged communications to uninterested third parties or (2) a disclosure to those parties whose interests may be adverse to the client. Case law has further held that disclosure of information through written or oral communications to representatives of related or affiliated corporations (subsidiaries) does not waive the attorney-client privilege or attorney work product privilege. Courts have viewed the parent corporation as the ultimate client and the subsidiary corporations to possess sufficient unity of interest to maintain the confidentiality of attorney-client communications and attorney work product privileged documents such as interoffice memoranda, and various and miscellaneous corporate reports.[1]

A corporate client generates a great deal of paper in the normal course and scope of its business operations. Some corporate housekeeping documents will naturally be accessible through document requests and subpoenas. A parent corporation with many subsidiaries will automatically generate a great deal of paper dealing with policies, procedures, and communications between the subsidiaries and the parent corporation. Most of these documents will not be privileged documents, and may not be the key documents that need to be protected from disclosure in litigation. Those documents which may be considered sensitive documents need to be protected in initial case preparation and at the onset of litigation to avoid having them become subject to disclosure through a document request or subpoena as discovery progresses in an action.

§ 6.6   Checklist for Protecting Corporate Documents

When you are representing a corporate client it is wise to establish ground rules from the beginning for communications between your law firm and the corporation, all of its agents, employees, directors, and department heads. This checklist can be very helpful in establishing the criteria for good, solid ground rules.

_____   1.   All letters, memoranda, interoffice communications, fax, letters, telegrams, and any other written communication that is to be exchanged between your office and the corporation (parent corporation and any of the subsidiaries) should be stamped at the top "CONFIDENTIAL—PREPARED AT THE REQUEST OF ATTORNEY JOHN DOE." The use of this stamp implies that the document is a confidential communication and that the author's intent was to make the document a confidential communication.

_____   2.   Confidential stamps should only be used on confidential documents and not overused, especially when a corporation has been trained to use a confidential stamp on their communications between your office and their office. For example, stamping a document "CONFIDENTIAL FOR ATTORNEY JOHN DOE" and then attaching a distribution list naming 25 individuals destroys the confidentiality of that document. It would be difficult to prove either that all 25 named individuals were necessary in order to convey that communication to the

---

[1] _See_ Hickman v. Taylor, 153 F.2d 212 (3d Cir. 1945); Insurance Co. of N. Am. v. Superior Court, 108 Cal. App. 3d 758, 166 Cal. Rptr. 850 (1980).

attorney or that all 25 individuals shared a community of interest in the information contained in the document. Of course, there are exceptions to every rule, and it may very well be that all 25 individuals named on the distribution list are presidents and vice-presidents of various subsidiaries and do share a community interest. However, it is difficult to establish that a document was intended to be a confidential communication when it is distributed to more than the attorney and one or two corporate spokespersons.

_____   3.   Communications between the corporate client and your office should be on a need-to-know basis. That is, copies of key documents should be routed only from the president of the corporation, or head of a particular division, to the attorney or paralegal working on the case. It is also wise to caution the corporate client not to create a paper trail. Corporate clients are used to reducing everything to writing and it is sometimes difficult for them to switch gears and phone their attorney or legal assistant with information that can be handled in a phone conference without creating a written document which may be discoverable.

_____   4.   A corporate client is usually a sophisticated businessperson who is somewhat organized and savvy at the rules of business negotiations and corporate game playing which are skills directly transferable to litigation. This type of client will need little encouragement in marking documents confidential, and may need to be less zealous in designating confidential documents. If a pattern can be shown by your opponent that all documents are routinely marked confidential without a true intent on the part of the corporate officer that the document is really meant to be treated in a confidential manner, the opponent can request confidential documents based on the argument that the stamp "confidential" on a document does not mean what it says. This type of client needs assistance in discerning those documents which are truly confidential from those documents which the client thinks should be withheld from discovery.

_____   5.   The agents and employees of a corporation, when moving down the chain of command, may be less sophisticated corporate game players. These individuals may have been very prominent in the prelitigation stage, and may have authored many documents which will be subject to a request to produce documents such as field notes, punch lists, reports of walk-throughs on construction projects, engineering logs, job site visit reports, construction diaries, and so forth. If these documents are requested by the opposition, and they will be if they are relevant to the litigation, they will have to be produced. Whether these documents need to be produced in their entirety is a strategic decision. Often, although the document itself is relevant and must be produced, portions of it may be considered privileged communications and may be excised from the document prior to production. Internal claims investigation reports which may have been authored by a foreman on a construction project, or engineer while troubleshooting an electrical wiring problem at the request of a risk manager, are privileged documents even though they originated in the prelitigation stage. The general rule is that any document prepared in anticipation of litigation is considered to be privileged, especially if it has been written or researched at the request of a corporate officer or insurance risk manager.

As investigation progresses in an action, it often becomes necessary for the paralegal to work with a project foreman or engineer regarding certain phases of construction. All communications regarding alleged defects, deficiencies, or deviations from plans and specifications should be documented in memorandum form with a caption at the top stating the case name, and the following: Prepared at the request of Attorney John Doe. Labelling each memoranda, letter, or communication in this manner clearly identifies these documents as part of an ongoing investigation and protects them from disclosure through a request to produce documents propounded by your opponent.

§ 6.7   Gathering Client Documents

Gathering documents from your client is one of the most important fact finding aspects of any case. It can be both time-consuming and frustrating, but it is the best opportunity for the legal team to meet with the client to explain the importance of the "due and diligent search requirement" of the statutes authorizing document requests. A meeting with the client should include all persons who will be working directly with you in assembling the responsive documents. It is important, at an initial client meeting, to learn the names of all the key players, that is, all persons who may have authored or received documents in the normal course and scope of business which may relate to any of the issues of the lawsuit. An initial meeting is an excellent opportunity to take a general inventory of your client's files, that is, all the paper in the client's possession. It is important to explain to the client that even though not every piece of paper in their possession will be relevant and/or requested by the opposition, it is important to know the extent of documentation which exists regarding each of the issues in the lawsuit. It is also important to have historical perspective on the issues in dispute. Frequently, in commercial litigation, a present dispute has its roots in prior misunderstandings, and a paper trail exists which will flesh out the issues in the lawsuit.

At an initial document gathering meeting with your client, speak to each custodian of records or head of specific departments, in the business organization. Ascertain whether the assigned custodian of records, or head of department, is really the person who maintains the files, or just the designated custodian of records in name only. The person who regularly maintains the files in the normal course and scope of business will be the most helpful when you need to respond to a document request. That person usually knows all contributors to the file, authors of various documents, and/or routing lists accompanying those documents. Every business has a pack rat who is frequently the employee with the greatest longevity with the business and has the best historical handle on the documents that have been generated in the normal course and scope of business.

Ask your client about their official document retention policy, and note any differences in that official policy with the documents presently in your client's files. If there are significant time gaps between what was generated and should have been retained and what actually exists in your clients files or is stored in the warehouse, take note of this and immediately alert your attorney of this discrepancy.

Take time at your initial visit to look at some actual document files to understand the client's organizational system. Is it chronological? Is it subject specific? Is it by project number? It is important to understand your client's organizational system and the types of documents which are generated in the normal course and scope of their business such as invoices, blueprints, bills of lading, and so forth, and it will help you to locate important documents when they are needed on short notice.

§ 6.8 Working with Your Client

Frequently we get caught up in the discovery process and are so busy requesting documents from the opposition and attempting to protect privileged documents from production that we fail to take time to understand our client's needs. It is important to make this process as smooth as possible for your corporate client. The following list of helpful hints are suggestions for how to make document production smoother from the corporate point of view:

1. Send discovery requests to the corporate client as soon as you receive them from the opposition to allow them sufficient time to locate documents in the requested categories. Do not wait to send the discovery request until it is accompanied by your draft response; because the draft response can be sent later.

2. Work with and through the in-house legal department, and allow them to make the initial contact with responsible parties in the business.

3. Learn some of the corporate vocabulary so that you will have a better understanding of the documents which are being produced.

4. Teach the corporate client some legal vocabulary so that they can understand the terminology of the requests better.

5. Use photocopies of files as often as possible, so that the original files can be left in the possession of the corporate client.

6. Respect the difference between active files and inactive files. Active files must remain within the business in order for the corporate client to carry on their day-to-day activities.

7. Respect the integrity of their files, especially active files. Return the files to the corporate client in the same manner of organization as you received them.

8. Use the documents already provided for your first draft response before sending the interrogatories or document request asking for further documentation and responses.

9. Copy the corporate client on the final written response to a document request, and include a list of all documents which have been produced.

10. Advise the corporate client which documents were not produced, and whether you will still need custody of them. If not, return them.

11. Return company files when they are requested, especially active ones.

12. Use the company organizational chart and list of approved abbreviations to help you understand the documents that the corporate client has given you.

§ 6.9   Criteria for Identifying Privileged Documents

Not all written communications between an attorney and client are privileged. For example, a simple cover letter or memoranda which does not contain comment or analysis does not necessarily qualify as a privileged document. Communication from an attorney to a client must be in a professional capacity, that of an attorney, not as a businessperson, a member of the business decision-making team, a member of the board of directors of the corporation, and so forth. Significant documents are those which contain comment or legal analysis.

This checklist is useful for an initial document screening. Those documents which should be classified as privileged communications and flagged for further review include the following:

_____ 1. Documents which offer any legal advice or opinion whether they are an informal memorandum, or on a law firm letterhead;

_____ 2. Documents evidencing a communication between an attorney and a corporate officer (or business client), unless the communication discusses nonlegal matters. Documents confirming legal proceedings such as "your deposition shall take place at 10:00 a.m. on May 1, 19__, and I will meet you at the office of defense counsel located at . . . " should not be considered privileged communications;

_____ 3. Documents prepared by an attorney recommending against or commenting on a particular course of business conduct, conduct of the officers or employees of the client corporation or business;

_____ 4. Any handwritten notes or marginal comments on any document which appear to offer advice, comment, or notation;

_____ 5. Documents which comment on, appear to have been prepared in connection with, or in anticipation of any proceeding in a court or an administrative agency of the state or federal government (Carefully examine the re: line on documents to determine the subject matter of the communication.);

_____ 6. Documents prepared by anyone in the client corporation or business which communicate or reflect the communication of any significant information to an attorney, or legal assistant, that is relevant to the subject matter of the action;

_____ 7. Internal documents reflecting, or commenting on, recommendations or legal opinions received from the in-house law department or outside counsel of a corporation or business;

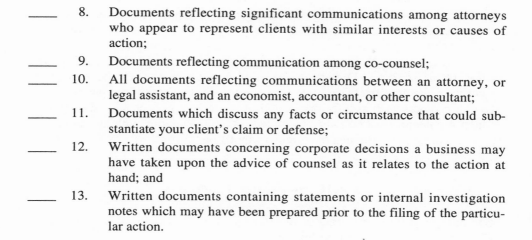

____ 8.   Documents reflecting significant communications among attorneys who appear to represent clients with similar interests or causes of action;

____ 9.   Documents reflecting communication among co-counsel;

____ 10. All documents reflecting communications between an attorney, or legal assistant, and an economist, accountant, or other consultant;

____ 11. Documents which discuss any facts or circumstance that could substantiate your client's claim or defense;

____ 12. Written documents concerning corporate decisions a business may have taken upon the advice of counsel as it relates to the action at hand; and

____ 13. Written documents containing statements or internal investigation notes which may have been prepared prior to the filing of the particular action.

§ 6.10 Inspection of Property

Federal Rule of Civil Procedure 34 authorizes the inspection of real property and objects or operations (facilities) located on real property. This method of discovery is not limited to a visual inspection of the property—it also authorizes the propounding party to measure, survey, photograph, sample, and conduct testing procedures on an opponent's land or property.

The party who makes a demand to enter onto and inspect an opponent's property also has the right to observe any operations conducted on the property. In product liability and employment discrimination cases, it may be helpful to watch a manufacturer's assembly line in operation or a piece of farm machinery, as well as observing the activities of those employees or customers who are users of the equipment.

The demanding party must notify the responding party not only when any related activity such as testing or sampling will be performed in addition to the actual inspection but also whether that activity could permanently alter, or destroy, the item tested. Reasonable tests and inspections may proceed without a showing of good cause; however, the responding party may object to any unusual testing, sampling, or other activity which could permanently alter or destroy the property or item. Stipulations may be agreed upon between parties to allow the inspection or testing to proceed only under specified terms and conditions.

When a request for entry onto land for purposes of inspections and/or testing is made, counsel for all parties should agree to work out the testing procedures so that a single site inspection and/or a single soil test is conducted. The responding party, and all owners of the property, should be present at the time of the inspection and/or testing, and any results or residue of the testing (such as soil samples) must be preserved by a neutral third party who has conducted the tests. Case law has held that to subject a party to numerous entries upon land or personal property and numerous tests is burdensome, oppressive, harassing, and generally unnecessary. Case law has further emphasized coordination of this discovery procedure with all parties to the litigation so that the interests of justice may be preserved in safeguarding the personal property rights of the respondent. Practical considerations in arranging inspections of personal property usually result in stipulations for a designated time and manner of inspection. A written stipulation to allow entry onto land and/or testing of land or personal property often includes certain protective provisions agreed upon by all parties such as tests being monitored, limited disclosure, or work not disrupted if the inspection is to occur on the premises where the items are usually kept and if the premises are a place of business such as a factory, chemical waste treatment plant, and so forth. A written stipulation must be signed by all parties to the litigation with the attorney for the demanding party retaining the original stipulation for trial.

§ 6.11   Stipulated Provisions

Stipulated provisions for inspection or entry onto land are beneficial to both sides. A party who has been served with a demand to enter upon land, or a demand for inspection, photographing, or testing may respond with an objection to that notice and a request for a protective order. This is a lengthy, cumbersome, and expensive court procedure which expends attorney and client time and money. A more practical solution is a stipulation which permits the inspection and/or testing, but contains protective language which provides safeguards for the responding party (See **Form 6–1**). There is a natural reluctance on the part of a litigant to give up custody of important demonstrative evidence, and it is always a difficult problem to conduct tests on articles or property that are in your opponent's custody or control. The danger of damage or loss is always present in considerations for arranging inspection and testing. For example, in a product liability case centered around the flammability of a particular article of clothing, such as children's pajamas, it may be necessary to obtain an identical pair of pajamas and test it to see if it is flammable. The type of proposed testing may ignite the pajamas and destroy them. If only a few pieces of the particular material used to make those pajamas are still in existence, and the proposed test would destroy those remaining pieces of material, a court order authorizing destructive testing is necessary before the proposed test can proceed. (See **§§ 6.13** and **6.14** for a further discussion on destructive testing.)

A sensitive issue also arises when a party demands an inspection of a factory, waste treatment facility, or manufacturing plant during operating hours. During the inspection, the requesting party may wish to photograph objects and activities on the land such as the operation of particular pieces of machinery (especially in product liability cases). Inspection and photographing of a manufacturing plant may be permitted on the condition that no secret processes are photographed, and that none of the photographs are made available to anyone outside of the interested parties in the action. The inspection may even be ordered on certain days during certain hours, when the responding party knows that no secret processes will be ongoing within the manufacturing plant, and when the inspection will cause the least amount of disruption to the normal business routine.

FORM 6–1
SAMPLE STIPULATION FOR INSPECTION

SUPERIOR COURT OF THE STATE OF [state name]
IN AND FOR THE COUNTY OF [county name]

[name], et al.,	No. [case number]
Plaintiff(s),	STIPULATION FOR INSPECTION
-vs-	
[name], et al.,	
Defendant(s).	

It is stipulated by the parties through [name], attorney for plaintiff, and [name], attorney for defendant, that defendant will permit plaintiff to enter the land and premises described as [specifically describe the land, using the legal description of the property as well as the complete street address, name of business if applicable, and so forth] for the following purposes:

[Describe the manner in which the inspection will be conducted and in particular any specific measuring, surveying, photographing, testing, or soil sampling that will be conducted.]

The stipulation may also include protective language at the request of the responding party such as:

. . . providing that the testing and analysis to be performed by the defendant's experts will not materially modify or otherwise damage the material to be analyzed; or . . . 10 days before performance of any test, defendant will notify plaintiff of which tests will be performed on the material, and plaintiff may designate a person to observe these tests. Furthermore, all reports of the results of these tests, and any remnants of the material tested, shall be made available to plaintiff on reasonable request. Nothing contained in this document requires defendant or defendant's expert to disclose the reasons why certain tests are being undertaken or the sequence or significance of those tests.

Protective language to be used if a factory, or place of business, is to be inspected:

. . . plaintiff shall indemnify defendant for the financial loss occasioned by the business interruption occurring during the cost of the operation and testing as follows: [state agreed upon method for calculating financial loss of business interruption if factory or business premises needs to be closed for one business day so that test and inspection may take place.].

Protective language to be used if the inspection or tests invade trade secrets and the disclosure of confidential information may be materially effected:

. . . provided that to preserve the commercial secrecy of the object tested, all notes, reports and photographs pertaining to the operation and testing of the object shall be delivered to the clerk of the court as soon as practical, and thereafter sealed and filed in this action with access to be limited to the plaintiff's attorney or an order of the court after due notice to all parties.

Protective language to be used if stipulation is to permit entry and surveying of real property (This is similar to an in camera inspection of documents.):

. . . provided that entry on and surveying of the above-described property shall occur only between the hours of [time] and [time], and provided further that plaintiff shall post a bond with this court in the amount of $ [dollar amount] as security for, and to insure indemnification of, defendant for financial loss on account of business interruption, alteration of property, or any other damage occasioned by the entry and survey.

The above-described entry and/or inspection will take place on [date], at [time] and may be monitored and supervised by [designate a representative of the party permitting the inspection and entry onto the land].

Counsel for requesting party shall file the stipulation with the court and request that an order incorporating its terms be issued without further notice or hearing.

Dated: [date].

_____
[attorney for plaintiff]

_____
[attorney for defendant]

§ 6.12   Inspection and Testing

Litigation of product liability cases, floods, earthquakes, and environmental cases has led to an increase in demands for inspection and testing pursuant to a Federal Rule of Civil Procedure 34 demand, which includes the right of the requesting party to arrange with a neutral third party, such as a professional contractor, soil engineer, termite expert, and so forth, to inspect and test the property and/or substances on the property. Federal case law has allowed a broad scope of activities and procedures pursuant to a formal Federal Rules of Civil Procedure demand including entrance to large tracts of unimproved acreage, livestock ranches, improved lots, gas and oil wells, piers, ships, offshore drilling rigs, prison facilities, mental institutions, and various manufacturing plants.

Examples of federal cases illustrating the wide variety of activities permitted under Rule 34 include the following:

1.   A company accused of discharging flourides from an aluminum plant onto a livestock ranch and into its water supply was served with a demand to enter onto the property for purposes of testing and sampling. A party was allowed onto the livestock ranch and allowed to take samples of the soil, water, air, forage, and cattle feed, to visually and physically examine the cattle, including the taking of urine samples, and testing of those samples. They were also allowed to conduct postmortem examinations on any dead animals.[2]

2.   A case in which a homeowner claimed that the homeowner's artesian well was being polluted by their neighbor's cesspool. Through service of a demand to enter onto the land, the plaintiff received permission to place a vegetable dye in that cesspool to test whether that same dye would later appear in his water supply.[3]

3.   A building contractor, who was being sued for installing defective materials in the roof of a school, served a demand to enter onto the school grounds for inspection and testing. The contractor was given permission to remove one of its insulroc panels so that experts could test it to evaluate whether it was defective.[4]

4.   A land owner claimed that a nearby oil well was drawing production from the subsurface of the landowner's property. The landowner served a demand to inspect the opponent's property including the oil wells and was permitted to make a directional survey of the path of the well.[5]

§ 6.13   Authorized Testing

Activities permitted under Federal Rule of Civil Procedure 34 relating to testing or sampling must be carefully spelled out in the actual demand for inspection and testing (See **Forms 6–2** and **6–3**). The responding party has the right to ask the court to intervene and to impose conditions to safeguard tangible items and to restrict the length of time they will be surrendered if they are removed from the property for testing. Most testing authorized pursuant to a Rule 34 request consists of routine examinations and tests which can be performed repeatedly. However, difficult issues concerning the permissible scope of inspection and testing arise when the requested testing procedure would either significantly alter the appearance of the item listed or destroy it completely. Destructive testing, or any testing which may alter material evidence cannot proceed without a formal court order. The concern of the court, in destructive testing, is generally towards preventing the party from being prejudiced in the pending litigation by the destruction of crucial evidence.

---

[2] Marking v. Reynolds Metal Corp., 297 F.2d 49 (9th Cir. 1961).

[3] Borland v. Dunn, 321 A.2d 96 (R.I. 1974).

[4] Kingsport v. SMC Corp., 352 F. Supp. 287 (E.D. Tenn. 1972).

[5] Williams v. Continental Oil Co., 215 F.2d 4 (10th Cir. 1954).

Testing is also sometimes sought that threatens to cause monetary damage to the item being tested. A practical solution to this problem has been for the court to require the party seeking the test to post an appropriate bond to protect against any damage that might be done to the article being tested. The court becomes involved in destructive testing upon either the motion of the parties seeking the test (to compel production of the article to be tested) or upon a motion for a protective order from the party holding the article to be tested.

FORM 6–2
SAMPLE DEMAND FOR ROUTINE INSPECTION AND TESTING

SUPERIOR COURT OF THE STATE OF [state name]
IN AND FOR THE COUNTY OF [county name]

[name], et al.,	No. [case number]
Plaintiff,	DEMAND TO ENTER AND INSPECT LAND OR
-vs-	PREMISES
[name], et al.,	
Defendant.	

DEMANDING PARTY: Plaintiff, [name]

RESPONDING PARTY: Defendant, [name]

Plaintiff, [name], demands that you permit plaintiff and plaintiff's attorney to enter the real property in your possession, custody, or control, located at [address], [city], [state] on [date] between [time] and [time] for the following purposes:

1. To make a visual inspection of the land to include surveying, photographing, and obtaining certain soil and mineral samples to be used in laboratory testing to determine the nitrogen content of such samples.

You are required under [cite statute authority] to serve a written response within 25 days from the date of service of this demand.

Dated: [date]

_____
[attorney for plaintiff]

FORM 6–3
SAMPLE DEMAND FOR INSPECTION OF TANGIBLE OBJECTS

SUPERIOR COURT OF THE STATE OF [state name]
IN AND FOR THE COUNTY OF [county name]

[name], et al.,	No. [case number]
Plaintiff,	DEMAND FOR INSPECTION OF TANGIBLE OBJECTS
-vs-	
[name], et al.,	
Defendant.	

DEMANDING PARTY: [plaintiff]

RESPONDING PARTY: [defendant]

SET NUMBER: [set number]

Plaintiff demands that you produce for the purpose of inspection and photographing by plaintiff or plaintiff's representatives the following tangible items in your possession, custody, or control on [date] at [time] at [name] Service Garage located at [address], [city], [state].

1. The bus belonging to defendant involved in the collision with the automobile of plaintiff on [date] at the intersection of [name] Street and [name] Street, [city], [state].

2. Any parts from either vehicle collected by defendant, or their agents, including but not limited to automotive repair personnel, salvage shops, insurance carriers, and other agents and representatives.

You are required under [cite statutory authority] to serve a written response within 25 days from the date of service of this demand.

Dated: [date].

_____
[name of attorney]

§ 6.14   Protective Orders for Testing Purposes

In attempting to balance the need of a party to obtain information regarding a particular article with an underlying concern for fairness to the owners of the article, the courts have generally either denied the right of a party to conduct destructive testing, or permitted testing under the provisions of a strict protective order which spells out the precise terms of the testing. Testing has then been authorized to proceed with a video record being made of everything which occurs during the testing, and a stipulation to the use of the video test as trial evidence.

The terms of a protective order authorizing destructive testing usually include the following safeguards:

1. A specific testing plan set forth in detail,
2. An opportunity, prior to testing, for all other parties to examine and photograph the article which is to be tested and possibly destroyed,
3. A notice to all parties with the time, date, and all particulars for the testing,
4. The right of any party to be present at the testing with any consultant or expert of their choice,
5. Careful and thorough written documentation of the test activities and test results along with a video tape of the actual test,
6. The availability of test results to all parties of the litigation,
7. The availability of reports by persons conducting the testing to all parties to the litigation, and
8. The right of other parties to take additional samples for similar testing, if the material is available at the time of the original test.

A case example taken from litigation in an Illinois product liability case involved a plaintiff who had alleged that a chip of metal from the hammer that the plaintiff was using in the course and scope of employment injured the plaintiff's eye. The manufacturer of the hammer was able to show the need for an expert to cut a piece of metal from the hammer for testing purposes. A demand for inspection and testing was served upon the supplier of the particular hammer. It was held to be in the discretion of the trial court in Illinois to permit an alteration of the hammer (as called for in the testing and inspection demand) once photographs and macrographs of the original condition of the hammer had been taken. The court in Farver v. Barrett Ace Hardware, Inc.[6] ruled that:

> The hammer will still be available for viewing by the jury after completion of the testing. While a small, pie-shaped wedge will have been removed from the hammer's striking face, the jury will still be able to observe the general condition of most of its striking face, and they will have macrographs of the hammer's face in its original condition.[7]

---

[6] 349 N.E.2d 28 (Ill. 1976).

[7] *Id.* at 30–31.

Form 6–4 could have been used in this case example. With modifications it can be adopted for use in any action in which requesting party seeks permission to perform product testing which may alter the original product.

FORM 6–4
SAMPLE DEMAND FOR DESTRUCTIVE TESTING

SUPERIOR COURT OF THE STATE OF [state name]
IN AND FOR THE COUNTY OF [county name]

[name], et al.,	No. [case number]
Plaintiff,	DEMAND FOR INSPECTION AND TESTING
-vs-	
[name], et al.,	
Defendant.	

DEMANDING PARTY: [plaintiff]

RESPONDING PARTY: [defendant]

SET NUMBER: [set number]

Plaintiff demands that you produce for inspection, photographing, testing, and sampling the following tangible things and/or categories of tangible things in your possession, custody or control on [date] at [time] at [place] located at [address], [city], [state].

1. The hammer manufactured by defendant, [name], and sold by defendant [name] to plaintiff [name] on or about [date].

2. The items that you produce will be subject to the following inspection, photographing, testing, and sampling:

(a) Photographing the hammer in the condition as received.

(b) Macroscopic examination and photographing of the hammer for areas of possible abuse.

(c) Drilling three 1/4″ holes approximately 1″ deep in the side of the hammer claw, just above the eye of the hammer, to obtain a sample of the metal for chemical analysis to determine steel composition.

(d) Cutting a wedge-shaped section from the striking face of the hammer for microscopic examination to evaluate the microstructure.

The item that you produce will be permanently altered to the extent described above by this testing and sampling. However, photographs will be taken of the item before it is altered and copies of all photographs and macrographs will be provided to you when the hammer is returned.

You are required under Federal Rule of Civil Procedure 34 [or cite applicable statute] to serve a written response within [number] days from the date of service of this demand.

Dated: [date].

_____

[name of attorney]

§ 6.15   Drafting Requests to Produce Documents

The drafting suggestions discussed in **Chapter 4** on interrogatories, along with the drafting suggestions discussed in **Chapter 5** for requests for admissions apply to drafting requests for document production. Document requests should be drafted with enough specifics to avoid allowing the other side to withhold some documents, while at the same time drafted with enough breadth of scope to make certain that no existing documents escape the confines of the request. Two different drafting techniques may be used to make the request escape proof and all-encompassing:

1.   Draft requests seeking both specifically designated items and generally described items; and

2.   Use specific definitions of categories and titles of specific documents, if known.

Requests to produce documents must specify a reasonable date, time, and place for the production. Federal Rule of Civil Procedure 34 requires that this be "reasonable." Written responses which specify objections, or agreements to produce documents only in particular categories are due 10 days before the actual production of documents. The actual time frame for production of documents is usually 30 days from the service of the request with extra time allowed for service by mail. Check local rules to be certain of the time frame for the response and actual production. Calendar the date for written responses so that a timely response can be made protecting your client's right to object, or seeking to limit the scope of a particular request.

Requests for document production must define and designate documents sought "with reasonable particularity." You can never be absolutely certain that your request meets the standard of reasonable particularity; therefore, common sense must govern. Materials should be described by the subject matter they contain, by particular classification, or by definite time periods. Case law has held that the standard of "reasonable particularity" is met if the request is drafted in such a manner as to allow a person of ordinary intelligence to say "I know what they want," and to permit a judge to determine whether all the requested items in a given category have been produced. Most courts allow discovery of general categories of items if the description is easily understood.

§ 6.16   Checklist for Drafting Requests for Production

This checklist can be very useful in approaching the logistics of drafting requests for production not only from an organizational point but also from the point of what documents to request.

_____ 1.   Know what documents are needed to prove your allegations, claims, and/or defenses before you begin drafting requests for document production. Review the pleadings which have been filed, read the correspondence in the file, and review the documents you have received from your client. Confer with your client. The client may know of the existence of key documents or may be able to provide you with the information necessary to describe specific documents by title or date.

_____ 2.   Review the depositions, interrogatory responses, and other discovery as a means of learning the existence of documents. Pay particular attention to documents which reference enclosures or attachments and request not only the specific document, but all enclosures and attachments as well. If deposition testimony or an interrogatory answer refers to a contract and/or agreement, request not only the original document but all drafts and revisions of the document.

_____ 3.   Request each and every document which was relied upon in preparation of interrogatory responses and any other discovery responses received from your opponent if you have not already done so.

_____ 4.   Request the minutes and agenda of the meeting, and any notes or memoranda reflecting discussions that occurred at the meeting if any discovery response or written statement refers to a meeting. If a reference is made to telephone calls, ask for telephone logs, diaries, appointment books, and so forth. Ask for all written material that has been mentioned in discovery responses that is relevant to the issues of the action.

_____ 5.   Describe the documents you are requesting by referring to the other party's pleadings, complaint, answer, demurrer, and so forth. For example, ask for all correspondence, communications, memoranda, documents, and other tangible evidence that refers to, relates to, or pertains to defendant's contentions in specific paragraphs in plaintiff's complaint.

_____ 6.   Be specific and describe the document by identifying its type (letter, agreement, contract), title, date, author, and addressee, if you know the title of the document you are requesting. For example, the original and all carbon or other copies of that letter written on May 1, 19__ to Jane S. from Roger B. which pertained to her employment at [name] Corporation.

_____ 7. Describe the documents by specific legal theories of plaintiff or defendant such as execution of contract, breach of contract, and damages. For example: "All correspondence, communications, memoranda, documents, and other tangible evidence pertaining to the alleged contract between the parties referred to in paragraph 3 of the complaint on file in this action."

_____ 8. Set forth each category of documents separately. For example, you may request all invoices and billing statements relating to transactions between Party A and Party B over a period of five years, and you may also request all receipts, cancelled checks, or money orders evidencing payment of the invoices between Party A and Party B for transactions conducted over the same time period. However, do not combine invoices and receipts in one request, because they must be set forth separately.

_____ 9. Set forth a relevant time period in the introductory paragraphs or instructions which accompany the request. For example, it is usually considered by the courts to be nonobjectionable to ask for a 5 to 10 year history in a particular request unless you reference a critical time period in a specific request. Certain requests, by their very nature, imply a particular critical time period, for example, the term of a contract, the term of employment, the length of a guarantee, and so forth. To request documents without setting forth a reasonable or particular time period renders the request ambiguous, unintelligible, and burdensome, and allows the responding party to raise objections to the production of the requested documents.

_____ 10. Request documents in all categories which are important to proving the allegations of your complaint or the affirmative defenses raised in your answer. The fact that a response to a particular request might be a privilege claim is not a reason to omit that request. It is important that privileged documents be requested, forcing your opponent to identify every document which exists in a specific category, even those in which they are privileged.

_____ 11. Direct requests to all categories in which documents may exist. They should be broad-based and all-encompassing, reaching into all categories in which relevant documents may exist. Caution must be exercised in drafting such requests to avoid objections that you are merely fishing for information. Requests which yield the response "no documents exist" are useful discovery tools. If a particular category of documents has been requested and the response is "no documents exist," it will be difficult for the responding party suddenly to discover documents in that category and seek to introduce them as evidence at time of trial.

_____ 12. Request realistic number of documents. A mistake frequently made in drafting document requests is to ask for more documents in each category than you need and can handle. In most cases, only about 5 percent to 10 percent of the documents produced are useful in discovery and trial preparation. Document discovery must be planned with real-istic goals and a budget that fits the economic boundaries of the case and your client's budget. If requests are carefully drafted based on information revealed in discovery, you can tailor document requests to specific items. For example, if only certain invoices in a particular, critical time period are relevant, do not ask for 5 to 10 years worth of invoices. Not only will it cost your client extra money to ask for more documents than you need, but also it may cause you to overlook important documents buried in a flood of unimportant documents. It is important to request documents in all categories, but it is not always prudent to ask for all documents in a specific category.

§ 6.17   The Use of Definitions in Drafting Requests

Definitions should be used in the introductory paragraphs of a request to produce documents for any terms which are unusual or unique to the specific litigation. For example, specific contracts should be named such as Contract for Employment between Jane S. and Roger B., Sales Transaction Contract for 44 Riverdale Drive, Escrow File No. 9536-1, bank account no. 003-005-896, commercial account of Jane S., and so forth.

Definitions in the introductory paragraph should also specify a time frame. The time frame stated should be broad-based enough to encompass two to three years prior to the incident or dispute, and two to three years subsequent to the incident or dispute. In some cases, the time frame of the request should be broadened to 5 to 10 years, for example, in cases where you are seeking accident, investigation, or prior incident reports, employment history, insurance policies covering continuing loss reports, and so forth.

"Document" should be defined to include all drafts, carbon copies, and revised copies of each document requested. The term "document" itself should be defined pursuant to Federal Rule of Civil Procedure 34 to include the following:

> The term "documents" means all writing of any kind including the originals and all non-identical copies, whether different from the originals by reason of any notation made on such copies or otherwise, including, without limitation, correspondence, mem-oranda, notes, diaries, statistics, ledgers, telegrams, minutes, contracts, reports, studies, checks, statements, receipts, returns, summaries, pamphlets, books, inter-office and intra-office communications, notations of any conversations, telephone calls, telephone logs, meetings or other communications, bulletins, printed matter, computer printouts, teletype, telefax, invoices, work sheets, all drafts, alterations, modifications, changes, and amendments of any of the foregoing; graphic or oral records or representations of any kind (including, without limitation, photographs, charts, graphs, microfiche, micro-film, videotapes, recordings, motion pictures) and any electronic, mechanical or electric records or representations of any kind (including, without limitation, tapes, cassettes, disks, recordings, and computer memories).

This all-encompassing definition of the word document is taken from Rule 34 and applicable federal case law. In addition to defining the word document in every conceivable aspect, Rule 34 also defines "communication" as it is always used in requests to produce. A definition of communication should include:

> Communication means any contact among or between two or more persons (any natural person, firm, partnership, joint venture, corporation, or any entity) and includes, without limitations, a written contract among two or more persons and includes letters, memoranda, telegrams, telefax, or any documents and/or oral contact as such may exist in face-to-face meetings or telephone conversations.

Form 6–5 is an example of the introductory paragraphs (with instructions) of a Request for Production of Documents.

FORM 6–5
SAMPLE DEMAND TO PRODUCE DOCUMENTS

UNITED STATES DISTRICT COURT
[judicial district] DISTRICT OF [state]

[name], et al.,	No. [case number]
Plaintiff(s),	DEMAND TO PRODUCE DOCUMENTS FOR INSPECTION
-vs-	AND COPYING
[name], et al.,	
Defendant(s).	

PROPOUNDING PARTY: [name]

RESPONDING PARTY: [name]

SET NUMBER: [set number]

Pursuant to Rule 34, of the Federal Rules of Civil Procedure, defendant requests you to produce all documents in your custody and control, your attorneys, agents, persons on whose behalf you are prosecuting this action or other persons acting on your behalf in the categories specified below. In searching for and producing said documents you must use all information which is known or available to you, including, but not limited to, information known of your own personal knowledge, information obtainable by a diligent search of sources of information available to you, and all information in the possession of or available to any person or persons acting on your behalf or under your control or under the control of any of your attorneys, agents, servants or representatives. Defendant requests that you produce said documents for inspection and copying at the offices of [attorney name], [address], [city], [state] on [date] at [time].

As an alternative to the means of production specified above, you may mail or hand deliver a true and correct copy of each document to be produced in response to this request to the requesting party's attorney ten (10) days before the date of production specified above.

This request is made pursuant to Federal Rule of Civil Procedure 34, which requires responding party to serve a written response subscribed under oath within the time specified in said section, and which further requires responding party to identify the documents falling within the categories specified below which are in the possession, custody or control of responding party; and to state that inspection and related activities will be permitted unless the request is objected to, in which event the reasons for each objection must be clearly stated.

<u>INSTRUCTIONS</u>

This request requires the responding party to produce all documents which are in the possession, custody, or control of the responding party, whether actual or constructive, including documents which may be in the physical possession of another entity holding the documents on behalf of responding party such as a business or law firm. If the responding party contends that any document requested is protected from disclosure by the attorney-client privilege or by the attorney work product doctrine, responding party should specify the nature of the privilege claimed, describe the precise ground for the protection, and identify the document with particularity, including its author, date, or recipients thereof, the subject matter and the number of pages therein.

This request requires the production of documents in the same form and in the same order as they existed prior to production. The documents are to be produced in the boxes, file folders, bindings, or other containers in which the documents are found. The titles, labels, or other descriptions on the boxes, file folders, binders or other containers are to be left intact.

Unless otherwise specified, for example, by the use of the phrase "at any time," the time period covered by this request for documents extends from [date] to the present.

Note: Be sure and use a reasonable length of time, never more than ten years, and, in many cases five years is more appropriate.

§ 6.18   Documents to Request (Standard Categories)

Form 6–6 illustrates standard categories which should be included in most requests/demands to produce documents.

FORM 6–6
SAMPLE DOCUMENTS TO REQUEST (STANDARD CATEGORIES)

1. All documents that reflect, refer, or relate in any way to written or oral communications between defendant and plaintiff concerning the incident which is the subject matter of the complaint on file in this action.

2. All documents that relate, refer to, or constitute demonstrative evidence that plaintiff plans to introduce at the time of trial in this action. This demonstrative evidence shall include, but is not limited to, the following: photographs, graphs, charts, diagrams, surveys, drawings and specifications, blueprints, tangible items, posters, and/or any visual representation of any item that is relevant to the subject matter of this action.

3. All documents that reflect, refer, or relate in any way to any evaluation, appraisal, or summary of damages which plaintiff contends were caused by defendant in plaintiff's complaint on file in this action.

4. All documents that reflect, refer, or relate to the allegations of paragraph [number] of your complaint on file in this action that defendants were "_____."

Note: Item 4 should be tailored to fit the allegations of each and every paragraph of plaintiff's complaint. The allegation should be quoted directly from the complaint word for word, and line by line.

5. All documents that reflect, refer or relate in any way to the affirmative defenses plead by defendant in paragraph _____ of the answer on file in this action that plaintiff . . . .

Note: Item 5 should be tailored to fit the affirmative actions of each and every paragraph of defendant's answer. The affirmative actions should be quoted directly from the answer word for word, line by line.

6. All internal memoranda, notes, or other documents that refer or relate to defendants, either collectively or singularly.

7. Any and all statements made or given by any person regarding any of the facts or circumstances relevant to the incident which is the subject of this lawsuit.

8. Any and all bills, invoices, receipts, estimates, appraisals, statements, documents or any type of writing which indicate, contain, or tend to prove any of the costs, expenses, losses, or damages claimed by you in this action.

Note: Use item 9 for all business, corporate, and partnership entities, whether plaintiff or defendant. Include 5 to 10 years as the relevant time period.

9. Each and every document created or maintained by (name of entity) in the normal course and scope of their business activities, including but not limited to: (list specific documents such as policy and procedures manuals, profit and loss statements, customer lists, telephone logs, or general categories such as those documents reflecting business procedures, business expenses, business management, employee relations, office procedures, and so forth).

10. Each and every document identifying, referred to, or used by plaintiff's/defendant's in their preparation of responses to plaintiff's/defendant's first set of interrogatories and/or first set of requests for admission which were served on (name) on (date).

11. Each and every document which has not been previously produced in response to a discovery request and which plaintiff/defendant intends to introduce as evidence at the trial of this action.

§ 6.19   Documents to Request (Construction Cases)

This list of documents is an overview of all documentation which is normally available in construction cases. It should be used as a guideline for the plaintiff in a construction defect case in the preparation of document requests to a general contractor, subcontractors, and/or other persons who have executed contracts dealing with the construction which is the subject matter of a dispute. The list groups documents in three chronological stages: precontract materials, contract documents, and construction documents. Not all of the items listed will be applicable to your specific request/demand for documents. Because construction litigation is almost always multiparty litigation, consider the specific party (defendant, cross-defendant, and so forth) to whom you are propounding the request in selecting the documents.

1. Pre Contract Materials
    a. Subsurface conditions
        (i)   Borings and other soil data
        (ii) Geodetic data
        (iii) Utility locations
        (iv) Preexisting tunnels, foundations, and so forth
        (v)   Hydrostatic data
    b. Surveys, site plans, topographical data
    c. Law, ordinances, regulations, and codes
    d. Material samples, laboratory tests, submissions to designer, and so forth
    e. Bids, estimates, and details, quotes, takeoffs
    f. Pertinent codes and standards
2. Contract Documents
    a. Invitation to bidders
    b. General and special conditions
    c. Plans and specifications
    d. Contract and addenda

    e.   Architects' or owners' written interpretations or clarifications to bidders

    f.   Site surveys, quantity estimates, soil conditions, and so forth contained in documents

3.   Construction Documents

    a.   Correspondence

        (i)   Owner, architect, consultants, contractor

        (ii) Contractor, subcontractor, supplier

    b.   Daily Reports

        (i) Owners, clerk of works, project manager

        (ii) Contractors, superintendent, foreman

    c.   Periodic Reports

        (i) Owners, architect, engineer, testing laboratory

        (ii) Contractors, engineer, testing laboratory, survey consultant

    d.   Progress Schedules

        (i) Bar graphs

        (ii) Construction Production Map (CPM), logic diagram, computer printout

    e.   Progress Photographs

    f.   Minutes of job meetings

    g.   Shop drawings

    h.   Shop drawings logs

    i.   Drawing revisions

    j.   Substitutions of materials

    k.   Field orders

    l.   Change orders and change order files

    m. Contractors' cost records (including equipment logs)

    n.   Trade payment breakdown

    o.   Requisitions

    p.   Financial statements of contractor including schedule of work in progress (percentage of completion or completed contract methods)[8]

§ 6.20 Documents to Request (Construction Defect)

Form 6–7 illustrates the categories of documents that should be requested in construction defect actions.

FORM 6–7
SAMPLE DOCUMENTS TO REQUEST
(CONSTRUCTION DEFECT)

   1. Any reports concerning alleged roofing (or any other alleged defect) deficiencies of the [name] Complex.

---

[8] This material was part of a presentation given at the American Bar Association Section Meeting on Litigation in 1981 by J.B. Grove, "Presentation of Documents and Exhibits" from a seminar called "How to Win a Construction Case."

2. Any estimates, bids, repair invoices, or writings of any kind pertaining to any repairs performed on the roof (or any other area, for example, floor, ceiling, windows, and so forth) of the [name] Complex.

3. All plans, drawings, specifications, and designs utilized in the construction of the [name] Complex.

4. Each and every contract which pertains in any way to work done by the general contractor, or any subcontractor, on the [name] Complex.

5. Each bid document submitted to the general contractor by any subcontractor for proposed work on the [name] Complex.

6. Any and all documents furnished to the general contractor, owner, or lender from an architect, consultant, professional, or any other person relating in any manner to any of the following phases of the development of the [name] project:

    a. Schematic design phase
    b. Design development phase
    c. Construction document phase
    d. Bidding or negotiation phase
    e. Administration of contract phase
    f. Actual construction phase

7. Each and every change order pertaining to a modification, alteration, amendment, or change made to those drawings or specifications utilized for the construction of the [name] Project.

8. Any and all "shop drawings," including drawings, diagrams, illustrations, schedules, performance charts, and/or brochures prepared by the contractor, any subcontractor, any manufacturer, supplier, or distributer hired by or through the general contractor which illustrates some portion of the work of the contractor on the [name] Project.

9. Any letters, correspondence, memoranda, or other written or oral communications between or among the contractor, the contractor's subcontractors, owner, and/or architect which in any manner relates to any of the contract documents or actual work performed on the [name] Complex.

10. Any and all field orders or other written interpretation by the owner, architect, or their representative in the form of drawings or otherwise which had the effect of interpreting any provisions of the contract.

11. Any and all progress reports, site inspections, or other documents prepared during the course of the construction of the [name] Complex.

12. Any and all itemized applications for payment submitted by the contractor to the owner or architect.

13. Any and all applications for building permits and building inspection reports evidencing work on the [name] Complex.

14. Any and all punch lists, memoranda reflecting walk-throughs or other notices of defective or nonconforming work.

15. Any and all final inspection reports and certificates of completion relating to the [name] Complex.

16. Any and all documents which refer, pertain, or evidence any guarantees or warranties of materials or products used by any contractor, subcontractor, or supplier on the [name] Complex.

§ 6.21   Checklist of Available Real Estate Documents

A general understanding of the types of commercial real estate transactions and the types of available documents is helpful in determining the specific documents to request in a real estate action. The types of commercial real estate transactions include:

_____ Acquisition loans
_____ Construction loans
_____ Permanent take-out loans
_____ Tax deferred exchange
_____ Sale/lease back transaction
_____ Purchase and sale transaction
_____ Equity participation—equity share

A basic list of documents to request from a lender in a real estate transaction are:

_____ Loan application/commitment
_____ Promissory note
_____ Loan agreement
_____ Deed of Trust
_____ Assignment of lease(s)
_____ Security agreement(s)
_____ Uniform Commercial Code UCC-1 financing statement(s)
_____ Warranties and guarantees
_____ Tenant estoppel and subordination agreements
_____ Legal opinions
_____ Corporate/partnership authorization documents
_____ Preliminary title report with copies of exceptions
_____ ALTA survey
_____ Appraisal documents

_____ Plans and specifications
_____ Construction progress schedule
_____ Construction budgets and loan budgets
_____ Cost breakdowns
_____ Cash flow projection documents
_____ Certified financial statements of borrower
_____ Certified financial statement of guarantor
_____ Certified financial statement of contractor
_____ Documentary evidence of compliance with applicable general plan
_____ Evidence of compliance with zoning ordinances
_____ Sewer availability letter (adequacy letter, permit, and/or license)
_____ Water availability letter (adequacy letter, permit, and/or license)
_____ Electricity availability letter (adequacy letter, permit, and/or license)
_____ Gas availability letter (adequacy letter, permit, and/or license)
_____ Engineer's report
_____ Construction contract with all addenda
_____ Subcontracts with all addenda and modifications
_____ Environmental impact report (when applicable)
_____ Soils report
_____ Architect's letter
_____ Engineer's letter
_____ Soil engineer's letter
_____ Architectural inspection report
_____ Architectural test records
_____ Architect letter and report
_____ Partnership agreement
_____ All insurance policies
_____ Errors and omissions policy for the architect
_____ Errors and omissions policy for all engineers
_____ Market feasibility study with pro forma cash flow
_____ Payment and performance bonds with all attachments
_____ Hazardous material report
_____ Uniform Commercial Code (UCC) search
_____ Documentary evidence of compliance with all requirements imposed by governmental authorities
_____ Permits and approvals
_____ Environmental report
_____ Architect's contract
_____ Engineer's contract
_____ Standard form lease and any variances
_____ Certified rent roll

_____ Property management agreement
_____ Maintenance, service, labor, and/or other contracts
_____ Certificates of occupancy

The following list of documents are often required by the lender in commercial real estate transactions, and may be adopted for use in document requests in your specific case after determining the requirements of the specific lender. All lenders require a clear title and request certain documents for title review to guarantee that there is no cloud on the title. The basic title review documents include:

_____ Preliminary title report commitment and/or pro forma title insurance policy
_____ Survey review
_____ Title insurance policy endorsements
_____ Escrow instructions
_____ Title insurance policy review
_____ Documentation of title exceptions
_____ Exceptions identified with recording information
_____ Easements plotted
_____ Documentary evidence of title for encroachments on adjoining property
_____ Modifications, revisions, or amendments to title insurance policy

§ 6.22   Documents to Request (Real Estate)

The list of documents in **Form 6–8** is appropriate for a defendant title company in an action by a plaintiff claiming a monetary loss of property/investment, fraud. misrepresentation, and so forth.

FORM 6–8
SAMPLE DOCUMENTS TO REQUEST (REAL ESTATE)

1. All documents relating to your [investment category] investment, including but not limited to promissory notes, deeds of trust, cancelled checks, checkstubs, receipts, accounts, and ledgers.

2. All policies of title insurance relating to property which allegedly was security for your [investment category] investment.

3. All preliminary or other title reports relating to property which allegedly was security for your [investment category] investment.

4. All documents received by you from [name] Title Company.

5. All documents received from any source, generated or allegedly generated by [name] Title Company relating to your [investment category] investment

or the property which allegedly secured your [investment category] investment.

6. All documents relating to _____ Title Company.

7. All documents relating to communications between you and [name] Title Company.

8. All documents relating to the value of any property, including appraisals, which allegedly were security for your [investment category] investment.

9. All documents relating to [name] Investment Company.

10. All documents relating to communications between you and any representative of [name] Investment Company.

11. All documents concerning communications with law enforcement officials, the district attorney, the Department of Real Estate, the Department of Corporations, or any other administrative agencies relating to your [investment category] investment, or the property allegedly securing your [investment category] investment or the investment company.

12. All documents relating to money paid or received from [name] Investment Company, including but not limited to cancelled checks and deposit receipts.

13. All documents received by [name] Investment Company pertaining to their financial condition.

14. Any documents received from [name] Investment Company purporting to be a prospectus or portfolio of the company.

15. All documents relating to your financial records, including but not limited to bookkeeping records, worksheets, financial statements, balance sheets, tax returns, or other documents which reflect information about or relate in any way to your [investment category] investment.

16. All documents relating to loans made by you to persons or entities in order to finance said investment.

17. All documents relating to your real estate transactions, whether a purchase, sale, refinance, or other transaction including but not limited to documents relating to escrow, title reports, appraisals, title insurance policies, promissory notes, and deeds of trust. (Note: The time frame here should include any real estate transactions for five years prior to the subject investment.)

18. All state and federal tax returns filed by you or on your behalf during any year in which you had an outstanding [investment category] investment with [name] Investment Company.

This can also be used with modifications by other possible defendants—real estate sales agents, brokers, and mortgage companies. In modifying this list, add those documents involving your client:

Listing agreements,

Escrow files,

Loan files,

Appraisals,

Marketing plans,

Property profiles,

Multiple listing agreements,

Reports from tours/open house (when property was viewed and evaluated by other real estate agents), and

Documents relating to the disposition of the sale proceeds of subject property.

§ 6.23   Documents to Request
(Invitee Business Premises—Plaintiff)

Form 6–9 is a sample request to be used by plaintiff when alleging a cause of action against a hotel, restaurant, convention center, cruise ship, and so forth, for negligence, inadequate security, failure to take reasonable safety measures and so forth.

FORM 6–9
SAMPLE DOCUMENTS TO REQUEST
(INVITE BUSINESS PREMISES—PLAINTIFF)

1. Any and all memoranda, correspondence, notes, reports, photographs, and tapes relating to defendant's investigation of the incident.

2. Copies of all contracts and/or agreements for security services entered into by defendant for safety and/or security for the [business premises] located at [address], [city], [state].

3. All notes, memoranda, and/or documentation reflecting complaints relating to safety and security made by trespassers, licensees, and invitees to defendant.

4. All notes, memoranda, and/or documentation reflecting the presence of security devices (mirrors, alarms, cameras, and so forth) present on the premises at the time of the incident and those placed on the premises subsequent to the incident.

5. Any and all memoranda, logs, correspondence, notes, manuals, directives, and/or instructions for security personnel, proprietary or contracted, related to safety and security plans, procedures, and practices at the [business premises].

6. Any and all memoranda, logs, correspondence, notes and other documentation relating to the performance by a qualified security/safety specialist of a security and safety risk exposure survey, analysis, and/or assessment identifying potential safety/security vulnerabilities and/or threats at the *Bluebird Lodge.*

7. Any and all records, memoranda, correspondence, and other documentation relating to the employment, training, and qualifications of all security/safety personnel, proprietary or contracted, employed by the [business premises] in crime prevention, security surveys, analysis, and assessments, physical security systems, security operations, and security and safety procedures.

8. Any and all documents, including but not limited to memoranda, reports, and correspondence consisting of any communications between the [business premises] and the contract security service regarding security matters.

9. Time sheets and logs for all security personnel physically on the premises at the [business premises] for the 24 hours prior to the date of the incident, the date of the incident itself, and the 24 hours subsequent to the incident.

10. Appointment books, logs, intraoffice memoranda or records of telephone or in person communications between defendant's security director, general manager, contract security service, and any other person regarding this incident.

11. Copy of the security budget, or other documentation, substantiating the percentage of the [business premises]'s total budget dedicated to the security and safety function.

12. A copy of the organizational chart showing the line of authority or chain of command for the security function at the [business premises].

§ 6.24   Documents to Request (Personal Injury/Medical Malpractice/Product Liability—Defendant)

In an action when plaintiff has damage claims relating to physical injuries, mental suffering, wage loss, property damage, and other miscellaneous damages, the documents in **Form 6–10** should be requested.

FORM 6–10
SAMPLE DOCUMENTS TO REQUEST (PERSONAL INJURY/MEDICAL MALPRACTICE/PRODUCT LIABILITY—DEFENDANT)

1. Any and all profit and loss statements, income statements, relating to your business for the period of [year] to the present (suggested time frame: 5 to 7 years).

2. Any and all balance sheets relating to your business for the period of [year] to the present.

3. Any and all accounts receivable or financial statements relating to your business for the period of [year] to the present.

4. Any and all accounts payable or financial statements relating to your business for the period from [year] to the present.

5. Any and all cash disbursement records or journals relating to your business for the period of [year] to the present.

6. Any and all sales or cash receipt records or ledgers relating to your business for the period of [year] to the present.

7. Any and all bank statements relating to your business for the period of [year] to the present.

8. Any and all bank statements of your personal accounts for the period of [year] to the present.

9. Any and all documents indicating or summarizing your business expenses for each year from [year] to the present.

10. Any and all documents indicating or summarizing your business income for the year from [year] to the present.

11. Any and all documents or business records relating to the identity, including the name and address, and wages paid to any employee of your business from [year] to the present.

12. The final transcripts from all high schools, vocational schools, or speciality training courses you attended.

13. Any and all transcripts from any college or university you have attended.

14. Any and all documents relating to your gross wages for each year from [year] to the present.

15. Any and all documents relating to your net wages for each year from [year] to the present.

16. Any and all documents relating to your earnings for each year from [year] to the present.

17. Plaintiff's state and federal income tax returns for each year from [year] to the present, including any attachments or schedules to such returns.

18. Any and all documents, not previously produced, which support your claim for loss of income or earning capacity.

19. Any and all documents pertaining to medical care received by you from any physician or health care practitioner for the years [year] to [year]. (Suggested time frame: 5 to 7 years.)

20. Any and all bills, invoices, receipts, statements, billing statements, documents, or other writings as defined in the pertinent evidence code which indicate, contain, tend to prove, or you will contend will indicate, contain or tend to prove any or all of the medical expenses alleged in your complaint on file in this action.

21. Any and all receipts, invoices, statements, earning statements, check-stubs, earning records, payroll records, documents or writings as defined in the Evidence Code which indicate, contain, or tend to prove or you contend will indicate, contain or tend to prove the wage loss and/or loss of earning capacity as alleged in your complaint on file in this action.

22. Any and all bills, invoices, receipts, estimates, appraisals, statements, documents or writings as defined in the Evidence Code which indicate, contain or tend to prove, or you will contend will indicate, contain, or tend to prove any or all costs, expenses, losses, or damages, not set forth in the categories above, which you contend were suffered or sustained as a result of the incident which is the subject of your complaint on file in this action.

23. Any and all bills, invoices, receipts, statements, billing statements, documents, or writings as defined in the Evidence Code which indicate, contain, tend to prove or you will contend will indicate, contend, or tend to prove any and all expenses associated with real property damage including but not limited to the cost, repair and/or improvement of real property, if any, is claimed as a result of this incident.

24. Any and all bills, invoices, receipts, statements, billing statements, documents, or other writings as defined in the Evidence Code which indicate, contain, tend to prove or you contend will indicate, contain, or tend to prove any and all damages associated with decreases in value of personal property, cost, repair, and/or improvement of personal property, or general personal property claimed as a result of this incident.

25. Any and all receipts, statements or other documents which indicate, contain, or tend to prove that plaintiff received any form of reimbursement for any of the expenses, losses, or damages which plaintiff contends were suffered or sustained as a result of the incident which is the subject of your complaint on file in this action.

26. Any and all receipts, statements or other documents which indicate, contain, or tend to prove that you received wages or salary from any source during the time that you have claimed a wage loss in your complaint on file in this action.

NOTE: For general wage loss, use 14 to 17 and 21. If plaintiff is self-employed, use 1 to 11, 17 and 21. Items 12 and 13 should be included in all cases where a wage loss or loss of earning capacity is alleged (self-employment or employer/employee).

§ 6.25   Documents to Request (Slip and Fall—Plaintiff)

Form 6–11 illustrates the types of requests that would be used in a slip and fall case, if you were representing the plaintiff.

FORM 6–11
SAMPLE DOCUMENTS TO REQUEST
(SLIP AND FALL—PLAINTIFF)

1. Each writing which refers, relates, or pertains to instructions for the inspecting and cleaning of the produce department at [name] Grocery Store.

2. Each writing which refers, evidences, or pertains to the duties and responsibilities of store personnel employed by [name] Grocery Store in the produce department.

3. Each writing which refers, evidences, or pertains to policy guidelines or operations manuals which were in effect on [date] for [name] Grocery Store.

4. Copies of sweeping logs and/or inspection reports for the produce department at [name] Grocery Store for the date of [date].

5. Each writing which refers, relates, or pertains in any way to the accident suffered by [plaintiff] on [date] at [name] Grocery Store.

6. Each writing which refers, evidences, or pertains to any statements taken by any [name] Grocery Store personnel from [plaintiff] regarding the accident of [date].

7. Each writing which refers, evidences, or pertains in any way to any statements and/or interviews of store personnel at [name] Grocery Store regarding the [date] accident.

8. Each writing which refers, evidences, or pertains to any reports of the [date] accident prepared by any agent or employee of [name] Grocery Store.

9. Any and all photographs, diagrams, reproductions, or sketches of any kind depicting the produce department at [name] Grocery Store, and specifically the area in which plaintiff slipped and fell on [date].

10. Each writing which refers, evidences, or pertains to any inspections of the produce department for [date] and [times] (list a total of 72 hours, include the 24 hours prior to the accident and the 24 hours subsequent to the accident).

11. Each writing which refers, evidences, or pertains to any memoranda or other in-store notices directed to [name] Grocery Store employees in general, and produce department employees specifically, dealing with store maintenance and/or inspection policies.

12. Each writing authored by any [name] Grocery Store manager pertaining to the need to perform inspections on a regularly scheduled basis in the produce department at [name] Grocery Store.

13. Any and all statements made or given by any person regarding the facts and circumstances relevant to the incident which is the subject of this lawsuit.

14. Any and all statements made or given by answering defendant, or any agent, servant, or employee of answering defendant, or any person who purports to be or you claim is or was an agent, servant, or employee of this answering defendant regarding facts, circumstances, or investigations relevant to the incident which is the subject of this lawsuit.

§ 6.26   Documents to Request (Partnership Disputes)

The documents in **Form 6–12** should be requested in actions involving a breach of partnership, dissolution of partnership, breach of fiduciary duty, and any dispute over partnership assets.

FORM 6–12
SAMPLE DOCUMENTS TO REQUEST
(PARTNERSHIP DISPUTE)

1. Each and every document that refers or relates in any way to the property located at [address] and known as The [name] Hotel.

2. Each and every document referring or relating to the management of The [name] Hotel for the years [year] to [year] (ten-year time span).

3. Each and every document referring, relating or pertaining to the allegations in your complaint on file in this action that [name]'s percentage of ownership of The [name] Hotel has diminished on a yearly basis for the years [year] to [year].

4. All expense, balance sheets, and profit and loss statements for The [name] Hotel for the years [year] to [year] (ten-year time span).

5. All accounting books and records for the [name] general partnership from [year] to the present.

6. All state and federal tax returns filed by the [name] general partnership from [year] to the present.

7. All bank account statements, records, cancelled checks, and loan documents for The [name] Hotel general partnership from [year] to the present.

8. All documents referring or relating in any way to refinancing and/or debt repayment by the [name] general partnership from [year] to the present.

9. All documents which have been filed with the Secretary of State which relate in any way to the [name] general partnership and/or The [name] Hotel for the years [year] to [year].

10. All documents which have been filed with the SEC including, but not limited to, prospectus, 10K, 8K, and all other documents filed as exhibits to those reports which related to the [name] general partnership.

11. Any and all annual reports, reports to shareholders, or general operating statements provided to shareholders by the [name] general partnership and/or The [name] Hotel for the years [year to year].

§ 6.27　Documents to Request (Limited Partnership Disputes—Defendant)

The documents in **Form 6–13** should be requested by a defendant in an action where limited partners allege monetary loss and other damages on investments made by a general partnership.

FORM 6–13
SAMPLE DOCUMENTS TO REQUEST
(LIMITED PARTNERSHIP DISPUTES—DEFENDANT)

1. Each document which refers, relates to, constitutes, or evidences an investment by you in [name] Power Company, a limited partnership.

2. Each document which refers to, relates to, constitutes, or evidences the purchases by you of any units of stock in the [name] Power Company.

3. Each document, including but not limited to, K-1 income tax forms, which refer, relate to, constitute, or evidence any income tax deductions generated as a result of your status as a limited partner in [name] Power Company.

4. Each document which refers, relates to, constitutes, or evidences any income tax credits generated as a result of your status as a limited partner in [name] Power Company.

5. Each document which refers, relates to, constitutes, or evidences your plan or intention to take a tax credit or tax deduction at any time in the future as a result of your status as a limited partner in [name] Power Company.

6. Each document which refers, relates to, constitutes, or evidences any monies received by you as a result of your status as a limited partner in [name] Power Company.

7. Each document which refers, relates to, constitutes, or evidences anything of value which you have received as a result of your status as a limited partner in [name] Power Company.

8. Each document which refers, relates to, constitutes, or evidences any payment or contribution in any form made by [name] Power Company to you.

9. Each document which refers, relates to, constitutes, or evidences any communications between [name] Power Company and you.

10. Copies of your federal tax and income tax returns for the period commencing [date] through and including the present (use a 5 to 7 year time frame).

§ 6.28   Documents to Request (Lender Liability—Plaintiff)

The plaintiff should request from the defendant bank, or savings and loan, the documents illustrated in **Form 6–14.**

FORM 6–14
SAMPLE DOCUMENTS TO REQUEST
(LENDER LIABILITY—PLAINTIFF)

1. All documents relating to, referring, or pertaining to any credit applications made by plaintiff during the relative time period.

2. All documents relating to, referring, or pertaining to any applications or requests by plaintiff for the opening of individual or commercial savings or checking accounts, or any other accounts at [name] Bank.

3. All documents relating to, referring, or containing communications of any kind between plaintiff and defendant [name] Bank.

4. Any documents received, created, or reviewed by you to evaluate and analyze any credit application of, the credit worthiness of, or credit line for plaintiff related to requirements for opening any accounts at [name] Bank and/or any loan applications.

5. Any documents relating to any written or oral communications between [name] Bank and plaintiff relating to the transaction of business on any account or loan maintained during [year] through [year] at [name] Bank by plaintiff.

6. Any documents relating to any payments, delinquencies, late charges, NSF checks, transfers from one account to another, or any irregularities in any accounts, individual or commercial savings or checks, opened or maintained by plaintiff from [year] to [year] at [name] Bank.

7. All documents relating, referring to, or reflecting [name] Bank's standard practice and/or policy manuals for customer relations, individual and commercial accounts, and loans.

8. All credit review memoranda related in any way to plaintiff's loans with defendant [name] Bank.

9. Any and all internal examination reports related to plaintiff's individual or commercial accounts or loans.

10. Any document which refers, relates, or pertains to any due or delinquent loan status reports regarding any loans between plaintiff and defendant [name] Bank.

11. Any appraisals of real and/or personal property of plaintiff.

12. Any documents reflecting the past or current status of any account opened and maintained by plaintiff at [name] Bank.

13. Any backup material and work papers relating to any business transacted on any account maintained by plaintiff, individual or commercial, during the years [year] to [year].

14. Any records relating to cashier's checks, certified checks, and/or money orders negotiated by plaintiff drawn on funds on any accounts maintained at [name] Bank from [year] to [year].

15. Any inspection reports related to plaintiff and/or any of their business operations.

16. Any foreclosure reports and/or liquidation analyses related in any way to plaintiffs and/or their business operation.

17. Any and all documents which relate to, pertain to, or constitute an agricultural operations budget prepared in relation to plaintiff's business operations. (This request should be used if the property involved is an agricultural lot, farm property, used for dairy products, and so forth.)

§ 6.29 Documents to Request
(Wrongful Termination—Defendant)

The documents in **Form 6–15** should be requested in a wrongful termination case when you are representing the defendant.

FORM 6–15
SAMPLE DOCUMENTS TO REQUEST
(WRONGFUL TERMINATION—DEFENDANT)

1. All documents which relate in any way to [name]'s employment with [name] Company during the time period from [date of hire] to the present time.

2. All documents such as any resumes prepared by plaintiff at any time, which show plaintiff's employment history for all or a portion of the time period from [year] (use 5 to 10 year time frame) to the present time.

3. All documents which relate to or in any way show the terms and conditions of plaintiff's employment with [name] Company during the time period from [date of hire] to [date of termination]. Included in this request are employment contracts, job descriptions, letters of agreement, memoranda or other written communications dealing with offer and acceptance of employment.

4. All documents which relate to or in any way refer to the circumstances of the termination of plaintiff's employment with [name] Company on or about [date of termination].

5. All documents which are part of the employment agreement which plaintiff contends existed between plaintiff and [name] Company which were not produced in response to request number 3.

6. All documents which refer to any attempt on plaintiff's part to secure employment during the period of [date of termination] through the present. Included in this response should be any inquiries plaintiff made to locate employment such as any employment advertisements to which plaintiff responded, any cover letters, any contacts with job search firms, or any other documentation concerning job searches made during this time period.

7. All documents which relate to or in any way show monies earned or received by plaintiff in employment and/or self-employment during the period

from [date of termination] to the present. If plaintiff has been engaged in any form of self-employment, included in this response should be all records showing the net profit of any self-employment endeavor.

8. All documents which relate to or in any way show that plaintiff was performing plaintiff's job responsibilities as project manager for [name] Company in a satisfactory manner.

9. All documents which relate to or in any way show that defendant falsely evaluated plaintiff's work performance as alleged in Paragraph [number] of the Complaint on file in this action.

10. All documents which relate to or in any way show that defendant "frustrated plaintiff's efforts to bring under control the product quality problems" of defendant [name] Company as alleged in Paragraph [number] of the Complaint on file in this action.

11. All documents which relate to or in any way show that defendant acted toward plaintiff with "malice" as alleged in Paragraph [number] of the Complaint in conjunction with either plaintiff's employment or the termination of that employment.

12. All documents which relate to or, in any way, show that defendant acted toward plaintiff in bad faith in the termination of plaintiff's employment as alleged by plaintiff in the complaint on file in this action.

13. All documents which relate to or in any way show that plaintiff received assurances and/or statements in the form of recommendations, or performance evaluations, that plaintiff was "competent, hard working, conscientious, honest, and knowledgeable" during the time period from [date of employment through date of termination].

14. All documents which relate to or in any way show the losses which plaintiff claims that plaintiff has incurred as a result of termination by [name] Company on [date of termination].

15. Each and every document identified, referred to, or used by defendant in preparation of their responses to plaintiff's first set of interrogatories and/or plaintiff's first set of requests for admissions which were served to defendant on [date].

§ 6.30   Documents to Request
(Wrongful Termination—Plaintiff)

The documents in **Form 6–16** should be requested in a wrongful termination case when you are representing the plaintiff.

FORM 6–16
SAMPLE DOCUMENTS TO REQUEST
(WRONGFUL TERMINATION—PLAINTIFF)

1. The complete employment file and all personnel files maintained by [name] Company on [name] from the date of plaintiff's first employment interview through the date of termination including any posttermination information that has been made part of any of plaintiff's personnel files.

2. Each document which refers to, relates to, or constitutes a written policy or procedure regarding employment discipline or termination which was in effect during the term of [name]'s employment with the [name] Company.

3. Each document which refers to, relates to, or constitutes a document signed by [name] regarding or concerning plaintiff's obtaining or continuing employment with the [name] Company.

4. Each and every document which refers to, relates to, or constitutes qualifications for employment, promotion, additional compensation, termination, or other disciplinary action concerning [name] that is in the possession and/or control of the [name] Company.

5. Each and every document which refers to, relates to, or constitutes correspondence or memoranda that confirms an offer of employment to [name] by any employee or agent of [name] Company.

6. Each and every document which refers to, relates to, or constitutes a letter of reference given out on behalf of [name] by any employee or agent of the [name] Company during the course of plaintiff's employment with the company.

7. Each and every document which refers to, relates to, or constitutes any specific commendations, compliments, or letters of recognition concerning [name] which were received by the [name] Company during the course of plaintiff's employment with the company.

8. Each and every document submitted by the [name] Company to the Employment Development Department or any other governmental agency concerning [name].

9. Each and every document which refers, relates, or constitutes a description of the job duties and responsibilities applying to [name] during the course of plaintiff's employment with the [name] Company.

10. Each and every document which refers to, relates to, or constitutes any communication, either written or oral, between [name] and the [name] Company during the course of plaintiff's employment with defendant.

11. Each and every document which relates, refers to, or constitutes written procedural guidelines of the [name] Company designed to provide employees with hearing in the context of disciplinary actions or terminations that was in effect during the course of [name]'s employment with the defendant.

12. Each and every document which refers to, relates to, or constitutes a "new employee packet" consisting of materials given to new employees to orient their employment with the [name] Company which was in effect at the time of [name]'s employment with defendant.

13. Each and every document which refers to, relates to, or constitutes a method of communicating management's production expectations for each department at [name] Company to their employees.

14. Each and every document which refers to, relates to, or constitutes a training manual for supervisory personnel at [name] Company that was in effect during the term of [name]'s employment.

15. Each and every document which refers to, relates to, or constitutes a listing of qualifications and job description for the project manager at [name] Company that was in effect during the term of [name]'s employment (Specify in this request the exact job title of plaintiff, and include any other job titles that plaintiff had during the course of employment from which plaintiff was either promoted or demoted).

16. Each and every document identified, referred to, or used by defendant in preparation of their responses to plaintiff's first set of interrogatories and/or plaintiff's first set of request for admissions which were served on defendant on [date].

NOTE: Request 16 is to be used as a standard form request in every document request regardless of the subject matter of the action (See request 10 in **§ 6.18**).

§ 6.31 Documents to Request (Construction Defect— from Homeowners Association)

The documents in **Form 6–17** should be requested from a Homeowners Association in a construction defect case.

FORM 6–17
SAMPLE DOCUMENTS TO REQUEST (CONSTRUCTION DEFECT— FROM HOMEOWNERS ASSOCIATION)

1. Minutes of all meetings of [name] Homeowners Association Board of Directors from its inception to the present.

2. Minutes of all meetings of [name] Homeowners Association from its inception to the present.

3. All writings between you and the developer regarding damages at the subject project for which you seek monetary damages herein.

4. All writings between you and any party herein regarding damages at the subject project for which you seek monetary damages herein.

5. All writings between you and any governmental entity regarding damages for which you seek monetary damages herein.

6. All writings between you and any management company regarding damages for which you seek monetary damages herein.

7. All writings including, but not limited to, invoices, bills, statements, and purchase orders regarding repairs to damage for which you seek monetary damages herein.

8. All writings that reflect maintenance to common areas at the subject project.

9. All writings that reflect landscaping/irrigation maintenance at the subject project.

10. All writings that reflect bids or proposals for repairs to any damage to the [name] project for which you seek monetary damages herein.

11. All writings to or from [name] Homeowners Association that describe, discuss, explain, evaluate, or otherwise pertain to any of the defective conditions at the subject project for which you seek monetary damages herein.

12. All writings from residents at the subject project that describe, document, or verify any complaints or deficiencies for which you seek monetary damages herein.

§ 6.32   Documents to Request (Construction Defect— from Insurance Company Plaintiff)

The documents in **Form 6–18** should be requested from the plaintiff Insurance Company in a construction defects case.

FORM 6–18
SAMPLE DOCUMENTS TO REQUEST (CONSTRUCTION DEFECT— FROM INSURANCE COMPANY PLAINTIFF)

1. All writings that describe the damages alleged to exist at the subject property.

2. All writing that describe repairs that have been performed or are anticipated to be performed at the subject property.

3. All cost of repair estimates regarding the subject property.

4. All contracts, bid documents, proposals, or agreements, that pertain to repairs proposed to be performed or that have been performed to the subject property.

5. All photographs depicting any damages alleged to exist at the subject property.

6. All bills, invoices, or any other written statements regarding monies incurred for repairs performed or to be performed at the subject property.

7. All writings that reflect payments made to your insureds for damages to the subject property.

8. The claims file pertaining to claims made by the insureds of the subject property.

9. All writings including, but not limited to, correspondence, notes, or memoranda pertaining to the damages that are alleged to exist at the subject property.

§ 6.33 Documents to Request (Construction Defect— from Developer)

The documents in **Form 6–19** should be requested from the developer in a construction defects case.

FORM 6–19
SAMPLE DOCUMENTS TO REQUEST (CONSTRUCTION DEFECT—FROM DEVELOPER)

1. Any and all preliminary, intermediary, and final plans, grading plans, as-built drawings, shop plans, soils reports, engineering studies, and written specifications relating to the subject project.

2. Any and all writings between any resident of the subject project and any director, agent, officer, or employee of [developer].

3. Any and all writings between any agent, officer, or employee of [developer] and any agent, officer, or employee of any property management company relating to the subject project from its inception to the present.

4. Any and all subcontracts relating to the supply, work, construction, installation, or repair of those deficiencies complained of by plaintiff herein.

5. Any and all written interoffice memoranda and memoranda of interoffice oral communications between any other officer, agent, or employee of [developer] and any other officer, agent, or employee of [developer] relating to the supply, work, construction, installation, and repair of those deficiencies complained of by plaintiff herein.

6. Any and all progress reports, progress notes, change orders, inspection notes, correction notices, and other reports, notes, and memoranda made by subcontractors relating to the supply, work, construction, installation, and repair of those deficiencies alleged to exist at the subject project by plaintiff herein.

7. Any and all project files maintained by [developer] relating to the construction of the subject project.

8. Any and all files relating to work performed by design professionals before, during, and after construction of the subject project.

9. Any and all writings between any member of the [name] Homeowners Association Board of Directors and any officer, agent, or employee of [developer].

§ 6.34   Supplemental Request for Document Production

Requests, or demands, for identification, inspection, and production of documents can be propounded to the opposing party at any time after formal discovery begins in an action. Successive sets can be propounded as discovery progresses and information is obtained through interrogatories, depositions, and further investigations indicating the likelihood of existing documents in particular categories. To insure that you have covered all bases and requested every discoverable document in a particular action, the sample catchall set of document requests in **Form 6–20** should be propounded within 65 days of trial. The use of 65 days allows not only for response time but also time for a motion to compel prior to the usual 30 days before the trial discovery cutoff date.

FORM 6–20
SAMPLE SUPPLEMENTAL REQUEST FOR
DOCUMENT PRODUCTION

REQUEST NO. 1:   Please provide copies of any and all documents and writings which were described or referred to in your responses to interrogatories, requests for admissions, or other written discovery propounded to you by [plaintiff/defendant] in the above-entitled action.

REQUEST NO. 2:   Please provide copies of any document reviewed or referred to in your preparation, and which reflects the specific information that you incorporated in your responses to interrogatories, requests for admissions, and other written discovery propounded to you by [plaintiff/defendant] in the above-entitled action.

Form 6–21 illustrates a sample supplemental demand for identification, inspection, and production of documents.

FORM 6–21
SAMPLE SUPPLEMENTAL DEMAND FOR IDENTIFICATION,
INSPECTION, AND PRODUCTION OF DOCUMENTS

[attorney for the plaintiff]
[address]
[telephone number]

Attorneys for Plaintiff
[plaintiff name]

IN THE SUPERIOR COURT OF THE STATE OF [state name]

IN THE CITY AND COUNTY OF [city/county name]

[name], Plaintiff, vs. [name] SHOPPING MALL, A LIMITED PARTNERSHIP, [defendant A] and [defendant B], as limited partners of [name] SHOPPING MALL, [defendant C], individually and (dba) [company D],	Case No. [case number] SUPPLEMENTAL DEMAND FOR IDENTIFICATION, INSPECTION AND PRODUCTION OF DOCUMENTS

and (dba) [company E],
and DOES 1 through 30,
inclusive,

    Defendants.

_____/

PROPOUNDING PARTY: Defendant, [name] SHOPPING MALL

RESPONDING PARTY: Plaintiff, [name]

SET NUMBER: [set number]

You are requested pursuant to [state] Code of Civil Procedure [section number] to identify, produce, and permit the inspection, copying, and/or photographing of the following documents in evidence at the Law Office of [attorney for the plaintiff], [address], [city], [state] on [date] at [time].

REQUEST NO. 1: Please review your responses to defendant [name] Shopping Mall's prior requests for production of documents in this action. If, for any reason, any response is no longer complete and correct, identify the response by the number, and provide whatever further documents are currently in your possession, custody, and control and are necessary to make this response correct and complete as of the date the response to this request is due.

REQUEST NO. 2: Each and every document, which has not previously been produced in response to a discovery request, and which plaintiff intends to introduce as evidence at the time of the trial of this action.

REQUEST NO. 3: All documents not previously produced which support your damage claims in this matter.

Dated: [date].

                               _____
                               [attorney for the defendant]
                               [name] SHOPPING MALL

This same supplemental request is appropriate to send to a defendant, using Request No. 1 and Request No. 2, and then adding:

REQUEST NO. 3: All documents not previously produced which support those facts stated in your First Affirmative Defense to the Complaint on file herein.

Continue with separate requests referring to each of the affirmative defenses raised in defendant's answer. For example, those facts stated in your Second Affirmative Defense, those facts stated in your Third Affirmative Defense, etc.

Note: Calendar this supplemental demand carefully to allow response time (30 days) and time to compel if the responses are inadequate while staying within the 30-day discovery cutoff for trial.

§ 6.35   Joinder in Document Request

When a party serves a request or demand for the identification, production, and inspection of documents on any other party in an action, copies of that request must be sent to all attorneys appearing on the proof of service list. When the responding party prepares a written response to that request or demand for identification of production of document, the written response must be served on all parties on the proof of service list. It is not axiomatic that all documents will accompany the written response. Local rules of civil procedure vary from state to state and court to court. In order to be certain that you receive copies not only of the written response to the document request but also copies of each and every document produced in response to that request, a Joinder should be served on all parties in the action. **Form 6–22** is a sample Joinder.

FORM 6–22
SAMPLE JOINDER

[attorney for plaintiff]
[address]
[telephone number]

Attorneys for Plaintiff
[plaintiff's name]

IN THE SUPERIOR COURT OF THE STATE OF [state name]

IN THE CITY AND COUNTY OF [city/county name]

[name]   Case No. [case number]

     Plaintiff,

vs.

[name] SHOPPING MALL, A
LIMITED PARTNERSHIP,
[defendant A] and
[defendant B], as limited partners
of [name] SHOPPING MALL,
[defendant C], individually
and (dba) [company D],
and (dba) [company E],

and DOES 1 through 30,
inclusive,

    Defendants.

_____/

AND RELATED ACTIONS

_____/

TO ALL PARTIES AND THEIR ATTORNEYS OF RECORD:

Please take notice that plaintiff [name] joins in defendant [name] SHOPPING MALL'S request for production of documents from cross-defendant [name] served on [date], and requests that a copy of each such document produced in response to that request be produced to plaintiff [name] at the time and place designated in the aforesaid Request for Production of Documents, along with cross-defendant's written response to said production.

    Dated: [date].

_____

[attorney for plaintiff]

§ 6.36 Coordinating Document Production with Interrogatories

Coordinated discovery produces the best results. Serving a request, or demand, to produce documents at the same time as a set of interrogatories, and referencing certain specific interrogatories as shown in **Form 6–23** illustrates this principle.

FORM 6–23
SAMPLE DEMAND FOR PRODUCTION OF DOCUMENTS COORDINATED WITH INTERROGATORIES

[attorney for the plaintiff]
[address]
[telephone number]

Attorneys for Plaintiff
[name]

IN THE SUPERIOR COURT OF THE STATE OF [state name]

IN THE CITY AND COUNTY OF [city/county name]

[name],   Case No. [case number]

Plaintiff,

vs.

[name] SHOPPING MALL, A
LIMITED PARTNERSHIP,
[defendant A] and [defendant B],
as limited partners
of [name] SHOPPING MALL,
[defendant C], individually
and (dba) [company D],
and (dba) [company E],
and DOES 1 through 30,
inclusive,

Defendants.

_____/

AND RELATED ACTIONS

_____/

DEMAND FOR
IDENTIFICATION,
INSPECTION, AND
PRODUCTION OF
DOCUMENTS

Dated: [date]
Time: [time]

DEMANDING PARTY:	Defendant [name] SHOPPING MALL
RESPONDING PARTY:	[plaintiff]
SET NUMBER:	[set number]

Pursuant to Code of Civil Procedure [section number], defendant [name] SHOPPING MALL demands that you produce for the purpose of inspection and photocopying the following documents and tangible items at the offices of [attorney for the defendant] on the above-stated date and time.

INSTRUCTIONS

This demand requires that you produce any and all documents or tangible items that are in your possession, custody, or control.

The word documents includes, but is not limited to, writings, drawings, graphs, charts, photographs, phono records, and other electronic data compilations from which information may be obtained as set forth in [state] Code of Civil Procedure [code section].

This requirement for production may be complied with by mailing photocopies of the requested documents five (5) days before the date indicated above, or by hand delivery on that date to this demanding party at their business address.

ITEMS TO BE IDENTIFIED AND PRODUCED:

REQUEST NO. 1: Any and all documents referred to in your response to Interrogatory No. 12 (Set One).

REQUEST NO. 2: Any and all documents referred to in your response to Interrogatory No. 14 (Set One).

Note: Be sure to key your document requests to those interrogatories which reference documents. Be careful not to request documents for responses to interrogatories which do not relate to documents, but ask for identification of persons or facts.

§ 6.37   Electronic Media Discovery

The 1990's is the electronic information age. It is a grave mistake in litigation to limit discovery requests to traditional paper searches, because to do so limits your effectiveness. Electronic media discovery (EMD) is a potent new legal weapon. It involves seeking information that can be read electronically and is found in data storage devices such as floppy disks, hard disks, tapes, optical disks. A responding party in discovery can truthfully produce all the paper documents requested which are in their "possession, custody and control" without handing over the most meaningful information. When preparing a document request/demand and/or subpoena, many law firms traditionally include in their definition of documents phrases such as "including but not limited to computer-readable media, machine sensible, electronic, or any other form of information." Few, if any, responding parties follow that definition and produce electronic information. In many cases, attorneys choose not to enforce their rights to obtain computer files or electronic media through motions to compel due to the absence of case law relating to the extent of the work product and attorney-client privileges applicable to electronic information.

Irrespective of the fact that privileges may apply to computer-generated materials, a motion to compel production or, in the alternative, an in camera inspection is an effective discovery tool. Electronic media discovery represents the cutting edge of discovery for the 1990's. As discovery disputes over the applicability of attorney-client and work product privileges in the discovery war over electronic media discovery reach the courts, case law will emerge to guide litigators in their attempt to discover information from the paperless office.

More and more corporations and public entities have adopted the use of electronic mail and computer networks to send and receive messages. The famous "E Mail" is standard is most large offices and has practically replaced what litigators used to look for in folders or boxes of memos, phone message slips, handwritten notes, calendars, telephone number rolodexes, ledgers, and other informal records kept in the course and scope of business. These informal records often provided leads to hot documents and other key issues such as whether someone within a commercial setting knew someone else, or had an appointment to meet that person, or perhaps sent an internal memo describing the meeting that took place.

In many commercial disputes, relevant information was most likely created or communicated by computers. Requesting information through EMD may preclude the need for your opponent to deliver truckloads of document boxes in response to discovery requests, thus streamlining discovery in terms of cost and time effectiveness.

§ 6.38   Electronic Media Discovery—Case Example

In a product liability case when you have become certain through investigation, witness statements, and other means that a certain executive knew about a product defect prior to the production of that product, and your opponent insists there are no documents reflecting this knowledge, your dilemma may be solved through electronic media discovery. A first step in your discovery strategy would be to discover through interrogatories or depositions the identity of that executive's secretary or administrative assistant, and then depose that person in order to establish the following facts:

1. That the deponent is the executive secretary or administrative assistant to the executive;
2. That the deponent understands the importance of preparing backup files on their computer and in the course and scope of normal business procedure does so;
3. The extent of time reflected in the deponent's backup disks;
4. The location of the backup disks—in the deponent's possession, closed files, archives, and so forth;
5. Whether the executive ever revises documents prepared in draft for signature and review;
6. Whether the original computer file for the draft document, before making the revisions, has been retained; and
7. The location of copies of earlier versions of key documents such as contracts, memos, letters, and so forth are stored (The answer will probably be "on my backup disks".)

Once you have established these facts regarding the use and availability of electronic media information it is important to:

1. Use as a deposition exhibit Plaintiff's or Defendant's First Request/Demand for Identification and Production of Documents to the plaintiff or defendant company;
2. Focus on that request, by using the deposition exhibit, which asks for the production of any responsive computer records reflecting earlier drafts, revisions, addenda, amendments, and so forth to the subject contract and/or document;
3. Request on the record that the backup disks (whose existence has just been discovered) be produced, if the defendant or plaintiff has responded to that request by producing the contract or document without producing earlier drafts, revisions, amendments, and so forth and has claimed that they no longer exist; and
4. Anticipate objections. Most likely a motion to compel will be necessary to obtain the backup disks. Arguments will be made that the information

contained on the backup disks is internal communications and is protected by the attorney-client and attorney work product privilege.

The requesting party will need to establish a chain of custody for the electronic data. Dates and times will be crucial in determining whether this material was prepared "in anticipation of litigation" and, as such, may be qualified work product, or whether the privilege has been waived by communication of information through electronic means to those persons who were not in the corporate control group.

EMD warfare is the latest weapon in discovery disputes, and as of this writing there are not many case law decisions and/or statutes to act as guideposts in this area. Each case law decision depends on the specific issues in dispute.

§ 6.39 Checklist for Protecting the Corporate Client

As a supplement to the discussion in § 6.5 and § 6.6 regarding protecting the corporate client in document production, the following checklist should be used to protect the corporate client from electronic media discovery requests.

Corporate clients should be advised to:

_____ Include electronic data in the company's overall document retention program. The company's document destruction schedule should be followed scrupulously so that electronic data is not unnecessarily retained or inadvertently destroyed.

_____ Segregate electronic versions of attorney-client or work product documents in a special file and store this information on a separate backup disk. Keep them away from access which could constitute a waiver of the privileged status of the information. Attorney-client and work product documents should be kept off multiple access systems and should require password security to gain access to those files.

_____ Store electronic versions of attorney-client or work product documents in separate directories on hard disks. This storage will enable documents to be identified readily to produce a privileged list. Use standard headings such as "Attorney-Client Privilege" for all documents so that they can be located with the use of retrieval software. This heading should be included in the description of the document when file names are created.

_____ Include dates, and the time of day, on all documents grouped under attorney-client or attorney work product privilege. The date may be crucial in establishing "prior knowledge" or "anticipation of litigation". Dates and authors of documents will be crucial in establishing a change of custody for the data to prove that the information was kept within the control group.

_____ Caution corporate employees about the overuse of E Mail, which is frequently used for off-the-cuff comments that can come back to haunt you at depositions and in trial testimony. Encourage them to make such off-the-cuff observations orally and not through E Mail! A mistake frequently made by employees within a corporation or business entity is that E Mail is perceived as their own personal mail. If a discovery request seeks all documents on a relevant issue including but not limited to computer readable media and electronic information, an objection based on confidential nature of an E Mail memo or based on invasion of a particular corporate employee's privacy, will frequently be overturned on the basis that the information is not discoverable through any alternative means and that the expectation of privacy did not exist at the time the communication was created. It is difficult, and almost impossible, to establish that confidential intent was present at the time that a specific E Mail message was sent.

§ 6.40   Electronic Media Information Vendors

Electronic public information consultants are public records search vendors who market their services as consultants with a specialization in accessing and analyzing corporate and government data bases.

A computer study (data base) can form the foundation of an investigation and produce discovery leads which can then be followed up on through traditional discovery devices such as depositions, interrogatories, requests for admissions, request/demand for documents, and subpoenas to gather documents from third parties.

§ 6.41   Sample Federal Data Bases

As discussed in **Chapter 2**, obtaining documents from the government is not an easy task. In addition to the traditional methods (for example, a federal Freedom of Information Act letter and, when appropriate, a subpoena), an electronic public information vendor can often afford you quicker access to federal data bases and obtain and analyze the information required for your case, saving time and money.

A sampling of federal data bases which may be accessed by an electronic public information consultant/vendor includes:

1. **National Highway Traffic Safety Administration Complaints Data Base, Recalls Data Base, Investigations Data Base, and Crash Test Data Base.** These data bases contain information about all consumer complaints, recalls, investigations, and crash tests of foreign and domestic automobiles and related parts since 1968. You may obtain information by writing to their Office of Defect Investigation, but an electronic public information vendor can provide quicker access of the entire data base on a specific subject.

2. **Food and Drug Administration (FDA) Medical Device Malfunction Data Base.** The Food and Drug Administration keeps records of every medical device malfunction which occurs in the United States. The data base includes the name of the device, the manufacturer, whether the malfunction resulted in injury or death, a brief narrative description of the event, and the FDA determination regarding causation. This data base goes back to 1984. Again, information can be obtained by writing directly to the FDA inquiring about a particular med-

ical device; however, to get a complete, comprehensive study, it is more efficient to use an electronic public information vendor.

3.   **FDA Adverse Reactions to Drugs Data Base.** This data base is extremely
     useful in product liability and medical malpractice cases against drug
     manufacturers. The FDA keeps records of every adverse reaction that occurs
     across the United States. In addition to basic information such as the name of
     the manufacturer, name of the drug, and description of the reaction, this data
     base also includes vast amounts of information including patient information
     and drug ingredients. The data base was started in 1968.

4.   **Occupational Safety and Health Administration (OSHA) Inspections
     Data Base.** This data base contains approximately 1.8 million records detail-
     ing every OSHA inspection ever done throughout the United States. The data
     base includes industrial safety violations, identifies on-site hazardous chemi-
     cals, names of victims, penalty amounts, the nature and causes of injuries and
     deaths, and so forth. Information in this data base would be helpful for anyone
     working in environmental law. Information on the data base goes back to 1970
     and is updated monthly.

5.   **Coast Guard Casualty Data Base and Safety Investigation Data Base.** This
     data base is maintained by the Marine Investigation Division of the Coast
     Guard and consists of two data bases including personnel and vessel casual-
     ties, safety violations, and pollution information for vessels. The data base has
     been maintained since 1980 and provides important background information
     for an environmental litigation query.

6.   **Environmental Protection Agency (EPA) Toxic Relief Inventory.** This
     EPA data base lists the source, nature, and quantity of every toxic chemical
     discharge of manufacturing facilities in the United States. Details include
     chemical names, discharge quantities, details about the source facilities, and
     other specific discharge information.

7.   **Federal EPA/Department of Justice Environmental Civil Enforcement
     Docket.** This docket sheet lists EPA suits filed against the worst or most per-
     sistent violators of environmental permits. The data base contains information
     on all these civil cases including names of the defendant companies, permit
     violations, penalty assessments, and much more information. The data base
     covers the past 20 years.

8.   **Federal Aviation Administration (FAA).** The FAA maintains records of
     every airplane safety inspection and mechanical difficulty. This data base can
     produce the entire malfunction and maintenance history of any aircraft. The
     FAA also maintains an aircraft registration file containing records of all U.S.
     civil aircraft registered with the FAA, including air carriers and general avia-
     tion aircraft.

9.   **Federal Procurement Data Base.** This data base contains information on all
     federal procurement actions from 1979 to the present when the total was
     $25,000 or more. It includes the purchasing or contracting office, date of the
     award, dollars obligated, principal product or service, name and address of the
     contractor, and other details.

State and local data bases may be accessed by an electronic public information vendor specializing in state government research. These data bases are useful for retrieving traffic accident information, fire department incident reports, and State Board of Pharmacy disciplinary actions. The data bases discussed in **Chapter 2** can be accessed through a computer search using a public records vendor or electronic public information consultant.

The major federal agencies and state agencies listed in **Chapter 2** respond to a request made pursuant to the Federal Freedom of Information Act or State Freedom of Information Act; however, it is, in most cases, more efficient, from the standpoint of cost and time, to select a public records vendor who has access to the appropriate data bases. In addition to the suggestions listed in **Chapter 2** for choosing a vendor for public records searches, consider those vendors billing themselves as electronic public information consultants. Contact them, and ask for a listing of all of their in-house data bases so that you can choose that vendor who has access to those data bases appropriate for your specific request.

§ 6.42   Responding to a Demand for Production of Documents

A party who has been served with a request for inspection and production of documents, a request for inspection and entry onto land, and/or a request for inspection of tangible items, must respond within the time constraints of applicable statutes. Pursuant to Federal Rule of Civil Procedure 34 and various state statutes, a written response is due within 20 days of service of the request with the actual inspection or production taking place within 30 days, unless the time is extended either by stipulation or agreement between the parties. The procedures for extending time for responding are identical to those procedures outlined in **Chapters 4** and **5** on interrogatories and requests for admissions. It is important to remember that a written response to a request to produce must be served on the demanding party within 20 days of service of the demand in order to protect your client's right to object to any part of the demand. Failure to serve this written response, even though the discovery sought may be totally objectionable, exposes your client to a waiver of objections and Rule 37(d) sanctions.

A response to a demand to enter onto land for inspection or testing purposes often takes the form of a stipulation permitting inspection or testing within certain parameters (See **Form 6–1** for a sample stipulation.) A demand for inspection of documents requires a specific written response to each demand or category of items stating:

1.   The responding party will comply with all of the specifics of the particular demand for inspection and production;

2.   The responding party lacks the ability to comply with the demand for inspection of a particular item, document, or category of items because of whatever specific reasons demonstrating that responding party has made a due and diligent search for the requested item(s) and is unable to comply because the documents are either lost, destroyed, or were never in the party's possession, custody or control;

3. All documents or things in a demanded category that are in the possession. custody, or control of the responding party, and to which no objection is made, will be produced (The responding party may also object to the particular demand by objecting to a specific item or category of items and specific objections must be set forth in the same manner as they are required to be set forth in objecting to any other discovery proceeding);

4. Which items will be produced and which items are objectionable, because objections may be made to part of a request, and other items in the same request may be produced (this type of response is frequently used in responding to a general, all-inclusive request asking for a variety of documents.); and

5. That the items sought are not relevant to the subject matter of the action, that they are privileged, that they are trial preparation materials, or that they are the work of an expert, thus the requested items do not fall within the scope of discovery permitted by Rule 26(b) (This objection to inspection must be supported with specific designations as to which, if not all, of the requested documents are privileged, and which specific privileges apply.).

§ 6.43 Objections

There are several possible grounds for objecting to a demand for inspection of documents. The grounds for objections (discussed in **Chapters 4** and **5**) relating to interrogatories and requests for admissions are valid grounds for objecting to requests for documents. Specific objections which may be raised in responding to a demand for inspection and production of documents include the following bases:

1. Expensive and oppressive.   The responding party may object on the basis that to allow inspection would be unduly expensive or oppressive. This objection may be made when the bulk of documents covered by the request have been previously produced, and/or made available to requesting party, or when the bulk of the documents covered by the request are equally available to the requesting party, within the public domain, or may be obtained by subpoena from a third party. In addition to stating an objection, a motion for a protective order should be made pursuant to Rule 26(c) of the Federal Rules of Civil Procedure.

2. Foreign documents.   In antitrust litigation involving corporations and entities with domestic and foreign offices, monumental difficulties are imposed upon the responding party when requesting the production of foreign documents. The requesting party may be required to narrow the issues and the amount of requested documents. Objections may be made that the request is overbroad, and that the documents requested have not been described with particular specificity.

3. Privilege.   Objections which are based on privilege must specifically state the particular privilege. Documents for which a responding party claims protection under the work product and attorney-client privileges must be specifically identified.

4. Inability to comply.   The representation of the inability to comply with a demand for inspection must specifically state that the responding party has made a diligent search and a reasonable inquiry in an effort to comply with the demand and must further state that the party is unable to comply because:

The particular item or category of items never existed,

The particular item or category of items has been destroyed in the normal course of business activities, and

The particular item or category of items has been lost, or is no longer in the possession, custody, or control of the responding party.

If responding party has knowledge of the person, entity, or organization known or believed to have possession, custody, or control of a requested item or category of items, it is their affirmative duty to identify by name and address, the particular custodian of the document(s)/item(s).

5. Noncompliance with procedure.   Objections to a demand for inspection may be made based on defects in procedure alleging that the demand, or set of demands, generally fails to comply with the requirements of the statute. For example, a request to produce documents must be served before a demand for inspection of documents may be served. This procedural step is frequently overlooked by a requesting party who feels that the response to its request to produce documents will be objections and noncompliance; therefore, they proceed to make a demand for inspection without having complied with the formal procedural step of first serving a request. Objections based upon a failure to comply with the procedural requirements of a statute will generally be upheld by the courts. The demanding party then must proceed to request the documents, wait for the response, and then make a motion to compel production of documents. The strategic value of this objection is to buy time for the party who must respond. This is beneficial when you are working with a corporate entity whose documents are stored in warehouses in many states, because it allows you time for the gathering and screening of requested documents. When the procedural defects have been cured and a demand is served, responding party may still assert the identical objections which would have been asserted in their response to a request to produce documents.

6. Particularity of description.   The responding party may also object, stating that a particular demand, or set of demands, fails to comply with statutory requirements when a description of a particular category of items does not give notice of exactly what is expected to be included within that category, that the documents have not been described with reasonable particularity. This type of objection has the effect of shifting the burden to the demanding party to move for a motion to compel documents describing the requested documents with the "particularity that would allow a reasonable person to know the documents or things that have been requested." This type of an objection is frequently raised, but it is difficult to sustain because courts have generally allowed a broad application of the reasonable person test, and in the interests of justice have permitted general descriptions of documents.

7. Annoyance, embarrassment, oppression, confidentiality.   An objection may be raised that the demand for inspection causes the responding party unwarranted annoyance, embarrassment, oppression, undue burden and expense, and/or requires the production of sensitive, confidential documents. Issues regarding confidentiality should be raised first in an objection for a second time in a motion for a protective order at the same time as the objections are served on requesting party.

§ 6.44   Response Preparation

The essential questions which must be considered before beginning to respond to a document request are:

1.   When are the documents due?

2.   When is our written response due?

3.   Do the documents which fall within the scope of each request exist and did they ever exist?

4.   Does our office have all of the documents or must we obtain them from the client?

5.   Which agents of our client (bookkeeper, auditors, payroll clerk, secretary) are the most knowledgeable regarding certain categories of requested documents?

6.   Will it be necessary for the client to retrieve the documents from others, (employees, corporate offices, and so forth)?

7.   How voluminous are the documents which comprise the universe of documents responsive to these requests?

8.   How many sets of documents will need to be photocopied before actual production?

9.   Will the client be able to gather the documents without assistance, or will it be necessary to go to the client's place of business and assist the client in gathering responsive documents?

10.   Can we get an extension on the production date if necessary?

§ 6.45   Response Production Checklist

Before beginning to respond to a request for production, it is useful to review your responses using the following checklist:

_____   Read the document production request carefully, paying particular attention to any overbroad statements or misleading definitions. Reread each sentence seeking the precise intent of each request. This will enable you to respond to the request in the narrowest possible manner.

_____   Review the relevant discovery statutes and local rules to see if the request is timely and procedurally correct. If not, there are procedural grounds for objections.

_____   Check the request for drafting errors. Are the requests overbroad and vague? Do the requests seek documents in different time frames (past and future), or different categories making them objectionable?

_____   Check the request for those items which are not in dispute and arrange for production of those documents.

_____ Are there protective orders in place which limit discovery and apply to any of these requests?

_____ Will it be necessary to seek a protective order before going forward with response to this document request?

_____ Can the opposition obtain the documents requested from sources other than your client (are they equally available, or available by subpoena to a third party, and so forth)?

§ 6.46   The Initial Steps in Preparing a Response

Requests for production of documents should be sent to your client as soon as they are received. The client should be instructed that they must make a due and diligent search for the requested items and must produce not only those documents which are under the client's direct custody and control, but also those items which are under the control of any of the client's agents, employees, insurance companies, subsidiary corporations and so forth. It is important that the universe of documents responsive to the request is gathered and screened as soon as possible. (*See* **Form 6–24.**)

Your client may have already provided you with many of the items and documents included in the request, and may mistakenly assume that they do not have a duty to look for any other documents. This is seldom the case because most document requests include production of 5 or 10 years worth of documentation in specific categories.

Each request should be carefully scrutinized so that a response may be made within the narrowest boundaries permitted by the request. Although it is not ethical to withhold documents from production if they have been properly requested, it is prudent to construe the request in the narrowest possible sense and not produce documents that have not been specifically requested. For example, a request that asks for that certain letter written on May 1, 19__ to John Smith, President of ABC Corporation by Mary Jones, President of XYZ Corporation, but does not specifically request drafts or attachments to that letter, should be construed as to be limited to the specific letter only. A request that asks for the policy and procedures manual of ABC Graphics Company that was in effect at the time of plaintiff Mary Smith's employment, but does not request the current policy and procedures manual and/or manuals in force for five years prior to the incident, or revisions to manuals, and so forth, is a narrow request. The proper response is to produce only the manual that has been requested. The responding party is not obligated to produce anything that has not been specifically requested or to interpret a request in favor of requesting party. It is not the duty of responding party to correct the drafting errors of the propounding party by producing, or even acknowledging the existence of, nonrequested documents.

If the requested documents merely repeat information which has been provided in prior discovery, such as deposition testimony or interrogatory answers, producing them again would duplicate efforts. The responding party may properly assert that there is no need for production of documents when deposition testimony, deposition exhibits, or responses to interrogatories have provided the identical information. The key here is the term "identical." It has been held by the courts that to object to the production of certain documents on the grounds that answers to certain interrogatories have furnished the same information are improper and have been generally rejected by the court. Documents which have become deposition exhibits, and are later requested in a demand for inspection of documents, are an example of a duplicative request that is objectionable.

FORM 6–24
SAMPLE LETTER TRANSMITTING A
DOCUMENT REQUEST TO A CLIENT

[name] Chief Executive Officer
[plaintiff] corporation
[address]

   RE: [plaintiff] Corporation v. [defendant] Corporation

Dear [name]:

   Enclosed for your review is a request to produce documents which has been propounded by counsel for the defendant, [defendant] Corporation, to plaintiff, [plaintiff] Corporation. The date scheduled for production of these documents is [date]. We must submit a written response to this document production 10 days before the actual date of production, [date]. In our written response, we may assert privilege claims for document(s) which are responsive to any of the requests but should be protected by the attorney-client, attorney work product, or trade secret confidential information privilege.

   You have provided our office with a great deal of documentation over the past few months to assist us in preparing the complaint in this action and responding to defendant's first set of interrogatories, and we will review those documents to see if they are responsive to any of the categories of this request. However, you will note that this document request addresses not only those documents within the possession, custody, and control of [plaintiff] Corporation, but those documents which [plaintiff] Corporation has access to through their agents, employees, subsidiaries, and other individuals who may have worked for [plaintiff] Corporation as independent contractors. It will be necessary for you to review each and every request and make a due and diligent search for all documentation responsive to that request. If there are documents which you will need to retrieve from storage or other corporate facilities, please make arrangements to do so immediately. If you anticipate any problem or delay in obtaining any of those documents, please notify us immediately so that we may seek an extension of time within which to respond to this document request.

   [name], my legal assistant, whom you met when we were preparing responses to your interrogatories, is available to assist you in gathering the "universe of documents" necessary to respond fully and completely to this document request. [name] will be contacting your secretary to make an appointment

to visit your offices and assist your staff in gathering all of the documents needed to respond to this request.

We need to receive documents in our office no later than [date], in order to allow adequate time for screening, reviewing, and indexing them prior to production. We will also want to Bates stamp each and every document to establish its identification in this action. Stamping will be done in the lower left-hand corner, and will not alter or destroy the document in any fashion. We highly recommend stamping original documents, as we have found this is the best way to preserve the integrity of the document and avoid evidentiary problems at time of trial. Should you have any questions about this numbering procedure, please do not hesitate to contact [name].

Thank you for your courtesy and cooperation.

Sincerely,

_____

[attorney for the plaintiff]

§ 6.47 Inspecting and Categorizing Documents

Before documents can be produced to the demanding party, they must be inspected, categorized, and screened for privilege. Factors which should be considered in inspecting documents which you have received from your client, or retrieved yourself from your client's place of business are:

Is the document clear and legible? If not, can you obtain a better copy?

If the document references attachments or enclosures, are they available and made part of the document?

If the document contains tables, charts, and other computer-generated data, is there a key for deciphering the material? Federal and state statutes now require that documents produced containing computer-stored data be translated into "reasonably useable form at responding party's reasonable expense."

If the document references pages in its numbering (for example, "2 of 10 pages"), make certain that all of the referenced pages are included. In any document of several pages, it is wise to check to make sure there are no missing pages.

Is the document a clean copy, that is, without annotations, initials, notes in the margin, or highlighted portions?

Is the document a draft or final? Be particularly careful in reviewing drafts to make certain that they are clean copies. Be careful to note designations on drafts such as "first draft," "seventh draft," and so forth. If there were twenty drafts and they have been requested, you must produce clean copies of each draft in sequence.

Production of 10 out of 20 drafts is not acceptable without a suitable explanation.

Once you have inspected the universe of documents, and can verify under oath that the client, with or without your assistance, has made a due and diligent search for any documents within the client's control and possession, you are ready to begin categorizing the documents as responsive or nonresponsive. Those documents which are deemed to be nonresponsive should be carefully set aside and labelled, for example, "Documents Not Produced in Response to Defendant John Smith's First Request for Production of Documents, January 12, 19__." After you have completed the document production, return to those documents which were not produced and briefly inventory them. Place a memo in the file indicating that you have reviewed certain documents which are not being produced at this time, but which are available and in the client's possession should they be requested at a second document production. This brief inventory and index of documents not produced will be useful and will save legal assistant time and client money as discovery progresses in the case and further document requests are propounded to your client.

The initial categorizing of documents as being responsive or nonresponsive is the first step in screening those documents which ultimately will be produced. Sifting through the responsive documents and screening them for confidential and privileged information is the second step in preparing documents for production. An initial inventory should be done of the responsive set of documents, that is, financial documents should be separated from telephone records, personal records from corporate records, correspondence and interoffice memos from narrative reports, and so forth. In inventorying responsive documents and separating them into distinct categories, remember to keep them in chronological order.

§ 6.48   Producing Redacted Documents

A responsive document may contain sensitive or nonresponsive information which should not be divulged. The document must be turned over and included in the production, but at the same time, the client must be protected from the production of confidential/sensitive materials and/or nonresponsive information. The procedure for producing such a document is to redact, or cover up, those portions which are either nonresponsive or sensitive. The following procedure should be followed in redacting a document:

1. Photocopy all of the documents that need to be redacted in their original state;
2. Use Liquid Paper Whiteout, Post-it Paper or self-seal labelling tape to redact. or erase, the portion of the document which you wish to redact;
3. Photocopy the redacted document (It may be necessary to photocopy it more than once so that it will look like every other document, and the areas which have been removed by label, post-it, or whiteout will not be seen);
4. Staple a photocopy of the original document to a photocopy of the redacted document for your files, so that you will have an exact record; and
5. Stamp or type on the document, prior to producing the redacted document, "Redacted Document, Privileged/Nonresponsive Information" (This label or stamp should be placed over the space which has been redacted.).

After redacted documents have been prepared for production, a list should be made identifying each document and explaining the reason for the redacting. A list of redacted documents is similar to a list of privileged documents.

The format for a list of redacted documents is illustrated in **Form 6–25.**

FORM 6–25
SAMPLE LIST OF REDACTED DOCUMENTS

Name of Document	Date	Redacted Portion	Reason for Redaction	Date of Production
Letter, Jim J., CFO [name] Corp. to Mary S., CFO [name] Corp.	[date]	3rd & 4th Paragraphs on pg. 5 detailing preacquisition financial history of [name] franchise.	Nonresponsive to request no. 7 of defendant's 1st request for production of documents served on plaintiff [date]. Additional objection, confidential financial information.	[date]

A separate file should be maintained for all redacted documents. Contents of the file should include the original and redacted pages, an exact copy of the document request and response, and the list of redacted documents. If redacted documents become the subject of either a motion to compel document production or an in camera inspection, it may become necessary to produce all original documents and redacted documents as they appeared at the time of production. Maintaining this separate file will save time and money in preparing for an in camera inspection.

§ 6.49   Numbering Documents

The numbering of all original documents is essential. Many clients, and some attorneys, may attempt to discourage the numbering of all documents, and insist on numbering only those documents which will be produced. This approach creates innumerable problems as litigation progresses. If your client, and/or attorney, is strongly opposed to numbering original documents, then a complete set of the universe of documents should be photocopied and numbered. This can be an expensive proposition if the volume of documentation is extensive. The usual objection raised by a client to numbering original documents is that they will be destroyed. This is simply not the case when documents are numbered discreetly in the lower right hand corner with a printed number from a Bates stamp, or any other of a variety of automatic numbering machine. The argument raised by most attorneys against numbering all documents in the universe of documents is that when certain documents are privileged and/or nonresponsive and are not produced, there will be a gap in the numbering indicating that certain documents have been withheld from production. Because, in virtually every case there will be documents withheld from production for purposes of a privilege claim, a gap in numbers will occur. In fact, if a gap does not occur, it often creates the suspicion that documents have been deliberately withheld from production. Because the responding party is required to furnish a list identifying those documents withheld from production pursuant to privilege, it is advantageous for responding party to place a number on each and every document as it preserves the integrity of each document and it gives the document an identity for purposes of the litigation. It is also a sign of good faith on the part of responding party to have numbered all documents in that it indicates that a due and diligent search has been conducted, and all documents have been identified and located. Finally, the numbering of all documents is a safeguard against the inadvertent production of any privileged document because numbering the documents provides one more opportunity for screening documents and guards against production of any miscellaneous bits of paper which do not have an identifying number.

Numbering documents consecutively creates a universal method by which all parties can refer to a particular document, and that is what gives a document its identity. No one can be expected to remember which of the 500 financial documents all dated January 1, 19__ is the one that is being referred to in a particular motion, deposition, or interrogatory; however, the code on the corners of the documents will assure all parties that they are referencing the same piece of evidence. Other advantages to numbering documents are that it facilitates the retrieval of an original document, safeguards against the loss of documents, and allows you to prepare an index indicating the source, current location, and type of a particular document.

If the litigation involves multiple parties, a numbering system should be established whereby each party is assigned a particular sequence of numbers or an alphabetical sequence. This avoids duplication of numbers and immediately identifies the source of documents. For example, the plaintiff may number documents 1000 through 7000. Defendant may number documents A through Z, AA through ZZ, and so forth. Co-plaintiffs and co-defendants could number their documents 15,000 through 30,000 and alphabetical numbers could be capital for one defendant and lower case for the second defendant. If there are many parties involved in the litigation, you will have to be creative in assigning particular number and letter sequences, and you may not be able to avoid duplication. Sequential numbering systems have proven to be the most useful. The numbering of documents should be accomplished with a Bates automatic numbering machine, and must be done carefully, assuring that each and every page of a document is numbered. For example, a 10-page prospectus for a particular project should receive 10 numbers, one for each page, and not one number for the entire document.

The numbering system to be used should be as simple as possible and yet sensible. The idea behind a numbering system is to allow an attorney, legal assistant, secretary, or office clerk to locate a particular document within the shortest amount of time. A numbering system which is so sophisticated and complicated that it can only be deciphered by the person who has created the system fails to answer the need for which the system was created in the first place.

§ 6.50   Document Production Status Checklist

As soon as a document request has been received in your office, a document production status checklist should be initiated to monitor each stage of the flow of documentation. This sample checklist serves as a guideline and may be adapted to the particulars of each case. Always include a column for the date a task is completed and for the initials of the person who completed the task. The categories which should be included in a document production status checklist are:

1.   Date document request received from opposing counsel (by mail or hand delivery)
2.   Document request sent to client with cover letter of instruction
3.   Documents received from client
4.   Initial review of document request by legal assistant as to all possible objections
5.   Initial screening of documents received by client by the case clerk
6.   Irrelevant documents pulled, sorted, and labelled
7.   All responsive documents numbered
8.   All responsive documents sent for duplicating
9.   Documents received from duplicating
10. Quality control check of documents received from duplicating versus original for legibility, accuracy, and so forth
11. Documents screened for privilege (There may be more than one screening.)
12. Preparation of privileged document list
13. Documents sorted per category of document request
14. Written draft of response with objections to attorney
15. Last day for written response to document production
16. Letter requesting extension on date of production to opposing counsel, if necessary
17. Attorney review of documents scheduled for production
18. Production date, copies mailed to requesting attorney and all other counsel in action

If the document production is too voluminous to allow you simply to mail the segregated documents, it may be stipulated between counsel to allow the opposing counsel to review the entire universe of documents which are responsive to the request, selecting those that the opposing counsel wishes copied. In this instance, you will already have gone through the initial steps of reviewing and screening documents in order to pull privileged documents and prepare a list of those documents being withheld from the production per privilege claim; however, it is not necessary to pull all nonresponsive documents. Strategically and economically, it is better to let the opposing counsel wade through thousands of boxes of documents and make their own decision as to whether certain documentation is, in their opinion, unresponsive to the request. It is not necessary for you to do opposing counsel's work by pulling nonresponsive documents that are harmless in and of themselves. It is also a sign of good faith and cooperation with the discovery process to allow opposing counsel the opportunity to view the universe of documents and realize that you are not withholding any documentation with the exception of those documents clearly identified on your privileged list.

§ 6.51 Checklist for Written Document Responses

Written document responses must comply with the following requirements:

_____ 1. A statement must be made that the responding party will use their detection devices at the reasonable expense of demanding party to translate the information into a useable format, if data compilations, computer records or electronic information are being produced in response to any of the requested categories.

_____ 2. A verification signed by an officer or agent of a corporation, partnership, or association must accompany the response. Attorneys may sign responses as officers or agents of an organization, but they cannot, by doing so, protect their client from additional discovery concerning the sources of information contained in the response. If an attorney signs the response on behalf of the client, the responding party waives attorney-client privilege and protection for work product for subsequent discovery from that attorney as to identifying the sources of the documents and specifics as to the due and diligent search made for documents not produced. It is a far better practice to have the client sign the verification.

_____ 3. The response must address, separately, each demanded item or category of items in the following fashion:
The party will comply with the particular demand for inspection and any related activities,
The responding party lacks the ability to comply with the demand for inspection of a particular item or category or items because of whatever listed reason, or
The responding party objects to the particular demand for the following reasons . . . .

If only part of a demand for a specific item or category is objectionable, the response must contain a statement of compliance or a representation of inability to comply as to the remainder of the demand.

_____ 1. Each statement of compliance, representation of inability to comply, and/or objection to a request must correspond directly to the numbered request and be in the same sequence as the corresponding item, or category, in the demand;

____ **2.** A representation of inability to comply must state affirmatively that the responding party has made a due and diligent search and a reasonable inquiry in an effort to comply with the demand, and must specify that the party is unable to comply because the particular item or category of items has never existed, has been destroyed, has been lost, or has never been in the possession, custody, and control of the responding party; and

____ **3.** An affirmative statement in the response should indicate that the documents produced represent the full extent of documents currently known to be in the possession, custody, and control of responding party. This caveat is essential to protect your client from the embarrassment of subsequently discovered documents and it also protects the client's right to use those documents at the time of trial.

§ 6.52 Sample Response to a Demand for Inspection (Documents)

The responding party is under a duty to produce documents as they are kept in the usual course and scope of business or to organize and label them to correspond with the categories of the demand. Similarly, a written response to a document demand must be prepared specifically addressing each category in the demand. **Form 6–26,** with variables, may be used as a guide in preparing written responses.

FORM 6–26
SAMPLE RESPONSE TO A DEMAND FOR
INSPECTION (DOCUMENTS)

SUPERIOR COURT OF THE STATE OF [state name]
IN AND FOR THE COUNTY OF [county name]

[name], et al.,   No. [case number]

    Plaintiff,   RESPONSE TO DEMAND
                                                  FOR INSPECTION
-vs-

[name], et al.,

    Defendant.

Responding Party: [defendant/plaintiff]

Demanding Party: [plaintiff/defendant]

Set No.:   [set number]

Plaintiff, [name], responds to Set No. 1 of Demands for Inspection of Defendant, [name], as follows: [specify]:

[statement of compliance] Item [number]

1. [Defendant/plaintiff] will produce and allow the inspection and copying of the document described in Demand No. 1.

[statement of compliance] [category]

2. [defendant/plaintiff] will produce and allow the inspection and copying of all items in the category described in Demand No. 2.

[representation of inability to comply]

3. After diligent search and reasonable inquiry [defendant/plaintiff] is unable to produce for inspection and copying the item described in Demand No. 3, because this item has [never existed/been destroyed/been lost/been misplaced/been stolen].

4. After diligent search and reasonable inquiry, [defendant/plaintiff] is unable to produce for inspection and copying the item described in Demand No. 4, because this item has never been in the possession, custody, or control of [defendant/plaintiff]. The item is believed to be in the possession, custody or control of [name], [address], [city], [state].

5. After diligent search and reasonable inquiry, [defendant/plaintiff] is unable to produce for inspection and copying the item described in Demand No. 5, because this item is no longer in the possession, custody, or control of [defendant/plaintiff]. The item is believed to be in the possession, custody or control of [name], [address], [city], [state].

[Objection to produce] [Item]

6. [Defendant/Plaintiff] has in [defendant's/plaintiff's] possession, custody, or control the following item described in Demand No. 6 for the production of documents: [identification of item]. [Defendant/Plaintiff] objects to producing this item for inspection and copying on the ground that [set forth specific ground for objection].

[Objection to produce] [category]

7. [Defendant/Plaintiff] has in [defendant's/plaintiff's] possession, custody, or control the following items in the category described in Demand No. 7 for the production of documents: [identification of items]. [Defendant /Plaintiff] objects to producing for inspection and copying these items on the ground that [set forth specific ground for objection].

I declare under penalty of perjury under the laws of the State of [state name] that each of the responses to [plaintiff's/defendant's] Demands for Inspection, Set No. [set number], is true and correct.

This declaration was executed on [date] at [city], [county name] County, [state].

_____
[signature of responding party]

Dated: [date].

_____
[attorney for responding party]

NOTE: In preparing a written response for a document production, add the caveat that plaintiff reserves the right to supplement this response up to and during time of trial to protect your client should subsequent documentation relevant to the subject matter of the request be located in a forgotten warehouse or by a subsidiary corporation. Procedures for supplementing a document request are identical to those procedures outlined for supplementing interrogatory and request for admission responses in **Chapters 4** and **5.**

If documents are attached to your response in substantial compliance with the Demand for Inspection, a general statement should preface your response:

All documents that are currently in the possession, custody, and control of [plaintiff/defendant], and to which no claim of privilege and/or objection(s) is being made, are attached.

§ 6.53 Sample Response to a Demand for Inspection (Tangible Items/Testing)

Form 6–27 illustrates a sample response to a demand for inspection of tangible items or testing.

FORM 6–27
SAMPLE RESPONSE TO A DEMAND FOR INSPECTION
(TANGIBLE ITEMS/TESTING)

SUPERIOR COURT OF THE STATE OF [state name]
IN AND FOR THE COUNTY OF [county name]

[name], et al.,	No. [case number]
Plaintiff,	RESPONSE TO DEMAND FOR INSPECTION
-vs-	

[name], et al.,

   Defendant.

   Responding Party: [defendant/plaintiff]

   Demanding Party: [plaintiff/defendant]

   Set No.:   [set number]

   [Defendant/Plaintiff] responds to Set No. [number] of Demands for Inspection of [plaintiff/defendant] as follows: [specify]

[statement of compliance] [Items]

1. [Defendant/Plaintiff] will produce and allow the inspection, testing, and sampling of all of the items described in [defendant's/plaintiff's] Demand No. 1.

[statement of compliance] [category]

2. [Defendant/Plaintiff] will produce and allow the inspection, testing, and sampling of items in the category described in Demand No. 2.

[Representation of inability to comply]

3. After diligent search and reasonable inquiry, [defendant/plaintiff] is unable to produce and allow the inspection, testing, and sampling of the item described in Demand No. 3 because this item [never existed/has been destroyed/has been lost/has been misplaced/has been stolen].

4. After diligent search and reasonable inquiry, [defendant/plaintiff] is unable to produce and allow the inspection, testing, and sampling of the item described in Demand No. 4 because this item has never been in the possession, custody, or control of [defendant/plaintiff]. The item is believed to be in the possession, custody, or control of [name], [address], [city], [state].

5. After diligent search and reasonable inquiry, [defendant/plaintiff] is unable to produce and allow the inspection, testing, and sampling of the item described in Demand No. 5 because this item is no longer in the possession, custody, or control of [defendant/plaintiff]. The item is believed to be in the possession, custody, or control of [name], [address], [city], [state].

[Objection to testing]

6. [Defendant/plaintiff] will comply with the inspection, testing, and sampling described in Demand No. 6 to the extent that it seeks production of [item requested], and inspection in the form of testing [type of testing, for example, its

rear passenger-exit door while the bus is in motion], but [defendant/plaintiff] objects to the portion of Demand No. 6 that includes [description of portion of demand such as the disassembly of the treadle step by] experts retained by [plaintiff/defendant] on the ground that [specify reasons such as such disassembling creates a substantial risk of damage to, or permanent alteration of, the mechanism, that would prevent a later demonstration of its actual condition at the time of the alleged injury].

I declare under penalty of perjury under the laws of the State of [state name] that each of the responses to [plaintiff's/defendant's] Demands for Inspection, Set No. [number], is true and correct.

This declaration was executed on [date] at [city], [county name] County, [state].

_____

[signature of responding party]

Dated: [date].

_____

[attorney for the responding party]

§ 6.54 Sample Response to a Demand for Inspection (Entry onto Land/Premises)

A written response to a request to inspect property, enter onto land and perform testing, and produce tangible items may use the format illustrated in **Form 6–1** or **Form 6–28.**

FORM 6–28
SAMPLE RESPONSE TO A DEMAND
(ENTRY ONTO LAND/PREMISES)

SUPERIOR COURT OF THE STATE OF [state name]
IN AND FOR THE COUNTY OF [county name]

[name], et al.,   No. [case number]

    Plaintiff,   RESPONSE TO DEMAND
                                                    FOR INSPECTION

  -vs-

[name], et al.,

Defendant.

Responding Party: [defendant/plaintiff]

Demanding Party: [plaintiff/defendant]

Set No.:   [set number]

[Defendant/plaintiff] responds to Set No. [number] of Demand for Inspection of [plaintiff/defendant] to enter the real property in possession, custody, or control of [defendant/plaintiff] located at [address], [city], [state], as follows: [specify]:

[statement of compliance]

1. [Defendant/plaintiff] will permit the inspection, testing, and sampling of the land and premises described in Demand No. 1.

(Representation of inability to comply)

2. [Defendant/Plaintiff] cannot permit the inspection, testing, and sampling of the land and premises described in Demand No. 2 because the land and premises have never been in the possession, custody, or control of [defendant/plaintiff]. The land and premises are believed to be in the possession, custody, or control of [name], [address], [city], [state].

3. [Defendant/Plaintiff] cannot permit the inspection, testing, and sampling of the land and premises described in Demand No. 3 because the land and premises are no longer in [defendant's/plaintiff's] possession, custody, or control. The land and premises are believed to be in the possession, custody, or control of [name], [address], [city], [state].

[objection to entry]

4. [Defendant/plaintiff] responds to Demand No. 4 of [plaintiff/defendant) under [state] Code of Civil Procedure [section number] for permission to enter [land/premises] and to inspect the operation of its [item] as follows: [specify method of inspection]. [Defendant/plaintiff] will comply with the demand to the extent that [plaintiff/defendant] seeks permission to enter [land/premises] and to observe the operation of its [item], but [Defendant/plaintiff] objects to that part of the demand that seeks permission to [specify part of demand] on the ground that [specify grounds such as such videotaping will distract its employees and disrupt the bottling and capping operations of its business].

I declare under penalty of perjury under the laws of the State of [state name] that each of the responses to [plaintiff's/defendant's] Demands for Inspection, Set. No. [number], is true and correct.

This declaration was executed on [date] at [city], [county name] County, [state].

_____

[signature of responding party]

Dated: [date].

_____

[attorney for the responding party]

§ 6.55 Production of Government Documents

The problem of production of documents in the hands of the government, particularly the federal government, has many facets. The rules against production of documents by state and federal governments are stricter when the litigation is between private parties, and a bit more lenient when the government is involved as a party. If the government is involved as a party, it has generally been held that there is a waiver of immunity except in unusual situations involving defense and national security. Rules 26 and 33 of the Federal Rules of Civil Procedure discuss governmental immunity in document production on the federal level. Specific government code sections in state statutes discuss production of documents from city and state governments.

Government corporations, which have the power to sue and be sued, have generally been held to have no more privileges than private corporations. They must abide by the same discovery rules as nongovernment corporations. The landmark case dealing with production of documents from a governmental corporation is _RFC v. J. G. Menihan Corp._, a 1941 case which continues to be the black letter case in this area).[9]

Document requests to governmental agencies must conform with Rule 34 governing production and must also demonstrate good cause in every case. Most federal refusals to produce documents are based on internal regulations of various governmental departments. Authority for this refusal stems from 5 U.S.C. § 22 which has been construed by the federal courts as permitting department heads to prescribe regulations governing the custody, use, and preservation of documents.

Documents from governmental agencies can be requested under a Federal Freedom of Information Act request (See **Chapter 2**). This is a much easier method of obtaining production of government documents and has the added advantage of not requiring a statement of good cause for the production. Congress has forbidden governmental agencies to withhold information from the public or limit the availability of records to the public except under certain conditions. Those conditions are discussed as exceptions to Federal Freedom of Information Act requests in **Chapter 2.**

Certain governmental agencies have specific regulations such as the Federal Trade Commission, the National Labor Relations Board, Securities and Exchange Commission, Selective Service, Veterans Administration, and so forth. Courts have

---

[9] 312 U.S. 81 (1941).

generally sustained governmental refusals to produce documents from these agencies in actions between private parties. When the government is not a party, the court's only power to compel production is to find the government official refusing production to be in contempt for their refusal, and this has rarely been done. Rulings have been on a case-by-case basis depending on the circumstances. Certain governmental agencies such as the Veterans Administration and Selective Services have been compelled to produce documents when it has been shown that there is an overriding public concern, such as a class action, and when no harm to national security or public well-being is involved in the production of the documents. The theories supporting disclosure have been that the information would have to be disclosed at trial anyway, and that the requesting party should have the opportunity to prepare for trial against whatever charges and/or defenses the government may be making.

Federal documents may be requested from a defendant government agency operating as a private corporation (for example, in breach of contract cases). In administrative procedures, such as Workers Compensation Appeal Board hearings, Social Security disability hearings, unemployment insurance matters, and other procedures which are governed by administrative law (when the hearing takes place as an administrative hearing rather than in the courtroom), different rules and regulations apply for the production of government documents. Administrative agency statutes and opinions should be checked for rules and procedures. Administrative hearings follow rules and procedures set forth for that particular agency. Necessary documents or records in the possession of the agency may be also obtained through a subpoena for the production of the record issued by the administrative law judge. An administrative law judge will issue a notice to produce certain designated documents to the administrative agency causing it to bring the requested records to the hearing. Records may be obtained before a hearing by a request to the administrative law judge. A request may be made before or after a case is set for hearing by any party. A request for a subpoena to compel a witness to attend and to produce books, papers, memoranda, or other records must be made by affidavit and must describe the matters desired with reasonable particularity setting forth their relevance to the issues in the case. The forms for subpoenas for records are available in most administrative field offices.

§ 6.56   Developing Discovery Plans with Government Attorneys

Recent amendments to the Federal Rules of Civil Procedure have increased the overall judicial supervision of pretrial proceedings, including discovery. These developments advocate the formulation of a custom-designed discovery plan worked out between private attorneys in coordination with the Assistant United States Attorney. If a discovery plan is negotiated early and put in place, it not only substantially reduces the chance of later disagreements but also increases the possibility of cooperation on the part of the government. It is natural for private attorneys, and most certainly legal assistants, to feel inhibition in seeking discovery against the federal government because, more often than not, you will be met with a closed door. Government attorneys tend to be more cooperative and reasonable if they are made aware of where the private attorney intends to go with their discovery plan, including scheduled depositions, interrogatories, and requests for production of documents. Federal Rule of Civil Procedure 26(g) allows for judicial scrutiny of discovery papers, including particular discovery demands. Under Rule 26(g), attorneys must attest in writing to the propriety, or good cause showing of the discovery demands being made.

Rule 29 allows that parties may, by written stipulation, modify discovery procedures and tailor them to their particular needs. This is most often used for an extension of time pursuant to Rules 33, 34, and 36 for interrogatories, requests for admissions, and document requests. Government policy favors providing discovery in stages. The identity of fact witnesses and underlying documents should be requested in interrogatories. Documents may then be requested in a request for production of documents. Rule 26(c) allows for the control of discovery by the government if that discovery is unfocused, out-of-sequence, or unduly intrusive. Restructuring a discovery plan and limiting the scope of documents requested from governmental agencies increases your chances of cooperation.

Generally speaking, the United States government is subject to discovery to the same extent as any other litigant.[10] However, this statement is subject to numerous exceptions developed to allow the government to transact public business without undue and intrusive interference by discovery requests. A party seeking discovery from the federal government must be aware of the particular department or agency's housekeeping regulations. To learn the regulations of the particular agency from whom you are seeking documents, consult the Federal Register. Department regulations normally give legal custody of all records to the department or agency head. If a subpoena is served upon an employee of that agency, the employee must decline to produce the subpoenaed documents unless the employee obtains the express approval of the department or agency head.

The government faces particular problems in responding to discovery requests in that search and retrieval from far-flung storage locations, along with the government bureaucracy will naturally slow their response. Certain agency's records, locally or regionally, as well as centrally, use different filing systems, making the retrieval more difficult. The attorney for the government in charge of a response may not be aware that requested documents are to be found in multiple locations. In today's computerized age, information sources are often frequently found in data bases making the retrieval of documents easier; however, the cost of computer searches for retrieval of documents must be borne by the requesting party. The government will gladly provide an itemized bill detailing the cost of their search.

Certain regulations, including 28 C.F.R. § 16.22, require that the agency head screen and authorize the release of discovery responses and documents even in cases when the government is not one of the parties. This requirement slows response time by adding an extra required step to the screening process.

§ 6.57　Government Privilege Claims

The government may invoke both traditional and unique privileges in response to certain discovery requests. Problems in obtaining government documents under a

---

[10] United States v. Proctor & Gamble Co., 356 U.S. 677, 681 (1958).

Federal Freedom of Information Act (FOIA) request are discussed in **Chapter 2.** These exceptions, as well as the traditional privileges, apply to the production of government documents. The government is entitled to attorney-client and attorney work product privileges which are the most frequently invoked privileges. In addition, there are privileges that only the government may raise, privileges which have been sustained by the courts because they are deemed to be essential for the proper functioning of the government (city, state or federal). Government attorneys must go through specified procedural hoops in order to assert unique government privileges. Generally, a department or agency head requests the privilege based on their personal consideration of the material and attests to that consideration in an affidavit supporting the privilege claim.

These unique privileges include:

1. The state secrets and national securities privilege,[11]
2. The deliberative privilege,[12]
3. The informant's privilege (The government has a duty to withhold information regarding anyone considered a government informant.),[13]
4. Privileges protecting law enforcement investigation files,[14] and
5. The privacy act (This has lead to a government policy not to release personnel files of government employees without a court order, and it is normal government procedure to request a protective order limiting access to all personnel files.).[15]

It is not impossible to obtain documents from the government. The key to obtaining them is to request them from the appropriate agency in the appropriate manner. Rule 26(s) of the Federal Rules of Civil Procedure provides for discovery conferences if you run into the problem of an unfocused response by a distracted, overworked government attorney. Propose your discovery plan to the court, schedule the discovery, and draft the discovery requests. Prior to asking for court intervention, you must, of course, make a reasonable effort to reach an agreement with the government attorney in the same fashion as all discovery disputes must be resolved by a meet and confer conference to negotiate a reasonable solution acceptable to both sides. Government attorneys are under a duty to participate in good faith in conferring with private attorneys regarding requests for government documents.

Finally, if the government refuses to release documents after many attempts, see if the same records are available from state public records, corporations, or the source that originally supplied the information to the government. Remember, in dealing with the government and its attorneys, that they are generally more concerned with policy and procedure than with time and money. Be persistent and be patient.

---

[11] United States v. Reynolds, 345 U.S. 1 (1953).

[12] NLRB v. Sears, Roebuck & Co., 421 U.S. 132 (1975).

[13] Roviaro v. United States, 353 U.S. 53 (1957).

[14] Black v. Sheraton Corp. of Am., 564 F.2d 531 (D.C. Cir. 1977).

[15] 5 U.S.C. § 522.

§ 6.58 Protective Orders

Grounds for seeking protective orders relating to requests for documents, tangible items, entry onto land, and permission to conduct testing or inspection of premises are similar to the grounds stated for seeking protective orders as they relate to interrogatories and requests for admissions (See **Chapter 5**). The protective order provision of Federal Rule of Civil Procedure 26 as it relates to document requests is most useful in resisting an inspection demand which seeks an inspection of and production of documents which are relevant to the subject matter of the case and which are not covered by any privilege, and not insulated from discovery by the work product doctrine. A protective order requests the trial court to exercise its broad discretionary power to override or to adjust an otherwise proper inspection demand when the operation of the demand in the particular case will cause responding party "unwarranted annoyance, embarrassment, or oppression, or undue burden and expense. . . ."

A protective order may be sought only after the formal response requirements have been fulfilled pursuant to Rule 34, or applicable state statutes. The responding party might seek a protective order when the request:

Seeks voluminous, marginally relevant background information on a particular business entity or individual;

Asks for information that is personally embarrassing, confidential, highly sensitive or a trade secret;

Sets a time for production that is unreasonable in light of the amount of material that must be produced, and all attempts at seeking an informal resolution of extending the time for production have failed; and

Does not make a provision for protecting the responding party's interests when there is a demand for destructive tests.

Other situations when a protective order might be sought include a demand for inspection of premises which is unduly disruptive to the employees' work being performed on the premises. In this instance, an argument for a protective order forbidding the inspection may suggest alternative discovery methods. It is frequently argued that the same information may be obtained in other less disruptive fashions, for example, a video.

The court, on a showing of good cause, can make any order that justice requires to protect against unwarranted annoyance, embarrassment, oppression, or undue burden or expense. The broad authority to shape a protective order to the individual circumstances of a case includes, but is not limited to, a court order which states that:

1. All or some of the items or categories of items in the inspection demand need not be produced;
2. The time to respond to the demand or to a particular item or category be extended to allow the responding party to gather the information;
3. The response may be made only on specified terms and conditions (In this instance, the party moving for the protective order frequently submits a stipulation and order, such as **Form 6–30,** with respect to the production of

confidential materials which has been submitted to opposing counsel in the hopes of avoiding a motion for a protective order.);

4. The trade secret or other confidential research, development, or commercial information not be disclosed, or disclosed only to specific persons, or as specified;

5. The items produced be sealed and thereafter be opened only on court order;

6. An in camera inspection be permitted of all documents requested, with the judge determining which documents will be released to opposing counsel.

A protective order (see **Form 6–29**) is a noticed motion which must comply with the specific notice requirements in your state or the federal jurisdiction in which the action is set. Notice must be served in a timely fashion allowing time for the opposition to respond with points and authorities. A motion for a protective order must include:

1. A notice and motion,

2. A memorandum of points and authorities,

3. Supporting declaration(s), and

4. A proposed order or stipulation with respect to the production of confidential materials.

There are no specific time limitations on when to move for a protective order, but it should be done promptly after service of an inspection demand. A motion for a protective order should be made immediately upon receiving an inspection demand accompanied by a simultaneous request to opposing counsel to extend the time to respond to the production demand until after the motion for protective order is heard. If opposing counsel refuses to grant an extension of time, the motion for protective order should be combined with an ex parte request to extend the time for the response to be served and for the inspection to occur after the motion for protective order has been heard. An ex parte motion may also be made for an order shortening the time for the hearing of the motion for protective order.

FORM 6–29
SAMPLE MOTION FOR A PROTECTIVE ORDER

SUPERIOR COURT OF THE STATE OF [state name]
IN AND FOR THE COUNTY OF [county name]

[name], et al.,	No. [case number]
Plaintiffs,	NOTICE OF MOTION FOR PROTECTIVE ORDER
-vs-	RESTRICTING DISCOVERY AND IMPOSING MONETARY
[name], et al.,	SANCTIONS

Defendants.

TO: [name], Defendant, and to their attorney of record.

NOTICE IS HEREBY GIVEN that on [date], at [time], or as soon thereafter as the matter may be heard in Department [number] of this Court located at [street address], plaintiff will move for a protective order that documents requested in defendant's First Request to Produce Documents and Tangible Things propounded by [name], defendant, and served on [name], plaintiff, on [date] need not be answered and no documents need be produced.

NOTICE IS ALSO GIVEN that if this motion for a protective order is opposed and substantial justification for that opposition is not shown, plaintiff also moves for a monetary sanction against defendant [name] and its attorney, in an amount equal to the attorneys' fees incurred by the moving party as shown by the attached declaration of [name], attorney for plaintiff.

This motion will be made on the grounds that the documents requested relate to confidential research, trade secrets, and business transaction information that plaintiff has in plaintiff's possession solely for the purpose of conducting plaintiff's business. In this particular case, this inspection demand causes unwarranted annoyance, embarrassment and oppression.

Plaintiff, [name], has made a reasonable and good faith attempt to resolve informally the issues presented by this motion.

This motion will be based on this notice of motion, on the declaration of [name], attorney for plaintiff, and on the memorandum of points and authorities set forth below, on the records and files herein, and on such other evidence as may be presented at the hearing of this motion.

Dated: [date].

_____

[attorney for the plaintiff]

This notice of motion and motion must be accompanied by a memorandum of points and authorities which clearly sets out the particular circumstances and issues in this case which have prompted the protective order.

If, as part of a good faith effort to resolve this dispute, the moving party has prepared a stipulation with respect to the production of confidential materials, a copy should be included as part of the moving papers. If the proposed stipulation has been refused by requesting party without substantial justification, that fact should be mentioned in both the memorandum of points and authorities and the attorney declaration. If alternative methods of discovery have been discussed between the plaintiff and the defense counsel, they should also be included in the declaration.

Sample attorney declarations supporting motions for a protective order, sample protective orders, and discussion of methods for opposing protective orders as they relate to inspection demands are similar to those discussed in **Chapter 5** as they relate to requests for admissions and **Chapter 4** as they relate to interrogatories.

§ 6.59   Stipulations

A stipulation to protect confidential information may be made at any time during the course of discovery as it relates to confidential information in the context of any discovery device.(See **Form 6–31.**) All discovery interrelates and information of a highly confidential or sensitive nature must be protected from the onset to guard against waivers of privilege. If confidential information has been discussed in deposition testimony or interrogatory responses without objections raised, it is difficult to claim that documents relating to the same information are privileged. A good waiver argument can be made based on earlier discovery responses.

The stipulation (**Form 6–30**) may be used with suitable variables at any stage in litigation, preferably the early stages of discovery, and it may be modified to relate to deposition testimony, interrogatory answers, request for admission responses, and/or production of documents.

FORM 6–30
SAMPLE STIPULATION (GENERAL FORM)
AND ORDER

SUPERIOR COURT OF THE STATE OF [state name]
IN AND FOR THE COUNTY OF [county name]

[name], et al.,	No. [case number]
Plaintiffs,	STIPULATION FOR PROTECTIVE ORDER
-vs-	AND ORDER
[name], et al.,	
Defendants.	

In the course of discovery in the above-entitled action, [plaintiff] [sent/will produce/receive from] [defendant], hereinafter referred to as "designated parties," certain valuable confidential and proprietary information. The designated parties intend that this information be kept confidential and not be used for any purpose other than in this action. The designated parties therefore agree, through their respective attorneys, as follows:

1. This stipulated protective order shall apply to all confidential information. Confidential information is defined as testimony, written or recorded materials,

and information in any other form, produced or disclosed by any designated party in connection with discovery proceedings in this case, in which the following is discussed or in any way referred to:

[Specify in detail the exact nature of the topic which is to be protected, for example, the exact recipe of the 11 herbs and spices used in the batter by the Colonel to make Kentucky Fried Chicken].

2. Confidential information shall be used by the party to whom it is disclosed only in this action. A designated party shall not use any confidential information for any business or competitive purposes.

3. Confidential information shall be produced only to counsel for the designated party seeking discovery of it and shall not be exhibited or disclosed to any person other than [name of judge] without the written consent of counsel for the party producing it. No person to whom this confidential information is disclosed shall discuss the information or disclose it to any other person other than those described in this paragraph, or for any purpose other than specified in paragraph 2.

4. Counsel to whom confidential information is disclosed or produced shall be responsible for insuring that the parties and other persons are informed of the terms of this stipulated protective order, but other than the persons specified in paragraph 3, that no one is informed of the substance of any confidential information disclosed or produced. Before disclosing confidential information to any other persons, counsel shall [specify disclosure conditions, for example, seek a modification of the agreement as provided to add names of persons to whom disclosure may be made].

5. Any document or tangible thing designated as confidential information that is identified as an exhibit in connection with testimony given in these proceedings shall be marked with the label "Confidential Information," and any testimony concerning the document or thing shall also be considered confidential information and shall be subject to the terms of this stipulated protective order. (Note: This provision applies specifically to deposition testimony.)

6. Counsel who seeks to file with the court clerk confidential information in the form of a document, interrogatory answer, deposition transcript, pleading, or other record or tangible item shall ask the court to direct that this confidential information be filed under seal, specifically marked as confidential information subject to the stipulated protected order and kept in a safe and secure place and not in files open to public inspection.

7. On final disposition of this action, counsel for any party having possession, custody, or control of confidential information produced in the course of discovery in this action shall promptly return all original documents and tangible items covered by this order to counsel for the designated party who produced

them, and shall destroy all copies, transcripts, notes, and extracts containing confidential information except those marked as exhibits during trial.

8. Nothing in this stipulated protective order, (a) effects in any way, the admissibility of any documents, testimony, or other evidence at trial; or (b) restricts the use of information obtained from sources other than discovery conducted under the terms of this stipulated protective order.

9. This stipulated protective order may be modified by the agreement of the parties, subject to the approval of the court.

Dated: [date].

By: [attorney for the plaintiff]

By: [attorney for the defendant]

ORDER

IT IS SO ORDERED.
Dated: [date].

[judge]

FORM 6–31
SAMPLE STIPULATION (CONF!DENTIAL DOCUMENTS) AND ORDER

SUPERIOR COURT OF THE STATE OF [state name]
IN AND FOR THE COUNTY OF [county name]

[name], et al.,	No. [case number]
Plaintiff,	STIPULATION AND ORDER WITH RESPECT TO THE
-vs-	PRODUCTION OF CONFIDENTIAL MATERIALS
[name], et al.,	
Defendant.	

It is hereby stipulated and agreed by and between the undersigned attorneys for the respective parties that documents responsive to any of the parties' discovery requests served or to be served informally or formally in this proceeding upon any of the parties shall be produced in accordance with the following terms and conditions:

1. Each party may designate documents containing or relating to competitive information as confidential. Confidentiality may be claimed with respect to documents of the following types, but this paragraph shall not be deemed to exclude any other types or classifications of documents for which confidentiality may be claimed by a party:

(a) Documents relating to customer information, negotiations, and quotations or bids;

(b) Documents relating to trade secrets, or other confidential research, development, processes, or commercial information;

(c) Financial statements, profit and loss statements, and summaries of financial data; and

(d) Corporate minutes, including any reports of officers or directors.

2. All documents to be produced as to which a claim of confidentiality is made pursuant to this stipulation and order will be marked with the stamp "CONFIDENTIAL."

3. Counsel who are currently appearing in this proceeding and any experts retained by counsel will be permitted to have copies of the confidential documents. Additionally, confidential documents may be disclosed to a reasonable number of senior executive officers, directors, and staff personnel of the parties necessary to aid counsel in the prosecution of the litigation of the above-entitled action. The identity of all such persons shall be furnished promptly to the supplying party together with the representation that those persons have been shown a copy of this stipulation and order, and that those persons have signed an acknowledgement of receipt of a copy of this stipulation and order and a copy thereof shall be provided to the opposing party in this litigation. Parties or persons who have signed such an acknowledgement of receipt found by the court to be in violation of this stipulation and order may be punished by contempt proceedings and such violation may be actionable for damages suffered.

4. Information obtained from the confidential documents will be used solely for the preparation and trial of the above-entitled action, and for no other purpose. At the end of the case, all confidential documents, including copies, portions and extracts, will be returned to counsel of record in this action.

5. In the event that any confidential documents or portions thereof are included with, or the contents thereof are in any way disclosed in any pleading, motion or other paper filed with the clerk of this court, such confidential material shall be furnished to the court and to counsel of record for the named parties, and a duplicate copy (with the confidential materials deleted therefrom) may be placed on the public record.

6. This stipulation is not intended to restrict counsel for the parties: (i) in their right to use any document designated as confidential in the taking of depositions, and any such documents shall only be used, and their confidentiality protected, as may be agreed upon by counsel at such deposition or, if counsel are unable to agree, as determined or directed by the court at trial or any pretrial hearing; or (ii) in their use of the information obtained from interviewing, deposing or otherwise communicating with any persons, including any persons identified in a confidential document; provided, however, that no counsel for any party hereto will disclose to any such persons the source of the information, or provide to any such persons copies of such documents.

7. The confidential documents and the substance of the information contained therein may be disclosed by counsel for any party hereto to other persons notwithstanding the conditions recited above, so long as counsel gives ten (10) days' written notice to counsel for all other parties of their intent to make disclosure or to seek a further protective order if deemed necessary. In the event that any party hereto gives notice of an intention to disclose confidential documents and that notice is challenged by a motion for a protective order, no disclosure will be permitted while the motion is pending and until a decision on that motion is issued by the court.

Dated: [date].

IT IS SO ORDERED.

[judge]_____

APPROVED AS TO FORM:
Dated: [date].

_____
[attorney for the plaintiff]

_____
[attorney for the defendant]

§ 6.60   Compelling Responses

If no response is made to a request, or if the response(s) object to all, or part, of the requested discovery, or if the responding party otherwise fails to permit discovery as requested (by providing documents, allowing inspection of tangible items, and allowing entry onto land and testing procedures); the party who propounded the request may move to compel a response pursuant to Rule 37(a) of the Federal Rules of Civil Procedure and further compel inspection in accordance with the request. The general source of most dissatisfaction with responses to document requests stems from the belief that the objections, which the responding party has cited, are unfounded, or that the objections stated are too general and are not particularized to the items which have been requested. You may have received a timely response but not be satisfied with some feature of it. The response may indicate that the inspection of documents or tangible items that will be provided is less than what has been demanded, or it may not factually support a claimed lack of possession or control of the item.

The procedure for compelling responses to an inspection demand includes an obligation on the propounding party to meet and confer in a good faith attempt to resolve the differences prior to making a formal motion. This good faith requirement of meeting and conferring is strictly construed by the courts and motions will not be heard unless this requirement has been satisfied. A motion to compel further responses to a document request must be accompanied by an attorney declaration executed under penalty of perjury detailing the exact steps taken to reach an informal resolution of the dispute.

To guard against overlooking the time frame within which a motion to compel further responses to document production must be filed, check local rules and calendar appropriately. For example, in California the statutory time limit is 45 days from receipt of the written response. Review the written response as soon as it is received to note and evaluate the privilege claims as well as those categories of documents which will be produced. Once you have received documents, review them to make certain that all relevant documents in a particular category have been produced. For example, the responding party may agree to produce the minutes of Board of Directors meetings of ABC Corporation for the calendar year 19__. In reviewing the minutes produced, you may find several months are missing. This is usually an oversight which can be corrected immediately by contacting counsel for the responding party. Frequently, in large document productions, there will be inadvertent gaps in the production due to clerical error. These mistakes can be easily corrected, if they are noticed promptly.

A motion to compel further responses to document production is a noticed motion and must comply with the formal requirements of all noticed discovery motions. The format of a motion to compel further responses to an inspection demand is the same as a motion to compel further responses to interrogatories and a motion to compel further responses to requests for admissions. In a motion seeking a further response to an inspection demand, the points and authorities accompanying the motion must set forth specific facts showing good cause justifying the discovery sought. The burden of showing the relevance of the information and the ability to produce the requested information/documents by responding party, rests on the one who seeks the discovery. It is within the discretion of the court to decide whether the documents sought are relevant and nonprivileged. The court also must determine:

1. Whether the items sought are properly discoverable,
2. Whether a showing of good cause for production has been made by requesting party, and
3. Whether the objections raised to the production are valid, because the objections to document production must be specific, generalized, unfocused objections to entire sets of document requests have been held to be invalid and sanctionable.

A motion to compel further responses to document inspection may be made concurrently with your opposition to a motion for a protective order. The claims that have been made in a protective order should be addressed in the points and authorities opposing the protective order; however, they should also be raised in the points and authorities accompanying a motion to compel further responses to a demand for inspection of documents. In ruling on an objection that claims privacy, secrecy, confidential records, or undue burden and expense, the courts consider the moving party's need for the inspection, and balance that need with the need to protect the information. The disclosure of documents may be refused as unduly burdensome when the information sought is only marginally relevant, but it may be ordered (at least as an in camera inspection) if a good cause showing substantiates that the information is important and directly relevant to the case.

When a demand for inspection of documents, tangible items, or entry onto land has been completely ignored by responding party, a motion to compel a response is usually routinely granted by the court (**Form 6–32**). Statutory authority based on federal and state procedures are straightforward in the requirement that a response must be served upon responding party within 30 days of their receipt of a demand for inspection. If you have received no response, and have not received a request for an extension of time within which to respond, a motion to compel should be made immediately upon the expiration of the statutory time period. Such a motion should seek sanctions and further state that all objections have been waived by responding party's failure to respond in a timely fashion. Therefore, all privilege claims have been waived, and responses should be full and complete. If you ever find yourself in this unfortunate circumstance, there is relief possible through a noticed motion for relief based on excusable neglect, mistake, inadvertence, death of attorney, serious illness, or some other unforeseen act of God which has prevented you from responding in a timely fashion. A motion for relief cannot be based on failure to calendar due dates, "my client was on an extended European trip," secretarial or paralegal mistakes, or other various "the check is in the mail" type of excuses.

This notice of motion and motion should be used when no responses have been received.

FORM 6–32
SAMPLE MOTION TO COMPEL RESPONSES TO A DEMAND FOR INSPECTION

SUPERIOR COURT OF THE STATE OF [state name]
IN AND FOR THE COUNTY OF [county name]

[name],	No. [case number]
Plaintiff,	NOTICE OF MOTION FOR ORDER COMPELLING
-vs-	COMPLIANCE WITH PLAINTIFF'S DEMAND FOR
[name],	INSPECTION AND FOR SANCTIONS

Defendant.

Date: [date]
Time: [time]
Place: [location]

_____/

TO: DEFENDANT, [name], AND TO THEIR ATTORNEY OF RECORD:

PLEASE TAKE NOTICE that on [date] at [time] or as soon thereafter as the motion may be heard in Department [judicial department] of the Superior Court located at [address], plaintiff will move the court for an order compelling defendant to respond to plaintiff's First Set of Demand for Inspection of Documents served on defendant on [date] and for an order for monetary sanctions against defendant and in favor of plaintiff pursuant to [cite applicable statutory authority for sanctions].

This motion is made pursuant to [cite applicable statutory authority] on the grounds that defendant was required by [cite applicable statutory authority] to serve on plaintiff a response to the demand for inspection no later than 30 days from the date on which it was served on defendant, and that defendant has failed, and continues to fail, to serve the required responses.

This motion is based on this notice, the pleadings, records and files in this action, the attached memorandum of points and authorities, and the attached supporting declaration of [name], attorney for plaintiff, such oral and documentary evidence and other which will be presented at the hearing of this motion.

Dated: [date].

_____
[attorney name]

The points and authorities for this motion need cite only statutory authority requiring a response when a properly served demand for inspection has been propounded. Points and authorities in this case need not argue the relevancy of the documents sought; merely that a demand has been made and a response has not been received.

The moving papers must be accompanied by a declaration as exemplified in **Form 6-33.**

FORM 6-33
SAMPLE DECLARATION IN SUPPORT OF A MOTION

DECLARATION IN SUPPORT OF MOTION
TO COMPEL RESPONSES AND FOR SANCTIONS

I, [name], declare:

1. I am the attorney for plaintiff, [name], in this action.

2. On [date] I caused to be served on defendant, [name], plaintiff's First Set of Demand for Inspection and Production of Documents. A copy of this demand and proof of service is attached to this motion as Exhibit "A" and made a part hereof.

3. Defendant, [name], failed, and continues to fail, to respond to this demand. Defendant, [name], has not contacted plaintiff, [name], to indicate that they are willing to comply with this demand, and/or to request an extension of time within which to respond.

4. I have spent 10 hours preparing this motion. This work has included legal research, telephone calls, and client conferences. I expect to spend an additional two hours completing work on this motion, including time spent in court. My customary billing rate is $125.00 per hour. My staff, consisting of legal assistants and secretaries, has spent an additional 4 hours on this motion, performing the following tasks: telephone calls to court, typing, xeroxing, and conferences with client.

I declare under penalty of perjury under the laws of the State of [state name], that the foregoing is true and correct.

Dated: [date].

_____

[attorney for the plaintiff]

In a motion to compel responses when no responses have been given, there is no requirement for a meet and confer good faith attempt to settle the dispute. That is, the burden is not upon the requesting party to contact the responding party and ask them why they have not offered a response. The burden is on the responding party to contact the requesting party to request an appropriate extension of time within which to respond. This, however, does not preclude attorneys from attempting to resolve this dispute on an informal basis, saving the client time and money and the attorney court time and aggravation. A common procedure is for the requesting attorney to send a warning letter to his opponent advising the opponent that considerable time has passed since the attorney served the demand for inspection, the statutory time period to respond has expired, all objections have been waived, and that the attorney would sincerely like to resolve this dispute by receiving documents directly from the opposing counsel rather than seeking court intervention and sanctions. This type of professional courtesy letter usually has very good results, because the party who owes the response is well aware that the motion will be granted and, the party may, indeed, be forced to pay sanctions for their failure to respond in a timely fashion.

§ 6.61   Sample Notice of Nonproduced Documents

The Notice of Nonproduced Documents in **Form 6–34** is similar to the sample Notice of Unanswered Interrogatories in **Chapter 4.** Prior to moving to compel documents, it is a common professional courtesy to follow up a meet and confer letter with a letter notifying opposing counsel that because efforts to meet and confer have not been successful, you will (within the next ten days) file a motion to compel documents. Prior to seeking court intervention in the discovery dispute, send a letter along with **Form 6–34.**

FORM 6–34
SAMPLE NOTICE OF NONPRODUCED DOCUMENTS

[attorney for the plaintiff]
[address]
[telephone number]

Attorneys for Plaintiff
[name]

IN THE SUPERIOR COURT OF THE STATE OF [state name]
IN THE CITY AND COUNTY OF [city/county name]

[name],
 	
     Plaintiff,
 	
vs.
 	
[name] SHOPPING MALL, A LIMITED PARTNERSHIP, [defendant A] and [defendant B], as limited partners of [name] SHOPPING MALL, [defendant C], individually and (dba) [company D], and (dba) [company E], and DOES 1 through 30, inclusive,
 	
     Defendants.
	Case No. [case number]
	
	NOTICE OF UNPRODUCED DOCUMENTS, WAIVER OF OBJECTIONS, AND REQUEST FOR PRODUCTION

_____/

AND RELATED ACTIONS
_____/

TO DEFENDANTS AND TO THEIR ATTORNEYS OF RECORD HEREIN:

PLEASE TAKE NOTICE that plaintiff, [name], served a First Demand for Identification, Inspection, and Production of Documents in the above-captioned matter on [date]. This demand required that a formal response be served within twenty-five (25) days or [date]. This propounding party has not received a formal written response, the requested documents, or any request for an extension of time in which to respond to the demand. Accordingly, any objections are deemed to have been waived.

Unless the documents are produced within fifteen (15) days of the date of this notice, plaintiff will file a motion to compel production, and will further request reasonable expenses and attorneys fees.

Dated: [date].

_____

[attorney for the plaintiff]

§ 6.62   Compelling Further Responses

The more usual situation in compelling responses is that of compelling further responses. It is rare that no responses at all are served. It is much more common that inadequate, evasive, and incomplete responses are served on the requesting party. The percentage of responses to demands for document inspection that are 100 percent complete with all documents produced and no privileges claimed is probably less than one percent. It is hard to imagine a case that does not have privileged documents, or documents which attorneys would like to claim as privileged to avoid having them subject to production.

Prior to preparing a motion to compel further responses for a demand for document inspection, review those documents which have been produced, noting carefully those pleas or categories in which objections have been raised. A motion to compel further responses to a demand for document inspection is similar to a motion to compel further responses to interrogatory or request for admission responses. It may not be necessary to compel further responses to each and every category of documents requested, just as it is not always necessary to compel further responses to each and every interrogatory or request for admission. Strategic decisions should be made as to the key categories and documents, and those should be the areas targeted for a motion to compel further responses. Possibly, many of the categories in the original document request were fishing expedition type categories, that is, you were not really certain documents existed in those categories and, if they did, they were of marginal importance. It is best to conclude that the fish simply were not biting in that category, and move on to more crucial categories of documents. Because all discovery serves as a catalyst for further discovery, you may have learned through deposition testimony or interrogatory answers that certain documents are not important, while other documents which you may have originally thought to be of lesser importance, have emerged as truly crucial or potential smoking guns. These are the documents that you wish to target in a motion to compel further responses. A motion to compel further responses (**Form 6–35**) that concentrates on one or two categories is usually more successful than one that seeks to compel in ten or twenty categories. Be selective and you will gain the favor of the courts. Your motion to compel will be viewed as being focused rather than scattered, which makes claims of relevancy more credible.

FORM 6–35
SAMPLE MOTION TO COMPEL FURTHER RESPONSES

SUPERIOR COURT OF THE STATE OF [state name]
IN AND FOR THE COUNTY OF [county name]

[name],	No. [case number]
Plaintiff,	MOTION TO COMPEL FURTHER RESPONSES TO PLAINTIFF'S
-vs-	FIRST DEMAND FOR INSPECTION
[name],	
Defendant.	Date: [date]
	Time: [time]
	Place: [place]

TO: DEFENDANT, [name], AND THEIR ATTORNEY OF RECORD:

PLEASE TAKE NOTICE that on [date] at [time] or as soon thereafter as the matter can be heard in Department [judicial department] of the Superior Court of [county name] County, [state], plaintiff, [name], will move the court for an order compelling defendant, [name], to provide further responses to plaintiff's First Demand for Inspection served on defendant on [date], and for an award of monetary sanctions pursuant to [cite statutory authority], against [name], attorney for [defendant], and in favor of moving party, to compensate for the reasonable cost and expense, including attorney fees, incurred in presenting this motion in the amount of $[dollar amount].

This motion is made pursuant to [cite statutory authority] on the grounds that the responses received were incomplete, inadequate, and evasive. The objections stated were generalized without merit and specific application to the requests. Further, good cause exists justifying the discovery sought, as more fully appears from the specific facts set forth in the declaration of [name], attorney for plaintiff, attached to this motion in that the documents sought relate directly to the [cite specific and relevant facts; for example, relate directly to the financial worth of defendant corporation, relate directly to the business transaction surrounding the critical time period of plaintiff's termination from defendant corporation].

This motion is based on this notice, the pleadings, records, and files in this action, the attached memorandum of points and authorities, and the attached declaration of [name], attorney for plaintiff, and all oral and documentary evidence which will be presented at the hearing of this motion.

Dated: [date].

_____

[attorney for the plaintiff]

This notice of motion must be accompanied by points and authorities setting forth specific causes for the production of the records sought, and a supporting declaration from the attorney of record setting forth a reasonable and good faith attempt at informal resolution of the issues presented. The original demand for inspection and the responses should be attached as exhibits to the attorney declaration. A separate document should also be prepared listing each demand, the response received, and an argument as to why that response is inadequate, evasive, incomplete, and so forth. Further, the factual and legal reasons compelling the response should be set forth individually as they apply to each requested category of documents. (See sample forms in **Chapter 4** (as they relate to compelling further interrogatory responses), and **Chapter 5** (as they relate to compelling further responses to requests for admissions)).

§ 6.63   Motion to Compel the Production of a Witness Statement

One of the most frequent problems in document production arises when, in addition to lodging objections, the responding party fails to produce documents which, in the opinion of requesting party, place them at a disadvantage in trial preparation because the documents requested provide information which cannot be obtained through alternate sources. The most frequently requested document in litigation is a witness statement. Parties who either anticipate or are actively preparing for litigation will almost always direct some of their efforts towards interviewing third persons who may have knowledge bearing on the subject matter of the case. These interviews may take place either before or after the filing of the lawsuit. They may have been conducted by the party itself (especially when a corporation is involved), by its insurance carrier, or by its attorney, either directly or through an investigator. The interview is almost always preserved verbatim and can be either tape-recorded or a signed statement.

Once litigation begins, the parties have the reciprocal and absolute right to discover (usually through deposition or interrogatories) the identity and location of persons having knowledge of any of the facts relevant to the subject matter of the action. There is also a reciprocal right to learn whether one's opponent has obtained an oral or written statement from any of these persons. Case law and statute authorize the discovery of "the existence, description, nature and custody of documents". A witness statement has been held to be a document within the meaning of the statute.

Access to these statements is a difficult discovery hurdle. A contention frequently encountered when a discovery witness statement is sought is that the statements themselves qualify as a form of confidential communication between attorney and client and hence are not discoverable because they are privileged. Case law has held that a witness statement taken by counsel, or their investigator, qualifies as a species of the attorney work product. If the opponents are given access to statements of independent witnesses, they will to that extent be " . . . taking advantage of their adversary's industry or efforts". The question then becomes what makes such advantage an unfair one, and when will the denial of discovery lead to unfair prejudice to the one seeking discovery. There is a need for a special showing of good cause to insure that the one seeking discovery is not simply trying to get a free ride on the opposition's industry and efforts.

The good cause requirement comes from civil procedure statutes governing requests/demands for production of documents. When a demand for inspection of a document has been refused, the demanding party is required to show specific facts showing good cause justifying discovery in order to obtain a court order compelling production of the requested document.

What constitutes good cause for discovery differs from court to court; however, the basic requirement for a showing of good cause focuses on the following elements:

1. A special need for the discovery, for example, to refresh a witnesses memory to resist potential impeachment; and

2. The inability to obtain a similar statement, or deposition testimony, because the witness cannot be located or no longer remembers the details.

The second element is the most compelling factor in formulating an argument based on good cause. If the requesting party can show the inability to obtain the evidence sought by any alternate means, including locating the witness and taking a second statement or issuing a subpoena for the deposition of that independent witness, the chances are the court will look favorably upon the demand for production of that witness statement.

Case law varies from state to state. Several cases in California have held that witness statements are not work product.[16] They are regarded as merely evidentiary in nature rather than derivative or interpretative material created by an attorney. California case law also states that witness statements should be regarded as work product because they reflect what the attorney deems important to the client's case in the questions asked of the independent witness. The ultimate test appears to be that the attorney work product is not discoverable ". . . unless the court determines that the denial of discovery would unfairly prejudice the party seeking discovery in preparing that party's claim or defense or will result in an injustice."

At best, it can be argued that a witness statement represents qualified work product rather than absolute work product. Assuming that the witness statement represents qualified work product, it is a rebuttable presumption that can be argued in a motion to compel which sets forth good cause that the witness statement is:

---

[16] *See* Rodriguez v. McDonald Douglas Corp., 87 Cal. 3d 626, 647, 151 Cal. Rptr. 399, 410 (1978); Craig v. Superior Court, 54 Cal. App. 3d 416, 126 Cal. Rptr. 565 (1976); Kadelback v. Amoral, 31 Cal. App. 3d 823, 107 Cal. Rptr. 720 (1973).

1. Relevant to the subject matter of the case,
2. Calculated to lead to the discovery of admissible evidence, and
3. Represents evidence which cannot be obtained through any alternative means.

§ 6.64 Sample Motion to Compel the Production of a Witness Statement (California)

Form 6–36 is a sample of a (California-specific) motion to compel the production of a witness statement. Included is a memorandum of points and authorities in support of the motion (**Form 6–37**), a declaration by the plaintiff's attorney (**Form 6–38**), and a declaration by the plaintiff's investigator (**Form 6–39**).

FORM 6–36
SAMPLE MOTION TO COMPEL THE PRODUCTION OF A WITNESS STATEMENT (CALIFORNIA)

[attorney for the plaintiff]
[address]
[telephone number]

Attorneys for Plaintiff
[name]

IN THE SUPERIOR COURT OF THE STATE OF CALIFORNIA
IN THE CITY AND COUNTY OF [city/county name]

[name],
 	
      Plaintiff,
 	
vs.
 	
[name] SHOPPING MALL, A LIMITED PARTNERSHIP, [defendant A] and [defendant B], as limited partners of [name] SHOPPING MALL, [defendant C], individually and (dba) [company D], and (dba) [company E], and DOES 1 through 30, inclusive,
 	
      Defendants.
	Case No. [case number]
	
	NOTICE OF MOTION TO COMPEL PRODUCTION OF WITNESS STATEMENT, MEMORANDUM OF POINTS AND AUTHORITIES IN SUPPORT OF MOTION, DECLARATION OF [attorney for the plaintiff]
	
	Hearing Date: [date]
	Time: [time]
	Court: [judicial department]

_____/

AND RELATED ACTIONS

_____/

TO ALL PARTIES AND THEIR ATTORNEYS OF RECORD:

NOTICE IS HEREBY GIVEN that on [date], at [time], or as soon thereafter as counsel can be heard in the Law and Motion Department of the above-entitled court, plaintiff [name] will move this court for an order compelling defendant [name] SHOPPING MALL to produce the witness statement of [witness name]. This motion is made on the grounds that defendant [name] SHOPPING MALL has secured a written and recorded statement from this percipient witness, that it has refused to produce this witness statement upon request of plaintiff [name], that diligent investigative efforts have been made to locate and secure a witness statement from witness [name] with no success, that witness [name] cannot be located, and that the statement is necessary to plaintiff in plaintiff's preparation of this case for trial and to prevent surprise at trial, as well as to facilitate settlement of this action.

This motion will be made and based upon this Notice, all the records, papers and pleadings on file in this action, the Memorandum of Points and Authorities filed herewith, and on the Declarations of [name of investigator], investigator, and [name], attorney for plaintiff.

Dated: [date].

_____

[attorney for the plaintiff]

FORM 6–37
SAMPLE POINTS AND AUTHORITIES IN SUPPORT OF THE
MOTION TO COMPEL

[attorney for the plaintiff]
[address]
[telephone number]

Attorneys for Plaintiff
[name]

IN THE SUPERIOR COURT OF THE STATE OF CALIFORNIA

IN THE CITY AND COUNTY OF [city/county name]

[name],   Case No. [case number]

     Plaintiff,

vs.

[name] SHOPPING MALL, A
LIMITED PARTNERSHIP,
[defendant A] and [defendant B],
as limited partners
of [name] SHOPPING MALL,
[defendant C], individually
and (dba) [company D],
and (dba) [company E],
and DOES 1 through 30,
inclusive,

    Defendants.

_____/

AND RELATED ACTIONS

_____/

MEMORANDUM OF POINTS
AND AUTHORITIES IN
SUPPORT OF MOTION TO
COMPEL PRODUCTION OF
WITNESS STATEMENT

STATEMENT OF FACTS

The subject accident arises out of an accident which occurred on [date]. [Plaintiff] was a business invitee at [name] SHOPPING MALL, and at the time of the accident, [time], was in the process of walking up an outside set of stairs which joined one section of the mall to the next. Suddenly and without warning, the step on which [plaintiff] placed plaintiff's foot collapsed, causing plaintiff to be hurdled 20 feet to the pavement below, causing plaintiff to sustain serious injuries.

Interrogatories were submitted to [name] SHOPPING MALL asking for the identification of percipient witnesses. Further interrogatories submitted to defendant [name] SHOPPING MALL asked whether statements had been secured from such percipient witnesses. Defendant [name] SHOPPING MALL responded by identifying as a percipient witness [witness name]. [Name] SHOPPING MALL further stated that [witness] had been an eye witness and had given a statement which had been reduced to written form. [Name] SHOPPING MALL then refused to produce the statement claiming it was part of their investigation of the accident and as such qualified for work product protection.

Immediately, [name], attorney for plaintiff, retained [name], a licensed private investigator, to attempt to locate witness [name] and to secure a statement from the witness regarding the witness' observations of the events surrounding the circumstances of [plaintiff]'s fall. Diligent efforts to locate [witness] are detailed in the accompanying Declaration of investigator [name] attached to this Motion and made part thereof. The witness could not be located and consequently a statement could not be secured.

A second Request for Production of Documents was served on defendant [name] SHOPPING MALL requesting production of the witness statement of [name]. Defendant [name] SHOPPING MALL responded by again objecting to the production of said witness statement on the grounds that the document was prepared for "the investigation and defense of the within matter, and as such is protected under the work product doctrine."

Additional interrogatories were served upon defendant [name] SHOPPING MALL seeking to determine the present address and phone number of witness [name] so that a statement could be independently secured from the witness by plaintiff's investigator, [name].

Defendant [name] SHOPPING MALL responded to the second set of interrogatories by stating that, "[Witness] is not a regular employee of [name] SHOPPING MALL and is not presently working for defendant. We have no information in our personnel files other than the address furnished to plaintiff in response to plaintiff's first set of special interrogatories, Interrogatory No. 12. [Witness] did not leave a forwarding address with our administrative offices."

No other eye witnesses to [plaintiff]'s accident have been identified by defendant, and plaintiff has not discovered any eye witnesses to this accident. Under the circumstances, production of the statement of [witness] will serve the ends of justice, will prevent surprise at the time of trial, will likely lead to the discovery and location of admissible evidence and/or other possible witnesses, and as an additional benefit, will lead to fruitful settlement negotiations.

Good cause exists to compel the production of the requested witness statement.

California Code of Civil Procedure § 2031 provides for the discovery of documents relevant to the litigation in question and further provides that a motion to compel production pursuant to a demand for documents properly served pursuant to the requirements of the statute. Good cause exists to compel the production of the witness statement of [witness]. A definition of good cause was stated in *Associated Distributor Co. v. Superior Court* 65 Cal. 2d 583, 586–587, 422 P.2d 332, 55 Cal. Rptr. 772 (1967):

> The history of the Code of Civil Procedure indicates that the legislative purpose was to prevent abuse of discovery by requiring the moving party to show that the document sought to be produced for inspection will aide in trial preparation of the case. The legislator did not provide that the document must be admissible as evidence, but only that the trial court be afforded the factual data necessary to make an informed ruling on the issue of good cause.

Clearly good cause exists for the production of the statement of [witness]. The major issue in this litigation is the respective liabilities between defendants. Liability is disputed. The only nonparty witness has been identified as [name]. Plaintiff is informed and believes that [witness] has given a statement to defendant [name] SHOPPING MALL. Because plaintiff was rendered unconscious due to the seriousness of plaintiff's injuries, which included a fractured skull, plaintiff is unable to recall the events of the accident and has been diagnosed with retrograde amnesia. Plaintiff [name] cannot adequately protect themself by giving plaintiff's own version of the occurrence. The witness statement of [name] will be invaluable in preventing surprise at the time of trial as well as assisting in both accident reconstruction and the preparation of this case.

The work product doctrine is superseded under the circumstances of this case and in the interests of justice.

The doctrine of work product protection was first established in the federal case of *Hickman v. Taylor,* 325 U.S. 495 (1947), and was intended to protect from discovery the work prepared by an attorney in preparation for trial. The doctrine is not inflexible. Courts have held that the doctrine does not apply where the effect is to severely prejudice an opposing party or to block the process of justice.

The work product doctrine was codified in California Code of Civil Procedure § 2016(b), which states in part:

> The work product of an attorney shall not be discoverable unless the court determines that denial of discovery will unfairly prejudice the party seeking discovery in preparing his claim or defense, or will result in an injustice . . .

The courts have refused to invoke this work product doctrine in situations in which a witness whose statement has been recorded by counsel is no longer available or cannot be located. In *Greyhound Corp. v. Superior Court,* 56 Cal 2d 385, 15 Cal. Rptr. 90 (1961), the California Supreme Court at page 400 stated:

> Where relevant and non-privileged facts remain hidden in the attorney file and where production of these facts are essential to the preparation of one's case, discovery may properly be had. Such written statements and documents might, under certain circumstances, be admissible in evidence or give clues as to the existence or location of relevant facts where they might be useful for purposes of impeachment or corroboration. <u>And production might be justified where the witnesses are no longer available or can be reached only with difficulty.</u> (Emphasis added)

In *Christy v. Superior Court,* 252 Cal. App. 2d 59, 90 Cal. Rptr. 85 (1967), at page 72, the court discusses the legislative purpose of enacting discovery statutes as they pertain to production of witness statements and stated, "elimination of surprise, preparation for examination and cross-examination, prevention of perjury, and the ascertainment of truth . . . are among such legislative purposes."

As will be shown in the Declaration of [name], plaintiff's investigator, the witness statement of [name] is needed to prevent the elimination of surprise at the time of trial and preparation for this litigation, as well as in preparation for examination and cross-examination of witnesses which may be called in this action.

The Declaration of [name], Investigator, is attached to this motion and sets forth in detail the investigator's efforts to locate witness [name]. The Declaration of [name], attorney for plaintiff, is attached hereto and details further efforts to obtain [name]'s witness statement from [name] SHOPPING MALL'S attorney, [name].

CONCLUSION

For all of the reasons set forth above, plaintiff [name] respectfully requests that the court order defendant [name] SHOPPING MALL'S attorney, [name], to produce the witness statement taken from [name], or in the alternative, to produce [name] at a deposition to be scheduled at a mutually convenient time for both counsel.

Dated: [date].

_____

[attorney for the plaintiff]

FORM 6–38
SAMPLE DECLARATION OF THE PLAINTIFF'S ATTORNEY

[attorney for the plaintiff]
[address]
[telephone number]

Attorneys for Plaintiff
[name]

IN THE SUPERIOR COURT OF THE STATE OF CALIFORNIA
IN THE CITY AND COUNTY OF [city/county name]

[name],	Case No. [case number]
Plaintiff,	
	DECLARATION OF
vs.	PLAINTIFF'S ATTORNEY
[name] SHOPPING MALL, A LIMITED PARTNERSHIP, [defendant A] and [defendant B], as limited partners of [name] SHOPPING MALL, [defendant C], individually and (dba) [company D],	

and (dba) [company E],
and DOES 1 through 30,
inclusive,

    Defendants.

_____/

AND RELATED ACTIONS

_____/

    I, [name], declare:

    1. That I am an attorney-at-law duly licensed to practice before all the courts in the State of California and am the attorney of record for plaintiff [name] in the action herein.

    2. In defendant [name] SHOPPING MALL'S responses to interrogatories, they have identified that they secured a written statement from [name], an eye witness to the accident complained of herein. Plaintiff [name] propounded a request/demand to produce documents and specifically requested the statement of [witness].

    3. Defendant [name] SHOPPING MALL has refused to produce the statement of [witness], claiming it is protected from discovery by the work product privilege. [name], attorney for defendant [name] SHOPPING MALL, has also stated that they do not have a current address for [witness], that the witness is no longer employed by [name] SHOPPING MALL, and that they have no forwarding address for [witness].

    4. After disclosure of the identify of [name] as an eye witness, I retained investigator [name] to contact and locate [witness]. The address of [witness], provided through defendant [name] SHOPPING MALL, was incorrect. Despite diligent efforts to locate the witness, as detailed in the attached Declaration of [investigator], [witness] cannot be located.

    5. It is essential that the statement secured by defendant [name] SHOPPING MALL be turned over due to the unavailability and inaccessibility of [witness] so as to avoid prejudice to plaintiff [name] in the preparation of plaintiff's case for trial. Further, production of this witness statement will avoid the potential for surprise at the time of trial and will also be of invaluable assistance in either cross-examination or examinations of witnesses. As a practical matter, the production of this statement may lead to settlement negotiations when all facts and versions of the accident will be available so that there will be no surprise regarding a person's position in this litigation.

    6. This showing of good cause is made to the court to show that attorney for plaintiff, [name], and their agent, [name], investigator, have made every effort

to locate this witness before attempting to secure defense counsel's statement. It is only because the witness is unavailable, and defendant [name] SHOPPING MALL refuses to produce the statement, that the subject motion has become necessary.

I declare under penalty of perjury that the foregoing is true and correct, and that if called as a witness I could testify competently to the foregoing. All of the facts contained in this declaration are within the personal knowledge of this declarant.

Executed on this [date], at [city], [state].

_____

[attorney for the plaintiff]

FORM 6–39
SAMPLE DECLARATION OF THE PLAINTIFF'S INVESTIGATOR

[attorney for the plaintiff]
[address]
[telephone number]

Attorneys for Plaintiff
[name]

IN THE SUPERIOR COURT OF THE STATE OF CALIFORNIA

IN THE CITY AND COUNTY OF [city/county name]

[name],	Case No. [case number]
Plaintiff,	
	DECLARATION OF
vs.	PLAINTIFF'S INVESTIGATOR
[name] SHOPPING MALL, A LIMITED PARTNERSHIP, [defendant A] and [defendant B], as limited partners of [name] SHOPPING MALL, [defendant C], individually and (dba) [company D], and (dba) [company E], and DOES 1 through 30, inclusive,	

Defendants.

_____/

AND RELATED ACTIONS

_____/

I, [name], declare:

1. That I was contacted by attorney [name] to locate and statementize witness [name]. I was provided with the address of [witness] as had been provided to plaintiff's attorney in responses to interrogatories submitted by defendant [name] SHOPPING MALL.

2. That I therefore went to the address of [witness] and after several attempts learned that the witness had moved from the witness' rental dwelling. Thereafter, I rang doorbells and made contacts with other occupants of the premises in an attempt to determine if anyone knew [witness] so that I could find some leads to this individual's present whereabouts.

3. I attempted to find out if any forwarding address had been filed by [witness] at the post office for that zip code, [number]. No forwarding address form is on file.

4. I checked all of the available investigative directories, including Bay Area Directories and Telephone and Informational Services. I have checked several data bases, but have been hampered in that search due to the unavailability of [witness]'s Social Security number. All of these efforts have proved to be negative with respect to locating [witness].

5. Ultimately I contacted one individual who suggested they may know a girlfriend or someone who might have been sharing the apartment with [witness]. I then attempted to track down this woman and was informed by this woman's father that she had left to join former classmates on an archeological dig somewhere in Africa. He had not heard from her since she left over three months ago.

6. I have further tried job checks and have been unable to locate the name and location of the employment of [witness], assuming the witness would still be working in the Bay Area.

7. At the present time, I feel I have used every available resource to locate [witness] in an effort to contact and statementize the witness. I have been unable to locate the witness, and the search has been a diligent one.

I declare under penalty of perjury that the foregoing is true and correct, and that if called as a witness I could testify competently to the foregoing. All of the facts contained in this declaration are within the personal knowledge of this declarant.

Executed on this [date], at [city], California.

_____

[investigator for the plaintiff]

An alternative to a motion to compel, in this particular case, is to compel [name] SHOPPING MALL to produce the witness' payroll information, which is sure to include her Social Security number. With the Social Security number, a professional investigator can access those data bases specific for searching for individuals (discussed **Chapter 2**). The witness was at the time of the incident an employee of [name] SHOPPING MALL, either salaried, hourly or an independent contractor, and the defendant [name] SHOPPING MALL would most certainly have the witness' Social Security number for tax purposes.

On the other hand, locating the witness through the witness' Social Security number will assist your investigator in locating the witness, taking a statement, and even serving a subpoena for the witness' appearance at a deposition; but, it will not enable you to obtain a copy of the earlier statement. The chances are that the first statement given by the witness was close in time frame to the accident, and the witness may not recall all the specific details at the time of giving a second statement or deposition.

Before preparing your Memorandum of Points and Authorities for a Motion to Compel Production of a witness statement, refer to **Chapter 2** and refer to case law in your particular state. Work product protection for witness statements is not statutory in California, but it is decided by case law depending upon the facts of each given case. It is important to locate a witness and take a statement and/or subpoena that witness for a deposition, but it is equally important to obtain an earlier statement given by that same witness for impeachment purposes at time of trial.

§ 6.65 Opposing Motions to Compel

Opposing motions to compel further responses to document production is similar to preparing an opposition to a motion to compel further interrogatory answers and further responses to requests for admissions (*see* **Chapter 5**). The main reason for opposing a motion to compel further responses to document production is to safeguard the privileges which you have raised on behalf of your client in protecting sensitive, confidential, and work product information. If objections have been served in a timely fashion in a written response to the demand, and a motion for protective order has been noticed, the preliminary steps in protecting your client have been taken. Your goal in preparing an opposition to a motion to compel further responses to document inspection is to prove those objections which have been set forth. The burden of proof that these objections are indeed valid rests with the party who raised them. The party who makes a motion to compel further responses to document production has a dual burden of proof. The party must demonstrate through a good cause showing that the documents are relevant, and must further demonstrate that the objections which have been claimed by the responding party are invalid. The burden of proof in opposing a motion to compel further responses is to show that the objections which have been raised are particular to the inspection demand and are valid.

The documents in question usually fall into the categories of attorney-client and attorney work product information and those are the privileges which are most frequently stated in general without specific case law examples. In preparing opposing points and authorities to argue the validity of a work product objection, case law should be cited with specific examples of the same type of document you are trying to protect. Courts have made distinctions between conditional and absolute work product and allowed discovery of many work product documents which have been held to be conditional work product. There is a great deal of federal and state case law on this privilege, so check the cases carefully.

Confidential information, secret processes of a manufacturer, and trade secret information, are usually the subjects of stipulations for exchange of confidential information, and not the subject of a motion to compel further responses to document inspection. (*See* **Form 6–31** for a sample form stipulation.)

The format for opposition to a motion to compel further responses to a demand for inspection is a memorandum of points and authorities and an attorney declaration. Exhibits to the attorney declaration should include attempts at a meet and confer informal resolution of the dispute such as letters to opposing counsel, the original demand for inspection, and the response. An exhibit to an attorney declaration may also include a proposed stipulation for exchange of confidential materials, or a stipulation for entry onto land, inspection, and testing. An argument can be made that the stipulation was prepared in good faith by the responding party, only to be met by a surprise refusal from requesting party, and an unsigned stipulation. The stipulation itself is evidence that the responding party has attempted a good faith substantial compliance with the request.

Each category of documents and specific documents which is addressed in a motion to compel further responses must be addressed in a motion to oppose providing further responses. Arguments set forth in opposition points and authorities should focus on proving that:

1. Each privilege claimed is valid (Specific case law should be used as examples.);

2. Each response provided was complete, in and of itself, and not incomplete, evasive, or nonresponsive;

3. Each and every category of documents has been addressed, and a due and diligent search has been made for documents responsive to that request (When a statement of inability to comply appears in the response, it should be completely documented by listing each attempt made to locate documents responsive to that request.);

4. The documents sought are simply not relevant to the subject matter of the action and are burdensome, harassing, and so forth (Arguments should be made as to why the documents are not relevant; fishing expedition, remote in time given date of incident, and so forth.);

5. The information sought is equally available to propounding party through public records, third-party custodians of record, and other discovery devices; and

6. The probative value of the inquiry is not justified in that the invasion of privacy outweighs the interests of justice; the documents sought invade your

client's privacy and have little or no direct bearing on the issues of the case; and the documents requested would only prejudice your client by revealing personal, confidential information.

§ 6.66 Motions for Compliance

Occasionally, the responding party will indicate in their response that they are prepared to comply with a particular demand for inspection, and at a later date may refuse or simply fail to do so. A dispute may also arise as to precisely what complete compliance actually entails. Documents may be produced which indicate to the responding party that there are gaps in the production and that certain documents have been withheld. In this instance, the attorneys should attempt to resolve this dispute informally, but are not usually required by statute to meet and confer before a motion may be made for compliance with the demand for inspection, (which is similar to a motion demanding responses when none have been given). The responding party argues that they have relied upon a statement of compliance received by requesting party, and in doing so expected to receive everything requested in the original demand for inspection. The responding party was not advised that certain documents might be withheld, certain privilege claims might be made, or certain interpretations of the word compliance would be made by opposing counsel which differed greatly from the original intent of the demand. The responding party should also argue that further discovery was defined and scheduled based on the anticipated document production, and that preparation of their client's case has suffered immeasurable harm. An argument may also be made that because of this bad faith and breach of professional ethics by opposing counsel, the client has been unfairly prejudiced and is unable to prepare for trial. Of course sanctions should be requested, and in most cases will be awarded.

A motion for compliance (**Form 6–40**) or demand for inspection is a noticed motion which must be accompanied by points and authorities and an attorney declaration. The format is similar to a motion to compel responses (**Form 6–34**) with slight variations.

FORM 6–40
SAMPLE MOTION FOR COMPLIANCE

SUPERIOR COURT OF THE STATE OF [state name]
IN AND FOR THE COUNTY OF [county name]

[name],	No. [case number]
Plaintiff,	MOTION FOR COMPLIANCE
-vs-	
[name],	

Defendant.

_____/

TO: DEFENDANT, [name], AND THEIR ATTORNEY OF RECORD:

PLEASE TAKE NOTICE that on [date] at [time], or as soon thereafter as this matter may be heard in Department [judicial department] of the above-entitled court located at [address], [city], [state], plaintiff will move the court under [cite statutory authority] for an order directing defendant to comply with plaintiff's First Demand for Inspection of Documents. The grounds for this order are that although the defendant, [name], served a response within the statutory time frame stating that it would comply with the demand for inspection, it has subsequently failed or refused to permit the demanded inspection.

PLEASE TAKE FURTHER NOTICE that if this motion for compliance is opposed and substantial justification for that opposition is not shown, plaintiff also moves for a monetary sanction against defendant, [name], and their attorney of record in an amount equal to the attorney's fees incurred by the moving party, as shown by the attached declaration setting forth the attorney's hourly rate and the number of hours consumed in preparing and presenting this motion.

This motion is based on the attached memorandum of points and authorities, declaration of [name], attorney for plaintiff, [name], and oral and documentary evidence as may be presented at the time of the hearing.

Dated: [date].

_____
[attorney for the plaintiff]

Noncompliance with inspection demands is becoming increasingly common. Frequently a party will state that they will comply with an inspection demand based on a review of the universe of documents as known to them at the time of their response. They may then receive forgotten documents from their client, which may have been stored in another warehouse or have been under the control of a subsidiary corporation. After reviewing these forgotten documents, the responding party may not be in a posture to allow them to comply substantially with the inspection demand. The responding party may then not produce any documents, or not produce all of them, or refuse to allow the demanding party to copy them claiming that it would disrupt the business operations of their client to allow crucial documents to be removed from the premises for copying purposes. The concept of acting with substantial justification in making a motion for compliance with an inspection demand, or in acting contrary to a previously stated intention to comply with the inspection demand is the determining factor that the courts look to in deciding this motion. If a motion is granted demanding compliance with an inspection demand, a date will be set by the court, and the party to whom the demand is directed will be sanctioned and face possible dismissal of the action, if they do not comply. If you are the unfortunate party who has been served with a motion for compliance, and you face the situation of several boxes of forgotten documents, a motion should immediately be made for relief based on excusable neglect, ignorance, and so forth. It is also wise to consider whether a motion to withdraw as attorney of record should be made. Communications between the client and your law office may have disintegrated, and there might be a dispute over the management of the case as well as ethical problems. Unfortunately, clients have been known to request that their attorney simply lose, or not produce, certain sensitive documents. This type of client is not one that you wish to keep.

§ 6.67   Obtaining Documents from Nonparties

In most cases, it will be necessary to obtain documents from nonparties in order to investigate the claims and/or defenses of a particular action fully. There are several methods of obtaining documents from nonparties, the most common of which is a subpoena. However, a frequently overlooked method of obtaining documents from nonparties, and more specifically entry onto nonparty land, is a motion made pursuant to Federal Rule of Civil Procedure 34(c). Subsection (c) of Rule 34 states clearly that the rules do not preclude an independent action against a nonparty for the production of documents and things and for permission to enter onto land. Federal courts have traditionally recognized the availability of such an action. Individual case circumstances may dictate proceeding under a Rule 34(c) action depending upon the scope of documents, the necessity of entering only the nonparty land, and the cooperation of the nonparty.[17] The expense and time involved in filing an independent action to obtain documents pursuant to this provision should be balanced against your client's budget, liability exposure, and the possible value of the documentation.

A subpoena issued pursuant to Rule 45 is the more common method of compelling production of documents and things from a nonparty witness. There are three methods of obtaining desired documentary materials from nonparties pursuant to Rule 45:

1.   A deposition of a nonparty witness can be scheduled and a subpoena served upon that person ordering them to bring designated documents and tangible objects to the deposition (see **Chapter 3**);

2.   A subpoena may be served upon a person ordering them to bring designated items to a hearing; and

3.   A subpoena may be issued by the court requiring the party to produce documents and tangible objects at a certain time and place.

Custodian of records deposition subpoenas may require a designated custodian of record to appear in person along with designated documents, records, and tangible items. However, when all you are really seeking is access to the records themselves,

---

[17] For a discussion of this method and a practical overview of proceeding to discover documents from a nonparty pursuant to Rule 34(c) of the Federal Rules of Civil Procedure, refer to *Discovery of Non-Party Land,* 85 Yale L.J. 112 (1975).

a Rule 45 subpoena may be used as a functional equivalent of an inspection demand to a nonparty. This becomes a records-only subpoena when a custodian of records is served (and they must be personally served) with the subpoena. They then have the option of sending a sealed copy of the records, accompanied by an affidavit attesting to their authenticity, to a designated deposition officer, or allowing an actual production of records.

A nonparty served with a subpoena pursuant to Rule 45 cannot refuse to obey because the documents asked for are irrelevant, immaterial, or privileged. In order to oppose producing documents, a formal motion must be made to quash the subpoena. This motion to quash must be prepared by the attorney of record for the party about whom records have been sought. The normal procedure is for a custodian of records for a nonparty (for example, hospital, bank, or mortgage company) to contact the attorney for the party and inform them that they have been served with a subpoena requiring the production of records which they feel are privileged and confidential. It is then up to the attorney representing the party about whom records are being sought to promptly notify the attorney who has caused the subpoena to be issued, informing that attorney that a motion to quash service of subpoena will be made.

§ 6.68   Protecting the Records (Subpoena Abuse)

Of all the available discovery tools in a personal injury, product liability, or medical malpractice action, subpoenas for the production of business records are unique in that they allow the defense counsel to obtain information from plaintiff's witnesses (often health care providers) without involving the plaintiff's attorney as a direct intermediary. Documents may be obtained from nonparties through the use of a subpoena for business records (see § 6.67), which, unlike other discovery requests, is served directly on the custodian of records, with a copy served on the plaintiff's attorney, along with a notice to the consumer (see § 6.75). This discovery process is subject to abuse more easily than other discovery devices. The plaintiff's attorney may request copies of those documents produced, but because the records themselves are not under the attorney's immediate control, the plaintiff's attorney may not scrutinize and object to the production of certain records. A subpoena for business records served directly on a custodian of records effectively forfeits the right of the plaintiff's attorney to restrict the scope of the information provided to the defendant unless immediate action is taken.

This type of subpoena routinely contains sweeping boiler plate classifications of those records required to be produced. Defense attorneys will argue that the scope of these subpoenas are "comprised of standard requests and all say the same thing." However, this standard subpoena language is frequently outrageously overbroad and clearly objectionable. For example, a routine subpoena for medical records may request ". . . all records and papers relating to plaintiff's medical and dental histories, complaints, symptoms, examinations, findings, diagnoses, prognoses, photographs, treatment, physical therapy, billings, health insurance and payment records from all time past to the present." This request is outrageously overbroad, boiler plate in format, and seeks to discover plaintiff's lifetime medical history, which is a violation of privacy and contrary to the case law and statutes governing personal injury litigation.

Another standard request which is similarly overbroad is to request from a custodian of records, "any and all medical records, charts, files, reports, papers, x-rays, and medical notations pertaining to plaintiff for any and all times whatsoever."

An example of an overbroad request in a subpoena for employment records when a wage claim has been made requires production of "all personnel files, employment files, earnings/wage records including, but not limited to, insurance coverage and claims, accidents and records of illnesses or injuries, sick leave, vacation requests, and medical reports for any and all times whatsoever." These requests would meet with immediate objections if contained in a request/demand for production of documents or asked as an interrogatory, but they may pass unchallenged in the context of a subpoena served on a custodian of records.

Each of the above requests are clearly subject to challenge. In California, Code of Civil Procedure § 1985.3(g) provides that a consumer whose personal records are subpoenaed may move the court under California Code of Civil Procedure § 1987.1 to quash or modify the subpoena. The same section empowers the court to make an appropriate protective order to protect the parties from unreasonable or oppressive demands, including unreasonable violation of a consumers right of privacy.

A party may not withhold information relating to a condition at issue which has been tendered by the Complaint on file in a lawsuit; however, the party is entitled to retain the confidentiality of all unrelated treatment undergone in the past. At a minimum, subpoenas for medical records should be limited to records concerning treatment for physical conditions related to the injuries claimed in the lawsuit. Properly, they should be limited to treatment for such conditions occurring on or after the date of the accident in question. Defense attorneys will argue that more extensive discovery is needed to determine any preexisting conditions which could relate to present injuries, but the existence of such conditions can be determined by deposition questioning or interrogatories, without allowing the defendant to go on a fishing expedition, rummaging at will through plaintiff's lifetime medical records.

When the plaintiff has made a wage claim in an action, the defendant is entitled to subpoena employment records relevant only to that claim. The defendant is entitled to receive earnings and wage records only. They are not entitled to receive a complete personnel file, insurance coverage, accidents, requests for vacation, records of illnesses for injuries, sick leave, or medical reports for any time taken off from work which does not correspond chronologically to the times relevant to the injuries claimed in the action on file. The plaintiff's earnings are certainly relevant to wage loss and future earnings capacity claims. However, a request for the plaintiff's personnel records clearly seeks a significant amount of information which is neither relevant nor calculated to lead to the discovery of admissible evidence at trial. The plaintiff has a protectable privacy interest which must be asserted promptly through plaintiff's attorney.

As soon as you receive a notice to consumer (accompanied by a business records subpoena), immediately write to each of the subpoenaed custodians of record, requesting that they voluntarily withhold production until a formal resolution of the problem has been attempted. **Forms 6–41** through **6–43** exemplify letters which may be used as guidelines in this process.

§ 6.69   Sample Letter (Custodian of Records)

FORM 6–41
SAMPLE LETTER (CUSTODIAN OF RECORDS)

[name] Medical Center
[address]

ATTN: Medical/Legal Department

RE: [plaintiff] v. [name] Shopping Mall

Dear Medical/Legal Department:

Our office represents [plaintiff] in a lawsuit for injuries that [plaintiff] received on [date]. We have received notice that the attorney for the defendant has subpoenaed records from your facility, specifically "all records and papers relating to plaintiff's medical history, complaints, symptoms, examinations, findings, diagnoses, prognoses, photographs, treatment, physical therapy, billing, health insurance form, and payment records." We believe that this request is legally overbroad and improper, and have requested that the defendant's attorney voluntarily modify the request for production of these records, confining it to those injuries related to the accident which is the subject of this lawsuit. Failing this, we intend to ask the court to quash this subpoena.

The medical records requested are confidential records of our client, for which there is some reasonable and legally-recognized exception of privacy.

We accordingly ask that you refrain from providing documents in response to this subpoena until the propriety of defendant's demand has been determined.

Once again, we reiterate that the requested information is overbroad, and goes beyond the issues and injuries sustained as a result of the accident complained of herein, which is the only issue to be decided by the above-referenced litigation.

Thank you very much for your prompt attention, and I urge that you contact me immediately if you feel you must produce documents pursuant to this improper, illegal, and overly broad subpoena, or if you have any questions.

Sincerely yours,

[attorney for the plaintiff]

cc: Major Copy Services (or whatever copy service has been designated as the deposition officer in the subpoena).

§ 6.70   Sample Letter (Copy Service)

FORM 6–42
SAMPLE LETTER (COPY SERVICE)

[name] Copy Services
[address]

    RE: [plaintiff] v. [name] Shopping Mall
          Your File Numbers [file number]
          and [file number]

Dear [name] Copy Services:

We have received notice that the attorney for the defendant, [name] Shopping Mall, has subpoenaed records from [name] Medical Center and Dr. [name]. We believe that these requests are legally improper and overbroad, and have requested that the defendant's attorney voluntarily modify the request for production of records, confining it to those records related to the injury giving rise to the action at hand. Failing this, we intend to ask the court to quash each of these subpoenas.

The requested medical records are confidential records of our client, for which there are some reasonable and legally recognized exceptions of privacy. We accordingly ask that you refrain from seeking documents in response to the subpoena from the health care providers identified above, until the propriety of defendant's demand has been determined.

Once again, we reiterate that the request for information is overbroad, and goes beyond the issues and injuries sustained as a result of the accident in the complaint on file in this action, which is the only issue to be decided by the above-referenced litigation. We intend to request that the defendant's attorney voluntarily modify the subpoenas to comply with our request. Failing voluntary compliance, we intend to ask the court to quash these subpoenas.

Thank you very much for your prompt attention and I urge you to contact me immediately if you have any questions.

                    Sincerely,

                    [attorney for the plaintiff]

§ 6.71   Sample Letter (Defendant's Attorney)

FORM 6–43
SAMPLE LETTER (DEFENDANT'S ATTORNEY)

[attorney for the defendant]
[law firm]
[address]

  RE: [plaintiff] v. [name] Shopping Mall

Dear [attorney for the defendant]:

We are in receipt of deposition subpoenas for the production of records from [name] Medical Center in [city] and Dr. [name] in [city], our client's health care providers. These subpoenas directed to our client's health care providers are overly broad and boiler plate in form requesting "all records and papers relating to plaintiff's medical history, complaints, symptoms, examinations, findings, diagnoses, prognoses, photographs, treatment, physical therapy, billings, health insurance, and payment records."

We call your attention to recognized [state] case law supporting the proposition that, "although a party may not withhold information relating to a condition at issue in a lawsuit, he or she is entitled to retain the confidentiality of all unrelated treatment undergone in the past." See *In re Lifschultz,* 2 Cal. 3d 415, 85 Cal. Rptr. 829 (1970), and *Britt v. Superior Court,* 20 Cal. 3d 844, 143 Cal. Rptr. 452 (1978).

In this regard, we believe that your request for medical records and reports concerning any and all care, treatment, and examinations that were given to our client is impermissibly overbroad and outside the scope of admissible discovery.

We are communicating our opinion on this matter to the health care providers concerned, requesting that they decline to produce these documents, and ask that you revise your subpoenas to request a narrower and more appropriate range of information. Failing such a voluntary limitation of your subpoenas, we will move the court for an order quashing or modifying these subpoenas and for a protective order limiting the scope of discovery in this area.

Please advise us promptly as to your intentions in this regard. Inasmuch as the documents sought are to be produced on [date of production listed on subpoena], I request that we receive your response to this letter within the next five (5) days, well before the scheduled production, in case we need to seek judicial intervention regarding your overbroad subpoenas.

Thank you very much for your anticipated courtesy and cooperation.

Sincerely,

[attorney for the plaintiff]

After these letters have been sent, the subpoena process is stayed until the defense counsel volunteers to modify and limit the scope of the subpoena or until the court has ruled on the proper scope of the subpoenas. Should a motion be necessary to modify, limit, or quash deposition subpoenas, be sure to include a request for a protective order as well, so the process will not have to be repeated if subsequent improper subpoenas are issued.

§ 6.72   Sample Motion to Quash, Modify, or Limit a Deposition Subpoena

A motion to quash, modify, or limit a deposition subpoena (**Form 6–44**) must include a memorandum of points and authorities in support of that motion (**Form 6–45**) and an attorney declaration in support of the motion (**Form 6–47**).

FORM 6–44
SAMPLE MOTION TO QUASH, MODIFY, OR
LIMIT A DEPOSITION SUBPOENA

[attorney for the plaintiff]
[address]
[telephone number]

Attorneys for Plaintiff
[name]

IN THE SUPERIOR COURT OF THE STATE OF [state name]

IN THE CITY AND COUNTY OF [city/county name]

[name],	Case No. [case number]
Plaintiff,	
vs.	NOTICE OF MOTION TO QUASH, MODIFY OR LIMIT DEPOSITION SUBPOENA
[name] SHOPPING MALL, A LIMITED PARTNERSHIP, [defendant A] and [defendant B], as limited partners of [name] SHOPPING MALL,	Date: [date] Time: [time] Dept: [judicial department]

[defendant C], individually
and (dba) [company D],
and (dba) [company E],
and DOES 1 through 30,
inclusive,

    Defendants.

_____/

AND RELATED ACTIONS

_____/

TO ALL PARTIES AND THEIR ATTORNEYS OF RECORD:

PLEASE TAKE NOTICE that on [date], at [time] in Department [judicial department] of the above-entitled Court, plaintiff [name] will move the Court for an order to quash defendant's deposition subpoena.

This motion is made pursuant to [code section(s)] of the [state] Code of Civil Procedure on the grounds that there is no good cause for the items sought, said documents are not calculated to lead to the discovery of admissible evidence, and their production would constitute a violation of plaintiff's right to privacy.

This motion is based upon all pleadings, papers and records in the Court's file, on the attached Memorandum of Points and Authorities, on the Declaration of [attorney for the plaintiff], and upon such other evidence as may be presented at the time of hearing.

Dated: [date].

_____
        [attorney for the plaintiff]

FORM 6–45
**SAMPLE MEMORANDUM OF POINTS AND AUTHORITIES
IN SUPPORT OF A MOTION TO QUASH**

[attorney for the plaintiff]
[address]
[telephone number]

Attorneys for Plaintiff
[name]

IN THE SUPERIOR COURT OF THE STATE OF [state name]

IN THE CITY AND COUNTY OF [city/county name]

[name],
 	
    Plaintiff,
 	
vs.
 	
[name] SHOPPING MALL, A
LIMITED PARTNERSHIP,
[defendant A] and [defendant B],
as limited partners
of [name] SHOPPING MALL,
[defendant C], individually
and (dba) [company D],
and (dba) [company E],
and DOES 1 through 30,
inclusive,
 	
    Defendants.
	Case No. [case number]
	
	MEMORANDUM OF POINTS
	AND AUTHORITIES IN
	SUPPORT OF MOTION TO
	QUASH
	
	Date: [date]
	Time: [time]
	Dept: [judicial department]

_____/

AND RELATED ACTIONS

_____/

I. FACTS

Plaintiff [name] was injured in an accident which occurred on [date]. Plaintiff has filed a Complaint against defendant [name] SHOPPING MALL, alleging that they failed to maintain properly the premises owned and controlled by them located at [address] in the City and County of [city/county name], State of [state name]. Their improper and negligent maintenance and control of these premises caused plaintiff to fall on a wooden stair which connected sections of the shopping mall. Plaintiff fell approximately six feet to a concrete walkway and sustained serious injuries including, but not limited to, a fractured skull.

On [date], defendant issued deposition subpoenas (attached hereto as Exhibits "A" and "B") to [plaintiff]'s health care providers, requesting that they produce "any and all" records, files, bills, hospitalization, exam notes, and so forth for "any and all times whatsoever."

On [date], plaintiff sent a letter (attached hereto as Exhibit "C") to defendant's counsel [name] requesting that defendant's counsel revise the subpoenas to request a narrower and more appropriate range of information relevant to the action at hand.

As of this date, plaintiff has not received a response from defendant's counsel as to their intentions in this regard.

II.   DISCUSSION

A. Defendant's Subpoena Is Not Sufficiently Particularized.

Under [state] Code of Civil Procedure Section [section number], a deposition subpoena must "designate the business records to be produced by either specifically describing each individual item or by reasonably particularizing each category of item." By this limitation, a party cannot go on a fishing expedition looking for evidence but must instead identify those precise items which it needs.

This point was addressed by the court in *Flora Crane Service, Inc. v. Superior Court,* 234 Cal. App. 2d 767, 786, 45 Cal. Rptr. 79 (1965), where the court stated:

> Identification may be inadequate . . . when the books and documents sought to be produced are designated by or included within so-called omnibus description (citation omitted). The unlimited characteristics of such a description may impair or destroy exactitude so that the custodian of records is not reasonably apprised of what he may produce.

The case of *Pacific Auto Insurance Co. v. Superior Court,* 273 Cal. App. 2d 61, 77 Cal. Rptr. 836 (1969), is also on point. In *Pacific,* the court held that a subpoena of all records and correspondence between an accident investigator and an insurance company from the date of the accident to the filing of a complaint was "too broad". Thus, the order quashing a subpoena similar to the one here was upheld. *Id.,* at 70.

Thus, it is clear in this case, when defendant has subpoenaed "any and all" of plaintiff's medical records for "any and all times whatsoever", that said subpoena is improper. The description provided has no reasonable limitation on what records need to be produced and is therefore invalid.

B. Defendant's Subpoena of Plaintiff's Health Records is a Violation of Plaintiff's Right to Privacy.

The [state] Constitution guarantees the inalienable right to have and pursue privacy. [specify constitution reference.] Before this constitutional right can be compromised by a discovery request, a litigant's privacy interest must be carefully weighed against the legitimate interests of the defendant in preparing the defendant's case. *See Jones v. Superior Court,* 119 Cal. App. 3d 534, 550, 174 Cal. Rptr. 148 (1981). As a result, defendants in personal injury actions may obtain medical records about only those conditions which are put at issue.

In *Britt v. Superior Court,* 20 Cal. 3d 844, 143 Cal. Rptr. 452 (1978), residents of homes located near an airport sued the public agency which owned the airport seeking compensation for diminution of property values, personal injuries, and emotional disturbance caused by the operation of the airport.

Defendants, in the court of discovery, propounded to plaintiffs detailed questions regarding their mental and emotional histories. In *Britt,* the California Supreme Court held that, in compelling wholesale disclosure of private association affiliations and activities, the discovery order worked an unconstitutional infringement of First Amendment rights of association and went far beyond any limited disclosures that defendant's legitimate litigation interests could justify.

As expressed in the case of *Britt,* and in the case of *In re Lifschultz,* 2 Cal. 3d 415, 85 Cal. Rptr. 829 (1970), it is clear that although plaintiff may not hold back information relating to conditions at issue, the confidentiality of all unrelated treatment is not abrogated. The unrestrained breadth of defendant's subpoena clearly violates this rule and unduly infringes on plaintiff's reasonable expectation of privacy in medical records unrelated to the injuries at issue in this case.

III.   CONCLUSION

For the foregoing reasons, plaintiff respectfully requests that the subpoena duces tecum to plaintiff's health care providers be quashed in this case, and that a protective order be issued restraining defendant from such improper and extensive inquiries in the future.

_____
[attorney for the plaintiff]

In most personal injury, medical malpractice, and product liability cases, the plaintiff claims a wage loss as part of their damages. The defendant may then subpoena employment records to help document this claim. If the defendant's subpoena for employment records is overbroad and seeks an entire personnel file including medical information, you should move to quash. **Form 6–46** can be used in place of paragraph A and paragraph B in the motion in **Form 6–45.**

FORM 6–46
SAMPLE PARAGRAPHS (EMPLOYMENT RECORDS)

B. Defendant's Subpoena of "Any and All" of Health Records in Possession of Plaintiff's Employer is Overbroad and Not Reasonably Calculated to Lead to Relevant Evidence.

Under [state] Code of Civil Procedure § [section number], any party may obtain discovery regarding any matter not privileged that is relevant to the subject matter involved in the pending action if the matter either is itself admissible in evidence or is reasonably calculated to lead to the discovery of admissible evidence.

Thus, when discovery calls for disclosure of matters remote from the subject matter of the action, such discovery is overbroad and an order to quash is proper. *Ryan v. Superior Court,* 186 Cal. App. 2d 813, 817, 9 Cal. Rptr. 147 (1960).

In the present case, defendant flatly attempts an unbridled hunt through "any and all of defendant's employment records . . . insurance records and sickness or injuries, since first employed", in the possession of defendant's employers. Defendant makes no attempt to limit the request for information regarding the subject matter of this action or matters related to this action. All of plaintiff [name]'s medical records in the possession of health care providers are not relevant to the subject matter in this action and forced production of said records is harassing, intrusive, and without any legal basis. None of this information is a proper subject of discovery in the instant case, and defendant is incapable of showing good cause in this regard. For this reason, the subpoena as to plaintiff [name]'s health medical records should be quashed.

FORM 6–47
SAMPLE DECLARATION IN SUPPORT OF A
MOTION TO QUASH

[attorney for the plaintiff]
[address]
[telephone number]

Attorneys for Plaintiff
[name]

IN THE SUPERIOR COURT OF THE STATE OF [state name]

IN THE CITY AND COUNTY OF [city/county name]

[name],	Case No. [case number]
Plaintiff,	
vs.	DECLARATION OF PLAINTIFF'S ATTORNEY IN SUPPORT OF MOTION TO QUASH, MODIFY, OR LIMIT DEPOSITION SUBPOENA
[name] SHOPPING MALL, A LIMITED PARTNERSHIP, [defendant A] and [defendant B], as limited partners of [name] SHOPPING MALL, [defendant C], individually and (dba) [company D], and (dba) [company E], and DOES 1 through 30, inclusive,	Date: [date] Time: [time] Dept: [judicial department]
Defendants.	

_____/

AND RELATED ACTIONS

_____/

I, [name], declare:

1. I am the attorney of record herein for plaintiff [name], and licensed to practice in the Courts of the State of [state name].

2. I have knowledge of the matters stated herein and if called as a witness, could competently testify thereto.

3. On [date], [name], attorney for defendant [name] SHOPPING MALL, caused to be issued a subpoena duces tecum to obtain "any and all" medical records from plaintiff's health care providers for "any and all times whatsoever."

4. On [date], my office contacted defendant's counsel by mail requesting that counsel revise the subpoena to address a narrower and more relevant range of information.

5. As I prepare this document, I have not heard from the defense counsel regarding counsel's intentions in this matter.

6. I am informed and believe, and therefore allege, that the subpoenas are overbroad and lack adequate specificity. If allowed to stand in their present form, they will cause plaintiff's health care providers to release to defendant and defendant's counsel documents that are irrelevant and infringe upon plaintiff's constitutional right to privacy.

I declare under penalty of perjury under the laws of the State of [state name] that the foregoing is true and correct, except as to those matters stated to be based upon information and belief; and as to those matters, I believe them to be true and correct.

Executed at [city], [state], on this [date].

_____

[attorney for the plaintiff]

§ 6.73 Consumer Records

The preparation of a subpoena calling for consumer records, requires special handling. In most states, a _consumer_ is defined as "any individual, partnership of five or fewer persons, association, or trust that has transacted business with or has used the services of the witness or for whom the witness has acted as agent or fiduciary." The reasons for seeking production of consumer's records include:

The witness has had a business or fiduciary relationship with the consumer;

The consumer's records are in the witness' possession and are relevant to your client's case; and

There is no alternative method for obtaining this information.

Personal or consumer records include originals, or copies, of books, documents, or other writings pertaining to a consumer that are maintained by one of the following individuals or groups:

Physicians, pharmacists, pharmacies, hospitals

State or national banks

State or federal associations (as defined by the Finance Code)

State or federal credit unions

Trust companies

Security brokerage firms

Insurance companies

Title companies, mortgage companies

Attorneys

Accountants

Institutions of the farm credit system (as specified in 12 U.S.C. § 2002)

Telephone and other public utilities, gas, electric, water, and so forth

Psychotherapists, licensed marriage and family counselors, licensed social workers, vocational social workers, private counselors

Private or public preschool, elementary school, secondary school, vocational school, college, and university records.

The service of subpoenas for personal consumer records requires a specific Notice to Consumer which must be served 10 days before the subpoena itself may be personally served on the custodian of records. (*See* **Chapter 3.**) This provision is designed to protect the consumer by allowing them time to contact the custodian of records and object to the production of the records. A consumer who wishes to object must file a motion to quash, or modify, the subpoena following the appropriate format for a noticed motion to quash service of subpoena.

Custodians of records for large financial or medical institutions routinely have their in-house counsel review subpoenas served upon them for production of consumer records to make certain that all procedural requirements have been met, in particular, that a notice to the consumer (**Form 6–48**) was mailed in a timely fashion demonstrated by a proof of service, and that a certificate of compliance (**Form 6–49**) with the required notice to consumer signed by the attorney issuing the subpoena is included in the moving papers.

Subpoenas for consumer records open involve production of records pertaining to nonparties. It is the duty of the responding custodian of records to safeguard the rights of privacy of those consumers who are not parties to the action. This often causes a delay in the production of records and a cost for clerical time required in redacting the records to safeguard the rights of privacy of other consumers serviced by the custodian of records. For example, in a lender liability action against a savings and loan, the plaintiff claimed that they had placed telephone calls over a period of six months to the loan officer attempting to arrange an appointment to review plaintiff's credit application. The plaintiff further stated that these telephone calls had been made from the homes of various children and other relatives. In interrogatory answers, the plaintiff listed the name, address, and telephone number of 10 individuals claiming that telephone calls had been placed to the savings and loan from each of their residences. In order to verify the facts that telephone calls had indeed been placed to the savings and loan, it was necessary to subpoena the telephone records of these 10 individuals. After a protracted dispute with Pacific Bell, there was an agreement to produce the telephone records of the 10 consumers in a redacted form. That is, Pacific Bell's clerical staff would go through the telephone bill eliminating all information with the exception of calls placed to two specific telephone numbers (the savings and loan main office and branch office). Production of these records was delayed by eight weeks from the original date of the subpoena. Additionally, Pacific Bell submitted a bill to the attorney in the amount of $975 to cover copy costs and clerical time. A custodian of records has the statutory right to bill for reasonable expenses incurred in responding to a subpoena. They also have the right to withhold the records until they receive your check. In this particular case, it was crucial to determine whether there had been contact between the plaintiff and the savings and loan during a particularly crucial time period; therefore, the time and expense were justified.

§ 6.74 Checklist for the Preparation of a Subpoena for Consumer Records

The preparation of all subpoenas to third-party custodians of records requires a thorough knowledge of statutory procedure to guard against procedural defects which will give rise to grounds for a motion to quash service of the subpoena. This is particularly true in the preparation of a subpoena for consumer records. Follow the guidelines set out below, making any modifications necessary to conform with your state statutes.

_____ 1. Calendar the largest margin of time possible for the receipt of records, including the extra time necessary for service of notice to consumer prior to the service on the custodian of records. The notice to consumer must usually be served 10 days by mail, or 5 by hand, before the subpoena itself may be personally served. The custodian of records then has 15 days from the date of service to produce the requested records. An extension of time may be requested. Check your local rules.

_____ 2. Check applicable statutes, if you are in doubt that the records you are seeking are consumer records. If you are still in doubt whether the records you are seeking are consumer records, play it safe and serve a notice to consumer.

_____ 3. Choose carefully, if you elect to use a process server. The average process server does not have the legal knowledge required to correct any mistakes in service. For example, most process servers do not know that they cannot serve the subpoena itself until 10 days have elapsed from your mailing of the notice to consumer.

_____ 4. Remember, subpoenas require personal service. This means a subpoena must be served upon the custodian of records or a designated agent for the custodian of records. Serving it on some girl in the office is not proper. Remember that if service of the subpoena is not procedurally correct, the third-party custodian of records does not have to comply. All defects in service of the subpoena must be corrected before you can even hope to see compliance with the subpoena.

_____ 5. Prepare all of the documents yourself and include a detailed letter of instruction when in doubt about your process server. Or use a process server, but hire a professional investigator to locate the correct person and handle the service.

_____ 6. Serve the notice to consumer by mail, as a safe procedure, and after the statutory 10 days have expired, contact the process server for personal service of the subpoena.

_____ 7. Allow at least 6 to 8 weeks for the records to be assembled, if you are requesting records which will require redacting by the third-party custodian of records to protect the right of privacy of other consumers (utility company, bank, mortgage company). Plan ahead. Do not subpoena records two weeks before a scheduled deposition and expect to receive them in a timely fashion.

_____ 8. Maintain a form file with exemplar copies of subpoenas as an efficient way of making subpoena preparation a routine task. The procedural aspects of preparing subpoenas for third-party custodians of record, including consumer records, are simple and straightforward. They are set out in your local rules, state statutes, or federal rules of civil procedure.

§ 6.75   Sample Notice to Consumer

FORM 6–48
SAMPLE NOTICE TO A CONSUMER

SUPERIOR COURT OF THE STATE OF [state name]
IN AND FOR THE COUNTY OF [county name]

[name], et al.,   No. [case number]

    Plaintiff,   NOTICE TO CONSUMER

-vs-

[name], et al.,

    Defendant.

  TO: [name]

PLEASE TAKE NOTICE that records pertaining to you are being sought by defendant, [name], from the witness named in the subpoena and declaration attached hereto. That witness is [name].

If you wish to object to this witness furnishing the records, you must file papers with the above-named court prior to the date specified for production of the documents on the subpoena.

You or your attorney may contact the undersigned, as the attorney for the party seeking to examine such records, to determine whether the undersigned is willing to agree in writing to cancel, limit, or modify the subpoena. If no such agreement is reached, YOU SHOULD CONSULT AN ATTORNEY IMMEDIATELY ABOUT YOUR INTEREST IN PROTECTING YOUR RIGHTS TO PRIVACY.

  Dated: [date].

               Respectfully submitted,

               _____

                  [attorney name]

§ 6.76   Sample Certificate of Compliance

A certificate of compliance with required notice to consumer must be signed by the attorney of record after the notice to consumer has been served by mail or hand. The following form (**Form 6–49**) should be used.

FORM 6–49
SAMPLE CERTIFICATE OF COMPLIANCE

SUPERIOR COURT OF THE STATE OF [state name]
IN AND FOR THE COUNTY OF [county name]

[name], et al.,	No. [case number]
Plaintiff,	CERTIFICATE OF COMPLIANCE WITH NOTICE TO CONSUMER
-vs-	REQUIREMENT PURSUANT TO [statutory authority]

[name], et al.,

    Defendant.

  TO: [name]

I certify under penalty of perjury under the laws of the state of [state name] that, with respect to the subpoena duces tecum attached hereto, notice has been given to [name] as required by [statutory authority]. Such notice is evidenced by the notice to consumer with proof of service by mail attached hereto.

  Dated: [date].

Respectfully submitted,

_____

[attorney name]

§ 6.77   Motion to Quash Subpoena Service

A motion to quash service of a subpoena is a noticed motion which must include a notice of motion, a motion, points and authorities, declaration of attorney of record, and proposed order. Grounds for quashing the service of a subpoena are similar to those grounds for opposing demands for inspection and production of records, documents, and things. Additional grounds include:

1. The requesting party can obtain the same documents and things from a party to the case and should use a Federal Rule of Civil Procedure 34 request for production before using a Rule 45 subpoena directed to a nonparty;
2. The nonparty's privacy outweighs the need for the information;
3. The requested documents will create unwarranted annoyance, embarrassment, oppression, undue burden, and expense to the nonparty;
4. The requested records will violate the privacy of parties not involved in the litigation (This is a common ground used in situations where a husband and a wife are co-signers on a loan, co-trustees of a bank account, or partners in a joint venture and at the time of the instant litigation are no longer husband and wife; however, to disclose the records simply because husband is a party to the action would violate the privacy of his ex-wife, who may have remarried and moved out of the jurisdiction of the court); and
5. The records requested in the subpoena are consumer records as defined by statute, and the proper notice to consumer has not been served.

In federal cases involving antitrust litigation, many factors will render an effort to inspect the records of a nonparty "oppressive, burdensome and harassing." The federal courts are influenced by the level of relevance of the items sought. When the information is only marginally relevant to the subject matter, judges have been slower to require nonparties to produce the records. A federal case on point, *Collins & Aikman Corp. v. J.P. Stevens & Co.,* indicated "quite strong considerations that discovery will be more limited to protect third parties from harassment, inconvenience, or disclosure of confidential documents. . . " than parties to an action who have a financial interest in the outcome.[18]

§ 6.78   Opposing a Motion to Quash Service of a Subpoena

The grounds for opposing a motion to quash service of subpoena may be based on the significance of the particular lawsuit: the fact that the outcome of this lawsuit will have a far-reaching effect on the general public, the fact that the documents sought have a significant relevance level, and the fact that the documents sought are directly related to the central issues of the lawsuit. Several federal cases can be cited to oppose a motion to quash service of a subpoena for relevant documents. *Covey Oil Co. v. Continental Oil Co.,*[19] a leading case concerning the relevancy level of documents subpoenaed, stated, "Judicial inquiry should not be unduly hampered. Inconvenience to third parties may be outweighed by the public interest in seeking the truth in every litigated case . . . ." The courts in general seem to be more than willing to require even nonparties to shoulder heavy burdens of inconvenience when a substantial sum of money is at stake and it has been demonstrated that the desired information will have a far-reaching effect on the interests of justice and the general public, particularly consumers.

The arguments, in a proposed motion to quash service of subpoena, that the records sought are voluminous and will cause a nonparty to undergo a costly, time-consuming search to obtain the documentation can be answered by citing Federal Rule of Civil Procedure 45(b)2, which authorizes the court in denying a motion to quash service of subpoena, to do so " . . . upon the advancement by the person in whose behalf the subpoena is issued of the reasonable cost of producing the books, papers, documents, or tangible things." In this instance, the court rejects the argument of oppression resulting from time-consuming and costly searches by providing that the witness who is not a party to the lawsuit need not bear the expense, and by requiring the one who issued the subpoena to bear the cost of the search.

§ 6.79   Inspection of a Nonparty's Land,
Business Premises, or Tangible Items

In many cases, a litigant preparing for trial may deem it necessary to conduct an inspection of the land or the premises of a nonparty. For example, employees injured on the job as a result of defective machinery may wish, in their product liability

---

[18] 51 F.R.D. 219, 221 (D.S.C. 1971).

[19] 340 F.2d 993 (9th Cir. 1965).

action against the manufacturer, to gain access to their employer's place of business for the purpose of examining and inspecting the machine itself. In most product liability cases, the employer will be named as a party because the employer purchased or leased the machine, inspected it, and maintained it. However, should the employer not be named in the action, it is still possible to gain access to the business premises to inspect the actual machinery. The article, *Discovery of Non-Party Land,* sets several examples of instances when it may be necessary to inspect nonparty land.[20] The notes and the decisions of cases involving these examples and others can be found in the legislative use note to Federal Rule of Civil Procedure 34(c). Examples include litigation arising out of an airplane crash, when either side may wish to inspect the site of the crash. In an environmental case, the parties may wish to test the soil or water of the adjacent land in an effort to trace the cause of the alleged toxic pollution. In condemnation cases, an appraisal of nearby land may be useful to establish the value of the land which is the subject of the action. In an ordinary slip and fall personal injury case, you may learn through discovery that the land or premises where the injury occurred is no longer under the control of the defendant; it may have been leased or sold to another entity who may have made repairs to the dangerous and defective condition which you allege caused the accident. Inspection of the premises in its postaccident site is very important when modifications, repairs, or any substantial changes have been made.

The 1970 advisory committee note to amended Rule 34 at Appendix G, states clearly that Rule 34 continues to apply only to parties: "While an ideal solution to the problem is to provide for discovery against persons not parties in Rule 34, both the jurisdictional and procedural problems are very complex. For the present, this subdivision makes clear that Rule 34 does not preclude independent actions for discovery against persons not parties." Rule 34(c) recognizes an independent action in the nature of an equity bill of discovery.[21]

§ 6.80   Protecting the Business Client from Subpoena Abuse

If your law firm regularly represents business clients in commercial transactions and related litigation, you may be called upon to advise your clients how to respond to a business record subpoena served on them as a nonparty. Records in their possession may be relevant in litigation in which they are not named as a party and do not have any interest in the outcome. Your client will be required to respond by producing those documents in their possession, custody, and control responsive to the specifics of the subpoena.

If the subpoena requests that your client produce several thousand documents at a deposition, you must advise them how to reduce the cost of responding to the subpoena while keeping within the required legal boundaries. Your client may tell you that the business/corporation's limited resources will be severely strained if it has to absorb the cost of producing these documents. What can the business/corporation do

---

[20] 85 Yale L.J. 112 (1975).

[21] The nature of an equity bill discovery is discussed in detail at 62 A.L.R. Fed. 935.

to minimize the financial impact of this document production? This is the question you must answer for your client.

The primary alternatives available to a nonparty witness to alleviate the potential financial burden of responding to a subpoena duces tecum for business records, include not only negotiating an agreement for payment of costs but also applying for an award of costs. An application for an award of costs will result in added expense for all parties, including your client, because it will involve attorney time for preparing the necessary documents and for appearing in court. Further, an application for an award of costs may be limited by state and federal statutes and rules, and also by judicial discretion.

The first step in negotiating an agreement for payment of costs by the requesting party is for the paralegal to meet with the client to assist in conducting a diligent search for the responsive documents, as well as the cost of responding to the request. After this cost has been determined, the attorney and paralegal should meet with the client to discuss whether the cost of responding to this subpoena does indeed amount to a financial burden. After the meeting, contact the requesting party to discuss payment of costs before directing your client to undertake the retrieval of the documents.

The requesting party is most likely to agree to some form of reimbursement if your client documents the effort and cost required to respond to the subpoena. The following information should be prepared:

1. The location(s) of the documents (Corporate clients frequently have documents in multiple locations such as warehouses, document retention areas, subsidiaries companies, and so forth),

2. The nature of the documents requested,

3. An estimate of the number of documents responsive to this subpoena,

4. A description of the personnel required to search for the documents (temporary employees, management level employees, consultants, legal team, and so forth),

5. An estimate of the time needed to conduct the search and review the documents for privilege prior to production, and

6. An itemization of the costs (for example, the estimated cost per hour of each person working on the request, transportation expenses, document retrieval expenses from warehouses, and office expenses).

This information should be assembled with great care so that it can be submitted to the court in the form of a declaration, if necessary.

The requesting party is usually amenable to reaching some accommodation on cost. The economics alone may dictate that the requesting party resolve the issue quickly, because the requesting party knows that, pursuant to statute or court order, it will be required to reimburse the responding party for at least some of the cost. The requesting party also knows that substantial attorneys' fees may be incurred in opposing a request for costs.

The most important factor of all to the requesting party is usually time. A motion to quash service of a subpoena on the grounds that it is overbroad, burdensome, harassing, and outside the scope of permissible discovery, or, in the alternative, to seek a protective order limiting the scope of the request will slow down the process. Valuable time may be lost in litigating these issues. If a motion to quash or a motion for a protective order is granted, the requesting party may be denied access to documents that would have been produced if the parties had reached an agreement on reimbursement of costs.

Both sides benefit from an agreement on costs. The requesting party obtains documents expediently. The disruption of business for the responding party is minimized, and each party incurs less expense.

§ 6.81   A Sample Agreement to Reduce Response Costs

The sample agreement in **Form 6–50** is useful as a guideline in preparing an agreement to reduce the cost of responding to a subpoena for business records.

FORM 6–50
SAMPLE AGREEMENT TO REDUCE RESPONSE COSTS

This Agreement is entered into by and between the parties listed below: _____[Name]_____ is the [plaintiff/defendant] in _____[plaintiff]_____ v. _____[defendant]_____, case number _____[case number]_____, in the _____[type of court]_____ Court, in and for the State of _____[state name]_____. [Defendant/Plaintiff] served a subpoena duces tecum on _____[name]_____ Corporation requiring that they produce certain documents pursuant to the attached subpoena (Exhibit "A") on _____[date]_____.

_____[Name]_____ Corporation contends that the documents identified in the subpoena duces tecum are relevant to its defense or claims in the above-entitled action. _____[Name of corporation]_____ is desirous of obtaining the requested documents as soon as possible to pursue its claims or defend the claims made against it.

_____[Name]_____ Corporation contends that the subpoena duces tecum is unreasonable, oppressive, and burdensome because it will sustain a financial burden if it is required to search for and retrieve the documents requested. _____[Name]_____ Corporation contends that it is entitled to payment of all costs incurred in responding to the subpoena duces tecum.

The parties to this agreement wish to settle any dispute existing between them with regard to the payment of costs that will be incurred by _____[name]_____ Corporation in connection with responding to the subpoena duces tecum.

THEREFORE, in consideration of the mutual covenants and agreements set forth below, the parties agree as follows:

1. By _____[date]_____, _____[name]_____ Corporation shall produce [identify category of documents or specific documents depending on the number of documents to be produced by date for the production of documents. The production may be staggered over a period of time] at _____[specify location]_____.

2. _____[Name]_____ party shall pay to _____[name]_____ Corporation the costs incurred by _____[name]_____ Corporation for [identify costs; for example, employees time, office expenses, copying expenses, transportation, document retrieval]. For each cost identified in this paragraph, _____[name]_____ party shall pay to _____[name]_____ Corporation the following: [specify agreed upon costs, for example, hourly rate for clerks and management level employees, legal staff, copying costs].

3. Two business days before [delivery/each delivery] of documents by _____ _____[name]_____ Corporation to _____[name]_____ party, _____ _____[name]_____ Corporation shall deliver by messenger to _____[name]_____ party at their offices an itemized statement identifying each service performed by the date and the cost incurred. _____[Name]_____ Corporation shall not be obligated to deliver the documents to _____[name]_____ party unless it has received payment of the costs specified in the itemized statement.

4. The parties understand that due to unforeseen circumstances, _____[name]_____ Corporation may not be able to deliver the documents on the date(s) set forth in Paragraph 1, above. Accordingly, if _____[name]_____ Corporation determines that it cannot deliver the documents as scheduled, no later than three business days before the date such documents are to be produced, _____[name]_____ Corporation shall so inform requesting party and shall have the right to an extension of _____[number]_____ days to produce said documents.

Dated: [date].

_____
[party]

Dated: [date].

_____
[party]

This document should be signed by the requesting party and its attorney of record, and by your business/corporate client and their attorney.

Remember that the requests/demands for documents can only be served on parties to an action. The business record subpoena is the only method of obtaining documents from nonparties. The term client corporation in this section refers to a business client that your office may represent whose records have been subpoenaed in an action in which they are not a party.

Nonparties have an obligation to respond to a business record subpoena, but they do not have an obligation to bear unreasonable expenses and/or disruption of their normal business activities in order to comply.

Because a nonparty does not have a real interest in the outcome of the litigation in which they are not personally involved, it is to the advantage of the requesting party to insure the nonparty's expedient compliance and cooperation by entering into a cost reimbursement agreement.

§ 6.82 The Legal Assistant's Role During Document Production

If there is one task that attorneys will gladly and routinely delegate to legal assistants, it is the task of orchestrating a document production. Indeed, many legal assistants are hired solely for the purpose of managing document production in complex litigation. The following checklist is meant as a guide for the legal assistant who is responding to a document production.

_____ 1. Follow the procedures outlined in § 6.47 and § 6.49 for screening and numbering documents.

_____ 2. Be absolutely certain, double check, and triple check, that your client has provided you with the entire universe of documents.

_____ 3. Be certain that each and every original document has been numbered and indexed prior to production.

_____ 4. Be certain that those documents considered nonresponsive to the production request have been completely segregated from those documents that will be produced. It is neither necessary nor recommended that nonresponsive documents be returned unless they are requested by your client (see § 6.8). Nonresponsive documents should be labeled and sent to the file room to avoid confusion at the time of production, and also to have them in your custody and control for reference in case they need to be produced at a subsequent production.

_____ 5. Be certain that photocopying has been done of all documents that will be produced, and that a quality control check for legibility and completeness has been done by a case clerk of the finished photocopies.

_____ 6. Segregate, file, and index privileged documents with two lists. The legal assistant privileged document identification list should be filed in the correspondence section of the file and not available at the time of document production. A bare bones list of privileged documents should be available at the time of production in case the opposing counsel requests such a list. If a request is not made, do not provide a copy.

_____ 7. Make photocopies and mail them to the opposing counsel if the volume of documents to be produced is manageable; a record should be made of those documents which have been produced. This record of actual production differs from the written response which has preceded the production. A simple transmittal letter with the documents can act as a record of production. (_See_ **Form 6–51.**)

§ 6.83   Sample Letter/Record of Production

FORM 6–51
SAMPLE LETTER/RECORD OF PRODUCTION

Dear Opposing Counsel:

Plaintiff, [name] Corporation, responds to defendant [name] Corporation's Request for Inspection and Production of Documents by enclosing documents numbered [beginning number] through [ending number]. These documents represent all documents which have been found to be responsive to the categories of items detailed in [name] Corporation's Request for Production of Documents served on [name] Corporation on [date]. Photocopies of these documents amount to [number] pages and comprise one Bekins box, which has been hand delivered to your office on this date by [name], legal assistant to [name], attorney for [name] Corporation.

Please examine these documents at your earliest convenience to confirm that you have received all numbered pages indicated in this transmittal letter, and that all numbered pages are legible and complete.

Thank you for your cooperation.

Sincerely,

_____

[legal assistant]

§ 6.84   Document Review Memo

As soon as a document production is completed and you have had an opportunity to review both the documents and evidence produced, prepare a memorandum to the file focusing on:

1.   The production. What has been produced? This should include a list of each document by dates, Bates stamp identification number, title, and author.

2.   The relationship of the documents to the allegations, claims, and/or defenses of your client.

3.   The discovery leads that have emerged based on your review of the documents. What depositions should be scheduled? Have new documents been identified which need to be requested?

4.   The other findings of interest, such as a lack of documents in a particular category (no marketing studies, no field test data, and so forth) should conclude the memo.

If the responding party has stated that no documents exist in a specific category, and that statement is part of their verified response to the document production, they are precluded from discovering documents in that category and attempting to introduce them as evidence at the time of trial. It is important to note in your memo that responding party has stated the lack of the existence of responsive documents to a specific category, and to confirm that no documents exist in that category by following up with a Supplemental Request/Demand for Documents (*see* § **6.34**) within 65 days of trial.

§ 6.85   Document Production at Your Office

If the documents, which have been determined to be responsive to the document request, are voluminous, it is easier to set up a convenient time and place for inspection and allow the opposition to come and choose those documents which they wish photocopied. If you have determined that at least, for example, 124 storage boxes contain responsive documents, the production may span several days or even weeks. It is more convenient for all involved to have the inspection take place at your office. Arrange for a conference room and plan on spending your time babysitting the documents and monitoring the production. The opposing counsel will most certainly send their legal assistant to inspect and view the documents you are producing. You should greet the legal assistant, explain the numbering system you have used, provide yellow tabs, paper clips, notepads, and coffee. Remain in the room at all times when the documents are out for inspection. Offer your assistance, be cheerful and helpful, and, without being obvious, take careful note of those documents in which opposing counsel's legal assistant shows a great deal of interest. Discuss with the legal assistant the method for making photocopies. It may be more efficient to have copying done by an outside vendor and billed directly to opposing counsel. However, if, after inspecting the documents and tabbing them with paper clips or yellow post-it notes, the volume of documentation that needs to be copied is small, it can be done in-house. Two copies of all documents should be made with one set, accompanied by the photocopying bill, going to opposing counsel and the second set going to a specially created file labeled "Documents Requested By Defendant XYZ Corporation After Inspection of Documents Produced by Plaintiff ABC Corporation in Response to Defendant's First Document Request. Date of Inspection and Production: February 23, 19__." The documents which have been inspected, but not chosen for photocopying, should be boxed and labeled, "Documents Provided for Inspection by ABC Corporation in Response to Defendant XYZ's Demand for Inspection and Production of Documents, First Request. Copies not Requested. Date of Production: February 23, 19__." These documents should be boxed separately to safeguard against problems which may arise regarding whether a document was ever produced for inspection.

§ 6.86   Checklist for Attending a Document Production

You may be the lucky person chosen to attend the production of documents of XYZ Corporation, who in responding to the first demand of inspection and copying of documents propounded on them by ABC Corporation, has discovered 795 boxes of documents responsive to the categories of documents requested in the demand. It may also be your good fortune that this assignment comes as a complete surprise to you because you have never worked on the *ABC Corp. v. XYZ Corp.* case and know nothing of the issues involved in this litigation. Advance warning of these document productions is usually limited to the night before the production, so you do not have a great deal of time to come up to speed on the issues of the case. Although your first reaction might be to advise the attorney that it would be simpler to copy each document and sort them out back in your office, this is neither cost-efficient nor time-efficient. It would be difficult to bill the client for duplicating charges for all of the documents when only a small amount may be directly relevant to the claims and/or defenses of your client. The following advice and guidelines are meant to preserve your sanity, and enable you to participate in a document production in a professional and competent manner.

_____   1.   Make every effort to find a partner or any associate attorney who has worked on the case as soon as you receive the assignment of attending a document inspection. Ask them to give you a five minute overview of the client's position. Request the file and obtain a copy of the document request. Meet with the attorney with the document request in your hand ready to ask questions about each category of documents referenced in the document request. Come prepared with questions regarding your client's allegations, liability exposure, important people, crucial dates, buzzwords (those words which immediately signal an area of interest), and so forth.

_____   2.   Go through the initial pleading file, answer, cross-complaint and answers to cross-complaints, if an attorney is not available to discuss the case with you. Prepare a rough draft of the cast of characters for reference so that you will be able to identify signatures on memos and other pieces of correspondence.

_____   3.   Review the correspondence file to help you gain a frame of reference, or time line, for the sequence of events giving rise to the incident which is the subject of the litigation. Review the memorandum file for an opening memo, client narrative, or case assignment memo. Add these to your cast of characters along with information you discover in the correspondence file.

_____   4.   Review the discovery, focusing on the interrogatory responses, noting names of people, places, and crucial dates. Revise your cast of characters according to information found in discovery responses which will help in matching job titles, dates, and other identifying information to the names you have listed.

____   5.   Do not take any client materials with you to the document production. Take the notes which you have made from your review of the client documents, and a copy of the complaint, answer and inspection demand. Taking these documents with you will give you a sense of confidence, and allow you to check documents you are reviewing against information contained in pleadings and discovery responses.

____   6.   Bring your portable dictaphone with you to the document production. Explain at the onset of the document production that you have been requested by your attorney to make a record of the inspection so that the attorney will know the extent of documents that were produced and made available for duplication. Also explain that, although you will be tagging some documents and requesting that they be duplicated today, you will be adding to the list of documents that you want duplicated after your attorney reviews your memorandum describing the documents.

____   7.   Begin dictating immediately, including the number of boxes, the manner in which documents have been produced, the file labels, markings on the insides of files, labeling of documents, and so forth. Paint a word picture of the document production so that your attorney may review your record of inspection memorandum and know that you have not overlooked a single piece of paper. In describing the documents produced per category, describe each document, even those that you are not requesting be duplicated. Your description can be simple. For example, "five page letter dated May 18, 19__ from Jane Smith to Robert Brown. Subject heading of letter: suggested advertising technique for biscuit campaign." Dictate this overview of documents memorandum in a straightforward, narrative way, without editorializing. When you stumble across a hot document and feel the need to editorialize on the value of this document, do not dictate your comments. Instead, write them out on your yellow notepad and keep them confidential.

____   8.   Request the correspondence and memorandum files because they are the most important files to examine in a document production. If the response is that correspondence and memorandum files are considered privileged documents and will not be produced, note this and inform your attorney immediately. Although certain documents contained within correspondence and memorandum files will most certainly be subject to attorney-client and work product privilege claims, it is rare that an entire correspondence or memorandum file can be considered a privileged file. Do not get into a discussion of what is privileged and what is not privileged with opposing counsel's legal assistant, rather, alert your attorney immediately to the situation and let the attorney handle it. You may be surprised to return the next day and either find out that the document production is to be continued while additional documents are reviewed, or find certain files which were not there the day before magically appearing within the stack of documents to be inspected.

_____   9.   Finish off your dictated record of inspection with any editorial comments you choose to make when you return to your office. Include in your comments approximately how much documentation is left to review and your best estimate of the time it will take for you to complete the document inspection and review. When you turn your dictation in to word processing, mark it for overnight transcription and routing to your attorney. This way, while you are attending the second day of the document production, your attorney can be reviewing your record of inspection from the first day noting those documents which the attorney wishes to have duplicated. If it is feasible to meet with the attorney after the attorney has reviewed the memorandum before going to your second day of the document production, do so as it will provide an opportunity for you to discuss questioned documents.

_____   10.   Establish with opposing counsel that the document production is to be considered continuing, and that you will be returning on as many occasions as necessary to complete your review of the documents. Also request that the documents be left available for inspection for a reasonable period of time, 3 to 5 days, after you have finished, so that your attorney may review your record of inspection and decide if there are additional documents that need to be photocopied.

§ 6.87   Making a Record of Inspection

Both the demanding party and the responding party should make a record of not only the items that were produced but also how the inspection was conducted. Such a record is useful in preventing and discouraging questions arising later as to what was in fact produced or made available for duplication at the inspection. The record should be made cooperatively with the parties agreeing on the scope of the production, for example, whether all items responsive to the demand were produced or whether certain specified items were withheld pursuant to a claim of privilege. When you attend a document production as the requesting party, be certain to ask at the onset whether certain documents are being withheld pursuant to a claim of privilege and request a copy of the privileged document list.

It is a good practice for the demanding party to follow up a production of documents with a letter to the opposing counsel listing, separately, the items that were produced and those that were not produced pursuant to each category of the request. The letter should conclude with a paragraph stating:

We rely on your production of [date] to be a complete production of all documents described by our demand. If you doubt whether certain documents or items withheld by you are required by our demand, please respond within 30 days to this letter by describing the specific documents or items withheld and stating why they should not be produced. We also expect you to deliver to us any documents or items described in our demand and later discovered by you. Should you attempt to introduce at trial any documents or items described in our demand and not produced for us, we will move to have them excluded from evidence.

It is also important to make a record of inspection activities such as sampling, testing, surveying, and measuring land or premises to protect both parties. Generally records will be made by the person performing the testing or inspection. Copies of this record of inspection, testing, sampling, surveying, and so forth should be made available to all parties in the litigation. If testing procedures have been worked out by stipulation, part of the stipulation should include the provision that a video record, in addition to a written record, be made of the actual testing (see § **6.11** for a sample stipulation).

§ 6.88   Document Management in Large Cases

The principles of document management remain the same whether the case is small, medium, or large and complex. The larger the case, the more documents that will be generated by your client and other parties in the action; thus, it is more crucial to have prompt and efficient document organization from the onset. It is a common practice for attorneys to appoint a legal assistant custodian of documents in large cases. Frequently, the task is shared by teams of legal assistants who become the document team. A document team in a large, complex litigation case can include case clerks, who will do an initial screening of documents, document coders, and various other legal support staff who will assist in computerizing an index system for the documents. Books are available on the preparation of computerized litigation support systems with specific software designed to assist in document organization. Many legal assistants have become independent contractors doing freelance consulting on large document productions and computerized legal support systems for the management of large document cases. If you have not previously had large document production management experience and you are faced with the task of document organization in a large multi-party action, it is a wise investment to call in a professional legal assistant as a consultant, so that a program of document management can be set up properly and designed for trouble-free maintenance by the legal assistants in your office.

In a complex litigation case, not only should a document index(es) and analysis of key documents be included in your case organization, but also all discovery responses should be included so that facts may be integrated into a computer-based system of document organization in such a way that discovery responses can be checked for contradictions and discrepancies as they relate to important issues of the action. Deposition summaries with key word indexes should be in your system along with interrogatory responses, requests for admission responses, and indexes of documents produced. With all of this information stored in your system, you may choose a particular key word and retrieve all information relating to that key word. For example, let us assume that Mary Smith, the president of ABC Corporation, is a key player in your case scenario. You would like to retrieve all information about Mary Smith; that is, every time her name was mentioned in deposition summary, interrogatory response, request for admission response, or documents produced by the opposition. If Mary Smith appeared on your key word list and was coded into the computer in that fashion, you could simply call up the name, Mary Smith, and retrieve all the information. The intricacies of document coding, preparation of key word lists, and retrieving information from a data base set up for complex litigation is beyond the scope of this chapter. It has become a unique area of specialization for legal assistants and there are many experts in the field available for consultation and hire.

§ 6.89 Conclusion

Documents play a major role in trial preparation of all cases, irrespective of size. The volume of documents will increase as the issues of a case increase. Your client's documents are important in planning an initial discovery plan, calculating damages and evaluating liability exposure. Original documents should be protected and kept in a safe place for use as exhibits at trial. Copies of client documents should be used for trial preparation work.

Document requests to your opponent and to third parties will provide the missing links in the chain of evidence needed to prove your client's claims and/or defenses. Once the floodgate of documents has been opened in discovery, you may receive far more than you ever expected or wanted. The role of the legal assistant is to wade through mountains of material digesting, categorizing, indexing, analyzing, and cross-referencing key documents to issues of the case. Discovery of the "hot document" or "smoking gun" in that mountain of paper is well worth the time and effort it takes to search for that needle in the haystack.

CHAPTER 7

EXPERT WITNESSES

§ 7.1   Introduction

Our litigious society has made "expert witnessing" one of the country's newest growth industries. Dozens of businesses have cropped up offering to match experts with attorneys. The evidentiary issues in complex litigation often require technical expertise in many diverse areas. Collecting information in technical areas is not a simple process. Numerous nonlegal sources must be consulted, some of which are readily available for manual searching, but others are found only on expensive and nonuser-friendly data bases. Keeping up with new sources of information is a constant challenge. Data base vendors add nonlegal information at an astounding rate. Tools used to profile an accident reconstruction today may be outdated tomorrow. The need to constantly be on the cutting edge of technology in numerous complex technical fields is the main reason why hiring a trial consultant is essential in complex litigation.

§ 7.2   Trial Consultants

It is important to understand the difference between a trial consultant and an expert witness. A consultant does not testify in court, and their identity is not subject to discovery under the Rules of Civil Procedure. The need for attorneys to work with specialized technological consultants for trial preparation has been recognized by case law and statutes in most states as work product and as such is considered privileged. It is important in the initial stages of investigation of a case to work with a consultant in gathering evidence to support theories of liability or affirmative defenses. A trial attorney may work with several consultants in this information gathering process in the preliminary stages of trial preparation. Not all of the consultants will become expert witnesses.

The advantages of using a consultant at the initial stages of investigation in complex litigation are as follows:

A consultant generally has a vast amount of scholarly knowledge in a particular field, and may have authored various scholarly writings;

A consultant may have worked in a particular field for several years prior to retiring which gives the consultant working knowledge along with technical expertise;

A consultant usually works at a more reasonable pay rate than expert witnesses;

A consultant usually knows all the important players in a given field, and can refer you to experts in the field.

A consultant may have a personal reason for not wanting to become involved formally as an expert witness in your case, but may be more than willing to provide information which can be relayed to your expert;

A consultant may provide you with information pointing out the holes in your liability theory and other unfavorable aspects of your case (In a situation like this the main value of the consultant is that he has taken on the role of a devil's advocate. The information you receive from this consultant will be extremely valuable and will allow you to focus your discovery and investigation on those holes in your theory of liability and/or defense.);

A consultant's main value early in the case is for learning all of the facts about your case, the good as well as the bad, and for focusing your investigation and discovery on those areas which need to be flushed out; and

A consultant helps with case evaluation, liability exposure, and damage assessment.

An expert witness is that person who is qualified to testify regarding a particular subject because they possess that degree of knowledge which is sufficiently beyond common experience. The expert witness may have been your trial consultant; however, this status changes the moment the consultant is designated an expert witness and named in a Disclosure of Experts.

§ 7.3   When to Use an Expert

The use of experts in litigation is so commonplace that it is hard to imagine a case going to trial without expert testimony on both sides. The impact of an expert in litigation is threefold:

1. They explain the logic of the mechanism involved whether it is mechanical, technological, medical, and so forth;

2. They give an authoritative opinion as to how the incident in dispute occurred, be it a defect, physical condition of a product, accident reconstruction, design defect, and so forth; and

3. They enlarge the importance of the issue, and thus the monetary value of the case by their presence.

Experts can and should be used:

To suggest to the litigation team sources of facts, literature, and opinions to consider before formal discovery begins;

To assist in investigation of facts and provide specialized analytical skills by reviewing public record materials and other evidence obtained through technical libraries;

To assist in discovery by helping to draft interrogatories and to uncover the basic evidentiary facts which will be helpful to an expert's analysis and evaluation of the case;

To assist in determining those documents or tangible items in the possession of third parties which should be subpoenaed and inspected;

To inspect documents and evidentiary facts as they are received from third parties via subpoenas and to note the irregularities or omissions in materials received from third parties;

To evaluate the opinions and credentials of the opponent's expert and to prepare an attorney to depose the opponent's expert;

To review discovery responses received from the opposition, pointing out nonresponsive or evasive answers and suggesting follow-up discovery;

To provide opinion testimony at trial (medical, liability, legal, and so forth); and

To create the implication that the case is important.

This list is not meant to be all-inclusive, but only to suggest why it is important to use expert testimony at trial. In today's litigation environment, the success of your client's position depends largely upon the experience and credibility of the expert witness. The right expert witness educates and persuades the trier of fact and the jury that your client should prevail. An expert is essential to proving your case or defending your client. The evidence which supports your major theories of liability and/or affirmative defenses must be presented in a logical, understandable manner to the trier of fact and the jury.

Experts do more than just present or explain evidence, they also rebut or counter the opinions of the opposition's expert. Many trials become a battle of experts. Experts can introduce evidence, providing both fact and opinion testimony that may be based on hypothetical theories or on evidence that would not otherwise be admissible as trial testimony. Experts may reach opinions based on evidence whether the evidence is admissible if it is "of the type that reasonably may be relied upon by an expert in forming an opinion on the subject to which his testimony relates" (California Evidence Code § 801). An expert may be utilized not only to offer opinion testimony on the ultimate issues of the case, but also to introduce evidence that may be otherwise inadmissible.

The main reasons for hiring an expert are for case:

1. Evaluation,
2. Settlement potential,
3. Education on liability theories/relevant issues, and
4. Discovery assistance.

§ 7.4   Locating an Expert

Locating expert witnesses has become extremely easy in today's litigious society because "expert witnessing" is one of the country's newest growth industries. Dozens of businesses have cropped up offering to match experts with attorneys. The Association of Trial Lawyers of America (ATLA) publishes directories of experts. Local bar associations and professional associations also publish directories of expert witnesses, all of whom are ready and willing to testify at trial. For example, the San Francisco Bar Association publishes the Northern California Register of Experts and Consultants, which is sent out as a membership benefit to seven Bay Area county bar associations. Their 1993 circulation was over 25,000 copies, and listed experts and consultants in over 360 categories.

Most directories of experts publish a disclaimer stating that their directories are based on information supplied by the persons and firms listed, but that the publishers do not review, investigate, or evaluate the accuracy or completeness of the information provided, or the qualifications or competency of those listed. Bar associations and other publishers of directories of experts always state that they will not recommend or endorse the services of those experts listed in their directory, and that the omission of others in particularized specialized fields from the directory does not imply any negative assessment or evaluation or recommendation. The persons and firms listed in the various directories have paid for the advertising and the right to be included in that directory. Directories of expert witnesses should be treated like the *Federal Yellow Pages* or any other informational directory, that is, as a starting point in your search to find the right expert for your case.

General sources of information for locating experts are available from your law librarian and/or public library. The following publications are extremely useful in locating specific biographical information on experts in a variety of fields, technical and nontechnical.

Lawyer's Desk Reference, Volumes I and II, Harry M. Philo, The Lawyer's Cooperative Publishing Company, Bancroft Whitney Company, publishers. *Lawyer's Desk Reference* is more commonly known as LDR and was first published 23 years ago. Most of the subject headings relate to tort practice in product liability, admiralty, railroad accident, construction injury cases, and environmental tort litigation. Information contained in the LDR is received from the Association of Trial Lawyers of America (ATLA) and its 65,000 members through seminars, newsletters, and conferences. The LDR does more than simply list experts in a given field. It also includes checklists of legal theories of liability, suggested discovery in particular areas, the mechanics of failure, the economic analysis of a case, and so forth.

Who's Who in America, Wilmett, Illinois. This is also available on WESTLAW and DIALOG, and is considered the granddaddy of biographical directories. This book contains a geographical and professional index covering 39 topical categories. There are several indexes for *Who's Who* publications to assist in focusing your search. The "Biography Master Index" is on-line and indexes approximately 630 different sources providing the name and title of the book where a particular biographical reference is located. The "Biography Master Index" is available on both DIALOG and WESTLAW.

The "Who's Who" title is also found on many derivative publications which may prove helpful depending on the specifics of your search. For example:

International Who's Who, Europa Publications, Ltd.

Who's Who in Insurance, The Underwriters Printing & Publishing Company.

Who's Who in Architecture from 1400 to the Present, Holt, Rinehart & Winston Publishers.

Who's Who in American Art, R.R. Bowkar Publisher (also available on DIALOG).

Who's Who in Finance and Industry, Marquis Who's Who.

Forensic Services Directory, The National Register of Experts, Engineers, Scientific Advisers, Medical Specialists, Technical Consultants and Sources of Specialized Knowledge, Princeton, New Jersey, published by the National Forensic Center, (Also available on WESTLAW and LEXIS). This directory has biographical data on a wide range of experts including names, addresses, telephone numbers, areas of expertise, education, professional licenses, affiliations, and other assorted data.

Encyclopedia of Associations, Gale Publishing Company, Detroit, Michigan. This is an annual publication which is also available on DIALOG and WESTLAW. This directory contains information on over 75,000 nonprofit organizations. It is a three-volume set and provides information about associations that certify doctors and lawyers, establish professional standards, provide business sources and contacts, publish newsletters, books and membership directories, exchange and announce technological breakthroughs, do professional research, survey salary levels, make economic forecasts, compile statistics, lobby, improve and develop standards of quality and safety, suggest ethical codes, and provide continuing education for their members and for the general public. It is an amazing source of information regarding professional and nonprofessional associations. It is especially useful when you are looking for an expert in an obscure field to begin your research with the *Encyclopedia of Associations.* The major categories into which the *Encyclopedia of Associations* divides associations include: trade, business and commercial, agricultural, legal, governmental, public administration and military, scientific, engineering and technical, educational and cultural.

Directories in Print—An Annotated Guide to Over 10,000 Business and Industrial Directories, Professional and Scientific Rosters, Directory Data Bases and Other Lists and Guides of All Kinds That are Published in the United States or That Are National or Regional in Scope of Interest, Gale Research Incorporated, Detroit, Michigan. This is an annual publication. Entries in this directory are divided in 16 broad topical areas. On-line sources for publications are also provided.

National Trade and Professional Associations of the United States, Columbia Books, Inc. This is another directory of a smaller group of the better known trade and professional associations.

Business Organizations, Agencies and Publications Directory, Gale Research Incorporated.

Consultants and Consulting Organizations Directory, Gale Research Incorporated. This directory is also available on-line on WESTLAW, LEXIS, and DIALOG.

National Directory of Experts, Consultants, and Advisers, Experts at Law, Inc.

National Directory of Certified Public Accountants, Peter Norbark Publishing Company.

American Medical Association's Directory of Physicians in the United States.

Mortgage Banker Association Membership Directory. The AMA publication and the Mortgage Banker Association Membership Directory are not readily available and must be purchased directly from the association. Check your professional business and trade library to see if they can access these directories for you on-line.

Directory of Product Liability Expert Witnesses, Lewis J. Laski, J.D., National Product Liability Data Base, Nashville, Tennessee. The first edition of this directory was published in 1991. It is organized categorically by specific product and design defect.

The Legal Expert Pages, Donald G. Haflam, Ed., San Diego, California. This directory is published privately by Mr. Haflam and can be ordered directly from him at (619) 487-6194. Experts are organized by category and subject matter.

§ 7.5   Expert Data Bases

Many of the publications mentioned in the preceding section can be accessed by an on-line search. The following expert data bases can also be useful in helping locate the perfect expert witness:

Expert Net, Chicago, Illinois, Expert Net, Ltd. This data base is available on WESTLAW, LEXIS, and DIALOG and provides biographical information on those medical malpractice and personal injury experts who are willing to serve as expert witnesses. The records include areas of specialization, education, certification, previous and current employment, geographic location, and fees. If you access Expert Net on DIALOG, in addition to the expert's name, address, and telephone number, their approximate age will be given. If you access through WESTLAW, you must call Expert Net at their main office to get personal information on an expert's identity. A referral fee is charged for using Expert Net services.

TASA (Technical Advisory Service for Attorneys) is available on WESTLAW. This data base contains biographical records of over 17,000 expert witnesses found in over 4,800 specialty areas. WESTLAW subscribers have access to brief biographical profiles and can call TASA directly for the identity of each expert. Information is available for a fee.

Defense Research Institute's Expert Witness Index, Chicago, Illinois, (312) 944-0575. The Defense Research Institute maintains a computerized biographical data base of plaintiff expert witnesses in medical and technical areas. You may only access this data base if you are a member of the Defense Research Institute (DRI). It is useful to obtain background information including resumes and depositions on plaintiff's expert witnesses. For defendants, this is valuable for obtaining data on adverse expert witnesses. DRI also notifies its callers of other members submitting data or requesting information on a particular expert.

IDEX, Overland Park, Kansas, 1-800-521-5596. IDEX has compiled a data base of plaintiff experts. They provide the names and telephone numbers of subscribers sharing biographical information, depositions, or resumes. Subscribers pay an initial membership fee and both annual and search fees. It is available through business and trade libraries, county libraries, and law libraries.

§ 7.6 Locating New Experts

The sincerity and unpolished testimony of a new expert can be remarkably impressive although their cost is usually below the charges of court-experienced professional type witnesses. Any person can qualify to be an expert based on their special knowledge, skill, experience, training and/or education. The right expert for your client is the person who possesses a successful combination of the proper credentials, ability to communicate to lay members of the jury, and credibility.

An individual may have impressive credentials, but if that person cannot communicate their opinion to the jury, the credentials are worthless. The quality of credibility is intangible, but it is also the most important. A battle of experts at trial is often won by the person who appears to the jury to be the more objective, knowledgeable, sincere, and ultimately more believable. Jurors are extremely sensitive to the cost of litigation and are particularly put off by the expensive hourly fees charged by the professional expert. An expert who has been qualified to testify in court and has testified on many occasions in a particular subject area may charge anywhere from $150 to $450 per hour. Because most members of the jury not only do not make that kind of money, but also do not know anyone in their immediate family, relatives, or circle of friends who earn that kind of money, it is understandable that they are somewhat put off at the expensive dollar sign attached to the expert's testimony.

The best source for finding an inexpensive and new expert is your local university. Universities and colleges are an excellent source of men and women who are singularly dedicated to their professional activities. Such a person testifying in court can truthfully answer the question regarding their occupation as, "I am a professor at San Francisco State University in the area of economics and I chair the department." Juries like teachers. Through the course of history, teachers have always occupied a place of favor in the minds of the American public. Most jurors respect teachers and appreciate the jobs they do with their students.

Another advantage in using a college professor is that their communication skills are usually excellent. They are used to speaking to groups of 30 to 40 students and lecturing on given topics. They know how to organize topics to highlight key points, and, most importantly, they know how to communicate technical knowledge to the lay person.

Last but not least, an advantage of using a college professor is the amount of their hourly charge. Usually, charges for expert testimony from a college or university professor will be commensurate with their loss of a paycheck for the time given to you to prepare for the testimony and testify in court. Paychecks of college and university professors are traditionally low. It is a safe bet that some members of the jury may earn more than your college professor expert. In a battle of experts charging $200 to $400 per hour, the college professor's charges will seem most reasonable to the jury.

Another area in which to look for inexpensive and credible experts is to look into retired government specialists and retired industry specialists. In many government and industrial areas, there are men and women who have raw life experience plus the educational background which they had to have in order to get their job in the first place. This will give your case a flavor of sincerity and reality, while holding the cost reasonably close to what the witnesses will actually lose as out-of-pocket expenses. Use the professional societies in a particular subject area, if you are looking for a retired industry specialist.

When looking for an expert, be sure to ask around. Ask other attorneys practicing in that particular field, and ask lay persons who may use experts. Banks, for example, use real estate appraisers and gemologists. If you represent a business or corporate client, start with them. Your client will be an excellent source of information regarding retired employees, ex-employees, and even their competitors.

§ 7.7   Reference Sources

In addition to the publications listed in **§ 7.4** and **§ 7.5,** another excellent and valuable source of information regarding experts is to locate jury trial information to determine the kinds of cases the expert has testified in, the substance of their testimony, and the outcome of the case. Jury trials are not officially reported. However, there are state and regional reporting services through the United States, such as:

Jury Verdicts Weekly, Santa Rosa, California. Summaries of jury verdicts in California, Arizona and Nevada. It is a semi-annual publication. Indexes are available. If you do not have access to the publication or indexes, call Jury Verdicts at (707) 539-5454 and they will conduct research for you at a nominal fee.

Verdicts and Settlements, Litigation Research Group, Chappaqua, New York, and San Francisco, California.

Jury Verdict Research, Inc., Salon, Ohio.

Verdictum Juris, O'Bruns, Evaluator, P. O. Box 100, Claremont, California, 91711, (714) 627-3345.

A call to Verdictum-Juris initiates a search of up to twelve years of trial history on expert data bases, and will tell you the number of times, and for whom a particular expert testified, along with the name of the attorney who hired the expert and a brief synopsis of the case. This source of information is invaluable when you are researching the adverse party's expert.

Another source of information is scholarly writings in a particular subject area or technical field. Research can be done through working with a reference librarian or through on-line searches. One of the best reference books is *The National Union Catalog: A Cumulative Author List* (Library of Congress, Card Catalog Division). This reference work includes copies of catalogs containing full records and often listing holding libraries. WESTLAW, DIALOG, and WILSONLINE have files containing Library of Congress records. Another good reference source for locating scholarly articles is *Books in Print,* R.R. Bowker Company. (Also available on WESTLAW and DIALOG.)

A search for scholarly articles is more complicated than for specific books due to the range of information needed. Searches in highly technical data bases, which are topical and full text, are often necessary to locate published articles. The following data bases are best when you need to explore a wide range of material:

The Readers Guide to Periodical Literature (available on WILSONLINE).

Chemical Abstracts, Columbus, Ohio, American Chemical Society. This data base includes books, journal articles, doctorate dissertations, conference papers, and reports.

Applied Science and Technology Index, New York, The H.W. Wilson Company (also available on WILSONLINE). This index is useful for articles in engineering, physical science, earth science, aerospace technology, and computer technology.

Academic Index, Foster City, California, Information Access Company (available on DIALOG). Indexes over 400 scholarly and general interest journals which are commonly found in academic libraries.

Business Periodical Index, The H.W. Wilson Company, New York (available on WILSONLINE).

Public Affairs Information Service Bulletin, New York, Public Information Service (available on WESTLAW and DIALOG). It indexes articles in political science, government, economics, and sociology.

Medline, Bethesda, Maryland, U.S. Library of Medicine (available on WESTLAW, LEXIS, and DIALOG). Medline, and its on-line version Medlars, is the primary source for biomedical articles. It is comprised of three print indexes: (1) Index Medicus, (2) Index to Dental Literature, and (3) International Nursing Index.

Compendex "Plus", New York, Engineering Information, Inc. (available on DIALOG and ORBIT). This data base is the on-line various of Engineering Index which includes entries from approximately 4,500 technical journals.

NTIS, Springfield, Virginia, National Technological Information Service, U.S. Department of Commerce (available on DIALOG and BRS). This multidisciplinary data base includes government sponsored research and analysis prepared by federal agencies or their constituents. Many of its holdings have a limited distribution.

This list is only a sampling of what is available on-line when you search for experts through scholarly writings in a particular field. DIALOG has over 220 data bases, many of which index various journals and periodicals. If you locate leading authorities in a particular field through their scholarly writings, write to them expressing an interest in arranging a meeting. They will be flattered by the time and effort you have gone through to research the area, and the fact that what they have said in their writing is pertinent and relevant to your case.

§ 7.8 Lay Expert Witnesses

A lay expert witness may testify in court as to the custom and habit in a particular trade. For day-to-day, nitty-gritty, practical realities of a product, place, or design with which you are involved, a lay witness who is steeped in the day-to-day practical aspects of the product may be just the right witness. To qualify their testimony, degrees and educational background are not as important as their long-standing continuous personal contact with the conditions involved within the pertinent community. Custom and habit in the trade, if it does not conflict with a legal or statutory duty, is extremely persuasive to a jury.

A lay expert witness who is qualified to testify may offer opinions as to the custom and usage of a particular product, but they cannot testify based on hypothetical situations. The witness must testify from firsthand knowledge. For example, if the accident resulted from an accident which occurred on a construction site, a lay expert construction foreman would be a good choice.

As an example, construction foremen who are responsible for carpenters, finishers, and other construction workers may be called upon to testify regarding fastening ends of boards to any part of the frame during the construction phase of a building. There is a recommended number of nails which must be used on the end of the board to fasten it safely to a joist. A construction foreman, or carpenter who has worked years in the field, could competently testify that roofing carpenters are always told to use three nails to fasten the ends of their boards to a joist. If you use less than three nails, the board ends will often split between the two nails, allowing the board to wobble and move when you walk across it on the roof. This type of explanation is extremely useful if your client walked across the roof on a particular construction project and fell through it in the course and scope of the client's employment.

Another example of the use of a lay expert happened on a case involving replacement fencing. The defendant had been ordered by the court to replace fences for several farmers whose fences did not survive weather conditions (wind storms, rain, snow) and accidents with livestock during branding when the animal would rush into the fence at full speed. The lay expert who testified as to the custom and usage within the fence building industry had apprenticed in his father's fence building company from the age of 16. The expert had worked during his high school years with his father in the fence building business. At the time of his testimony, he was in his early 40's and could easily say he had built millions of miles of fences in rural areas over a span of close to 30 years. Our lay expert had a high school diploma and had not gone to college, but he was an expert on how to build a fence that would last through inclement weather and survive livestock accidents. He testified that he had built fences for private farmers and ranchers on the freeway and on state-owned property. He had contracted with businesses as well as private parties building many different types of fences depending on the terrain and usage. He further testified that he had never been called back by any of his customers to replace sections of fencing unless either the materials had been defective or the fence had been exposed to an unusual trauma. He defined an "unusual trauma" as fire, lightning, acts of God, tractors going out of control, and so forth.

The lay fence expert was extremely popular with the jury. He was able to speak to them in lay language about how one built a fence. He further did not charge an excessive amount for his testimony, billing only his hourly labor charge, which was $35 an hour. This expert's opinion was particularly appropriate because of the subject matter of the testimony. It was sufficiently beyond the common experience of the jury and was based on specialized, firsthand knowledge.

§ 7.9   In-House Experts

Business and corporate clients routinely rely on certain designated individuals within their business to advise them and provide them with information normally used in the course and scope of their business. This in-house expert in reality is a lay expert who can testify at time of trial as to the customs and habits of a particular business. If a company bookkeeper, appraiser, accountant, risk manager, and so forth, reports on a particular incident in anticipation of litigation, and that report is transmitted to the Chief Executive Officer (CEO) or corporate counsel, the report is privileged and considered work product. The in-house expert generally functions in a consultant capacity and may be called upon at trial to give an opinion based on the subject matter of the expert's work. For example, a bookkeeper may present an opinion at trial based on their analysis of accounts receivable and accounts payable for the business for which the bookkeeper keeps the books. This opinion is viewed as lay expert or factual testimony. The basis for the opinion is personal knowledge gained from personal experience.

An in-house expert may not give an opinion based on a hypothetical situation, hearsay facts, or data of which the in-house expert does not have firsthand knowledge. The expert may offer testimony, including opinion testimony, on data and documents that they have studied if those documents were necessary for the preparation of accounts payable and receivable reports, profit and loss statements, or any other documents that the expert was required to prepare in the course and scope of their employment.

An in-house expert may testify regarding those documents which have been entered into evidence pursuant to the business record provisions of the state evidence code. The expert may also authenticate business records so that they can be admitted into evidence if the expert knows from firsthand knowledge how those documents were prepared.

An in-house expert may also testify regarding matters that explain their state of mind when certain documents were prepared. An important distinction is usually made by the judge by way of instruction to the jury as to how they should consider this testimony. This type of testimony is not admitted for the truth of the matter itself, but merely for the state of mind of the witness at the time of the preparation of a certain document.

Although the in-house expert's reports prepared in the course and scope of business are usually done in anticipation of litigation and as such qualify for work product protection, those documents which will be introduced as exhibits at the time of trial must be made available to the opposition prior to that witness's testimony. In order to protect earlier reports prepared in the anticipation of litigation, the in-house expert may prepare a final version of a profit and loss statement or financial memo to be used as a trial exhibit. As a consultant, or in-house expert, the earlier reports remain protected pursuant to the work product privilege. The fact that the final document which becomes a trial exhibit may contain some of the information from the earlier reports does not remove the work product protection from the actual reports—at least in California. Because case law varies greatly on work product protection (see **Chapter 2**), be sure to check your state and local statutes and rules of admissibility of evidence at trial in order to determine the extent of work product protection afforded an in-house consultant.

§ 7.10   Expert Witness Services

Expert witness services which match attorneys with experts can be extremely useful when you are either looking for an expert in an obscure field or when the best available expert in your field has been hired by the opposition. An expert witness service will prescreen experts for you and furnish you with resumes, fee schedules, and biographical information on selected experts in a given area of specialization. Some of the services such as Technical Advisory Service for Attorneys, Forensic Technologies International Corporation, and Case Assessment Screening and Expert Services, Inc. specialize in particular areas of practice and have a national pool of experts who are available for evaluation and testimony in a wide variety of claims. Experts who work for expert services are unbiased, objective, and generally work for both plaintiff and defendant law firms. Credentials sought by expert services include academic affiliations and an active practice in a given area of specialization. Some services boast rosters of more than 6,000 experts in over 3,000 fields. Many retired college professors join expert services as a means of augmenting their retirement income. Some experts consult on a full-time basis and work through an expert service as well as advertising on their own.

The decision of whether to use an expert service depends upon:

The complexity of the case,

The amount of liability exposure,

The amount of potential recovery,

The availability of a specific expert in a specific technical field,

The client needs and desires, and

Whether the case has become a battle of experts, eliminating many of the more well-known experts in a given field.

An expert witness service functions as a middleman or matchmaker in the selection process of an expert witness suitable for your particular case. Consulting an expert witness service does not oblige you to hire one of their experts. You may receive resumes from several experts and the case may settle, eliminating the need for expert testimony. Or, you may receive resumes from several of their prescreened experts, and decide that none of them are exactly right for your specific needs. The expert witness service will bill for the time spent searching for an expert for you; however, this amount is usually nominal. If your law firm decides to retain an expert recommended by the expert witness service, payment of the expert fees is made directly to the expert, not to the service.

§ 7.11   Selecting the Right Expert

What to look for in an expert varies with the specific facts of any given case as well as the number of other experts who will be disclosed to testify on behalf of your client. General considerations when selecting an expert are:

Integrity

Objectivity and lack of bias on the specific subject

Academic qualifications, professional licenses, and so forth

Ability to testify to a jury in lay language

Experience as an expert witness

Publications authored, lectures given, seminars, and so forth

Teaching experience, if any

Personality—will the jury like this person and, therefore, listen carefully to their testimony?

Credibility—Does this witness sound believable and sincere?

Costs—Is the amount this expert charges on an hourly basis appropriate given the expected nature of recovery in this case?

Acceptability to client—This is particularly important when you are representing a business or corporate client who should be involved in the process of selecting experts.

Conflict of interest—This should be checked out immediately, because if there is even a hint of a potential conflict because of prior testimony given by this expert, this is not the expert you wish to hire.

Independent thinking—This is an important characteristic to look for in an expert witness because an independent thinker will provide critical analysis and point out weaknesses in the opposition's expert opinions so that you can access the merits of the claim or defense and consider the appropriateness of settlement.

Focus on the issues—Can the expert put aside their ego and focus on the issues of the case?

Specific Expertise—Be sure your expert is an expert in that specific field because you are not looking for general expertise, but specialized expertise in a given area.

Nature of Expertise—Has the expert testified in many fields? If so, are they related fields? Or is your expert an "expert in everything"?

Communication—Can your expert explain their opinion to you in lay language without lapsing into expert language? It is necessary in presenting some opinions on scientific and technical issues to use words that will be beyond the knowledge of the lay jury, and that expert language is permissible and required in those circumstances; however, beware of the expert who describes seat belts as "restraining devices" and the lighting at an accident scene in terms of "candle power" or "kilowatts."

Clear and Concise Presentation—The expert's ability to articulate, analogize, and simplify scientific and technical data in a manner that presents the material clearly and concisely without talking down to the jury is the expert who the jury will listen to and trust.

§ 7.12 Sample Letter to an Expert

An expert search often begins with a wide-based general search in a field of expertise before it narrows into a specific area of specialization. The following letter (**Form 7–1**) is a sample which can be sent to several experts to gather information regarding their specific expertise:

FORM 7–1
SAMPLE LETTER TO AN EXPERT

[name of expert]
[address]

   RE: Title of Case

Dear [name of expert]:

   Our office has been retained by the family of a gentleman who was killed in a pedestrian motor vehicle accident which occurred in [city]. Our client had exited a [name of transit authority] station and was about to cross [name] Street when the client was struck by a pickup truck. It is unknown whether the client was struck on the left side or the right side. We are interested in retaining an expert who can assist us in recreating the physics of this particular accident in so far as recreating where our client was struck, what direction our client was facing, and the relative speed of the vehicle involved in the accident.

   Your name has come to our attention through a search of Jury Verdicts which indicates you have previously testified as a Biomechanical Engineer in various motor vehicle accidents.

Please forward a resume and the terms and conditions of your employment, including your current fee schedule. Please let us know if you are available for consultation and/or testimony in this matter.

We look forward to hearing from you at your earliest possible convenience because we are in the process of beginning discovery in this matter. If you have any questions, or need further information, please do not hesitate to contact our office.

> Very truly yours,
>
> [name]
> Legal Assistant

After you receive resumes in response to this letter, telephone contact should be made to discuss case specifics and rule out conflicts of interest.

§ 7.13   Qualifying Experts for Trial

In order for an expert witness to testify at trial and present evidence that will be admissible to the jury, the witness must be qualified as an expert in accordance with Evidence Code requirements. Federal Rule of Evidence 702 states the law of most jurisdictions pertaining to the admissibility of expert testimony as follows:

> If scientific, technical or other specialized knowledge will assist the trier of fact to understand the evidence or to determine a fact in issue, a witness qualified as an expert by knowledge, skill, experience, training, or education, may testify thereto in the form of an opinion or otherwise.

A witness with specialized knowledge or skill can help the jury understand complex issues. Concisely stated, an expert is an explainer of facts. The purpose of qualifying an expert witness is to persuade the trier of fact that the findings and opinions presented by this expert are accurate and should be accepted.

Expert opinion testimony based on other than the expert's own perceptions is admissible if the field is one in which expert testimony will be helpful to the trier of fact, and if the witness is an expert in that particular area in question. To establish expert qualifications, it is necessary to examine the witness regarding the witness' field of expertise, education, and/or training. A statement of qualifications is intended to convince the judge of this witnesses qualifications to testify as an expert in this particular field. A statement of qualifications is also beneficial in that it instills in the jury a sense that this witness is competent (in fact, more competent than the opposition's expert) and credible to testify.

In some instances a well-documented list of credentials and scholarly achievements is advisable and required to qualify an expert in a particular field such as a complex business case. In other instances, hands-on experience is much more impressive. University degrees, publications, and professional recognition help establish competency; however, skill, experience, and training can be as valid as a means of qualifying a witness. It is important to realize that there is no single criteria by which to measure expertise. The most effective expert is one who combines scholarly achievement and hands-on experience.

The standard method of qualifying an expert witness to the judge and jury is for the lawyer presenting their expert witness to voir dire the expert by asking leading questions concerning qualifications, progressing from the general to the specific and covering the following topics:

General education, advanced degrees, training;

Education and/or training concerning matters both specific and relevant to the issues of the case on trial;

Experience and specific type of professional activity which has equipped the witness to render authoritative opinions on the specific subject matter of the case;

Articles, books, and technical papers written by the expert with emphasis on the subject matter relevant to the litigation;

Professional internships, apprenticeships, and teaching activities;

Offices and memberships in professional societies or associations relevant to the subject matter;

Previous experience as a witness. This is especially effective if the witness has testified for both plaintiff and defendant;

Special qualifications which qualify the witness to give an opinion on an ultimate issue in the case. Ask about the tests, examinations, experiments performed, and the fact and data reviews undertaken in coming to those specific conclusions (Follow guidelines set forth in Federal Rule of Evidence 801(b).);

Certification in certain fields (for example, board certified, medical doctor, and so forth), and an explanation of both the significance of the certification and the requirements to obtain that special recognition; and

Continuing professional training outside the context of the job (such as courses taken at continuing education programs, vocational programs, lectures, symposiums, and so forth).

§ 7.14   Qualifying the Hands-On Expert

In certain cases, a hands-on expert is the best person to testify in a particular area. For example, in a case involving a defective drill bit, a carpenter with 20 years experience using the same type of drill on various construction jobs may indeed be the expert appearing the most credible in the eyes of the jury. Qualifying the hands-on expert is somewhat different than qualifying a scholarly expert, because this witness derives their expertise from extensive practical experience and should be asked questions about the following:

Present job or position, name of employer, nature of employer's business, and type of duties performed on the job;

Professional licenses issued by a State Board of Examiners for a particular trade or occupation, the name of the license, description of its requirements, and a discussion of the examination or experience required before license is awarded;

Total amount of time in which the witness has been engaged in the trade, occupation, or craft from which their expertise derives;

The stages in the witness' practical experience, together with a statement of the knowledge required at each stage from apprenticeship through journeyman, and so forth;

Various jobs held from the lowest apprentice clerk job through the stages of career development in the particular trade, occupation, or craft; and

Previous practical experience, and what the witness learned from each previous job experience that contributes to their qualifications to render an opinion in the case at issue.

A hands-on expert commands serious respect from the judge and the jury if they are used to testify in areas where they are explaining how things actually work. This expert can be more impressive to a jury than a scholarly expert who provides a laboratory or computer-generated analysis of how things are supposed to work.

§ 7.15   Voir Dire by Opposing Counsel

When the plaintiff or the defendant has finished qualifying their expert witness, they may move the court to rule that the witness is an expert and permitted to give expert opinion testimony in the present case. This gives the jury the impression that the expert has the court's stamp of approval. However, it is not axiomatic that opposing counsel will respond that they are satisfied with the expert's qualifications. Opposing counsel also has the right to examine, or voir dire, the witness regarding their qualifications in advance of that witness' opinion testimony. This is important for the following reasons:

1. To lay a foundation for a successful motion that the witness not be permitted to give an opinion;
2. To demonstrate to the jury before the witness testifies that the opinion they are about to hear should be given little weight because of the expert's lack of experience or education;
3. To break the flow of an effective presentation of that expert's testimony; and
4. To challenge the witness' expertise in a particular specific area by limiting the witness' testimony to a more generalized area.

This is frequently done in an attempt to exclude from evidence an expert's particular test, computer diagram, video simulation, or other data prepared by the expert to illustrate and explain a disputed issue germane to the case. The expert is then qualified to testify only in a limited manner, and they may not be allowed to testify in an area for which they have prepared a report as part of their original testimony. This trial strategy, when successful, creates problems that can poke serious holes in your opposing counsel's case.

§ 7.16   Percipient Experts

A percipient expert is similar to an in-house expert. The distinction between a percipient expert and a designated expert witness is that the percipient witness may give opinions based only on personal observation, as opposed to opinions based on information provided by the attorney. Percipient witnesses are considered fact witnesses and are very important in laying a foundation for factual evidence admissibility at the time of trial. Examples of percipient witnesses include police officers, fire officers, treating health care providers, government employees acting in their capacities as directors of particular departments or divisions, and so forth.

There are several advantages to using percipient witnesses. First, they help lay a factual foundation for testimony elicited from a retained and disclosed trial expert. Percipient witnesses' names and addresses must be listed on an expert witness disclosure to give notice to the other side that the witness will be giving an expert factual opinion at trial. The witnesses must also be made available for deposition, if noticed.

A percipient witness has a built-in air of believability on the witness stand because they were involved before the litigation. This total familiarity with not only the issues of the case but also the persons involved in the prelitigation stage is the main reason why percipient witnesses should be used at trial.

A percipient expert witness may be light in terms of education, training, and qualifications, but their testimony can always be supplemented with a retained trial expert. Consider the percipient witness' on-the-job training, particularly when using police officers, firemen, emergency rescue team members, and so forth. On-the-job training in specific procedures relating to natural disasters, police emergencies, treatment for trauma victims, securing the scene of an incident, obtaining physical evidence, and related safety training learned in the course and scope of a percipient witnesses employment more than qualifies them to provide factual opinion testimony at trial. This type of on-the-job training used to qualify a percipient expert impresses a jury because of its hands-on nature.

The percipient witness, who is a treating health care provider, is very important in cases involving physical, emotional, and mental injuries. If the treating health care provider is a family doctor who has known and treated the plaintiff over the years, the doctor's testimony is extremely valuable in demonstrating the before and after physical, mental, and emotional condition of the plaintiff. Treating health care providers are often experienced in trial testimony and may have even testified as experts in other cases. From a believability standpoint, the treating health care provider is in the best position to assess the effects of the accident/incident on your client, especially if she provided initial treatment to your client.

Percipient fact expert witnesses are most valuable because of their prelitigation, firsthand knowledge of the facts and/or people involved in the case. Police officers, firemen, sheriffs, city marshals, or government employees acting in their official capacity are generally viewed by the jury as authority figures who frequently testify upon reports written at the time of the incident. These witnesses can authenticate these reports so that they can be admitted into evidence as a trial exhibit and used with other witnesses.

§ 7.17   Researching the Opposition's Expert

It is just as important to learn everything about the opposition's expert witnesses as it is to locate, learn about, and work with your expert. Preparation of an expert witness profile includes a careful review of any prior testimony given by that expert such as depositions, reports, lectures, and so forth. It also includes reviewing anything the expert has authored on your specific subject which will prevent embarrassment at trial and enhance the qualifications and believability of your expert witness.

Collecting information to prepare a profile of an adverse expert witness is not always a simple process, but it is necessary in order to prepare your attorney to depose, cross-examine, and discredit effectively the opinion testimony of the opposition's expert. Many of the references and bibliographic sources listed in § **7.5** and § **7.7** relating to locating expert witnesses to testify for your case can be used to locate information regarding the adverse expert witness. Witnesses are found in many areas and numerous legal and nonlegal sources may be consulted in the search for information about the adverse expert.

Begin your research on an adverse expert with on-line data base searches such as WESTLAW, LEXIS, newspaper data bases, and special trial court survey data bases. The most useful information you can find on an adverse expert is former trial testimony. Unfortunately, there is no easy way to obtain a comprehensive listing of previous trials. You must access several data bases and trial court decisions. Many trial court decisions are not reported. The Jury Verdict Research, Inc. network compiles surveys of personal injury, medical malpractice, and product liability verdicts for many states. Consult your local law library to see if Jury Verdict Research, Inc. is available on-line. (See also § **7.7** regarding state and regional reporting services.)

Newspaper data bases will often report actual testimony if it is a major or sensational trial (most frequently criminal trials). WESTLAW, LEXIS, and DATATIMES often contain reports of actual testimony.

Occasionally an expert witness will be mentioned within an appellate court opinion which can be found on either WESTLAW or LEXIS. Also, you will find on WESTLAW, LEXIS, and LEGI-SLATE testimony of witnesses who have spoken before Congressional committees. The Congressional record is available in full text on WESTLAW, LEXIS, and LEGI-SLATE. If you are seeking to obtain information on an adverse witness in environmental litigation, it is highly probable that the witness may have spoken before a Congressional committee or administrative agency.

One of your goals in compiling a profile on an adverse witness is to locate prior deposition testimony as well as prior trial testimony. Compiling a case list of those actions when the expert has previously testified can be used to locate law firms and individual attorneys who may have depositions of the adverse expert. Bar associations and trial lawyer associations have established expert deposition banks. The purpose of these banks is to provide ready access to association members the depositions of expert witnesses, both plaintiff and defense. Association members may access the bank and request the depositions of a given expert, and are provided with copies at a nominal charge. Public information vendors also have deposition banks and furnish copies of transcripts to members upon request and payment of copy charges.

In addition to researching prior testimony of an adverse expert, prepare a bibliography of articles written, books published, chapters in text books, and so forth, and obtain hard copies of those articles or chapters which relate specifically to the issues of your case. It is important not to overlook publications where the adverse expert is named as a co-author or contributor. In order to impeach an adverse expert effectively, you need to obtain all written opinions on a disputed issue so that inconsistencies and contradictory information can be highlighted and used by your attorney in deposing and cross-examining that expert.

If the adverse expert has authored many publications, or contributed to various definitive textbooks in their subject of expertise, it is a safe bet that they have presented some of their work at conferences and symposiums. Searching for conference and symposium papers is a challenge because many of them are never cataloged. Technical conference papers may be found within certain data bases such as COM-PENDIX PLUS, or Nursing and Allied Health (CINAHL), Conference Papers Index, Bethesda, MD, Cambridge Scientific Abstracts. This is available on DIALOG and includes papers presented in the areas of life sciences, chemistry, physical sciences, and engineering.

Topical full text data bases which contain an expert's actual publications will frequently be able to locate any articles citing the expert's works. These articles are an excellent source of locating a critical analysis of the adverse expert's publication. This information is useful in deposing the adverse expert or cross-examining them at trial, and it can also be used to locate the best opposing expert witness who may have written a critical analysis of the adverse expert's publication. On-line searches which will assist in this type of a search include the LEXIS Library, GENMED for medical journals in full text, and various directories such as *Book Review Index: A Master Compilation,* published by Gale Research Company, and *Book Review Digest,* published by the H.W. Wilson Company.

Compiling an adverse expert witness profile is not an easy task; it is, however, an investigative challenge and the benefits far exceed the time and effort expended.

§ 7.18   Sample Letter Retaining an Expert

After potential experts have been identified, they should be contacted by telephone not only to determine their availability, but also to rule out conflicts of interest. You should then follow up with a commitment letter verifying that the expert has agreed to be a consultant on your case. The following letter (**Form 7–2**) is a sample letter sent subsequent to telephone contact verifying the expert's commitment:

FORM 7–2
SAMPLE LETTER RETAINING AN EXPERT

[name of expert]
[address]

   RE: [plaintiff] v. [defendant]

Dear [name of expert]:

   We represent [plaintiff], who was injured on [date], at a residence located at [address], in [city], [state]. [Plaintiff] was an invited guest at a party held by the tenants of that property for a group of students celebrating the end of the academic semester. [Plaintiff] was one of many guests. [Plaintiff] and several other guests were outside on the back deck visiting and enjoying the fresh air. [Plaintiff] remembers leaning back against the railing on the back deck when it suddenly and without warning gave way, hurtling her and four other people to the concrete driveway. Our client, [plaintiff], sustained serious injuries, including multiple fractures.

   My paralegal, [name], spoke with you on [date], regarding our desire to retain you as an expert consultant in this case. I understand that your consulting fee is $250 per hour. I understand that you and [paralegal] discussed the potential defendants, insurance carrier, and possible Doe defendants [include here names of all known defendants, potential Doe defendants, and if known, insurance company and claims adjuster]. It has been determined that you do not know any of these named individuals and would have no conflict of interest in assisting us on this case.

   We will attempt to obtain a piece of the wood railing that gave way and broke causing the plaintiff's fall. Please contact my paralegal, [name], so that we can schedule a meeting to discuss what needs to be done to develop liability in this case.

   I am looking forward to working with you on this case, and welcome your input regarding the need to add additional consultants to develop our theories of liability.

                       Sincerely,

                       [attorney for plaintiff]

§ 7.19 Providing Experts with Case Materials

In order to prepare your consultant/expert adequately to form an opinion regarding liability issues in your case, it is necessary to provide them with adequate resource material to understand the facts of the incident/accident as known to you. Providing materials to the expert also helps to define the scope of their work. Expert consultants need to be aware of the identities of all other experts that you have hired to work on your case. This will minimize duplicate efforts, and is also necessary when one expert's testimony depends upon the facts and findings of another expert or percipient witness. For example, an economist testifying in a personal injury or product liability action cannot present their opinion on future economic loss without reviewing information found in medical records along with information on the client's work history, family background, and life style. All of these individual factors are then correlated by the expert economist to future costs that the client will likely incur as a result of their injuries. The expert economist presents their opinion on future costs per year based on the client's anticipated life expectancy.

In order to get full value out of an expert witness, it is wise to choose that person early in the case and use them as a consultant on your case as well. An expert witness functioning as a consultant can help in planning discovery, anticipating defenses, and in identifying and selecting other necessary experts by providing personal referrals regarding other experts that they have worked with in the past. Your expert is also a good source of information in helping develop the adverse expert witness profile discussed in § 7.17.

Materials which should be sent to your expert include the following:

All material relevant to the basis of their opinion including information obtained through discovery, public records, subpoenas to third parties, or client files;

Depositions, answers to interrogatories, responses to requests for admissions, exhibits to depositions, and answers to requests for production of documents, along with the documents;

Medical records and physical evidence such as police reports, accident reports, photographs, autopsy reports, x-rays, and other experts' reports; and

Factual data relating to the incident which may include information obtained through the Federal Freedom of Information Act (FOIA).

Just as it is appropriate and necessary to furnish your expert consultant with all of the necessary documents and tangible items, it is inappropriate and not advised to give the expert case summaries, including deposition summaries, or any document which could be considered attorney work product. If the expert places any of these documents in the file that they have opened for work on your case, they will be subject to disclosure at the time of that expert's deposition. If an expert even reads deposition summaries and returns them, they may be questioned at deposition or trial as to the content of those summaries. The rule in working with an expert is not to furnish them with any information that you do not want subject to your opponent's inquiry and view.

Impressions and opinions of an attorney and paralegal working with a trial consultant are privileged as work product pursuant to federal and state statutes (in California, see California Code of Civil Procedure § 2018). It is best to communicate with an expert witness orally and to put as little as possible in writing. If you prepare summaries of conversations with an expert consultant, do so in your own handwriting and place them in your case file. The presumption of confidentiality will then be preserved and they will not be discoverable under any circumstances pursuant to statute. They will be considered the mental impressions of an attorney or someone working under the supervision of that attorney and qualify for absolute work product protection.

When you are transmitting materials to an expert witness for their review, make your transmittal letter extremely brief. A good practice pointer is to call the expert consultant and tell them in a telephone conversation what you are sending to them, why it is being sent to them, and any specific instructions for use of that material. After you have completed this phone call, record a summary of that conversation in your own handwriting and place it in the file. Your transmittal letter can then simply state, "Dear Expert: Enclosed please find materials relevant to the Smith vs. Jones case."

It is important to keep a working list in your file of all materials sent to an expert for their review, along with the date those materials were sent. This type of a list is a valuable trial preparation tool for several reasons. It allows you to see at a glance what materials have been sent to the expert for review, so that additional materials may be sent to fill in any gaps; it helps avoid sending duplicate materials to an expert; and it is also a valuable reference for compiling trial exhibit lists.

§ 7.20   Trial Exhibits

The old expression "a picture is worth a thousand words," is never more true than it is in the courtroom. It is almost mandatory that an expert witness testifying in a complex litigation matter illustrate the technical and scientific aspects of their testimony through the use of trial exhibits. Demonstrative evidence includes documentary evidence such as letters, manuals, memoranda, maps, photographs, three-dimensional models, computer-generated video programs, photographs, overhead transparencies, xerographic enlargements, and simply writing facts and figures during testimony on a white board with felt markers. The goal of a good trial exhibit is to support the case strategy and enhance the jury's understanding of the facts, figures, and theories advanced by the expert witness through their opinion testimony.

A chart or graph communicates complicated data to the jury. Many jurors find numbers hard to swallow and understand. Graphs make them palatable and understandable. A chart or graph used to illustrate numbers can be a line graph, bar chart, pie chart, or table. It is important to choose the right graphic to illustrate the expert's opinion. For example, line graphs and bar charts both plot changes: Line graphics usually emphasize progression, and bar charts are the most impressive when they highlight individual changes. If an expert wishes to illustrate an entire theory and divide that theory into its parts, a pie chart is especially effective. Pie charts can show a large amount of information that would not fit into any of the other formats, and can be used to illustrate various sections or pieces of an expert's testimony.

Paralegal involvement with experts in the preparation of demonstrative evidence presents many challenges. Some experts provide the paralegal with an 8 × 10 inch or smaller pencil drawing illustrating the subject matter of their testimony. It then becomes the job of the legal assistant to work with an outside graphics firm or in-house graphics department and translate the expert's illustration into a meaningful trial exhibit. The major problem with most illustrations provided by experts is that they provide either too much information in a confined space or too little information, because the expert understands the main issues and does not see the need for explanation through their illustration.

The basic rule of all trial exhibits can be summarized as the "ten-foot rule." To test the effectiveness of a trial exhibit, stand back from your graphic or illustration at least 10 feet and see if you can read the writing and/or numbers on the graphic. If you cannot read your trial exhibit clearly when standing back 10 feet from it, the jury will not be able to read the exhibit. In an average superior courtroom, the optimum size for a trial exhibit is 36 × 48-inches or greater. In a federal courtroom, the trial exhibit should be 40 × 60-inches or greater. Using anything smaller defeats the purpose of a trial exhibit.

Some expert witnesses who testify on a regular basis have graphic artists with whom they have worked in the past and will prepare their own trial exhibits. This is a very workable solution if the trial exhibits go from the graphic artist back to the expert for their review for accuracy, and then are forwarded on to your office well in advance of trial. This type of quality control assurance check is necessary to prevent surprises at trial, and to make sure that the graphics are consistent with the facts, opinions, and conclusions that the expert will testify to at trial.

The admissibility of graphics at trial varies depending upon local rules and customs. Generally speaking, the best evidence rule governs the identification and admissibility of all demonstrative evidence. California Evidence Code § 140 defines demonstrative evidence as "material objects or other things presented to the senses that are offered to prove the existence or nonexistence of a fact." This leaves it to the discretion of the judge to rule on the admissibility of an exhibit.

In federal court, admissibility of graphic exhibits is similar to that in state court. The trial judge retains the discretion to admit or exclude a particular exhibit. However, in federal court there is a requirement that the source of each document used to make the trial graphic is listed directly on the exhibit. Without this identification, the exhibit is inadmissible.

§ 7.21   Choosing Graphic Consultants

Demonstrative evidence experts/graphic consultants specialize in much the same way as trial experts. A demonstrative evidence directory lists subdivisions for those consultants specializing in animation, charts, computer animation, computer graphics, exhibit boards, medical illustrations, and photography. The best source for locating a graphics consultant is to contact the Demonstrative Evidence Specialist Association (DESA).[1] DESA is a national organization of graphic specialists whose expertise lies in presentation of materials for litigation. Members of DESA have graphics studios that have developed a working knowledge and relationship with attorneys and their expert witnesses. DESA membership includes illustrators, animators, designers, videographers, and model makers who blend artistic and communication skills to create trial exhibits for use in state and federal courts. DESA

---

[1] The telephone numbers for the Demonstrative Evidence Specialist Association (DESA) are 800-555-DESA or 214-871-1908.

maintains a referral system based on your geographic location and/or trial needs and is an excellent source of information for choosing graphic consultants.

Another excellent source of information when working with an expert in the preparation of trial exhibits is the book, *What Makes Juries Listen?:* by Soyna Hamilton.[2] The chapter on visual aides is both fascinating and educational. Ms. Hamilton states in Chapter 8 of *What Makes Juries Listen?:* "research has shown that we get up to 90% of our knowledge from visual sensory impressions and that these are the most memorable and lasting impressions."[3] The challenge is to incorporate the main theories of your case into a trial exhibit that will be memorable and lasting.

§ 7.22   Hypothetical Questions

The purpose of an expert witness is to interpret technical and scientific matter for the jury, and offer an opinion on a theory that can reasonably be deduced from the evidence. A method frequently used in direct examination of an expert witness is to set up hypothetical situations similar to the real case situation and then, through a series of hypothetical questions, elicit opinion testimony. Hypothetical questions are tricky, and incomplete hypotheticals can create holes in case strategy. Problems with hypothetical questions include omitting essential factors (lack of foundation for the hypothetical situation) or that the hypothetical question contains facts inconsistent with facts in evidence.

Paralegals can assist in preparing hypothetical questions for trial by listing relevant facts from witness statements, discovery responses, relevant records, and so forth, and including the source of each fact. If technical terms are used in hypothetical questions, include the definitions in lay language of those terms. A sound hypothetical question should focus on each element that needs to be proven and include as many pertinent facts as possible.

Hypothetical questions are permissible on both direct and cross-examination. A special jury instruction should be given when hypothetical questions have been used with an expert witness. A sample jury instruction is as follows:

> An expert witness was asked to assume that certain facts were true and to given an opinion based upon that assumption. This is a hypothetical question. If any fact assumed in such a question has not been established by the evidence, you should determine the effect of that omission upon the value of the opinion based on that fact.[4]

§ 7.23   Expert Jury Instructions

Special jury instructions address expert testimony and how the jury should view that testimony in their deliberations. The starting point in working with an expert should

---

[2] Law and Business, Inc., Clifton, N.J. (1985).

[3] *Id.* at 375.

[4] Book of Approved Jury Instructions § 2.42 (7th ed. 1986).

be those instructions that the jury will hear just before their deliberations. A sample jury instruction regarding qualifications of experts follows:

> A witness who has special knowledge, skills, experience, training or education in a particular subject has testified to certain opinions. In determining what weight to give the opinion, you should consider the qualifications and believability of the witness, the facts or materials upon which opinion is based, and the reasons for each opinion.
>
> An opinion is only as good as the facts and reasons on which it is based. If you find that any such fact has not been proved, or has been disproved, you must consider that in determining the value of the opinion. Likewise, you must consider the strengths and weaknesses of the reasons on which it is based.
>
> You are not bound by an opinion. Give each opinion the weight which you find it deserves.
>
> However, you may not arbitrarily or unreasonably discard <u>(medical, scientific, technical, economic)</u> opinion testimony in this case which was not contradicted. Therefore, unless you find that it is not believable, it is conclusive and binding on you.[5]

The purpose of this instruction is to alert the jury that if the subject matter of the expert opinion testimony is not within the common knowledge of laymen, and is within the knowledge of experts only, expert opinion testimony which is built, uncontradicted, and unimpeached is conclusive on the jury.

This instruction also tells the jury to consider the qualifications and believability of the expert. You want a qualified expert that will be believed by the jury. It is important that the expert has sound, logical, and conclusive facts for each reason and opinion presented to the jury.

Experts are used at trial by both the plaintiff and the defendant. Once one side designates an expert in a particular area of specialization, it becomes incumbent upon the other side to find an opposing expert to refute that testimony. Complex litigation cases are frequently termed battles of experts. A special jury instruction is almost always given regarding how the jury should weigh conflicting expert testimony:

> In resolving the conflict in the testimony of expert witnesses, you should weigh the opinion of one expert against that of another. In doing this, you should consider the qualifications and believability of each witness, the reasons for each opinion, and the matter upon which it is based.[6]

§ 7.24   Exchanging Expert Witness Information

Discovery of the identity and the anticipated testimony of designated experts is addressed in Rule 26(4) of the Federal Rules of Civil Procedure which states in part that, ". . . discovery of facts known and opinions held by experts and acquired or developed in anticipation of litigation for trial may be obtained through various discovery methods."

---

[5] *Id.* § 2.40.

[6] *Id.* § 2.41.

The Federal Rules of Civil Procedure differ significantly from the California Rules of Civil Procedure regarding discovery of identity of expert witnesses, the subject matter of their testimony, their opinions, and the basis for those opinions. According to Federal Rule of Civil Procedure 26(4)(a), interrogatories may be drafted requiring the identification of:

> each person whom the other party expects to call as an expert witness at trial and the subject matter on which the expert is expected to testify and the substance of the fact and opinions to which the expert is expected to testify and a summary of the grounds for each opinion.

Under California Civil Procedure § 2018, the discovery of materials used by the expert in formulating the substance of the facts and opinions to which the expert is expected to testify is not unrestricted after interrogatory responses have been served on the requesting party. The Work Product Doctrine protects certain documents or reports from disclosure if they are opinion work product and/or that material which would ordinarily qualify for absolute work product protection pursuant to statute and case law. The scope of protection for work product depends on the type of work product involved. Those matters which would ordinarily be classified as conditional work product may not qualify for protection pursuant to Federal Rule of Civil Procedure 26(4)(a)(1). Documents and/or reports which are entitled to only qualified protection open the door for the court to allow disclosure if good cause is shown. The party seeking discovery must show a substantial need for the materials in the preparation of that party's case for trial. The requesting party must also show that they are unable, without undue hardship, to obtain the substantial equivalent of the materials sought.[7] *Hickman v. Taylor*[8] and *Upjohn Co. v. United States*[9] are the ruling cases regarding determination of good cause for discovery of qualified work product documents.

Different rules apply to discovery of "facts known and opinions held" by those experts who are expected to testify at trial and those who are not (for example, trial consultants, or lay experts). Rule 26(b)(2) and Rule 26(b)(4) of the Federal Rules of Civil Procedure discuss in detail discovery of "facts known and opinions held."

According to Federal Rule of Civil Procedure 26, a party in the course of discovery may propound interrogatories asking for:

1. The identity of expert witnesses whom the opponent expects to call at trial, complete with name, address, phone number, and area of specialization;
2. The subject matter, as well as the substance of the facts and opinions, of which the expert is expected to testify;
3. A precise statement of the subject matter;
4. A precise statement of the theories the expert will use when testifying;
5. The opinions that the expert is expected to express in trial testimony; and
6. The reasons behind the expert's opinion, and an explanation of any technical terms used in that opinion.

---

[7] Federal Rule of Civil Procedure 26(b)(3).

[8] 329 U.S. 495 (1947).

[9] 449 U.S. 383, 399 (1981).

Generalizations regarding expected expert testimony as to "substance, facts known and opinions held" are not permitted pursuant to Federal Rules of Civil Procedure, proclaimed most recently in the case of *URESIL Corp. v. Cook Co.*[10]

In addition to the stringent requirements the Federal Rules of Civil Procedure and case law, the responding party is under a statutory obligation in federal court to update interrogatory answers. (See **Chapter 4** regarding supplementing interrogatory responses in federal court.)

In litigation at the federal level, the responding party is under a duty to supplement its responses to an interrogatory seeking permitted information about experts who will testify at trial. This supplementation must include any change either in the experts who will testify at trial or on the matters, facts, and opinions on which they will testify. The supplemental response must conform to those requirements set forth in Federal Rule of Civil Procedure 26(e)(1)(b) and affirmed in *Bradley v. United States.*[11] (5th Circuit) (1989) 866 F.2d 120.

§ 7.25   Exchanging Expert Witness Information (California)

California Code of Civil Procedure § 2034, which sets forth the requirements for simultaneous discovery of expert witnesses in legislation in California State Courts, is far less demanding than the requirements set forth at Rule 26(4) of the Federal Rules of Civil Procedure.

In California, and in many other states, the Rules of Civil Procedure govern disclosure of expert witnesses expected to testify at trial. Interrogatories sent out during the course of litigation asking for identification of expert witnesses may be objected to on the grounds that they seek premature disclosure of experts and that discovery relating to expert witnesses is governed specifically by the California Code of Civil Procedure § 2034.

The standard answer given to interrogatories requesting the identity of expert witnesses and their opinions regarding liability issues of the case is as follows:

Investigation, discovery and trial preparation are continuing in this case. Responding party has not determined those person(s) who will be designated as expert witnesses and offer opinion testimony at the time of the trial of this action. This discovery request is premature, in that case preparation is continuing as facts, opinions, and analyses are ascertained through depositions, interrogatories, subpoenas, and other means of discovery. Accordingly, responding party refers you to California Code of Civil Procedure § 2034 which governs the disclosure of expert witnesses and discovery of their opinions after service of a demand for disclosure pursuant to statute is received.[12]

The service of a supplemental interrogatory (see **Chapter 4** for form) is always recommended as a way to clean up discovery matters. However, because there is a

---

[10] 135 F.R.D. 168, 173 (N.D. Ill. 1991).

[11] 866 F.2d 120 (5th Cir. 1989).

[12] The author has used this response herself in answering Interrogatories.

30-day cutoff on discovery before trial, a response to this interrogatory may not include the names of expert witnesses if they have not yet been retained. Without a special procedure to discover the identities and opinions of experts hired shortly before trial, there really would be no effective manner of discovering the opposition's experts and deposing them in order to prepare the case for trial effectively.

California Code of Civil Procedure § 2034 calls for a mutual and simultaneous exchange of expert witness information by all parties in the litigation. Any party may obtain discovery by serving a § 2034 demand on all parties. A demand made pursuant to CCP § 2034 achieves the following:

It prevents surprise at trial;

It is effective in barring testimony from experts whose names and opinions are not properly disclosed;

It is self-executing;

It entitles you to discovery of the other side's experts as a matter of right; and

It allows you to obtain this information without a motion, hearing, or court order.

The greatest advantage of serving a demand for the exchange of expert witness information pursuant to § 2034 is that in addition to the names and qualifications of the expert, statutory requirements must be met and you must be provided with the general substance of their testimony and copies of their discoverable reports and writings. Obtaining discoverable reports and writings of the adverse expert is extremely important in order to prepare your expert fully to refute those opinions offered by the adverse expert at the time of trial.

Discovery of expert witnesses' identities and writings pursuant to § 2034 is somewhat of a mixed blessing in that it is a reciprocal exchange, obligating you to disclose the very same information: your own expert witness identities, their opinions, and discoverable reports and writings. An additional problem occurs when the expert witness, who is designated to testify at trial, has previously been a consultant on the case generating writings and reports which could result in unfavorable disclosures if they do not qualify for absolute protection as work product documents.

Because today's litigation relies increasingly on expert testimony, it is necessary to prepare for trial by knowing which experts will testify for the other side and what they will have to say. Expert witness discovery is an integral part of case preparation and, irrespective of the mutual and simultaneous exchange required by § 2034, it is a necessary discovery tool to be used in the final countdown to trial. An important distinction between preparing a case in California for trial at the superior court level and the federal court level is that demand for exchange of expert witness information in § 2034 of the California Code of Civil Procedure is optional, not mandatory, whereas expert witness disclosure is mandatory at the federal level pursuant to Federal Rule of Civil Procedure 26(4).

§ 7.26   Sample Demand for Disclosure of Expert Witness Information (California)

This form (**Form 7–3**) conforms to the requirements of California Code of Civil Procedure § 2034(a) in asking for:

1. A brief narrative statement of the expert's qualifications and the general substance of the expert's expected testimony;

2. Representations signed, under penalty of perjury by the trial attorney, that the expert has agreed to testify and will be sufficiently familiar with the action to submit to a meaningful oral deposition concerning the expert's opinion and the basis of that opinion; and

3. A statement of the expert's hourly and daily fee for providing deposition testimony and trial testimony.

FORM 7–3
SAMPLE DEMAND FOR EXCHANGE OF EXPERT WITNESS INFORMATION

[attorney for plaintiff]
[address]
[telephone number]

Attorneys for Plaintiff
[plaintiff name]

IN THE SUPERIOR COURT OF THE STATE OF CALIFORNIA
IN AND FOR THE COUNTY OF [county name]

[name],	No. [case number]
Plaintiff,	DEMAND FOR EXCHANGE OF EXPERT WITNESS
vs.	INFORMATION (CCP § 2034)
[defendant], et al.	

_____/

Plaintiff, [name], hereby demands pursuant to California Code of Civil Procedure § 2034 that all other parties to this action exchange:

1. A list containing the name and address of each person whose expert opinion testimony that party expects to offer at trial, whether orally or by deposition testimony; and

2. An expert witness declaration for each such person in conformance with the requirements listed in California Code of Civil Procedure § 2034(f)(2).

DEMAND IS ALSO MADE for the production for inspection and copying of all discoverable reports and writings, if any, made by each expert listed in the course of preparing that expert's opinion.

The time and date for the exchange of information and production of reports shall be [date], fifty (50) days before trial of this action which has been set for [date].

The place for such exchange and production shall be at the Law Offices of [attorney for the plaintiff], [address], [city], [state].

Dated: [date]

[attorney for plaintiff]_____

§ 7.27   Protective Orders

Protective orders may be sought in connection with a Demand for Expert Witness Disclosure just as they may be sought in any area of discovery (depositions, interrogatories, requests for admissions, requests for protection of documents, independent medical examinations, subpoenas, and so forth). The general purpose and concept of a protective order is to protect any party from unwanted annoyance, embarrassment, oppression or undue burden and expense.

The grounds for a protective order, as it relates to expert witness disclosure, are somewhat different than the grounds would be if you were seeking a protective order in connection with interrogatories or a demand for document production. The mere exchange of a list identifying experts and setting forth requested information regarding the witness' opinions can hardly be considered oppressive and burdensome. Examples of those grounds which might give rise to the need to seek a protective order regarding expert witness disclosure are as follows:

1. The demand was not served in a timely fashion, and the requesting party wants to obtain a ruling to this effect rather than run the risk of consequence of failure to exchange expert witness lists in a time; and
2. One attorney is relying on an expert witness retained by another attorney but is having difficulty in obtaining the information required for the expert witness declaration, given the time constraints of the disclosure.

The most common relief sought by way of a motion for a protective order, as it pertains to expert witness disclosure, is to request that the opposing party reduce the number of expert witnesses designated to testify at trial. Grounds for this type of a motion usually include duplication of information and specific expertise commonly known as stacking the deck. A common trial tactic is to disclose multiple experts in a specialty area, forcing your opponent into noticing and taking depositions of all of the disclosed experts in order to prepare for trial adequately. This is time-consuming and extremely costly. Also, the party designating multiple experts may at the last minute withdraw experts by simply amending its original expert witness list.[13] No prior notice or leave of court is required for the amending of an expert witness list.

§ 7.28   Designation of Expert Witnesses

A Designation of Expert Witnesses and an attorney Declaration must be filed in response to a demand made for expert witness disclosure. All of those experts who are expected to testify at trial must be disclosed. This includes a party to an action, an employee of a party, or an expert retained by a party for the purpose of forming and expressing an opinion. Designated experts are those individuals who have been retained for the purpose of either forming and expressing an opinion in anticipation of the litigation or in preparation for trial, and will testify to their opinion at trial.

Independent witnesses, such as fact and percipient witnesses such as treating physicians and others discussed in **§ 7.16** must be disclosed by their name and address. It is not necessary to discuss in detail what information or opinion they will offer at the time of trial because they have not been retained for the purpose of giving expert testimony, but rather they will be rendering opinions based on firsthand knowledge.

In setting forth information regarding expert witness qualifications, you must provide enough information to enable the opposing party to gauge the credibility of that expert. Information set forth should cover the expert's general area of expertise, relevant education, relevant employment and/or experience within the industry, and professional society memberships and honors.

Immediately upon the receipt of a Designation of Expert Witnesses and Declaration, check to see that the resumes and/or curricula vitae's of each expert have been attached. If they have not been attached, contact opposing counsel and ask for them. You are entitled to receive that information. Resumes are not confidential documents and will most likely be submitted as trial exhibits at the time that expert qualifies to testify in court. Obtaining a resume in advance of the deposition of the adverse party's expert is extremely valuable. From that resume you can begin assembling a profile of the adverse expert witness as discussed in **§ 7.17** as a means of preparing your attorney for the deposition of that expert. Generally speaking, expert witness resumes are routinely attached to a Designation of Expert Witness. If they have not been, ask for them immediately because it will save hours of research and preparation.

§ 7.29   Sample Designation of Expert Witnesses and Declaration Forms (California)

The following Designation of Expert Witnesses Form and Declaration (**Form 7–4**) is a sample form for use in California.

---

[13] California Code of Civil Procedure § 2034(f)(1).

FORM 7–4
SAMPLE DESIGNATION OF EXPERT WITNESSES FORM
AND DECLARATION (CALIFORNIA)

[attorney for the defendant]
[address]
[telephone number]

Attorneys for Defendant
[name] Corporation

IN THE SUPERIOR COURT OF THE STATE OF CALIFORNIA
IN AND FOR THE COUNTY OF [county name]

[name], Plaintiff, vs. [name] CORPORATION, et al. _____/	No. [case number] DESIGNATION OF EXPERT WITNESSES AND DECLARATION Date: TRIAL: [date] Time: [time] Dept: [judicial department]

Defendant [name] CORPORATION designates the following expert witnesses for testimony at the trial of this matter.

1. [witness A], [name] Consultants, Inc., [address], [city], [state], [telephone number]. [witness A] is a retired [name] Corporation engineer with 40 years experience. [witness A] will testify regarding the transmission interlock system, its use and application in [name] Corporation's cars and in particular the vehicle being operated by the plaintiff, and on all factors surrounding the decision by [name] Corporation to use the device in question on its vehicles. Charge: [hourly rate].

2. [witness B], [university name], [city], [state], [telephone number]. [witness B] will testify as a bio-mechanic expert and as to the effect of the deceased plaintiff's failure to wear a seatbelt. Charge: [hourly rate].

3. [witness C], [address], [city], [state], [telephone number]. [witness C] will testify as a seatbelt expert and as to the effects of plaintiff's failure to wear a seatbelt.

Defendants reserve their rights pursuant to California Code of Civil Procedure § 2034 with regard to other experts who may be called as witnesses in this matter.

Defendants also reserve their right to call any and all persons designated as experts by any other party.

Defendants also reserve their rights to call any and all persons disclosed in the subpoenaed records.

Defendants also reserve their rights to call additional expert witnesses for purposes of rebuttal or impeachment, if necessary, at the time of trial, whose names are not now known.

Defendants also reserve their rights, at their option, to exclude an individual herein as an expert.

Defendants request that should plaintiff desire to take the depositions of any potential expert witnesses, that plaintiffs tender a fee as prescribed by § 2034 of the California Code of Civil Procedure based on the anticipated length of the deposition.

Dated: [date].

[attorney for the defendant]

DECLARATION OF [attorney for the defendant]

I, [attorney for the defendant], declare and affirm:

I am an attorney at law licensed to practice before all the courts in the State of California.

I am the attorney representing defendants in this matter.

The qualifications of the experts and the subjects of their testimony are listed above, and each expert will be sufficiently familiar with the action to submit to a meaningful oral deposition concerning their opinion and its basis.

I declare under penalty of perjury that the foregoing is true and correct. Executed on [date], at [city], [state].

[attorney for the defendant]

Proof of service on the above Designation of Expert Witnesses and Declaration included not only all counsel to the action, but also all those experts designated by the defendant corporation. It is a good idea to send the Designation of Expert Witnesses to your own expert witnesses because it enables them to see how they have been described and more importantly, the specific specialization and area of expertise you have included. It also enables them to see what has been said regarding the opinions and conclusions they will offer at time of trial. It is also good deposition preparation for your expert to review this designation.

§ 7.30   Disclosure of Discoverable Expert Reports

An expert witness demand should always include a request for all discoverable writings.[14] It is a mistake to limit the request for only those writings deemed discoverable pursuant to California Code of Civil Procedure § 2034(h). You will receive more information about the adverse party's expert if you request that expert's entire file and not just the expert's reports and writings. The entire file of an expert should be defined pursuant to the California Evidence Code § 250, which includes all writings, time records, and other physical material the expert considered, referred to, relied on, or prepared in connection with work on the case. Good cause for the production of the expert's entire file is that they are materials needed for effective trial preparation, and will assist opposing counsel in determining how best to prepare their case for trial. It is important to receive time records to know how many hours the expert has spent working on the case, the date that the expert was first hired to consult on the case, and the amount of time devoted to the research of outside materials in reaching the expert's opinion.

Certain reports may be consultant advisory reports and not be considered discoverable writings pursuant to California Code of Civil Procedure § 2034. To rule on claims of work product protection for trial consultant (expert witness) reports, the court considers the following criteria:

Does the report reflect, in whole or in part, the attorney's impressions, conclusions, opinions, or theories? If so, such information qualifies for absolute privilege and cannot be discovered under any circumstances including designating that trial consultant as an expert witness.

Are the contents of the report/memo, particularly those portions of the trial consultant/expert witness' writings which are not absolutely privileged, advisory to the attorney? If so, it qualifies for conditional privilege and cannot be discovered unless preventing its disclosure results in unfair prejudice to the party seeking discovery. If the trial consultant has been designated as an expert witness, those materials receiving conditional privilege are frequently deemed discoverable once the trial consultant has been designated as an expert witness.

Does good cause for discovery as to advisory reports outweigh the policies supporting work product protection? Could the advisory report serve as possible impeachment of the expert's testimony at trial? This potential for impeachment of the expert's testimony qualifies as good cause for the party seeking discovery of the advisory report.

Disputes frequently arise over what constitutes discoverable writings, and what qualifies as protection pursuant to the Work Product Doctrine. If a report's existence is known before trial, it can be either subpoenaed for production at the expert's deposition or subpoenaed to be produced when that expert testifies at trial. If the court finds that reports withheld as privileged were truly discoverable, that expert's testimony or a significant portion of it, may be excluded at time of trial.

---

[14] *Id.* § 2034(h).

§ 7.31   Scheduling Expert Witness Depositions

The scheduling of expert witness depositions within the time constraints of trial and expert witness' schedules is a frustrating but necessary duty frequently assigned to the paralegal who has assisted in trial preparation. Use the following recommended guidelines for best results:

1.   Meet with the trial attorney to determine the attorney's order of priority in terms of deposing the adverse party's witness. For example, it is usually more important to depose liability experts than damage experts, and they should be scheduled first.

2.   Call each of your experts as soon as possible after the disclosure has been served on opposing counsel. Discuss with them their availability, including those dates which are absolutely impossible as well as those dates which could be arranged if necessary. Also discuss with the expert the location for their deposition. Whether an expert's deposition is taken at the expert's office, the adverse attorney's office, your office, or a mutually convenient location frequently determines availability.

3.   Be prepared for the fact that each side will wish to depose the other side's experts before making any of their experts available for deposition. It is unfair and unreasonable to expect one side to produce all of their experts for deposition before taking any of the other side's expert witness depositions. Usually this matter can be resolved by adopting a "one of your's, one of mine" approach. If this cannot be resolved between paralegals from respective plaintiff and defendant offices, it may become necessary for the attorneys to become involved in an exchange of correspondence and/or conference calls.

4.   Confirm the depositions in writing with your expert and with all other opposing counsel who will attend the deposition after all depositions have been scheduled.

5.   It is rare that the depositions will go forward on the dates they were originally noticed, so a confirmation letter is necessary to avoid any ambiguity as to date, time, and place.

6.   Communicate immediately in writing to the person noticing the deposition if your expert requires an expert witness fee to be paid 24 or 48 hours before the date of the deposition. If your expert does not receive their fee in advance of the deposition (after you have notified the other side of the requirement), the deposition may not go forward on the date scheduled, and will have to be continued.

7.   Make certain, if the adverse party's expert requires payment in advance of their deposition, that you have requested a check for that expert's witness fee and mailed it in accordance with the requirement (24 or 48 hours in advance), or have given it to your attorney to bring with them to the deposition.

8.   Have your expert witness send to your office their entire file and any other writings which may be considered discoverable reports and writings in advance of the deposition so that you can make two complete copies of any writing which may be used as an exhibit at the expert's deposition. Send one complete copy

with your attorney to the deposition, and keep the other complete copy in a witness file for that expert safely tucked away in an office file drawer.

9. Order an expedited transcript, if necessary, depending upon the proximity in time of the expert's deposition to the actual trial date (which is frequently only a matter of days). Be sure to give copies of any expedited transcripts of adverse experts to your expert prior to their depositions. For example, your liability expert testifying regarding accident reconstruction should immediately be given a copy of the adverse expert's deposition testimony regarding accident reconstruction. It is sometimes not possible to obtain a copy of the adverse expert's deposition transcript in advance of your expert's deposition. In that case, it is helpful if you have attended the deposition and can give a copy of your notes to your attorney so that they can be conveyed to the expert.

§ 7.32   Sample Notice of Taking Expert Deposition and Request for Production of Documents (California)

Form 7–5 is a sample Notice of Taking Expert Deposition combined with a Request for Production of Documents. This combination is essential for effective trial preparation.

FORM 7–5
SAMPLE NOTICE OF TAKING EXPERT DEPOSITIONS AND REQUEST FOR PRODUCTION OF DOCUMENTS (CALIFORNIA)

[attorney for the defendant]
[address]
[telephone number]

Attorneys for Defendant
[name] Corporation

IN THE SUPERIOR COURT OF THE STATE OF CALIFORNIA

IN AND FOR THE COUNTY OF [county name]

[name],   No. [case number]

    Plaintiff,   NOTICE OF TAKING EXPERT
                                               DEPOSITIONS AND REQUEST
vs.   FOR PRODUCTION OF
                                               DOCUMENTS AT DEPOSITION
[name] CORPORATION,
et al.

_____/

TO: PLAINTIFF AND PLAINTIFF'S ATTORNEY OF RECORD:

PLEASE TAKE NOTICE that on the dates, time, and places indicated below, defendant [name] CORPORATION will take the depositions of the following experts:

Deponent	Date	Time
[expert A]	[date]	[time]
[expert B]	[date]	[time]
[expert C]	[date]	[time]
[expert D]	[date]	[time]
[expert E]	[date]	[time]
[expert F]	[date]	[time]

The depositions will take place at the offices of [attorney for the defense], [address], [city], [state].

The depositions will be taken on oral examination before a Notary Public authorized to administer oaths in the State of California pursuant to § 2034 of the California Code of Civil Procedure.

Each expert is required to produce for inspection and copying by defendant at that time and place of the deposition the following documents and things. As used herein, the term "documents" refers to all writings of any kind or nature whatsoever in their actual or constructive possession, custody, care or physical control, including, without limitation, correspondence, memoranda, agreements, messages, notes, contracts, or extracts or excerpts from any of the foregoing:

1. Their entire file concerning their work on this case, including, but not limited to, all correspondence, notes, reports, draft reports, charts, diagrams, computer programs and disks, instrument recordings, testing data, pleadings, depositions, statements, and any other documents or evidence which have ever been part of the experts' files.

2. All photographs taken or reviewed by the expert that relate to this case.

    (Note: [name] Corporation requests that a copy of all photographs be provided at the deposition. [name] Corporation will pay for photographic copies.)

3. All documents, including, but not limited to, reports, books, notes, computer programs and disks, photographs, tests, and other similar documents or information which they have utilized for their opinions in this case.

4. Billing and time records that relate to their work as a consultant/expert in this case, including the dates of work, time spent, and amount charged.

5. Hard copies of all computer work they have done that relates to their work in this case.

The undersigned is informed and believes that the above-described documents, matters, and things are in the deponent's custody, possession or control, are not privileged, and are relevant to the subject matter of this action or reasonably calculated to lead to the discovery of admissible evidence in this action. The undersigned also believes that the writings described above are required to be produced pursuant to the provisions of California Code of Civil Procedure § 2034(j).

Expert deponents will be tendered their deposition testimony fee prior to commencing their depositions, unless otherwise requested in writing 24 hours prior to the date scheduled for the deposition.

Dated: [date]

>[attorney for defendant]
>[name] Corporation

§ 7.33   Expert Fees

Certain experts are entitled to be paid reasonable and customary fees for time spent in giving a deposition. Fees are also required when experts are subpoenaed to appear at trial. Payment of fees must be made by the party who notices a deposition. Fees are to be paid to any expert listed in the Designation of Expert Witnesses other than parties or employees of parties. Treating physicians who are asked to express expert opinions are entitled to be paid a deposition fee. Architects, engineers, and surveyors involved with an original construction design, project design, or road survey on which they will be asked to express an opinion at the time of trial are considered expert witnesses, are designated as such, and are entitled to an expert witness fee.

If an expert's fee has not been paid by the time of their deposition, or in advance of that time which has been set in writing and conveyed to the party who noticed the deposition, the expert may not be deposed at that time.

The subject of expert witness fees is a touchy subject because all attorneys feel that the adverse expert charges way too much and that their expert fees are most fair and reasonable. It is difficult to attack a fee based on a "reasonable and customary hourly or daily fee" disclosed in an Expert Witness Declaration. Various rates are permitted, and it is not unreasonable for one expert to charge more than another expert. It is also not unreasonable for an expert to charge more for deposition testimony and court appearances than for ordinary services and consultations. Case law has stated that. " . . . the process of giving formal testimony under oath is an obviously more stressful and tense activity than consulting with your client in his office."[15]

---

[15] Rancho Bernardo Development Co. v. Superior Court, 2 Cal. App. 4th 358, 362, 2 Cal. Rptr. 2d 878 (1992).

It is sometimes difficult to anticipate the length of a deposition, and the fee initially tendered to an expert may not be sufficient to pay for the entire deposition. The actual time consumed in the deposition is billable to that party who noticed the deposition. However, an expert cannot refuse to continue a deposition merely on the grounds that the amount tendered is insufficient because the estimate of the anticipated length of the deposition was inaccurate. It is permissible to send the additional money for the expert's fee for completing the deposition after the deposition is concluded.

There are occasions when the amount demanded by an expert is deemed excessive. For example, the expert demands a full day's pay for a deposition, and the deposition is concluded in one hour. In extreme cases such as that, the attorney scheduling the deposition of the expert may move the court for an order setting the compensation of that expert. This is a touchy matter and should be handled with grace and diplomacy. It is best not to alienate the adverse expert prior to the expert's testimony at trial. A good faith attempt to settle the dispute usually results in a compromise fee.

§ 7.34   Supplemental Expert Witness Lists

Within 20 days after serving the Designation of Expert Witnesses and Declaration, a party may submit a Supplemental Expert Witness List. This list includes the name and address of any expert witness who will express an opinion on a subject covered by an expert witness designated by an adverse party, if you have not previously retained an expert to testify on that subject. This permits a plaintiff or defendant an opportunity to add additional expert witnesses if it is discovered that opposing counsel is naming expert witness concerning issues you did not originally intend to cover with expert testimony. When a Supplemental Expert Witness List is served, you must be ready to make those experts available for deposition immediately. The Designation of Supplemental Expert Witnesses must also include all discoverable writings and reports, if any, made by them.

Supplemental expert witnesses are most frequently added when you receive an expert witness designation from opposing counsel naming experts in an area or subject matter in which you had not previously retained an expert to testify, requiring you to locate and retain an expert to refute the adverse party's expert opinion. The supplemental expert witness list may be served upon all parties in the action without seeking a motion, or permission of the court to do so in California pursuant to California Code of Civil Procedure § 2034(h).

To supplement expert witnesses designated to testify at trial at the federal court level, a supplemental interrogatory response may be served providing expert witness information pursuant to Rule 26(e) of the Federal Rules of Civil Procedure. The provisions of Rule 26(e) require the supplementing of any prior response by the person giving that response any time that new information has been discovered (in this case the name of a new expert).

The need for supplemental expert witness lists is most frequently occasioned by long procedural delays between the trial setting conference, assignment of first trial date, and the actual trial date. In most superior courts at the state level, it is not unusual for a case which does not qualify for early setting due to statutory preference to be set for trial on three or four different occasions before it finally gets a definite date and goes to trial. These long delays give both sides the opportunity to do further investigation and case preparation. Formal discovery procedures close pursuant to court rule in most state superior courts 30 days before the first scheduled trial date; however, both sides have ample opportunity to confer with trial consultants due to the rescheduling of trial dates, and may wish to retain additional experts.

In federal court, Rule 26(e)(1)(b) of the Federal Rules of Civil Procedure, and case law as established in *Bradley v. United States,*[16] states unequivocally that should a party wish to supplement their expert witness list, they are obligated to provide the opposing counsel with supplemental disclosure including sufficient detail so as to provide the opposing party with information about the significance of the new expert's testimony.

The consequences for failing to provide supplemental information regarding experts are severe. If new experts are not properly disclosed, the court has the discretion to exclude their testimony at trial. The court must consider the importance of the testimony, the prejudice to the opposing party for the failure to disclose the expert. The court will consider the explanation, if any, for failing to disclose this information in a timely fashion.

In federal court, a court order is necessary to take a late deposition of a trial expert disclosed through supplemental disclosure;[17] however, in most cases, both parties stipulate or agree that the experts for each side can be deposed.[18]

The fact that the supplemental expert witness must submit to a meaningful deposition to prepare both sides adequately for trial is usually not at issue. It does, however, become an issue sometimes to supplement, augment, or amend an expert witness list if the additional testimony by the new expert will be on the same subjects raised in the original expert witness information list. It is usually a given that a party has the right to serve a supplemental expert witness list within the time constraints dictated by the Code of Civil Procedure for your state. However, where the additional testimony from the new expert relates to subjects originally disclosed in the adverse party's exchange of expert witness information, the party seeking to supplement, or augment, the expert witness list must seek leave of court through a formal noticed motion for permission to amend, or augment, the earlier information.

An example of a need to amend or augment earlier information given on expert witnesses may include not only the need to add a new expert to rebut information expected to be given by an adverse expert witness, but also an augmenting or expanding of the general substance, facts and opinions of a previously disclosed expert. This type of supplementing usually must be done through a formal noticed motion explaining the reasons for augmenting or changing the area of expertise or expected opinions and conclusions of a previously disclosed expert.

The effect of a Designation of Expert Witnesses and an attorney Declaration is to state unequivocally, under oath, that this particular expert specializes in the differences between apples and oranges and at the time of trial will offer an opinion based upon the differences between apples and oranges. If that expert at the time of trial attempts to discuss lemons along with apples and oranges, and if that expert attempts to offer an

---

[16] 866 F.2d 120 (5th Cir. 1989).

[17] Federal Rules of Civil Procedure 26(e)(4)(a).

[18] *Id.* Rule 29.

opinion on the differences between lemons and apples and oranges, the expert will not be permitted to so testify due to the parameters of the expert witness designation.

In order to avoid the problem of the necessity to augment or amend an expert witness list to allow your expert to testify and offer opinions in those areas not previously disclosed, describe their testimony in a general sense, mentioning specifics regarding their testimony in the main areas of liability or damages, and including additional areas of subspecialization where the expert may offer fact and opinion testimony depending upon testimony from other witnesses during the course of trial.

Remember that your opposing counsel may limit your expert's testimony through a motion in limine if the expert declaration does not accurately reflect the " . . . general substance of the testimony that the expert is expected to give at trial."[19] It is important that your declaration covers each of the areas which your expert intends to cover at the time of trial testimony. It is essential that you review with your expert all of those areas in which it is expected they will have an opinion based on study, research, or use and customs within the industry. It is also important to consider that an expert can only testify in those areas where they have that special knowledge, skill, experience, training, or education to offer admissible opinions.

It is permissible for an expert to say at the time of their deposition that they are prepared to testify in areas A, B, and C; but that they have been asked to do additional work in areas D and E. The expert can then further state that that additional work is continuing and they have not yet come to a point in their research and/or study which will allow them to give a final opinion. It should also be stated that whether the expert testifies on subjects D and E will depend upon testimony from adverse experts. The purpose of that additional testimony from your expert is then considered rebuttal.

§ 7.35 Motion to Supplement/Amend/Augment an Expert Witness List

Should a formal motion to supplement and/or amend and/or augment an expert witness list become necessary, the moving party must show the following facts:

1. The subject of this motion could not have been expected in the exercise of "reasonable diligence." (It was not expected that there would be a need to call this new expert, or offer the additional testimony of a previously disclosed expert at the time that the original exchange was made.)

2. The failure to include the expert or the additional testimony in the original exchange was the result of "mistake, inadvertence, surprise or excusable neglect."

3. There are exceptional circumstances requiring the necessity of supplementing, amending, and augmenting this expert witness list.

4. All information regarding the supplementing, amending, or augmenting of the original witness list has been served on all other parties in the action.

---

[19] California Code of Civil Procedure § 2034(f)(2)(b).

5. The moving party will make this witness available immediately for deposition at the convenience of the adverse party.

6. There will be no prejudice to the opposing party in their ability to maintain their action or defense on the merits of the case.

7. The new expert will not give testimony that is cumulative of other expert testimony.

8. Other parties in this action have already designated experts in the area of the new expert and they have already anticipated the issue and opinion upon which this new expert will testify, and they have prepared their case accordingly.

9. The issue upon which the new expert will testify, or the expanded issues upon which a previously disclosed expert will testify, are key to the liability and/or damage issues of this case. The determination of these issues requires expert analysis; therefore, to deny moving party the right to augment, amend, and/or supplement their expert witness designation to include this new expert will be detrimental to their case.

A motion to supplement, augment, or amend an expert witness designation is a noticed motion requiring all of the elements needed according to statute and local court rules: a notice of motion and motion, a memorandum of points and authorities, a declaration of moving party, and a proposed order. The most important part of this motion is the meet and confer section which must show that parties have informally attempted to resolve this matter. Frequently attorneys will stipulate to the supplementation making the motion unnecessary.

To deflate the other side's claims of prejudice, the party seeking to augment, supplement, or amend an expert witness disclosure may offer to stipulate to the following:

No more than one new expert will be added and/or no more than one expert's previously disclosed area of specialization will be augmented;

Not only will the new expert be made available for deposition, but the deposition will be at the office of opposing counsel with all deposition expenses to be paid by the party seeking to augment and/or change the expert witness designation; and

All opposing counsels will be provided with a list of all cases in which the new expert has consulted or given expert opinion in the past three years, complete with a list of the names and addresses of all opposing counsel.

It is this last concession by the moving party that usually convinces all adverse parties to stipulate to the supplementing, augmenting, or amending of the expert witness designation. Given the information promised by this concession, it can hardly be argued that they have inadequate time to prepare for the deposition and testimony of the new expert.

§ 7.36 Videotaped Expert Witness Depositions

It is becoming increasingly common to videotape depositions of expert witnesses or treating or consulting physicians, even though that deponent may be available to testify at the time of trial. (A sample form Notice of Video Deposition of a trial expert is included in **Chapter 3.**) A videotaped deposition may be used at time of trial in lieu of live testimony by the expert.

Include in a video deposition notice for an expert the following information:

1. The address where the deposition will be taken;

2. The date and time of the deposition;

3. The name of the deponent, and the address and telephone number of any deponent who is not a party to the action; and

4. The name of the designated videotape reporter, and a statement that the deposition will also be recorded stenographically with the name and address of that reporter (Remember it is essential if you are noticing this deposition to confirm with both the videotape reporter and the court reporter that they will be present at the time and date. It is necessary to have both reporters present before the deposition may go forward.);

5. Specific description of any materials the deponent must produce at the time of deposition (Refer to the Notice of Taking Expert Deposition and Request for Production of Documents in **§ 7.32** for an example of a specific description of materials.);

6. A statement of the intention to record the expert witness' and/or treating or consulting physician's testimony by videotape;

    A statement of an intention to reserve the right to use this videotaped deposition of this expert witness and/or treating or consulting physician at the time of trial.

    A sufficient description to identify the witnesses and the specific matters upon which they will testify if the name of the deponent is not known (This is necessary when you have noticed the deposition of an officer, director, managing agent, employee, or agent of a corporation or public entity.).

The court and all parties must be notified in writing of the intention to take a videotape deposition of an expert, allowing sufficient time for any objections to be made and resolved.

The opposing party may seek a protective order postponing the videotape deposition of an expert until the moving party has had an opportunity to take a discovery deposition. There must be a reasonable and good faith attempt made to resolve the matter by making that expert available for a discovery deposition.

The party noticing the videotape deposition reserves the right to offer into evidence only certain parts of the deposition rather than the entire deposition, but the noticing party must keep in mind that any other party may introduce any other portion of the deposition at the time of trial.

The advantages of taking a videotape deposition of an expert include the fact that you do not have to accommodate testimony dates into the expert's schedule at the time the case goes to trial. The disadvantage of videotaping an expert witness is that if they are a very good expert witness, you lose the spontaneity of their personal appearance and their ability to communicate with the jury.

§ 7.37   Withdrawal of an Expert Witness

The parties occasionally change their mind as to which expert to call at trial. This occurs when a previously disclosed expert witness performs further studies and analyses which changes their original opinion. This presents a problem for the party who has designated this person as their expert witness. It then becomes necessary for a party to redesignate someone previously designated as a testifying expert witness as a nontestifying consultant. This redesignation prevents the opposing party from discovering the expert's opinions. If the redesignation of the expert occurs before the expert is deposed, the unfavorable or unhelpful opinion testimony will be protected from disclosure. Work product protection is reinstated if the expert is now retained in a consultant capacity and will not give expert testimony at trial.

Once experts have been designated as potential witnesses, their opinions and reports are discoverable; however, if a party seeks to withdraw a particular expert and return them to the consultant status, it does effectively shield them from discovery. An exception, of course, may be made by the courts if it can be proven that the party seeking to withdraw the expert is doing so in return for a payoff for suppression of evidence.

The opposing party may still seek to notice the deposition of the withdrawn expert, and depending upon statutory provisions may succeed. For example, in California pursuant to California Code of Civil Procedure § 2034, a designated expert's deposition may be noticed. However, by withdrawing the expert and returning them to consultant status, advisory reports and other such written materials are protected from disclosure and are considered work product. The leading case in California on this point is *County of Los Angeles v. Superior Court (Hernandez)*.[20]

§ 7.38   Conclusion

Dealing with expert witnesses is a challenging and exciting part of trial preparation. Paralegal duties in regard to the selection, retention and preparation of expert witnesses for deposition and trial include, but are not limited to:

_____ Locating an expert.

_____ Researching your own and adverse party's experts in order to prepare expert witness profiles.

_____ Working with your expert in the preparation of demonstrative exhibits, reports, photos, graphs, and so forth, to enhance their testimony.

_____ Working with your expert in the "care and feeding" capacity to help them to translate scientific and technical data into common everyday phrases and language that will be understandable to the lay jury. This is perhaps the most important role a paralegal plays in preparing an expert witness.

_____ Attending expert witness depositions to take notes and provide information to your expert concerning the adverse expert's testimony.

---

[20] 222 Cal. App. 3d 647, 271 Cal. Rptr. 698 (1990).

_____ Arranging for expert witness depositions, scheduling, and so forth.

_____ Arranging for expert witness trial testimony, scheduling, and so forth.

The importance of expert witness testimony at the time of trial cannot be diminished. Rarely are there cases being tried in the state superior courts and federal courts of this country without expert testimony. The complex issues of liability, causation, and damages are best understood by a jury when they are presented by an expert witness.

INDEX